HISTORY OF
BRITAIN
& IRELAND
THE DEFINITIVE VISUAL GUIDE

HISTORY OF BRITAIN
& IRELAND

THE DEFINITIVE VISUAL GUIDE

2019 EDITION

DK LONDON

Senior Art Editor
Helen Spencer

US Editor
Megan Douglass

Pre-production Producer
Robert Dunn

Producer
Nancy-Jane Maun

Senior Managing Art Editor
Lee Griffiths

Managing Editor
Gareth Jones

Associate Publishing Director
Liz Wheeler

Art Director
Karen Self

Design Director
Philip Ormerod

Publishing Director
Jonathan Metcalf

DK INDIA

Senior Art Editor
Chhaya Sajwan

Senior Editor
Anita Kakar

Project Art Editor
Pooja Pipil

Editor
Aadithyan Mohan

Managing Art Editor
Sudakshina Basu

Senior Managing Editor
Rohan Sinha

Pre-production Manager
Sunil Sharma

DTP Designer
Umesh Singh Rawat

2011 EDITION

CONTRIBUTORS
R.G. Grant, Ann Kay, Michael Kerrigan, Philip Parker

EDITORIAL CONSULTANTS
Sir Barry Cunliffe, Eric Evans, Kenneth Morgan, Miri Rubin

DORLING KINDERSLEY

Senior Art Editor
Edward Kinsey

Project Art Editor
Amit Malhotra

Art Editors
Kaberi Hazarika, Mansi Nagdev,
Zaurin Thoidingjam, Shreya Anand Virmani

Assistant Art Editor
Mini Dhawan

Cartographers
Ed Merritt, Simon Mumford

Managing Art Editor
Owen Peyton Jones, Ashita Murgai

Consultant Art Director
Shefali Upadhyay

Art Director
Philip Ormerod

Senior Editor
Pip Morgan

Project Editors
Nicola Hodgson, Peter Preston, Alka Ranjan

Editors
Brishti Bandyopadhya, Shatarupa Chaudhuri,
Sudeshna Dasgupta, Dharini, Rahul Ganguly,
Bincy Mathew, Karishma Walia

Picture Researcher
Karen VanRoss, Sakshi Saluja

Managing Editor
Julie Ferris, Rohan Sinha

Production Manager
Pankaj Sharma

DTP Designers
Neeraj Bhatia, Arjinder Singh, Jagtar Singh,

Associate Publisher
Liz Wheeler

Reference Publisher
Jonathan Metcalf

This American edition, 2019
First American edition, 2011
Published in the United States by DK Publishing
1450 Broadway, Suite 801, New York, NY 10018

CONTENTS

1

BRITONS AND INVADERS
UP TO 1066

Introduction — 8

Timeline — 10, 12

Britain's First People — 14
Arrival of first humanlike species in Britain
and colonization by modern humans around
15,000 years ago.

Stone Age Britain — 16
Settlers build stone monuments and
agriculture develops.

■ STONEHENGE — 18

Iron Age Britain — 20
Warrior elites in hillforts dominate Britain,
maintaining strong links with Europe and
producing art of great beauty.

Caesar's Invasion — 22
Julius Caesar establishes treaty relations with
British tribes, drawing Britain into the orbit
of Roman political ambitions.

Conquest and Resistance — 24
The Romans, under Emperor Claudius,
conquer much of Britain, despite bitter
resistance in Wales and the north
of England.

■ HADRIAN'S WALL — 26

A Distant Province — 28
Much of Roman Britain prospers as towns
grow and roads encourage trade and
communication.

Outside the Empire — 30
By the 5th century, communities in Ireland
and remote parts of Scotland lay the
foundations of independent kingdoms.

Life in Roman Britain — 32
Rome profoundly affects British life with its
military organization, urban lifestyle, new
religious beliefs, and novel foods.

End of Empire — 34
In 410 CE, Roman rule over Britain comes to
an end, leaving Britain exposed and at the
mercy of Germanic barbarians.

**■ THE SUTTON HOO
SHIP BURIAL** — 36

Holy Ireland — 38
Rapid growth in Ireland's Christian Church
in the 5th century, as abbots of the main
monasteries become powerful and send
missionaries abroad.

Anglo-Saxon Rulers — 40
Between the 5th and 8th centuries,
Anglo-Saxon invaders establish the powerful
kingdoms of Mercia, Northumbria, and Wessex.

■ FRANKS CASKET — 42

Christian England — 44
Missionaries sent by Pope Gregory I convert
Anglo-Saxons to Christianity, transforming
England into a vibrant and thriving Christian
culture, largely based on monasteries.

Viking Raiders and Settlers — 46
Anglo-Saxon kingdoms succumb to Viking
raiders, armies, and settlers, leaving Wessex
to stand alone, weak and beleaguered.

■ BOOK OF KELLS — 48

■ ALFRED THE GREAT — 50

Wessex Takes the Lead — 52
In the 10th century, several able kings of
Wessex progressively conquer Viking-held
areas of England, uniting the country as
far north as the border with Scotland, and
becoming kings of the English.

Ireland in the Viking Age — 54
From their port-enclaves in Ireland, the
Vikings, without conquering the country,
play a major role in shaping Irish culture.

Triumph of the Danes — 56
At the turn of the first millennium, the
Danes successfully invade England and take
over the throne for a quarter of a century.

Independent Realms 58
In the 9th and 10th centuries, Scotland is more successful than Wales at achieving unity and independence from England.

King Edward's World 60
Edward the Confessor struggles to contain the country's internal tensions.

2

MEDIEVAL BRITAIN
1066–1485

Introduction 62

Timeline 64

Norman Conquest 66
William the Conqueror installs an Anglo-Norman rule, introduces a feudal society, and reshapes England.

■ **BATTLE OF HASTINGS** 68

Norman Realm 70
Henry I's reign manages to establish the institutional bureaucracy that realizes the Norman kings' desire to dominate their new realm.

■ **DOMESDAY BOOK** 72

Reign of a Powerful King 74
King Henry II fights the Church and his sons, conquers Ireland, and reforms the English legal system.

■ **MURDER IN THE CATHEDRAL** 76

Invasion of Ireland 78
Irish infighting opens the way for Henry II to move in and establish English rule over Ireland.

England in the Crusades 80
Richard I and other kings of England embark on a series of crusades, as they heed papal calls to regain Jerusalem and the Holy Land.

Challenging Royal Authority 82
Royal concessions to the barons of England lead to a Parliament that has to approve any new taxes the monarch wishes to levy.

■ **MAGNA CARTA** 84

A Prosperous Realm 86
In the 12th and 13th centuries, England prospers, which improves the social and economic life of some of the people.

Subduing Wales 88
The powerful princes of Gwynedd try to create an independent Wales, but Edward I subdues them.

Scotland's Independence Struggle 90
Led by Edward I, an English invasion to crush the Scots ends in failure as Robert the Bruce and his army expel the occupiers.

■ **BATTLE OF BANNOCKBURN** 92

Hundred Years' War Begins 94
The English and the French fight over the throne of France, starting a series of costly wars that will last more than a century.

Knights and Bowmen 96
During the medieval period, advances in infantry warfare throw a challenge to the central role of heavily armored cavalry.

■ **BATTLE OF CRÉCY** 98

The Black Death 100
A deadly infection wipes out half of the population within a year, causing profound social changes.

The Peasants' Revolt 102
A heavy poll tax causes many people to rebel against king and government, but the killing of the rebel leaders brings the revolt to an end.

■ **LUTTRELL PSALTER** 104

Religious Enthusiasm 106
Monasteries and pilgrimage play a major role in English life, though religious reformers are brutally suppressed.

Poets of the People 108
Geoffrey Chaucer pioneers vernacular writing in a form of English, poetically revealing everyday contemporary life in his *Canterbury Tales*.

■ **ELY CATHEDRAL** 110

Change of Dynasty 112
As Richard II is deposed, a new Lancastrian dynasty under Henry IV lays the seeds of a conflict that would burst into civil war.

Invasion and Revolt 114
In the 15th century, Scotland proves to be far more troublesome for England than Wales, except for the revolt of Owain Glyn Dwr.

The Later Hundred Years' War 116
Henry V's bid for the French throne almost succeeds after Agincourt, but a French revival sees the English kings lose almost all their lands in France.

Merchants and Guilds 118
Craftsmen and tradesmen form guilds in British cities and towns during the prosperous but sometimes turbulent 15th century.

The Wars of the Roses 120
The houses of Lancaster and York embark on a long period of civil strife as they fight bitterly for the throne of England.

■ **MEDIEVAL WEAPONS** 122

3

TUDORS AND STUARTS
1485–1688

Introduction 124

Timeline 126

The Early Tudors 128
Henry Tudor centralizes the state and concentrates power on the monarchy, an enduring legacy he passes on to his successors.

■ **HENRY VIII** 130

Religious Upheaval 132
The Protestant Reformation of the Church radically changes the lives of the British people, both religiously and culturally. The spirit of theological self-reliance changes the political landscape as well.

Scottish Troubles 134
The tragic life of Mary Queen of Scots epitomizes the dangers Scottish power struggles posed to the English monarchy.

■ **ELIZABETH I** 136

English Society under the Tudors 138
The country prospers as trade and agriculture flourish, but in the rapidly expanding cities hunger and crime stalk the streets.

■ **TUDOR LIFE** 140

Sailors and Privateers 142
Inspired by the skill and daring of several English seafarers, the Royal Navy is founded and British naval power expands with a renewed spirit of exploration and discovery.

The War with Spain 144
England battles remorselessly with her Spanish foe, finally overcoming its fearful shadow and ushering in a golden age.

■ **THE DEFEAT OF THE SPANISH ARMADA** 146

The English Renaissance 148
Arts and philosophy flourish, with great theater, wonderful music, evocative poetry, striking Tudor portraits, and far-reaching humanist thinking.

■ **WILLIAM SHAKESPEARE** 150

Conquest and Plantation 152
English power savagely puts down several fierce revolts in Ireland, followed by colonization and settlement in the north of the country, which sets the stage for future conflicts.

The Union of the Crowns 154
James I's accession effectively unites the kingdoms of Great Britain under the rule of a Scottish dynasty, the House of Stuart.

■ **THE GUNPOWDER PLOT** 156

Colonial Expansion 162
English colonists gradually establish settlements along much of North America's eastern seaboard and on many islands of the Caribbean.

■ **LONDON AND THE THAMES RIVER** 164

Charles I and Parliament 166
Political turbulence unsettles the country as an absolutist King collides with an increasingly confident Parliament.

The Civil War 168
Desperate terror, death, and suffering sweep across the country as rival supporters of the King and Parliament fight a vicious war that eventually divides the entire British Isles.

■ **THE EXECUTION OF THE KING** 170

The Commonwealth 172
As the country ceases to be a kingdom, many start to build a better society while others feel excluded by the righteousness of the new elite.

Scotland and Ireland Subdued 174
Scotland and Ireland are drawn into the life-and-death struggle of the English Civil War, bringing their destinies closer together.

The Restoration 176
The monarchy is restored, bringing fashion, fun, and color at first, then the King starts to revert to his father's old absolutist ways.

Commerce and War 178
As the world enters a new and more dangerous age, successive governments of England are prepared to fight for their commercial interests.

Pepys's London 180
Samuel Pepys vividly records the political gossip, pioneering ideas, and cultural pursuits of Britain's global commercial center.

■ **THE GREAT FIRE OF LONDON** 182

Inquiring Minds 184
Modern science is born as new institutions and scholars champion reasoned knowledge and experimental methodology.

■ **ST. PAUL'S CATHEDRAL** 186

The Glorious Revolution 188
Parliamentary democracy succeeds in overthrowing James II, preventing the King's despotic attempts to shape the religious beliefs of the nation.

4
RISE OF POWER
1688–1815

Introduction 190

Timeline 192

Succession Wars 194
Rival Protestant and Catholic factions fight each other in Ireland and then engage in wars of supremacy that spread across Europe.

■ **TREATY OF UNION** 196

The House of Hanover 198
A German dynasty succeeds to the British throne and rules over a people whose patriotism is increasingly linked to the Protestant cause.

Scottish Jacobites 200
Jacobite rebellions in Scotland by Catholic Stuarts rock the Protestant Hanoverian state.

■ **BATTLE OF CULLODEN** 202

Politics and Prime Ministers 204
Robert Walpole and William Pitt the Younger use their new position to transform British politics.

Power of the Pen 206
New tracts, journals, and newspapers dissect every aspect of British politics, manners, and thought.

Commercial Expansion 208
The Royal Navy gives protection to seaborne trade, while the slave trade flourishes from English ports such as Bristol and Liverpool.

Colonial Conquests 210
The Seven Years' War gives Britain control of Canada, while the East India Company begins the gradual British takeover of India.

America is Lost 212
The 13 colonies of America rebel against Britain, which fails to suppress the rebellion in a costly and prolonged war.

■ **SURRENDER AT YORKTOWN** 216

Georgian Society 218
In the 18th century, the better-off worked, played, shopped—and revelled in the social season.

■ **LANDED GENTRY** 220

Disorder and Religious Revival 222
Social turmoil brings crime and disorder to many English cities, causing thousands to turn to religion for help and guidance.

Scottish Enlightenment 224
Edinburgh becomes a center for a flourishing intellectual, scientific, and artistic life.

New Horizons in the Pacific 226
Voyages of exploration bring many scientific and geographical discoveries, and help to extend Britain's imperial horizons.

■ **GEORGIAN TRADE** 228

Modernizing Agriculture 230
Parliamentary enclosures and landowners seeking increased productivity transform British agriculture.

Inventors and Entrepreneurs 232
Invention and entrepreneurship enable the Industrial Revolution to transform the British landscape, social assumptions, and sense of identity.

The Anti-Slavery Movement 234
The campaign to abolish slavery gradually succeeds despite powerful vested interests.

Reaction to the Revolution 236
The British establishment worries that the revolution in France will cross the Channel and undermine its tradition and the rule of law.

Rebellion in Ireland 238
Inspired by the French Revolution, the Irish people rise up against the British, but face defeat.

Napoleonic Wars 240
Britain, with other European countries, attempts to control the vaunting ambition of Napoleon Bonaparte, the "Little Corporal."

■ **ADMIRAL NELSON** 242

The War of 1812 244
Land and sea battles between the United States and Britain end inconclusively for both sides.

■ **BATTLE OF WATERLOO** 246

5
INDUSTRY AND EMPIRE
1815–1914

Introduction 250

Timeline 252

The Regency 254
Celebrated for its fashions, art, and architecture the Regency and reign of George IV had political and social repercussions.

■ **BRIGHTON PAVILION** 256

Steam and Speed 258
In 19th-century Britain, the unquenchable quest for speed creates locomotives and ships that broaden everyone's horizons.

■ **ISAMBARD KINGDOM BRUNEL** 260

■ **ROYAL ALBERT BRIDGE** 262

Years of Change 264
The Industrial Revolution brings new ways of working that alter everything from timekeeping and housing to family dynamics and class relations.

The Irish Famine 266
A potato-destroying fungus causes a widespread famine in Ireland, which the authorities do little to alleviate—a million people die.

The Triumph of Reform 268
As Britain's economy booms, profound reforms take place to improve the fairness of the way governments are elected and society is run.

■ **QUEEN VICTORIA** 270

■ **THE GREAT EXHIBITION** 272

The Crimean War 274
War with Russia dents Britain's self-confidence and questions its competence, while newspapermen have a field day at the front.

Workshop of the World
Britain becomes the world's first industrial power, successfully manufacturing a range of goods for international markets.

Victorian Values
Britain's expanding middle class espouse hard work, progress, self-improvement, and a high moral tone.

■ **VICTORIAN ENTERTAINMENT** 280

Cultural Conflict
Currents of dissent unsettle British self-confidence, with new cultural, religious, and artistic ideas that challenge the status quo.

■ **VICTORIAN WORKHOUSE** 284

Exploring the World 286
British explorers and missionaries venture into many corners of the world, including the dark heart of Africa, the blazing heat of Australia, and the icy poles.

■ **CHARLES DARWIN** 288

British India 290
Britain gradually takes over of the Indian subcontinent and the Indian Raj becomes the country's jewel in the crown.

■ **INDIAN MUTINY**

Dominions and Emigrants
The white colonies in Canada, New Zealand, and Australia develop as self-governing dominions, attracting many emigrants from Britain.

Imperialist Muscle
Britain's bellicose imperialism triggers wars against the Chinese, Zulu, and Ashanti.

■ **RAILROAD STATION**

Irish Home Rule
As Parnell and Gladstone try to get Home Rule legislation through Parliament , the Fenians and Invincibles resort to terrorism.

The Boer War
South Africa plunges into a bitter guerrilla war in which a much-relieved Britain defeats the Boers.

The Edwardian Age 304
A brief age of extravagance and elegance witnesses a range of modern novelties, from motorcars and tabloid newspapers to airplanes and cinemas.

■ **SINKING OF THE TITANIC** 306

The Suffragettes 308
Parliament's failure to give women voting rights propels them into a campaign of demonstrations and escalating direct action.

Trade Unionists and Socialists 310
Political radicals voice the concerns of the working classes, organizing their collective strength.

The Road to War 312
Despite Britain's economic leadership and imperial authority, the rise of German power casts a long shadow of war over the country.

6
MODERN TIMES
1914–present

292 **Introduction**
294 **Timeline**

Britain Enters the Great War 320
The war that would be "over by Christmas" becomes a terrifying stalemate of pointless
296 trench warfare and a merciless war of attrition.

Victory through Slaughter 322
With patriotism, courage, and stoical endurance, troops from Britain and its allies
298 finally triumph over their German foes,
300 but victory comes at the cost of almost a million lives.

■ **FIRST DAY OF THE SOMME** 324

302 **The Home Front** 326
Propaganda and censorship force British citizens to support the war, yet the social solidarity helps to make the country more democratic.

■ **WAR GRAVES** 328

Peace and After 330
The enormous human cost of victory and the difficult path to a durable peace casts a long
306 shadow over the disillusioned people of Britain.

Irish independence 332
Southern Ireland finally gains independence from Britain as the island is partitioned, with Northern Ireland receiving Home Rule.

Crisis and Depression 334
Britain experiences the decline of Victorian industries, a general strike, a worldwide depression, financial crisis, and mass unemployment.

■ **THE JARROW MARCH** 336

Life in the Twenties and Thirties 338
Despite the misery of unemployment, many Britons enjoy picture palaces, dance halls, and the wireless, and some even buy homes and cars.

■ **DOMESTIC APPLIANCES** 340

Imperial Issues 342
The British Empire reaches its greatest extent, yet it is challenged by a vigorous independence movement in India led by Gandhi.

The Abdication of Edward VIII 344
A constitutional crisis is averted when King Edward VIII abdicates, choosing love and exile over the throne.

Slide to War 346
Britain tries to appease Hitler's aggressive Nazi regime, but in the end war becomes inevitable.

Britain Alone 348
Britain finds itself alone in Europe as it upholds the cause of freedom and survives through epic endurance, loyally supported by its Commonwealth.

■ **WINSTON CHURCHILL** 350

■ **THE BLITZ** 352

Life in Wartime Britain 354
During the war, Britons endure rationing, air raids, flying bombs, American GIs, evacuation, and an all-controlling government.

■ **THE BATTLE OF BRITAIN** 356

An Allied Victory 358
Britain's alliance with the United States and the Soviet Union triumphs over Germany and Japan, but the war exhausts the nation's resources.

The Post-War Years 360
In 1945 the newly elected Labour government starts to rebuild a country devastated by war and creates a welfare state.

The Modern Monarchy 362
Queen Elizabeth II's reign is long and stable, yet witnesses great changes in the world and in the country's attitudes to the monarchy.

Retreat from Empire 364
Britain all but ceases to be a colonial power and its Commonwealth is an international organization of limited practical importance.

■ **THE SUEZ CRISIS** 366

The Cold War 368
Britain lives with the risk of nuclear annihilation as it joins America in a Cold War confrontation with the Soviet Union.

Never Had It So Good 370
Britons buy houses and spend on cars, TVs, and other consumer goods as their rising wages bring security and prosperity.

Britain Goes Pop 372
Britain loses its stuffy image in the Swinging Sixties with the flowering of popular culture, fashion and music, stylish art, and loose morals.

■ **BEATLEMANIA** 374

Conflict in Society 376
Social and political conflicts dominate the 1970s and 1980s as Britain experiences high inflation and rising unemployment.

Troubles in Northern Ireland 378
IRA terror and the presence of British troops on the streets of Ulster fuels a bitter sectarianism and a collapse of law and order.

Turn to the Right 380
Party politics assumes a more right-wing identity in Thatcher's Britain as wealth and enterprise replace the belief in solidarity and security.

■ **MARGARET THATCHER** 382

Wars in Peacetime 384
Britain defends the Falklands, British aircraft bomb Serbia, and the country's forces join the United States in waging wars in Afghanistan and Iraq.

Facing the Future 386
Globalization, Europe, and financial meltdown are key concerns in Britain's future.

Monarchs and Rulers 388

Index and Acknowledgments 390

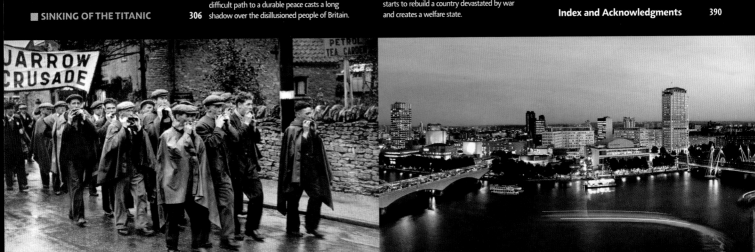

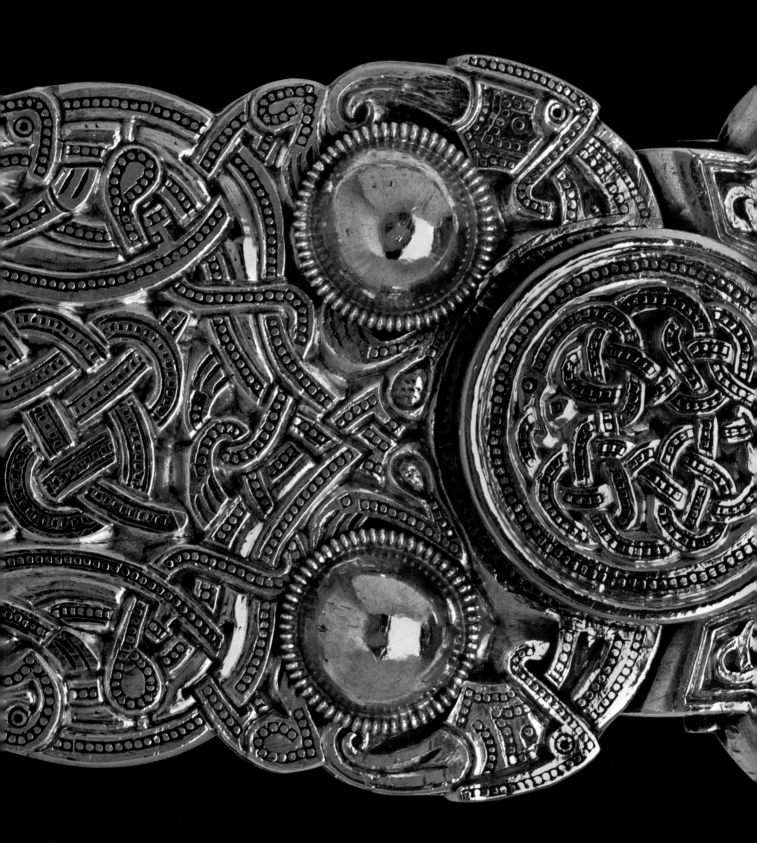

1

BRITONS AND INVADERS
Up to 1066

The islands of Britain witnessed wave after wave of settlements and invasions that brought wealth, faith, and conflict, while helping to shape the flourishing arts, languages, and destinies of the peoples of England, Wales, Scotland, and Ireland.

Sutton Hoo belt buckle
This gold belt buckle was among the many treasures that accompanied the man who was buried in the Anglo-Saxon ship found at Sutton Hoo. Writhing snakes and birds' heads with curved beaks adorn the buckle, its hollow interior a place to safely store a relic.

age from around 3000 BCE, when stone monuments appeared throughout Britain and Ireland. Political entities did exist, but their development is hard to trace. It is only from immediately preceding the first Roman invasion of Britain in 55 BCE that we begin to know names: Cassivellaunus, Caratacus, and Boudicca, native British leaders in the struggle against the Romans.

New identities

The separate destinies of England, Scotland, and Ireland now became apparent. Ireland was never invaded by the Romans, and its Iron Age chieftains developed a political culture untainted by imperial rule. The final limit of the Roman province of Britannia, at Hadrian's Wall (built around 120 CE), marked out a southern entity that would broadly develop into England and Wales, and a northern one that would ultimately become Scotland. Roman Britain lasted 367 years until 410 CE, and gave the area a long period of peace and prosperity not known until early modern times. Yet its ending heralded a troubled time, particularly for England, as successive invaders swept through the south. In the 5th century CE, Anglo-Saxons arrived from northwestern Europe. They gradually progressed westward and

First arrivals

About 800,000 years ago, the first human ancestors reached the British Isles from continental Europe. In 1066, their descendants once more encountered European migrants, in the shape of the Norman conquerors of England. Over the intervening vast span of time, all parts of the isles of Britain and Ireland were settled, with Norfolk in England showing the first scant evidence, Scotland being reached around 14,000 years ago, and Ireland about 7000 BCE. When agriculture arrived, in about 4000 BCE, people began to modify the landscape in ways which can be recognized today. Ards (primitive plows) scarred the land and great earthworks and causeways were constructed, culminating in a fully fledged megalithic northward, expunging many residual elements of Roman culture, and supplanting England's Celtic (and Latin) with a Germanic dialect. The Anglo-Saxon invasions divided southern Britain between a Germanic east and a Celtic west, ultimately creating Wales—a western haven that remained largely unconquered and was ruled by the descendants of the displaced Britons. Christianity joined these two halves (and Ireland and Scotland, too) in a common faith from the 6th century CE, while petty kingdoms in each of these realms began to coalesce into something larger. Viking invasions from Scandinavia from the late 8th century CE, decided, by a process of elimination of their weaker opponents, who would inherit the isles.

End of the beginning

England's survivor was the kingdom of Wessex, which merely endured under Alfred the Great, but expanded in the 10th century CE under his successors, until Athelstan in the 920s CE could call himself, with some justification, "king of the English and ruler of all Britain." In Scotland, the Dal Riatan ruler Kenneth MacAlpin conquered the Picts in 842 CE to create the kingdom of Alba, the forerunner of Scotland. In Wales, the struggle against the Vikings threw up rulers such as

Rhodri Mawr and Hywel Dda, who briefly united the country. Only Ireland remained disunited, with no one kingdom able to establish anything but the most fleeting hegemony. England suffered another brief period of foreign rule by the Danes from 1016 to 1042, but by 1066 it possessed an increasingly sophisticated royal administration, and produced works of literature and art that came close to matching its longer-established European rivals, such as France. In Scotland, Wales, and Ireland, royal rule was much less secure, with government still more closely resembling that of migration-age chieftainships.

The British Isles were about to be changed forever. England and Wales sooner, Scotland and Ireland later, but all profoundly, would be shaped by the Norman invasion of 1066.

End of an era
The Bayeux Tapestry commemorates the end of Anglo-Saxon England in 1066. It also marks the moment when the Normans, themselves descended from the Vikings, became the last successful invaders of England.

BRITONS AND INVADERS
800,000 BCE–1066 CE

800,000–54 BCE	53 BCE–250 CE	251–448

800,000–54 BCE

3000 BCE
First stage of Stonehenge is built.

2400 BCE
Beaker-style pottery appears in Britain, a style possibly imported from Iberia.

≪ Paleolithic stone tool

800,000 BCE
Flint tools in Suffolk are the first signs of human habitation in Britain.

40,000 BCE
Modern humans arrive in Britain across a land bridge from Europe.

2100 BCE
Knowledge of bronze-working arrives in Britain.

700 BCE
Iron begins to come into regular use in Britain.

4000 BCE
Neolithic Age begins in Britain as agriculture arrives from Europe.

3800 BCE
Earliest megalithic monuments are built; also earthwork enclosures and causeways.

3100 BCE
The first henge monuments are built.

3000–2500 BCE
Stone village at Skara Brae in the Orkneys, Scotland, is built.

⌃ The Battersea shield

400 BCE
"Developed" hill-forts appear, with more complex defenses.

55 AND 54 BCE
Roman general Julius Caesar mounts two invasions of Britain.

≫ Stone house at Skara Brae

53 BCE–250 CE

139–143
Frontier of Roman Britain moves north to new line of Antonine Wall from Firth of Forth to the Clyde.

C.160
Pull-back from Antonine Wall to Hadrian's Wall begins.

⌃ Roman Emperor Claudius conquering Britannia

10–40 CE
Cunobelinus, king of the Catuvellauni, builds a powerful kingdom in southern England.

43
Emperor Claudius dispatches invasion force to Britain under Aulus Plautius.

51
Caratacus in captivity after Queen Cartimandua gives him to the Romans.

60–61
Boudicca leads revolt of the Iceni; Londinium (London), Verulamium (St. Albans), and Camulodunum (Colchester) burned before the uprising is suppressed.

74–78
Roman conquest of most of Wales carried out by Julius Frontinus.

78–83
Campaigns of Agricola in Scotland end with defeat of Caledonians at Mons Graupius.

⌃ Roman helmet

208–211
Campaigns of Septimius Severus in Scotland; on his death, new emperor Caracalla terminates the war.

213
Roman province of Britannia becomes Britannia Superior and Britannia Inferior.

90
Roman withdrawal from most of north and eastern Scotland.

122–123
Construction begins on Hadrian's Wall after visit by Emperor Hadrian to Britain.

≫ The Manse stone

251–448

396
Roman general Stilicho visits Britain to restore order.

≪ Mildenhall treasure

260–274
Britain forms part of the Gallic empire of Postumus and his successors.

260–330
Building of the Saxon Shore forts (coastal defensive line between Solent and Wash).

286
Revolt of Carausius, who declares independent British empire.

C.312
Roman provinces divided into two again, so Britannia now has four provinces.

367
The "Great Barbarian Conspiracy": Picts, Scots, and Saxons attack Britain.

383
Revolt of Magnus Maximus; many British legions accompany him to Gaul.

407
Constantine III chosen as emperor by the British army: he removes most of the troops to Gaul.

410
British leaders rise up and expel remaining Roman officials from the towns.

432
St. Patrick arrives in Ireland to begin his mission there.

⌃ Roman agriculture

446
"Groan of the Britons" plea by British notable to Roman commander Aetius, asking for his help against barbarian raiders.

"I had horses, **men, arms, and wealth**… If you wish to command everyone, does it really follow that everyone should **accept your slavery**?"

CARATACUS, BRITISH CHIEFTAIN, AT THE TRIBUNAL OF CLAUDIUS IN ROME

449–792	793–990	991–1066

449
Traditional date for arrival of Hengist and Horsa, legendary first Saxon rulers of Kent.

477–491
Aelle is King of Sussex: the first of the Bretwaldas.

> Anglo-Saxon claw beaker

793
First Viking raid in British Isles on monastery of Lindisfarne.

794
Vikings raid Iona, first recorded attack in Scotland.

878
Alfred flees into Somerset marshes but then wins Battle of Edington against Vikings.

892–896
Alfred the Great fights off a new Viking invasion, aided by network of burhs and reformed army.

991
Battle of Maldon; new force of Vikings defeats and kills the ealdorman of Essex; invaders paid 10,000 pounds of danegeld to withdraw.

> Wulfstan psalter

633
Battle of Hatfield: Edwin of Northumbria killed by British King Cadwallon of Gwynedd.

664
Synod of Whitby convenes to settle differences between Celtic and Roman Christian traditions.

« Saint Bede

909
Edward the Elder of Wessex beats Vikings at Tettenhall, beginning reconquest of the Five Boroughs.

917
Vikings retake Dublin (having lost it in 903).

1012
King Aethelred forced to pay a danegeld of 48,000 pounds of silver.

1013
Aethelred flees to Normandy; his son Edmund Ironside continues the anti-Danish resistance.

1035
Death of Cnut; succeeded by his son Harold Harefoot.

1040
Duncan I deposed by Macbeth, the mormaer of Moray.

C. 520
Battle of Mount Badon. British check Saxon advance in the west (victory ascribed to "King Arthur").

547
Foundation of Kingdom of Bernicia by Ida.

669
Theodore of Tarsus becomes Archbishop of Canterbury and begins reform of English Church.

694
Ine of Wessex gives the kingdom its first law code.

> Statue of King Alfred

937
Battle of Brunanburh: alliance of Constantine II of Scotland, Vikings, and Strathclyde Britons defeated by Athelstan of Wessex.

939
Death of Athelstan leads to resurgence of the Viking kingdom of York.

1042
On death of Harthacnut, the Anglo-Saxon dynasty is restored as Edward the Confessor becomes King.

1053
Harold Godwinson becomes Earl of Wessex.

« Dumbarton Castle

577
Battle of Dyrham: Saxon victory opens up southwest to invaders.

597
Mission of St. Augustine arrives in England and converts Aethelbert of Kent.

≫ Emly reliquary

716
Aethelbald becomes King of Mercia (to 765), beginning period of Mercian supremacy.

757–796
Offa becomes King of Mercia: he dominates the other Anglo-Saxon kingdoms.

795
Viking Age in Ireland begins with an attack on the monastery of Rechru.

841
Vikings establish a naval base at Dublin (the origin of the city).

850
Viking army overwinters in England for first time (on Thanet).

1014
Cnut of Denmark becomes king in the Danelaw portion of England.

1014
At the Battle of Clontarf, the army of Brian Boru and Máel Sechnaill defeats the Dublin Vikings and their allies.

1065
Revolt of the northern earls; Harold's brother Tostig is replaced as Earl of Northumbria.

1066
Edward the Confessor dies and is replaced as king by Harold.

865
The Great Viking Army arrives in England under Ivar the Boneless, Halfdan, and Ubba.

869
Vikings conquer East Anglia.

874
Vikings put an end to Mercian independence.

⌃ Anglo-Saxon reliquary

954
Death of Eric Bloodaxe leads to final conquest of York by the kingdom of Wessex.

973
Edgar of Wessex receives submission of six kings, symbolizing his dominion over Britain.

1016
Death of Aethelred. Cnut is acknowledged as King of all England.

1023
Gruffydd ap Llywelyn becomes King of Gwynedd (he annexes Deheubarth in 1039).

> King Edward the Confessor with Harold

« BEFORE

From around 1 million years ago, the Earth experienced extreme cooling. Ice caps advanced to and from the poles in periods known as glacials. This was the Ice Age.

GLACIALS AND INTERGLACIALS

Britain's last three **glacial periods** (the Anglian, Wolstonian, and Devensian) were divided by two warmer interglacial periods (the Hoxnian and Ipswichian). The **last ice sheet** retreated around 10,000 BCE, but today is probably an interglacial (the Flandrian), and glaciers may one day return.

Neanderthal skull
Neanderthals had protruding brow ridges, big teeth, and wide nasal cavities, which may have helped warm the air when breathing.

During the glacial periods of the Ice Age, when much of the Earth's water was locked up in polar ice and average sea levels fell, Britain was connected to the main European landmass and was not a separate island. It is not clear precisely when humans first took advantage of this land bridge and arrived in Britain, but they certainly did so before the Anglian glaciation, which began around 470,000 years ago. Flint tools found at Happisburgh, Norfolk, may date from around 900,000 to 800,000 years ago, and throughout the rest of southern England there is a scattering of other sites where flint hand-axes have been unearthed.

The largest such site is Boxgrove, in West Sussex, dating from around 500,000 years ago, where evidence of both tool-making and the butchering of animals such as deer, bison, and rhinoceroses has been found. The inhabitants of Boxgrove belonged to a hominin (humanlike species) group known as *Homo heidelbergensis*. They lived as hunters and scavengers in small groups across the southern part of England.

Around 470,000 years ago, one of the coldest phases of the Ice Age began—the Anglian glacial. The ice sheets advanced as far south as Bristol, the Cotswolds, and the Thames Valley. As far as is known, Britain was uninhabited at this time. Only in the succeeding Hoxnian interglacial (425,000 to 360,000 years ago) did humans return to Britain.

Tools and hand-axes

Finds from the Hoxnian are far more plentiful than those in the pre-Anglian period, and belong to two different groups, distinguished by the types of tools they made. The Clactonian culture is characterized by flint flake tools, made by striking a core of flint with a hammer stone. The people of the Acheulian culture made hand-axes of many shapes and sizes, as well as stone scrapers and knives. The best-known Clactonian site is at Swanscombe, Kent, where the inhabitants hunted elephants, deer, horses, and rhinoceroses. At Hoxne, in Suffolk, a quantity of Acheulian

hand-axes made of black flint has been excavated. Evidence of deforestation may indicate early peoples deliberately burned off forest to encourage the growth of scrub, which would be an attractive habitat for the animals they wished to hunt.

Neanderthals in Britain

Relatively few sites of the Wolstonian glacial era (360,000 to 130,000 years ago) are known, but one of them, dating from around 200,000 years ago,

> **PALEOLITHIC** The name given to the Old Stone Age period, or the first period of tool making, lasting from before 1 million years ago to about 10,000 years ago. It covers about 99 percent of the time that humans have used technology.

is at Pontnewydd Cave, in Flintshire. It contained bones of an early form of a new species, known as Neanderthal, or *Homo sapiens neanderthalensis*. The

Britain's First People

Humanlike species arrived on the British Isles around 800,000 BCE, but periods of abandonment followed as ice alternately advanced and retreated across the landscape of the islands. Modern humans finally colonized Britain about 14,000 years ago.

Ice Age landscape
The maximum glacial advance covered Britain as far south as the River Thames. Even to the south of this, a tundra-like landscape prevailed in which only small groups of hunters would have been able to survive the harsh living conditions.

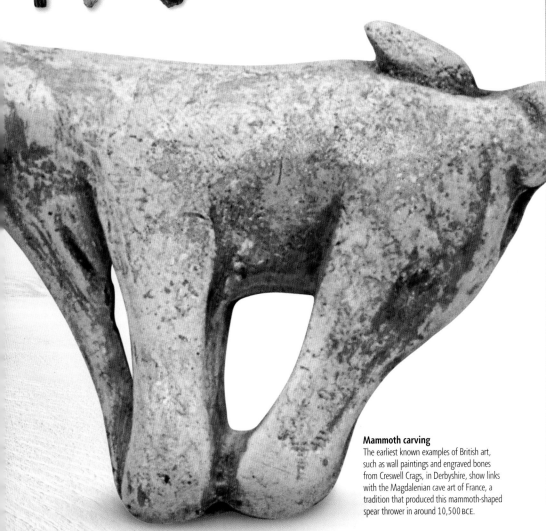

Neanderthals were thicker set and more heavily built than contemporary humans, with prominent brow ridges and an average brain size larger than their modern counterparts. They were also capable of some cultural sophistication. For example, in the Middle East, Neanderthal burials have been found where the bodies were deposited with grave goods and daubed with red ocher, indicating a sense of care for their dead.

Neanderthals replaced

Warmer temperatures saw rising sea levels cut off the land bridge with continental Europe during the Ipswichian interglacial, from 130,000 to 115,000 BCE. Britain was

Hand-axes and flint tools
For thousands of years, hand-axes were the main tool used by humans. Attaching a stone head to a shaft was a later development.

recolonized once more by Neanderthals during the early Devensian glacial period. Their tools included flint points that may have been used on spearheads to hunt the plentiful game—including mammoth—which roamed southern England at the time.

99 The percentage of time during the total period of human habitation in the British Isles in which nomadic hunting and gathering, rather than agriculture in fixed settlements, was the main means of subsistence.

The Neanderthals lived as hunter-gatherers in small groups, which probably ranged over large territories. However, no evidence has been found of them living in the north or west of Britain, and the earliest sign of any human settlement in Ireland is as late as 10,500 BCE, a long time after the Neanderthals had been supplanted by *Homo sapiens sapiens*, the first modern subspecies of human.

AFTER ≫

After the arrival of modern humans, the climate cooled and the ice sheets advanced southward and covered much of Britain, forcing people to leave the region and leaving the island uninhabited.

MODERN HUMANS ARRIVE

Modern humans arrived in Britain a little after 40,000 BCE, having **crossed the land bridge** with Europe. Only 20 or so sites of this mid-Devensian era are known; many seem to have been temporary camps or shelters for bands of hunters. They show some **technological advances**, with hand-axes being replaced by more specialized tools, such as "leaf-point" blades and scrapers. One of the most **spectacular sites**—dating from around 31,000 BCE—is the "Red Lady of Paviland" burial in Goat's Cave, on the Gower Peninsula, near Swansea. The deceased, who was in fact a man, was 5 ft 9 in (1.75 m) tall, his bones sprinkled with red ocher and set in a **shallow grave**, with around 50 mammoth ivory rods, ivory bracelets, and perforated seashells.

ENDINGS AND BEGINNINGS

Around 25,000 BCE, the **climate cooled** dramatically once more and the ice sheets advanced as far south as the Bristol Channel. It appears that Britain became **uninhabited** during this Late Devensian Discontinuity, which lasted some 10,000 years. Around 15,000 BCE, the climate **warmed again** and the ice sheets began to melt; **sea levels rose** and the reshaping of the coastlines of northwestern Europe to something like their modern appearance began with the creation of the **North Sea**. About 13,000 BCE, groups of mammoth-hunters returned, followed 1,000 years later by neolithic elk- and deer-hunters, whose DNA indicates they may have originated in northern France or Spain. After a false start, the **continuous occupation of Britain** began **16–17 ≫**

NEOLITHIC CAUSEWAY, WILTSHIRE

Mammoth carving
The earliest known examples of British art, such as wall paintings and engraved bones from Creswell Crags, in Derbyshire, show links with the Magdalenian cave art of France, a tradition that produced this mammoth-shaped spear thrower in around 10,500 BCE.

Stone Age Britain

The arrival of agriculture allowed communities to live a more settled life. Permanent villages were established and great stone monuments, or megaliths, were erected as tombs or for other complex ritual purposes. By the end of the Neolithic Age, in around 2400 BCE, parts of Britain were densely inhabited by a farming folk whose chieftains were able to accumulate great material wealth.

Agriculture arrived in Britain around 4000 BCE, marking the start of the Neolithic Age, or the New Stone Age. Knowledge of agricultural techniques seems to have been acquired from groups of people arriving from continental Europe. Settlements from as far back as the early 4th millennium BCE show signs of the cultivation of emmer and einkorn, which are early forms of wheat, as well as some barley. They also show the bones of domesticated animals such as cattle, pigs, and sheep, providing clear evidence that an agricultural way of life was being established at this time.

Early farming sites were principally single, isolated farmsteads, although larger, timber-framed longhouses up to 88 ft (27 m) in length have been found.

BEFORE

The resettlement of Britain around 13,000 BCE, proceeded from south to north, followed by almost 10,000 years of gradual cultural development before agriculture started.

FROM ART TO BOATS
The first **evidence of art** in Britain, such as a rib bone inscribed with a horse, found in Robin Hood's Cave, in Derbyshire, comes from the Creswellian culture around 12,000 BCE. With warmer temperatures after 10,000 BCE, new **hunting techniques** developed and bows and arrows became widespread. At Star Carr, Yorkshire, more than 200 barbed antler points were found, as was a wooden paddle, indicating the **use of boats**.

SETTLEMENT IN IRELAND
Ireland was **first settled** around 7000 BCE, as is indicated by Mesolithic tool finds in the valley of the Bann River. The land passage between Britain and continental Europe had finally been flooded by this time, **transforming Britain into an island**.

PALEOLITHIC STONE TOOL

In some of these, carbonized grains have been unearthed. Although evidence of plowing (with a simple ard or scratch plow) has been found near Avebury, Wiltshire, in southern England, from around 3900 BCE, early farmers at this time probably still supplemented their diet from hunting and gathering. Also, rather than go to the extent of actually clearing large areas of woodlands for cultivation, they may have used glades, or areas already thinned out by cattle grazing, for planting crops.

Stone continued to be the most sought-after material for making tools, and flint mines from the period have been found at Cissbury, West Sussex, from around 4000 BCE. Here, shafts as deep as 49 ft (15 m) were sunk in the search for the best seams of flint, largely using antler picks and ox-bone shovels.

Large-scale monuments
As society became more settled, Neolithic people began large-scale constructions, which required enormous effort in moving huge quantities of earth and clearing extensive woodlands. Among the earliest of the monuments constructed, around 3800 BCE, are large earthwork enclosures (often called "causewayed camps"). More than 100 of these enclosures have been identified and they may have been used as sites for festivals or religious ceremonies. At Carn Brea, Cornwall, a huge stone wall 6 ft 6 in (2 m) high erected about 3700 BCE enclosed an area exceeding 2½ acres (1 hectare) in size may have housed as many as 200 people living inside. Many of the causewayed camps remained in use for centuries—the later Iron Age hillfort at Maiden Castle, Dorset, was built on top of a 4th-millennium BCE camp.

Neolithic people erected the first stone monuments for the dead at around the same time. At first, these were simple settings of stone, but later more complex portal dolmens, or single-chamber megalithic tombs, were built using several stones to form a passage. By around 3500 BCE, a wide variety of burial monuments were in use, including simple round barrows (or earth mounds), long barrows (some of which had chambers inside and could measure up to 328 ft/100 m in length, as at West Kennet, Wiltshire), and passage graves (in which an internal stone chamber in the mound was connected by a passage to the outside). The latter type was particularly prevalent in Ireland, where the covering circular mounds were up to 280 ft (85 m) in diameter.

By about 3400 BCE, even more elaborate monuments, known as long mounds and cursuses (long enclosures created by boundary ditches) were being built. The cursus that was built at Dorchester-on-Thames, Oxfordshire, is 1 mile (1.6 km) long. The society that produced these monuments was prosperous, but life was hard; diseases were rife, with tooth decay and arthritis being particularly widespread, and average age at death

Neolithic pottery
Neolithic cultures are often named after the principal types of pottery found in graves or settlements, but this does not mean that the users of different sorts of pottery belonged to different ethnic groups.

was about 30 years. The average height (for males, about 5 ft 3 in–5 ft 11 in/1.6 m–1.8 m) was probably only a little shorter than that of today's adults. There is evidence of early conflict; a few graves contain burials of people who had clearly been killed by arrows, while at Crickley Hill, in Gloucestershire, hundreds of flint arrowheads seem to indicate that the camp was stormed by a hostile force and was then burned. Beside the Thames River at Chelsea, a number of wooden clubs have been found dating to around 3500 BCE, which were also probably weapons for use in battle. The total population of the British Isles

around 3000 BCE may have been as high as 200,000, which is dense enough to mean that competition over scarce resources might often turn violent and descend into warfare.

Complex means of exchange were developed to keep communities supplied with goods that they could not produce themselves. Evidence for this includes wooden trackways that have been found in marshy areas; the "Sweet Track" in Somerset crosses 1¼ miles (2 km) of marshes and dates from around 3800 BCE. Across these wooden

Newgrange passage tomb
The passage tomb at Newgrange, in Meath, Ireland, was built around 3200 BCE. Its inner chamber was illuminated by light from the rising sun during the winter solstice. Several stones were decorated with spirals.

The mid-3rd millennium BCE saw the beginning of profound changes in Britain with the arrival of new types of pottery, indicating strong cultural ties with Europe.

THE BEAKER PEOPLE

From around 2400 BCE, a **new type of pottery vessel** appeared in Britain. They were known as Bell Beakers from their characteristic bulb-shaped bowl and upward curve. In Ireland, these are found in the earliest copper mines and are associated with a type of wedge-shaped tomb. In Britain, they were much more widespread, especially in coastal areas. The dispersion of Beakers across the Atlantic coast of Europe suggests **an Iberian origin**. Beaker burials were often inhumations (as opposed to cremations), one of the most lavish being the "Amesbury Archer" at Stonehenge, who died around 2300 BCE. His grave goods included Beakers and copper knives, while analysis of his teeth revealed that he had grown up in Alpine Europe, possibly Switzerland.

RELIGION

Although gold sun disks of the type common in central Europe have not been found in Britain, the consistently circular shape of the great stone monuments of the later 3rd millennium BCE indicates an **interest in the sun**, with the circular shape possibly symbolizing the sun's course through the sky. Older monuments, such as Avebury and Stonehenge, were embellished by the people of the Beaker Culture; **Stonehenge was completely remodeled** with the erection of massive trilithons (two upright stones with one laid across on top).

Skara Brae
The Neolithic village at Skara Brae, on Orkney's mainland, was built to a surprisingly uniform pattern. Each of the dozen or so houses had a central hearth, stone beds on each side of the entrance, and stone boxes on the floor, possibly used to contain water.

trackways, goods such as grindstones, flint axes, and fine pottery (often with very distant origins) would have traveled; axes from as far away as Scandinavia and the Italian Alps have been found.

Radical changes
Around 3200 BCE society seems to have undergone radical changes. The older style of burial monuments fell out of favor and many of the long barrows and passage graves were blocked up. Around 3000 BCE a distinctive type of pottery known as Grooved Ware emerged. Grooved Ware was characterized by pots with incised spirals, lozenges, and wavy lines. Originating in northern Britain, the best preserved early settlement of the culture that developed this type of pottery is found at Skara Brae, in the Orkneys, Scotland. Here, a partly underground village of about a dozen houses was built between 3000 and 2500 BCE. Similar clustered villages made of wood have been found as far south as Wiltshire.

18 MILLION The estimated man-hours **needed to construct the Neolithic mound at Silbury Hill, Wiltshire.**

Other new types of monuments begin to appear at this time, including circles of wooden posts, such as at Seahenge, Norfolk, and large enclosures, such as the first stage of Stonehenge, in Wiltshire, built around 2950 BCE. Circular enclosures bordered by a ditched bank (the classic henge monuments) were also first built, ranging in size up to the colossal example at Avebury, Wiltshire, which has a diameter of 1,148 ft (350 m). Passage graves seem to have spread from Ireland to parts of Britain, such as north Wales. In a localized variant of this in the Orkneys, such as at Maes Howe, built in about 2750 BCE, the mound of the passage grave was actually built within the stones of an earlier henge monument. The exact purpose of the larger monuments is still unclear, but they may have had an astrological significance, with stones being lined up in the direction of the sun at key moments, such as the summer and winter solstices.

Central authority
The resources required to build the larger henge enclosures were prodigious; the construction of a large timber building within the South Circle, at Durrington Walls, near Stonehenge, required the clearing of 8.6 acres (3.5 hectares) of woodland. This implies that there were chieftains, or some other local form of powerful central authority, to command and coordinate the local population in the planning and erection of such extravagant monuments. Grave goods, which become increasingly elaborate after this period, with the inclusion of lavish jewelry in many burials, go some way in supporting this idea. It all adds up to a picture of Britain and Ireland in 2500 BCE, at the end of the Neolithic Age, in which the landscape was far more marked and shaped by human endeavors than it had been at its start. Where once there had been small groups of hunter-gatherers, now there were clustered villages of stone dwellings, extensive forest clearances, plowed fields, and elaborate monuments of banked earth and stone, all overseen by powerful political structures.

Henge monument, Avebury
Like many British Neolithic monuments, Avebury was constructed in stages: the North and South Circles were built around 2800 BCE, the Outer Circle around 2600 BCE, and the two avenues were built about 200 years later.

Stonehenge
The famous monument at Stonehenge is part of a larger sacred
landscape which developed from around 4000 BCE and includes
hundreds of burial mounds. The site that is seen today was
built from around 2150 BCE using at least 85 stones from the
Preseli Hills in Wales, more than 135 miles (217 km) away.
Other stones came from the Marlborough Downs nearby.

Iron Age Britain

The Iron Age, which began around 800 BCE, witnessed a gradual political consolidation. The warrior elites dominated the countryside from their hillfort strongholds. They also maintained strong links with their European counterparts, which ultimately proved to be their undoing.

As the Iron Age began in Britain, many areas saw a rise in the number of defended enclosures. The population was increasing and early chiefdoms were coalescing into larger political units. As this process continued, hillforts began to appear, particularly across southern, central, and western England, as well as in north Wales and the Welsh borders. Often with simple ramparts reinforced with timber and a single line of defenses, hillforts such as Danebury, Hampshire, and Maiden Castle, Dorset, probably acted as the residences of local kings or chieftains. From around

650 BCE to 300 BCE, more than 3,000 hillforts were built. The society that was shaped by these new centers of population has conventionally been termed "Celtic." The term was first used by Greek writers, such as Herodotus, in the 6th century BCE to describe the barbarian groups living on the fringes of the Greek world. Certainly, people of the cultures later termed by archaeologists as La Tène and Hallstatt—who were Celtic speakers—spread from a central European homeland into France, the middle Danube, and Asia Minor. They even threatened to capture Rome in 390 BCE. Yet, "Celt" was not a term that the people of Britain used to describe themselves; nor did the Romans who encountered them in the 1st century BCE refer to them as Celts. The traditional theory that large-scale migration or invasion from Europe brought a Celtic hillfort society into Britain has been modified in favor of the view that it was a process of assimilation, rather than conquest, which led

Bronze torc
Torcs (neck rings) were worn largely by men and were usually meant for ceremonial use. While the rich wore gold torcs, poorer men had to make do with bronze ones.

7 The area in square miles (19 square kilometers) enclosed behind the defensive earthworks of the Iron Age settlement at Colchester.

the elites of Iron Age Britain to adopt many of the same political and cultural practices that were found in mainland Europe.

Hillforts and fields

From around 400 BCE, many of the earlier Iron Age hillforts were abandoned, but others were rebuilt and developed in more sophisticated fashion. These more complex structures tended to exploit natural features to enhance their defenses, and they often had more substantial ramparts. Developed

The Battersea Shield

This 1st-century CE bronze shield may have been deposited in the Thames River as a ritual offering. It is decorated with spirals in the La Tène style and is inlaid with red glass, which may have been imported from Italy.

« BEFORE

Tin mining in Cornwall contributed to the introduction of bronze—an alloy of tin and copper—to Britain around 2200 BCE, and ironworking arrived from Europe in 1000 BCE.

ARRIVAL OF IRONWORKING

Funeral monuments became less grand, with barrows beginning to be replaced from 1500 BCE by cemeteries containing cremations, often in urns. Society became **more stratified**, with an increase in rich personal ornaments such as arm-rings and spiral torcs of gold, together with new weapons, such as swords and shields, around 1300 BCE. **Trade between Britain and Europe** grew stronger. Around 1000 BCE **knowledge of ironworking** also crossed over from Europe, but the British Isles did not really use iron extensively until 800 BCE.

hillforts could be very large, covering areas of up to 25 acres (10 hectares). Evidence of storage pits and dwellings at some, including Danebury, suggests that they were permanently occupied and not just used as refuges in times of danger. The huge resources necessary to build and maintain such structures indicate that in this phase of the Iron Age, kings and chieftains exercised great power, although the presence of a large number of hillforts points to the territories that they ruled over being quite small. Not everyone lived in hillforts, though, and other smaller enclosures and open settlements have been found in their vicinity. In eastern England and East Anglia very few hillforts have been identified, and on the Atlantic fringes of Britain, fortified

Horned helmet
This bronze helmet found in the Thames River near Waterloo Bridge dates from the late 1st century BCE. It may well have been made specifically as a votive object, rather than for wearing on the battlefield.

to the tin required for making bronze, aided this spread, and iron ax-heads, spears, and tools become more common in archaeological finds dating from around 700 BCE onward.

The appearance of iron weapons and the number of hillforts has been taken by archaeologists to mean that Iron Age Britain was dominated by the warrior elite, who engaged in frequent minor warfare and raiding. Scattered finds of weapons, and evidence of burning or

Shield, with stylized birds in the central roundel, showed a love of curves and flowing lines, which were essential features of Celtic art of this time.

Trade and grave goods

The Iron Age elites also took advantage of increasing trade connections with continental Europe, particularly with regard to luxury goods, which included amber, glass, and coral. The main avenues of trade were across the English Channel to northern Europe and along the Atlantic coastlines as far as Iberia. It is also from this time that the first written accounts of Britain appear, including those by the Greek adventurer, Pytheas of Massilia (Marseilles). He visited the islands in around 320 BCE and called them Prettania, a name which, modified into Britannia and then Britain, has survived to this day.

Iron Age burials were often surprisingly modest; from around 800 BCE barrows went out of fashion. In some areas, such as Yorkshire, the corpse was placed with the body flexed (the legs bent) and with comparatively few grave goods. Some richer graves included iron swords and spears for the men and jewelry for the women, while a few spectacular graves of the 3rd century BCE contained the remains of chariots. Elsewhere, the normal mode of disposal was excarnation (either leaving the body to be scavenged by wild animals or removing the flesh before burial). By around 200 BCE, the

AFTER

As the 2nd century BCE progressed, centers even larger than hillforts began to be built, mirroring developments in Europe. At the same time, international trade in Britain also increased.

THE DEVELOPMENT OF OPPIDA
Larger centers, called *oppida*, from the Latin word for "town," were defended by complex earthworks. Some had their own mints for the production of coins. Their **permanent populations**, however, may not have been large and they occupied a middle ground between hillforts and true towns. The largest *oppida* at Colchester was a royal center and would later become an important town in the Roman province **28–29 ≫**.

INTERNATIONAL TRADE
After a hiatus in trade with Europe between 300 BCE and 150 BCE, **new ports were built** in the south of England, including Hengistbury Head and Poole Harbour in Dorset. **Imported goods** including Mediterranean glass, Italian wine, and bronze vessels came through them.

BRONZE
DAGGER
SHEATH

population of Britain had probably reached around 2 million, with the landscape studded with larger settlements, including hillforts that might contain a population of 200 or more. Britain's comparative political isolation would soon, however, come to an end, as its growing wealth and overseas trade contacts made it an attractive asset to a potential invader.

> ## "The island is **thickly populated** and it is extremely cold."

DIODORUS SICULUS, *LIBRARY OF WORLD HISTORY*, 1ST CENTURY BCE

homesteads rather than hillforts made up the main defensive structures.

The division of the land into fields continued through this period and, although there were variations in different parts of Britain, most people derived their sustenance from barley, spelt, or emmer wheat, with cattle providing the bulk of the meat that was consumed. Surprisingly, even in river and coastal areas, fish played a comparatively small role in the British Iron Age diet.

The spread of ironworking

Although the techniques of ironworking had reached Britain by about 1000 BCE, it was only around 800 BCE that the metal really came to be more widely used. The greater availability of iron ore compared

destruction at sites such as Danebury, together with the later evidence of writers at the time of the Roman invasions of Britain in the 1st century BCE and 1st century CE, tend to confirm this impression. Finds of large cauldrons and cauldron chains at hillfort sites are also suggestive of a society that placed value on feasting, possibly for ritualistic reasons, but also to establish the primacy of the king or chieftain, the feast-giver. In their weaponry, too, the Iron Age warriors showed their love of display. Swords of the 3rd century BCE (the weapon had fallen out of fashion in the preceding centuries) showed lavish adornment and intricate curvilinear designs. Much of the decoration shows evidence of the influence of the La Tène cultures of northern Europe. These and the intricate ornamentation on finds, such as the Battersea Shield and the Witham

Iron Age broch

From the 6th century BCE, large roundhouse towers known as brochs began to appear in the Scottish Isles. They were part home and part fort. This one at Mousa in the Shetlands is more than 66 ft (20 m) high.

Caesar's Invasion

In 55 and 54 BCE Julius Caesar mounted two expeditions against Britain. Although he met with only limited success and did not establish a permanent Roman presence on the British Isles, he did establish treaty relations with many British tribes and drew Britain into the orbit of Roman political ambitions.

An anti-Roman revolt by the Veneti of Armorica (in modern Brittany) in 56 BCE, which probably received some support from Britain, led Julius Caesar to turn his attention northward. To enter Britain, an island that lay impossibly far off, beyond "the bounds of ocean," would have brought him immense prestige. However, political difficulties delayed his invasion plans for a year. Finally, in 55 BCE, Caesar prepared to cross the Channel with a small expeditionary force. His principal opponent was to be Cassivellaunus, who was probably king of the Catuvellauni, a tribe that had been expanding from its base

Roman sword
Roman soldiers were exceptionally able infantry fighters. They used the gladius (a short sword), to thrust upward at close quarters and inflict terrible wounds on their enemies.

at Wheathampstead in Hertfordshire to dominate much of southern England.

Preparation
Caesar received envoys from a number of other British tribes who were eager to show their submission and thus avoid having their lands invaded. He also despatched a small reconnaissance force under the tribune (a senior military officer), Volusenus, to scout out suitable landing beaches. In addition, he sent out a diplomatic mission under the Gallic chieftain Commius to further rally pro-Roman opinion. Unfortunately, though, both failed—Volusenus was unable to locate a sheltered harbor for the Roman fleet and Commius was promptly arrested. On August 26, Caesar set sail with

a force composed of two legions—the Seventh and Tenth. The cliffs and beaches around Dover were occupied by British defenders and the Roman ships were forced to run aground somewhere near Deal in Kent. The legionaries had to disembark in relatively deep waters under a constant hail of missiles. Although the legions managed to establish a beachhead, disaster struck four days later when a severe storm scattered the ships that had been bringing more than 500 cavalry as reinforcements, and also badly damaged many of the landing craft.

Deprived of cavalry support, Caesar was vulnerable, and after the Seventh Legion was severely mauled in an ambush, he chose to declare the expedition a success and returned to Gaul accompanied by a number of British hostages.

A new expedition
Preparations were soon underway for a new expedition. Caesar had learned lessons from the comparative failure of his first incursion into Britain. This time he decided to bring five legions—amounting to more than 30,000 men—and some 2,000 cavalry. The latter were a critical component in countering the battle tactics of the Britons who, unlike their counterparts in mainland Europe, still used chariots in battle to harass infantry units, which lacked mounted support.

On July 6, 54 BCE, Caesar set off for Britain once more. His flotilla of 800 ships landed near Deal, this time unopposed, apparently because the Britons were so intimidated by the size of the force that they chose not to resist it. Once more, however, the Roman fleet was battered by a

> | **800** The approximate number of boats in the fleet that carried the invading Roman army to Britain in 54 BCE. Of these, 28 were warships and most of the rest were troop transports.

serious storm and the 10 days delay in building a rampart extensive enough to allow the remnants of their naval force to be beached, emboldened the Britons. They were then able to offer a more effective defense under the leadership of Cassivellaunus.

The Romans won a series of engagements. They captured a hillfort at Bigbury near Canterbury, overcame an attempt at entrapping a Roman foraging force, and then pushed on toward the Thames. Diplomatic pressure also began to tell now, as Caesar had with him one of Cassivellaunus's arch-enemies, Mandubracius of the Trinovantes. Some British chieftains who were afraid that Cassivellaunus might use success against Caesar to increase his own power also began to waver in their support for the campaign against the Romans. The capture of Cassivellaunus's chief stronghold—probably the *oppidum* at Wheathampstead—led to a desperate attempt to stir the Kentish tribes into a final uprising against Caesar. It was to no avail and Cassivellaunus sued for

Caesar's coin
Julius Caesar is shown on this gold aureus wearing the laurel wreath of a victorious general. The coin commemorates his conquest of Gaul.

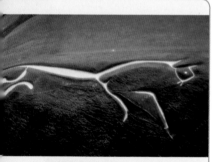

UFFINGTON WHITE HORSE

The inhabitants of southern Britain had long-standing relations with the tribes across the Channel. Through them, they would have heard of the northward progress of the Roman army.

PRE-ROMAN BRITAIN
The landscape of Iron and Bronze Age Britain was littered with sites of ritual importance, which the Romans would encounter after their invasion. The White Horse at Uffington, in Oxfordshire, is one such site. It may be 3,000 years old and have been part of a ceremonial complex.

CONQUERING GAUL
Julius Caesar conquered much of Gaul (modern France) between 58 and 52 BCE. He was able to derive political advantage from **British exiles who sought his protection**, such as Mandubracius, of the Trinovantes tribe, who was sent to him on his second invasion of Britain.

> "… Britons **dye themselves** with woad … and as a result their **appearance in battle** is all the **more daunting**."
>
> JULIUS CAESAR, *THE GALLIC WARS*, C. 47 BCE

Britain's invader
Julius Caesar had far less success as a politician than as a military commander. In this sculpture, which stands in Rome, he is making a gesture of peace.

peace. Caesar readily accepted, as he had already decided not to overwinter in Britain, fearing that a revolt might break out in Gaul during his absence. He accepted British hostages and fixed a tribute to be paid by Cassivellaunus

at least twice, in 34 BCE and 26 BCE, but suspected revolts elsewhere in the Empire caused him to call off the expeditions both times. Instead, the Romans, who in any case regarded the "whole of the island

> "**Leap**, fellow soldiers, **unless you** wish to **betray your eagle** to the enemy."

JULIUS CAESAR, *THE GALLIC WARS*, C. 47 BCE

before returning across the Channel some time in the middle of September. The Trinovantes became, in effect, a client-kingdom of Rome. In addition, Cassivellaunus was forbidden to interfere in their territory. Whatever his intentions regarding a third and more decisive invasion of Britain might have been, Julius Caesar was distracted from taking any action until 51 BCE by a major uprising in Gaul and thereafter by his involvement in the Roman civil wars, which led to his appointment as Dictator in Rome in 47 BCE.

Attempts by Augustus

Caesar's adoptive son and successor, Augustus, who also became the first Roman emperor, made plans to invade Britain

as Roman property" (according to the historian Strabo), supported client-kings, such as Tincommius and Verica, who ruled over a Belgic kingdom in southern England, against the growing power of the Catuvellauni, who overran the Trinovantian capital of Camulodunum (Colchester) around 9 CE. The Romans maintained their influence in Britain by involving themselves in its politics.

AFTER

Julius Caesar was assassinated in 44 BCE and the conquest of Britain was not an immediate priority for his successor Augustus.

INVASION BY CLAUDIUS
It was nearly 100 years after Caesar's first invasion that **Britain became a Roman province 28–29 ≫**. There was an abortive expedition in 40 CE under Caligula, but Britain was **finally invaded on the orders of the Emperor Claudius** in 43 CE. Thereafter, it remained under Roman control for almost four centuries until 410 CE, when the Empire was nearing its final collapse in the west **34–35 ≫**. **Hadrian visited Britain** in 121 CE and ordered a wall to be built to protect the northern limit of the Empire **26–27 ≫**.

EMPEROR HADRIAN

Conquest and Resistance

The Romans began their conquest of Britain in 43 CE. After initial success they were dogged by bitter resistance in Wales and the north and by revolts in the south. Forty years after the landing, however, their armies stood on the borders of the Scottish Highlands, the furthest north that they would reach.

Legionnaire's backpack
Each Roman legionnaire had to carry entrenching tools in his backpack to help build temporary camps.

« **BEFORE**

Cunobelinus, the ruler of the Catuvellauni, expanded his kingdom, encroaching on the territory of the pro-Roman Atrebates.

EXPANSION OF THE CATUVELLAUNI
Cunobelinus maintained a friendly stance toward the Romans. After his death in 40 CE, **his sons expanded the kingdom** further and were unfriendly to Roman interests. Another son fled to Rome, attempting to provoke a Roman invasion.

Defensive ditches
The remains of Ardoch Fort, built by the Romans in c. 80 CE during Agricola's campaigns, is one of the best preserved forts in Roman Scotland.

The immediate pretext for the Roman invasion of Britain was the appeal by Verica, the exiled king of the Atrebates, to the Emperor Claudius to help restore him. As a result, four Roman legions—more than 20,000 men—embarked for England in late April 43 CE.

The Claudian invasion force, under Aulus Plautius, established its main base in the sheltered harbor of Richborough in eastern Kent and moved westward. The British, under Caratacus and Togodumnus, the leaders of the Catuvellauni, opposed the advance but were pushed back to the Thames. The Romans found a way across and in the ensuing fighting Togodumnus was killed. A pause in the campaign allowed for the arrival of Claudius himself. The emperor was thus able to direct in person the capture of the capital of Camulodunum (Colchester), before he returned to Rome, basking in the glory of his new conquest.

Roman expansion

The next four years saw the expansion of the Roman-controlled area, as the remnants of the Catuvellaunian kingdom were absorbed, while the future Roman emperor Vespasian mopped up resistance in the south and southwest. By around 47 CE, the Romans had secured a line that ran roughly along the future Fosse Way (from the Devon coast to Lincolnshire) and established a series of forts to cement their control. They then tried to push west into Wales, vigorously opposed by Caratacus, who had escaped to lead a renewed British resistance. He was finally captured in 51 CE after he had fled to the imagined safety of the court of Cartimandua, queen of the Brigantes, who handed him over to the Roman authorities.

Boudicca's revolt

In 60 CE, the Romans faced a serious revolt that almost drove them from Britain. Boudicca, the queen of the Iceni, fearing her territory being incorporated into the Roman province after the death of her husband, King Prasutagus, revolted and marched on Camulodunum. The Roman governor, Suetonius Paulinus, was away in north Wales. By the time he returned, Camulodunum had been razed to the ground, and a detachment of the Ninth Legion cut to pieces. Londinium

(London) and Verulamium (St. Albans) were burned to the ground by Boudicca's marauding army. Finally, Paulinus's legions faced the Iceni somewhere in the Midlands. The Roman victory was total; some 80,000 Britons were said to have died, a figure that matches the tally of 80,000 Romans (mostly civilians) who perished during Boudicca's campaign of destruction. The Icenian queen died soon afterward, allegedly by poisoning.

The northern frontier

By the mid-70s, the Brigantian kingdom and the rest of Wales had been annexed, but it fell to Julius Agricola, who arrived in Britain as governor in 77 or 78 CE, to project Roman power far into the north of Scotland. Within four years, Agricola had reached the Forth-Clyde line, where he established a number of forts. He then pushed further northward, launching a combined land and naval assault against the Caledonians. In the summer of 83 CE, he won a crushing victory at Mons Graupius (probably somewhere near Inverness).

Resistance to the Romans crumbled and Agricola established a legionary fortress at Inchtuthill on the Tay. However, within a few years almost all of his conquests were abandoned.

AFTER

Northern Scotland was evacuated by Domitian and the garrisons in southern Scotland were also reduced.

REMOVAL OF A LEGION
Emperor Domitian needed troops to conduct a war in Dacia in the mid-80s. Scotland was not a high priority for him and **the legion which should have formed the garrison at Inchtuthill was withdrawn** and sent to Moesia on the Danube River by 92 CE.

NEW DEFENSIVE BORDER
During the reign of Trajan (97–115 CE), **Roman garrisons in southern Scotland were thinned out** and most forces became stationed in the forts along the Tyne-Solway isthmus between Carlisle and Newcastle. **Hadrian's Wall was built close to this line** in the 120s CE **26–27 »**, forming a **new defensive border** for Roman Britain.

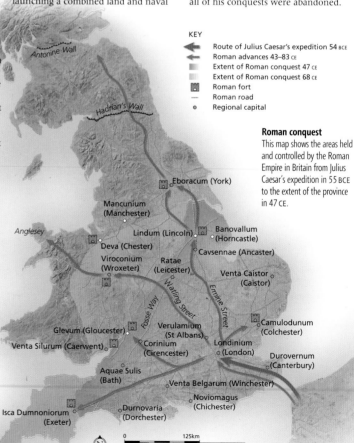

KEY

←	Route of Julius Caesar's expedition 54 BCE
←	Roman advances 43–83 CE
▨	Extent of Roman conquest 47 CE
░	Extent of Roman conquest 68 CE
⌂	Roman fort
—	Roman road
●	Regional capital

Antonine Wall

Hadrian's Wall

Eboracum (York)

Mancunium (Manchester)

Lindum (Lincoln)

Banovallum (Horncastle)

Anglesey

Deva (Chester)

Cavsennae (Ancaster)

Viroconium (Wroxeter)

Ratae (Leicester)

Venta Caistor (Caistor)

Glevum (Gloucester)

Verulamium (St Albans)

Camulodunum (Colchester)

Venta Silurum (Caerwent)

Corinium (Cirencester)

Londinium (London)

Durovernum (Canterbury)

Aquae Sulis (Bath)

Venta Belgarum (Winchester)

Noviomagus (Chichester)

Isca Dumnoniorum (Exeter)

Durnovaria (Dorchester)

Fosse Way

Watling Street

Ermine Street

Roman conquest
This map shows the areas held and controlled by the Roman Empire in Britain from Julius Caesar's expedition in 55 BCE to the extent of the province in 47 CE.

0 ___ 125km
0 ___ 125 miles

N

The Roman conqueror
This marble relief from Aphrodisias in modern-day Turkey shows Roman Emperor Claudius conquering Britannia. Claudius arrived in Britain in 43 CE to see for himself the defeat of the Britons at Colchester.

Hadrian's Wall
Stretching from Wallsend to Bowness-on-Solway,
Hadrian's Wall was almost 75 miles (120 km) long. It was
built over a period of years, following a visit to Britain
by the Emperor Hadrian in 122 CE, and covered some wild
terrain. Forts along the length of the wall housed Roman
army garrisons, which protected the northernmost border
of the Empire.

BEFORE «

Britain came under military authority in the very early stages of the conquest, but was soon organized as a regular Roman province. The northern frontier moved several times in the 2nd century CE.

HADRIAN'S WALL
In 122 CE, **Hadrian visited England**, the first reigning emperor to do so since Claudius and, according to one historian, "set many things right." In the north, the Romans had pulled back to a line from the Solway Firth to the Tyne. Here, Hadrian **ordered the building of a fixed barrier**, a wall « **26–27**. Under the governor, Aulus Platorius Nepos, Hadrian's Wall was begun almost at once and completed several years later. Though the Romans continued to occupy a number of outpost forts to the north of the line, the wall effectively formed the northern border of the Roman province for some 40 years.

EXTENDING THE NORTHERN FRONTIER
Hadrian's successor **Antoninus Pius ordered the evacuation of Hadrian's Wall and the building of a new defensive line** about 100 miles (160 km) to the north. The Antonine Wall was constructed of turf and spanned some 37 miles (60 km) between the Firth of Forth and the Clyde. A series of outpost forts north of the new wall were also occupied, once more establishing a **Roman military presence in central Scotland**. Around 161 CE, a new emperor, Marcus Aurelius, ordered the abandonment of his predecessor's advance, and by the mid-160s Hadrian's Wall once more marked the northern boundary of the province.

A **Distant Province**

During the 2nd and 3rd centuries CE, Roman Britain enjoyed a peaceful and largely prosperous period. Towns grew and a network of roads facilitated trade and communication. Rarely at the center of Roman political life, until the late 3rd century Britain avoided the instability of other parts of the Empire.

The period of peace following the withdrawal from the Antonine Wall until the 280s CE allowed the Roman province of Britannia to develop into a place with a complex road network, flourishing towns, and the full governmental system of a Roman province.

Pax Romana
The most important Roman official was the governor, who was responsible to the emperor and held authority over the civil and military administration. Initially based at Colchester, the governor moved to London toward the end of the 1st century. He was normally of senatorial rank, drawn from the elite of Roman society (although from the 3rd century, men of equestrian rank, the next rung down in the social hierarchy, were appointed). The other chief official of Britannia was the procurator, who was in charge of financial affairs. In 213 CE, the province was split in two: Britannia Superior (covering southern England and Wales) with its capital at London; and Britannia Inferior (northern England, including Hadrian's Wall), whose

governor resided at York. Some time before 312 CE, both provinces were further subdivided into two, leaving

> **LEGATUS AUGUSTI The official title of the Governor of Britannia. By the 3rd century this was replaced by titles such as Consularis and Praeses.**

Roman Britain with four and, later, five provinces. The result was that each governor, although he had his own staff and bureaucracy, wielded less power and so was unlikely either to mount an effective challenge against the emperor, or to implement policies which might be beneficial to Britannia as a whole.

The army's influence
The presence of the Roman army in the shape of three legions (after the 80s CE), amounting more than 16,000 men and

a roughly equivalent number of auxiliary troops, played a key role in the Romanization of Britain. The units shaped the local economy near the frontier as they needed grain and other supplies for the troops. The army also helped native Britons gain citizenship, as soldiers automatically acquired that privilege after 25 years of military service. Those joining the army would also have had to learn Latin, the language of command, which, because it was also used by the civilian administration, became firmly established in Britain.

The growth of towns
At the heart of Roman Britain lay its towns. Colchester, Lincoln, Gloucester, and York fell into the category of *coloniae*, established for legionary veterans who had full rights of

> " The Britons took up … **baths**, and **magnificent feasts**. The unsuspecting natives called these new habits 'culture' when they were in fact **part of their enslavement**. "
>
> TACITUS, *AGRICOLA*, C. 98 CE

citizenship, with a full town council and constitution. Other towns, such as St. Albans and London, held a lesser rank of *municipium*, where only town councillors and their families received Roman citizenship, but they were also important centers for the Romanization of the province. Many other towns, such as Silchester, started out as tribal centers (*civitates*) that became urbanized in Roman times, or as civilian settlements that grew up outside Roman forts (such as Cirencester). The presence in most towns of typical

The ruins of Viroconium
Viroconium (Wroxeter) is one of the best-preserved Roman towns. It was established in 129 CE as the *civitas* capital for the Cornovii tribe.

Roman buildings, such as baths, basilicas, and amphitheaters, shows the spread of Roman culture within Britain. Towns also served as regional markets and the base for small-scale industries and craft production; there were, for example, workshops for the production of the floor mosaics that adorned Roman villas.

The Romans built a network of roads linking the towns and villages, such as Watling Street running from Dover to Wroxeter and the Fosse Way from Exeter to Lincoln, which facilitated the transportation of bulky trade goods. Although Britain became integrated into the larger economy of the Roman Empire, it did not provide the gold and silver that had been hoped for. Apart from tin, lead, and iron, whose mining provided some income, Britain's main exports were leather and textiles. In return, Britain imported luxury goods, such as glass vessels, fine Samian ware pottery, and garum, the fish sauce much beloved of Roman cooks.

Romanizing rural Britain
The vast majority of people did not live in towns. At the top of the social scale, lavish villas, which were often surrounded by farming settlements, colonized the countryside, particularly from the 2nd century CE. Most people, however, continued to live in traditional roundhouses or rectangular aisled houses. Here, the penetration of Roman ideas was much weaker, and there is evidence of the persistence of traditional beliefs. Priests of the Imperial Cult and devotees of exotic mystery cults such as Isis and Mithras could be found in towns, but in the countryside Celtic deities such as Coventina or Cocidius held sway. Frequently, the identities of Celtic and Roman gods merged—such as Sulis with Minerva at Aquae Sulis (Bath).

Trouble in the north
Emperor Septimius Severus conducted the last major expedition into Scotland in 208–211 CE. A group called the Maeatae, in alliance with the Caledonians, had been menacing positions on the frontier for a decade. Bringing elements of the elite Praetorian Guard and contingents from the army units in western Europe, Severus began to prepare for a full-scale attack against them. The Maeatae sued for peace, but Severus launched his strike anyway, pushing northward. It was a hard-fought campaign in difficult terrain. Severus, by then seriously ill, accepted peace terms when they were offered again. Caracalla cut short a later campaign so he could return to Rome to secure the imperial throne, after Severus had died.

Life in the province of Britannia continued as before, but Roman armies did not attempt another reconquest of Scotland. Several emperors did visit Britain in the 3rd and 4th centuries, but it was to put down a revolt or deal with trouble on the borders, rather than in an effort to push further northward.

Lead curse tablet from a temple
Tablets like this one from Uley, Gloucestershire, were inscribed with messages and left at shrines by people seeking help from the gods in personal matters, such as finding a thief.

AFTER

The 3rd century was a time of grave instability for the Roman Empire, with a series of short-lived emperors unable to cope with the growing threat of barbarians from beyond the frontiers.

INDEPENDENT EMPIRES
In 260 CE, Postumus, governor of Gaul, declared his **independence from central control** and established a Gallic Empire. Britain formed a part of this until the reincorporation of the rebel provinces by Emperor Aurelian in 274 CE. In 286 CE a military commander, Carausius, declared himself emperor. He looked set to establish an **independent Roman state of Britain** but was assassinated in 293 CE and Constantius, one of the official Roman emperors, took control.

THE SURVIVAL OF LATIN
It is not clear whether Latin fully replaced the native Celtic languages of Britain during the Roman occupation. Germanic invaders in the 5th century CE **46–47 ≫** occupied Romanized areas in the south and east where Latin was widespread. Other areas had retained their native languages and so Latin more or less died out as a living language. It continued to be **the language of education and culture** for centuries. As the **universal language of the Christian Church**, Latin experienced a revival in Ireland and areas of western Britain which were converted by Celtic missionaries **38–39 ≫** and in parts of Britain converted from Rome by the mission of St. Augustine **44–45 ≫**.

Face from the past
This stunning example of Roman metalwork found in Cumbria dates from the 1st–2nd centuries CE. It would have been worn for display rather than in battle.

Brand of authority
This wooden writing tablet bears the stamp of the procurator, Roman Britain's chief financial officer, and may have originated in his office. Unfortunately, the wax-inscribed letter it contained has perished.

Outside the Empire

Little is known about the early political histories of Ireland and the part of Scotland not conquered by the Romans. By the 5th century CE, the first historical figures emerged and the core of later Irish and Scottish kingdoms had developed.

Ptolemy's map of the British Isles
The Alexandrian geographer Claudius Ptolemaeus (Ptolemy), working in the 1st century CE, produced a world map, which included the British Isles and showed a reasonably accurate outline of the Irish coast.

« **BEFORE**

The failure of the Romans to complete the conquest of Scotland after 83 CE and their decision not to invade Ireland left large areas of the British Isles outside the Empire.

EDGE OF THE EMPIRE
Although the Romans under **Agricola defeated the Caledonians** at Mons Graupius in 83 CE, and established the position for a fortress at Inchtuthill **« 24**, they pulled back. By 110 CE, the area north of a line from the Solway Firth to the Tyne lay outside the Empire.

DEVELOPMENTS IN IRELAND
Ireland continued to develop after the Bronze Age. Knowledge of ironworking may have reached there by the 6th century BCE and the La Tène culture reached Ireland by about 200 BCE. By the 1st century CE Ireland was **materially rich, but too remote** to invite Roman invasion.

Reconstructed Scottish crannog
Crannogs, houses constructed on artificial islands in lakes, first appeared in the late Bronze Age. Fairly common in Scotland, they were more prevalent in Ireland and may have been high-status dwellings.

The Roman withdrawal from northeast and central Scotland after 90 CE did not mean that the rulers of the Empire lost interest in the area. Outpost forts, such as the one at Trimontium (Newstead, near Melrose) continued to be occupied, while for 20 years under Antoninus Pius the Romans advanced to the Antonine Wall line between the Clyde and the Forth, with outpost forts even beyond that.

North of the frontier
Such a prolonged period of close contact with the Roman frontier is likely to have had an impact on the tribes who lived just beyond it. While some hillfort sites beyond the frontier experienced a reduced level of occupation (such as at Castle Law in Midlothian), one, at Traprain Law in East Lothian, evidently prospered greatly during the Roman period. This was the capital of the Votadini, a pro-Roman tribe, whose chieftains may have played a similar role to barbarian client kings beyond the Rhine and Danube in Germany, acting as a buffer against more distant groups and as a conduit for Roman influence in Scotland. Abundant Roman pottery and coins were found at Traprain Law in East Lothian—as well as an astonishing hoard of silver plate— and occupation continued into the 4th century. The inhabitants of the site were to some extent literate, as inscriptions in Latin have been found on pottery fragments there.

Similar finds at the western end of the Roman frontier, at Dalry in Ayrshire, may reflect the presence of another client kingdom. The penetration of trade into these areas is revealed by finds of large hoards of Roman coins, such as the 1,900 silver coins found near Falkirk. The appearance of stone huts and villages in central Scotland around the 2nd century (sometimes on the ruin of hillfort sites) may also have occurred as a consequence of

> **25** **The number of letters in the Irish ogham alphabet.**

Roman influence. Elsewhere, traditional crannogs (lake houses) continued to be built, even in the lowlands (such as at Milton Loch). In the Western and Northern Isles, huge stone-built broch towers persisted until the 2nd century CE, after which stone round houses replaced them.

The Picts
By the 4th century, new tribal federations had emerged in Scotland. Prominent in the "barbarian conspiracy" of 367 CE against Roman Britannia were the Picts (from the Latin *picti* meaning "painted folk"). At the height of their power in around 500 CE, the Picts occupied almost all of mainland Scotland north of the Clyde-Forth isthmus. A type of underground earth structure called a souterrain was very widespread in this area—although they may have been stores or cattle shelters rather than human dwellings. Very little is known of the Pictish language, but it may have been a relative of the Celtic P-dialect (or Brythonic) later spoken in Wales. The few examples of written Pictish that have been found are a little later in date. They are inscribed picture stones employing the Irish ogham alphabet, which was probably introduced into Pictland in the 8th century. Not much is understood of early Pictish society, although classical sources imply that they practiced polygamy. Bede, writing in the 8th century, states that the royal line of the Picts was matrilineal, with the succession to the throne passing through the female line.

Writing and stories in Ireland
Julius Agricola, the Roman conqueror of Scotland, is said to have mused that the conquest of Ireland would be a simple affair requiring just one legion. Despite this, no Roman army crossed the Irish sea and relations with Roman-occupied Britain were largely confined to trade. Artistic trends do seem to have crossed the Irish Sea, though, evidenced by finds of brooches and

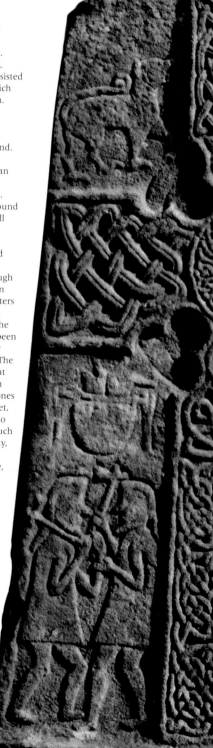

horse bits showing the influence of Romano-British style. Perhaps the most significant cultural import was knowledge of writing. The Irish ogham script, possibly developed around 400 CE, may have taken the Latin alphabet as its model. Ogham characters are written with incised lines along a central stem and are seen on inscriptions from Ireland and parts of Scotland and Wales.

Evidence from the sagas

Ireland possesses a wealth of orally transmitted sagas and histories almost unequaled in northern Europe. Tales such as the *Cattle Raid of Cooley* paint a picture of the country in the late Iron Age, while legendary figures in the histories such as Cormac mac Airt, who was said to have been king of Tara from 227–266 CE, may have a real historical basis. The *Cattle Raid* portrays an Ireland divided into four kingdoms: Ulaid (Ulster), Connachta (Connaught), Laigin (Leinster), and Mumu (Munster). These divisions persisted

The Manse stone

This 8th-century stone slab carving from Glamis with its interlaced stone cross and fabulous animals drew from an earlier tradition of Pictish symbol stones, whose abstract symbols and fantastic beasts have so far defied interpretation.

Irish flesh hook

This bronze object, dating from around 1000 BCE, set with ravens and a family of swans, and with a curved hook at the end, was probably a flesh-hook for retrieving chunks of meat from a stew.

into the Middle Ages and as administrative regions to the present day. The traditions related in the story predate the rise of the Uí Néill dynasty, whose founder Níall Noigiallach (Niall of the Nine Hostages) is thought to have ruled around 400 CE. The Uí Néill would dominate much of early medieval Irish history. They are said to have descended from the Milesians from Spain. This—or the subsequent arrival in legend of the "Black Gaels" around 600 BCE—may reflect a distant memory of the immigration into Ireland, which brought the Q-Celtic (or Goidelic) dialect there some time in the late 1st millennium CE or earlier.

The emergence of these very early dynasties may be reflected in the development during the Iron Age of the complex of enclosures and buildings at Tara, Navan Fort (County Armagh), and Dún Ailinne (County Kildare). The huge size of these—the internal enclosure ditch at Tara encircles 17 acres (7 hectares) of land—indicates the rise of rulers with sufficient power to command the vast resources necessary to construct them.

Irish settlers

By the 5th century CE, as the Roman grip on the west coast of Britain slackened, raiders from Ireland began to seize land there. An area in southwestern Wales was occupied by a group from Leinster, and Irish settlements dotted the coast as far north as Caernarvon. At about this time, a king called Cunedda is said to have established himself in north Wales, having transferred from beyond

Hadrian's Wall at the invitation of the emperor "Macsen Wledig" (or Magnus Maximus). Behind this story may lie a real movement of a Roman military unit, but the fact that many subsequent dynasties traced their descent from Cunedda is a sign that the Welsh were beginning to exercise political independence, even if this was a position forced on them by the Roman inability to defend their territories on the fringes of Britain. Of similar significance was the settlement, in Argyll in southwest Scotland, of another wave of Irish immigrants around 500 CE. By about 575, this group was firmly established in what became the kingdom of Dal Riata, under King Aedan mac Gabrain, with their capital in the fortress of Dunadd.

Alphabet stone

This stone from inside the Gallarus Oratory in Ireland shows ogham marks. Several hundred ogham inscriptions have been found in Ireland, and parts of Wales and Scotland.

AFTER

From the 5th century, definite kingdoms started to emerge in Ireland and Scotland, but it would be several centuries before the bulk of Scotland was united.

COMPETING DYNASTIES

Ireland was not united before the English conquest in the 12th century. Instead, the Uí Néill, Uí Briúin, Uí Fiachrach, and other local **dynasties competed for dominance** and recognition as *Ard Rí* (High King) **55 》**, a title that was mainly symbolic.

SCOTTISH COMPETITION

By the late 7th century in Scotland, **the Pictish kingdom faced competition** from the Irish incomers in Dal Riata, from the residual British kingdom of Strathclyde, based around Dumbarton, and from the Anglo-Saxon kingdom of Northumbria.

> **"** Ravens shall pick the necks of men. **Blood shall gush** in wild combat. **"**

THE CATTLE RAID OF COOLEY, 7TH–8TH CENTURIES

BEFORE

In the 1st century BCE, life in Britain was beginning to change. Contact with Rome in the century before the Claudian conquest of 43 CE modified it further.

URBAN DEVELOPMENT
A few **settlements like those beneath** St. Albans, Colchester, Canterbury, and Chichester **began to develop into oppida** (proto-towns). Many of these became true urban centers in Roman times. The presence of smaller denomination coins shows that they were used as **trading places**, rather than simply being royal or ceremonial centers.

COIN EVIDENCE
Some coins minted in Britain in the 1st century BCE are inscribed with names in **the Latin alphabet**, indicating evidence of contact with Rome.

TRADE GROWTH
An increase in **trade between Britain and the Continent** is indicated by the growth of new ports at places such as Hengistbury Head (near Bournemouth) and the **importation of goods** including pottery, wine, and glass.

Life in Roman Britain

The Roman rule of Britain, spanning nearly 400 years, introduced new ways of governing and an urban way of life with new architecture and religious beliefs. However, many Britons outside the urban centers continued to live in much the way they always had done.

The organization of an official Roman province of Britannia affected the higher levels of British society most. Some Britons became full Roman citizens and committed to a new way of life. For many people living outside the towns, however, life remained relatively unchanged after the Roman conquest.

Organized taxation
One aspect of Romanization that was hard to avoid was organized taxation. The province became subject to the

Temple of Mithras
These ruins of a Roman temple to an eastern god, Mithras, at Carrawburgh, a fort on Hadrian's Wall, date to the early 3rd century CE. Mithras was popular with soldiers.

tributum capitis (poll tax) and a tax on the productivity of the land based on periodic censuses. The poll tax caused particular upset and played a part in fueling the revolt of Boudicca (see p.24). Another unaccustomed imposition was a sales tax, levied on certain transactions, such as the sale of slaves, and on goods entering the province from elsewhere. Those who were Roman citizens—from 221 CE all freeborn inhabitants became citizens—were also liable to pay a five percent inheritance tax.

The organization—and the taxation—of Britain was made possible by the growth of urban centers connected by a network of roads. The well-constructed Roman roads also allowed movement of troops and supplies in the province.

Urban growth
The first official foundation at Camulodunum (Colchester) was in 49 CE.

The head of Serapis
The worship of Serapis, a Greco-Roman version of the Egyptian god Osiris was popular among Roman army units in Britain. This statue of the god was found in London.

This *colonia* was established for legionary veterans on the site of a long-standing native British *oppidum*, a pattern repeated in other places. The story of Londinium (London), which became the capital of the province, is rather different, as there is little trace of a settlement before 43 CE. A town grew up on the north bank of the Thames with a central forum and military fort in the northwest of the town, together with a palace. A major suburb grew up on the south side of the river crossing at Southwark.

The 20 or so large towns of Roman Britain housed about 500,000 people, about 10 percent of the total population. Smaller settlements

5 MILLION
The probable number of people living in the territories of Roman Britain at its peak.

clustered near major roads, or lay in the shadow of Roman military installations.

The wealthier Romanized elite owned villas—country estates surrounded by agricultural holdings. Built in the same style as villas found throughout the Empire, usually either in a courtyard or corridor style, these buildings are concentrated in the counties of the southeast, particularly in Somerset and the Cotswolds, usually within reach of

Slave manacles
Leg irons such as these were used to restrain captured slaves. Thousands of Britons were probably enslaved during the conquest.

an urban center. The most elaborate examples such as Lullingstone in Kent and Fishbourne in Sussex are evidence of a fully Romanized way of life. Even villas on a more modest scale show a level of everyday luxury that had not been seen in Britain before. Under floor heating, tiled floors, and plastered and painted walls are commonly found.

Town life
The towns of Roman Britain (see pp.28–29) evolved over time and types of buildings found throughout the Roman world became widespread in the province. These included public baths, temples, and theaters. The best preserved bath site is at Aquae Sulis (meaning "the waters of Sulis") in the modern city of Bath. Dedicated to the goddess Sulis, the bath complex used a natural hot spring already in use in the pre-Roman era. Classical temples in the Roman style are quite rare in Britain; the Temple of the Deified Claudius established in Colchester in the mid 1st century CE was probably the earliest established. As a center for the Imperial cult it acted as a focus for Romanization. Other public buildings included forums and basilicas, the judicial and administrative centers of many towns.

Theaters and amphitheaters are less common than temples and baths, which were found in most urban centers. However, the remains of a theater at Verulamium (St. Albans)

shows that Roman entertainments such as plays, dancing, and wrestling were enjoyed there from around 140 CE.

Most temples built in Britain were in the Celtic style. These often had a rectangular *cella* or inner room, which housed sacred images of the gods, around which was an enclosed area. Many Celtic deities seem to have become equated with similar Roman gods, such as Mars with the god Loucetius. Sulis, the traditional goddess of the healing springs, became identified with the Roman goddess Minerva since both shared similar characteristics. Other Celtic gods were not integrated into

Samian pottery
The finest pottery found in Britain was imported red-slip Samian ware, featuring potters' names stamped on it. Samian ware was produced in vast amounts in Gaul from the 1st century to the early 3rd, when the industry collapsed.

Mosaic pavement
Images from classical mythology, such as this head of Medusa from Cirencester, were a common theme of Roman mosaics, even after the coming of Christianity.

the Roman pantheon. These included the Matres, mother goddesses, and the Cucullati, a triad of mysterious hooded beings, whose statues have been found in Britain.

Health and well-being
The Roman period in Britain provides the first evidence for an interest in hygiene and sanitation. Aqueducts, such as the one at Lindum (Lincoln), were built to provide running water. The discovery of dentists' and doctors' instruments shows that surgery, albeit at a rudimentary level, was being practiced. Diseases like leprosy are also believed to have arrived in Britain for the first time with the Roman army.

Plowman and his team
This bronze model shows a Roman plow, one of many agricultural improvements brought to Britain. Vast amounts of grain were needed for the Roman army, turning large areas of land into cultivable spaces.

AFTER »

The economy and society of the province began to show signs of strain in the 4th century, collapsing as Germanic settlers (the Anglo-Saxons) arrived in number.

DECLINE IN THE CITIES
In the 3rd century, many British towns, including London, were walled, perhaps a sign of an increasing **sense of insecurity**. From the 4th century the towns went into decline and few or no new buildings were constructed. The villas underwent a **brief period of renewal**, as the urban dwellers may have retired to their country properties when life in the towns became less agreeable.

THE EMPIRE RETREATS
As the Roman **army was progressively withdrawn** in the 4th and early 5th centuries, economic activity diminished still further. No official supply of coins reached Britain after the reign of Constantine III (407–411); those that did were probably brought by individuals. Trades and crafts stagnated, and there was a notable decline in the quality of locally produced pottery.

THE EMPIRE RETREATS
By the time the Anglo-Saxons invaded Britain in force in the second half of the 5th century, the towns were already ghosts of their former selves. The newcomers **did not have an urban culture** and, unlike the Franks in Gaul, did not find a fully functioning one on which to graft themselves. Many **important Roman towns**, such as Silchester and Wroxeter, became **uninhabited** and when the Anglo-Saxons did begin to develop a more urban way of life, it was **often on new sites**.

LATIN CONNECTIONS
When Anglo-Saxon monarchs wrote to their fellow monarchs in Europe, **they did so in Latin**, a tongue that died out centuries before as a living language in Britain.

BEFORE

By the 360s new challenges were emerging for the Roman rulers of Britain. Picts from beyond Hadrian's Wall became more active and Saxon pirates from northwest Europe started to raid the east coast.

SAXON SHORE FORTS

A series of forts was built along the south coast, from the Solent to the Wash, between about 260 and 310. They are known as the Saxon Shore forts, after the Count of the Litus Saxonum (or Saxon Shore), a 5th-century military official who had responsibility for the defense of the region (presumably against the Saxons). What had been one of the more tranquil parts of Britain was now **in effect a frontier zone**. Some, including Pevensey, were well built and fortified and remained in use by the post-Roman defenders of Britain against the Saxons. Some were **refortified in Norman times**.

THREAT FROM IRELAND

Fourth-century Roman forts in western England, such as at Cardiff and near Lancaster, are an indication that **Roman Britain was also being threatened from across the Irish Sea.**

There are signs that Britain was entering a period of economic decline by the mid-3rd century CE. Industrial activity in towns slackened and high-quality imported pottery disappeared. Elsewhere in the Empire, in northwest Europe, towns were experiencing similar difficulties as the elite tried to escape the onerous duties of being a town councillor (which could be financially ruinous) and retired to their rural villas. Something similar may have occurred in Britain, although even large villas there seem to have suffered economic strains in the 4th century.

Barbarian threats

In 343 CE the Emperor Constans was forced to visit the province, to deal with an unspecified threat, but in 367 a more serious "barbarian conspiracy" broke out in which the Picts are said to have coordinated their attacks with the Irish and another group called the Attacotti. The Emperor Valentinian sent over a senior officer, Count Theodosius, who by 369 had scattered the invaders. He also restored a number of forts along Hadrian's Wall and in the east of England, and added a fifth province

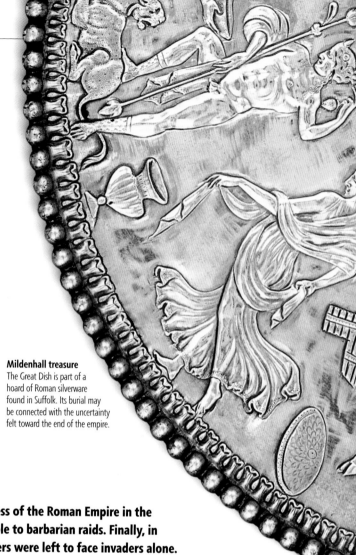

Mildenhall treasure
The Great Dish is part of a hoard of Roman silverware found in Suffolk. Its burial may be connected with the uncertainty felt toward the end of the empire.

End of Empire

In the early 5th century CE Britain suffered from the general weakness of the Roman Empire in the west. The withdrawal of much of the British garrison left it vulnerable to barbarian raids. Finally, in 410 CE Roman rule over Britain came to an end and native British rulers were left to face invaders alone.

LEGENDARY KING (c. 500 CE)

KING ARTHUR

King Arthur is a legendary ruler in Britain in the period following the collapse of the Roman Empire. The idea that he was a defender of the Britons against Saxon invaders owes much to the *History of the Kings of Britain* written around 1138 by Geoffrey of Monmouth. Given that the Britons do seem to have stemmed the Saxon advance in the early 6th century, the figure of Arthur may be based on a real leader or leaders of around that time.

(Valentia). In doing so, he established the last brief period of stability Britain would enjoy for centuries.

Withdrawal of troops

Britain's economic difficulties were exacerbated by the steady diminution of the Roman garrison in the late 4th and early 5th centuries. In 383 a usurper, Magnus Maximus, was proclaimed emperor in Britain. Taking at least a part of the Roman army of Britain, he crossed over to Gaul, where he defeated and killed the official emperor Gratian. Maximus himself ultimately suffered the same fate in 388 and it is likely that a portion of the soldiers he brought from Britain never returned (or were killed in the civil war). It was probably at this time that the Twentieth Legion was removed from Chester, leaving the western part of England vulnerable to raiders from across the Irish Sea.

Richborough fort

The Saxon Shore fort at Richborough (Rutupiae) was built in around 280 CE to boost the defenses of the south coast. The triple ditches date from defensive works constructed a few decades earlier.

The reduction in troop levels appears to have encouraged further barbarian incursions. In 396 Stilicho, the military strongman who dominated the government in the early reign of Honorius (395–423), was forced to come in person to restore order. He did so, but by 400, he, too, seems to have withdrawn yet more military units from the British provinces.

The steady decrease in the numbers of Roman soldiers reduced security and further damaged the economy. Supplies, which had been needed to support the army, were no longer required and the coin to pay its wages stopped being imported. After about 407, bronze coins, which were the only ones really useful for day-to-day transactions, were no longer in

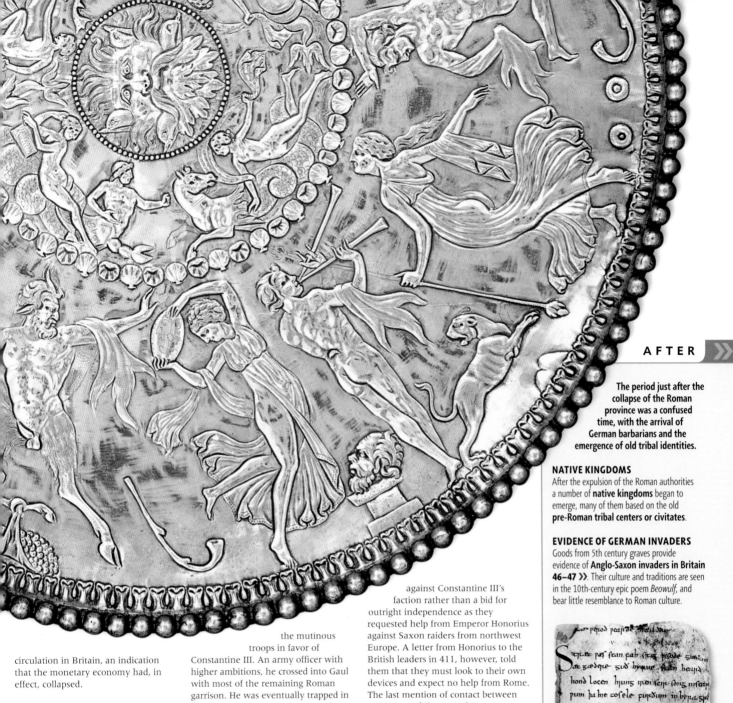

The period just after the collapse of the Roman province was a confused time, with the arrival of German barbarians and the emergence of old tribal identities.

NATIVE KINGDOMS
After the expulsion of the Roman authorities a number of **native kingdoms** began to emerge, many of them based on the old **pre-Roman tribal centers or civitates**.

EVIDENCE OF GERMAN INVADERS
Goods from 5th century graves provide evidence of **Anglo-Saxon invaders in Britain 46–47 »**. Their culture and traditions are seen in the 10th-century epic poem *Beowulf*, and bear little resemblance to Roman culture.

BEOWULF MANUSCRIPT

circulation in Britain, an indication that the monetary economy had, in effect, collapsed.

> **407** The last year that Roman coins found in Britain were made.
>
> **367** The number of years of Roman occupation in Britain.

The groans of the Britons

The end of Roman rule came with surprising rapidity. In December 406 a horde of barbarians—Alemanni, Vandals, and Burgundians—crossed over the Rhine (which had frozen solid during a harsh winter) and penetrated deep into Gaul. The army in Britain responded by raising another usurper, Marcus, to defend their interests. In rapid succession Marcus was overthrown and replaced by Gratian, who was, in turn, removed by

the mutinous troops in favor of Constantine III. An army officer with higher ambitions, he crossed into Gaul with most of the remaining Roman garrison. He was eventually trapped in 411 during a siege at Arles in southern Gaul and executed; his troops never returned to Britain.

Even before this, in 410, however, the Britons are said to have risen up and thrown out all the Roman officials and set up their own rulers. This, however, was probably a revolt

The last Roman coins
This gold solidus of the Emperor Constantine III was issued by the last Roman emperor to be proclaimed in Britain. After his departure for Gaul in 407, almost no more Roman coins are found.

against Constantine III's faction rather than a bid for outright independence as they requested help from Emperor Honorius against Saxon raiders from northwest Europe. A letter from Honorius to the British leaders in 411, however, told them that they must look to their own devices and expect no help from Rome. The last mention of contact between Britain and the central Roman authority comes in about 446 when the British leaders addressed a plea to Aetius, the western Roman Empire's last effective military commander, to hear "the groans of the Britons" and send them assistance against the increasingly predatory Saxon raiders. Aetius had enough problems of his own, however, with Hunnish invaders led by Attila and he ignored the Britons' plea (if, indeed, he ever received it in the first place).

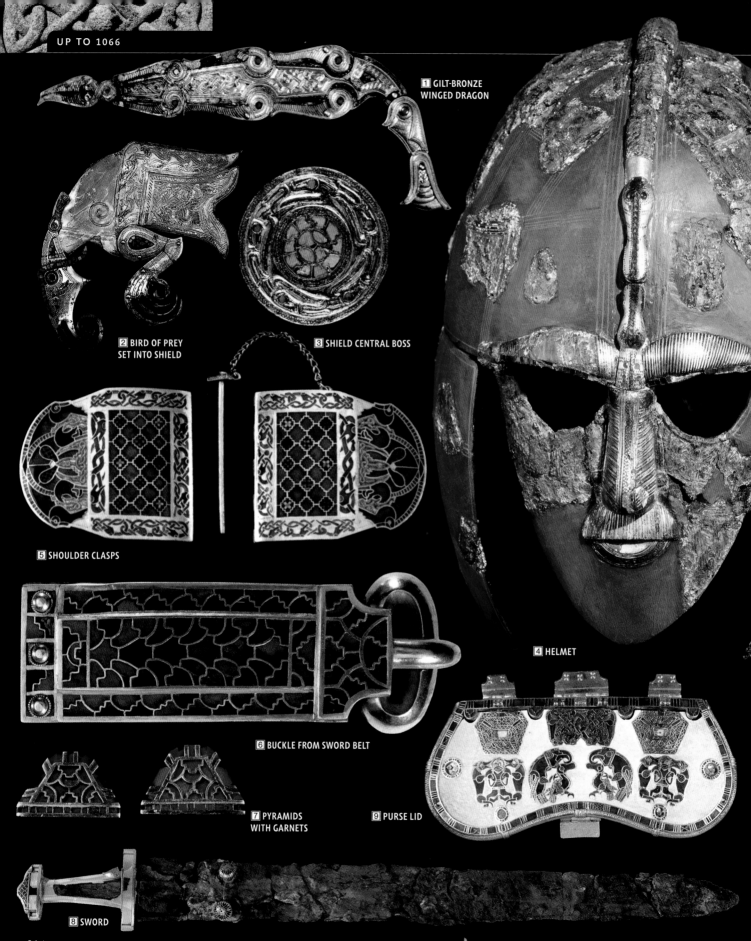

1 GILT-BRONZE WINGED DRAGON

2 BIRD OF PREY SET INTO SHIELD

3 SHIELD CENTRAL BOSS

5 SHOULDER CLASPS

4 HELMET

6 BUCKLE FROM SWORD BELT

7 PYRAMIDS WITH GARNETS

9 PURSE LID

8 SWORD

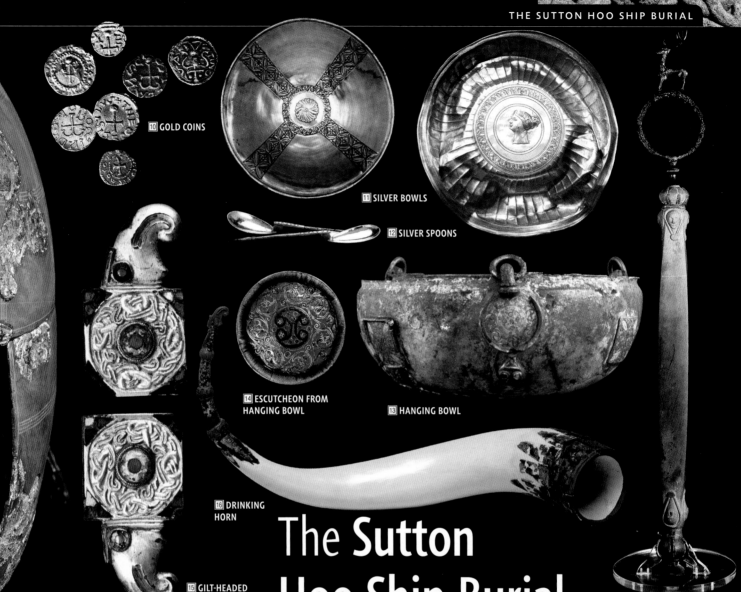

10 GOLD COINS

11 SILVER BOWLS

12 SILVER SPOONS

14 ESCUTCHEON FROM HANGING BOWL

13 HANGING BOWL

16 DRINKING HORN

15 GILT-HEADED BIRDS FROM HARP

17 WHETSTONE

The Sutton Hoo Ship Burial

The Sutton Hoo ship burial, discovered in 1939, is probably the last resting place of King Raedwald of East Anglia (599–c. 624). One of only two full ship burials found in England, its fabulous treasures show the wealth of the East Anglian royal dynasty.

1 Gilt-bronze winged dragon, set to one side of the shield boss, its eyes made of cabochon garnet. **2 Bird of prey set into shield**, made of gold foil set into alderwood. The head and leg are gilt-bronze. **3 Shield central boss** made up an animal frieze, surrounding a garnet disk. **4 Helmet**. The cap was forged from a single piece of iron, with iron ear-flaps and a neck-guard attached. Bronze plates stamped with animals and scenes from mythology were then added. **5 Shoulder clasps**, based on Roman prototypes, are curved to fit the shoulder, and have a pattern of garnets and millefiori glass. **6 Buckle from sword belt**, inlaid with gold and garnet fittings. **7 Pyramids with garnets** surrounded by a gold frame, originally attached to a sword knot, possibly to tie the sword into its scabbard. **8 Sword** is pattern-welded from eight bundles of iron rods. It was once mounted with gold and garnet fittings. **9 Purse lid**, with an ivory base enclosed by gold frame, is set with seven decorative plaques, four of them of interlaced animals. **10 Gold coins**, minted in Gaul between 575 and 625 CE. **11 Silver bowls**. The fluted bowl (right) shows a lady, with a diadem in the center. The cross on the bowl (left) was not necessarily intended as Christian. **12 Silver spoons** stamped with the names "Saulos" and "Paulos", a possible reference to St. Paul. **13 Hanging bowl**, made of bronze, probably in the eastern Mediterranean and then imported. **14 Escutcheon from hanging bowl**, enameled and set with millefiori glass, originally attached to a handle. **15 Gilt-headed birds from harp**. Originally attached to a six-stringed harp. **16 Drinking horn**, one of a pair set with silver-gilt end fittings. **17 Whetstone**, set with a beautifully carved bronze stag on top of an iron ring, believed to be a scepter. **18 Burial ship**. This 1939 picture of the excavation shows the lines of the ship's original planking.

18 BURIAL SHIP

Iona Abbey
Iona Abbey occupies the site of the monastery founded in 563 by Saint Columba. Iona remained an important center of Irish monasticism for four centuries.

Holy Ireland

From tenuous beginnings in the 5th century CE, Christianity in Ireland spread rapidly. Monasteries came to wield great power within Church and society, and missionaries were dispatched to the Continent. But secular Ireland saw struggles between the Uí Néill of the north and southern groups.

BEFORE

The Christianization of Ireland occurred during the 5th and early 6th centuries CE. Distant from papal authority in Rome, it later developed an independent identity.

PALLADIUS
The **first evidence of a Christian mission** to Ireland comes in 431, when Pope Celestine I sent the deacon Palladius to Ireland. It is uncertain exactly where he went—he may have also visited Irish-settled areas of Scotland—but it is likely his mission concentrated on the south and east coasts. It clearly **did not prosper**, as no records of its work survived in Ireland.

SAINT PATRICK'S BELL

SAINT PATRICK
The **conversion** of the Irish was achieved by Saint Patrick, who came from a rich family in northern Britain. His own account relates that his father was a town councillor and his grandfather a priest, and that, aged 16, he was seized by Irish pirates and taken to Ireland. After six years he escaped back to Britain, but resolved to return to Ireland to **bring Christianity** to the people there. Unfortunately, Patrick does not provide any clear indications of the dates of his mission. His return to Ireland has traditionally been assigned to 432 (the year after that of Palladius) but it may well have been any time between 400 and 450. The **early years** of the mission were **precarious** and Patrick was forced to make payments to local kings to secure protection. By the time of his death, traditionally given as 492, Christianity had a sufficiently **secure base** in Ireland to ensure its survival.

By the early 6th century, Irish Christianity had established itself much along the lines of the Christian churches in Gaul or Britain, divided up into dioceses, with bishops as the principal church leaders. After this, however, the balance of power in the Irish Church began to shift toward monasteries so that abbots exercised administrative power, and a network of daughter houses of the main establishments, rather than traditional parishes, came to be the characteristic feature of Church organization. The abbot was seen as the comarba, or heir, of the original founder of the monastery and the property was legally vested in him and not in the wider Church. It mirrored the organization of aristocratic families, and it is no surprise that many of the early monastic founders came from the nobility.

Remote monasteries
Men such as Finnian of Clonard and Ciarán of Clonmacnoise established monasteries in the 530s and 540s, followed by a spread of the monastic life into the most remote reaches of the island. Saint Brendan, ranked with Finnian and Ciarán among the "Twelve Apostles of Ireland," set up a monastery on Inishglora, off the coast of Mayo, in western Ireland, before taking off on a series of sea voyages in search of even remoter monastic retreats, possibly as far as Iceland and even North America.

Missionaries, culture, and unity
The next monastic generation included Comgall, who founded the monastery at Bangor around 558, and Saint Columba, who, after establishing a string of monastic houses, departed Ireland under a cloud after a dispute over ownership of a Gospel manuscript led to a pitched battle. His exile, however, led to the foundation of the great abbey of Iona, off the west coast of Scotland, in 563, and the beginning of a tradition of Irish evangelization abroad that would culminate in the career of Columbanus (see BOX). Columba himself continued to be held in high regard in his homeland, as shown by the Convention of Druim Cett in 575, when he returned to Ireland in the company of King Aidan of Dal Riata to a meeting of royalty and clergy, called to settle relations between the Dal Riatans and the Uí Néill clan.

From early on, the monasteries were centers of learning. In 536, 50 European students traveled to the monastery at Lismore.

Emly reliquary
Reliquaries housing the bones of saints or other sacred relics were often lavishly adorned. This house-shaped shrine, from Emly, Tipperary, was portable with a strap attached to hinged mounts.

MISSIONARY (540–615)

SAINT COLUMBANUS

Columbanus was born around 540 CE in Leinster, Ireland. Attracted to a monastic life, he spent 25 years under Abbot Comgall of Bangor. Around 590, he was allowed to go on pilgrimage, traveling through Britain, Gaul, and Burgundy. There, he established numerous monasteries, including at Annegray and Luxeuil. However, Columbanus fell foul of ecclesiastical politics—he had not placed himself under the obedience of the local bishop—and made an enemy of King Theuderic II of Burgundy. Expelled in 610, he went to Italy, settling at Bobbio, in the Apennines, where he built yet another monastery and developed what would become one of the more influential early monastic rules.

The Irish monasteries also produced numerous manuscripts. These were often greatly embellished with illuminated pages that are spectacular examples of Celtic art.

By around 700, the Irish Church was rich and powerful, and filled in part a vacuum in the secular political sphere, where no one region or dynasty exercised complete dominance over Ireland. Leinster was probably the most powerful early province, ruled first by the Dál Messin Corb and then, by the mid-7th century, contested by the Uí Dúnlaige and Uí Cenneslaig dynasties. However, from the 6th century, the Uí Néill dynasty began to become the most important group in Ireland, first dominating Ulster after

Book of Durrow
Produced around 675, probably in Ireland, but possibly in Northumbria or Iona, the Book of Durrow is one of the earliest surviving complete Gospel books.

victory over the Cruithin at Móin Dairi Lothair in 563, and then driving the Ulaid into the east of the province. The Uí Néill claim to the kingship of Tara, by long tradition the most venerable kingdom in Ireland, was a symbolic means of asserting primacy over all the other competing dynasties. However, it would be several centuries before anyone came even close to uniting Ireland.

> "The Lord **ordained clerics** everywhere through **my unworthy person**."
>
> SAINT PATRICK, *CONFESSION*, 5TH CENTURY CE

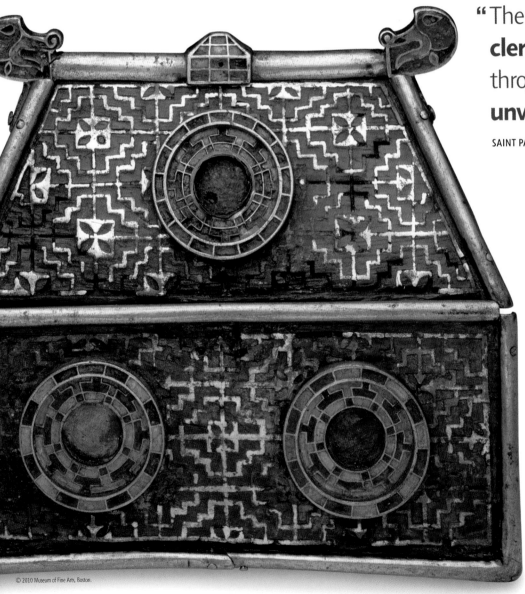

AFTER

When Saint Patrick arrived in Ireland in 432 CE there were few Christians there. By 700 CE the Church was well established and had passed its first, missionary phase.

SECULARISM AND REFORM
Monasteries became **increasingly secularized**, with some abbots marrying. They were even sending **armed raids** against each other by the 8th century. In 764, 200 monks from Durrow died in battle against their rivals from Clonmacnoise. Revulsion at this gave rise to a **reformist movement** of *culdees* ("vassals of god") who founded new houses, such as Tallaght in Dublin.

MISSIONARY AMBITION
Irish **missionary efforts expanded**, led by men such as Saint Gall, a disciple of Saint Columbanus, who converted the Alamanns (in modern Switzerland) before his death. From around 700, Irish scholars flocked to Europe, attracted by conditions at the courts of the **Frankish rulers**: Dungal was consulted by Charlemagne after a solar eclipse in 810, while Dicuil wrote the first medieval geography treatise in which he mentioned an island called "Thule" (almost certainly Iceland), and Sedulius Scotus advised Charles the Bald on government around 850.

Anglo-Saxon Rulers

Germanic invaders arrived in Britain in the middle of the 5th century CE and quickly pushed the Britons into fringes of the island. They established a series of kingdoms, which by the 8th century became increasingly sophisticated with rulers who were among the most powerful in Europe.

Lead weights
Trade and commerce played an important role in the prosperity of Anglo-Saxon England. Lead weights such as these were used by merchants to test the weight of precious metals and other small trade items.

◀◀ BEFORE

Evidence for early Anglo-Saxon kingdoms is obscure and much of our understanding comes from significantly later sources.

VORTIGERN AND THE SAXONS
Writing in the 8th century, the monk Bede **44–45 ▶▶**, dated the **arrival of the Saxon invaders** in England to 449. The British King Vortigern is said to have invited their leaders Hengist and Horsa to bring a troop of mercenaries to protect his kingdom against other barbarian marauders. A Gallic chronicle dates a Saxon victory to 440 and it is probable that somewhere around this time the nucleus of the groups who would form the later Anglo-Saxon kingdoms **began to settle in England**.

THE GERMAN HOMELAND
The invaders, whom Bede divided into **Angles, Saxons, and Jutes,** are believed to have come from northwestern Germany and the Frisian coast of the modern Netherlands. It is not clear why they began to migrate, but the **lack of a central authority in Britain** after the collapse of the Roman province **◀◀ 34–35** must have made the island a tempting target.

The Anglo-Saxons made rapid territorial gains in the century after their arrival in England. There was a pause in around 500 CE when, according to the near-contemporary Gildas, the Britons won a great victory at Mons Badonicus, led by a war-leader whom later tradition identified with King Arthur (see p.34). By 550, however, the Anglo-Saxon advance had resumed and a decisive victory at Dyrham in Gloucestershire in 577 opened most of the West Country to them. By around 600, the Britons had been reduced to control of the area known as Dumnonia (Devon, Cornwall, and Somerset), Wales, Cumbria, and Scotland.

Seven kingdoms

Gradually the tribal war-bands coalesced into a series of kingdoms, with the seven principal among them being collectively termed the Heptarchy (Kent, Sussex, Essex, East Anglia, Wessex, Mercia, and Northumbria). *The Anglo-Saxon Chronicle*, compiled in the 9th century, names the founders of several other kingdoms, although there is little independent historical evidence for any of these figures. Cerdic is said to have arrived in what would become Wessex (in western England) in 495, while Aelle of Sussex enjoyed a brief period of preeminence among the Anglo-Saxon chieftains from 477–491. Among his reported exploits was the capture of Anderida, the former Roman

Offa's Dyke

Running almost the entire border between England and Wales, this defensive earthwork, built by King Offa of Mercia had a 26-ft (8-m) high rampart, ditch, and forts to defend it.

Saxon Shore fort at Pevensey, which the Britons were still clearly using as a stronghold. In East Anglia, a dynasty called the Wuffingas ruled from the late 6th century (although Germanic settlers arrived there more than a century earlier), while in the northeast of

Anglo-Saxon claw beaker
Claw beakers like this originated in northwestern France and Germany. They were made by applying "claws" of glass and molding them. Examples imported to England would have been treasured possessions.

England, Ida founded a kingdom called Bernicia in 547 which, together with its neighbor Deira, probably originated as a British kingdom taken over by Anglo-Saxon war-bands. The Tribal Hidage, a tax-collection assessment drawn up for an 8th-century Mercian ruler, mentions others, such as the Hwicce and Magonsaete in the Midlands, so the reality was probably more like a kaleidoscope than a neat-fitting jigsaw of seven pieces.

Warrior kings

Anglo-Saxon kingship had its roots in north European Germanic custom. The king was a source of patronage and wealth, who gave feasts in his hall attended by a retinue of warriors. He was predominantly a war-leader, and the portrait painted of kings by the epic

of *Beowulf*, one of the most important surviving pieces of Old English literature, probably reflects the reality reasonably closely. The poem gives us an insight into the passionate and dangerous lives led by the kings of this period in a way that the scant archaeological evidence cannot. "It is always better to avenge dear ones than to indulge in mourning" is a line that several kings clearly took to heart, as in the Northumbrian ruler Oswy's campaigns against Penda, responsible for the death of his brother Oswald.

Archaeological evidence for this period has come from sites including Yeavering, near Bamburgh in Northumbria, where a series of royal halls were built in the 6th and 7th centuries. One of them—presumed to be that of King Edwin—was more than 82 ft (25 m) long.

Power of the Bretwalda

Bede, writing in the 8th century, refers to the office of Bretwalda, a ruler who wielded power over a far greater area than his own kingdom and sometimes over the whole of Britain. The first of these was Aelle of Sussex in the late

3,182 The number of lines in the epic Anglo-Saxon poem *Beowulf*, written in Britain by an anonymous author between the 8th and the 11th centuries.

5th century. Another Bretwalda was Aethelbert of Kent (560–616), the first royal Christian convert. Under him, Kent was open to influences from Merovingian France and seemed set to dominate the constellation of Anglo-Saxon kingdoms in southern England. However, the next Bretwalda, Raedwald of East Anglia (who died c.624) who was a pagan and the presumed occupant of the Sutton Hoo ship burial (see pp.36–37), denied Aethelbert and his successors the opportunity to expand into East Anglia and relegated Kent to a permanently subordinate position.

The rise of Mercia

Reflecting a shift in power northward the next three Bretwaldas, Edwin (616–633), Oswald (634–642), and Oswy (642–670) were all kings of Northumbria. By now, however, the kingdom of Mercia was on the rise.

Kings of Anglo-Saxon England

This medieval genealogy of the kings of Kent shows Aethelbert, under whom Kent was converted to Christianity, and his son Eadbald, who became king in 616 and under whom there was a brief pagan reaction.

The pagan Penda (626–655) defeated and killed both Edwin (in a battle near Hatfield in 633) and Oswald (near Oswestry in 642), although he himself died in battle against Oswald's successor Oswy in 655. Mercia's position was consolidated by a series of Penda's successors, including Aethelred, who defeated Ecgfrith of Northumbria in 679 and put an end to the northern kingdom's ambitions to expand into the Midlands. Aethelred felt secure enough to abdicate in 704 to become a monk,

1,200 The number of British monks said to have been slain by King Aethelfrith of Northumbria before the Battle of Chester, 616 CE.

a choice also made by his immediate successor Cenred in 709. King Aethelbald of Mercia (716–757) consolidated Mercia's position, absorbing territory as far south as London, and even went so far as to style himself king of the "southern English" as well as the Mercians.

The Mercians, though, faced rivals in the south in the shape of the growing power of Wessex, beginning with Caedwalla who took control of Kent in 686 and Ine (688–726) who, though he lost Kent, maintained control over the formerly independent kingdom of Sussex. Ine gave Wessex its first law code in 694, a useful source of evidence for the social structure of Wessex at the time: it lays down separate penalties for his Anglo-Saxon and British subjects, showing that the two groups were not yet fully integrated; and it sets an obligation on certain groups to provide *fyrd* or military service, indicating that the defense of the kingdom was a constant preoccupation. It was probably during Ine's reign that the great trading center at

Hamwic (near modern Southampton) was established, a sign of the growing economic strength of Wessex. In the 8th century, a series of more obscure kings ruled Wessex, which increasingly struggled to compete with Mercia. A new Mercian king, Offa, seized ground

a monastery, while his replacement Aethelred (790–796) was also murdered to make way for Osbald, whose reign lasted for only a few months.

Offa maintained a network of international connections, in part through the agency of the scholar

> " The Angles or **Saxons** came to Britain at the **invitation** of King Vortigern in three **longships** … "
>
> BEDE, *ECCLESIASTICAL HISTORY*, C. 731

in Berkshire and around Bath. It would be a century before Wessex was able to establish itself as the most powerful Anglo-Saxon kingdom.

Offa of Mercia

Offa (757–796) was the most powerful king of his day, being the first to style himself simply as "king of the English." He extinguished the royal dynasties of Kent and Sussex and seems to have ruled there directly. He had the East Anglian ruler Aethelberht put to death in 794 and in Mercia he installed his own son Ecgfrith on the throne in 787. Only Northumbria resisted his overlordship, and here a period of dynastic instability ensured that it did not pose him any real threat; King Aelfwald (779–788) was murdered and his successor Osred II (788–790) was forcibly placed in

Alcuin, who originally came from York, but who became one of the leading intellectuals at the court of the great Frankish king Charlemagne. He sent a yearly tribute to the Pope in Rome and received papal legates (including Alcuin) at his court in 786. In 795 he corresponded with Charlemagne over a commercial dispute and he clearly viewed himself as the equal of the Frankish ruler, as he asked for a Frankish princess as a bride for Ecgfrith. Offa also began the minting of a new penny coinage for Mercia, which was issued from Canterbury, Rochester, London, and Ipswich. He commanded sufficient resources to build a huge defensive work—Offa's Dyke—between western Mercia and the surviving British kingdoms in Wales. He left Mercia sufficiently stable and powerful for its hegemony to survive into the 830s when it collapsed under the twin pressures of Wessex and Viking invaders.

The Witham pins
This 8th-century set of interlinked dress pins, engraved with winged animals shows the Anglo-Saxon taste for elaborate personal ornaments.

AFTER »

Northumbria endured a time of prolonged political instability in the 8th century, while Mercia enjoyed a last period of supremacy before its final eclipse by Wessex after 800.

COLLAPSE OF MERCIA'S HEGEMONY
Concerned at the **rising power of Wessex**, King Beornwulf of Mercia marched against Egbert in 825 but was defeated at the Battle of Ellendun. As a result Egbert was acknowledged as king in Kent, Surrey, Sussex, and Essex.

VIKING PRESSURE
While Wiglaf recovered Mercia's independence in 830, it never recovered the preeminence it had enjoyed under Offa. An uneasy situation prevailed in the 830s and 840s with power balanced between Wessex and Mercia. This equilibrium, however, was destroyed by the **onset of severe Viking raids** which would ultimately result in the destruction of all the Anglo-Saxon kingdoms save Wessex **46–47** ». The raid at Lindisfarne in 793 CE is remembered in the Lindisfarne Stone erected there.

LINDISFARNE STONE

Franks Casket

Franks Casket gives a unique insight into early Anglo-Saxon culture. Likely made in the first half of the 8th century in Northumbria, it is an ornately carved, whalebone box and shows scenes from history and mythology, including the sack of Jerusalem by the Roman Emperor Titus, the Adoration of the Magi, and the legend of Romulus and Remus. This panel depicts the legend of Egil the Archer seen defending his castle and wife from attackers.

Christian England

Missionaries sent by Pope Gregory I converted the first Anglo-Saxon kingdom at the end of the 6th century CE. Despite early setbacks, within just over a century all the rest had become Christian, and England became the home of a vibrant and thriving Christian culture, largely based in monasteries.

In around 560 CE, King Aethelbert of Kent married Bertha, the daughter of Charibert, the Merovingian ruler of a Frankish kingdom based around Paris. Like her father, Bertha was a Christian and in her entourage came a bishop, Liudhard, who was allowed to establish a church in Kent.

Despite any intentions Charibert may have had of cementing Frankish influence in England by effecting the conversion of Aethelbert, the Kentish king found it far less politically

Kingston Brooch
Made of gold, inlaid with garnet and blue glass, the 7th-century Kingston brooch, found in Kent, is a testament to the great wealth of the area around the time of King Aethelbert.

constraining to accept missionaries from a much more distant source, Pope Gregory I in Rome.

In 597, a group of clerics despatched by Pope Gregory and led by Saint Augustine arrived in Thanet in Kent. They were warmly received and Aethelbert soon accepted Christian baptism. Whether he truly understood the significance of the new religion or utterly rejected the pagan beliefs of his forefathers is unclear, but he probably saw that the support of a powerful Church would provide him with a strong additional underpinning of his royal authority. Aethelbert was active in the propagation of his new religion and effected the conversion of King Saberht of Essex. East Anglia, too, fell rapidly into the Christian fold. Its king, Sigebert, had converted to Christianity while he was in exile in Gaul.

Pope Gregory intended the headquarters of the English Church to be in London, but this was under the political control of Essex and Augustine found it more convenient to remain under the protection of Aethelbert. So, the first archbishopric in England came to be

established in Canterbury, the Kentish royal capital, with the cathedral initially in the church that Bertha had used.

The death of Aethelbert

The cause of Christianity in England suffered a rapid setback on the death of Aethelbert in 616, for his successor reverted to paganism (as did the heirs of Saberht of Essex). Kent was rapidly gained back, and around 628 the Christians won a major victory with the conversion of Edwin, King of Northumbria and the appointment of

40 The number of clerics who went with Saint Augustine to Kent.

Paulinus as the first Bishop of York. The fragility of the Christian cause, however, was shown by the effect of the death of Edwin in battle against the pagan Penda of Mercia in 634; Northumbria relapsed into paganism for several years.

The Christian position in Northumbria was restored by King Oswald (634–653), while elsewhere Christianity again made rapid advances, with the conversion of Wessex in around 635 and of the last major pagan kingdom, Mercia, in 655.

Significantly, Oswald had not sent to Canterbury for missionary support, but to the Celtic monastery at Iona. The bishop he received, Aidan, established his see on the island of Lindisfarne, and from here a strong Celtic presence developed, often at odds with the "official" Church based in Canterbury and York.

Despite these advances, by 664 the Church in England faced a crisis. The acute tensions between the Celtic and Roman wings of the Church were largely resolved at the Synod of Whitby (see BOX). However, the Church outside Kent was in a parlous

Ruthwell Cross, Northumbria
A striking example of Anglo-Saxon sculpture, the Ruthwell cross illustrates the *Dream of the Rood*, a poem in which the narrator has a vision of Christ's cross.

state, with few bishoprics there paying more than lip-service to the authority of the Archbishop of Canterbury. To revive the flagging English Church, in 669 Pope Vitalian appointed a new archbishop, Theodore of Tarsus.

Theodore moved quickly to assert his authority over the Church in England, elevating the Northumbrian nobleman Wilfrid to the see of York in 669 (he was a spiritual powerhouse who converted one of the last pagan areas, Sussex, to Christianity in 679). The new archbishop also reorganized the bishoprics in England, sending

◄◄ **BEFORE**

Roman Britain must have had a substantial Christian population, but evidence of the survival of the religion in the areas the Anglo-Saxons conquered is very slight.

SHRINE OF SAINT ALBAN

GERMANUS OF AUXERRE
In 429, Germanus, Bishop of Auxerre (in Gaul), came to counter the **spread of a Christian heresy** called Pelagianism, which had taken root in Britain. He visited the shrine of Saint Alban at Verulamium—evidence that at least one Christian place of worship was still functioning.

CELTIC CHRISTIANITY
In areas the Germanic invaders did not conquer ◄◄ **40–41**, Christianity flourished. Monasteries such as Whithorn (established c. 432) and Iona (established in 563) became **centers of a Celtic church** with a distinct identity and bases for the **reconversion of northern England** and missions to pagan parts of Europe.

Saint Bede

Bede (673–735) spent most of his life in monasteries at Monkwearmouth and Jarrow. Despite this, he produced the most significant literature in England between Roman times and the Norman Conquest.

"Study, teaching, and writing have always been my delight."

THE VENERABLE BEDE, 673–735

The early history of the Anglo-Saxon Church was chronicled by Bede, a monk at Jarrow, in his *Ecclesiastical History* (completed in 731). Bede's narrative was intended to portray the triumph of the Church and the heroic endeavors of its founders and missionaries. However, in a separate letter to the Archbishop of Canterbury in 734, he did complain that the clergy of his day were illiterate in Latin and so could not conduct services properly, and that the standards of conduct in many monasteries were nothing short of scandalous. Despite this, references in his main work to the enormous library of manuscripts that Benedict Biscop had built up—an enormous achievement at a time when all books had to be copied by hand—and the extensive range of classical works quoted by Bede himself, indicate an environment in which scholarship was able to flourish.

In the visual arts, too, Christianity (and the monasteries in particular) made a huge contribution. Buildings, including the 8th-century church at Brixworth in Northamptonshire, and carvings such as the Ruthwell Cross, with its delicately interlaced vine-leaf

> **SCRIPTORIUM** The office in a monastery where the monks produced and copied manuscripts.

patterns, show the great skill of Anglo-Saxon craftsmen. The beautifully painted illustrations in books including the *Lindisfarne Gospels* (dating from around 698) also show a mastery of technique that matches the best of continental European art.

By the late 8th century, the English Church was well-established and confident. This is demonstrated by the foundation of the cathedral school at York by Archbishop Egbert (732–766) and the gifting of large tracts of land to churches and monasteries, attested in contemporary charters. Following Augustine's first small mission 150 years earlier, England had truly become a Christian country.

new bishops to many which had lain vacant, and subdividing others which had gained too much power and independence from Canterbury.

A flourishing Church

The later 7th century was a period when the English Church, now on a firmer footing, began to produce exceptional churchmen and flourished spiritually and culturally. Many new monasteries were established; Whitby as early as 657, and the great houses at Monkwearmouth in 674 and Jarrow in 682 (both founded by another

Northumbrian former nobleman, Benedict Biscop). The English Church was now self-confident enough to send missionaries of its own to evangelize among the pagans of Europe. One of the most prominent of these was Saint Boniface, who preached in Frisia and unconverted parts of Germany for 35 years from 719.

KEY MOMENT

SYNOD OF WHITBY

By 660, tensions between the Celtic and Roman traditions in England were becoming explosive. One issue was calculating the date of Easter (sometimes the celebrations were weeks apart in Celtic and Roman areas). To resolve the issue, a synod (church council) was held at Whitby, presided over by King Oswy of Northumbria. On the Roman side Wilfrid was the chief protagonist, while Colman, Abbot of Lindisfarne fought for the Celtic cause. Wilfrid was an able debater, and, with roots in the local nobility, had aristocratic support. King Oswy declared that the Roman method of calculating Easter should be adopted. Colman and many of his monks decamped to Ireland, weakening the Celtic cause in Northumbria.

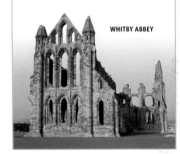

WHITBY ABBEY

AFTER

Between the 9th and 11th centuries, the missionary zeal of the Church in England faltered, due to the depredations of Viking raiders and an increasingly secular clergy.

THE VIKINGS AND THE CHURCH
The Vikings often **attacked monasteries**—such as Lindisfarne—in the initial phases of their attacks **46–47 »**. They were easy targets, undefended, and very wealthy. Later the Vikings **kidnapped senior churchmen**, such as Archbishop Aelfheah of Canterbury, who was seized by Viking raiders in 1011, and killed after he refused to allow himself to be ransomed.

THE CHURCH IN THE 10TH CENTURY
Wulfstan, Archbishop of Canterbury during the reign of King Aethelred II (979–1016), helped bolster anti-Viking resistance in England. He decreed a remarkable national series of fasts and prayer vigils in August 1009 and wrote the *Sermon of the Wolf* to the English in which he blamed the current plight of the kingdom on the English **neglect of their religion** and on the **lack of discipline** in many monasteries. Wulfstan's calls for reform were, however, swept away in the **political storms which engulfed England** over the next 60 years.

Viking Raiders and Settlers

At the end of the 8th century CE, Viking raiders began attacking vulnerable coastal settlements in England. Within 50 years, larger armies overcame the Anglo-Saxon kingdoms and started dividing the land between them. Finally, Wessex stood alone, weak and beleaguered.

Lindisfarne Abbey
Although probably the work of a small raiding party, the attack on Lindisfarne in 793 CE was the first in a series of Viking attacks that shocked the entire Christian world.

« BEFORE

Scandinavia was home to a rich and complex culture in the centuries before the Viking age. The political, technological, and economic changes which then took place here may have triggered the Viking raids.

RICH SCANDINAVIAN CULTURE
The Vendel culture flourished in Sweden in the 6th and 7th centuries, when **lavish weapons and jewelry were deposited in burial mounds**. Denmark seems to have developed a powerful centralized monarchy relatively early. Both here and in Sweden, trading settlements grew (at Ribe, Hedeby, and Birka), where **merchants exchanged Scandinavian goods** (such as furs, amber, walrus ivory, and locally produced pottery or combs) for more exotic imports.

OPPORTUNISTIC RAIDING
Long-distance trade was facilitated by the development of **new types of ships** (built with overlapping planks) and sails to supplement rowing power. However, trade could rapidly turn into opportunistic raiding, especially when periods of instability or political centralization constrained opportunities for young warriors at home. For these reasons, the **first small-scale Viking raids** on the coast of England, France, and Scotland began at the end of the 8th century.

GILT-BRONZE BRIDLE MOUNT

The *Anglo-Saxon Chronicle* of 793 CE speaks of "dire portents" that appeared over Northumbria, including "fiery dragons seen flying in the air." These seemed to be omens of the dragons set on the prows of the Viking longships that raided the monastery of Lindisfarne on June 8 that year. While the effects of this first raid were probably exaggerated by Alcuin of York, who wrote that the Lindisfarne church was "spattered with the blood of the priest of God," it was shocking nonetheless.

There was some uncertainty regarding the raiders' origins: they were alternately described as Danes and *nordmanni* ("northmen") in contemporary accounts, regardless of which part of Scandinavia they came from. The term "Viking" itself was rarely used in the early stages of the raids. Its origin is much debated; it may derive from the Viken, a part of the Oslo Fjord in Norway. In English, it has come to mean little more than a pirate.

Viking attacks
The years following the attack on Lindisfarne were punctuated by intermittent attacks in the surrounding regions: one on the monastery at Jarrow in 794, another in Iona, Scotland, in 795, and then on the monastic community at Rechru, Ireland, in 795. England was then almost free of raids for the next 40 years.

During this time, the Vikings started establishing bases in France, where the successors of Charlemagne had indulged in a series of civil wars, weakening the country and leaving it vulnerable to the Scandinavian predators. It was probably one such Viking group that appeared in Kent in 835, attacking the Isle of Sheppey.

The frequency of the raids rose rapidly after this; the following year the Vikings attacked Wessex and in 838 King Egbert had to face a combined

Raids and settlements
The Vikings raided almost the whole of northwestern Europe, and established long-lasting settlements in England, the Scottish Isles, parts of Ireland, and Normandy.

Viking-Cornish army at Hingston Down. In 840 the great trading center of Hamwic fell victim to a Viking raid.

The Vikings were highly mobile. They could pull their shallow-bottomed warships onto beaches without the need for a proper harbor, and even sail them up rivers to raid far inland. They were also able to travel quickly on land by horseback.

A new Viking host
As long as the Vikings returned to Scandinavia (or bases in Scotland or France) each winter, the threat from them could be contained. But in 850 a Viking army overwintered for the first time in England, on the Isle of Thanet. The following year, they stormed

[Map of British Isles and North Sea with dates: Shetland Islands 700, Orkney Islands, North Sea, Dublin, Waterford, York, Lincoln, Nottingham, Derby, Leicester, Stamford, Thetford, London, and dates 803, 795, 794, 853, 793, 796, 796, 860, 841, 865, 834–870, 841, 870, 793–850, 868, 800, 840, 840–860; 0 250km, 0 250 miles]

longship was built of fine oak

secure sail was attached to the mast

15 oar ports were located on each side

Oseberg ship
The Oseberg ship dates from around 820 CE. Viking ships were built using a skeleton of keel with bow and stern, to which a series of planks were connected, overlapping, and fastened with nails, creating a strong, flexible hull.

KNIFE

WAR AX

KNIFE SHEATH

SWORD

KEY
- Area of settlement
- Viking raid
- Viking fatherland
- Viking base

bow and prow were
elaborately decorated
with complex
wood carvings

350 The number of ships in the Viking raiding fleets that were recorded as having arrived in England in 850 CE, according to the *Anglo-Saxon Chronicle.*

It was, therefore, a depleted Viking army that crossed into Mercia in 878 with a new leader, Guthrum. Nonetheless, it was enough to force King Alfred, who had spent most of his reign either facing or worrying about Viking invasions, to flee to the Somerset marshes (see pp.52–53) to rally his followers. With Northumbria, East Anglia, and East Mercia in their hands, the Viking position in Anglo-Saxon England was unassailable.

Viking weapons
Only the richest Viking warriors possessed swords. The ax was a more common weapon of war and the most humble raiders may have been equipped only with knives or modified agricultural instruments.

an abortive assault on Wessex in 870, but it had petered out after a series of engagements. Despite the arrival of

"Never before has **such terror** appeared **in Britain**."

ALCUIN OF YORK, DESCRIBING THE 793 CE ATTACK ON LINDISFARNE

Canterbury and London, defeating King Berhtwulf of Mercia. The raids then intensified over the next decade. Yet worse was to come, for in 865 a new Viking host, called the "Great Army" by the *Anglo-Saxon Chronicle*, landed in East Anglia. Led by brothers, Ivar the Boneless, Halfdan, and Ubba, it may have numbered in the thousands and stayed for 13 years, extinguishing the Anglo-Saxon kingdoms.

After plundering in East Anglia and making peace with the East Anglian king, the Viking army headed north and captured York, throwing King Aelle into a pit filled with venomous snakes. They returned to East Anglia in 869, when King Edmund was defeated and killed.

Settling in Britain
Viking reinforcements (the "Summer Army") arrived in 871 and put an end to the independence of Mercia by 874. The Vikings had engaged in

the Summer Army, the unity of the raiders seems to have been fractured by this time. Ivar returned to Ireland, and in 874 the army under Halfdan split into two groups. One of these retired to Northumbria, and shared out the lands of the Northumbrians—this was the first recorded Viking attempt to settle in England. The remainder invaded Wessex in 875, with some success, but after this another faction elected to halt in Mercia and divide the land there among themselves.

ARM RING

BROOCH

Viking jewelry
Viking craftsmen were exceptionally skilled metal workers. Although fine pieces in gold were rare, many everyday items for personal adornment were decorated with twists, spirals, and fantastic beasts.

AFTER

The areas where the Vikings established settlements in England became known as the Danelaw. Eventually, the Viking raids ceased, but the Danelaw continued to retain a strong identity, distinct from the south in many ways.

VIKING LANGUAGE
The number of Vikings who settled in central, northern, and eastern England may not have been very large, but the **effect of their settlement was significant**. Some legal customs in the Danelaw persisted long after its reconquest by the kings of Wessex. Also, much of the **basic vocabulary of modern English** (words such as "eye," "bread," and "sky") comes from Old Norse, the Viking language, and place-names ending in -by and -thorpe also betray a Scandinavian origin.

SCANDINAVIA TURNS INWARD
The **Christianization of Denmark**, which began under Harold Bluetooth from 950 (commemorated by a magnificent runestone at Jelling), and that of Norway, brought Scandinavian monarchs into the mainstream of European rulers. In part with the aid of the Church, they built increasingly strong states with little room for the kind of freelance raids conducted by the Vikings. Although Christian Scandinavian monarchs **sought to conquer and absorb England** into their realms, by the late 11th century, the Viking Age had come to an end.

JELLING RUNESTONE

CUM PRETEXERANT FRATER TULLRETH

Book of Kells
One of the most lavishly illustrated manuscripts to survive from the Anglo-Saxon era, the *Book of Kells* contains the first four gospels in Latin. It is believed to date from around c. 800 CE and to have been created by the monks on Iona or in a monastery in Northumbria itself. The first page of each gospel was decorated with an ornate initial capital. Here, Saint Matthew is shown opposite the Virgin Mary and baby Jesus.

Alfred the Great

> **"He overthrew the pagans** with great slaughter, **smiting the fugitives**, and he pursued them as far as the fortress."

ASSER'S *LIFE OF ALFRED*, ON THE BATTLE OF EDINGTON, 878 CE

The statue of Alfred
This iconic statue of King Alfred was set up in 1899 in Winchester, a city with Roman origins, but which was revived by Alfred as one of his burhs.

Alfred, who became one of the most renowned kings of Wessex, spent most of his life under the shadow of the Viking threat. Born in 849 CE he was the fourth son of King Aethelwulf of Wessex. He may not have expected to become a king, although he was trained in the art of warfare, supporting his older brothers in battle against the Viking raiders (see pp.46–47). At the age of six he was too young to be considered for the throne on his father Aethelwulf's death in 855.

It was only after his brothers Aethelbald and Aethelbert died that Alfred became the heir to another brother, Aethelred. Alfred does not seem initially to have been given much responsibility by his brother, and so did not share in the abortive campaign of 868 when Aethelred and Burgred of Mercia failed in an attempt to trap Ivar the Boneless's Great Army in Nottingham.

Death of Aethelred
Wessex had not, up until then, been directly threatened by the Great Viking Army, but in 870 the Viking host crossed into Wessex, rapidly taking the important royal center of Reading. Although Alfred and Aethelred won an engagement at Ashdown, Halfdan, the Viking leader, made up for this by subsequent victories at Basing and at Merton on March 22, 871. Aethelred may have been wounded in one of these engagements, as he died in the middle of April, leaving Alfred undisputed ruler of a kingdom that seemed likely to be dismembered by an overwhelming force of Norse invaders.

After Alfred was defeated at Wilton in May, he paid off the enemy, buying nearly five years of peace in which there is little evidence of his making any further provision for the defense of his realm. Another Viking force, this time led by Guthrum, surged into Wessex in 876. Alfred was only saved by the destruction of the fleet intended to reinforce the invaders in a storm.

The making of a legend
In 878, he was not so lucky. Caught unawares at the end of the Christmas celebration on January 6, 878, Alfred was forced to flee and took refuge in the damp haven of the Athelney Marshes. It was the making of the King, and of his legend. It was from this time that the famous tale of Alfred and the burned cakes came into existence (see TIMELINE). Alfred began a guerrilla resistance and gathered his supporters to a meeting at "Egbert's Stone." Around 4,000 came and it was now Guthrum's turn to be caught unprepared as the Anglo-Saxon levies bested his veteran warriors at Edington. Barricaded in Chippenham, Guthrum was forced to accept

The Alfred Jewel
The inscription on the jewel states "Alfred made me" and it was probably commissioned by the King himself. It consists of a gold backing inset with a rock crystal into which is inscribed a figure that may represent the wisdom of Christ.

Christian baptism, together with most of his leading followers. Under the peace settlement, Alfred retained Wessex and took western Mercia, while Guthrum held the eastern portion of Mercia and East Anglia.

Army reforms

After getting the royal council, the witan, to swear that his sons would inherit the throne after him, so ensuring the line of succession, one of Alfred's first acts following the peace settlement with the Vikings was the building of a sea fleet. Although the armies of Wessex had, on occasion, been able to beat the Vikings on land, they had never

Coin from Alfred's reign
This silver penny of Alfred, issued around 880, post-dates reforms in which he restored the silver content of the coinage to 90 percent.

but was divided into two, so that one half could remain on their farms while the other half were fighting.

Alfred's defenses were put to the test in 892 when a massive Viking invading force landed in Kent, while another made its way up the Thames estuary. In four years of campaigning, which ranged across the country from the Welsh borders to Essex, the Vikings were unable to secure a permanent foothold in the face of the new network of burhs that now enmeshed Wessex. Having suffered a series of setbacks, and with their numbers severely diminished, in 896 they sailed back to France in the hope of easier plunder.

Alfred himself, who only learned to read when he was 12 and Latin even later, translated a series of books into Anglo-Saxon, beginning with the *Pastoral Care* of Pope Gregory I and the *Consolations of Philosophy* by the late Roman philosopher Boethius. These works were intended to provide firm moral examples for their readers. It was also around this time that the *Anglo-Saxon Chronicle* was begun, providing an invaluable near-contemporary source for his reign.

By the time of his death in 899, Alfred had restored the cultural life of Wessex, reformed its administration and, against all odds, seen off the Viking threat. By ensuring Wessex's survival, the only one of the Anglo-Saxon kingdoms to weather the storm, he had also ensured that when England was united, it was the kings of Wessex that would become its rulers.

- **849** Alfred is born in Wantage to King Aethelwulf of Wessex and his queen, Osburh.
- **853** Alfred, aged three, travels to Rome as his father's representative on a pilgrimage. He returns three years later with his father, who, on the return journey marries Judith, the daughter of the Frankish ruler Charles the Bald.
- **856** Alfred's brother Aethelbald revolts against their father and secures a share in the kingdom. Aethelwulf dies in 858.
- **860** Death of Aethelbald, who is succeeded by Aethelbert.
- **865** Aethelbert dies, and is succeeded as king by Aethelred, Alfred's full brother.
- **868** Alfred marries Ealhswith, the daughter of a Mercian nobleman. Although Alfred's wife did have some royal blood, it was not the most prestigious marriage, a sign perhaps that Aethelred did not intend his brother to succeed him. At the wedding ceremony Alfred is struck down by a mysterious malady, whose exact nature is unclear, but which will afflict him on and off for the next 25 years, inflicting excruciating pain on him at each reoccurrence.
- **871** Alfred, in command of part of the Anglo-Saxon army, is caught by the main Viking force at Ashdown. It is only the arrival of his brother in the thick of the fighting that saves him. Aethelred had allegedly been delayed by the need to wait until the end of Mass before joining the battle. Aethelred dies some weeks later of battle wounds, and Alfred succeeds him as King of Wessex.
- **878** Alfred flees to Athelney Marshes in Somerset after a surprise Viking attack. There he rallies a new Wessex army. Later legend has it that he took refuge in a peasant woman's house and when asked by her to look after the loaves (sometimes translated as "cakes") in her oven, he neglectfully allowed them to burn. More a parable about the consequences of neglecting the kingdom's defenses, the tale is almost certainly apocryphal.
- **May 878** Alfred's supporters meet at Egbert's Stone. The *fyrd* rallies and defeats Guthrum at Edington (or Ethandun).
- **882** Alfred's fleet wins a naval engagement against the Vikings, capturing two of their ships.
- **885** A Viking force attacks Rochester, but is beaten off; the first fruit of Alfred's army reforms.
- **886** Alfred makes a new treaty with Guthrum, defining the limits of their respective territories and setting the borders of the Danelaw. Alfred occupies London.
- **892** New Viking armies land in England. One part, led by Haesten, is temporarily bought off, but the armies unite by 893.
- **894** Haesten's men are besieged in Chester, but escape and attack north Wales.
- **895** The Vikings return to Essex and finally agree to leave England.
- **October 26, 899** Alfred dies and is buried in Winchester. His nephew Aethelwold revolts in a failed attempt to prevent the throne passing to Alfred's son, Edward the Elder.

> " He was **superior to all of his brothers**… both in wisdom and in all good habits, and furthermore because he was **warlike beyond measure** and victorious in almost all battles."

ASSER'S *LIFE OF ALFRED,* 893 CE

been able to challenge them at sea. The naval victory of 882, in which the Wessex fleet captured two Viking ships, was a sign the Scandinavians would not in future be able to raid the English coastline unmolested.

27,000 The number of men available for military service from Alfred's burhs. Calculated from a version of the *Burghal Hidage*, which documented the military obligation of the burhs' inhabitants.

In the early 880s, Alfred also boosted the land defenses of his realm by ordering the construction of a series of new fortified towns or burhs ("boroughs" in modern English), each around 20 miles (32 km) apart. These provided a network of strongpoints which would hinder any subsequent Viking invasion and whose inhabitants were obliged to provide a certain amount of military service. Alfred also reorganized the army, so that the *fyrd*, the peasant levy, did not have to serve all at once,

Spreading literacy

Alfred had saved Wessex, but it was not only for this that he is remembered as "the Great" (the only English king to receive such an accolade). From the 880s, the King sponsored a revival of learning in Wessex, attracting to his court men such as Waeferth, the Mercian Bishop of Worcester; Asser, a Welsh monk from St. Davids who would become Alfred's biographer; and Grimbald of St. Bertin, a leading Frankish scholar. He established a school at court to educate the children of the nobility, setting aside a portion of the royal income to fund this, although his aim of bringing literacy to all free-born men was not achieved.

Commemorative tower
The tower, built in 1770 by a wealthy banker, was set up near the supposed site of Egbert's Stone, the rallying point for Alfred's remaining supporters in the spring of 878.

BEFORE

Alfred the Great saved Wessex from conquest by the Vikings, but the Scandinavian invaders still occupied large portions of England's north and the Midlands.

VIKING SURVIVORS

The survivors among the Vikings of the Great Army of 865 CE and the Summer Army of 871 had mostly settled down in Mercia, East Anglia, and Northumbria, establishing bases in **strongholds at York and in the Five Boroughs** (Lincoln, Derby, Nottingham, Leicester, and Stamford).

VIKING REINFORCEMENTS

The campaigns of Alfred the Great **≪ 50–51** caused some difficulties for the British Vikings. By 900, **they were looking to the Viking settlements** in Ireland, the Isle of Man, and the Scottish Isles **for support and reinforcements**. In addition to western Mercia and Wessex, the Vikings faced opposition from what remained of the English kingdom of Northumbria, around Bamburgh.

VIKING SWORD

Wessex Takes the Lead

In 900 CE, the kingdom of Wessex had only recently secured its independence from the Viking threat. Over the next half-century a series of able kings progressively conquered the areas of Viking England, until their lands bordered with Scotland. Now the Wessex rulers' claim to be "kings of the English" was no hollow boast.

Edward the Elder, the son of King Alfred, hardly had a smooth path to succession. After Alfred's death in 899 CE, Aethelwold, his nephew, attempted to seize the throne. He failed, fleeing to Viking-held Northumbria, where the Scandinavians installed him as their king. Edward spent the next four years trying to defeat Aethelwold, who finally perished at the Battle of the Holme in 903.

Taking Viking territories

Edward launched raids into Danish territories in 909, but it was only during a Viking counterstrike southward the following year that he won his first significant victory, at Tettenhall, where three Danish kings perished, together with huge numbers of their men. The death in 911 of Aethelred, who had been ealdorman of Mercia, further strengthened the Wessex king's position, as his replacement was his widow Aethelflaed, the "Lady of the Mercians," who just happened to be Edward's sister.

Aethelflaed secured their position in Mercia by fortifying Chester in 907 and then transforming the ancient royal center of Tamworth into a burh, or defensive fortification, in 913. She created a series of further burhs, including Stafford, Warwick, Eddisbury, and Runcorn. Meanwhile, Edward campaigned to the north and the east, forcing the Viking kingdoms of Essex, Bedfordshire, and Northamptonshire, to surrender by 916. The Scandinavians of the Five Boroughs did not present a common front and had not had time to establish a centralized kingship such as grew up in York within a few years. When Aethelflaed captured Derby in 917, the only remaining Viking forces south of the Humber were based in Leicester, Stamford, Nottingham, and Lincoln. By the end of the

The Danelaw divisions

Before Edward the Elder began his reconquest of the Danish-controlled areas of England around 910, the Scandinavians controlled East Anglia, the East Midlands, an area around York, and a block of territory in the northwest.

KEY
■ Danelaw
■ Kingdom of the English

SCOTIA
STRATHCLYDE
NORTHUMBRIA
York
Chester Lincoln
DANISH MERCIA
Derby Nottingham
Shrewsbury Lichfield Stamford EAST ANGLIA
Leicester
ENGLISH KINGDOM OF GUTHRUM
MERCIA Cambridge
WALES
Wantage London
Bath Chippenham Canterbury
Wedmore WESSEX
Athelney Winchester
Exeter

N
0   200 km
0   200 miles

following year all of these were in Edward's possession, while York itself had submitted to Aethelflaed.

Edward's setbacks

Edward then suffered two setbacks. Firstly, Aethelflaed died, opening up the question of the succession to Mercia at a less-than-convenient moment. Edward had Aethelflaed's daughter, Aelfwynn, seized and removed to Wessex, where she could not provide the focus for any resistance to his rule over Mercia.

Ecclesiastical revival

This 10th-century reliquary cross, which contained the finger of an unidentified saint, epitomizes the progressive ecclesiastical revival that followed the Wessex kings' recapture of English lands.

Potentially more serious was the rise of a new Viking power in the north of England. The weakening of the Danes of the Five Boroughs had opened up opportunities for ambitious adventurers from other Viking lands and so in 918, Ragnall, the grandson of Ivar the Boneless, descended on northern England. After an indecisive battle at Corbridge, he moved south and seized York, establishing a Viking kingdom, which acted as a block to Wessex's interests in the region. Edward reacted by constructing a series of fortresses in the northwest and Midlands (including Nottingham) to prevent any further expansion from York. By 920 Ragnall felt it politic to accept Edward as his overlord (joining the Welsh kings of Gwynedd and Dyfed, who had done so in 918). Although this and the submission of

Site of the witenagemot

These chapel ruins at Cheddar, Somerset, are on the site of an earlier chapel and near the site of an Anglo-Saxon palace where three meetings between the kings of Wessex and their council (witan) took place.

After the fall of York in 947 CE, England experienced more than 30 years of peace in which the strengthening of royal administration and monastic reform were the main developments.

EDGAR'S REIGN

Edgar was Eadred's younger son and became king of Wessex in 959. His reign was largely peaceful and in 973 **he received the submission of six kings** (including those of Scotland, Strathclyde, and Gwynedd), who are said to have taken oars and rowed him on the Dee River. He supported a **series of Church reforms** undertaken by his Archbishop of Canterbury, Dunstan, and **improved the coinage** by insisting that all coins be recalled for reminting every six years. During his reign the custom of appointing *ealdormen* to larger areas (such as the whole of East Anglia) rather than individual shires became established.

REMAINING VIKING POWER

The Vikings remained in control of Dublin, the Isle of Man, and parts of Scotland **54–55 »**. At the end of the 10th century, **new Viking leaders** with the resources of whole kingdoms behind them launched fresh raids. Men such as Sweyn Forkbeard of Sweden commenced **a new Viking Age in Britain** in the 990s.

Ealdred, Earl of Bamburgh, and the kings of Strathclyde and Constantine gave Edward notional lordship over virtually all of Britain, he exercised no real control in those areas. By the time of Edward's death in 924, Mercia was fully incorporated into Wessex. Athelstan, the new king, moved to secure the position on his northern border by a marriage alliance between his sister and Sihtric, the Viking ruler of York. When Sihtric died in 927, Athelstan took the opportunity to drive out his successor, Olaf, and take York for himself, razing its fortifications in an effort to neutralize any possible future threat. In the afterglow of victory, he arranged a meeting at Penrith at which he received the submission of King Constantine of Scotland, Hywel Dda of Dyfed, the King of Strathclyde, and the Earl of Bamburgh.

King of all Britain

In 934 Athelstan felt strong enough to invade Scotland, pushing deep into the central part of the country. King Constantine reacted by building an

> " The king of Scots … and Ragnall and sons of Eadwulf and all who live in Northumbria … and also the king of the Strathclyde Britons … **chose him as father and lord**."

ANGLO-SAXON CHRONICLE ENTRY RECORDING THE SUBMISSION OF THE NORTH TO EDWARD THE ELDER, 920 CE

this ground, at which point York itself fell prey to factional infighting, resulting in a rapid succession of kings in no position to reassert themselves against the armies of Wessex. Even so, Edmund was forced to grant Cumbria to Malcolm I of Scotland, in exchange for his support against the Vikings.

Final defeat at York

A final threat from York emerged in 947, when Eric Bloodaxe, son of King Harald Fairhair of Norway, and a refugee from Scandinavia, was recognized as king. Six years of confused campaigning followed before Eadred—Edmund's brother and successor as king of Wessex—invaded

WITENAGEMOT A meeting of the Anglo-Saxon royal council, the witan. It was not a formal institution, including the secular and ecclesiastical nobles the king chose to summon. Its role was to give advice on policy, but the king was not constrained to follow it.

ANGLO-SAXON KING (c. 893–939 CE)

KING ATHELSTAN

Athelstan was the eldest son of Edward the Elder. His upbringing in Mercia—he had been raised by his aunt Aethelflaed—made him acceptable as a sovereign to the Mercian nobility there, and there was relatively little resistance to his rule. Although much of his reign was occupied with the struggle against the Vikings of Northumbria (his success at Brunanburh, setting a seal on his dominance of the north) he also absorbed Lancashire and drove the Britons out of Exeter. Athelstan's prestige as a result of these victories was high, and on his coins he styled himself as "King of the English and Ruler of All Britain," and he was able to arrange important diplomatic marriages for his sisters, to Charles the Simple and Emperor Otto I. His network of alliances was also boosted by foreign nobles, who were fostered at his court, including Louis d'Outremer (the future Louis IV of France) and Haakon, son of King Harald Fairhair of Norway. Athelstan's unexpected death in 939, almost caused the loss of everything he had achieved.

alliance of all those who feared the expansionist power of Wessex: the Scots, the Strathclyde Britons, the Dublin Vikings, and Scandinavians from the Western Isles. The allied army invaded England in 937 and, at Brunanburh (possibly in Cheshire) suffered a catastrophic defeat in which five kings of the anti-Wessex alliance died (though Constantine himself escaped). Athelstan now referred to himself as Imperator Orbis Britanniae (emperor of the whole world of Britain), but his death in 939 showed that the paramount position of Wessex was far from secure.

Athelstan's brother Edmund succeeded to the throne of Wessex, but almost at once lost most of the gains of the preceding 30 years, as Olaf Guthfrithson rode the tide of a Northumbrian revolt to become Viking king of York, seizing, in addition, most of the land of the Five Boroughs. It took until 942 for Edmund to recover

Northumbria. The citizens of York, seeing the cause was lost, expelled Erik, who was murdered while fleeing northward. After half a century of warfare, the kings of Wessex had finally, or so they thought, rid England of the threat of Viking conquest, and had emerged as undisputed rulers of all England.

Ireland in the Viking Age

The Vikings never succeeded in conquering Ireland, instead establishing a series of port-enclaves along the Irish coastline from the 840s CE. From these, the Vikings alternately allied and fought with a succession of native Irish kings, until they finally lost their political independence in the early 11th century. Although their kingdoms did not last, the urban culture they established survived.

Viking gold ring
Some of the treasures plundered from Irish monasteries and churches were melted down and made into jewelry such as this ornate spiral ring.

« BEFORE

The early Viking raids on Ireland began in the 790s CE. They were comparatively small scale and it was more than 40 years before larger groups came to settle.

EARLY VIKING ATTACKS
The first reported Viking attack came in 795 against the monastery of Rechru (Raithlin) which was "laid waste." Raithlin lay off the northeast coast of Ireland, an easy journey for marauders making their way from Scotland, but soon **the Vikings swept south**, attacking Inis Pátraic off the coast of County Dublin in 798 and smashing the much-revered shrine of Do Chonna. Just as they had in England, **the Viking raids caused outrage**, increased by the fact that **monasteries and churches**, with their easily portable treasures, were the raiders' principal targets.

THE RAIDS CONTINUE
By 807 Viking raiders reached the west coast of Ireland, **burning monasteries** as they went. Occasionally the Irish fought back successfully; an annal entry for 811 speaks of a **"slaughter of pagans"** by the men of Ulster. The *Book of Kells* was brought to Ireland after a raid on the monastery at Iona in Scotland.

BOOK OF KELLS

The main accounts of the early Viking raids come from chronicles such as the *Annals of Ulster*, which were compiled in monasteries. The writers reserved particular venom for the Norsemen, referring to them as *geinti* ("heathens") and holding up the Viking raids as an example of divine wrath against an Ireland that had turned away from God.

Early attacks

The early attackers, who seem to have come from Norway, gradually expanded the field of their operations, in the south reaching Cork by 822 CE, and in the north plundering the monastery of Bangor in 824, where they scattered the relics of Saint Comgall from its shrine, in a shocking act of sacrilege.

Unlike in France and England (see pp.52–53), there was no centrally organized resistance to the Vikings in Ireland, which may have encouraged the Scandinavians to mount further raids. In the 830s, these became more serious, sometimes penetrating deep inland; in 837 two large Viking fleets appeared carrying thousands of warriors (probably from the Norse settlements in Scotland), one on the Boyne and another on the

> **1,200** The number of Vikings said to have been killed at the Battle of Castledermot (848) against Ólchobar, King of Munster, and Lorcán, King of Leinster.

Liffey (near the site of present-day Dublin). The army of the Uí Néill kings, which tried to resist them, was cut to pieces.

In 839, a Viking fleet stayed over the winter for the first time in Lough Neagh, and remained for two years. If this was a grim development, far worse was to come. For in 841 the Vikings began to establish fortified naval bases, or *longphorts*, first at Linn Dúachaill in County Louth and

Saint Conall Cael's bell

This iron handbell from the 7th–9th centuries may have belonged to Saint Conall Cael. It later became enshrined as a relic. Such items were a common target of Viking raiders.

at Dublin and then, in the following decade, at a number of other points including Lough Ree (845) and Cork (848). The main leader of the Viking raiders in the 840s was Turgéis, who operated from the *longphorts* at Lough Ree, and whose attacks ranged widely through Connaught and Meath, including the abbey of Clonmacnoise. At the latter, his wife Ota is said to have performed a pagan divination rite called *seidr*, while draped across the high altar. Finally, in 845, Turgéis was captured by Máel Sechnaill, the king of Tara, and drowned in Lough Owel.

The Irish kings, who had expended so much effort in fighting each other, now realized that the Vikings posed a much greater threat to their survival. In 848, Máel Sechnaill won another victory near Skreen, County Meath, in which he is said to have killed 700 Vikings. An embassy sent by the Irish to the Frankish King Charles the Bald the same year announced that they had driven the pagans out of Ireland.

Viking Dublin

The Vikings had not, however, been removed, although they were weakened by internal disputes and the

"The Irish, falling upon the Northmen, **with the help of Our Lord Jesus Christ** were victorious and drove them from our country."

ANNALS OF SAINT BERTIN, RECOUNTING THE IRISH ENVOY'S ACCOUNT TO THE FRANKISH COURT OF THEIR RECENT VICTORIES, 848 CE

arrival of a new group from Denmark which sacked Dublin in 851. The Scandinavians were only saved from tearing themselves apart by the arrival of Amlaíb from Scotland in 853, who allied himself with Imar, another Viking leader, and reestablished the supremacy of Dublin. He made it the main Norse center in Scotland, the Isle of Man, and England. For the next half-century the dynasty that Amlaíb and Imar founded held sway in Dublin and across the Irish Sea. Frequently, however, the Dublin dynasty's interest in Britain weakened their position in Ireland, as in 866 when the Uí Néill king Áed mac Néill sacked a series of Viking *longphorts*, burning the Viking fort in Dublin the following year. In 873 Imar died, and for the next 30 years, the Dublin Vikings were riven by a series of dynastic feuds, until finally, in 903, the Irish recaptured Dublin.

The Viking return

Ireland's gain was Britain's loss, as an exodus of Dublin Vikings descended on northwestern England and parts of Wales. It was not long, however, before the Vikings returned to Ireland with the appearance in 914 of "a great sea-fleet of pagans" in Waterford. In 917, Imar's grandson, Sihtric Caec, and Ragnall, a Dane from Northumbria, arrived with a new force. Níall Glúndub, the King of Tara, saw the danger and moved against the Norsemen, a campaign which ended in a heavy defeat and the retaking of Dublin by Sihtric.

The Vikings established a second settlement at Dublin close to the first *longphort* of 841. This phase of the Viking town has been excavated, revealing a network of streets and lanes divided by boundary fences of wattle, defining plots containing well-built houses. Remains have been found of a variety of industries, including comb-making, blacksmiths and other metalworkers, wood- and amber-working. At this time, Dublin's population was probably several thousand, and it was clearly a prosperous place.

The Second Age

This Second Viking Age in Ireland from 917 saw an attempt by Sihtric and his kinsman Godfrid to create a Viking kingdom in Ireland to match that of York in northern England. However, this effort was undermined by their continued involvement in England, as first Sihtric, then Godfrid succeeded to the throne of York and abandoned their Irish possessions to deputies. Godfrid's successor, Amlaíb, also became entangled in English affairs, fighting against King Athelstan of Wessex at the Battle of Brunanburh in 937. Amlaíb escaped the defeat of his allies at the battle, but he became King of York, as did his successor in Dublin, Amlaíb Cuaran in 944–945.

On his return from England, Amlaíb Cuaran threw himself wholeheartedly into trying to restore the Viking position in Ireland. By now, however, the Norse were more like another fractious Irish kingdom than a foreign power to be feared. In 980, they were thoroughly crushed by Máel Sechnaill of the southern Uí Néill, who then forced Dublin to come to terms, including the release of all Irish slaves in the territory ruled by the Vikings.

Rise and fall of Brian Boru

By the 980s, the Dál Cais dynasty under Brian Boru had established itself in Munster, beginning a bitter struggle with Máel Sechnaill for the high-kingship of Ireland. In 997, the two Irish kings divided the island between them, with Brian becoming the nominal overlord of Dublin. He married his daughter to the leader of the Dublin Vikings and married himself into the same family to strengthen his position.

A desperate final bid by the Vikings for independence from the Irish rulers took place in 1014, when the Dublin Norse recruited an army, including Vikings from Orkney and the Hebrides, to help them throw off Brian's rule. On April 23, 1014, the Vikings faced

4,500 The number of men in Brian Boru's army at the Battle of Clontarf in 1014.

1,000 The number of men fighting under Sigtrygg at the Battle of Clontarf in 1014.

the troops of Brian Boru and Máel Sechnaill at Clontarf to the north of Dublin. Although Brian was killed, the Irish were utterly victorious. After 1014, Dublin remained a fundamentally Scandinavian town for more than a century, but the Viking Age in Ireland was over.

Kilmacduagh tower
Kilmacduagh monastery was founded by Saint Colman in the early 7th century. Its round tower may have offered a refuge against Viking raiders.

AFTER ≫

Scandinavian influence on the art and language of Ireland lived on even after the Viking defeat at Clontarf in 1014.

VIKING STYLES
The Ringerike style, with its spirals and tendrils in the shape of leaves, and the Urnes style, with its fantastic beasts and sinuous snakes, spread widely throughout Ireland, appearing both in **metalworking** and on **stone sculpture**.

LANGUAGE AND TOWNS
A few Viking terms made their way into modern Irish, such as *accaire* ("anchor"), *margad* ("market"), and *sráid* ("street"). The most enduring Viking legacy of all, however, is the **establishment of the first towns in Ireland**, including Dublin, Limerick, and Waterford.

IRISH KINGS
The **death of Brian Boru at Clontarf was a disaster** for his family, the Ua Briain. Máel Sechnaill once again became the most powerful king in Ireland until his death in 1022. Thereafter, Diarmait of Leinster was supreme in 1042–1072, using the remaining Viking fleet of Dublin in campaigns in Wales in the 1040s. His court was a **magnet for disaffected English and Welsh princes,** and in 1066 he **gave refuge to the sons of Harold Godwinson** after their father's defeat at the Battle of Hastings **70–71 ≫**.

King Canute
Despite being Danish, Canute, shown here in a 13th-century manuscript, was widely accepted in England. His rule brought peace, because his rule over the lands from which the Vikings originated meant no new raiders would attack England's shores.

Triumph of the Danes

Aethelred the Unready proved incapable of fending off a new wave of Viking raiders in the 990s CE. By 1016, these raids had turned into an invasion and the Danish king, Sweyn, seized the English throne. His son Canute and his grandsons presided over a quarter century of Danish rule in England.

Maldon causeway
Ealdorman Byrhtnoth allowed Olaf's Vikings in 991 CE to cross this causeway leading from Northey Island. Although the Anglo-Saxons fought bravely, most of them paid for Byrhtnoth's decision with their lives.

BEFORE

Following the final collapse of the Viking kingdom of York in 954 CE, England experienced around 30 years free of significant Viking raiding.

REMAINING VIKING POWER
Political **changes in Scandinavia** at the end of the 10th century boded ill for the ruling English House of Wessex. The Danish king, Harold Bluetooth, consolidated his political control over his kingdom and was among the first of the Viking rulers to accept Christianity. Harold's building of great round forts at Trelleborg, Fyrkat, and Nonnebakken in Denmark, around 980, shows he was **able to command considerable resources**.

NEW RAIDS
From the 980s Viking raids began once more against the coast of England. There was a **political crisis** caused by the **murder of King Edward** in 978 (at the instigation of Aelfhere, Earl of Mercia) and the new king, Aethelred, was at first uncertain of his throne.

OLD BASES
Although the Viking raiders of England came principally from Denmark and Norway, the Vikings retained their bases in Ireland, the Isle of Man, and the islands of Scotland, where **the last great raid** took place under Magnus Barelegs of Norway in 1098–1099.

RECONSTRUCTION OF A LONGHOUSE AT TRELLEBORG

A ethelred—whose nickname means "Ill-Advised"—was relatively untroubled by the first, small-scale Viking raids. In 991 CE, however, a much more dangerous Viking army made its way from Scandinavia under the command of

> **48,000** The number of pounds of silver paid by Aethelred to Sweyn as part of the Danegeld of 1012.

Olaf Tryggvason. Landing near Maldon in Essex, the raiders were at first bottled up on an offshore island by Byrhtnoth, the local *ealdorman* (high-ranking official). He then unaccountably let them across the narrow causeway to give battle and found his army cut to pieces.

Paying Danegeld
On the advice of Archbishop Wulfstan, Aethelred paid out a Danegeld of 10,000 pounds of silver to be rid of the invaders, a bribe which merely attracted more Scandinavian armies in search of a similar payoff. Progressively higher Danegelds were paid in 994, 1002, 1007, and 1012, when they reached a colossal sum nearly five times that of the 991 payment.

The strain caused in England by the Vikings led to panic measures being taken. On St. Brice's Day (November 13) 1002, the King ordered the massacre of all Danes in England. This only prompted a fresh invasion in 1003 led by King Sweyn of Denmark, bent on vengeance (Olaf had made peace with Aethelred and agreed not to return to England). From then until 1013, Sweyn and the Danes returned again and again, aided by the wavering loyalty of several Anglo-Saxon ealdormen.

There was a brief respite in 1012 when the Viking leader Thorkell the Tall defected to the English, disgusted at the murder of Archbishop Aelfheah

of Canterbury after his capture by a Viking band. Thorkell returned to Sweyn's side and in 1013 the Danish king landed at Sandwich, Kent, with an enormous force. The rapid submission of Earl Uhtred of Northumbria led to the collapse of Anglo-Saxon resistance. Aethelred fled to the court of his brother-in-law, Richard of Normandy, and by October Sweyn was recognized as king of England.

Canute takes power
Sweyn's early death in February 1014 breathed false hope into the English cause, prompting Aethelred's return. However, Sweyn's son Canute, once he had secured his position in Denmark, returned to England in 1015. Although he briefly acknowledged Aethelred's son, Edmund Ironside, as king of southern England in 1016, both Aethelred and Edmund died within six months of each other and by December, Canute was unchallenged king of the whole country. England was now part of a vast realm that spanned the North Sea and included Denmark, Norway, and part of Sweden. The lack of any credible Anglo-Saxon pretender made Canute's rule secure, and his rapid marriage to Emma, Aethelred's widow, cemented his position both in England and in respect of his new father-in-law, the Duke of Normandy.

Canute's main change to the governance of England was to establish the new large earldoms of Northumbria, Mercia, East Anglia, and (in the 1020s) Wessex. He rewarded his leading followers, making Thorkell earl of East Anglia (until his exile in 1020 for

Wulfstan Psalter
Archbishop Wulfstan of York was one of the leading intellectuals at Aethelred's court, and a noted writer of sermons. His tenure saw the production of beautiful liturgical manuscripts, such as this illustrated psalter.

rebellion) and Eric earl of Northumbria. He also appointed native Anglo-Saxons, giving Mercia to Leofric (whose wife was Lady Godiva), and Wessex to Godwin, whose son would later become King Harold II. Canute established his main court in England, at Winchester, which became the capital of his huge northern empire. At the time of his death in 1035 it seemed the triumph of the Danes was complete.

AFTER

Canute's death led to the dissolution of his empire, but Danish rule over England continued under his sons.

RULE OF HAROLD HAREFOOT
Although Canute had probably intended his son Harthacnut to inherit the English throne, the heir was in Denmark when his father died. This allowed **Harold Harefoot**, his half-brother, **to seize the throne of England** with the assistance of Godwin Earl of Wessex.

THE LAST DANISH KING
Harthacnut came to the English throne in 1040. His two-year reign was the last by a Danish king and was followed by the **restoration of Anglo-Saxon rule** under Edward the Confessor **60–61 »**. A Viking fleet **invaded England** under Harald Hardrada of Norway in 1066, and as late as 1085, Cnut IV of Norway planned (but did not dispatch) an expedition to England.

Runestone
This runestone from Uppland in Sweden commemorates Ulf, who is said to have received three payments of Danegeld from Viking leaders, including from Canute.

Independent Realms

After several false starts, Scotland became a united nation in the 9th century CE, excluding some areas on the fringe. Wales was almost united several times before the 10th century, but the attempts failed. It was, therefore, less well placed than Scotland to resist the aggressive intentions of English kings.

St. David's shrine
Reverence for the 6th-century monk St. David, who died in 589 CE, spread until he was recognized as the patron saint of Wales. The shrine stands in St. David's Cathedral, built on the site of the monastery the saint founded.

BEFORE

In the centuries following the Anglo-Saxon invasions of England, new kingdoms emerged in Wales and Scotland.

EARLY KINGDOMS
Early Welsh kingdoms had their **origins in the tribal groups** of Roman and pre-Roman times such as Dyfed, which derived from the Demetae. In Scotland, the emergence of **rival kingdoms of the Picts**, the Dal Riatan Scots from Ireland, the Strathclyde Britons (whose stronghold was at Dumbarton Castle), and an **area ruled from Northumbria** led to a struggle for power.

DUMBARTON CASTLE

Historical developments in Wales in the 6th century are rather obscure. Gildas, in his *De Excidio*, inveighs against the evils perpetrated by the "Five Tyrants," including Maelgwyn of Gwynedd who died in the late 540s, and Vortepor, ruler of the Demetae (or Dyfed). Also around the late 6th century, the kingdom of Powys emerged in central Wales. It was principally these three kingdoms that struggled for supremacy over the next three centuries.

A brief hope of reuniting the Welsh lands with the Britons of the southwest and Cumbria, from whom they had been cut off by the advancing Anglo-Saxons, occurred in the reign of Cadwallon of Gwynedd. Cadwallon defeated and killed Edwin of Northumbria in the battle of Hatfield in 633. The triumph was short-lived, however, for in 635 Cadwallon perished in battle against Edwin's brother Oswald at Heavenfield near Hexham.

It was two centuries before another ruler of note took power. Merfyn Frych became king of Gwynedd in 825. During his 19-year reign, he consolidated the kingdom and passed on a strong position to his son, Rhodri Mawr or Rhodri the Great.

Rhodri expands Gwynedd
It was a moment of opportunity for Gwynedd as the kings of Mercia, who had long harried the Welsh principality, were under extreme and fatal pressure from Wessex to the south and Viking invaders. Rhodri, too, had to face the Viking threat, and in 856 he defeated them in a great battle on Anglesey.

He also succeeded in expanding his power to the south. Cyngen of Powys died in exile in Rome in 856, probably having been driven out by Rhodri, and the last known independent ruler of Ceredigion, Gwgan, drowned in 872, after which it was annexed by Gwynedd. Rhodri died in 878 and power was divided amongst his six sons. The most active

Welsh ruler
This manuscript depiction of Hywel Dda stresses the idea of his kingship, showing him crowned and bearing a scepter. His successful military campaigns, issuing of a law code, and minting of coinage bolstered the image of a successful and benevolent king.

of them, Anarawd, struggled to contain the twin threats of Alfred the Great's Wessex and resurgent Viking groups who established themselves in Anglesey in 903.

Welsh unity under Hywel
It was Anarawd's nephew Hywel Dda, or Hywel the Good, who achieved the next near-unification of Wales. He became ruler of Dyfed in 910 and strengthened his claim by his marriage to Elen, niece of Rhydderch, the last king of the native Dyfed dynasty. By 920, he united Dyfed with the smaller territory of Seisyllwg to create a new kingdom of Deheubarth.

Although he submitted in 927 to Athelstan of Wessex, it may have been a means of gaining advantage against his great rival Idwal Foel of Gwynedd, who adopted a more openly aggressive anti-English policy. Hywel maintained a more diplomatic stance, visiting the English court several times and even making a pilgrimage to Rome in 929.

In 942 Idwal launched an attack against England in which he died, and Hywel took advantage to invade Gwynedd before Idwal's sons could

Constantine II
Constantine built a coalition of those interested in weakening the power of Wessex. His defeat at Brunanburh in 937 could have been a disaster, but his kingdom was strong enough for Alba to endure.

35 The number of Welsh rulers who died violent deaths between the end of Hywel Dda's reign in 949 and the Norman conquest of England in 1066.

(642–70), prevented this. In fact, Oswy may have exacted tribute from Picts.

In 671, the Picts seem to have revolted against Northumbria's hegemony and as a result, their king, Drest, was expelled. His replacement, Bridei mac Beli, came and exacted Pictish revenge at the Battle of Nechtansmere in 685. In this battle, King Ecgfrith of Northumbria perished along with the prospects of an Anglo-Saxon dominance of southern Scotland.

Disunity among Picts
The Picts themselves were divided into various clan groups and kingdoms. The ruler of one of these in the south, Óengus mac Fergus (Onuist in Pictish), defeated a rival, Elphin, at Moncreiffe near Perth in 728 and conquered northern Pictland and parts of Dal Riata by the late 730s.

A defeat inflicted by the Strathclyde Britons in 740 briefly threatened Onuist's dominance, but in 746 they

Scotland remained united, but none of the Welsh rulers succeeded in restoring anything like Hywel Dda's kingdom until the beginning of the 11th century.

KENNETH'S LINE REIGNS
Scotland was ruled by the descendants in the male line of Kenneth MacAlpin until the reign of Mael Coluim, or Malcolm II (1005–1034). At times, they were **strong enough to intervene in England**. Malcolm II invaded the country while it was weakened by the Viking invasions, and won a victory at Carham on the Tweed River in 1018. Malcolm's grandson Duncan I was deposed by Macbeth, the *mormaer* of

Moray in 1040. From the 1060s, Duncan's restored descendants faced a greater threat from Norman England **72–73** ≫, which culminated in **a series of bitter wars** in the 13th century **92–93** ≫.

WELSH INSTABILITY
After Hywel Dda's death, Wales became unstable and suffered Viking raids—St. David's monastery was sacked in 999. Gruffydd ap Llywelyn **90–91** ≫ restored the power of Gwynedd from 1023, defeating an English army at Welshpool in 1039 and annexing Deheubarth. However, under pressure from Harold II of England, his support fell away, and he was murdered in 1063. **Wales was annexed** by Edward I in 1283.

claim the throne. This helped him become the king of most of Wales, save Morganwg and Gwent in the southeast. The rest of his reign was peaceful. On

> ## "So then also … came in flight, to his northern land, **Constantine**, the hoary warrior."

THE ANGLO-SAXON CHRONICLE'S *BRUNANBURH POEM* RELATING THE DEFEAT OF CONSTANTINE II AND HIS ALLIES AT THE BATTLE OF BRUNANBURH, 937 CE

his death in 949 it looked as if the prospects for Welsh unity were bright.

Scottish campaigns
By the late 6th century CE, the Dal Riata kingdom in southwestern Scotland, which was established by immigrants from northern Ireland over the preceding century (see p.31), was beginning to make inroads into the lands of the previously dominant Picts.

King Áedán of Dal Riata, who came to the throne in 576, launched far-flung campaigns in Orkney, the Isle of Man, and central Scotland as far as Stirling. These campaigns, as well as Áedán's possession of ancestral Dal Riatan lands in Ireland, created a precocious empire that straddled the Irish Sea.

The defeat and death of Áedán's grandson, Domnal Brecc, at Mag Rath in County Down in 639 led to the total eclipse of the Dal Riatan position in Ireland, and an opportunity for the Pictish kings to reassert themselves in Scotland. However, the growing power of the English kingdom of Northumbria, beginning in the reign of King Oswy

submitted to him in a treaty at Clyde Rock. Instability in Pictland after the death of Onuist in 751, together with the destabilizing effect of the Viking raids that began in 795 with an attack on Iona, made the Dal Riatans of the southwest much better placed to assume the mantle of Scottish unity in the 9th century.

Getting Scotland together
In 839, the Vikings won a great victory in which Uuen, ruler of the Pictish kingdom of Fortriu, was slain along with Aed mac Boanta, the king of Dal Riata, and "others almost beyond counting." As the grip of the descendants of Onuist over Pictland collapsed, the way was open to new men. One such, Cinaed mac Ailpin, or Kenneth MacAlpin, succeeded in adding the crown of Pictland to his existing domain of Dal Riata in 842, thereby uniting the two rival kingdoms for the first time.

Kenneth is conventionally regarded as the unifier of Scotland, but it was by no means certain that his achievement

would be any more lasting than those of Áedán or Onuist, and a separate Pictish identity persisted for at least 50 years. Kenneth's brother Domnal (858–862) and nephew Constantine I (862–876) were both still referred to as "Kings of the Picts" in the annals.

Constantine had to face a worsening threat from the Vikings as Amlaíb, king of Dublin, embarked on a three-year campaign of plunder. This concluded with the capture of Dumbarton, the main stronghold of the Strathclyde Britons in 870. Constantine died in 877 in a battle against the Vikings and for a decade, the MacAlpin family was excluded from power.

When Constantine's son Domnall regained the throne in 889, it was not as the ruler of the Picts and Scots (Dal Riatans) but as the King of Alba. The long-term survival and unity of this new kingdom of Alba was secured by Domnall's successor, his cousin Constantine II. Over his 40-year reign, Constantine saw the demotion of the former Pictish client kings of Athol, Angus, and Mar to the status of royal stewards (or *mormaer*) and an increasing confidence in external diplomatic affairs.

Constantine's achievements
It was Constantine II (900–943) who built an alliance of Viking, Strathclyde Britons, and Scots to stem the tide of advance of Athelstan of Wessex in northern England. The fact that the defeat of the alliance at Brunanburh in 937 did not lead to the collapse of Alba is a testament to Constantine II's achievement in securing its permanence.

Pictish stone
Sueno's Stone in Scotland, at approximately 21 ft (6.5 m) high, is the tallest surviving Pictish monument. It is filled with battle scenes commemorating an unknown conflict, possibly a victory by southern Picts over a more northerly group from Moray.

2

MEDIEVAL BRITAIN
1066–1485

Fierce rivalry for land and power dominated the centuries following the Norman conquest of the nascent English realm. The ubiquitous feudal system, emerging departments of state, and a strong Church dominated an often prosperous nation, while fruitless wars with France drained the exchequer and frequently divided the country.

Becket's reliquary
This ornate casket, known as a reliquary, is thought to
have contained the relics of Thomas Becket. The sides of
the casket are decorated in enamel and show scenes
of his murder in Canterbury Cathedral in 1170, his
burial, and his ascent into heaven assisted by angels.

Kidwelly Castle
After the Norman conquest, the country's new rulers created a network of castles to consolidate their hold over the land. Originally made of wood, they were, over the next generation, replaced by imposing stone fortresses, such as this one at Kidwelly, in Carmarthen, Wales.

A new kingdom

The Norman conquest in 1066 was a watershed in English, and, by extension, Welsh, Scottish, and Irish history. England joined a realm spanning the English Channel, and the aspirations of English kings to maintain or extend their French lands meant they did not consolidate the monarchy as a purely English affair. The later acquisition by Henry II, through marriage and inheritance, of a vast Angevin Empire, give him control of up to half of modern France, with the result that English monarchs often spent much of their reign outside England. It seemed that a dual monarchy might emerge, balanced between England and France. All this changed, however, with King John's loss of all his inheritance, save Bordeaux, after 1214.

As well as French lands, the Norman conquest gave England a feudal system of landholding, which mirrored that in northern France. The growth in royal authority—and in the financial resources available to the king—after 1066, led to tensions in this feudal system. The king tried to assert control over the country's resources without passing through the barons and the Church, who controlled access to those lower down the feudal hierarchy. Although England's civil wars of the 1140s—when Henry I's heir, Matilda, and his nephew, Stephen, fought over the Crown—had involved the barons, these conflicts were over who had the right to rule. The later conflict between John and the barons in 1215–1217 was over how the king should rule.

Parliament and conquest

Although intended to protect baronial rights, Magna Carta (1215) was the first occasion when an English king's freedom of action was diminished by agreements forced on him by his subjects. Civil war in the 1260s saw a further deterioration in the royal position. Although the barons, under Simon de Montfort, were defeated, the Parliament they summoned at Oxford, in 1258, heralded a platform in which the great men of the realm could organize nonviolent resistance to royal demands, and to which, by 1376, the king had to defer if he wanted to raise taxation. One reason kings needed additional funding was the increasing sophistication of royal administration, which had been transformed from a few key officials in 1066, into the nucleus of the great departments of state by the 15th century. Money was also needed by successive English kings as they attempted to conquer their neighbors. In Ireland, this was largely successful after Henry III's invasion in 1171, and in Wales, after a brief renaissance under the kings of Gwynedd in the 13th century, the process was completed by 1283. Scotland looked likely to fall into English hands in the 1290s, but a Scottish revival and the defeat of Edward I's army at Bannockburn in 1314 secured Scottish independence.

The English kings' attempts, from Edward III to Henry V, to reestablish an English empire in France came to nothing. Victories at Crécy (1346), Poitiers (1356), and Agincourt (1415) are established in the English imagination, but by the end of the Hundred Years' War in 1453, England held only Calais. All this was at ruinous cost, which further undermined royal authority and increased that of Parliament. Elsewhere there had been peace. By the mid-15th century, Ireland lay uneasily divided between a disunited group of native lords in the west and the lands of the English Crown in the east. Wales was mostly subdued under English dominion, while Scotland was no longer threatened with conquest from England.

Another civil war

After 1455, the Wars of the Roses threatened to overturn this equilibrium. A long battle between the Lancastrian and Yorkist descendants of Edward III over who had the right to rule the country, left the authority of the Crown in ruins. The man who emerged to claim what was left came from an unexpected quarter. Henry VII, the ultimate victor in the war, was the first Welshman to rule over any portion of England since the 7th century.

Battle of Barnet
In 1471, the Battle of Barnet marked the final defeat in the Wars of the Roses of the Lancastrian king, Henry VI. Just 14 years later, the Yorkist king, Richard III, was ousted by Henry VII, the first Tudor king of England.

MEDIEVAL BRITAIN
1066–1485

1066–1153	1154–1215	1216–1272

△ Bayeux Tapestry depicts the Battle of Hastings

1066
William of Normandy becomes King of England.

1086–1087
The Domesday Survey and compilation of the Domesday Book.

≫ Domesday Book

1106
Battle of Tinchebray; defeat of Robert Curthose by Henry I leads to English annexation of Normandy.

1120
Wreck of the *White Ship*; William, heir to Henry I, is killed.

1128
Henry I's daughter, Matilda, marries Geoffrey of Anjou.

1135
Accession of Stephen.

1139–1153
Civil war in England between Matilda, her son Henry, and Stephen.

1087
Accession of William II Rufus.

1093
Anselm becomes Archbishop of Canterbury.

1100
Accession of Henry I after William Rufus is killed in the New Forest.

1149
David I of Scotland takes Northumbria.

1152
Marriage of Henry and Eleanor of Aquitaine.

≫ Eleanor of Aquitaine

1154
Henry II becomes king on death of Stephen.

1157
Henry II regains Northumbria from the Scots.

1162
Thomas Becket becomes Archbishop of Canterbury.

1164
Assize of Clarendon leads to Becket's exile.

1169–1171
Conquest of Ireland by Anglo-Norman knights under Strongbow (later by Henry II).

△ Cross of Cong

1200
Beginning of ascendancy of Llywelyn the Great in Gwynedd.

1203–1204
Loss of Normandy to Philip II Augustus of France.

1170
Murder of Archbishop Becket in Canterbury Cathedral.

1173–1174
William the Lion of Scotland invades northern England.

△ Joinville's *Chronicles of the Crusade*

1214
Battle of Bouvines; loss of most of remaining English territory in France.

1215
Baronial revolt forces John to sign the Magna Carta.

1189
Death of Henry II and accession of Richard I.

1193–1194
Richard I imprisoned in Germany on his way back from a crusade.

1199
John becomes king.

≫ Murder of Thomas Becket

1216
Accession of Henry III.

1224
Henry III loses Poitou to Louis of France.

1232
Henry III dismisses Hubert de Burgh as his justiciar.

≫ 13th-century map of British Isles

1237
Treaty of York by which Alexander II renounces Scottish claims to border counties.

1240
Death of Llywelyn the Great of Gwynedd.

1265
Death of Simon de Montfort at Evesham and the end of the baronial uprising.

1266
Treaty of Perth with Norway secures the Western Isles for Scotland.

△ Conwy Castle, Wales

1258
Baronial revolt led by Simon de Montfort. Issuing of the Provisions of Oxford.

1264
Henry III captured after the Battle of Lewes.

1267
Treaty of Montgomery recognizes Llywelyn ap Gruffudd as Prince of Wales.

1272
Accession of Edward I.

> **"No free man** shall be seized or imprisoned, or stripped of his rights and possessions, or outlawed or exiled … except by **the lawful judgement** of his equals …**"**

MAGNA CARTA, CLAUSE 39, JUNE 1215

1272–1327		1328–1399		1399–1485	

1291
Edward I asserts his right to decide Scottish succession at Norham Parliament.

1297
Battle of Stirling Bridge; William Wallace defeats the English.

« King Edward III

1328
Death of Charles VI of France leads to Edward III claiming the French throne.

1333
English victory over Scots at Halidon Hill.

1337
Start of Hundred Years' War between England and France.

1366
Statutes of Kilkenny forbid intermarriage between English settlers and native Irish.

1376
Edward, the Black Prince, dies.

1377
Death of Edward III and accession of Richard II.

1400
Beginning of revolt of Owain Glyn Dwr.

1403
Death and defeat of Henry Percy ("Hotspur") at Shrewsbury.

» Trading document

1276–77
Edward I invades Wales.

1282–83
Defeat of Llywelyn ap Gruffudd and conquest of Wales by Edward I.

1298
Wallace defeated at Falkirk.

1306
Robert the Bruce begins his rebellion against Edward I.

1307
Edward I dies and is succeeded by his son, Edward II.

≫ Depiction of Battle of Bannockburn

1381
The Peasant's Revolt begins.

1387
Rise of the Lords Appellant in opposition to Richard II.

1388
The Merciless Parliament indicts Richard II's allies.

1408
Earl of Northumberland defeated and killed at Bramham Moor.

1413
Henry IV dies and Henry V accedes to the throne; defeats the French at Agincourt in 1415.

1453
Loss of Gascony to the French.

1455
Battle of St. Albans marks start of Wars of the Roses.

1461
Henry VI deposed and Yorkist leader Edward IV becomes king.

⚞ Ivory carving relief of a castle under siege

1340
English naval victory over French at Sluys.

1346
English victories against French at Crécy and the Scots at Neville's Cross.

⚞ Battle of Neville's Cross

1420
Treaty of Troyes between England and France.

1422
Death of Henry V and accession of Henry VI. He attains age of maturity in 1436.

» Joan of Arc

1284
Statute of Wales issued by Edward I.

1290
Death of Margaret, Maid of Norway, leaves Scottish succession open.

1314
Battle of Bannockburn; the English lose and are driven from Scotland.

1315–1318
Edward Bruce invades Ireland.

1348
Outbreak of the Black Death in England. A second outbreak follows in 1361.

1360
Peace of Brétigny between England and France.

≫ Bloodletting instrument

1449–1450
English lose Normandy to France.

1450
Rebellion of John Cade.

1469
Revolt of Earl of Warwick reignites the civil war. Henry VI becomes king again.

1471
Battle of Barnet; final deposition of Henry VI.

1320
Declaration of Arbroath—formal statement of Scottish independence.

1321–1322
Civil war in England leads to deposition of Edward II in 1327, when Edward III succeeds him.

« Coronation throne of Edward I

1389
Richard II declares himself to be of age; Lords Appellant are dismissed.

1394–1395
Richard II's expedition to Ireland.

1399
Richard II deposed; Henry Bolingbroke becomes king.

1483
Edward IV dies; accession of Richard III.

1485
Richard III dies at the Battle of Bosworth Field. Henry Tudor becomes king as Henry VII.

« Tudor Rose

Norman Conquest

The Norman invasion of 1066 overthrew six centuries of Anglo-Saxon rule in England. William the Conqueror, the Norman duke, faced early rebellions, but once he had overcome them he radically reshaped England, replacing its old ruling class with an Anglo-Norman aristocracy and bringing the feudal system of landholding prevalent in Normandy to England.

The Norman invasion force that set sail from Saint-Valéry-sur-Somme on September 27, 1066, to enforce Duke William's claim on the English throne was probably no more than 8,000 strong, yet it succeeded in conquering one of the most established monarchies in Europe. William had luck on his side, in that he landed near Pevensey in Sussex while King Harold Godwinson was away in the north dealing with an invasion led by Harald Hardrada, King of Norway. Harold Godwinson had already defeated the Norwegians and their Anglo-Saxon allies at Stamford Bridge, four days before William's landing, but it was not until October 1 that he heard of the Norman invasion and, after forced marches, it was some two weeks more before he approached the new invaders near Hastings.

> ## "[Normans] built castles … oppressing … people, and things went … from **bad** to **worse**."
> ### ENTRY FROM *ANGLO-SAXON CHRONICLE*, 1066

« BEFORE

HAROLD OFFERING ALLEGIANCE TO WILLIAM

Duke William of Normandy had, on the face of it, a stronger claim to the English throne than Harold Godwinson, who succeeded Edward the Confessor in 1066.

SUCCESSION RIGHTS
William based his claim **on being Edward's cousin: « 60–61 Edward the Confessor's** mother, Emma, was the daughter of **Duke Richard I of Normandy**, who was William's great-grandfather. Edward also owed his throne to the assistance William had given him to return to England in 1042, and in 1051 Edward the Confessor is said to have **made William his heir**. Furthermore, William claimed that **Harold Godwinson** had paid him homage while in Normandy in 1064.

William had a fortnight to prepare, but acted cautiously, fortifying the old Roman Saxon Shore fort at Pevensey, but declining to move on the royal centers of Winchester or London. Harold's death in the subsequent Battle of Hastings (see pp.70–71) on

8,000 The number of troops in the invasion force that William brought over from France in 1066.

October 14 removed William's main obstacle to the throne, but the Anglo-Saxon nobility did not submit at once, for one remaining alternative candidate survived; Edgar Aetheling, the great-grandson of Aethelred the Unready, who had a better claim by blood than William.

Crowning a Norman king
The Norman army advanced slowly, first to Dover, and then via Canterbury toward London. The main surviving Anglo-Saxon leaders, such as Earls Edwin and Morcar, and Stigand, Archbishop of Canterbury, at first declined to recognize William, but when it became clear William was too strong to be defeated by their remaining forces, they paid him homage, beginning with Stigand on November 15. Edgar Aetheling was pushed aside and on Christmas Day 1066, William of Normandy was crowned King of England

Norman helmet
The head protection worn by the Norman knights at the Battle of Hastings in 1066 was not as all-covering as that of their successors two centuries later, but it was flexible, allowed good visibility, and warded off glancing blows.

in Westminster Abbey, using much the same form of ceremony as had been employed for Harold's coronation barely a year before.

William went to East Anglia in the New Year, where he received the submission of Earls Edwin and Morcar. He then returned to Normandy in March, taking with him Edwin, Morcar, Edgar Aetheling, and Archbishop Stigand, so depriving, as he thought, the Anglo-Saxons of any focus for resistance. He left in charge his half-brother, Odo of Bayeux, whom he had made Earl of Kent, and William FitzOsbern, the Earl of Hereford. The two regents were heavy-handed in their exercise of power, and a rebellion broke out in the west under Edric the Wild. Although this was put down, another one promptly erupted in Kent.

William was therefore forced to return to England in December 1067, only to find yet another revolt had begun, led by the men of Exeter. William's rule was dangerously threatened and the situation deteriorated in early 1069 when a much more serious uprising occurred in the north. This time Earls Edwin and Morcar joined in, together with Edgar Aetheling. Although William quickly dispersed the rebels, in the summer the north revolted once more, now with the assistance of a Danish fleet led by the sons of King Sweyn Estrithson. York itself fell on September 20, and the whole Norman venture in England seemed in peril.

Stamping out resistance
William acted swiftly, striking first west to defeat Edric the Wild, who had rebelled once more, and then north, devastating the land in a "harrying of the north" that was remembered for centuries. York—or at least its smoldering ruin—was retaken by Christmas, and then the last rebel stronghold at Chester. There, and at Stafford and other key towns,

NORMAN RULER (1028–1087)

WILLIAM THE CONQUEROR

William was the illegitimate son of Duke Robert II of Normandy and a tanner's daughter. He became duke in 1047, aged 19. His early rule was insecure, with a revolt that year almost unseating him, and it was not until he defeated Henry I of France at Mortemer in 1054 that he was sure of survival. Continued trouble with rebels plagued him until 1060, and only then could William turn his attention to England. Yet, while his ally and cousin Edward the Confessor was on the throne, the battle-hardened Norman duke chose not to press his claims.

COIN FROM WILLIAM'S REIGN

Granting of fiefs
William I accepts the homage of Alain le Roux, his cousin, who probably led the Bretons at Hastings and received more than 400 manors as a reward.

William built new castles to reinforce the Norman control of the northern counties. First made of wood, these would be replaced over the coming century by imposing stone fortifications.

Although a residual Anglo-Saxon resistance continued in the East Anglian fens until 1072, William rounded the campaign off with an attack into Scotland to chastise King Malcolm III, who had aided the northern rebels. He was never again seriously threatened and felt able to spend most of the rest of his reign in Normandy, where he faced wars in Maine (1073), with Brittany (1076) against the Counts of Anjou (1077–1078 and 1081), and against Philip I of France (in 1087).

French nobility

After the revolt of the north, William adopted a conscious policy of replacing the remaining Anglo-Saxon magnates with Frenchmen. The process was so thorough that by 1086 only two Anglo-Saxons held land directly from the King himself (Thurkell of Arden and Colswein of Lincoln). William took for himself a large portion of the confiscated property, and for the rest established a system of feudal tenancies which mirrored the one that was already established in Normandy. As native influence waned, so English came to be replaced as the language of government, with charters and writs being issued largely in Latin.

The use of Latin

Latin became the language of the Church as well as the government, and the old Anglo-Saxon bishops were largely replaced by Normans. In 1070 William had Stigand deposed as Archbishop of Canterbury and replaced by Lanfranc, the Abbot of St. Stephen's Monastery in Caen, Normandy. Lanfranc, in turn, consecrated Thomas of Bayeux, another supporter of William, as Archbishop

17 The percentage of English land that William kept for himself, worth £12,600. The proportion held by the Church remained at 26 percent, the same as it had been before the Norman Conquest.

of York and set about reforming the English Church, beginning with the replacement of all the English bishops, save those of Worcester and Rochester, as well as the abbots of major monasteries. In the field of Church discipline Lanfranc enforced clerical celibacy. He also supported a program of cathedral building, which resulted in the construction of basilicas at sites including Canterbury and Winchester.

Surveying the land

Shortly before his death in 1087, William ordered the compilation of a great survey of landholding in his English domains, which formed the basis of the Domesday Book (see pp.74–75). By recording who had held the land at the time of Edward the Confessor and who held it at the time of the Domesday Survey, it showed the extent and scale of the Norman achievement. They had conquered the kingdom and occupied the land.

The later part of William's reign was occupied mainly with wars against Normandy's neighbors, who were concerned that the acquisition of England had made the Duke of Normandy too powerful.

A LAND DIVIDED

William had decided to divide his territories between his eldest son Robert Curthose, who was to receive Normandy, and Richard his second son, who was to get England. **Impatient and provoked** by Philip I of France, **Robert rebelled** in 1078 and 1083 **72–73 》**, but was on both occasions reconciled to his father. The link between Normandy and England, however, was weakened.

TUMULTUOUS REIGN

Richard died in 1081 and a third son, **William Rufus, inherited the English throne**. He initially faced a coalition of barons, prominent among them Odo of Bayeux, who wanted to see England and Normandy united under Robert's rule. The revolt was put down and Odo captured in 1088. William invaded Normandy in 1091, forcing his brother's submission. A campaign in Scotland followed in 1091–1092 to **punish** Malcolm III, who had been **sheltering Edgar Atheling**.

ADVENT OF ANSELM

In March 1093, William II fell dangerously ill and, in the hope of divine favor, appointed Anselm, an Italian monk, Archbishop of Canterbury. Anselm was an uncompromising supporter of reform and **quarrels broke out** between King and Archbishop. In 1097, Anselm went into exile in Rome and stayed there until William's death.

ANSELM'S CHAPEL AT CANTERBURY

> "William in the **fullness of his wrath** … ordered the **destruction of all** that could serve for the support of life … beyond the Humber."

ORDERIC VITALIS, *ECCLESIASTICAL HISTORY*, C. 1140

The Battle of Hastings

Hard on the heels of his victorious encounter with a Norwegian army in the north, King Harold Godwinson marched his weary army southward to face the invading force of Duke William of Normandy. On October 14, 1066, the two armies faced each other in a battle that would determine the fate of Anglo-Saxon England.

The Anglo-Saxon army drew near to the south coast at Hastings on October 13. Duke William had been harrying Anglo-Saxon garrisons in Sussex and it was imperative that Harold prevent the Normans from approaching London. Harold's army was around 8,000 strong, composed of a mixture of elite royal bodyguards called housecarls and part-time peasant soldiers. William commanded about the same number of men, with a stronger component of cavalry and, crucially, a larger force of archers.

The battle commences

Harold took up position on a hill called Senlac, with the housecarls forming a wall of interlocking shields. For William to win, he would have to dislodge the shield wall. The Normans reached their opponents' position around 9 a.m., beginning the battle with a thick rain of arrows intended to break up the shield wall. Both this and subsequent attacks up the hill failed. Disheartened, some of the Bretons—the non-Norman forces who made up William's right wing—fled, and wild rumors began that the Duke himself had been killed or wounded. Seeing their opponents seemingly in retreat, part of the Anglo-Saxon shield wall surged forward, but it was soon surrounded and cut down.

Flight and aftermath

William now ordered a series of feigned retreats, hoping to entice more of the housecarls down from Senlac Hill. Although some of the Anglo-Saxons fell into this trap, it was not enough. Rapidly running out of options, the Norman Duke commanded his archers to pour a stream of arrows into the enemy line. One of these may have hit Harold in the eye—he certainly suffered a mortal wound. Thinking that their king was dead, the Anglo-Saxons' morale collapsed and many of Harold's part-time soldiers fled.

The collapse of part of the shield wall allowed the Normans to storm the hill. Despite a last stand there and at the Malfosse (a steep ditch on the outskirts of the battlefield) the Anglo-Saxon army was soon utterly crushed by the Normans. With Harold now dead and his main army defeated, William was free to march on to London.

> **"** I am **still alive** and with God's help **I shall be victorious**. What madness leads you to flee?**"**
>
> WILLIAM OF POITIERS, *GESTA GUILLELMI*, RELATING WILLIAM'S RALLYING CRY TO HIS TROOPS

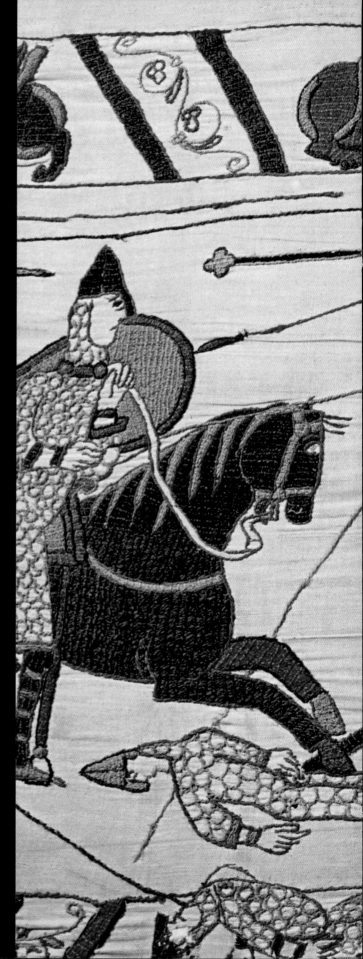

The Bayeux Tapestry
Commissioned after the Battle of Hastings to glorify the events leading up to and including the Norman invasion and conquest of England, this section of the Bayeux Tapestry shows the Norman cavalry assaulting the Anglo-Saxon shield wall at Hastings.

Norman Rule

At the start of the reign of Henry I in 1100, the transformation of Anglo-Saxon England into an Anglo-Norman realm was well underway. By its end, in 1135, a set of bureaucratic mechanisms had been developed which gave institutional reality to the Norman kings' desire to dominate their new realm.

Duke of Normandy
Robert Curthose, elder son of William the Conqueror, became Duke of Normandy in 1087. He was a weak ruler who failed to unite his duchy with England.

« BEFORE

From the 12th century, the Anglo-Norman government of England developed ever more sophisticated instruments of government to rule their disparate subjects.

BATTLE FOR THE CROWN
When **William Rufus died suddenly** in 1100 **« 57** he was unmarried and childless. His brother, Henry, was nearby when he died. He seized the opportunity to take power, riding to Winchester to claim the treasury and on to London for the Crown. His older brother, Robert, would later attempt to depose Henry.

DEVELOPMENT OF BUREAUCRACY
The **Burghal Hidage** drawn up in the reign of Alfred the Great's son, Edward the Elder **«52–53**, around 914 was an assessment of what each fortified burh needed to contribute for its defense. Anglo-Saxon charters recorded grants of land by the kings to their retainers and to the Church. The **Domesday Book** of 1086 **« 74–75 went further**, revealing the scale of the land held by the French elite. The reign of Henry I would see further administrative reforms.

Henry I, the fourth son of William the Conqueror, was the first Norman king to be born in England. However, his elder brother Robert Curthose reigned as Duke of Normandy and most of Henry's barons held lands on both sides of the English Channel, so the destinies of the two territories remained firmly intertwined. At Henry's accession he issued a solemn charter promising to restore the laws of his father William the Conqueror (see pp.68–69) and those of Edward the Confessor. Furthermore, his wife Edith was a descendent of Edmund Ironside (see p.57) and so their marriage symbolically united the English and Norman peoples of the realm.

Abortive coup

Henry's attempt to portray the reign of his brother William Rufus as a period of unrestrained oppression and rapacity backfired. One of William's chief advisers, Ranulf Flambard, persuaded Robert Curthose that the English barons would support an attempt by the Norman duke to depose Henry. Robert duly landed in England, but he was easily bought off with the promise of an annuity of 3,000 marks, leaving his baronial supporters to face Henry's justice. Only the ringleader, Robert of Bellême, escaped.

The King and the Church

Henry's relationship with the Church was troubled, too, as Archbishop Anselm returned from exile and refused to pay homage to Henry for his Canterbury lands. He also insisted that the King give up his right to invest bishops, a practice known as "lay investiture," which had, in theory, been outlawed by the Pope in 1059. The dispute led to the collective excommunication of those bishops who

Rochester Castle
Work on replacing the earlier wooden motte and bailey castle at Rochester, Kent, began in 1128, with the encouragement of Henry I. This was one of the earliest stone-fortified castles in Britain.

> "He was a **good man**, and there was great awe of him. In his day **no man dared harm** another."

THE PETERBOROUGH CHRONICLE, ON HENRY I'S CHARACTER, 12TH CENTURY

took Henry's side in 1105, and renewed exile for Anselm. An agreement was finally reached at a meeting between Henry and Anselm in 1106, when the King agreed to give up his power to invest bishops, but reserved the right to receive their homage.

England and Normandy united

In 1104, the exiled Robert of Bellême joined forces with Count William of Mortain to attack Henry's interests in Normandy. Not willing to give up his possessions or abandon his supporters there, Henry arrived at Barfleur in 1105 and moved cautiously inland. His brother, Duke Robert, had too little money to raise reinforcements, and in September 1106 at Tinchebray the army of Normandy was defeated by

> **237** The number of surviving documents from Henry I's reign issued at Westminster (as opposed to 127 at Winchester, 92 at Woodstock, and 71 at Windsor).

Henry's force. Normandy and England were reunited under Henry's rule. In an act of clemency that he would later come to regret bitterly, Henry allowed Robert's son, William Clito, to remain in Normandy, where he became the focus for dissent and the pretext for a series of wars with France from

Tally sticks

Wooden sticks like these were used by accountants and officials during Henry I's reign. They were marked to keep track of transactions and then split between the two parties involved.

recorded with notches on a tally stick, one half of which was kept by the official, and the other by the sheriff as a record of what his county was to raise. A more permanent record of each year's revenues was set down in Pipe Rolls. The court itself became known as the Exchequer after the checkerboard cloth on which the royal accountants made their calculations.

Loss of an heir

Henry's later years were marred by sadness. In 1119, Louis VI was finally defeated in the war over Normandy and he accepted the homage of

AFTER

The peace and tranquillity of England under Henry I was rapidly replaced by a bitter civil war lasting 19 years.

BITTER CIVIL WAR
Henry I's nephew, Stephen, **seized the treasury** with the help of his brother Henry of Blois, Bishop of Winchester, and he and leading barons **renounced their oath to Matilda**. In 1138, her half-brother, Robert of Gloucester, defected from Stephen's side and in 1139, she landed at Arundel in an attempt to unseat Stephen from the throne. **Matilda defeated and captured Stephen at Lincoln** in 1141. However, Stephen was freed in exchange for Robert of Gloucester, who was also a captive. After **years of damaging warfare**, Matilda finally left England in 1148.

PLANTAGENET RULE
During the civil war, **Matilda's second husband**, Geoffrey Plantagenet, Count of Anjou, **took towns in Normandy**, leading to his acceptance as Duke of Normandy in 1144. Henry I's legacy of bringing order and prosperity to England, and uniting the country once more with Normandy, lay in ruins.

> " He preferred to **contend by council** rather than **by the sword.**"
>
> WILLIAM OF MALMESBURY ON HENRY I, *GESTA REGUM ANGLORUM*, C. 1125

1111–1114 and 1116–1119, as Louis VI attempted to make him into a puppet Duke of Normandy.

Justice reforms

The power of the barons in England had grown dangerously since the death of William the Conqueror, and on his return from Tinchebray in 1108, Henry I enacted a series of reforms aimed at curbing their power. He began by forbidding members of the royal household to plunder or extort money, on pain of blinding or castration. Henry then stamped down on the practice of county sheriffs who were holding extra sessions of courts to extract profit on their own account. He also began sending royal judges on circuit to hear pleas. As fines from these cases went to the Crown, it was a useful extra source of revenue for the royal coffers, too.

Henry's most important minister was Roger, Bishop of Salisbury, and it may have been Roger who devised one of the key administrative advances of the reign. Each year from 1110, officials met at the royal court, normally at Winchester, and prepared a list of the revenues expected to be collected by the county sheriffs. The sums were

Henry's son William Adelin as Duke of Normandy. However, on the return journey to England in 1120 the *White Ship*, the vessel carrying the young prince, was wrecked and Henry's only legitimate son drowned. For a while Stephen of Blois, Henry's nephew, looked likely to succeed. Then in 1125, Henry's daughter Matilda, who had married the Holy Roman Emperor

> **66** The percentage of property owners in Winchester with foreign names in 1148. At the time of the Norman conquest the figure was 29 percent.

Henry V in 1110, was widowed and returned to England.

Henry doted on Matilda and at Christmas 1126 the Royal Council was made to swear allegiance to her as heir to the throne. Henry's reign was prosperous and peaceful for the next decade, with his administrative reforms bearing fruit in increased revenues and a smoother operation of justice. However, his decision to leave his crown to Matilda ended in catastrophe. For at Henry's death in 1135, Stephen refused to accept Matilda as queen.

INNOVATION

FEUDALISM

The Norman conquest of 1066 brought a set of landholding practices to England, which together have been termed feudalism by later generations. The king, in theory, held all land and tenants-in-chief held parts of it from him as *fiefs*. In return, they were obliged to provide military service when the king needed it. These tenants, in turn, had their own tenants who had a similar set of obligations right down to the peasants, or *villeins*, at the bottom of the hierarchy, who owed labor instead of military service to their lord. As a sign of their loyalty, feudal landholders would swear an oath, known as fealty, to their overlord.

CLERIC, KNIGHT, AND PEASANT

In Burgo MALMESBERIE habet rex xx.vi. masuras hospitatas. 7 xx.v. masuras in qb; st dom que n reddut gel' plusqua uasta tra. Una quaq; haru masuraru redd. x. den de gablo. hoc e simul xl.iii. sol 7 vi. den. / Scrutati reddit.

De feudo epi baiocis. e ibi dimidia masura uasta. que nulli Abb malmesbie he. iiii. mas 7 dimid. 7 foris burg. xx. coscez q geldat cu burgsib. Abb Glastingbiens he. ii. masur.

Eduuard. iiii. masur. Radulf de mortem. i. 7 dimid. Durand de Glouuec. i. 7 dim. Wills de ow. i. Hunfrid de insula. i. Osbn Gifard. i. Alured de Merleberge. dimid mas uasta. Goisfrid simile. Iou. i. 7 qrta parte uni mas. Drogo.f. ponz. dimid. Uxor Edric. i. Rog de berchelai. i. mas de firma regis. 7 Ernulf. i. simile de firma regis. qua incaute accep. he due nullu scrutati reddut.

Rex ht una uasta masuram de tra qua Azor tenuit.

HIC ANNOTANTUR TENENTES TRAS IN WILTESCIRE.

.I. REX WILLELMUS.	.xxxvi. Walscinus de Dowai.
.II. Eps Wintoniensis.	.xxxvii. Walran uenator.
.III. Eps Sarisberiensis.	.xxxviii. Willelm filius Widonis.
.IIII. Eps Baiocensis.	.xxxix. Henricus de Ferieres.
.V. Eps Constantiensis.	.xl. Ricard filius Gisleba.
.VI. Eps Lisiacensis.	.xli. Radulf de Mortemer.
.VII. Abbatia Glastingberiens.	.xlii. Robertus fili Giroldi.
.VIII. Abbatia Malmesberiens.	.xliii. Robertus fill Rolf.
.X. Abbatia Westmonasterii.	.xliiii. Ogerius de Curcelle.
.X. Abbatia Wintoniensis.	.xlv. Rogerius de Berchelai.
.XI. Abbatia Greneburnensis.	.xlvi. Bernard pancewolt.
.XII. Abbatissa Scefteberiens.	.xlvii. Berenger Gifard.
.XIII. Abbatissa Wiltuniensis.	.xlviii. Osbernus Gifard.
.XIIII. Abbatissa Wintoniensis.	.xlix. Rogo filius ponz.
.XV. Abbatissa Romesiensis.	.l. Hugo lasne.
.XVI. Abbatissa Ambresberiens.	.li. Hugo filius baldrici.
.XVII. Ecclesia Beccensis.	.lii. Hunfrid camerarius.
.XVIII. Giraldus pbr de Wiltune.	.liii. Gunfrid maldutch.
.XIX. Canonici Lisiacenses.	.liiii. Aluredus de Ispania.
.XX. Comes Mortoniensis.	.lv. Aiulfus uicecomes.
.XXI. Comes Rogerius.	.lvi. Nigellus medicus.
.XXII. Comes Hugo.	.lvii. Osbernus pbr.
.XXIII. Comes Albericus.	.lviii. Ricard puingiant.
.XXIIII. Eduard de Sarisberie.	.lix. Robtus marescal.
.XXV. Ernulf de Hesding.	.lx. Robertus flauus.
.XXVI. Aluredus de Merlebergh.	.lxi. Ricardus Sturmis.
.XXVII. Hunfridus de Insula.	.lxii. Rainald canud.
.XXVIII. Milo crispin.	.lxiii. Aci de Moretania.
.XXIX. Willelmus de Breteuile.	.lxiiii. Gozelin Riuere.
.XXX. Durand de Glouuecestre.	.lxv. Godescal.
.XXXI. Walterius Gifard.	.lxvi. Herman 7 alii sequentes.
.XXXII. Wills de Ow.	.lxvii. 7 alii taini regis.
.XXXIII. Wills de Braiose.	.lxviii. Herueus 7 alii ministri regis.
.XXXIIII. Wills de Molun.	
.XXXV. Wills de Faleise.	

Rex habet de Burgo Wiltune. l. lib. Qdo herueus recepit ad custodiend' reddeb. xxxii. libras.

De Wiltescire he rex x. lib p dacipre 7 xx. solid p sumario. A seno. c. solid 7 v. oras.

De denario molino ap Sarisberie ht rex xx. solid ad pensum.

De tcio denario Sarisberie. he rex vi. lib. De tcio denar Merleberge. iii. lib. De tcio denar cricchelade Bade. xi. lib. De tcio denario Malmesberie. vi. lib.

De Creneur. lx. lib ad pondus. h reddut Eduuardus.

Walterius de iii. partib; burgi Malmesberie redd. vii. lib regi.

TERRA REGIS.

Rex tenet CALNE. Rex. E. tenuit 7 nunq; gel' dauit. Ideo nescit quot hide sint ibi. Tra. e xxvi. car. In dnio sunt. vii. car. 7 viii. serui. Ibi xxx. vi. uilli 7 xxvi. bord. 7 x. colib. hntes xi. car. Ibi xl. v. burgenses. 7 vii. molini reddut. iiii. lib 7 xii. sol 7 vi. den. 7 l. ac pti. pastura ii. leu lg. 7 una leu lat. h uilla redd firma uni nocas cu omib;

Hui co eccla ten Nigell de rege. cu vi. hid 7 dim 7 cu uad. Tra. e. v. car. In dnio e. i. 7 vi. serui. Ibi. vi. uilli. ii. bord 7 xi. cozets. Ibi. ii. molini de. xx. sol. 7 xx.v. burgses redd. xx. sol. Silua. ii. qa lg. 7 una qa lat. xxiiii. ac pti. Pastura iii. qrent lg. 7 ii. qa lat. Tot ual. viii. lib.

Alured de hispania ten. v. hid 7 dim. qs Nigell calum. h tra testimonio scire panuit ad ecclam. T.R.E.

Rex ten BEDUINDE. Rex. E. tenuit. Nunq; gel'dauit nec hidata fuit. Tra. e qd xx. car una min. In dnio sunt xii. car. 7 xiii. serui. Ibi qd xx. uilli. 7 lx. cozets. 7 xxv. colibti. Ibi viii. molini redd. c. sol. Due silue hntes iiii. lg. 7 una leu lat. Ibi cc. ac tra. 7 xii. qa pasture lg. lo uic co parc. xx.v. burgenses.

h uilla redd firma uni nocas cu omib; csuetudinib. In hoc co fuit. T.R.E. lucus hns dimid leu lg. 7 ii. qel. 7 erat in dnio regis. Modo tenet eu henric de ferieres.

Rex ten AMBLESBERIE. Rex. E. tenuit. Nunq; gel'd nec hidata fuit. Tra. e xl. car. In dnio sunt. xvi. car. 7 lx. serui. 7 ii. colib. Ibi qa xx. v. uilli 7 vi. bord hntes xxiii. car. Ibi viii. molini redd. iiii. lib. 7 x. sol. 7 lxx. ac tra. Pastura. iiii. leu lg. 7 ii. leu lat. Silua vi. leu lg. 7 iiii. leu lat.

hoc co cu appendic suis redd firma uni nocas. T.R.E. In hoc co numerant tra iii. tainorum qui ibi serui. T.R.E. has ded Wills com in Amblesbie p mutatione Boue me. De hui co tra. ii. hid ded rex. E. in sua infirmitate abbatisse Wiltuniensis. qs nunq; antea habuerat. postea u eas tenuit. 7 Wills com ded Quintone 7 Suindone. 7 cheurel que erant tainlande. p tra de insula de Wt que pane ad firma de Amblesberie.

Rex ten COLENE... Rex. E. tenuit. Non gel' nec hidata fuit. Tra. e xl. car. In dnio e. vi. car. 7 xxiiii. serui. 7 xii. porcarii. Ibi. xv. uilli 7 viii. ca rf. 7 xiiii. colibti. cu xxx. vi. car. Ibi. vii. molini de ... lib. 7 qd xx. ac tra. pastura. i. leu lg. 7 dim leu lat. Silua. ii. leu lg. 7 ii. lat. Ibi xxx. burgses.

hoc co reddt firma uni nocas cu omib; csuetudinib.

Rex ten CHEPEHA. Rex. E. tenuit. Non gel'dauit nec hidata fuit. Tra. e. c. car. In dnio sunt. xvi. car. xx. serui. Ibi. xl. vii. uilli 7 xv. bord. xx. colib. 7 xx. ptari. int oms hnt. lx. vi. car. Ibi xiii. molini de. lxiiii. fol. 7 c. ac tra. Silua. iiii. leu In lg. 7 lat. pastura. ii. leu lg. 7 una leu lat. hoc co cu append suis redd firma uni nocas cu omib; csuetudinib. ual. c. x. lib ad numeru.

Hui co eccla cu. ii. hid ten Osbn eps ex T.R.E. Una uirt int ecc 7 mnt 7 una alter pan eccle. Tot ual. l. vi. fol.

Huic co pan una tra qua rex. E. dedit Uluiet suo 7 erat de dnio suo. h in firma regis e m. 7 una beruit tra. ii. car. 7 ipse ibi ii. serui. 7 uii. uilli 7 iiii. cozet cu. i. car. pastura. iii. qa lg. 7 una qa lat. Val. iii. lib. In firma hui co e dimid hide que fuit tainlande. Edricus tenuit T.R.E.

Domesday Book

On Christmas Day 1085, according to the *Anglo-Saxon Chronicle*, King William I resolved to send commissions of inquiry all over his realm to determine who held the land and how much money it should yield in dues. The results were collated together to create the Domesday Book, the most famous document from medieval England.

King William I's purpose in ordering the inquiry has been much discussed. However, it seems to have been clearly to the King's advantage to know how much revenue he commanded, and to establish the absolute ownership of land, which would facilitate its redistribution, as well as aid him to resolve property disputes.

The Great Inquest
During the survey, also known as the Great Inquest, commissioners collected oral answers from sheriffs in each shire, from barons, and even from reeves and peasants in villages to know more about the land-holding system. They asked several questions, such as who held the land now and who had held it earlier, how many plows there were on the manorial demesne (estate land), and how many men there were. The inquiry was conducted with speed and thoroughness. The *Anglo-Saxon Chronicle* laments that "so very narrowly did he have it investigated that there was no ... one ox nor one cow nor one pig which was there left out." The data collected was compiled for each of the seven large survey districts and these were then sent to Winchester, where they were summarized and consolidated into the form seen in the final Great Domesday book. One example of the regional surveys survives in the "Little Domesday," which covers Essex, Norfolk, and Suffolk, and which was never added to the final version.

Remarkable record
The preliminary results were presented to the King in September 1086 and it seems the work was completed before William I died in September 1087. The book included a record of almost every manor in England—from the majority, which yielded around 20 shillings in annual revenue, to certain ecclesiastical estates in East Anglia, which had an income 100 times that. It has been estimated that some 10,000 people took part in its compilation—an extraordinary achievement for a medieval administrative apparatus.

> "We have **called** this book 'The **Book of Domesday**' ... because **its decisions**, like those of the **last judgement**, are **unalterable**."
>
> RICHARD FITZ NIGEL, *DIALOGUES DE SCACCARIO*, c. 1180

Domesday Wiltshire
The first page of the Domesday Book listing for Wiltshire contains the names of the 66 principal landowners in the county. The King is listed first; followed by 19 bishops, monasteries, and churches; and then the secular nobility. Tellingly, Anglo-Saxon names only appear among the subtenants in the main entries.

Reign of a Powerful King

Henry II's inheritance of England and vast areas of France made him one of the most powerful rulers in Europe. He expanded his possessions further in Ireland and made important reforms to the English legal system. However, his reign was marred by a troubled relationship with the Church and the revolts of his sons.

Henry's marriage at the age of 19 to Eleanor, heiress of the duchy of Aquitaine (and the former wife of Louis VII of France) in 1152, made him the most powerful man in France, lord of a domain that historians came to call the Angevin Empire. Yet there was still no certainty he would inherit the English Crown. It was only the sudden death of Stephen's son, Eustace, in August 1153, which opened the way to him (see pp.72–73). By the Treaty of Winchester, Stephen recognized Henry as his successor, on the condition that he was left in peace on the throne of England. However, Stephen did not enjoy this respite long, for he died in October 1154, and within six weeks Henry II had been crowned at Westminster Abbey.

Lasting power
Although he spent only one-third of his 35-year reign in England, Henry's impact there was profound and long-lasting. The wars under Stephen had left England prey to the ambitions of the warring barons and also caused it considerable loss of territory. In 1157, Henry forced Malcolm IV of Scotland to hand back Cumberland, Westmorland, and Northumbria, which the Scots had acquired amid the chaos of the civil war. In 1174 Scotland was reduced to a fief of the English Crown in exchange for Henry's release of its king, William I, from captivity. Attempts to improve the English position in Wales failed in the face of dogged resistance from Owain of Gwynedd and Rhys of Deheubarth from 1157 to 1165.

At home, Henry removed key supporters of Stephen, demolished castles that had been built illegally during the civil war, and garrisoned others with royal troops. By 1155, some 52 castles (one-fifth of the total) were controlled by the Crown. To further strengthen his position, Henry replaced two-thirds of the county sheriffs with men loyal to him and restored the application of "forest laws," which provided a lucrative source of revenue by levying fines on those who cleared forest land. He also restored the currency with the issue of a new coinage in 1158.

The justice system
A key component in the program to restore royal authority was the strengthening of the system of justice. Previously, competing jurisdictions had made the administering of justice a haphazard affair. By the Assize of Clarendon in 1166, Henry replaced a system whereby sheriffs might hear cases in the absence of royal justices with one in which "justices in eyre" visited each locality on a regular basis. They tried serious crimes and

> **£23,000** The average royal expenditure in the last eight years of Henry's reign, according to the Pipe Rolls (compared to £10,000 in the first two years).

BEFORE

Henry II's route to the English throne was a long and tortuous one, involving civil war and the death of his main rival. His French domains fell to him more easily.

BEGINNINGS OF A DYNASTY
Henry II was the son of Matilda, daughter of Henry I, and Geoffrey Plantagenet, heir to the Count of Anjou. **Matilda's failure to secure the English throne** after the death of Henry I in 1135, and her defeat by King Stephen in the civil war of the 1130s and 1140s **« 73** left Henry to fall back on his French inheritance. First, he **became Duke of Normandy**, conquered by his father in 1144, and then, on Geoffrey's death in 1152, Henry succeeded him as Count of Anjou.

GEOFFREY PLANTAGENET

> " The **French crown has five duchies** and, if you count them up, there are **three missing**."
>
> FRENCH TROUBADOUR BERTRAN DE BORN, REFERRING TO THE POSSESSION OF NORMANDY, BRITTANY, AND AQUITAINE BY HENRY II, 12TH CENTURY

1162, it seemed an obvious move to appoint Becket as his successor. It was a terrible mistake, for Becket was both inexperienced in Church matters and inflexible. Far from supporting him, Becket opposed Henry at almost every turn, particularly over the issue of criminous clerks whom Henry wanted tried in the civil rather than ecclesiastical courts. Becket refused and fled England in 1164. The dispute between the two men seemed to have been resolved and Becket returned in 1170. However, the ill-feeling caused by the King's coronation of his son earlier that year without the customary presence of the Archbishop of Canterbury and by Becket's procurement of the excommunication of many of those bishops who had attended, caused it to explode again. The end result was the murder of

> **CRIMINOUS CLERK** A member of the clergy who had committed a serious offense, and who traditionally would be tried by an ecclesiastical court.

Becket in Canterbury Cathedral in December 1170 (see pp.78–79). Henry made a public apology in return for absolution and in 1176 revoked the Constitutions of Clarendon, which had decreed criminous clerks must be tried in secular courts.

Ambitious conquests

The King's territorial ambitions had not been satisfied by his Angevin and English inheritance, and as early as 1155 he seems to have planned to conquer Ireland, having secured a papal bull, *Laudabiliter*, from Pope Adrian IV permitting him to seize it.

The King and the Archbishop

This painting from 1350 shows Henry II and Thomas Becket in conversation. A relationship that had been cordial when Becket was chancellor soured when he became Archbishop, and ultimately turned violent.

In 1171, the activities there of a group of Anglo-Norman knights from the Welsh Marches, led by Gilbert de Clare, Earl of Pembroke, attracted his attention and he led a royal force to secure the lands they had occupied, claiming the island for the English Crown.

A family at war

Henry's later years were marred by worsening relations with his sons. By the 1170s, he had planned to partition his realms between the three eldest, with Henry receiving Anjou, Normandy, and England; Richard inheriting Aquitaine; and Brittany (which Henry II had acquired in 1166) going to Geoffrey. His sons were impatient for their inheritances and Prince Henry rebelled in 1173 (with the support of many English barons disgruntled at the King's financial exactions). It was a particularly dangerous moment. Henry made common cause with Louis VII of France, who persuaded his English ally to grant a variety of French nobles large tracts of land in France, and with William the Lion in Scotland. Yet the revolt petered out: Henry II won a major victory by capturing the castle of Dol in Brittany in August 1173. In England, another of the young Henry's principal supporters, the Earl of Leicester, was decisively defeated at Fornham on October 17, while the Scots fared even worse: William the Lion was captured outside Alnwick in July 1174. The young king made terms with his father in September, and was granted two castles in Normandy. Undeterred, he rebelled again in 1182. Prince Henry died in 1183 and Geoffrey in 1186. This should have ended the family dispute, but Henry II had developed a preference for John, and Richard suspected he was being pushed aside. He rose up in open revolt against his father. Sick and defeated, Henry died at Chinon castle on July 6, 1189.

SCOTLAND

IRELAND
Dublin

York

ENGLAND

WALES
Bristol

London

NORMANDY
MAINE
BRITTANY
ANJOU
FRANCE
AQUITAINE

GASCONY

0   250km
0   250 miles

N

KEY
☐ Land ruled by Henry II

Extent of Angevin Empire

Henry II acquired Anjou from his father, England through his agreement with Stephen in 1152, Aquitaine by his marriage to Eleanor, and Ireland and Brittany through his own conquest.

AFTER »»

The absence of Richard I on the Crusade and the weakness of King John caused the loss of most of the Angevin Empire.

A DIMINISHING KINGDOM
Richard I's **absence from England** on the Crusades from 1191 **82–83 »** allowed Philip II of France to take back some of the Angevin lands held by England. Under King John, **Normandy fell to the French king** in 1204, and in 1214, Poitou and most of the English-held lands in southern France **were also lost**.

KING RICHARD ON THE CRUSADE IN 1194

established assizes, court sessions under which pleas to the Crown concerning serious cases would be answered with a royal writ ordering the local sheriff to assemble a jury to hear the case at the next judicial session. Justice became faster, more effective, and the power of the barons was diluted, as their tenants discovered that an appeal to the Crown might offer rapid relief with a lessened danger of baronial retribution.

Trouble with the Archbishop

Henry's key ally in implementing these reforms was his chancellor, Thomas Becket, and when Theobald, Archbishop of Canterbury, died in

---

QUEEN CONSORT OF FRANCE AND ENGLAND (1122–1204)

ELEANOR OF AQUITAINE

Eleanor became Duchess of Aquitaine in her own right in 1137, at the age of 15, and soon after married Louis VII of France. The marriage produced no sons, and Louis divorced her in 1152. Within months, though,

Eleanor had made another politically astute marriage, to Duke Henry of Normandy (the future Henry II of England) to whom she bore five sons and three daughters. Courageous and resourceful, Eleanor retained her own independent court in Aquitaine and was not afraid to oppose Henry, as when she supported the rebellion of their son, Prince Henry, in 1173. She and the King became estranged and he placed her under house arrest for 15 years. Eleanor acted as regent for Richard I while he was on the Third Crusade, outlived him, and survived to see her youngest son John become king.

Murder in the Cathedral

When Thomas Becket was enthroned as Archbishop of Canterbury in June 1162, Henry II hoped that his former chancellor would protect the interests of the Crown against excessive ecclesiastical interference. However, Becket proved to be inflexible and his stubbornness ended in his brutal murder inside his own cathedral.

Things turned rapidly sour between King and Archbishop. Disputes concerning the rights of jurisdiction over clerics who had committed criminal acts led to the Archbishop's escape into exile in October 1164. Becket stayed away for six years, until mediation involving Pope Alexander III and King Louis VII of France bore fruit and the Archbishop and King met at Fréteval for a reconciliation in July 1170. But in June, Henry II had his son Prince Henry crowned in a ceremony at which the Archbishop of Canterbury should have been present. Offending both ecclesiastical practice and Becket's pride, this action was at the root of the disaster which then unfolded.

At Becket's request, the Pope suspended Archbishop Roger of York and excommunicated the bishops of London and Salisbury for taking part in the coronation. Becket then provocatively sent the letters of excommunication ahead of his own return to England on December 1.

So as the Archbishop arrived back in Canterbury in triumph, Roger of York and the two bishops reached Bures in Normandy to present their case to the King. Henry was beside himself with rage, inveighing against his treacherous former friend. Hearing him, four knights slipped away, eager to win favor with the King.

The four reached Canterbury on December 29 and found Becket. After a brief confrontation, Becket's entourage persuaded him to go to the cathedral as he might be safer there. The knights, though, took up arms and followed him into the church. With most of his followers having fled, Becket resisted attempts to drag him from the cathedral and in the confusion he was struck on the head. Bleeding, profusely, he was finished off in a rain of blows.

Henry denied all responsibility for the murder and in May 1172 was publicly pardoned by the Pope. Becket was canonized as a saint in March 1173, less than 18 months after his death.

> "Here I am, **not traitor to the king**, but a priest of God. Why do you want me?"

THOMAS BECKET ADDRESSING HIS MURDERERS, DECEMBER 29, 1170

A fatal stab
This stained-glass window inside Canterbury Cathedral depicts the moment of Becket's murder. The four knights, William de Tracy, Richard le Bret, Reginald FitzUrse, and Hugh de Morville, came upon the Archbishop as Vespers was being said.

Invasion of Ireland

The English conquest of Ireland happened almost by accident, when the deposed Irish king of Leinster recruited a band of Norman adventurers to restore him to his throne. Their success and the involvement of King Henry II led to the establishment of English rule over Ireland, which endured for 750 years.

Holy Cross Abbey
The abbey, founded as a Cistercian monastery by King Domnall Mór O'Brien in the 12th century, is one of Ireland's most venerated places of worship. Its architecture marks the pinnacle of the late Gothic style in Ireland.

> **"At the creek of Baginbun, Ireland was lost and won."**

TRADITIONAL IRISH RHYME REFERRING TO THE LANDING BY STRONGBOW'S ADVANCE GUARD AT BAGINBUN IN 1170

A rivalry over the lordship of Dublin brought about the English invasion of Ireland in 1171. Dermot MacMurrough, King of Leinster, claimed to be king of Dublin, but he was unpopular there. Rory O'Connor, King of Connaught, took advantage of this in 1166 to send his ally, Tighearnán O'Ruairc, against MacMurrough. Driven into heavily wooded territory around Ferns, County Wexford, the Leinster King was unable to rally support and took ship for Bristol.

MacMurrough traveled to Aquitaine in France, to offer homage to Henry II in the hope of securing the English King's assistance. But Henry, caught up in a quarrel over his Archbishop of Canterbury, Thomas Becket (see p.79),

at Waterford had, in theory, papal sanction, for in 1156, Adrian IV (the only English Pope) had granted a papal bull, *Laudabiliter*, giving Henry permission to invade Ireland. Although this may have been a pretext, Henry was probably in reality more concerned with gaining control of the large lands his notional vassals were carving out for themselves in Ireland. Henry regularized the situation by appointing his own man, Hugh de Lacy, as constable of Dublin and placing garrisons loyal to him in key towns such as Cork and Limerick.

Although Henry returned to England in spring 1172, de Lacy and Strongbow continued to build up their holdings in the face of sporadic Irish resistance. In 1175, Rory O'Connor acknowledged that the English could not be expelled and agreed the Treaty of Windsor with Henry II, by which he was recognized as High King in the western part of Ireland, although he was to pay a tribute to the English King, while the eastern portion, including Leinster, Meath, Waterford, and Dublin was to remain in the hands of the Anglo-Norman barons.

English possession
Neither the barons nor the other Irish kings paid much attention to the treaty, and warfare continued between them. The death of Strongbow in 1176 brought a greater involvement by the English Crown and in 1183, Henry II had his son Prince John crowned as King of all Ireland, following the death of Rory O'Connor.

With the English in possession of the east and north of Ireland, colonization from England over the next few centuries changed the character of the area to resemble the feudal lordships on the other side of the Irish Sea. The English-controlled area (known as the Pale of Settlement) gradually expanded, with the conquest of most of Connaught by 1235. Royal control, meanwhile, strengthened as the liberties of the barons were restricted. By 1300, the remaining Irish kings ruled reduced domains and were the feudal tenants of English barons.

Kilkenny Castle
The castle was an important stronghold of the Anglo-Norman barons in Ireland from its construction by the earls of Pembroke at the end of the 12th century. The original wooden castle was built by Strongbow.

was in no mood to take on a costly campaign in Ireland. Rebuffed, Dermot turned to other ambitious members of the Anglo-Norman minor nobility.

Norman power
The effect on the MacMurrough cause was electrifying. The Norman force that answered Dermot's call took Wexford within two days. MacMurrough handed the city over to his allies in return for their acknowledging him as their overlord. The allies endured a few difficult moments in 1169, as the Leinster King's enemies, Mac Gilla Pátraic of Osraige and the High King Rory O'Connor, tried to combine their forces to crush them, but in August 1170 they were reinforced by MacMurrough's most powerful Norman ally, Richard fitzGilbert de Clare, Earl of Pembroke (nicknamed "Strongbow"). The new arrivals soon took Waterford, drove out Askulv, the Viking lord of Dublin, and took possession of the city.

Henry's arrival
The astonishing success of such a comparatively small group of Norman knights finally attracted the attention of Henry II. The English King's landing

300 **The number of Norman knights who came to Ireland in the first three ships under Robert Fitzstephen on May 1, 1169.**

THE EXCHEQUER OF IRELAND, 15TH CENTURY

The capture of Jerusalem from the Christian Byzantine emperor by Muslim Arab armies in 638 CE was a disaster for the Christian world.

THE FIRST CRUSADE

It was centuries before any serious attempt was made to recover Jerusalem. Pilgrims continued to reach the Holy City. Yet anecdotal accounts of the restrictions of Muslim authorities on Christian pilgrims in Palestine, and the effects of the **disastrous defeat in 1071** of the Byzantine army at Manzikert by the Muslim Seljuk Turks, **reignited efforts to regain the Holy Land**. In 1095, Pope Urban II began to preach a Crusade—a holy war—to reconquer Jerusalem.

POPE URBAN PREACHING THE CRUSADE

KING OF ENGLAND (1157–1199)

RICHARD I (LIONHEART)

Known as "Lionheart" due to his skill as a warrior, Richard I gained early military experience while rebelling against his father Henry II. He spent only three months in England in 1189, just long enough to claim the throne after his father's death and raise finances for the Third Crusade. While returning overland from Palestine, he was seized by Duke Leopold of Austria and held prisoner until a large ransom was paid in 1194. Another brief sojourn in England followed to restore the damage done by his brother John, who had seized power in Richard's absence, but he then spent the last five years of his life in France, where he built Gaillard castle (below) in 1196.

England in the Crusades

As Christian monarchs, the kings of England were bound to take the papal calls to crusade seriously. Over two centuries, scores of English nobles, thousands of ordinary soldiers, and one reigning king took the Cross and embarked for the Holy Land to save it from the advance of Islam.

With cries of *Deus le Veult* ("God wills it"), the crowds responded to Pope Urban's sermon at Clermont in France in 1095. Many knights and nobles pledged themselves to an armed expedition to seize Jerusalem from its Muslim rulers.

The First Crusade (1096–1099) was a largely French affair, but the closely interlinked landed and political interests of the nobility of Normandy and that of England meant that there was an English dimension of sorts; William II's brother, Robert Curthose, Duke of Normandy, took part, as did others, such as Eustace of Boulogne, who held large estates in England. A small English fleet also made its way to the Levant, and English sailors may have been present at the fall of Jerusalem on July 15, 1099.

Paying for the Crusade

The First Crusade had another impact on England, a financial one that was to recur during later crusades. Robert Curthose pledged the Duchy of Normandy as surety for a 10,000-mark loan his brother gave him to fund his crusading effort. To raise this money, William II in turn levied a crusading tax of 4 shillings to the hide on his kingdom, an imposition so severe that monks were said to have been forced to melt down sacred ornaments to pay for it.

The popularity of crusading as an idea was undimmed by these financial impositions, and the English chronicler Henry of Huntingdon described the preaching of the First Crusade as the

The Crusade assault on Jerusalem

The capture of the Holy City of Jerusalem on July 15, 1099, was a great triumph. It was accompanied by the massacre of large numbers of its inhabitants, both Muslim and Christian.

most important event since the Resurrection of Christ. There was a good response to the first preaching of a crusade in England when the founder of the Templar Order of knights, Hugh de Payens, visited England in 1128. Henry I gave money, and soon the Templars and the Hospitallers (the other military monastic order) were receiving widespread grants of land and other property in England.

The Second Crusade

The Second Crusade (1147–1149) saw a large contingent of English crusaders. The motives of men such as Waleran, Earl of Worcester, William of Warenne, Henry of Glanville, and William Peverel of Dover were varied. Some felt a genuine religious desire for the recovery of Jerusalem, others sought glory or coveted the lands which might be won, while some, such as Peverel, found it a convenient means to escape their political

enemies or a reputation for violence.

The Crusade itself, whose aim had been the recovery of the strategic city of Edessa in Syria, seized by the Muslim emir Zengi in 1144, was largely a failure. Its one lasting result came in October 1147, with the capture of Lisbon by a crusading force en route to the Holy Land, prominent among whom were the English crusaders.

Between the Second and Third Crusades, Englishmen took the Cross and made their way to "Outremer" (the term for the Christian states established in Palestine). In 1169, Saladin came to power in Egypt and between then and 1187 he chipped away at the crusader kingdoms. In 1185 Heraclius, the Latin patriarch of

5,023 The amount in pounds spent by Henry of Cornhill acquiring ships for Richard for the Third Crusade (at a time when a sailor's average daily wage was two pence).

Jerusalem, traveled west to appeal for aid, but the response was muted. Henry II of England made a donation, but no further promises.

The fall of Jerusalem

A few English crusaders, such as Hugh of Beauchamp, made their way to the Holy Land, arriving just in time to die at the Battle of Hattin in July 1187, when Saladin overwhelmed the army of the Kingdom of Jerusalem, leaving the Holy City defenseless. When it fell in October, shock waves reverberated throughout Europe and a new crusade was launched. Henry II of England took the Cross, but died before he could leave for Palestine, and it was left to

Knight's effigy
This monument to a crusader knight can still be found in Temple Church, London—the headquarters of the crusading order of the Templars.

his son Richard I to lead the English contingent.

The German Emperor Frederick Barbarossa drowned on the way to the Holy Land, leaving the Third Crusade as an Anglo-French venture, with command shared between Richard and Philip II. Richard got to Syria in June 1191, and was present when Acre fell in July. Philip left soon after, leaving Richard in command, a challenge he took up with resounding success by defeating the previously invincible Saladin at Arsuf in September. Despite this, the war then settled into stalemate, and in August 1192 Richard agreed a three-year truce with Saladin. Two months later Richard set sail from Acre, ending the campaign of England's only crusader king.

This was the only crusade in England with something like mass participation; Richard's army was at least 6,000 strong and included magnates, citizens, and groups of archers.

Later crusades

The crusades of the early 13th century attracted a much lower level of English participation, as the Anglo-Norman aristocracy was preoccupied with the civil war that only ended in 1217 (see pp.84–85). Richard of Cornwall, the younger son of King John, launched his own crusade to Syria in 1240 and, while Henry III took the cross three times (in 1216, 1250, and 1271) he never actually went to the Holy Land. His eldest son Edward (the future Edward I) did do so in 1270, joining the expedition of Louis IX of France against

Tunis and then making his way to Palestine in 1271. He again achieved little, save the reinforcement of the garrison at Acre.

Lasting effects

If the military importance of English crusading was largely spent by 1192, its cultural effects were more long-standing. Many knights sold their lands to raise money for the long journey to Palestine and the Church, and in particular monasteries, which possessed the largest source of ready cash, benefited by greatly extending their landed properties when many failed to return to redeem their estates. Those who did come back had experienced a lifestyle with which Europe had long been unfamiliar. A taste for luxuries such as silk and spices, which could only be obtained through Muslim intermediaries, came back with the returning crusaders. This helped promote an interest in trade with the area which long outlasted the fall of Acre, the last Christian outpost in Palestine, in 1291.

AFTER

The loss of Acre in 1291 did not mark the final end of European attempts to retake lands in Palestine and elsewhere from their Muslim rulers.

RISE OF THE OTTOMAN EMPIRE
Minor crusades were launched in an effort to stop Constantinople, the capital of the Byzantine Empire, falling into Muslim hands, but the Crusades of Nicopolis (1396) and Varna (1444) were all crushed by a newly rising Muslim power, **the Ottoman Empire**. Crusading taxes—such as one of £1,000 raised in 1446—were levied in England, and the proceeds were sent to help finance the fight against the Turks, but even **the fall of Constantinople** to them in 1453 did not prompt a new crusade.

FALL OF CONSTANTINOPLE, 1453

> **"We have not come seeking wealth … we have come for the sake of God** and for the salvation of our souls."

KING PHILIP OF FRANCE AT THE SIEGE OF ACRE (IN WHICH RICHARD I OF ENGLAND WAS TAKING PART), 1191

Challenging Royal Authority

King John of England signed the Magna Carta in 1215. This marked the first of a series of concessions by which English monarchs ceded parts of their power in the face of baronial challenges to their authority. By 1277, Parliament had become established in England and kings could no longer levy new taxes without its consent.

In 1200, King John became involved in a drawn-out war with France. His failures in France, especially the defeat at Bouvines in 1214, tarnished his prestige. His quarrel with Pope Innocent III over his refusal to accept the appointment of English cardinal Stephen Langton as Archbishop of Canterbury in 1207, was also damaging, as England was placed under an Interdict, which theoretically forbade the holding of almost all church services in the country. In November 1209, the Pope excommunicated

John, absolving all his subjects—including the barons—of their oath of allegiance to him.

The increasing level of financial exactions needed to pay for the unpopular French war crystallized opposition to John around a group of northern nobles, including William de Mowbray. A meeting between John and his tenants-in-chief in November 1213 did little to resolve the situation, and by the time John returned to England in October 1214, three months after Bouvines, the demands for a

scutage (a tax paid in place of military service) of three marks for each knight's fief (land) had further inflamed matters.

Magna Carta

The baronial revolt looked likely to be settled without violence when the Magna Carta was accepted by King and barons on June 15, 1215 (see pp.86–87). The charter protected the barons from undue exactions by the Crown, but certain of its provisions, such as the choice of 25 of their number who could, in the event of the King breaking the terms of the

Magna Carta, seize the King's castles and lands, were never likely to be allowed to stand by John. The King did everything he could to wriggle out of the agreement, asking for a papal condemnation of it; and in late September 1215, a papal bull absolving John of his promises duly arrived in England.

135,541 The sum in marks (£90,370) that Henry III had to pay the Pope for the appointment of Edmund as King of Sicily.

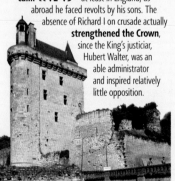

The kiss of peace
John is seen here giving a fraternal kiss to his arch-enemy Philip II Augustus of France. John was defeated many times by Philip, which fatally undermined his power to control the English barons.

Map of Britain
The 13th-century Benedictine monk Matthew Paris compiled a series of chronicles covering the history of England in the 1240s and 1250s. His works include maps, such as this representation of the British Isles.

Civil war erupted as an assembly of barons declared John deposed and invited Louis, son of King Philip II of France, to take over the English throne. The French prince arrived in Kent in May 1216, and he and the rebel barons soon controlled the whole of southeast England. When John died in October 1216 and his nine-year-old son, Henry III, succeeded him, it looked as though the triumph of the rebels would be complete. The young King was supported by a group of loyalists led by William Marshall, Earl of Pembroke. Marshall secured the support of the papal legate Guala Bicchieri and won crucial victories at Lincoln in May 1217, and at Dover in August. The barons' enthusiasm for rebellion evaporated and a formal peace was signed in November.

Henry's regency council acted quickly to restore royal authority, as the barons had seized much royal land and the King's revenues had collapsed. Under Marshall's direction, justices were sent to the localities to hear all pleas, in the most comprehensive display of royal authority since 1176. As a gift to the barons, the terms of Magna Carta were reaffirmed in 1216, and again in 1217.

The reign of Henry III
After Henry was declared of age in 1223, and especially after his marriage to Eleanor of Provence in 1236, he came to depend on foreign advisors. The barons, feeling excluded, began to chafe once more.

Meanwhile, with little sign of the success in France he craved, Henry sought prestigious ventures elsewhere, and in 1255, had his son Edmund appointed titular King of Sicily by the Pope. The price that the papacy demanded for this was exorbitant and the King was forced into new measures to raise funds. One means of doing this was increasing the amount local sheriffs were expected to exact from their counties. The sum had increased by £2,500 in 1258 compared to the start of his reign and it is no coincidence that Robin Hood stories started to circulate during Henry's reign. The King also turned to Parliament, the assembly of barons and advisers that had replaced the role of the Anglo-Saxon *witenagemot*. The barons were not cooperative,

> **£40,000** The sum spent by Henry III in building a shrine to Edward the Confessor at Westminster Abbey— the equivalent of two years' revenue.

> " You English want to **hurl me from my throne** as you did my father."

MATTHEW PARIS, QUOTING HENRY III IN *CHRONICA MAJORA*, C. 1260

however, and of the 14 assemblies where Henry asked for new taxation between 1232 and 1257, Parliament refused it on 12 occasions.

Growing opposition
The demands of payment for Edmund's elevation to the Kingdom of Sicily were the last straw and on April 12, 1258, seven magnates took an oath to stand by each other in opposition to royal oppression. They included Richard de Clare, Earl of Gloucester, and Roger Bigod, Earl of Norfolk. The man who emerged as their leader was Simon de Montfort, a former protégé of Henry's. By the end of April, many other barons and knights had taken the oath and on

May 2, Henry was forced to agree to their demands for radical change. The Provisions of Oxford covered a wide range of judicial reforms and established a council of 15 persons to administer their implementation. They were formalized by the Provisions of Westminster in 1259.

Having agreed, Henry decamped to France and tried to put off the reassembly of the Parliament in February, which in theory could not take place in his absence. Following the tactics of his father John, in 1261 Henry got Pope Alexander to absolve him of his oath to the barons. With both sides unwilling to yield, Henry managed to persuade de Montfort to agree to

AFTER

The growing complexity of royal administration and the need to raise money to pay for it led to an increasing reliance on Parliament, which was acknowledged as the only body that could raise the funds.

TAXES AND PARLIAMENT
Henry III died in 1272, and his successor Edward I summoned at least two Parliaments every year from 1275–1286 to provide funds. He found **new means of taxation**, including a **levy on people's movable goods,** which raised £117,000 in 1290. In 1297, Edward declared that a proposed tax had been granted by the barons of the kingdom, but a group of nobles denounced this, as no summons to attend Parliament had gone out to the barons, knights, and burgesses. Edward had to issue a **Confirmation of the Charters** acknowledging that taxation could only be levied with Parliament's approval.

CONSULTING PARLIAMENT
Later kings had to ask Parliament to raise taxes, until **Charles I sought to levy taxes without parliamentary consent** from 1629–1640, making use of archaic royal rights to gather funds. This was only resolved by the English Civil War **168–169 ≫** and Charles I's execution in 1649 **170–171 ≫**.

KING EDWARD I

arbitration by Louis IX of France. At Amiens in January 1264, the French King listened to both sides' cases and then ignored the barons by declaring Henry vindicated on all points.

The result was civil war. At Lewes on May 14, 1264, de Montfort's forces crushed the royal army, and Henry III and Prince Edward were imprisoned. De Montfort then tried to enlarge his base of support. He had already summoned four knights from each shire to his Parliament of 1264, widening representation from the previously dominant baronial class. In 1265, he summoned burgesses from the towns as well, so that the London Parliament resembled for the first time the later House of Commons.

Prince Edward, however, escaped from captivity in May 1265 and three months later, at Evesham, he trapped de Montfort with a small force. The baronial leader was killed and the rebellious barons melted away or were hunted down. Although their challenge to the King was temporarily at an end, Parliament, whose power it had established, became permanent.

Magna Carta

King John's growing unpopularity with his barons, aggravated by his financial demands and defeat in France, finally led to open revolt in the spring of 1215. At Runnymede, near Windsor, the King and his rebellious subjects met and agreed to Magna Carta, a charter of liberties. Some of the clauses would endure for centuries.

John's authority was fatally damaged by the comprehensive defeat of his army by Philip II of France at the Battle of Bouvines in July 1214. To make matters worse, the Justiciar, Peter des Roches, who had administered England in John's absence, had levied a scutage (feudal due payable in lieu of military service) of three marks per knight. After widespread resistance to his oppressive tax throughout the fall of 1214, a coalition of barons came together and produced a charter of liberties, which had—they said—been granted to the English by Henry I.

Rebellion and agreement

The barons demanded John confirm his charter, but he fobbed them off with a promise of a reply after Easter, while himself appealing to Pope Innocent III. Given that John had vowed to go on a crusade to the Holy Land, the Pope's reply was predictable and he ordered the barons to pay the scutage. Furious, the barons mustered an army and marched south toward the King's position at Wallingford, in Oxfordshire. On May 5, they renounced their homage, so entering a formal state of rebellion. The loss of London to the rebels on May 17 concentrated John's mind, and he ordered Stephen Langton, the Archbishop of Canterbury, to act as a go-between. Langton arranged the meeting at Runnymede between the two sides on June 15, although the terms had probably been largely agreed beforehand. Magna Carta ("Great Charter") was dated that day, and on June 19 it was "made firm."

Failure and symbolism

The terms of this extraordinary 63-clause agreement largely confirmed the barons' feudal rights, particularly with regard to inheritance, and restricted the royal right to tax them. Those clauses that seemed to enhance the rights of free men were strictly subsidiary to this main purpose. Although it endured for centuries as a symbol of England's constitutional liberty, in the short term, Magna Carta was a failure. Neither the more extreme barons nor John were satisfied with it, and civil war broke out again in September. It was still rumbling on when John died in October 1216.

> "No **free man** shall be taken or imprisoned… except by… lawful **judgment of his peers** …"
>
> MAGNA CARTA, CLAUSE 39, 1215

Magna Carta
Four copies of the Great Charter of 1215 have survived. It was reissued with modifications in 1216, 1217, and 1225, under John's successor, Henry III. While most clauses were repealed or became redundant, the right to a fair trial has remained a cornerstone of English law.

Working in the fields
The Luttrell Psalter (c. 1320) shows a farmer broadcasting seed from a basket held on a strap round his neck, while his dog chases off the birds. The narrow field strips were sown in the spring.

A Prosperous Realm

The 200 years following the Norman conquest were troubled times politically, but a time of stability for the kingdom. The population grew, new land was taken into cultivation, trade increased, and urban life flourished.

BEFORE

The old aristocratic Saxon and Anglo-Danish families were swept away after the Norman invasion, and their lands taken over by William the Conqueror, his family, and his Norman and French followers.

FEUDAL LIFE

The Normans were organized for war. They introduced a new type of landholding, **feudalism**, designed to keep them in a state of battle readiness. King William I took all the land into his own hands and **granted large estates** to his main supporters in return for specified military service **« 72–73**. These "great men," the tenants-in-chief of the King, granted land to their own supporters who undertook to give **military service as knights**, the battle-winning armored cavalry of the 11th and 12th centuries.

The men and women who worked the land for their lords, either as free peasants or as **unfree tenants**, made up the greater part of the population. The rhythm of their lives remained relatively unchanged, subject to the seasons.

The ruling class, the king, his family, the leaders of the Church, bishops and abbots, and the great landowners, were all Norman or French. After the conquest (see pp.68–69), the largest estates went to William's family and to his companions in battle. William's half-brother Odo, the Bishop of Bayeux, was given the bishopric of Winchester and lands in Kent. Families such as the FitzOsberns and the de Warennes were granted landholdings across several counties. French was their language. From their estates they had access to the best food, and acquired the best horses, armor, and the finest clothes and jewelry from the revenues they collected.

Kings and aristocrats

The Norman kings established "The Forest," large areas of land reserved for royal hunts, and subject to special laws designed to preserve these habitats. Game such as deer, wild boar, and birds could be caught in The Forest for sport and to supply aristocratic tables with meat. Indeed, hunting and hawking were important features of aristocratic society, teaching skills that would be useful in war.

The great families were part of an international society and had as much contact with their kin in Normandy, France, or Flanders, as with the tenants to whom they granted land. When they were not obeying the king's summons to attend him, they were constantly on the move between their estates.

Life in the countryside

The majority of people lived in the countryside, which was divided into thousands of landholdings called manors. A manor usually included a village and its surroundings, although some manors incorporated several

> " There stretch before you the **most fertile fields**, flourishing meadows, broad swathes of arable land … "
>
> DESCRIPTION OF ENGLAND BY GOSCELIN OF ST. BERTIN, C. 1100

settlements. Fields were open, long, narrow strips of land. The peasants who worked the land paid part of their annual harvest to the lord of the manor as rent, another part went to the Church. Some peasants were free tenants, others were unfree (villeins), who worked the lord's own fields. They were required to give the lord labor and to pay certain fines (fees) such as *heriot*, when inheriting a landholding, and *merchet*, on the marriage of a daughter. The lord of the manor protected his tenants in times of war and acted as judge in disputes between neighbors.

Some knights owned only one or two manors, but most had several, and managed them through an agent called a reeve. Large estates consisting of numerous manors, often widely scattered around the country, were known as honours. Abbeys and cathedrals owned manors, as did secular lords.

Population growth
During the Norman period, the population rose from around 2,250,000 in 1086 to an estimated 5,750,000 by 1220. To meet this increase, forests were cleared to bring new lands called "assart" into cultivation, reducing the amount of woodland in England from 15 to 10 percent of the total land surface. Some changes in landholding took place, too, as land farmed directly by the lords of the manor

Salisbury Cathedral
Towns grew up around large abbeys and cathedrals, such as that at Salisbury. Building work never ceased as bishops and abbots rebuilt their churches in the new Gothic style with pointed arches.

60 MILLION The number of silver pennies in circulation in 1216. The silver penny was the only coin minted at this period and weighed 0.05 oz (1.4 g). The king kept strict control over its minting.

was turned into smallholdings for freemen and villeins who paid cash rents. The expansion of economic life led to changing social bonds. Many obligations of service, whether providing a knight, or working on a lord's land, were commuted into cash payments, and the use of coins became more important.

Sheep were an increasingly profitable commodity. As well as providing meat and milk for cheese, their skins were used for parchment. They were most valued for their wool, which was exported in bulk to the weavers of Flanders during the 12th and 13th centuries. Many of the great monasteries became specialists in sheep farming.

Urban centers
Growing population and increased agricultural production went hand in hand with a rise in the number and size of towns. The Domesday Book (see pp.74–75) identifies 112 towns. Approximately 150 years later this number had grown to 240, all founded by royal charter. The greatest of these were London, Lincoln, Norwich, York, and Winchester. From a population of 15,000 in the days of William I, London had grown to 80,000 inhabitants in 1300. All the major towns were religious centers, often cathedral cities, but they were also market towns and centers of manufacture.

Surplus agricultural produce was brought from country estates to be sold in the towns, and merchants found a ready market there for goods such as wine and furs. The most common urban trades were those involved with the supply of

Artistic riches
Wealthy monasteries produced highly accomplished works of art. This portrait from the Eadwine Psalter (c. 1160), one of the great treasures of medieval England, portrays a monk at his desk in a scriptorium.

food and drink—brewers, bakers, and butchers. Every town had at least one tailor, ironsmith, carpenter, shoemaker, and weaver. Only the large centers would have had more specialized craftsmen.

Town dwellers
Besides the king, other landowners granted charters to build new market towns. These were a source of profit for those who established them and for the merchants and artisans who lived there. Anyone, whatever his origin, who could prove he had lived in a town for a year and a day was a freeman. If he held land in a town, he would have burgage rights, which meant he could subdivide, sell, mortgage, and bequeath it freely. The royal boroughs were governed by the king's officials, but the richer merchants also played a major part in the administration.

Clergy of every rank and type lived in the towns, and schools for the education of boys were attached to cathedrals and monasteries. The universities of Oxford and Cambridge came into being. Instruction was always in Latin, the language of the Church. Books were still rare objects; texts were copied and illustrated by hand.

AFTER »

This period of prosperity, population growth, and increased economic activity came to an end at the beginning of the 14th century.

END OF THE GOOD TIMES
In 1314, a **bad harvest** hit Britain, and for the next seven years (1317 was the only exception) repeated violent winds and rainstorms destroyed crops and caused disease in livestock. As crop yields fell, landowners found themselves without grain surpluses to boost their incomes. In parts of southern England, the harvest was 55 percent below normal, and some areas suffered famine. **Town life stagnated** as demand for manufactured goods fell, and exports of cloth and wool declined. In 1304, 46,000 sacks of wool were exported from England; 15 years later this figure fell to 30,000.

There is evidence that villages began to be abandoned early in the 14th century, as the amount of cultivated land contracted, a crisis that deepened after the widespread devastation and depopulation of the **Black Death 102–103 »**.

WHARRAM PERCY, A DESERTED VILLAGE

‹‹ BEFORE

The new Norman lords of England after 1066 were a far more dangerous adversary for the Welsh than the Anglo-Saxon kings.

CASTLE BUILDERS

After the Norman conquest of England, Norman lords established themselves on the borderlands and made inroads into Welsh territory. **A series of castles**, such as Chepstow and Caerleon, were built, diminishing Welsh autonomy. **The Welsh struck back** in 1094 and almost all of these were destroyed. For some time after this, English kings were preoccupied elsewhere.

CHRONICLE

Gerald of Wales, a cleric of Norman-Welsh heritage, visited Wales in 1191 and **recorded information** about the history of Wales.

GIRALDUS CAMBRENSIS MANUSCRIPT

Subduing Wales

In the 13th century, a series of powerful princes of Gwynedd emerged to unite much of Wales. It seemed as though the principality could establish a political identity separate from England, but in the end the English kings were too powerful and Welsh independence was extinguished by Edward I in 1282.

By 1218, Llywelyn ap Iorwerth of Gwynedd—known as Llywelyn the Great—had united Gwynedd under his rule and swept away much of the English royal control in the south. At first, King John had found Llywelyn a useful counterbalance to the earls of Chester, but while John was preoccupied with a civil war against the barons in 1215–1217 (see pp.86–

An "iron ring" of castles

Beginning in 1283, Edward I had a number of castles built in north Wales to protect England's gains. Designed by master mason James of St. Georges, Harlech Castle, shown here, was completed in four and a half years.

87), Llywelyn formed an alliance of Welsh princes and seized the royal castles of Cardigan and Carmarthen, as well as occupying southern Powys.

Although the Treaty of Worcester (1218) allowed Llywelyn to keep his gains, in 1223 William Marshall seized Cardigan and Carmarthen. Montgomery was also regained for the English. Llywelyn, however, recovered most of these losses in the early 1230s, and after this Wales was mostly at peace until his death in 1240.

Llywelyn's successor Dafydd paid homage to Henry II for the whole of Gwynedd, but his authority was undermined by the

4,000 The number of workmen employed by Edward I to build Harlech, Caernarvon, and Conwy castles in Wales in 1283–1284.

attempts of his half-brother Gruffudd to unseat him. Dafydd reached out to Louis IX of France, offering to hold Wales from the Pope (and thus independently of Henry III) and implicitly offering support to the French King in his wars against the English. Henry's reaction was weak, even failing to take advantage of Gruffudd's death in 1246 to make advances. Instead, he made the Treaty of Woodstock (1247) with Gruffudd's

"Can you not see that **the world is ending**?"

GRUFFUDD AB YR YNAD COCH, LAMENT FOR LLYWELYN AP GRUFFUDD, C. 1282

two sons Owain and Llywelyn, by which the strategic Four Cantrefs (land divisions) between Conwy and the Dee were ceded to England.

Llywelyn ap Gruffudd—often known as Llywelyn Fawr, "the Last"—had pushed his brother aside and in 1258 he seized the Four Cantrefs back and assumed the title Prince of Wales. Henry III who had problems enough with the barons' revolt led by Simon de Montfort was again in no position to react. In 1267, the Treaty of Montgomery finally acknowledged Llywelyn's right to the princely title, in exchange for a fee of 25,000 marks.

The end of Welsh independence

It looked as though Welsh independence under the overlordship of Gwynedd was secured, but disputes over the treaty led to Llywelyn's repudiation of it in 1271. Henry III died in 1272 while his heir, Edward I, was away on crusade, so it was not until 1276 that the new English King invaded. Llywelyn Fawr had made himself unpopular with other Welsh rulers whose lands he had absorbed, and they rapidly submitted to Edward.

With the English King advancing on Deganwy with an army of 15,000, and an English fleet landing at Anglesey, Llywelyn submitted.

He was stripped of all his territories outside Gwynedd, but even then, native rule might have survived there had it not been for his brother Dafydd, who felt himself slighted by the claims of an English lord, Reginald de Grey, to the part of the Four Cantrefs he had received as a reward for fighting on Edward I's side. On March 22, 1282, Dafydd attacked Hawarden Castle, while his confederates among the Welsh princes seized a number of other key Norman castles. Llywelyn hesitated, but felt he had no choice other than to join his brother's insurrection. Early successes were followed by a disastrous battle near Builth on December 11, where the Welsh army was cut to pieces and Llywelyn killed. Most of the Welsh princes were dispossessed and Edward I took control of virtually the whole of Wales.

Falling prince
Henry III kept Dafydd of Gwynedd's half-brother Gruffudd captive in the Tower of London, hoping to use him to his advantage, but in 1244 Gruffudd died in a fall while trying to escape.

AFTER

The conquest of Wales in 1282, and the deposition of most of the native princes, opened the way for direct English rule over Wales, which lasted until the union of the two countries in 1536.

THE LAST WELSH PRINCESS
Llywelyn's daughter, Gwenllian, was born in 1282. She was taken to a nunnery in Lincolnshire by Edward I, where she remained until her death in 1337.

THE STATUTE OF WALES
Edward I moved quickly to organize his new dominion, issuing the Statute of Wales in March 1284, by which he extended **the English shire system into Wales** and established a number of officials to administer the principality.

LATER REBELLION
Rebellions, including that of Rhys ap Maredudd of Ystrad Tywi, one of the few Welsh princes allowed to keep his lands in 1283, and by Madog ap Llywelyn in 1294–1295 **were put down**.

ENGLISH PRINCE
In 1301, Edward I's son, Edward of Caernarvon, was made **Prince of Wales**, a title that is used by members of the British royal family to this day. Wales was largely quiet until the **rebellion of Owain Glyn Dwr** in 1415 116–17 》.

EDWARD OF CAERNARVON

Scotland's Independence Struggle

Edward I's invasion of Scotland in 1296 began a 30-year struggle, which at first saw the English occupy almost the whole of Scotland. Then, just as the spark of Scottish independence seemed extinguished, the English were expelled from Scotland by a new king, Robert the Bruce.

Scotland was almost undone by a piece of dynastic bad luck. At peace with England for nearly 70 years, the Scottish Crown had gradually expanded its area of control beyond the central lowland core, suppressing Galloway's autonomy by 1245, and in 1266 acquiring the Hebrides from Norway by the Treaty of Perth. In 1286, however, Alexander III was killed by a fall from his horse. His three children had already died, leaving the only obvious heir his three-year old

Coronation chair
Edward I had this chair made for the coronation of English kings. As a snub to Scottish sentiment it contained the Stone of Scone, on which the Scottish kings had by tradition been crowned.

BEFORE

A long struggle between the Scottish and English kings over the northern counties seemed to settle down in the 13th century.

KINGDOM OF SCOTLAND
A **program of reform** by King David I of Scotland (1124–1153) created a **medieval kingdom of Scotland**.

BORDER DISPUTES
Malcolm IV was forced to **withdraw from the northern counties** of England in 1157 **« 76**. Alexander II of Scotland brought stability by renouncing claims to the Border counties in 1237.

JEDBURGH ABBEY, BUILT BY DAVID I IN 1138

granddaughter, Margaret, the "Maid of Norway." The infant Queen was sent for from Norway, and her planned engagement to Edward I of England's son Edward of Caernarvon (the future Edward II) seemed to presage a union of the English and Scottish crowns, albeit one that was supposed to guarantee Scottish autonomy.

The kingship of John Balliol

In September 1290, Margaret died while on her way from Bergen in Norway to Scotland, throwing the Scottish nobility into disarray. Edward I summoned an Anglo-Scottish parliament on the border at Norham, in May 1291, and demanded that the Scottish lords acknowledge his right to decide the process by which their next king would be selected. One by one they did so, first Robert Bruce of Annandale and last John Balliol, who had an independent claim to the throne as a descendant of David I. Finally, in November 1292, a commission with 24 jurors and the English King as judge selected Balliol to rule Scotland, but he was not an independent monarch since he owed his position entirely to the favor of Edward I.

John Balliol tried to assert himself, but his refusal to attend Parliaments in York and his maneuvering for a French alliance brought the wrath of Edward ("Longshanks" as the Scots came to call him) down upon Scotland. The Scots were defeated at Dunbar in late April, and in early July, John surrendered. Edward had him summarily stripped of his royal vestments, giving rise to Balliol's unfortunate nickname of "Toom Tabard" (empty surcoat).

The siege of Berwick

As Edward III's army marched north in 1332 to support Edward Balliol's bid for the Scottish Crown, it laid siege to the Castle of Berwick, long contested between England and Scotland. It fell after the Scots defeat at Halidon Hill in July 1333.

Having placed garrisons in many Scottish castles, Edward I then left for Gascony in August 1296. Already the rumblings of resistance were growing louder and a series of risings broke out in spring 1297, with an able leader emerging in the shape of William Wallace, who defeated the English at Stirling Bridge in 1297. Wallace

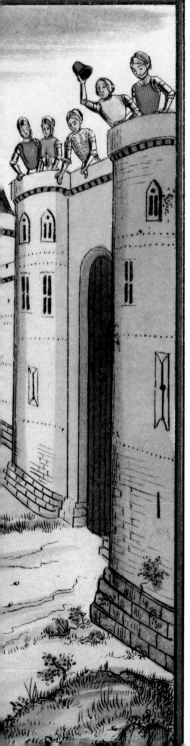

overreached himself and risked another pitched battle at Falkirk in July 1298, where he was soundly beaten.

For a while, the protection of their French ally Philip IV kept Longshanks at bay, but the French defeat at Courtrai in 1302 and the subsequent Peace of Amiens, which excluded Scotland, gave Edward I free rein once more. In 1303, the English came north again and by early 1304 the Scottish leader John Comyn had surrendered. At a meeting called at Greyfriars' Church in Dumfries in February 1306 to discuss their tactics, Robert Bruce struck Comyn dead and assumed the leadership of the anti-English party. On March 27, 1306, he declared himself King at the traditional royal coronation site of Scone, but it was an inauspicious first year and by early 1307, he was a fugitive in western Scotland.

7,000 The number of inhabitants of Berwick killed by Edward I's army on his way north to Scotland in March 1296.

Return of Robert Bruce

King Robert's comeback began with a victory at Loudon Hill in May 1307, and from then he won an uninterrupted string of victories, aided by the accession of Edward II to the English throne in 1307, a man who

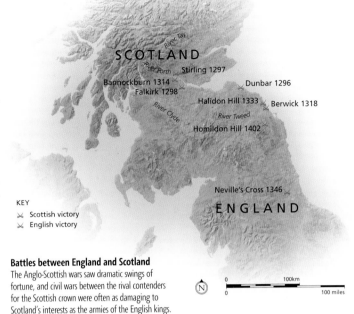

SCOTLAND

River Tay

Stirling 1297
Bannockburn 1314
Falkirk 1298
River Forth
Dunbar 1296
Halidon Hill 1333
Berwick 1318
River Clyde
River Tweed
Homildon Hill 1402

Neville's Cross 1346

ENGLAND

KEY
⚔ Scottish victory
⚔ English victory

N

0 ——— 100km
0 ——— 100 miles

Battles between England and Scotland
The Anglo-Scottish wars saw dramatic swings of fortune, and civil wars between the rival contenders for the Scottish crown were often as damaging to Scotland's interests as the armies of the English kings.

lacked the firm resolution of his father and who did not adequately fund the Scottish garrisons. Aberdeen fell to the Scots in July 1308, and in 1309 Bruce felt able to call his first Scottish Parliament at St. Andrews.

By spring 1314, only Stirling Castle remained in English hands, and it was to save this last redoubt of English power in Scotland that Edward II finally stirred himself to a counterstrike. This ended in disaster, with the English army being cut apart at Bannockburn on June 24, 1314 (see pp.94–95).

By 1315, Robert had taken the offensive against northern England, besieging Carlisle. In the same year his brother Edward landed in Ulster in an attempt to topple English rule in Ireland. The invasion bogged down, and though Edward was declared High King of Ireland in 1316, it was a hollow title and the Scots occupation was largely confined to the north. By the time Robert recovered Berwick, the last Scottish possession occupied by England, in 1318, Edward Bruce's forces were nearly exhausted and in October 1318 he was killed in battle near Dundalk.

The declaration of Arbroath

A succession crisis ensued as Robert still had no direct heir, and he feared that Edward II, who was grooming John Balliol's son Edward for the Scottish throne, might invade. These anxieties led to a formal Scottish statement of independence by the Declaration of Arbroath in 1320, and the choice by Robert of his grandson Robert Stewart as his successor. The failure of an attempt by Edward II to invade Scotland and the weakening

of the English position by an outbreak of civil war there in 1326–1327 finally brought about a negotiated peace. In spring 1328, by the Treaty of Edinburgh, Edward III renounced his claim to lordship over Scotland. The country's independence seemed finally secured.

AFTER ≫≫

The English invaded Scotland shortly after the Treaty of Edinburgh. However, Scotland retained its independence until the Union of the Crowns in 1603.

ENGLISH GAINS IN POWER
Robert died in 1329, but in 1324 he had fathered a son, David, who became king. In 1332, **Edward Balliol**, the son of John, **invaded Scotland** with the encouragement of Edward III. He defeated the army of Bruce loyalists and had himself crowned King at Scone. A **victory at Halidon Hill** in 1333, led to Edward III taking much of southern Scotland. The young King David II was sent to France for safety. Robert Stewart rallied and **drove the English out** by 1341.

COIN OF DAVID II

THE STEWART RULERS
Robert became king in 1371 after the death of David II without an heir. The Stewarts ruled Scotland until **James VI succeeded his cousin** Elizabeth I of England in 1603 **158–159 ≫**, and became king of both countries. As a result, a descendent of Robert Bruce ruled over England.

SCOTTISH LEADER (C. 1272–1305)

WILLIAM WALLACE

Wallace emerged to lead the Scottish resistance movement in 1297, following his murder of the English sheriff of Lanark. His defeat of the English against the odds at Stirling Bridge in September 1297 cemented his reputation, but his luck did not hold, and after losing at Falkirk the following year he never led another Scottish army. Wallace left on a diplomatic mission to France, but after his return to Scotland, he was betrayed and handed over to the English. He was hanged, drawn, and quartered in London.

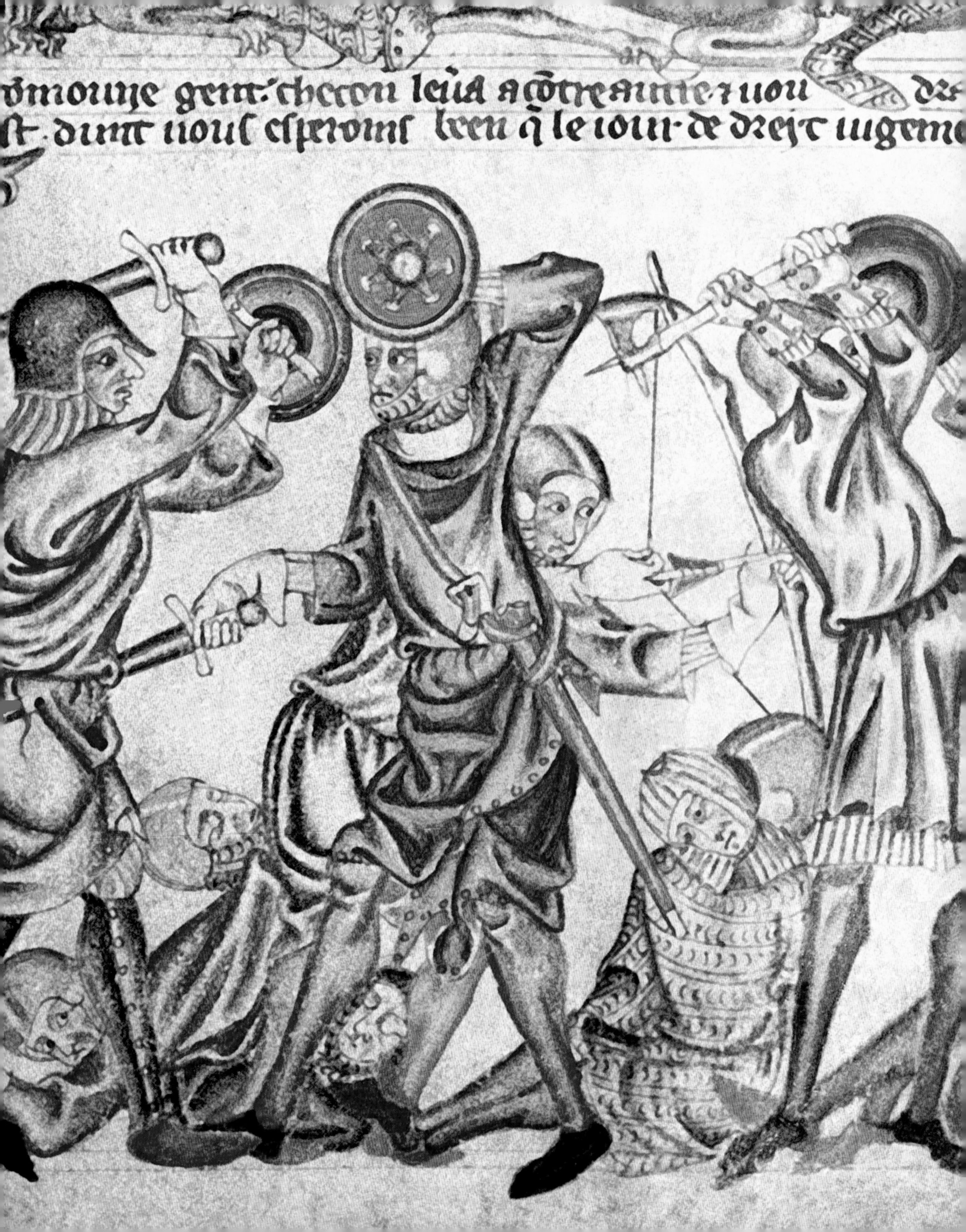
dunt nous esperoms bien q le iour de dreit iugeme

The Battle of Bannockburn

Following the loss of Edinburgh Castle to the forces of King Robert the Bruce in March 1314, King Edward II of England launched an invasion to relieve Stirling Castle, the last English possession in Scotland. The subsequent encounter at Bannockburn would have a decisive bearing on Scotland's fight for independence.

The army that Edward mustered in Berwick in June 1314 was around 15,000 strong, including 10,000 infantry, 2,000 heavy cavalry, and a large force of archers. Pushing north, on June 23, the English arrived just south of Stirling, where King Robert's army lay in wait. Robert commanded around 5,000 men, mainly infantry armed with long spears, organized into shield formations known as schiltrons, and a small force of light cavalry. He set anti-cavalry pits and spikes along the road to Stirling, and deployed the bulk of his forces in the wooded New Park, which blocked the English army's progress. A premature English attack on June 23, was caught in the cavalry traps.

The English then forded the Bannock Burn, a stream to the south and east of the Scottish position. A difficult crossing left the English tired, and they camped for the night just across the Burn in an open space. Probably not expecting a direct attack, Edward gathered his forces in a constricted space that made it difficult for them to maneuver in the face of any unexpected assault.

At dawn on June 24, upon Robert's orders, the Scottish infantry charged from New Park, to the astonishment of the resting English troops. The Earl of Gloucester roused them with a cavalry charge, but with little room to move, its impact against the Scots was limited. Archers attacked the Scottish flanks, but with Robert unleashing his light cavalry, the English scattered.

Scottish victory

Robert then inflicted the killing blow against the disheartened English by throwing forward his reserve of Highlanders, while the emergence of the "small folk," untrained Scottish levies, spread panic through the English ranks. Edward fled the scene, first to Stirling Castle, which did not admit him, and finally to Berwick. Back on the battlefield, a massacre took place as the Scots cut down the disordered, escaping English. The blow to Edward's prestige in Scotland was huge, although the war would drag on for another 14 years before Scottish independence was finally recognized by England.

> **"These barons** you see before you, clad in armor, **are bent** upon **destroying … our whole nation**. They **do not believe we can resist."**

ROBERT THE BRUCE, ADDRESSING HIS TROOPS BEFORE THE BATTLE OF BANNOCKBURN, JUNE 24, 1314

Carnage of close combat
The Holkham Bible's depiction of Bannockburn vividly illustrates the violent chaos of the battle. At its end, the Bannock Burn was bloated with bodies as the fleeing English were butchered in their thousands. Most survivors were captured; very few made it back to England.

Battle of Crécy

Edward III's invasion of France in the summer of 1346 was within 19 miles (30 km) of Paris. With his army tiring, Edward decided to risk a pitched battle with Philip VI of France. The outcome of this engagement at Crécy would determine the future of the French Crown and mark a pivotal moment in the Hundred Years' War.

On the morning of August 26, the English—some 12,000 strong, half of them longbowmen—marched out of the forest of Crécy and took up position on a long ridge between Crécy and Wadicourt. The sloping terrain offered them some protection. The French—around 40,000 strong, including 6,000 Genoese crossbowmen—had halted around 9 miles (15 km) short of the English position. The French commanders could not decide whether to delay the attack until the following day. However, some of the men headed of their own accord toward the English. Soon, the rest of the army followed suit.

Victory of the longbowmen

The Genoese crossbowmen were the first to attack. But with the sun in their eyes, and deceived by the ridge's slope, their usually lethal volley proved ineffective. The response of the English longbowmen was more telling; swathes of Genoese fell and the rest pulled back. The Duke of Alençon in the French forward division regarded the Genoese action as cowardice, and ordered them cut down as they retreated.

A hasty retreat

The French knights charged, but were pushed toward the enemy line. When the English knights advanced down the slope, the French retreated to their second division. Soon, English archers poured further volleys into its flanks and the French dissolved into chaos.

Despite mounting up to 15 charges that day, the French were beaten back by the unscathed English knights. Toward midnight, King Philip withdrew to the castle of Labroye, abandoning his army to flee or die.

Edward chose not to march to Paris, but instead headed to Calais, which he hoped would fall quickly to him. The siege lasted until August 1347 and the impetus of the English victory was lost.

> **"The French did not advance in any regular order** ... some came before and some came after."**

JEAN FROISSART, *CHRONICLES*, c 1373

A one-sided battle
This illustration from Jean Froissart's *Chronicles* shows the English longbowmen facing the Genoese crossbowmen at the Battle of Crécy. Around 10,000 Frenchmen perished at Crécy, including many leading nobles; about 500 Englishmen were lost.

BEFORE «

The Black Death was not the first pandemic to cause great mortality. Others had been recorded in ancient times.

ANCIENT PLAGUES

The Greek historian Thucydides gave a detailed account of an **epidemic that struck Athens** from 430 BCE, describing its symptoms in detail. It is likely that neither this, nor the **great Antonine Plague,** which afflicted the Roman Empire in 165 CE, was the bubonic plague widely believed to be the cause the Black Death. However, the **Justinianian Plague** of 541–542 CE, which devastated the Byzantine Empire, did have similar symptoms to those of the 14th-century plague.

EMPEROR JUSTINIAN

The **Black Death**

The "Great Pestilence" that struck Britain in the spring of 1348 killed up to half of the population within a year. Inspiring helpless terror as it passed through the land, the epidemic contributed to profound and long-lasting social changes in the British Isles.

England in the 1340s was a society vulnerable to economic and social stress. Bad harvests in the 1310s and 1320s led to a high mortality rate, as grain prices more than quadrupled. On Halesowen Manor in Worcestershire some 15 percent of adult males died in 1315–1316.

Time of disease

Outbreaks of smallpox and measles were also well-known killers in late medieval society, but their victims were most often children and their impact did not seriously disturb the social order or damage the economic productivity of the land. Nothing, therefore, had prepared the British Isles for the scourge that descended upon it from the east in the spring of 1348.

> "The Great Pestilence … raged so terribly that **it cleared many villages** … of every human being." *CHRONICLE OF GEOFFREY LE BAKER OF SWINBROOK*, C. 1357

The traditional view is that the Black Death—as later historians called what contemporaries labeled the "Great Mortality" or the "Great Pestilence"—was caused by *Yersinia pestis,* an organism passed into the human blood stream by the bite of fleas endemic in certain species of rat. Some historians now suggest that the Plague was in fact a viral disease. Although the cause is not certain, what is clear is that a terrible disease emerged, most likely in Mongolia around the 1320s, which then spread eastward to China (where successive outbreaks killed up to two-thirds of the population) and west through central Asia. By 1347, it had reached Crimea.

Plague scene

This 14th-century manuscript shows plague victims being carried from a city to be buried in mass graves. Such scenes would have been seen in many European cities.

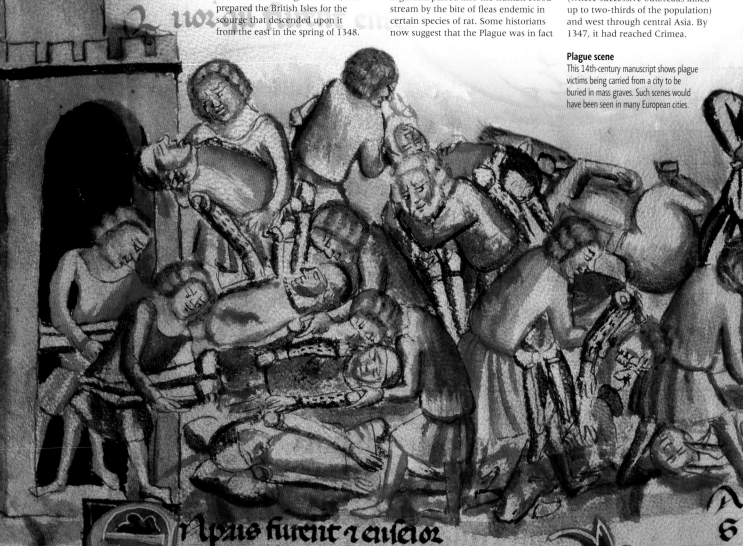

Medical care
Late medieval doctors plied their art using the Roman physician Galen's theory of the "humors" in the body, which could be rebalanced by the application of poultices or other equally ineffective measures.

The disease manifested itself first with a high fever, convulsions, and vomiting. Within a few days the victim's lymph glands swelled up dramatically in the characteristic lumps, or buboes, whose black discolored appearance gave the plague its name. In the final phase of

6.5 The amount in pence that a Somerset reaper could earn in 1350, compared to the 3 pence per acre he was able to charge in 1348.

the illness, the buboes split apart and the patient died soon after. Contemporary medicine, dependent on the theories of 1st-century CE Roman physician Galen, was virtually useless in the face of such a virulent affliction, and around 70 percent of those who contracted the illness died.

The plague probably reached Europe through Kaffa in Crimea in 1347. Genoese sailors, escaping the siege of the city by the Mongols of the Golden Horde, then spread it by ship throughout the ports of the Mediterranean. The first reports of the plague in England came from Melcome Regis in Dorset, where a ship carrying some Gascon sailors is said to have brought the infection just before the Feast of John the Baptist (June 24), 1348. Before long, the plague was

spreading throughout the southwest, reaching Bristol on August 15, moving north and west to the Midlands and Wales soon after, and making relentless progress toward London in the late fall.

There are varying estimates of the death toll by the time the epidemic had run its course in 1350, but the proportion of beneficed clergy (those who had a stipend) who died was 40 percent and this group probably suffered somewhat less than the general population. In the end, probably somewhere between a third and a half of Britain's population perished in the plague. In England this amounted to up to 2.5 million of the pre-plague population of 5 million in around 1300.

The pestilence in London
London fell victim to the pestilence before All Saints' Day (November 1), by March 1349 cases were recorded in East Anglia, and York succumbed on Ascension Day (May 21). The losses in London alone may have amounted to 25,000, or half the pre-plague population. Reactions to the plague were varied, but always tinged with panic and terror. Many fled their homes, further spreading the disease; others threw themselves into prayer and devotional literature. The art of the period dwells on death and the allegorical *Danse Macabre* (Dance of Death) story in the 15th century is an apt reflection of the preoccupations of the age.

No social class was spared. Three successive archbishops of Canterbury died of the plague in 1348 and 1349, leaving the Church leaderless. As the plague touched Wales and Ireland in 1349, and Scotland in 1350, it seemed as though the death would never end.

Taking blood
A method employed by doctors following the methods of Galen was to bleed the patient to remove a perceived excess of blood. Some used leeches, others used more invasive instruments, such as this one, known as a fleam.

Plague saint
Saint Roche of Montpellier is said to have ministered to the victims of a plague in northern Italy before his death in 1327, afterward becoming the patron saint of plague sufferers.

Yet the Black Death simply ran out of victims, and by 1350 in England the death toll fell.

A changed society
The plague left a radically altered social landscape in its wake. The 1348 harvest had been planted for a population double the size of that left the next year. Food prices fell and the price laborers could charge for their work rose as a labor shortage hit landowners. Although the Great Pestilence had for the moment passed, the imbalances created meant that landowners would be forced either to adopt more oppressive measures to secure labor or pay more for it.

AFTER ⟩⟩

More outbreaks of the Black Death struck from the 1350s, destabilizing attempts to deal with the aftermath of the 1348 attack.

WAGE RISES
The Statute of Labourers in 1351 established the maximum wage reapers could earn at 2 pence per day and set ceilings for craftsmen such as master carpenters, who were to be paid no more than 3 pence per day. But in 1361, an outbreak of the **pestilence killed about 20 percent** of the population and the maximum wages had to be revised upward (to 4 pence per day for master carpenters). Further attacks followed every 10–12 years thereafter.

THE GREAT PLAGUE
The final English outbreak of the Black Death struck in 1665 **181 ⟩⟩**, when some 100,000 people died in the capital. **Medicine had advanced little** and elaborately dressed plague doctors did little more than administer placebos and collect their pay.

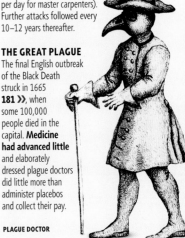

PLAGUE DOCTOR

BEFORE

The economic and social consequences of the Black Death continued to cause grave difficulties for the English Crown decades after the main outbreak had ended.

LABOR SHORTAGE

In the immediate aftermath of the plague of 1348 ❮❮ 102–103, peasants demanded **higher wages** and improved conditions of land tenure, including fixed tenancy and employment terms. The nobility and Parliament moved to counter this, with the **Ordinance of Labourers** in June 1349 decreeing that all physically fit men and women under 60 be available for work. Some landowners began to **enclose strips of land**, which could then be farmed more easily and with fewer laborers.

CORRUPT COURT

The last years of Edward III's reign were marred by his dementia, and the dominance of the court by a cabal of **corrupt favorites**, including his mistress Alice Perrers. The war against France was also proving costly, with little gain, and in 1376 there was a real **fear of invasion**.

ROYAL LANDOWNER (1340–1399)

JOHN OF GAUNT

By the age of 22, John of Gaunt, the third eldest surviving son of Edward III, was Duke of Lancaster and one of England's leading landowners. He was associated with the failing government of his father in the 1370s, and his lack of battlefield success in France and his dominance of the unpopular regency councils of Richard II's early reign made him a target of the 1381 revolt. In 1386, he became King of Castile (through his wife Constanza) but was driven out in 1389, returning to England. He was sidelined by an increasingly tyrannical Richard, and did not quite live long enough to see his son Henry become king.

The **Peasants' Revolt**

For a week in June 1381, England seemed on the edge of a revolutionary change, as rebels, angered at the imposition of a heavy poll tax, marched on London and threatened to unseat the government. The moment soon passed with the killing of the rebel leadership and the restoration of Richard II's power.

Edward III's death in 1377 was followed by the succession of the 10-year old Richard II. As a result, England was ruled for the next three years by a series of regency councils, which lacked the firm will to divert the country from its ruinously expensive war with France. One expedition alone, in December 1379, under Sir John Arundel, cost £15,000 and was dispersed by a storm in the Channel without achieving anything at all.

In rural areas resentment simmered at the land enclosures, extortion by landlords, and the successive royal attempts to drive down wages, which had taken place over the 30 years since the Black Death. The Crown's need for extra funding for the French campaign was the spark that set this anger ablaze.

A tax for all

Traditionally the king relied on "lay subsidies" for funding, assessed at around 6 percent of a household's movable property, which raised correspondingly more money from the rich.

> **36** The percentage of those eligible to pay the poll tax in the county of Essex who disappeared from the poll tax rolls between the first tax in 1377 and the punitive poll tax levy of 1381.

In 1377, however, Parliament voted a poll tax of 4 pence from every male and female over the age of 14, irrespective of income. This raised £22,000 and there was no widespread resistance to it. In 1379, a second poll tax was approved by Parliament, levied according to an elaborate set of rules that included 50 gradations, with dukes at the top paying £6, and barons 50 shillings, down to the poorest at the bottom, who were assessed at 4 pence. This more progressive tax raised only £18,600 and with tension simmering on the Scottish border and little sign of success in the war against France, Chancellor Sudbury (who was also the Archbishop of Canterbury) returned to the House of Commons with a demand for a poll tax that would raise an astonishing £160,000. The Commons finally assented and the new tax was levied at a flat rate of 12 pence per head on all over the age of 15—three times

the level of the 1377 tax. Evasion was instant and widespread. The poll tax rolls compiled to show who had paid the imposition, show that 450,000 fewer people paid in 1380–1381 than in 1377, meaning one-third of taxpayers had vanished. The royal council ordered inquiries into the massive evasion in January 1381, and in March, new commissions were sent into the counties to track down those who had refused to pay.

Growing resentment

The heavy-handed actions of the commissioners fueled the resentment of the peasantry, which was already reaching dangerous levels. Within three days of the arrival of John Bampton's commission in Essex on May 30, some 50,000 peasants (probably an exaggerated figure) are said to have risen under a certain Thomas Baker of Fobbing. In Kent, the arrest of a man claimed as a serf by Sir Simon Burley proved the immediate spark for revolt, and on June 5, the Kentishmen gathered at Dartford and then marched on Maidstone, which fell to them the next day.

Centers of unrest

The Kent rebels first marched to Canterbury, then on to London, where they were joined by rebels from other farming counties of the southeast.

It is at this point that Wat Tyler emerged as leader of the revolt. Little is known of him—other than he seems actually to have been a tiler—but for the next 10 days he acted as the figurehead for the rebels, together with a radical preacher named John Ball, who espoused a radical (for medieval times) form of egalitarianism, and an even more shadowy figure named Jack Straw, whom some sources claim was no more than an alias of Wat Tyler.

Targets of the rebellion

The rebels next marched on Canterbury, the seat of the hated Archbishop-Chancellor, where they burned the poll tax rolls. They then moved on London. At an early stage the rebel tactics were clear. They directed their attacks at the King's ministers and sought to extract concessions from Richard himself. On June 13, with the rebels at Greenwich, the King came in person to meet them. Tyler demanded

KEY

⬅ Principle peasant marches
○ Centre of unrest
▪ Area affected by peasant violence

CAMBRIDGESHIRE & ISLE OF ELY

NORFOLK
Norwich
Yarmouth

Leicester

HUNTINGDON & PETERBOROUGH

Cambridge
Bury St Edmunds
SUFFOLK
Sudbury

ESSEX
Colchester

HERTFORDSHIRE
St Albans

Brentwood
MIDDLESEX
Highbury
London
Mile End
Dartford
Rochester
Canterbury

SURREY
Maidstone
KENT

Winchester

0   100km
0   100 miles

"When **Adam delved** and **Eve span**, who then was the **gentleman**?"

PEASANTS' REVOLT LEADER JOHN BALL, c. 1380

the surrender of John of Gaunt, the King's uncle; Chancellor Sudbury; Treasurer Hales; and a clutch of other especially despised notables. The King refused and tried to trap the rebels into a meeting at Windsor where royal forces might more easily hunt them down. Wat Tyler was not fooled and the rebels, up to 60,000 strong according to some sources, marched on Southwark where they opened the Marshalsea Prison, burned Sudbury's palace, and razed John of Gaunt's Savoy Palace.

Rebel manifesto

On June 14, the rebels, who had trapped the King and his ministers in the Tower

Tyler's death

The meeting between Tyler and Richard II descended into an argument and the rebel leader may have drawn a dagger. He was then struck by Mayor Walworth, before being killed by Ralph Standish, a royal esquire.

of London, issued a manifesto. It demanded the punishment of traitors to the Crown, the abolition of serfdom, the establishment of a mandatory rent of 4 pence per acre, and the legalization of negotiations between masters and servants on contracts.

On the same day, Richard met once more with the rebels at Mile End. He issued a charter proclaiming the end of serfdom, and many of the rebel bands, with one of their key demands satisfied, started to break up and return home. The men of Kent were more stubborn and refused to disperse, breaking into the Tower and murdering Sudbury and Hales, whose severed heads were displayed on poles to the assembled mob.

Royal fracas

Richard met again with the remaining rebels on June 15 at Smithfield.

Historical sources are hostile to the

Kentishmen, but it seems that Tyler was insolent in the royal presence and some kind of scuffle broke out with Richard's retainers. In the fracas, Tyler was fatally wounded. It was a moment of profound danger that might have descended into a massacre, but Richard kept his head. He persuaded the rebels to move on to Clerkenwell.

The rebellion collapses

The momentum of the rebellion was lost and Jack Straw, who seems to have replaced Wat Tyler as leader, failed to keep the remaining rebels together. Straw was executed the same day and the Great Rebellion collapsed.

14 The age of King Richard II when he rode out to meet Wat Tyler and the rebels in a field near Mile End in 1381. The country was ruled by councils, with Richard's uncle John of Gaunt hugely influential.

It was time rather than violent action that ultimately gave the peasantry what they demanded. The reprisals in the aftermath of the peasants' poll tax rebellion were relatively slight, while over the next century the vestiges of the legal servitude Wat Tyler's men had so dramatically rebelled against gradually withered away.

The Peasants' Revolt was not the last major rural uprising in late medieval England. Economic and political grievances continued to provoke rebellions well into the 15th century.

REBEL PARDON

The Parliament of November 1381 passed a **general pardon for the rebels**, except those who had been involved in the killing of ministers (and the men of Bury St. Edmunds who were singled out for special punishment). Those who survived the end of the Great Rebellion were **hunted down**, such as John Wrawe of East Anglia, who was executed in May 1382.

FURTHER REVOLTS

The next major rising was that of Jack Cade in 1450–1452, when again the men of Kent **marched on London** (though their expressed objectives were political rather than economic). In 1489, opposition to **Henry VII's tax raising** led to violence in Yorkshire, and a major revolt by Cornishmen in 1497 again reached Blackheath, in London. After this, the rural risings of the 16th century had a more **religious and political component**.

no: terram autem

um

Luttrell Psalter
This illuminated book of psalms is named after Geoffrey Luttrell, lord of the manor of Irnham, Lincolnshire, who commissioned it between 1320 and 1340. It contains an array of depictions of contemporary rural life. Here, servants prepare food and carry it to the lord's table. Such depictions mask a grim reality, for in 1315, 1316, and 1321, the harvests failed in England's worst agrarian crisis for centuries, and disease killed many cattle and sheep in 1317 and 1319–1321.

Religious Enthusiasm

A matter of concern for people in the Middle Ages was knowing what to believe and how to live the Christian life so as to avoid going to hell. However, criticism of the Church grew in some quarters, and many individuals sought salvation in personal devotion and charitable work.

During the 13th century, the Church in England, as in the rest of Europe, increased in power, organization, and influence. The Lateran Council of 1215, convened by Pope Innocent III in Rome, set out standards of reform for the behavior of the clergy, which the English bishops sought to follow. For example, Robert Grosseteste, the Bishop of Lincoln from 1235–1254, instructed that the clergy in his diocese should preach regularly to their parishioners. The century also witnessed a new development as religious orders of Franciscan and

" I believe that in the end the truth will conquer."

STATEMENT OF JOHN WYCLIFFE TO JOHN OF GAUNT, 1381

Dominican friars arrived in England. The friars were committed to a life of poverty and because, unlike monks, they chose to live in rather than apart from the communities in which they served, the friars brought the practice of the Christian religion to the people of England's growing towns. They also came to dominate teaching in the newly established universities of Oxford and Cambridge.

Service and criticism

In the centuries that followed the new orders' arrivals, influential churchmen, such as William of Wykeham and William Waynflete, each in turn Bishop of Winchester, and Henry Chichele, the Archbishop of Canterbury, founded schools and university colleges to provide a source of educated clergy to act as skilled administrators for both the King and the Church.

Christ in judgement

This painting, known as a doom, shows Christ sitting in judgement over the living and the dead. St. Peter (on the left) admits the righteous to heaven, while St. Michael (on the right) dispatches the wicked to hell.

For lay people, religious observance was expressed in many ways. For the rich, endowing a chantry chapel, where priests would say mass and pray in perpetuity for the founder's soul after death, was considered to be a path to avoiding their eternal damnation. Lay people also showed their piety by giving sizeable donations or legacies to charitable institutions for the care of the sick, aged, and indigent. Pilgrimage, which was a journey

to the shrine of a saint, was also seen as a means of gaining spiritual merit. Geoffrey Chaucer's poem, *The Canterbury Tales*, written in the late 14th century, tells of a group of pilgrims on their way to Canterbury, Kent, to visit the shrine of the saint and martyr, Thomas Becket (see pp.78–79).

However, the growth of the Church as a worldly and powerful institution caused unease among many clergy and lay people. One churchman who tried to improve the situation was

« 84–85

BEFORE

The Anglo-Norman kings sought to strengthen the independence of the English Church. This brought them into frequent conflict with the papacy.

THE KING AND THE CHURCH

William I was crowned King of England with the **papacy's support**. He appointed churchmen from Normandy as bishops, and initiated the construction of great stone cathedral churches and abbeys in the Romanesque style.

Relations between the King and the Church deteriorated in the 12th century. Henry II's Archbishop of Canterbury, Thomas Becket, was **murdered at the king's behest** for refusing to put the interests of the Crown before the Church. A further crisis came when **King John rejected the Pope's nominee**, Stephen Langton, as Archbishop of Canterbury, leading to his excommunication by the Pope « 84–85.

New religious orders, such as Cistercians and Carthusians, were established in Britain before 1200, to meet the need for greater monastic spirituality.

CARTHUSIAN PRIORY OF MOUNT GRACE, NORTH YORKSHIRE

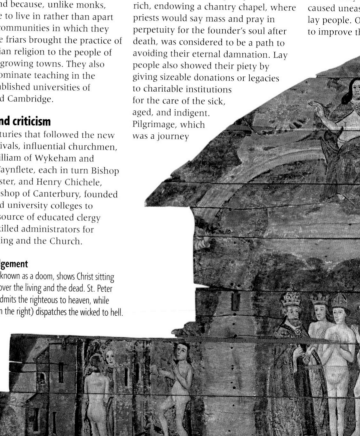

JOHN WYCLIFFE

John Wycliffe was born in Yorkshire. As a teacher of theology at Oxford University, he came to believe that the claims of the Pope to be the supreme authority of the Church were unjustified. He escaped persecution in his lifetime, but after his death his body was exhumed and burned, and his ashes thrown into a river.

Monks praying

This stained-glass window in Canterbury Cathedral shows monks praying. Monks devoted their lives to God within the confines of their monasteries, while friars, living a life of poverty, preached to people in the streets.

Archbishop Thorseby, who as Archbishop of York in 1352–1373 set about reforming the clergy in his province, and put together a catechism in Latin and English for the instruction of lay people. William Langland's long narrative poem in English, *Piers Plowman*, written in c. 1360–1387, is a critique of the Church and its practices, as well as an exploration of how to discover the true meaning of the Christian life.

The Lollards

The most open and subversive expression of this mood of discontent with the Church came from the Lollard movement, which rose to prominence in the second half of the 14th century.

EXCOMMUNICATION A decree by the Pope excluding a Christian from the sacraments of the Church. It was used to punish those who flagrantly rejected the Church's teachings or authority.

Reflecting the controversial teachings of the Oxford theologian, John Wycliffe, the Lollards challenged the wealth of the Church, its involvement in the secular world, its doctrine of the Eucharist (the central rite of the Christian Church), and the exclusive role of the priesthood in the administration of the sacraments.

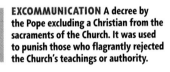

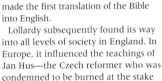

Most importantly, to give ordinary people access to, and understanding of, the Bible, Wycliffe and his collaborators made the first translation of the Bible into English.

Lollardy subsequently found its way into all levels of society in England. In Europe, it influenced the teachings of Jan Hus—the Czech reformer who was condemned to be burned at the stake as a heretic by the Council of Constance in 1415—and also foreshadowed many of the theological teachings of Martin Luther, Ulrich Zwingli, and other later Protestant reformers. Although the Church condemned his theological writings, John Wycliffe himself was protected by Oxford University. His followers also found protection, initially from John of Gaunt, Duke of Lancaster, who was also an uncle of King Richard II. In the 15th century, Henry IV and Henry V, who ruled as the first Lancastrian kings of England, supported the Church in its opposition to Lollard heresy, and regularly persecuted its adherents.

AFTER »

The 14th and 15th centuries saw an increasing quest in England for both personal spiritual devotion and a direct relationship with God.

JULIAN OF NORWICH

The real name of **Julian of Norwich** (1342–1416) is uncertain. It is known that she lived as a hermit in a cell attached to the Church of St. Julian, in Norwich. In *Sixteen Revelations of Divine Love,* believed to be the first book in English written by a woman, she describes a series of intense visions she had of Jesus Christ.

MARGERY KEMPE

Julian's writings greatly influenced **Margery Kempe** (1373–1438), a married woman who had several children, but all her life felt called to Christ, and made extensive pilgrimages throughout Europe. *The Book of Margery Kempe* describes both her **journeys and the inner mystic conversations** she had with Christ.

Poets of the People

Britain in the 14th century saw the emergence of a body of vernacular writing—in the spoken language, English, rather than in Latin—that laid the foundation for a richly expressive literary tradition. Geoffrey Chaucer was the major, masterful pioneer among early vernacular writers.

The quest for the Grail
Tales of King Arthur and a holy quest were influential in medieval times. In this painting from c. 1470, Gawain attempts to remove a magical sword lodged in a rock.

« BEFORE

Vernacular English literature grew out of a fertile mix of traditions including Anglo-Saxon and Norman literature.

EARLIER WRITINGS
The **Germanic meter** of Anglo-Saxon tradition influenced the 7th-century *Creation Hymn* of the monk-poet, Caedmon, and *Beowulf* **« 35**. The prose of Aelfric (10th–11th centuries), had a clear, **direct vernacular style**. The Anglo-Norman strand included 13th-century romances such as *Floris* and *Blancheflour* and the classic French courtly love poem, *Roman de la Rose*.

Four terms help in understanding the writers of Chaucer's time: Old English, Germanic, Middle English, and vernacular. Old English, or Anglo-Saxon, was an early English form used between the 5th and 12th centuries. It grew out of the dialects of Germanic peoples—including Angles, Saxons, Jutes, and Scandinavians—who settled in Britain. Middle English evolved from Old English after absorbing French influences from the Norman conquerors. Vernacular languages are those spoken every day by ordinary people.

Chaucer's world
Geoffrey Chaucer (c. 1343–1400) was born the son of a prosperous London wine merchant. He made a good marriage and held a succession of important posts for king and country, including being made customs controller for the port of London in 1374 and clerk of the king's works in 1389. He wrote and translated throughout his career and was said to have adorned the English language with new words, most directly borrowed from French.

Chaucer was in the right place at the right time. At the court of Richard II, a great patron of literature and art, English was replacing Anglo-Norman. Chaucer was already well steeped in vernacular French and Italian literature, partly thanks to diplomatic trips abroad. He translated some of the French courtly love poem *Roman de la Rose* into the Middle English *Romaunt of the Rose* and was knowledgeable about the Italian writers Dante (1265–1321), Petrarch (1304–1374), and Boccaccio (1313–1375). His story *Troilus and Creseyde* has an Italian flavor.

A very English tale
Chaucer blended all of these traditions to develop a rich, flexible language that culminated in his late Middle English

Edward III
The reign of Edward III (see pp. 96–97), shown here in a 13th-century painting, saw the flourishing of a mix of literary traditions, and important writers such as Chaucer, William Langland, and John Gower.

masterpiece, *The Canterbury Tales* (c. 1387–1400), with its bawdy humor and unforgettable cast of characters drawn from right across 14th-century English society.

This collection of lively tales, told in rhyming couplets, was influenced by the multiple tales of Boccaccio's *Decameron* (c. 1350). It features a group of diverse pilgrims, from an outwardly pious but bigoted prioress to a lusty miller, on their way to Thomas Becket's shrine at Canterbury. They tell tales to pass the time, with settings ancient and modern, and embracing every tradition from bawdy comedy to courtly romance. These showcase the keen sense of drama, humor, vivid storytelling, and stimulating ideas that make Chaucer's vernacular writing so effective. A line from the knight's tale:

A mantelet upon his shuldre hanginge,/ Bret-ful of rubies rede, as fyr sparklinge.

This translates into modern English: "A short mantle hanging on his shoulders/was brimful of rubies, sparkling like fire."

Important influences
Chaucer and his contemporaries used certain devices to make their work immediate, distinctive, and of their place and time. One is the use of English Midlands dialects, widespread at the time, which evokes ordinary people rather than a classics-educated elite. Another is the medieval tradition of courtly love and romance. This was a popular European fashion, developed in France, for tales of a knight's noble love for an aristocratic lady. First told by troubadours, these stories followed strict rules. A third strand is the importance of rhetoric. Part of any educated person's skills, this was the ability to speak or write in a persuasive way and make an impact.

Another major strand was the use of an alliterative style—standard in English literature at this time. This was a Germanic/Old English meter, using a marked pattern of stresses within "half lines," in verse that was typically unrhymed and was markedly different

> ## "[the] well of **English undefiled**"
>
> **EDMUND SPENSER'S DESCRIPTION OF CHAUCER, IN *THE FAERIE QUEENE* (1590–1596)**

GERMANIC The peoples of northern Europe speaking languages including English, Dutch, German, and Scandinavian.

to other rhyming forms from abroad. The later 1300s saw a Middle English alliterative revival.

Creating an English tradition
Other important writers contributed to the vernacular tradition. The poem *Piers Plowman* possibly by William Langland, (c. 1330–c. 1400) told a tale, in a down-to-earth style, of the search for truth. It is a classic of the Middle English alliterative revival, as is the more courtly *Sir Gawain and the Green Knight* (by an unknown contemporary of Chaucer) and the epic narrative poem *Morte Arthure*, about King Arthur. The English, French, and Latin work of John Gower, author of the allegorical tales *Confessio Amantis* (1386–1393) was also influential.

AFTER »

The pioneering work of Chaucer and his contemporaries made possible the great body of English literature that has appeared since his death.

LATER VERNACULAR WRITING
In the 15th and 16th centuries, **vernacular writing gained increasing ground**. A French-style courtly influence also persisted, for example in the work of poet Sir Richard Ros (b. 1429), who probably translated Alain Chartier's *La Belle Dame Sans Merci*.

THE CHAUCER EFFECT
Chaucer influenced writers such as Spenser **152–153 »** and Shakespeare **154–155 »** who inherited Chaucer's love of contemporary language, and John Dryden **180–81 »**

JOHN DRYDEN

Geoffrey Chaucer
This portrait of Chaucer appears in a manuscript of *The Canterbury Tales*, dated c. 1413–22. He is often said to be the main founder of literature in modern English.

So priketh hem nature in hir co[rages]
Than longen folke to gone on [pilgrimages]
And palmeres for to seeke str[aunge strondes]

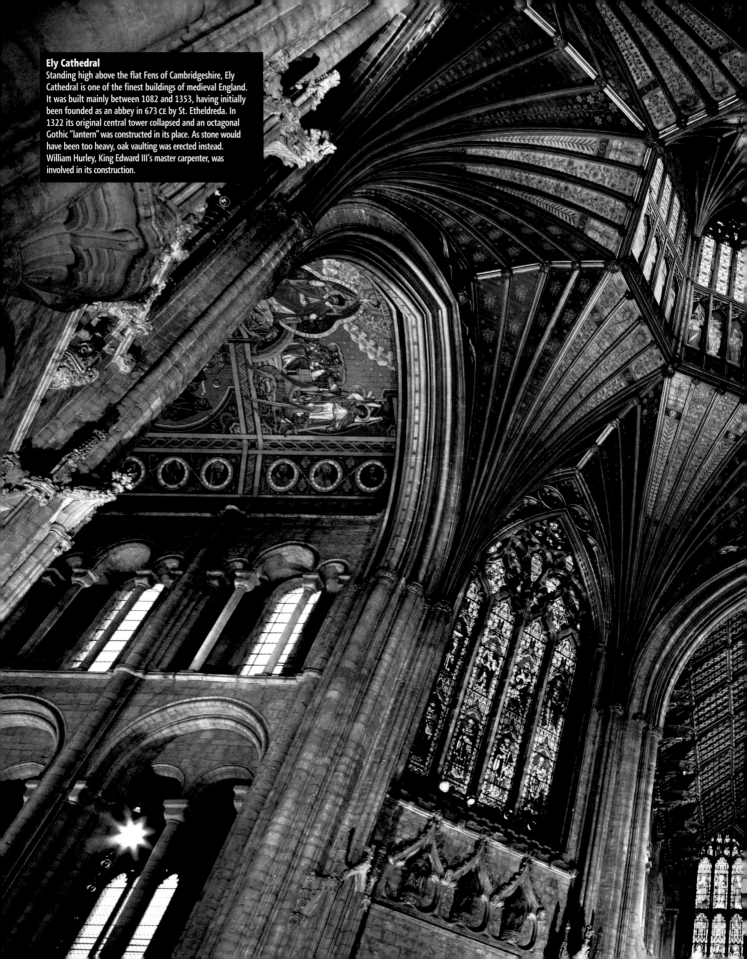

Ely Cathedral

Standing high above the flat Fens of Cambridgeshire, Ely Cathedral is one of the finest buildings of medieval England. It was built mainly between 1082 and 1353, having initially been founded as an abbey in 673 CE by St. Etheldreda. In 1322 its original central tower collapsed and an octagonal Gothic "lantern" was constructed in its place. As stone would have been too heavy, oak vaulting was erected instead. William Hurley, King Edward III's master carpenter, was involved in its construction.

The succession of Richard II in 1377 left England with a 10-year old king. Despite early crises, he survived to take power in his own right in 1389.

THE YOUNG HEIR
Edward, the Black Prince, who had shown so much promise at the Battle of Poitiers (1356), died one year before his father King Edward III of England, in 1376. Upon the death of Edward III, the throne passed to his grandson Richard II, a minor. England faced its first **royal minority** since 1216.

A "continual council" was appointed to **administer the regency** until Richard was of age to rule. A power struggle between Richard's uncles—the Duke of Lancaster (John of Gaunt) and the Earl of March—marred the first year of Richard's reign, although in the end Gaunt prevailed. It was Gaunt's and the council's decision to raise more money for the war in France by levying a poll tax that sparked the **Peasants' Revolt** in 1381 **≪ 104–105**.

GROWING OPPOSITION
Although Richard took the reins of power in 1382, the **Duke of Lancaster dictated policy** until he left England in 1386. The King increasingly relied on a small coterie of aristocrats, principal among them Robert de Vere, Earl of Oxford, and Sir Simon Burley, Receiver of the Chamber. An **opposition party** began to form around disenchanted magnates such as Thomas Beauchamp, Earl of Warwick, and Thomas of Woodstock, Duke of Gloucester.

Change of Dynasty

Richard II's quarrels with his magnates aroused such opposition that he suffered the indignity of being only the second English king to be deposed since the Norman conquest. The change to the Lancastrian dynasty under Henry IV laid the seeds of a conflict that would grow into civil war 50 years later.

Rebel seat
Alnwick Castle in Northumberland became the seat of the Percy family in 1309. It was the base for the 1st Earl of Northumberland's rebellion against Henry IV, which ended with the Earl's death in 1408.

The Parliament that met in 1386 marked the second major crisis of Richard II's reign (after the Peasants' Revolt). This time it was Richard's own actions that were to blame. The assembly condemned Richard's advisers, in particular Robert de Vere, whom the King had just appointed Duke of Ireland, and demanded the dismissal of the Chancellor, Michael de la Pole. Although Richard protested, he was forced to back down, and de la Pole was removed and imprisoned.

Richard's opponents, including the Duke of Gloucester, the Earl of Arundel, and the Bishop of Ely, established a Commission of Government to take over. In November 1387, these "Lords Appellant," as they

Face of a king
The tomb effigy of Richard II—which was carved during his lifetime—lies in Westminster Cathedral beside that of his beloved first wife, Anne of Luxemburg, who died in 1394.

became known, published an "appeal" against five of Richard's supporters, including de la Pole and de Vere, accusing them of treason.

Fighting back
De Vere tried to raise an army, while Richard played for time in Parliament. His cause was undermined by de Vere's defeat at Radcot Bridge in 1387. The army of the Appellant marched on London and it seemed for a while as though Richard might be deposed. The resulting Merciless Parliament was dominated by the Lords Appellant and most of Richard's leading loyalists were sentenced to death. Many escaped abroad, but Nicholas Brembre, the Mayor of London, was put to death on Tower Hill in March 1388.

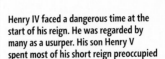

> " A **wonderful land** is this …
> which has exiled, slain,
> destroyed, or **ruined so many**
> kings, rulers, and great men. "

RICHARD II, WHILE A PRISONER IN THE TOWER OF LONDON, SEPTEMBER 1389

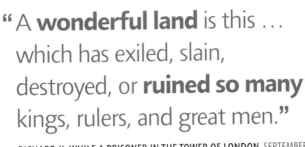

Henry IV faced a dangerous time at the start of his reign. He was regarded by many as a usurper. His son Henry V spent most of his short reign preoccupied by the war with France.

REIGN OF HENRY IV

Henry IV faced **a number of revolts** early in his reign, initially by supporters of Richard II. After a plot to assassinate Henry at Windsor Castle in December 1399, **Richard mysteriously died** at Pontefract Castle where he was being held prisoner. Several further conspiracies centered around the Earl of Northumberland. In 1402, offended that the King had not permitted the Earl's son, Sir Henry Percy ("Hotspur"), to ransom the Scottish prisoners he had taken at the Battle of Homildon Hill, the **Percy clan rose in revolt**. Hotspur perished at the Battle of Shrewsbury in 1403 and the King had his **body pickled in salt** so the corpse could be displayed for longer as a **deterrent to potential rebels**. In 1408, at Bramham Moor, the Earl of Northumberland's army was defeated and he was killed.

UNRESOLVED ISSUES

The **rebellions were over** and Henry V succeeded the throne without opposition. With England largely at peace, Henry V devoted himself to renewing the **war with France** from 1415–1420. His early death, and the accession of his baby son, left England facing a long royal minority. **Unresolved claims to the throne** set the scene for the outbreak of a new civil war and the Wars of the Roses **122–123 ≫**.

in 1392 when the city refused to loan him money, and the imposition of a £10,000 fine on its citizens, gradually lost him friends. In 1394, Richard's expedition to Ireland revitalized the English position there. A truce with France, sealed by the King's marriage to Isabelle of Valois in 1396, offered the hope of an end to the expensive war with France.

Rebel army

In 1397, Richard decided to act against his remaining enemies. He manipulated Parliament into declaring the supporters of the 1387 rebellion as treasonous, and levied fines on them.

In February 1399, John of Gaunt died, and Richard, rather than permitting Gaunt's exiled son Henry Bolingbroke to succeed to the title and lands, seized them for the Crown. Bolingbroke made contact with his supporters in England, and the departure of Richard for a new expedition in Ireland in May gave him just the opportunity he had been waiting for. In early July he landed at Ravenspur at the mouth of the river Humber.

As the rebels advanced, Richard's officials scrambled to mobilize men and strengthen defenses in the south. By mid-July, Bolingbroke reached the Midlands, his support growing all the time. At the end of May the regent, the Duke of York (who was also Bolingbroke's uncle), defected to the rebel cause. Richard hurried back from Ireland and tried to assemble a new army in south Wales, but it soon melted away and, faced with an enormous rebel army, he surrendered to Bolingbroke at Flint Castle on August 19.

A new beginning

Richard was transported to London as a prisoner and a parliamentary commission was set up to decide what to do next. Although it ruled that Richard had broken his own coronation oath and had lost the right to rule, it did not hand the throne to Bolingbroke by right of descent. Instead, Richard was induced to abdicate on September 30, and Parliament passed the Articles of Deposition, which indicted Richard on a series of misdemeanors, accepted his abdication, and acknowledged Bolingbroke as king. King Henry IV addressed Parliament in English, not Norman French, to inaugurate the start of the new Lancastrian dynasty.

Royal symbolism
The *Wilton Diptych* glorifies the kingship of Richard II. The King is portrayed gazing at the Virgin Mary and Child Christ, and kneeling beside his patron saint John the Baptist, and the English royal saints Edmund the Martyr and Edward the Confessor.

A lack of success in France and the English defeat against the Scots at Otterburn in August dented the prestige of the Lords Appellant, enabling Richard to construct an

100,000 The size of Henry IV's army that forced the surrender of Richard II at Flint Castle in 1399.

alliance opposed to them. The Cambridge Parliament of September was more sympathetic to the King and by May 1389 he felt strong enough to march into council, declare that he had attained his majority, and dismiss the Lords Appellant.

High-handed rule

For the next few years, Richard managed to retain control. Yet his high-handed actions, such as the removal of the Mayor of London

Surrendering the crown
Richard II is seen handing over his crown to Henry Bolingbroke. It was an important part of the propaganda surrounding Henry IV's accession, that his predecessor had voluntarily relinquished his throne.

Invasion and Revolt

The wars between Scotland and England erupted several times in the 15th century, but Scottish troubles were caused more by weak kingship than foreign intervention. Wales, in contrast, remained subject to the English Crown save for a brief 15-year period during the revolt of Owain Glyn Dwr.

David II secured his release from England in 1357, in exchange for a hefty payment to Edward III. He found his kingdom devastated, because the core regions of Scotland had suffered badly during the wars, and Lothian had been ravaged by the English as recently as 1356 during the "Black Candlemas." The King's authority was much reduced, and he was forced to impose heavy annual land taxes to restore the royal income. Robert Stewart, the King's nephew and William, 1st Earl of Douglas, who had safeguarded the kingdom in David's absence, felt unrewarded for their loyalty and rebelled in 1363. Robert and David II were reconciled, and Robert was still the heir to the throne, but it led the King to consider appointing one of the sons of Edward III of England as heir to the Scottish throne.

The Stewart dynasty

Despite these problems, Robert Stewart did become King of Scotland on David's death in 1371, the first of the Stewart dynasty. His early appointments shaped the rest of his reign, with his son John, Earl of Carrick, becoming lieutenant of the English marches and his brother Robert, Earl of Fife, appointed to run the royal treasury.

In 1384, the Earl of Carrick removed his father from active rule. Carrick was also the architect of the Scottish invasion of England in summer 1388. With the prospect of the renewal of the Anglo-French war making England an appealingly weak target, the Scottish army struck south, encountering the

> **100,000** The ransom paid in marks (£66,000) to Edward III to secure David II's return to Scotland in 1357.

English under Sir Henry Percy ("Hotspur") at Otterburn, in Northumberland on August 5. The Scots were victorious and Hotspur was captured, but Carrick's joy was tempered by the death of his key ally, the 2nd Earl of Douglas, in the battle. This loss so weakened his position that in December Carrick was summarily pushed aside by his younger brother Robert of Fife, who was to dominate Scottish politics until 1420, latterly as the Duke of Albany. A half-hearted counterinvasion by Richard II in 1389, came to nothing and in September the two sides made peace.

The Earl of Carrick succeeded to the Scottish throne in 1390 as Robert III, but his health was so poor that the real ruler was the Duke of Albany; in 1399 he was officially declared unfit to rule. Albany engaged in a more aggressive foreign policy toward England, which culminated in an invasion in September 1402. At Homildon Hill in Northumberland, the English avenged themselves for Otterburn; on the Scottish side, the 4th Earl of Douglas was killed and the death or capture of many other Scottish nobles severely dented Albany's reputation. Although he remained in power until 1420, it would be almost a century before there was another major encounter between English and Scottish armies in the field.

The rise of Owain Glyn Dwr

The Welsh revolts of the late 13th and early 14th centuries (see pp.90–91) were followed by a period of quiet. The effects of the Black Death (see

Battle of Neville's Cross

The defeat and capture of King David II of Scotland at Neville's Cross in 1346 was a disaster for Scotland. He was held prisoner in England for 11 years following the failed attempt to invade England.

pp.102–103)—which struck as hard in Wales as in England, bringing with it wholesale changes in land tenure system and a move to a monetary economy—led to deprivation in the countryside and a distinct rise in Welsh resentment at English rule.

There was no focus for resistance, however, until the emergence of Owain Glyn Dwr in 1400. He was descended from the royal houses of both Powys and Deheubarth, but was also a member of the Anglicized aristocracy, who had learned law and fought with the English army in Scotland in 1385.

In 1400, a land dispute arose between Glyn Dwr and Lord Grey of Ruthin, a supporter of Henry IV. With little prospect of resolution from an unfriendly Crown, Glyn Dwr called a meeting on September 16 and was proclaimed Prince of Wales. The rebellion rapidly spread and Glyn Dwr's men captured Conwy Castle. In 1402, he seized two important English prisoners, Lord Grey and Edmund Mortimer.

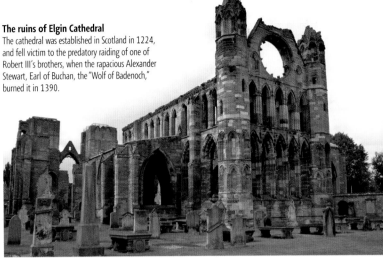

The ruins of Elgin Cathedral
The cathedral was established in Scotland in 1224, and fell victim to the predatory raiding of one of Robert III's brothers, when the rapacious Alexander Stewart, Earl of Buchan, the "Wolf of Badenoch," burned it in 1390.

> " He is a **worthy gentleman** … valiant as a **lion** and wondrous affable, and as **bountiful as mines** in India … "

SHAKESPEARE DESCRIBING OWAIN GLYN DWR IN *HENRY IV*, 1598

The latter was the uncle of the Earl of March, who had a stronger claim to the throne than Henry IV, and the King declined to ransom him. Mortimer became Glyn Dwr's son-in-law. The Welsh rebel leader extended his network of friends by allying himself with Sir Henry Percy.

The end of political freedom
Glyn Dwr's first real setback was Percy's defeat and death at Shrewsbury in 1403, as he marched south to link up with the Welsh. The following year, he captured Harlech and Aberystwyth, while the English were reduced to a handful of strongholds. Glyn Dwr established all the trappings of government, with a Welsh Great Seal and a Welsh Parliament summoned to meet at Machynlleth. In 1405, he signed a Triple Indenture with the Earl of Northumberland and Mortimer, by which England and Wales were divided into three. Glyn Dwr was to receive Wales and a portion of west England.

However, events were moving against the Welsh. A French army landed at Milford Haven, but failed to engage the English and slipped away. In 1408, Glyn Dwr lost Harlech and Aberystwyth. By 1410, he was reduced to fighting a guerrilla campaign in the hills and in 1412 he is mentioned in the sources for the last time. Glyn Dwr's exact fate is unknown, but when his surviving son

Maredudd accepted a pardon in 1421, all hopes for a revival of the revolt and Welsh political freedom were finished.

AFTER

Wales remained under English rule from the 15th century, while the Stewart kings continued to rule Scotland until 1603, when James VI's accession to the English throne led to the union of Scotland and England.

THE EMERGENCE OF THE TUDORS
After Glyn Dwr's defeat, Wales subsided into **an uneasy calm**. The **rise of the Tudor family**, starting with Jasper Tudor, Earl of Pembroke, a key supporter of the House of Lancaster, would lead to the **accession of a Welsh noble** to the English throne, when Henry VII became king in 1485 **122–123 ≫**.

SCOTTISH KINGS
In 1406, Robert III sent his son James to France, but he was captured and held prisoner until 1424. His assassination in 1437 left Scotland ruled by his son James II.

JAMES II OF SCOTLAND

The later **Hundred Years' War**

By 1413, it seemed the Hundred Years' War between England and France had reached a stalemate that might even lead to peace. The accession of Henry V, a martial king with ambitions for glory, changed that. Soon England once more ruled half of France, but once again the French recovered and, with the aid of new weapons and tactics, chased the English out of France for good.

In 1388, Charles VI of France came of age, and the next year, Richard II of England managed to rid himself of the Lords Appellant, who for three years had kept him sidelined and persecuted his leading supporters. Both monarchs now ruled personally and turned to the relations between them. Aquitaine had long been a running sore that kept the Hundred Year's War alive.

In particular, the matter of whether the King of England should render homage to the French King was still unresolved. Discussion raged between 1389 and 1392 and, though no agreement was reached, an exchange of lands was agreed, by which the English acquired lands bordering Aquitaine in exchange for Poitou, Limousin, and

BEFORE

England gained little in the first third of the Hundred Years' War, despite all its victories. The prospects for improving the position under Richard II seemed slight.

EARLY VICTORIES
Edward III's **claim to the French throne** triggered the outbreak of the Hundred Years' War in 1337 **‹‹ 96–97**. Despite **great English victories** at the Siege of Calais (1346), where they used weapons such as trebuchets to capture the port, Crécy (1346) **‹‹ 100–101**, and Poitiers (1356), the gains slipped away.

INTERNAL REVOLTS
The war continued after the 1381 Treaty of Guerande, but both sides were plagued by **internal revolts**. In France, the Duke of Burgundy, Philip the Bold, was quick to intervene in an uprising by the burghers of Ghent, a sign of his growing interest in gathering a share of French territory.

TREBUCHET

Ponthieu. The French also demanded Calais, but the English royal council refused point blank to relinquish the site of the lucrative Wool Staple and it seemed as though war might break out after all. Only the intervention of Richard II, who requested the hand in marriage of Isabella, the daughter of Charles VI, averted conflict. A truce was agreed, which should have meant peace between the two countries until 1420.

Power struggles

Several events helped reignite the war before then. The first was that Charles VI had a violent fit that sent him mad in 1392. Periodically thereafter he would descend into madness, convinced he was made of glass and might shatter at the slightest touch.

A power struggle broke out between Philip the Bold of Burgundy (and John the Fearless, his successor from 1404) and the King's brother Louis, Duke of Orléans. Louis' murder on a Paris street in 1407 sent France into a state of near civil war.

If France was in no state to continue the war, neither was England. Henry IV, who had usurped Richard II's throne,

> **£170,000** The annual cost of the Hundred Years' War to the English by 1435, which was approximately six times the normal annual royal revenues.

had to deal with revolts in England led by the Percys of Northumberland and a Welsh uprising under Owain Glyn Dwr, which was subdued in 1410.

Henry V's demands

Shortly after Henry V came to the throne in April 1413, the Burgundians were driven from Paris and so John the Fearless was particularly receptive to the

Warrior king
Henry V was intent on the conquest of France almost from his accession in 1413. Even his marriage to Catherine, the French King's daughter, in 1420, did not turn him aside. Yet his death from dysentery in 1422 fatally undermined the English position in France.

new English King's overtures regarding a renewed war with France. Both he and Charles VI, however, were taken aback by the scale of Henry's ambitions: he demanded nothing less than to be recognized as the heir to the French throne. Negotiations broke down in February 1415, and Henry prepared for war. The House of Commons granted Henry a large grant in taxation; even the bishops gave him a loan of £44,000. Knights and archers were recruited from across the land.

Despite a last-minute French peace offer, Henry was set on war. On August 11, he sailed from Southampton with 10,000 men—including 2,000 knights and men-at-arms, 8,000 archers, and 75 gunners. He landed at Harfleur but took until September 22 to force the town to surrender.

Meanwhile, the French had been gathering their forces. Three divisions under Charles d'Albret, the Constable of France; Jean Boucicaut, the Marshal of France; and the King himself converged on Henry V's army. The English had lost 2,000 men at the siege of Harfleur and Henry could muster a mere 7,000 men, less than one-quarter the size of the French army approaching him.

Victory at Agincourt

The English struck out toward the Somme, in a desperate attempt to evade their pursuers and cross the river at Blanchetaque, just as Edward III had done before the Battle of Crécy (see pp.100–101). However, they found the crossing

blocked by Marshal Boucicaut and 6,000 men, and were forced far to the south. Henry desperately tried to avoid a pitched battle and find a way through to Calais, but then, three days later, he discovered his way barred by the entire French army.

Brought to bay, Henry made the best of his position, drawing his troops in such a way that the French could only advance along a narrow front hemmed in by the castle woods of Agincourt. At around 11 a.m. on the morning of October 25, the English archers erected

Longbowmen
English archers were key to almost every major victory in the Hundred Years' War, from Crécy to Agincourt. Yet by the end of the war, at Formigny in 1450, they were outclassed by French gunners.

15 The number of musicians who were recorded as accompanying King Henry V at his landing at Harfleur (along with 13 chaplains, 12 armorers, 6 bowyers, and 20 surgeons).

a makeshift barrier of stakes and then loosed a murderous volley into the French line. The French knights charged but, felled by arrows, they crashed into each other and were run into from behind by their own men coming forward to reinforce them. Their line collapsed into a writhing chivalric muddle. The English men-at-arms fell on the French survivors, cutting those who resisted to pieces. D'Albret was killed, and the Duke of Orléans and Marshal Boucicaut

captured. A late French rally only had the effect of causing Henry V to order the killing of all French prisoners, save the great lords. French losses were catastrophic: 8,000 dead and 1,600 prisoners, against just 500 English casualties.

Leaderless
Throughout 1415, the English, led by the Earl of Dorset, and John the Fearless's Burgundians gradually choked off French royalist resistance. In 1417, Henry returned with a new force of 8,000. He took Caen in September, and then reduced the

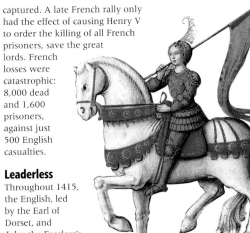

Joan of Arc
The 17-year-old "Maid of Orléans" presented herself at the French court claiming she could raise the siege of Orléans, an endeavor in which, against all the odds, she succeeded.

rest of Normandy until Rouen fell to him in January 1419. In the meantime, John the Fearless had seized Paris. France was leaderless, with the Constable dead and the King insane. Charles VI's eldest son died in 1416; the new Dauphin, Charles, was 15 years old. In 1420, the French faced the inevitable and Charles VI signed the Treaty of Troyes, by which the Dauphin was declared illegitimate and Henry V became heir to the throne. Supporters of the Dauphin continued to resist, but Henry and Philip the Good, the new Duke of Burgundy, advanced remorselessly.

All change
Henry V's death from dysentery in August 1422, changed the position radically, as his heir was just nine months old. The regent, John, Duke of Bedford, campaigned ably, but the English Parliament was increasingly unwilling to grant large subsidies for the war. The Duke of Burgundy opened negotiations with the Dauphin about

switching sides, and in 1427, the Duke of Brittany defected to the Dauphin's side. It was against this background that the English, under the Earl of Salisbury, moved south in 1428, and reached Orléans in October. If he could seize this great citadel, the Earl reasoned, he might be able to throttle the French revival at birth.

Divine mission
The Earl reckoned without two things. The first was the cannonball that struck him on October 24, causing him to die of gangrene a week later. The second was a peasant girl, Joan of Arc, who arrived in the French camp in March, convinced she had a divine mission to set the Dauphin on the French throne. Joan's religious charisma and reckless impetuousness worked and the French army were inspired to chase the English from Orléans by May 8.

Unstoppable Charles
Charles was crowned King of France at Rheims on July 18, 1429, and the French armies, now seemingly unstoppable, swept northward taking a string of cities. Even Joan's death in 1431 did not stop the French revival. At a peace conference in Arras, in 1435, the Burgundians switched sides, and by 1436, Paris had fallen to them.

Charles reorganized his armies, setting up *compagnies d'ordonnance* that were strictly drilled and trained, and which helped him gradually reduce the English territories in Aquitaine. His commanders' effective use of field artillery was not matched by the English and, despite a two-year truce that was signed at Tours in 1446, Henry VI's armies were driven from Normandy in 1449. It looked very much as if the war would end with the English in precisely the same position they had been in 1381.

CANNON
The earliest effective guns were large cannons, or bombards, which shattered town walls or defended them (though they did not entirely supplant traditional siege engines such as mangonels and trebuchets). At the siege of Harfleur in 1415, Henry V faced a dozen guns that could hurl lethal stone balls up to 220 lb (200 kg) in weight. By the mid-15th century, artillery was more varied, with field guns that could shoot balls of around 22 lb (10 kg) in weight. Under Jean Bureau, Charles VII's Master Gunner from 1439, the French artillery won them the key engagements of the last stages of the Hundred Years' War, including Formigny in 1450 and Castillon in 1453.

AFTER

From 1450 to 1453, the English were swept from their territories in Aquitaine, leaving only Calais in their hands.

END OF THE WAR
In 1450, the French invaded Aquitaine. At the Battle of Formigny on April 15, French **cannon fire cut through the English defenses** and destroyed the last English field army in France. English fortunes looked as though they might revive when a new English army under John Talbot landed in October 1452. However, at Castillon on July 17, 1453, this force was **torn to pieces** by the combination of **French cannon** and the discipline of the *compagnies d'ordonnance*. Bordeaux surrendered in October and the Hundred Years' War was at an end.

Calais resisted as a **solitary outpost** until its loss to the French in 1558, during the reign of Queen Mary. To all intents and purposes, however, the **English territorial involvement in France, which had begun in 1066, was over**.

BATTLE OF FORMIGNY

> " Sire, there are enough **to kill**, enough **to capture**, and enough **to run away**."
>
> THE ENGLISH ARMY'S SCOUT DAFYDD GAM WHEN ASKED HOW LARGE THE FRENCH ARMY BLOCKING THE ENGLISH ROUTE WAS, OCTOBER 23, 1415

BEFORE ◀◀

The agricultural crisis of the first two decades of the 14th century was followed by the Black Death, which reduced the population by more than one-third. This led to a sharp decline in economic activity.

RURAL UNREST

The remaking of feudal bonds and obligations, already underway before 1350, continued as the **countryside was depopulated**. In some places, labor became so scarce that **wages rose** and **villeins left their manors** to find paid work in the towns or become tenant farmers ◀◀ **88–89**. However, because there was no one to sell goods to, prices fell and landowners **imposed harsher conditions** on their tenants.

RESENTMENT AND REVOLT

The **Peasants' Revolt** in 1381 ◀◀ **104–105** saw these factors coalesce into an outbreak of **popular resentment against wealthy churchmen** and royal administrators. Urban centers also suffered. After 300 years of steady growth, **towns declined** as the **volume of trade was reduced**. Some small towns reverted to being farming communities or disappeared.

PEASANTS STACKING SHEAVES OF WHEAT

1400, and remained low into the following century. Towns and cities found new ways of coping with these difficulties. Overall, the urban-based population swelled as large numbers of landless peasants and the unemployed moved into the towns looking for work.

All towns would have maintained the trades necessary for daily life—bakers, butchers, tanners, leather workers, and blacksmiths—but some towns and regions developed specialized trades and areas of economic activity. Birmingham was known for its manufacture of scythe blades; Burton-on-Trent was already famous for brewing.

Medieval guilds

Within the towns and cities, each trade was organized into a guild—an association of merchants or craftsmen. Guilds were run by masters and served many functions. They offered professional training, agreed standards

a fee by his family. He was contractually bound to his master and could not leave his master's household or work for anyone else during his apprenticeship (usually five to seven years from the age of about 10). At the end of this time, he became a journeyman, or a "day-worker," again working for a master. The ultimate aim of a journeyman was to become a master himself. For this, he would need to prove himself a skilled craftsmen and a successful businessman, and win

Signed and sealed

The four wax seals attached by linen ribbons to the bottom of this 14th-century trading document gave this agreement legally binding force.

and jewelry, also provided banking services. London grocers dominated the import and sale of spices such as ginger and pepper from Asia—by now considered essential to flavor the food of the wealthy. The Bishop of Carlisle bought his spices in London and had them carried north as he knew the quality and range of products were better than any he could acquire locally. Among other specialized crafts, London was also known for the casting of church bells.

Urban success story

Richard "Dick" Whittington (1354–1423) was a younger son with no prospect of inheriting land in his home county of Gloucestershire, so he went to London to learn the trade of mercer (a dealer in cloth). His success as a merchant selling English fabrics to Europe led to him becoming a master of his guild and then a councilman of London, part of the government of the city. He subsequently served as Lord Mayor of London four times during the reigns of Richard II, Henry IV, and Henry V, frequently lending large sums of money to the royal exchequers. He gave money for the rebuilding of the London Guildhall, where the leading merchants could meet to discuss business, and for several churches. He also paid for drainage and sanitation works. In his will he made donations for the construction of almshouses and the repair of St. Bartholomew's Hospital, as well as two prisons.

Merchants and Guilds

Economic activity in towns remained at a low ebb for many decades during the 15th century. Responsible for keeping it alive were the guilds—associations of merchants or craftsmen who managed the trade in a particular commodity or product and regulated employment.

A survey of Gloucester in 1455, a hundred years after the Black Death, presented a gloomy picture of urban decline—houses in ruin, not tenanted, or turned into stables. Gloucester was one of several formerly prosperous wool-exporting ports that had suffered badly as sales of wool and woven cloth to Europe fell away and stayed low. Even so, the wool industry remained the most valuable business in England and Scotland, providing a major source of revenue, through its taxation, for the king and his administration.

Urban decay was not confined to the wool towns. In Canterbury, the rents received by landlords for houses fell by 33 percent between 1350 and

of quality and measurement, and provided a network of mutual support for everyone involved in a particular trade. Above all, they were protectionist, designed to exclude outside competition. As commerce recovered, the guilds became wealthy institutions with their own churches and buildings, and they supported their own charitable foundations.

To enter a trade, a young man had to be accepted as an apprentice by a master, perhaps on payment of

> **HABERDASHERS** People dealing in needles, buttons, and other small items of dress. Other guilds connected with the cloth trade were mercers, drapers, clothworkers, and dyers.

the acceptance of the masters of his guild. Although the vast majority of apprentices were male, some girls were able to train in crafts, including seamstressing, baking, and cordwaining (shoe making).

Growth of London

By the end of the 14th century, London was becoming preeminent in trade and manufacturing. Many businesses concentrated their activities here, including the goldsmiths who, as well as making high-value objects

Uniform weights

The guilds regulated the weights and measures used by traders to ensure they were of uniform standard. This iron weight was probably used on a balance arm or steelyard.

Builders at work

The masons who built the great cathedrals and abbeys were skilled craftsmen who moved as work demanded. The apprenticeship for a stonemason was seven years, and master masons, such as Henry Yevele (c. 1320–1400), could make considerable fortunes.

English merchants, including the likes of Whittington, traveled to annual trade fairs in the cities of Europe to buy and sell goods. The fairs of Flanders in Europe were particularly important for the wool trade, but English merchants would also travel to fairs in Germany, Italy, and as far away as Constantinople (Istanbul). European merchants established guilds in English cities. The most famous of these was the Hansa, the association of German merchants, who had their own walled community in London, at the Steelyard. Elsewhere in the city, Lombard Street was named after the area where goldsmiths and bankers from northern Italy (Lombardy) were concentrated.

Recovery of the towns

By the end of the 15th century, town life was recovering throughout England. Towns and cities were more than just places of trade and manufacture. They remained important religious centers, with numerous churches and religious foundations. It is estimated that the City of London had more than 100 religious buildings and Norwich had 60. At the same time, the royal administration and courts of justice, which in earlier medieval times had been peripatetic, moving from place to place, came to be permanently based in towns.

London's rise in relation to the other towns and cities of England, Wales, and Scotland continued inexorably throughout the 16th and 17th centuries.

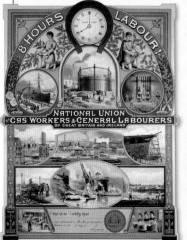

TRADE UNION BANNER, 1889

MEDIEVAL LEGACY

In 1400, the population of London was 50,000; by 1550, it had risen to 120,000. Although the **Great Fire of London** (1666) **182–183** ≫ swept away most of its medieval buildings, **reminders of the old city** are still to be found in street names such as Cheapside and Poultry. The greatest **legacy of the medieval city** are the City Livery Companies such as the Goldsmiths, Mercers, Vintners, Skinners, Haberdashers, and Fishmongers—successors of the guilds, which still support educational and community charities in the city.

TRADE UNIONS

In the 19th century, **socialist idealists** such as William Morris and C.R. Ashbee attempted to **revive the medieval guild-craft tradition** in the arts and crafts movement. Others have sought to trace a connection between the medieval guilds that protected the interests of artisans, and the trade unions that sprang up in the industrial cities of the 19th century as **workers' organizations** bargaining for better working conditions.

" I thank God and ever shall. It is the **sheep** hath **paid for all**."

MOTTO IN THE WINDOW OF A RICH WOOL MERCHANT OF NEWARK, c. 1480

« BEFORE

A royal usurpation, which took place 56 years before the Wars of the Roses began, set the scene for the longest period of civil strife England has ever known.

RIVAL CLAIMS

The dynastic claims underlying the Wars of the Roses date back to Henry IV's **seizure of power** from his cousin Richard II in 1399 **« 114–115**. Though Richard died without children, another heir **had a better title** than Henry's to succeed him.

RICHARD II (C.1390)

Henry's Lancastrian line stemmed from his father, John of Gaunt, created Duke of Lancaster by Richard; the rival Yorkists traced their claim back to Henry's uncle, Edmund, Duke of York. All the future Lancastrian and Yorkist **claimants were descended** from one of these two siblings.

17 The number of battles during 30 years of war, with fewer than 13 weeks of fighting in total.

3 How many kings were supplied by each of the royal houses of Lancaster and York.

IMPOSING LANCASTRIAN RULE

Henry gained the **support of most of the barons**. Moreover, his claim was accepted by Parliament. His son, Henry V, united the nation through military victories, most notably at Agincourt **« 118–119**, leaving little appetite for internal dynastic feuds. In the long reign of his son and successor, Henry VI, **military defeat**, combined with the King's weak governance and frequent bouts of ill health, allowed the **feud to resurface** and the Wars of the Roses to begin.

QUEEN CONSORT OF HENRY VI (1430–1482)

MARGARET OF ANJOU

Born in the Duchy of Lorraine in 1430, Margaret married Henry VI of England at the age of 15. Her decision in 1455 to exclude the Yorkist faction from court provoked the outbreak of war. For the next 16 years, while Henry suffered repeated bouts of insanity, she led the Lancastrian cause. She contested the ambitions of Richard, Duke of York, first in his role as Lord Protector of England and then in his attempts to establish himself as heir to the throne in place of her own son, Edward. In 1460 her army defeated the Yorkists at Wakefield, where Richard was killed. She was unable to capture London, though, and her star finally waned in 1471 when she in turn was defeated at Tewkesbury and Edward was killed.

The Wars of the Roses

The bitter dynastic struggle for the throne of England, waged by two branches of the royal house of Plantagenet—the houses of Lancaster and York—led to 30 years of rebellions and civil wars. These ended with the victory of Lancastrian Henry Tudor, who founded the House of Tudor.

Henry VI succeeded to the throne of England before he was a year old. The first three decades of his long reign were marked by military defeat in France, whose armies, under the inspiration of Joan of Arc, won back most of the French lands that his father, Henry V, had conquered. Meanwhile, financial overstretch led many in England to question his governance at home.

Henry suffered a mental breakdown in 1453. Richard, Duke of York, was appointed Lord Protector of England until the King regained his wits. As the Yorkist champion, Richard was bitterly opposed by the Lancastrian faction at court and particularly by Henry's wife, Margaret of Anjou. Once the King's

The Coronation of Henry IV
Henry was crowned king in 1399 after his uprising against his cousin Richard II. His military success allowed him to override the claim of Richard's heir presumptive, Edmund de Mortimer, who began the Yorkist line.

health returned, Richard was dismissed. Supported by much of the nobility and in particular by the influential Earl of Warwick, he raised an army and defeated the Lancastrians at the First Battle of St. Albans in 1455, the first battle of the wars. The Lancastrian leader, the Duke of Somerset, was killed, so Richard resumed his old position as de facto ruler of the nation, although he did not press his own claim to the throne.

A precarious status quo held for four years until 1459, when both sides again took up arms. This time Richard and his ally Warwick were outmaneuvered and declared traitors, forcing them both to take refuge abroad. But their exile did not last for long. The following year Warwick returned to England to lead Yorkist forces to victory at the Battle of Northampton. Henry was captured, but Queen Margaret managed to escape to Scotland. Richard once more resumed his former position as Lord Protector.

The wheel of fortune

Richard's triumph was brief. Margaret rallied the Lancastrian forces in the north of England, defeating and killing Richard at the Battle of Wakefield. Margaret won another victory at the Second Battle of St. Albans, freeing the captive King Henry in the process. London, though, remained fervently Yorkist, and Richard's son was crowned there as Edward IV, the first Yorkist king.

Edward and Warwick marched north, gathering a vast army as they went. They met an even larger Lancastrian force at Towton in Yorkshire on March 29, 1461. Edward won the ensuing battle, the bloodiest ever to occur on British soil. Margaret and Henry fled to Scotland, but their remaining hopes were dashed at the Battle of Hexham in 1464. Henry was again captured, and imprisoned in the Tower of London the following year.

Warwick the kingmaker

With the 23-year-old Edward secure on the throne and his Lancastrian rivals defeated or in exile, the future looked bright for a long and peaceful reign.

The Battle of Barnet, 1471
Fought just north of London, the Battle of Barnet marked a turning point in the Wars of the Roses, restoring the fortunes of the Yorkist King Edward IV. His opponent, the Earl of Warwick, was killed during the fighting, as shown in this manuscript illumination.

"England hath long been mad, and scarr'd herself."

FROM WILLIAM SHAKESPEARE'S PLAY, *RICHARD III*, 1591

Any such hopes were dashed, though, when it was revealed that the King had married a commoner, Elizabeth Woodville, in secret. His main supporter Warwick, who had been negotiating a match for the King with a French princess, was infuriated. He became even more so when Elizabeth set about obtaining influential positions in the King's administration for her own family members. The rift between the two men grew until 1469, when Warwick deserted the Yorkist cause and joined with his old enemy Margaret of Anjou, who had been raising a fresh Lancastrian army in France. When she crossed to England, the isolated Edward fled to Flanders. Henry VI, now aged 48, was reinstated on the throne.

It was Edward's turn to plot abroad. In 1471, with an army supplied by his brother-in-law, the Duke of Burgundy, he confronted his one-time ally Warwick at Barnet. Edward was victorious and Warwick was killed. Edward then defeated Margaret's troops at Tewkesbury. Captured for a third time, King Henry was taken to the Tower of London, where he was murdered. His son and heir had also been killed during the battle, leaving Edward almost unchallenged on the throne. The only remaining Lancastrian with credible aspirations to rule was Henry Tudor, a distant cousin of the King who was living in exile in Brittany.

Richard's usurpation

Once restored to power Edward proved himself an able ruler, and the country enjoyed a period of peace and prosperity. Then, in 1483, aged just 41, King Edward died suddenly, leaving his 12-year-old son Edward V as his heir and his brother Richard of Gloucester as Lord Protector until the boy king reached adulthood. In fact the young Edward was to remain on the throne for only two months before Richard had him seized and placed in the Tower of London. It was then announced that the boy's father's marriage to Elizabeth Woodville had been illegal, invalidating the youngster's right to rule. Richard had himself proclaimed king in Edward's place, being crowned that July in Westminster Abbey. Edward and his nine-year-old younger brother Richard, the "princes in the tower," were never seen again, seemingly having been killed on Richard's instructions.

20,000 The number of men that died at the Battle of Towton, the biggest recorded loss of life in a single day on English soil.

5,000 The number of Lancastrian troops that defeated 10,000 Yorkists at Bosworth, the decisive battle that ended the wars.

Richard's seizure of the throne was badly received, and Henry Tudor was able to take advantage of the ensuing disaffection. In 1485 he landed with a small force in Wales, where he soon attracted further support. His army came face to face with Richard's troops at Bosworth in Leicestershire, where Richard was defeated and killed. The victor took the throne as Henry VII, inaugurating the Tudor dynasty. Five months later he married Edward IV's daughter Elizabeth, thereby uniting the warring houses of Lancaster and York, and finally bringing the Wars of the Roses to an end.

AFTER

Henry VII's defeat of the last Yorkist King, Richard III, at the Battle of Bosworth ushered in the Tudor dynasty, which would rule England for the next 118 years.

PROFOUND SHIFT
The accession of Henry Tudor marked **the end of the Middle Ages** in England and signaled a change in the relationship between the monarchy and the nobility **132–133 ≫**. Thirty years of sporadic fighting had severely **weakened the might of the barons**, allowing the Tudor kings to wield far more power than their Plantagenet predecessors. They also sat more **securely on the throne**: not one of the five Tudor monarchs would be murdered or deposed. Except during the short reign of the boy king Edward VI (1547–1553), no aristocrat was ever allowed to grow so strong as to **threaten royal power**, and Parliament was **kept under firm control**.

A TIME OF CHANGE
Tudor absolutism formed a backdrop for **major social, economic, and cultural change**, most notably the flowering of a class of merchants and manufacturers, as well as Henry VIII's break with the Catholic Church **136–137 ≫**. Culturally, the Tudor years would set the scene for the **English Renaissance** in architecture, literature, and the arts **152–153 ≫**, exemplified above all by the works of Shakespeare **154–155 ≫**, whose history plays would paint **vivid portraits of the preceding Plantagenet kings**.

TUDOR ROSE

123

Medieval Weapons

Soldiers often fought with metal axes, swords, daggers, and halberds, while wearing helmets, chain mail, or cumbersome suits of armor. Archers could turn the tide of a battle—longbows, though hard to master, were unerringly accurate.

1 **English sword** from the 14th-century with a double-edge, a pommel on the handle, and a shallow groove, or fuller, on the blade. **2** **Dagger** of the late 15th-century with a round, disklike guard. **3** **Broadsword** with double-edged blade with a long, flat pommel, thin hilt, and thick cross guard. **4** **Rondel dagger** of an English longbowman with a spiral tang on the handle. **5** **Long-handled ax** with a curved blade, which would have been wielded with both hands. **6** **Mace** with a circular bronze head with vertical ridges, or flanges, from the 14th century. It would have been carried by a horseman. **7** **Mace** with steel pointed ridges, or flanges, which could penetrate armor and helmets. **8** **Suit of armor** of plate mail and broadsword. It belonged to a knight. **9** **English crossbow** that fired a projectile that could penetrate a knight's armor. **10** **English longbow** made of yew, which could fire an arrow more than 1,000 ft (300 m)

with good accuracy. **11** **Longbow arrows** with fletchings made from goose feathers. **12** **Chain mail helmet**, or coif. It was worn under a plate helmet, giving added protection. **13** **Basinet helmet** that reached down the sides of the head, giving good protection and mobility. **14** **Chain mail shirt**, or hauberk, which extended down to the knees, and had a slit to make it easier to ride a horse. **15** **Breastplate**, or cuirass. This is pointed with a sharp vertical ridge down the center. **16** **Poleax** with a sharp spike and an ax blade. **17** **Bill** was a combination of a spear and an ax. **18** **Halberd** from the late 14th century with a steel ax head, a sharp, thrusting point, and a metal strip, or langet, part of the way down the haft. **19** **Glaive** with a single blade on the end. Used by infantrymen fighting at close quarters.

5 LONG-HANDLED AX

1 ENGLISH SWORD

3 BROADSWORD

2 DAGGER

4 DAGGER

6 MACE

7 MACE

8 SUIT OF ARMOR

9 ENGLISH CROSSBOW

12 CHAIN MAIL HELMET

13 BASINET HELMET

14 CHAIN MAIL SHIRT

11 LONGBOW ARROWS

15 BREASTPLATE

16 POLEAX

10 ENGLISH LONGBOW

17 BILL

18 HALBERD

19 GLAIVE

3
TUDORS AND STUARTS
1485–1688

The Tudors brought controlling leadership to the country, but their break with Rome caused religious strife, just as a renaissance in art, science, and culture was taking shape. The Stuarts' belief in their divine right to rule turned the people against them and unified Parliament, Protestantism, and the constitution.

English gold coin
A rare English gold coin dating to the last half of the 16th century depicts Queen Elizabeth I, a sailing ship, and the Tudor rose. It celebrates the prowess of the English navy and the monarchy.

Arthur, Prince of Wales
This stained-glass illustration of Arthur, Prince of Wales, is from a window at Great Malvern Church. In 1501, he married Catherine of Aragon. He died within a year, however, leaving his widow to marry his younger brother, the future Henry VIII.

The strength of the Tudor monarchy

Henry VII scrambled on to the throne in 1485, having triumphed in a winner-takes-all struggle among England's aristocratic houses. He was absolutely determined to achieve something that no other king had done. His motives for shoring up his own royal power were primarily self-serving, but in hindsight he can be seen to have served the cause of modernization, too. Magna Carta, signed by King John in 1215, is celebrated as a statement of what might be seen as "people power"—albeit that of already extremely powerful people. Yet the Wars of the Roses had all too clearly illustrated the converse danger: that an absence of a strong monarch at the center might cause the structures of the state to fly apart.

Henry VII's reign established a pattern that can be seen running through the history of the next two centuries, in which the reigning monarch's actions produced an outcome that was both unintended and unexpected. Even the Reformation of the Church in this context can be seen as having stemmed only from Henry VIII's desire to control every aspect of life and law-giving throughout his realm. Henry VIII's break with the Roman Catholic Church in the 1530s subjected the country to a century or more of religious strife, but the monarchy itself stayed strong, whether under Catholic Mary in the 1550s, or her Protestant successor, Elizabeth I.

Who should rule the land?

The Tudors' instinct to preserve their power was essentially (if often ruthlessly) pragmatic. It was not something they appear ever to have had to think about—still less to philosophize over. Elizabeth I's Stuart successor, James I (James VI of Scotland), however, adduced learned arguments and scriptural references in support of the idea that kings were "God's lieutenants upon earth." His son, Charles I, insisted so adamantly on his "divine right" in the face of mounting parliamentary opposition that the country slid into civil war in the 1640s.

How much better off the people of Britain were once the pendulum of power had nominally swung their way has to be doubted, given the drabness of life under the Commonwealth of the 1650s. Its leader, Oliver Cromwell, supposedly the savior of the nation's freedoms, soon installed himself as a stern Puritan dictator.

A new return
When the pendulum swung back the Stuarts' way and Charles II was restored to the throne in 1660, the mass of the people seem to have reacted with relief. He too was soon alienating influential subjects. Little seemed to have changed.

If Charles II's absolutism was hard to bear, that of his younger brother, James II, was utterly impossible—especially because it was coupled with his Roman Catholicism—now considered un-English and completely taboo. When James was toppled from the throne in the Glorious Revolution of 1688, his successor, William III, was chosen both for his readiness to reign constitutionally alongside Parliament and for his Protestant beliefs.

However, for most of the people most of the time, such exalted issues barely impinged: they worked the land, and carried out their trades in the way they always had. Yet they were affected: Tudor taxation influenced everything from land use to the export of wool, while the Stuarts further extended taxes into the towns.

The power of the individual
Along with kings, there were all those anonymous individuals who had walk-on parts in the great dramas of the age: not just the Shakespearean player, but the sailor who helped stop the Spanish Armada in 1588, and the Jamestown colonist of the early 1600s. All of these individuals made their contributions to one of British history's most exciting periods; one whose conflicts were to do so much to shape the modern age.

The Great Fire of London
One of the major events of Stuart England, the Great Fire of London destroyed about 80 percent of the City of London in 1666. However, rebuilding helped turn London into a modern capital city. This unattributed illustration dates from 1667.

Scottish Troubles

Intensifying power struggles around the Scottish throne affected not just that nation, but its neighbor to the south, holding over successive English monarchs the threat of instability and worse. The dangers were vividly dramatized in the tragic life of Mary Queen of Scots, who was deemed too sympathetic a figure to be allowed to live.

The Auld Alliance with France had been central to Scottish diplomatic policy since the 13th century, and central to the Auld Alliance had been enmity with England. Times were changing though. In 1502, James IV signed a Treaty of Perpetual Peace with Henry VII's England. James married Henry's daughter, Margaret Tudor, the following year. The peace was not quite perpetual: it broke down in 1513 when Henry VIII invaded France. The loyalties of the Auld Alliance reasserting themselves, James led an invading army south.

On September 9, Thomas Howard, Earl of Surrey, met them with an English force at Flodden Field, in Northumberland. His victory was a catastrophe for Scotland. In just a few hours up to 17,000 Scots were killed. They included the flower of the nation's nobility—and their King.

« BEFORE

A diplomatic force since the 13th century, Scotland's Auld Alliance with France had been founded in the old enmity both nations had for their neighbor, England.

ENGLISH WARS
Scotland fought England in **numerous battles** over the centuries, including Stirling Bridge in 1297 and Otterburn in 1388, but it was the **victory of Robert Bruce** at the Battle of Bannockburn in 1314 that had won Scotland her **independence from England « 94–95.**

BATTLE OF OTTERBURN, 1388

James' successor, James V, was only 30 when he died—after a further defeat by Henry VIII at Solway Moss in 1542. His daughter, Mary I, was just six days old.

Mary Queen of Scots

While James Hamilton, Earl of Arran, governed Scotland as regent, Mary was brought up in France. Growing up to personify the Auld Alliance, in 1558, she married the French Dauphin and future Francis II of France.

Within a couple of years, however, she was widowed. Mary returned home to Scotland in the midst of its Reformation, though she herself was Catholic. Her marriage in 1565 to the Catholic Henry Stuart, Lord Darnley, sent out an unmistakable signal to Scotland's Protestant nobility, provoking a rebellion that Darnley had

The Osprey
Beautifully embroidered with gold, silver, and silk in tent stitch, this design was created by Mary Queen of Scots; Elizabeth, Countess of Shrewsbury; and other members of Mary's household.

(subsequently her private secretary) David Rizzio. For all the scurrilous gossip, theirs seems not to have been an adulterous affair, but Mary clearly felt closer to Rizzio than to her rough-and-ready husband or her Scottish lords. When Rizzio was murdered right in front of her, at Holyrood Palace in 1566, she blamed Darnley.

In her grief and rage, she then appears to have plotted Darnley's assassination with another noble, James Hepburn, Earl of Bothwell. He is believed to have murdered Darnley on her behalf. Having established a hold over her, however, Bothwell was able to compel the Queen to marry him before a fresh revolt by the Scottish lords saw her deposed and imprisoned in Loch Leven Castle, Fife.

> **Execution of Mary Queen of Scots**
> Mary died a martyr's death at Fotheringhay Castle, Northamptonshire. It is said her executioner begged, and received, her forgiveness.

KINGS OF SCOTLAND (1371–1603)

THE HOUSE OF STUART

The Stewart family were so called as they had held the hereditary High Stewardship of Scotland since the 13th century. Robert Stewart (born 1316) served David II so well that, on the King's sudden death in 1371, he was anointed his successor as Robert II, becoming the founder of the Stewart (later Stuart) line of Scottish kings. Their claim on the English throne resulted from James IV's marriage to Margaret Tudor, daughter of Henry VII of England. Their son, James V, followed his father as Scottish king. His daughter, Mary, thus had a claim, as the granddaughter of Margaret, to the English throne, especially if Elizabeth I was illegitimate, as her father, Henry VIII, had claimed.

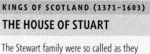

ENGRAVING OF ROBERT II

AFTER »

After all the tumult, the conflicts were resolved when Elizabeth I died childless and the succession passed smoothly to Mary's son. James VI of Scotland reigned simultaneously as James I of England.

UNION OF ENGLAND AND SCOTLAND
Although the Union of the Crowns **158–159 »** brought harmony, in practice Scots remained resolute **against English domination**, as Charles I found when he tried to **impose an Anglican hierarchy** on the Scottish Kirk (Church) **166–167 ».** Resistance to full political union with England (from 1707) strengthened the unsuccessful **Jacobite Rebellions 202–203 ».**

> " Look to **your consciences** and remember … the theater of the **world is wider** than …England. "
>
> MARY QUEEN OF SCOTS, AT HER TRIAL FOR TREASON IN ENGLAND, 1587

difficulty in putting down. Their marriage had implications for England, too, given that both Mary and Darnley could make claims to Elizabeth I's English throne. Insecurity had been bred into the Tudors since Henry VII seized the Crown (see pp.122–123) and Elizabeth's own succession had not been without its controversial aspects.

Unhappy attachments

Mary and Darnley also had their own difficulties with one another. The Queen distrusted her husband's ambitions. Darnley resented his wife's friendship with the Italian-born court musician

At Her Majesty's pleasure

Mary escaped to England but was imprisoned by Elizabeth for 18 years. Elizabeth was sympathetic to helping Mary regain her throne, but when it was proven that Mary had been involved in the Catholic Babington Plot against her in 1585, she ran out of patience and Mary was executed on February 7, 1587.

Message in a barrel

These beer barrels were used by Mary Queen of Scots, to smuggle messages out of Fotheringhay Castle to her fellow plotters.

‹‹ BEFORE

The Domesday Book documented a society in which plots of land were held in grant from the lord of the manor. Common land was open to all for grazing. This was to change during the Tudor period.

A SHORTAGE OF LABOR

The Black Death left a shortage of serf labor **‹‹ 102–103**. Growing discontent with the feudal system was an important factor in precipitating the Peasant's Revolt **‹‹ 104–105**. Although it failed, the rebellion served notice that **popular attitudes were changing**.

SERFS WORKING THE LAND

GROWTH OF THE GUILDS

A drift to the cities was already under way by the beginning of the Tudor period: merchants and craftsmen in the cities **protected their privileges** by establishing livery companies and guilds **‹‹ 128–129**.

English Society under the Tudors

The Tudor period was a time of far-reaching change for England and its people. Trade and agriculture flourished, and the country prospered, but at a cost. Thousands were cast adrift; many of these went hungry or turned to crime. The rapidly expanding cities were places of opportunity, not just for those who could come by honest work, but also for a growing underworld.

Good housekeeping was the overriding goal of Henry VII's domestic policy (although it also led to his own enrichment). The King set about reforming the Exchequer to make it more efficient. A Privy Chamber was established to manage the costs of the royal court. Named for Henry's own private bedchamber, in which these officials attended the King, reported to him, and received his orders, the Privy Chamber had overall charge of the costs and expenditures of the monarchy.

Taxing policies

Taxation in the country took two forms: ordinary and extraordinary. The first included regular rents from Crown lands, customs duties, and legal fines; the second was in the form of special levies imposed in time of war or crisis. Henry VII was entitled as King to the properties of anyone who died without a will. Since traitors were not allowed

Tudor architecture

Many Tudor houses were built in brick and stone, but the timber-framed building style of Little Moreton Hall in Cheshire is seen as typically Tudor. Around the world it is now seen as quintessentially English.

by law to make wills, he was able to use Acts of Attainder both as a way of boosting wealth and of keeping the nobility in line. These Acts allowed the King to confiscate the lands of those he accused of treason (once he had stated his belief in their wrongdoing, their conviction was merely a formality).

Under Henry VIII, Lord Chancellor Thomas Wolsey drove through a tough taxation policy, which raised vast revenues for the Crown. It was graduated according to income,

10 **The percentage of the population categorized as "vagabonds" by the 1570 census. The able-bodied unemployed or "sturdy beggars" were whipped or placed in the stocks and moved on.**

so payments from the poor were drastically less than those demanded from the rich aristocracy. Wolsey also introduced laws enforcing a "Just Price," to regulate the price of certain foodstuffs. On top of this, the Crown bought up large quantities of grain after poor harvests and issued it to those who were going hungry.

Balance of trade

The encouragement of trade was a natural extension of fiscal policy. Customs dues were key. At least partly with this end in view, Henry VII encouraged trading ties with France and Spain. The cash economy grew in importance as long-distance commerce supplanted local exchange. Textiles, leather, wine, and other items all raised handsome revenues for the Crown. But wool was overwhelmingly the most important product, accounting for 90 percent of England's export trade in the reign of Henry VII. It made for a completely different economic map from anything recognizable today. Places like Cirencester and Stroud in Gloucestershire and Lavenham

in Suffolk were wealthy centers, exporting to the manufacturers of Flanders and Renaissance Florence. Some manufacturing took place in England, too, much of it in Yorkshire. It was in order to protect this trade by sea, that Henry VII started building a Royal Navy, although this was always to remain small by the standards of his son's reign. Henry VII was more interested in encouraging merchants to build big ships, which he could then commandeer when he needed them.

Henry VIII's religious Reformation (see pp.136–137) was not only a religious event, but also an economic one, and it brought the Crown a windfall twice over. The first came when wealth was directly confiscated from the monastic houses; the second when the property of religious houses was sold to landowners.

Agrarian revolution, social change

Already underway illegally, enclosure of agricultural land won approval from the Crown in the reign of Henry VII, since it allowed important economies of scale. So, too, did the turning over of previously cultivated land to grazing. Sheep were the most important livestock: their meat was sold locally, but their wool exported in great quantities—and at vast profit to the big landowners and the Crown. Some selective breeding took place to produce larger and more heavily fleeced sheep. This, in turn, fed through into fashion, in the luxurious "New Draperies" of the early Elizabethan era, which were made using lighter-weight combinations of linen, silk, and wool.

Enclosure also broke the already much-weakened link between the peasantry and the land. The early

Tudor pitchfork

Tools like this remained unchanged over centuries. The agrarian revolution of Tudor times allowed for important economies of scale, but weakened the bond between the rural population and the land they worked.

A fete at Bermondsey
As feudal ties weakened, fetes like this one painted by George Hoefnagel in c. 1569 helped foster social cohesion. They provided a chance to let off steam— and for local magnates to demonstrate their largesse.

Tudor period saw the final replacement of the old-style serf with the independent yeoman-farmer and the tenant farmer who paid his landlord rent in money, rather than in free labor. Laborers were increasingly working for payment in cash, speeding the overall transition to a cash economy.

On the move

Enclosure meant that large numbers of families were evicted from their land. This left them without income, sustenance, or home and uprooted from the places and communities they knew. The growing numbers of the homeless and landless roaming the country also represented a problem for society as a whole, which had to cope with the resultant issues of public nuisance, begging, and petty crime. Successive Poor Laws from 1536 introduced a carrot-and-stick approach with, on the one hand, food or cash relief for the hungry, and job creation through public works. On the other, however, there were severe punishments for vagabondage, including public flogging

and the piercing of the ear as a mark of shame. While every village experienced the comings and goings of groups of vagabonds, the period saw a steady transfer of population to the towns.

Urban centers were growing quickly now, the push factor of landlessness augmented by the pull of growing prosperity through trade. People felt that there were opportunities in the cities; chances to earn money working for a flourishing new middle class of merchants and skilled craftsmen.

Elizabethan crime

A colorful underworld was well established by Elizabeth I's time, and to some extent was showcased by the drama of the day. Footpads—what we might now call muggers—lay in wait along the main highways and cutpurses stalked the city streets. The equivalent of modern pickpockets, they used sharp knives to cut the leather thongs which

people used to hang their purses from their belts. Vice was rife: pimps and prostitutes figure prominently in the popular humor of the time, including that of Shakespeare's plays, as do confidence-tricksters or "coney-catchers." A coney was a rabbit—a meek and innocent person: there was no shortage of sharp operators eager to profit from such vulnerable people. The authorities, on the face of it, had draconian powers to crack down on crime: the punishments at their disposal ranged from placing in the stocks through flogging, branding, and mutilation to hanging. However, woefully inadequate law enforcement meant that they were for the most part fighting a losing battle. Local "watches," set up by each parish, had poor or little organizational structure, and were staffed by men who could get no other work. With no training, and generally no appetite for the job, the constables were one of Elizabethan society's biggest jokes.

Tudor coin
England had been gradually moving toward a cash economy since the reign of Henry VII. Here, his son Henry VIII sits enthroned on a gold half-sovereign coin dated around 1545.

AFTER

The economic changes of the Tudor Age had a lasting influence. Industry, trade, and urbanization increased over the following centuries.

TRADE WARS
Reliance on trade led the country into war in the 17th century **178–179 》**, although this did not stop the **drive toward trade and enterprise** in the period that followed.

EXPLORING THE COLONIES
Colonial expansion opened up **new sources of raw materials** while at the same time creating market opportunities **162–163 》**. **New financial institutions** and mechanisms made it easier to do business **210–211 》**.

URBAN CRIME AND UNREST
Crime and disorder became common **222–223 》** as **urbanization increased**. The agricultural revolution changed country life **230–231 》**, while clearing the way for **the Industrial Revolution 232–233 》**. The belief of many people that they were missing out on Britain's prosperity—and its democracy— provoked **widespread unrest** in the early decades of the 19th century **264–265 》**.

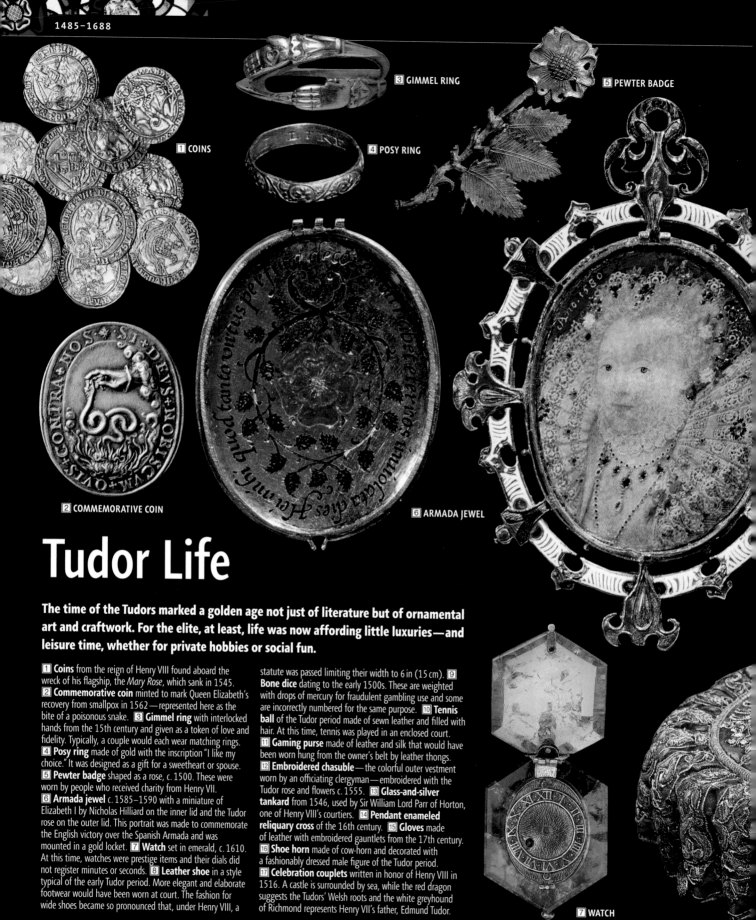

1 COINS

3 GIMMEL RING

5 PEWTER BADGE

4 POSY RING

2 COMMEMORATIVE COIN

6 ARMADA JEWEL

Tudor Life

The time of the Tudors marked a golden age not just of literature but of ornamental art and craftwork. For the elite, at least, life was now affording little luxuries—and leisure time, whether for private hobbies or social fun.

1 Coins from the reign of Henry VIII found aboard the wreck of his flagship, the *Mary Rose*, which sank in 1545.
2 Commemorative coin minted to mark Queen Elizabeth's recovery from smallpox in 1562—represented here as the bite of a poisonous snake. **3 Gimmel ring** with interlocked hands from the 15th century and given as a token of love and fidelity. Typically, a couple would each wear matching rings.
4 Posy ring made of gold with the inscription "I like my choice." It was designed as a gift for a sweetheart or spouse.
5 Pewter badge shaped as a rose, c. 1500. These were worn by people who received charity from Henry VII.
6 Armada jewel c. 1585–1590 with a miniature of Elizabeth I by Nicholas Hilliard on the inner lid and the Tudor rose on the outer lid. This portrait was made to commemorate the English victory over the Spanish Armada and was mounted in a gold locket. **7 Watch** set in emerald, c. 1610. At this time, watches were prestige items and their dials did not register minutes or seconds. **8 Leather shoe** in a style typical of the early Tudor period. More elegant and elaborate footwear would have been worn at court. The fashion for wide shoes became so pronounced that, under Henry VIII, a

statute was passed limiting their width to 6 in (15 cm). **9 Bone dice** dating to the early 1500s. These are weighted with drops of mercury for fraudulent gambling use and some are incorrectly numbered for the same purpose. **10 Tennis ball** of the Tudor period made of sewn leather and filled with hair. At this time, tennis was played in an enclosed court.
11 Gaming purse made of leather and silk that would have been worn hung from the owner's belt by leather thongs.
12 Embroidered chasuble—the colorful outer vestment worn by an officiating clergyman—embroidered with the Tudor rose and flowers c. 1555. **13 Glass-and-silver tankard** from 1546, used by Sir William Lord Parr of Horton, one of Henry VIII's courtiers. **14 Pendant enameled reliquary cross** of the 16th century. **15 Gloves** made of leather with embroidered gauntlets from the 17th century.
16 Shoe horn made of cow-horn and decorated with a fashionably dressed male figure of the Tudor period.
17 Celebration couplets written in honor of Henry VIII in 1516. A castle is surrounded by sea, while the red dragon suggests the Tudors' Welsh roots and the white greyhound of Richmond represents Henry VII's father, Edmund Tudor.

7 WATCH

8 LEATHER SHOE

12 EMBROIDERED CHASUBLE

15 GLOVES

9 BONE DICE

10 TENNIS BALL

13 GLASS-AND-SILVER TANKARD

11 GAMING PURSE

14 RELIQUARY

16 SHOE HORN

17 CELEBRATION COUPLETS

Sailors and Privateers

The skill and daring of its seafarers was to be England's salvation several times over the centuries, and an inspiration to the country as a whole. Yet that tradition was late in developing: not until Tudor times was the Royal Navy founded or the possibilities for naval power realized.

Elizabethan cannon
Merchant vessels were routinely armed so as to double as fighting ships. The aggression of English privateers in the 16th century did much to provoke war with Spain.

BEFORE

Britain had been an island since the last glaciation, and the maritime tradition had historically been strong. The sea was both highway for trade and barrier to attack.

INVASION
The barrier had been broken: by Romans **《 22–23** and by Saxons **《 34–35**. From the 9th century, Vikings had often raided Britain **《 46–47**. The **Normans** landed

BATTLE OF SLUYS, 1340

in 1066 in a huge force from across the Channel **《 68–69**. But since medieval times naval warfare essentially meant **land battles** fought **at sea**. English archers decided the outcome of the Battle of Sluys in 1340, just as they had at Agincourt **《 118–119**.

The 15th century had introduced the Age of Discovery. European seafarers set out to explore the wider world. First, under the patronage of Prince Henry the Navigator, in the 1420s Portugal's seafarers started charting the Atlantic, venturing ever further south down the coast of Africa. In 1487, Bartolomeu Dias rounded the Cape of Good Hope. A decade later Vasco de Gama pushed on to India.

Following on from Columbus' first famous voyage of 1492, Spanish navigators opened up a New World in the Americas. Portugal created its own American colony in Brazil.

A late start

Surprisingly, given their reliance on overseas commerce, the countries of Britain played little part in this exploration. Their maritime tradition meant it could only be a matter of time, however, and Henry VII sponsored the voyage of John Cabot to Newfoundland

301 The number of African slaves captured from a hijacked Portuguese ship and subsequently sold for profit in Santo Domingo, in the Caribbean, by English privateer John Hawkins on his first major voyage.

in 1497. He also established a navy, but his son, Henry VIII, is regarded as the Royal Navy's founder, expanding a fleet of five ships by building, buying, and capturing almost 100 ships in his reign. These vessels were designed to protect existing seaborne trade. Soon, however, the possibilities were realized for promoting aggressive policies abroad.

Privatizing war

It was not Henry's official Royal Navy that would be the main motor of either exploration or war. Both were advanced a great deal more by "privateering," in which the King granted a charter to a captain to carry out piratical actions against vessels of an

Francis Drake
England's seafaring spirit was epitomized by Francis Drake. He was both patriotic servant and maverick adventurer, out for himself.

enemy state. The privateer and his investors kept the profits they made from any ships or cargoes they could capture, allowing a cash-strapped monarchy to both devolve the costs of fighting a war and keep offensive actions at a diplomatic distance.

Merchant adventurers

Privateering was a matter for individualists. In 1563, Plymouth's John Hawkins, whose father had preyed on French ships in the 1540s, took slaves from west Africa to the Caribbean in return for trade goods in a forerunner of the "triangular trade" (see pp.234–235).

Another instinctive adventurer to whom privateering offered a ready-made role was Martin Frobisher. In 1576 he sailed to the Arctic in search of the fabled Northwest Passage to the Indies but found only Baffin Island. He returned with a shipload of shiny, yellow iron pyrites, learning the hard way that "all that glisters is not gold."

State-sponsored piracy to inflict economic damage on an enemy, however, saw successful attacks on Spanish ships in the 1570s. With a permit from Elizabeth I, Francis Drake sacked Nombre de Dios, Panama, in 1572; the following year, venturing inland, he ambushed a Spanish mule train bringing 22 tons of gold from the mines of Peru. His circumnavigation of the globe (1577–1580) was as much about enrichment as exploration. And as well as numerous Spanish treasure ships, Drake captured the great galleon

20,000 The number of gold ducats offered by King Philip II of Spain as reward for the life of the English privateer Francis Drake. The King considered Drake a common pirate.

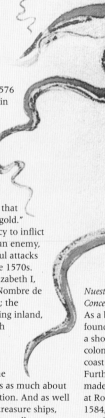

Nuestra Señora de la Concepción. As a base, Drake founded Nova Albion, a short-lived English colony on the Pacific coast of North America. Further colonization was made by Walter Raleigh at Roanoke, Virginia, in 1584, but deprived of supplies in the Armada crisis (see pp.150–151) it died out. The appetite to attack was still strong, however, and in 1586 Drake and Frobisher sacked Spain's great Colombian cities of Santo Domingo and Cartagena de las Indias.

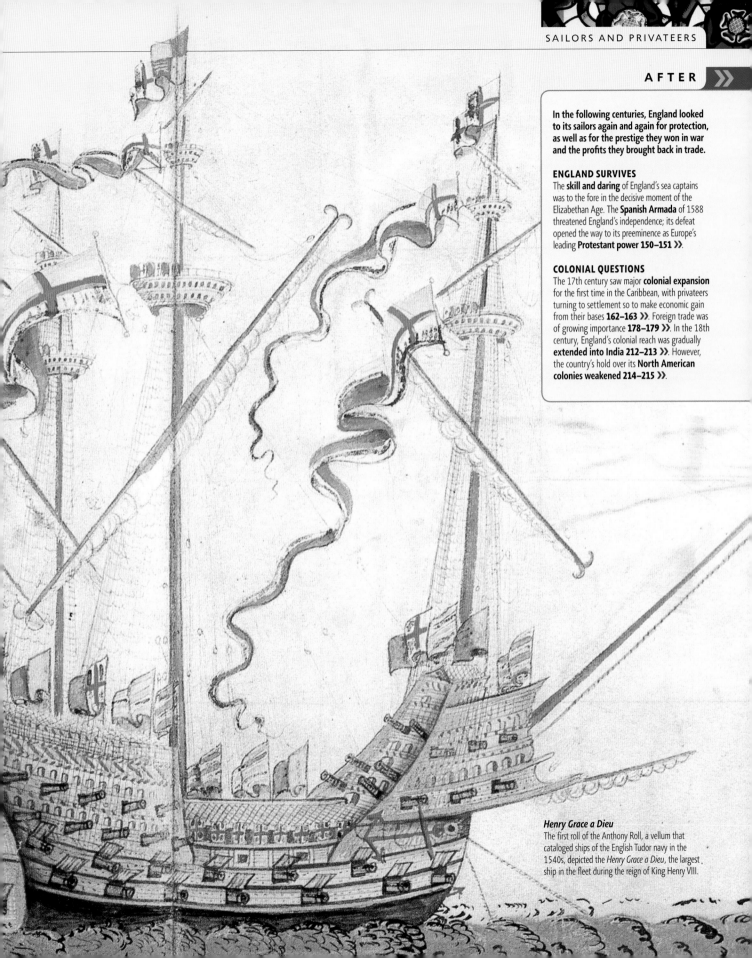

AFTER »

In the following centuries, England looked to its sailors again and again for protection, as well as for the prestige they won in war and the profits they brought back in trade.

ENGLAND SURVIVES

The **skill and daring** of England's sea captains was to the fore in the decisive moment of the Elizabethan Age. The **Spanish Armada** of 1588 threatened England's independence; its defeat opened the way to its preeminence as Europe's leading **Protestant power 150–151 »**.

COLONIAL QUESTIONS

The 17th century saw major **colonial expansion** for the first time in the Caribbean, with privateers turning to settlement so to make economic gain from their bases **162–163 »**. Foreign trade was of growing importance **178–179 »**. In the 18th century, England's colonial reach was gradually extended **into India 212–213 »**. However, the country's hold over its **North American colonies weakened 214–215 »**.

Henry Grace a Dieu
The first roll of the Anthony Roll, a vellum that cataloged ships of the English Tudor navy in the 1540s, depicted the *Henry Grace a Dieu*, the largest ship in the fleet during the reign of King Henry VIII.

« BEFORE

Spain had been a key ally of England against France in medieval times. Since then, however, the situation had been slowly changing.

SEAL OF MARY TUDOR
AND PHILIP OF SPAIN

RELATIONS WITH SPAIN

Henry VII worked hard to maintain **good diplomatic relations** with Spain, marrying his eldest son, Arthur, to Catherine of Aragon, daughter of Spain's king and queen—and then, when that prince died, to his younger brother, Henry « **134–135**. The 16th century had seen Spain emerge as **Europe's major power**, enriched by its New World empire: it made sense to keep relations as cordial as they could be. As king, however, Henry VIII had broken with Rome « **136–137**. Inevitably, this had **soured relations** with Spain, which saw itself as the custodian of Catholicism and its values.

ATTEMPTS TO RESTORE RELATIONS

Rapprochement was made possible by Mary I's **restoration of the old religion**. She even married the future Philip II of Spain. He attempted to renew the alliance when she died, seeking the hand of Elizabeth I, despite her Protestantism. However, this **offer was rejected** by the young Queen « **140–141**.

The **War** with **Spain**

Spain was the dominant European power of Elizabeth I's day, and war with that country was the dominant reality of her reign. The fear of this great enemy cast a shadow over England through several decades of the 16th century. Spain's defeat was seen as ushering in a golden age.

England's place as Europe's preeminent Protestant power conferred prestige on the kingdom, but it also brought the enmity of both Catholic France and Spain. Fortunately, the two great Catholic powers were dogged by a rivalry of their own, but even so, their attitude toward England was hostile. One of Elizabeth I's first acts on ascending the English throne was her refusal to accept Philip II of Spain as suitor for marriage. The death of Mary I, which had made Elizabeth queen, had of course left the Spanish king a widower.

Elizabeth's rejection

Philip is unlikely to have taken it personally, of course, but the symbolism was still clear to him. If Philip's marriage to a second successive English queen would have sealed the continuation of good relations between their countries, Elizabeth's rejection underlined the differences between them. This was especially so when her relationship with his rebellious Dutch subjects seemed to be so warm.

Spain had inherited the Netherlands through the ancestral connections of the then Spanish king, Charles I, with the House of Burgundy. It had proved to be a valuable possession, with its grain exports and woolen-textiles industry. However, as elsewhere in prosperous northern Europe, the people had been receptive to Luther's Protestant message, and Reformation values very quickly took hold. In 1566, there was an explosion of iconoclastic anger in the Netherlands. Protestant rebels sacked churches, smashing stained-glass

Massacre of the Dutch
Drawing inspiration from a biblical event, when Herod massacred every newborn boy in Judea, *Massacre of the Innocents*, by Peter Brueghel the Elder, struck a bitterly contemporary note, clearly commenting on Spanish atrocities in the Netherlands in the 1560s.

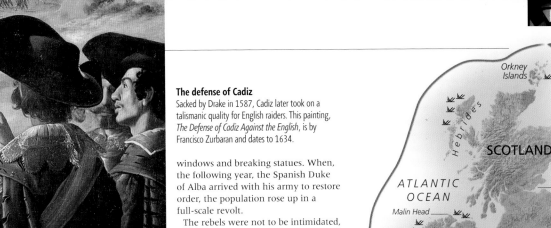

The defense of Cadiz

Sacked by Drake in 1587, Cadiz later took on a talismanic quality for English raiders. This painting, *The Defense of Cadiz Against the English*, is by Francisco Zurbaran and dates to 1634.

windows and breaking statues. When, the following year, the Spanish Duke of Alba arrived with his army to restore order, the population rose up in a full-scale revolt.

The rebels were not to be intimidated, but they saw that numbers and strength were not on their side, so they naturally looked to Europe's foremost Protestant monarch for support. Elizabeth was cautious, in fact; conscious of the risks of antagonizing Spain. In reality, she had already done that by engaging with the Dutch. By signing the Treaty of Nonsuch on August 20, 1585, offering them men, horses, and financial support, she had effectively declared war, Philip believed.

Leicester the loser

Elizabeth still hoped to steer a middle course. She quarreled with her favorite, Robert Dudley, Earl of Leicester, about how the situation should be handled. With considerable misgivings, she backed his expedition to the Netherlands in 1585, but was adamant that it should not engage directly with the Spanish. Leicester disobeyed her, and, worse, under his leadership the English came off decidedly second best against the Spanish. He had to resign in 1587, when it became clear that his campaign was not succeeding.

Of battleships and beards

The campaign had enraged Philip II. He was smarting, too, from the continuing irritation of privateer attacks in the Americas (see pp.146–147). Philip began building what was to be an "Invincible Armada"—a huge war fleet (see pp.150–151). This would enable him to invade and conquer Elizabeth's kingdom, and put an end to his English problem once and for all. As the conflict heated up, however, Francis Drake and his fellow privateers took the war to Spain itself: in 1587, they stole into the ports of Cadiz and La Coruña, and sacked them both. The episode was memorialized by the gleeful English as the "Singeing of the King of Spain's Beard." It was an expression that nicely caught both the boldness of Drake's attack and the humiliation it caused Spain. A furious Philip launched his Armada attack the following year. On paper, it represented an irresistible force. Its

COURTIER (1554–1586)

SIR PHILIP SIDNEY

"Thy necessity is yet greater than mine …." Sir Philip Sidney's words as, fatally wounded, he passed his water-bottle to a dying Spanish soldier, marked him out as a model of a new and specifically Protestant brand of knightly chivalry. Born in 1554, he grew up an accomplished writer and poet, an elegant courtier, and a valiant and noble soldier, embodying all the greatness and the grace of Elizabeth's England. He died at the Siege of Zutphen in 1586, during the Earl of Leicester's failed expedition to the Spanish Netherlands.

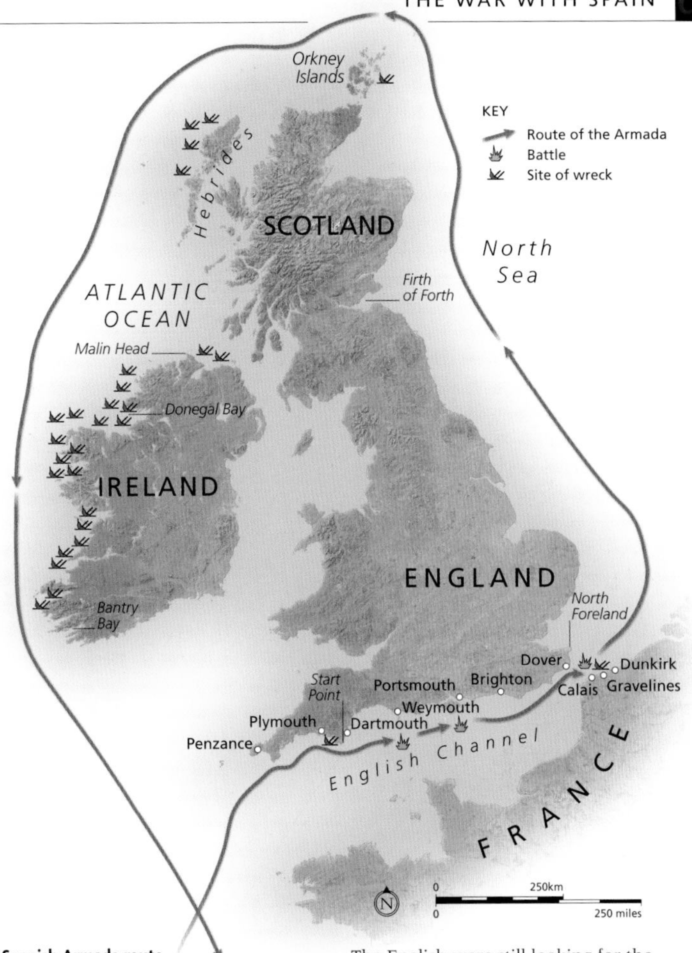

Spanish Armada route

English ships harassed the Armada as it sailed up the English Channel to pick up the Spanish invasion force in Flanders. A strong wind then destroyed the Spanish fleet.

failure was a disaster for Spain and a much-celebrated high point of English patriotic history (see pp.150–151).

A long slog

It was all anticlimactic for England from this point on. An attempt to counterstrike with an English armada in 1589 did not succeed. The fleet, commanded by Francis Drake and carrying a land force led by Sir John Norris, was inadequately equipped and unfocused in its aims. Considerable casualties were sustained in both men and ships. (Robert Devereux, the Earl of Essex, took part against the Queen's orders; though still a favorite, he was now living on borrowed time.)

Sir Richard Grenville's attack on Spain's Azores in 1591 fared little better, and Drake's assaults on San Juan, Puerto Rico, were thwarted. So, too, was an attempted "Second Singeing" in 1596: Essex, Lord Howard of Effingham, and Walter Raleigh arrived at Cadiz, but found the Spanish ready, their treasure ships scuttled for later recovery. A nominally successful raid had brought no appreciable gains.

The English were still looking for the great victory that would humble the enemy, but Philip changed strategy. Rather than renew his all-out assault, he was content to give continuing support to those Irish rebels whose war of attrition was exhausting England's armies and finances. The euphoria of 1588 was ebbing steadily away.

AFTER

At the beginning of the 17th century, England's Protestants, fearful that their new king, James I, had inherited the Catholic sympathies of his mother, Mary Queen of Scots, were quickly reassured by the determined realities of his reign.

A PROTESTANT KING
The King, simultaneously reigning as James VI of Scotland and James I of England, brought a **union of the Crowns** to the two nations 158–159 ≫. Raised as a Scottish Protestant, the King cracked down on Roman Catholics—especially after the **Gunpowder Plot** of 1605 160–161 ≫. He did, however, make **overtures to Catholic Spain**, by attempting to marry his eldest living son, Charles, to Maria Anna, daughter of Philip III. Charles eventually married Henrietta Maria of France, a Catholic 166–167 ≫.

Map labels: Orkney Islands, Hebrides, SCOTLAND, Firth of Forth, North Sea, ATLANTIC OCEAN, Malin Head, Donegal Bay, IRELAND, Bantry Bay, ENGLAND, North Foreland, Dover, Dunkirk, Brighton, Calais, Gravelines, Portsmouth, Start Point, Weymouth, Plymouth, Dartmouth, Penzance, English Channel, FRANCE

KEY — Route of the Armada, Battle, Site of wreck

The **Defeat** of the Spanish Armada

King Philip II of Spain resolved to free himself from the English irritation once and for all. But his "Invincible Armada" turned out to be all too vincible in the face of skilled and daring English and Dutch seamanship, supported by a cooperative "Protestant wind."

Philip planned for his Invincible Armada to sail up the English Channel to Flanders, where it would pick up the Duke of Parma's invasion force and take it to England. The Armada, comprising 24 warships and around 40 armed merchantmen, along with many other smaller craft, was led by the Duke of Medina Sidonia. An English fleet led by Francis Drake sailed from Plymouth to harass them as they sailed past, but had little impact. On August 6, the Armada reached its intended anchorage off the coast at Gravelines, near Dunkirk, in safety.

Armada adrift
However, Parma's force had been blockaded on shore by patriotic Dutch privateers, so the Armada was left stranded at anchor. As night fell on August 8, it was at the mercy of England's "fireships" (drifting ships deliberately set on fire). As these loomed out of the darkness, the Spanish cut their vessels free in panic. They escaped the fireships, but their line lost coherence. The English ships, led by Lord Howard of Effingham, then wove in and out of them at will.

Deadly return
What defeated the Armada was the loss of initiative, not ships (just four sunk). The fracas had been inconclusive, but the longer it went on the further the strong winds dragged the Spanish ships into the North Sea and toward the point of no return. Given the shoals and sandbanks along the Dutch coast, they could not cut inshore to pick up Parma's army. By August 12, the moment had passed, and the Armada was forced to head home in a perilous journey around the Scottish and Irish coasts. Sixty ships and thousands of lives were lost. A Spanish fleet never seriously threatened England again.

"One of the most notable **disasters** ever to happen in **Spain** and one to **weep** over all one's life."

FRAY LUIS DE SEPÚLVEDA, SPANISH FRIAR, ON THE DEFEAT OF THE ARMADA

The Armada is attacked
When the two fleets finally met in force, off the Flanders coast, the Spanish ships lost their discipline allowing the English ships to move in among them, attacking at will. The painting shown here, by an unknown English artist, was completed soon after the battle that it depicts.

The **English** Renaissance

Arts and philosophy flourished from the early 1500s to the early 1600s. This was the era of Shakespeare and Webster's dramas, the development of the madrigal and sonnet, far-reaching humanist thinking, and Holbein's striking portraits of the Tudor ruling classes.

Hans Holbein's portraits of Tudor nobility, including his iconic painting, *The Ambassadors*, and images of Henry VIII, have become the perfect symbols of this age. Holbein was German but lived in England after 1532, and by 1536 was Henry's court painter, which placed him at the heart of the English Renaissance. Holbein's lavish portraits are statements of affluence and power designed to impress. They reflect the self-confidence that drove Henry's aggressive foreign policy, at a time when exploration was starting to build an empire, which made the King break with Rome in 1531 and place himself at the head of the English Church (see pp.134–135).

Hilliard's self-portrait
This miniature of Hilliard from 1577, aged 30, shows him looking every inch the Elizabethan courtier. His use of line was considered to be one of his talents.

« **BEFORE**

The English artistic Renaissance was less cohesive in nature than the Italian one, comprising a disparate mix of elements from home and abroad.

ITALIAN FORERUNNERS
The Italian Renaissance influenced the English one, but started earlier, in the 1400s.

EARLY ENGLISH CONTRIBUTIONS
Some aspects of the English Renaissance arts also **contained features from earlier English traditions**. These included: Chaucer and the growing body of **English vernacular literature « 110–111**; medieval mystery, miracle, and morality plays; and the Gothic style, seen in art such as the Wilton Diptych **« 114–115**.

This break, and Henry's Dissolution of the Monasteries and destruction of churches, effectively destroyed the development of religious church painting in England. The aristocratic portraiture that dominated the English Renaissance went on to become extremely important in British art.

Elizabethan glories
Elizabeth's reign did much to keep the country's self-confidence riding high and underpin a flourishing period for the arts. One of the leading portraitists of the day—who was working for the Queen by 1572 and went on to work for James I—was Nicholas Hilliard. His particular talent was for exquisitely detailed and elegant miniatures. He produced images of key figures of the time such as Walter Raleigh, famed explorer of the Americas and a favorite at Elizabeth's court. Other notable painters included George Gower, leading portraitist and Elizabeth's "serjeant-painter," and William Segar, another portraitist and Garter King-of-Arms under James I.
Elizabeth and James's reigns were also a golden age for English drama.

> " For all **knowledge and wonder** ... is an **impression of pleasure** in itself.

FRANCIS BACON, *THE ADVANCEMENT OF LEARNING* 1605

Southwark, on London's south bank across the river from the City, became a center for rowdy entertainment. It was home to the Globe and the Rose theaters, where William

William Byrd
Pioneer of English vocal and keyboard music William Byrd (c 1542–1623) wrote almost 500 pieces of music over the course of his career.

Shakespeare's new plays were staged. He also performed at court, which was a great patron of the theater. Shakespeare and Christopher Marlowe were the pioneers of drama in creative blank verse, new to England at this time (see pp.154–155). Another leading playwright was Ben Jonson whose plays included *Every Man in his Humour* (1598), a "comedy of humors," in which each character has a dominant trait, and *Volpone* (1607).

Jacobean theater
James's reign witnessed a rich seam of powerful Jacobean dramas in which extreme tragedy and satire were major

The Ambassadors
Holbein's 1533 portrait of two diplomats is full of symbolic objects that display their success. The skull in the foreground representing death only appears recognizable when viewed from a certain angle.

Jacobean classic. Other Jacobean playwrights include Thomas Middleton, who collaborated with Thomas Dekker on the comedy *The Honest Whore* (1604) and with William Rowley on the tragi-comedy *The Changeling* (1622). Shortly after James's reign, John Ford took the Jacobean drama to extremes with his tale of bloody incest, *'Tis Pity She's a Whore* (c.1633).

The courts of the English Renaissance are also famed for their patronage of poetry, and the sonnet was developed by writers such as Sir Thomas Wyatt. Edmund Spenser produced a key masterpiece of Elizabethan poetry with his *The Faerie Queene* (1590–1596). In praise of Elizabeth I, this drew inspiration from Italian poet Ludovico Ariosto's *Orlando furioso*, and used complex allegory and vivid description to tell the story of a succession of knights' adventures. Using iambic pentameter (see pp.154–155), he created the "Spenserian stanza": verses of eight five-stress iambic lines, followed by an iambic line of six feet, with a rhyming scheme of a b a b b c b c c.

> **MADRIGAL** An unaccompanied form of music for voices that began in 14th-century Italy and involved more voice parts as time passed. During the English Renaissance, London and Chester were two major madrigal-composing centers.

John Donne, one of the metaphysical (exploring emotional states via complex imagery) poets of the time, was another central figure, penning his famous love poems, as well as *Satires and Elegies* (c.1590–1599), while Sir Philip Sidney produced the Renaissance classic, *Arcadia* (1590), a pastoral prose romance filled with poetry.

Sweet music
Some comparisons between the Italian and English Renaissances suggest that the English version was less about art and architecture and more about literature and music. The madrigal came of age, with the light style especially popular in the 1580s and 1590s. The "ayre," a song-form with less counterpoint than a madrigal, was also favored. Madrigals were often played on the lute. The virginal was another key instrument in this period. Leading composers included

Thomas Morley, Thomas Tallis, William Byrd, and John Dowland, whose music includes *Lachrimae*.

Questioning the world
Underpinning much of the artistic outpouring was an English form of humanism—a philosophical outlook central to the Italian Renaissance. Humanism was a system of thought that placed human beings at the center of things, in contrast to the more remote scholasticism that characterized typically medieval thought. Humanist thought drew ideas from ancient Greek and Latin classics, and asserted the dignity and worth of humans and their ideas and beliefs. Thomas More, Lord Chancellor under Henry VIII, was a leading humanist. His *Utopia* (1516) explored notions about the ideal city-state and was the first time this word was used.

The lute
Most popular during the 16th and 17th centuries, the lute was often played at stately dances. Elizabeth I enjoyed playing the instrument and John Dowland was its leading contemporary composer.

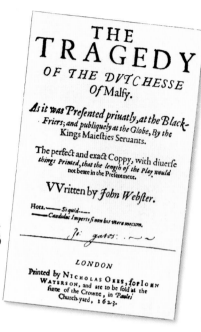

Title page of *The Duchess of Malfi*
John Webster's influential 1623 Jacobean tale of tragedy, passion, bloodshed, and retribution was partly influenced by Philip Sidney's *Arcadia*.

Thinker, essayist, and statesman Francis Bacon was an influential philosophical figure. He attempted to move thought on from the logic of Aristotle toward a more empirical approach—one based on the idea that knowledge comes from experience, received through our senses. This contributed to the growth of modern experimental science, with its stress on causes, which gathered pace in the 17th century (see pp.184–185). Bacon discussed the notion of cataloging useful knowledge in his seminal 1605 work, *The Advancement of Learning*.

features. The "revenge tragedy," featuring bitter vengeance invariably accompanied by graphic carnage, was very popular—Thomas Kyd's *The Spanish Tragedy* (1592) is an earlier example, while John Webster's *The Duchess of Malfi* (1623) is a

Una and the lion
This 1847 Minton model shows Una from Edmund Spenser's *Faerie Queene*, who is saved from a dangerous fate by a lion.

AFTER

> Forms explored during the Renaissance were responsible for many of the major subsequent developments in the English arts.
>
> **POETICAL INSPIRATION**
> The blank verse developed by Shakespeare, Marlowe, and others was **used by later writers**. Examples of its use include John Milton's epic poem, *Paradise Lost* (1667), Wordsworth's *The Prelude* (1850), and *Ulysses* (1842) by Tennyson. The stanza-form found in Spenser's *Faerie*
>
> *Queene* was subsequently used by the Romantic poets John Keats, Percy Shelley, and Lord Byron.
>
> **THE MADRIGAL**
> Madrigal societies were **popular in the 18th century**. Vaughan Williams (1872–1958), a reviver of historic English music, composed his **homage to English Renaissance music**, *Fantasia on a Theme* by Thomas Tallis, in 1910.
>
> *PARADISE LOST* ILLUSTRATION BY WILLIAM BLAKE

PLAYWRIGHT Christened 1564 Died 1616

William **Shakespeare**

"He was **not of an age**, but **for all time**!"

BEN JONSON, IN HIS POEM *TO THE MEMORY OF MY BELOVED, THE AUTHOR MR. WILLIAM SHAKESPEARE: AND WHAT HE HATH LEFT US*, 1623

William Shakespeare is regarded as Britain's, and perhaps the world's, most important writer. While some may disagree with this, it is certain that this highly influential poet and playwright had a gift for language that seems as remarkable now as it did in his day. Shakespeare's work was much loved by a wide range of people in his time, and it has continued to enthrall all kinds of audiences since his death.

A start in Stratford

The details of Shakespeare's life and works are patchy and much contested. He was born into a provincial middle-class family in the town of Stratford-upon-Avon in Warwickshire. His father was a glover, who served as Stratford's mayor, but also descended into serious debt. Shakespeare was the third of eight children. Three siblings died young and only one outlived him.

Shakespeare probably received a good classical education at the town's grammar school—his work is full of classical references. Growing up, he may

Anne Hathaway's cottage

The childhood home of Shakespeare's probable wife, Anne Hathaway, is in the outskirts of Stratford. Her father was a well-to-do yeoman farmer and so was able to provide this substantial house.

well have accompanied his father to see the many traveling theater troupes that stopped off in Stratford. This early experience could have sparked his later interest in theater. At 18, he probably married Anne Hathaway. He had three children, one of whom died in childhood—some say that passages in *Twelfth Night* reflect this tragedy.

The King's man

After years about which very little is known, Shakespeare turned up in London in the 1590s as a well-established actor-dramatist. *Venus and Adonis* (1593) was an early poetic success and the *Henry VI* trilogy and *Richard III* were probably among his first plays. By the early 1600s, Shakespeare and his plays were leading the King's Men (named after their patron King James I) to glory as England's greatest theater company. In demand at court, with a home at London's Globe, the most famous contemporary theater, their dramas starred legendary actor Richard Burbage. Shakespeare was now mixing with everyone from royalty to the era's leading dramatists.

From the 1590s, Shakespeare produced a huge body of plays, as well as his beautiful sonnets. Born into the culturally rich Elizabethan age, with influences including the ancient classics and traditional English folk and mystery plays, Shakespeare made the most of his sources. His settings ranged from the ancient world of *Anthony and Cleopatra* to the contemporary Danish court of tragic *Hamlet*. His characters, too, span the farcically incompetent theatrical troupe in *A Midsummer Night's Dream* to the hot-headed Katharina in *The Taming of the Shrew*.

Vibrant verses

Shakespeare's towering achievement was his lyrical and powerful use of iambic pentameter—typically a line with ten syllables where five unstressed syllables alternate with five stressed ones (in bold below). A common form in English verse, Shakespeare used it very expressively in his sonnets:

> Shall **I** compare thee **to a** Summer's day?
> Thou **art** more **lovely and** more **temperate:**
> Rough **winds do shake the** darling **buds** of May,
> And **Summer's** lease hath all too **short a** date …

His extraordinary talent, however, was an unusually clever use of blank (unrhymed) verse—specifically nonrhyming iambic pentameter—in his plays. Blank verse was a new craze in 16th-century England, which Shakespeare and Marlowe (see BOX) adapted for plays, often using it in unorthodox, subtle ways. Shakespeare used blank verse to express all kinds of emotions and information among the histories, comedies, and tragedies into which his plays are grouped. His plays include: histories such as *Henry V* and *Richard III*; comedies such as *A Midsummer Night's Dream* and *As You Like It*, and more complex comedies such as *All's Well that Ends Well* and *Measure for Measure*; the great tragic plays, *Hamlet*,

Memorial to Shakespeare
A statue of Shakespeare, designed by William Kent, stands in Westminster Abbey. It shows the playwright leaning on a pile of books and pointing to a scroll with lines from *The Tempest*.

Macbeth, *Othello*, and *King Lear*; the Greek and Roman works, including *Julius Caesar* and *Antony and Cleopatra*; and the mature tragi-comedies at the close of his career, such as *The Winter's Tale* and *The Tempest*.

His work is loved for its dazzling wit, poetry, clever turns of phrase, and word-play. From coarse humor and an evocative use of everyday contemporary English to exquisite poetry, Shakespeare explored the spirit of his times and the human condition in a newly approachable way, using language to conjure varied moods and control complex plots full of mistaken identities and misunderstandings. He is admired for his probing psychological studies (unusual at the time) of complex characters, such as the ambitious King Macbeth. His work often contains a central character with a fatal flaw that causes their downfall, an idea common to ancient classical philosophy and writing. Othello's jealousy is just one example of this.

Shakespeare's *Othello*
A title page from Shakespeare's *Othello*, which was probably first performed in 1604. The story was taken from one by 16th-century Italian writer, Cinzio.

Mysterious to the end

Many mysteries have attached themselves to Shakespeare's life. His early years may have seen him fleeing to London to escape a deer-poaching charge. He may have been a secret lover to the "Dark Lady" of his sonnets, whose identity has also been hotly debated. Many have even suggested that he did not actually pen his plays and this has become a contentious issue. Others believe that he collaborated with the likes of Ben Jonson, Sir Francis Bacon, Edward de Vere, and Sir Walter Raleigh.

Shakespeare and Southwark
This stained-glass window in London's Southwark Cathedral depicts characters from Shakespeare's plays. Southwark was (and is) home to the Globe Theatre, where many of Shakespeare's plays were first performed.

Shakespeare's final years are equally mysterious. It is widely believed that by 1610, he was embarking on a peaceful retirement in one of the several properties in Stratford-upon-Avon that he owned. There is little evidence to support this, although Shakespeare did die in Stratford. The cause of his death is uncertain. One popular theory is that it was from a fever brought on by a night's carousing with friends including artistic rival, Ben Jonson, probably the next most successful playwright of the age after Shakespeare.

POET AND PLAYWRIGHT (1564–1593)
CHRISTOPHER MARLOWE

Shakespeare's contemporary, Christopher Marlowe, was a poet, playwright, and probable government spy, whose plays include *Tamburlaine the Great* (1590) and *Doctor Faustus* (c. 1590). He was associated with the Admiral's Men theater company. Like Shakespeare, Marlowe was a master of blank verse and populated his plays with human characters. This led many to believe that he was the real author of Shakespeare's plays. Most scholars disagree with these theories but admit that parts of Shakespeare's plays might have been written in collaboration with others.

TIMELINE

- **April 26, 1564** Shakespeare is baptized at Stratford-upon-Avon, Warwickshire, as the first son of Mary Arden and John Shakespeare, glover and burgess.

- **1570s** Shakespeare most likely attends Stratford's grammar school, the King's New School, where he would have taken part in the classical rhetorical declamation (the art of using speech to persuade an audience), which was part of a good education in his day. He probably watches traveling theater shows with his father. John Shakespeare gets involved in dubious trade dealings and serious debt, and drops down the social scale.

- **1582** An 18-year-old Shakespeare gets married—very probably to Anne Hathaway.

- **1583–1585** Shakespeare and his wife have a daughter, Susanna (1583) and twins, Hamnet and Judith (1585).

- **1590** It is thought he starts writing plays.

- **c. 1591–1595** Shakespeare writes the three parts of *Henry VI* and *Richard III*.

- **1592** A pamphlet provides evidence that Shakespeare is established as an actor-dramatist in London.

- **June 1592–1594** London's theaters close due to plague, causing a temporary break to Shakespeare's career.

- **1595** Shakespeare has a share in the theater company known as the Lord Chamberlain's Men (founded in 1594). The company performs plays by leading dramatists of the time, including Ben Jonson, and gives most of Shakespeare's plays their first outing.

- **1596** John Shakespeare is granted a coat of arms, probably testifying to his son's success by this time.

- **1597** Shakespeare buys an impressive house in Stratford called New Place.

- **1599** Cuthbert Burbage builds the Globe Theatre at Bankside, Southwark; most of Shakespeare's plays from this point onward premiere here.

THE GLOBE THEATRE

- **1603** Elizabeth I dies and James I ascends to the throne. The Lord Chamberlain's Men become known as the King's Men, under the direct patronage of the King.

- **1609–1611** Writes his more mature plays: *The Winter's Tale*, *Cymbeline*, and *The Tempest*.

- **1613** The Globe burns down. Shakespeare buys a property in Blackfriars, home of the Blackfriars Theatre, where the King's Men perform during winters as the Globe is roofless.

- **1614** A rebuilt Globe reopens for business.

- **April 23, 1616** Dies at Stratford-upon-Avon, possibly as a result of a heavy drinking session, and is buried in the Holy Trinity Church, Stratford.

Conquest and Plantation

A series of revolts against English rule erupted across Ireland in Tudor times. They were put down with the utmost savagery, and with some considerable difficulty. The Nine Years' War cast a lengthening shadow over Elizabeth's otherwise illustrious reign—and sowed the seeds for conflicts yet to come.

Siege of Kinsale
Franz Hogenberg's engraving of 1602 shows Spanish and Irish rebel forces defending the County Cork port in the concluding action of the Nine Years' War.

Ireland's Hiberno-Norman families resented the Tudor monarchs' attempts to regularize land-use and taxation. The Gaelic chieftains became emboldened and Ireland "beyond the Pale" (the areas outside the well-settled and defended area around Dublin) grew increasingly restive and wayward. From 1541, Henry VIII and his Chief Minister Thomas Cromwell tried to Anglicize the authority of the Gaelic chiefs through the policy of "Surrender and Regrant." Each chief would surrender his authority and be regranted an English aristocratic title in its place. Up to a point, it worked. Conn O'Neill, in Ulster, accepted the title of Earl of Tyrone, for instance. But somehow, the "regrant" part seemed more appealing than the "surrender."

Plantation of Munster
In 1569, the Desmond Rebellions flared up in Cork. Quelled in 1573, they erupted again six years later. They were suppressed and the southwest pacified by the Plantation of Munster. New English settlers were planted

Sir Arthur Chichester
A veteran of the Nine Years' War, Chichester had little sympathy with the Irish. As Lord Deputy from 1605 to 1616, he oversaw the plantation policy.

BEFORE

Ireland had been "English" since the 12th century, in that the Norman lords of England also ruled Ireland. England's emergence as one of medieval Europe's preeminent powers had left Ireland the subordinate.

ARISTOCRATIC RIVALRIES
England's hold weakened as its **aristocratic rivalries spiraled into war ❮❮ 122–123**. The problem to begin with was not with the Gaelic Irish but with the Hiberno-Normans and "Old English." They had arrived in the first colonizing wave **❮❮ 80–81** but had "gone native" in the centuries since, adopting Gaelic dress, language, and customs. Like the Gaelic Irish, moreover, **they were faithful to Catholicism**, so the English Reformation drove a further wedge between the two countries **❮❮ 136–137**.

Cahir castle
Situated on an island in the Suir River, this medieval stronghold was captured by the Earl of Essex in 1599.

> "A **million swords** will not do them so much harm as **one winter's famine**."

SIR ARTHUR CHICHESTER, 1600

there to domesticate and (as the English saw it) civilize the place. In 1593, Conn's successor Hugh O'Neill, and allies including Hugh Roe O'Donnell of Donegal, rebelled against Elizabeth. The Nine Years' War that followed pitted the English against lightly armed Irish kerns and more heavily equipped Scottish "redshank" mercenaries, too.

Irish ascendancy

The rebels won the early rounds at Clontibret (1595) and Yellow Ford (1598). In 1599, the Lord Deputy of Ireland, the Earl of Essex arrived in Ireland with almost 20,000 troops, only to be defeated by O'Donnell at Curlew Pass. Having agreed a truce, Essex was recalled by a furious Queen Elizabeth. He tried to topple his former protector from power in 1601. Failing in his coup, he was tried and executed.

English attrition

His successors fought more effectively, gradually wearing down resistance. By 1600, O'Neill and his rebels were exhausted. The arrival of a Spanish army in 1601 appeared to offer a last-minute respite, but the newcomers were cornered after landing at Kinsale. The Irish surrounded the army of Essex's successor, Baron

Londonderry map

The city seems an outpost in this Survey of the Estate of Londonderry prepared by Thomas Phillips in 1624.

Mountjoy, only to be outmaneuvered at the Battle of Kinsale. The Spanish withdrew; the rebellion was quashed. In 1607, the defeated O'Donnell and O'Neill led the "Flight of the Earls" leaving for the Catholic countries of Europe.

Colonization of Ulster

The north of Ireland had been left relatively untouched by Old English settlement. The population was unsettled with communities of herders and the least tractable chiefs.

Around 1610, a program of plantation (or colonization) was launched. Lands were granted to English and Scottish landowners, who brought tenants from their estates to settle the country. Towns were established to provide administration and promote commerce. The City of London guilds were pressed to send tradesmen and their families.

They were given lands to develop around Derry, which was renamed Londonderry.

Separate lives

The Gaelic population, rather than being expelled, moved to the margins, remaining there in poverty and helplessness. The "civilizing" mission never got beyond a policing role, as Protestant settlers and the Catholic populace lived parallel lives. England was storing up trouble for the future.

AFTER

Oppression bred rebellion in a rancorous, self-perpetuating cycle, which was to shape the unhappy history of Ireland for centuries.

RELIGIOUS DIFFERENCES

The entrenchment of religious differences made the Irish seem even more alien to the Protestant English. **Oliver Cromwell rejoiced in their destruction** and drove them from ancestral lands **174–175 ≫**. Religious considerations ensured that the Irish backed the "wrong" side in the wars which followed William III's accession to the throne of England in the Glorious Revolution **188–189 ≫**.

IRISH REVOLUTION

At the end of the 18th century, Protestants and Catholics made common cause as United Irishmen, attempting a French-style **revolution in Ireland 238–239 ≫**. The revolution failed, but did enough to persuade some in England that those who starved in the Great Famine of the 1840s were getting no more than they deserved **266–267 ≫**.

HOME RULE

The Home Rule movement of the late-19th century won sympathy—but little more **300–301 ≫**.

CROMWELL AND HIS TROOPS STORMING DROGHEDA, 1649

The **Union** of the **Crowns**

The death of Elizabeth I left a vacancy on the English throne. There was only one viable successor— the son of her one-time rival, Mary Queen of Scots. James I's accession effectively united the kingdoms of Great Britain under the rule of a Scottish dynasty, the House of Stuart.

The infant James became James VI of Scotland in 1567, after his mother's ousting. His father had been murdered (see p.138).

Questions of control

James's tutors brought him up a learned man—and a committed Protestant. Yet he had absolutist instincts. Casting envious glances southward at the hierarchical structure of the Church of England, he tried to bring back bishops to introduce order to an overly democratic Scottish Kirk.

Catholics constituted a still more frightening enemy within. James's mother had been Catholic, and some had plotted to topple Elizabeth I in her favor. For this reason, some English Catholics had high hopes for his reign—while Protestants had corresponding fears. As King of England, he calmed the latter by taking a hard line against Catholics.

There was a degree of desperation in the Catholic response: early attempts to topple James only strengthened his Protestant position. The conspiratorial ferment intensified in its turn: hence the plan to blow up the House of Lords during the State Opening of Parliament, on November 5, 1605.

The English Parliament was potentially another enemy. What James saw as its obstructionism was a spur to his writings on monarchy and his theory of the "divine right of kings." Paradoxically, the Gunpowder Plot (see pp.160–161), and the crackdown on Catholics that followed, helped ease relations between King and Parliament.

Spanish stalemate

The religious question reared up again in the affair of the "Spanish Match" when James tried to marry his son Charles to the Infanta Maria, for diplomatic reasons. The episode was famously satirized by Thomas Middleton's play *A Game at Chess* (1624). The wooing of Spain and her infanta was deeply unpopular.

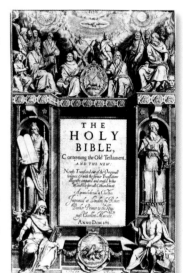

King James I Bible
A Protestant and indefatigable scholar, James was fascinated by the challenges of scriptural translation. He commissioned an "Authorized Version" of the Bible (1604–1611) that is still relevant today.

Tracts against witchcraft
James VI helped ferment the hysteria about witches, claiming innocent lives in Scotland. His *Daemonology* (1597) offered a learned justification for the persecution. He is shown here examining convicted witches.

The Sutherland portrait of James VI/I
James's kingships of Scotland and England were separate. However, many saw him as the King of Great Britain—a title that he would occasionally use himself.

> " What God hath conjoined **let no man separate**. I am the husband and the whole isle is my lawful wife… " JAMES I OF ENGLAND, 1603

‹‹ BEFORE

Relations between the countries of Britain had been fractious for centuries. Wales's princes had been put down by England's Edward I, who also rejoiced in his nickname of "Hammer of the Scots."

SCOTTISH BATTLES
Gains made by Edward I in Scotland were eroded by Robert the Bruce **‹‹ 93**, who helped Scotland win its independence at the Battle of Bannockburn in 1314 **‹‹ 94–95**. Further skirmishes occurred between the two nations **‹‹ 116–117**. England inflicted a **terrible defeat** on Scotland at Flodden in 1513 **‹‹ 138**.

SCOTTISH ROYAL COAT OF ARMS

QUEEN WITHOUT A SUCCESSOR
Elizabeth I had **Mary Queen of Scots** executed **‹‹ 138**. However, her lack of an heir left the way clear for Mary's son, James, to succeed.

Fears of secret Catholic sympathies were allayed by his marriage to the unimpeachably Protestant Princess Anne of Denmark. In 1603, James succeeded Elizabeth and was warmly welcomed by the English people as he progressed triumphantly south.

An uneasy union

His coronation was momentous in bringing about a "Union of the Crowns," since James I of England was still James VI of Scotland. His promise to return regularly to his homeland was soon neglected. Even so, the system seemed to work. James wanted more general union, with harmonized laws, trade tariffs, and taxation, although neither the English nor the Scottish Parliaments were enthusiastic.

Enemies within

James was formidably clever, but an apparent lack of common sense saw him labeled "the wisest fool in Christendom." His denunciations of witches seem tragically misguided. Antiwitchcraft legislation dated back to 1563 in Scotland, but it was with James's encouragement that large-scale persecution began in 1590. Hundreds of women (and some men) were killed after summary show-trials.

AFTER ›

The countries of the British Isles retained their own identities, but English dominance was to remain in the ensuing years.

CROMWELL'S TREATMENT
Cromwell cruelly **suppressed the Irish**, bullying the Scots into an unequal union **174–175 ››**.

DANGEROUS ABSOLUTISM
England and Scotland shared much—not least their Protestantism. James's son, Charles I, **upset the Scots** by trying to impose his Anglican hierarchy on the Kirk **166–167 ››**. His absolutism **engulfed England in the Civil War 168–169 ››**.

THE LAST CATHOLIC MONARCH
James II's Catholic and autocratic leanings lost him his throne in the Glorious Revolution of 1688 **188–189 ››**. An Act of Union followed a few years later in 1707, bringing about the creation of Great Britain **202–203 ››**. Bonnie Prince Charlie's **bid for the Crown** in 1745 menaced the Union briefly, resulting in the Battle of Culloden **204–205 ››**, but most Scots and English united against the Stuart threat.

The Unification of the Crowns
The Union of England and Scotland was given an allegorical spin when Peter Paul Rubens made it the centerpiece of his ceiling painting (1632–1634) at the Banqueting House in Whitehall. It shows James's son Charles being brought to the throne by personifications of England and Scotland.

The **Gunpowder Plot**

The plot to kill the King and bring the Houses of Parliament crashing down helped shape British history for generations. Yet the ineptness of Guy Fawkes and his coconspirators did little to console those who had hoped for a new monarch to safeguard their freedom and loosen the grip of Protestantism.

Guy, or Guido, Fawkes is the most notorious of a clique of Catholic conspirators who plotted to blow up Parliament and King James I during the State Opening of 1605. They meant to strike a blow against a state whose laws had deprived them, they believed, of their just rights. Led by Robert Catesby, a veteran of Essex's Rebellion of 1601 against Queen Elizabeth I, they included the Earl of Northumberland's cousin, Thomas Percy, and Francis Tresham. Fawkes, a former soldier, provided the military experience.

Catholic uprising
Percy's ties with Northumberland, a Catholic sympathizer, were crucial. Though there is no clear evidence that the Earl was involved, the conspirators relied on him to rally support. For, shot through with wishful thinking, the plot did not stop at the assassination of the King: the attack was to spark a general uprising. The King's young daughter, Princess Elizabeth, was to be installed as a Catholic queen. But the Catholic powers on the Continent were skeptical. Spain disliked the idea of overturning the monarchical order, and the Pope was worried that the plan would rebound on English Catholics.

Clumsy conspirators
Preliminary meetings between the conspirators began in May 1604. Later that year, they bought a cellar in a nearby property that ran underneath the precincts of Parliament. They also rented rooms in a house just across the Thames River, so they could carry gunpowder across at night.

They were discovered when an anonymous letter—from Tresham, it is suspected—warned Lord Monteagle, brother-in-law of Tresham, to stay at home. A search of Parliament by the authorities on the eve of the opening found Fawkes in the midst of his preparations. The others were quickly caught. Two were killed resisting capture and the remainder were interrogated, perhaps tortured, and finally tried and condemned to death.

> " … devise some excuse to **shift off your attendance** at this Parliament, for God and man hath concurred **to punish the wickedness** of this time."
>
> ANONYMOUS LETTER TO LORD MONTEAGLE, OCTOBER 26, 1605

Executed for treason
Guy Fawkes and three coconspirators were executed outside Parliament on January 31, 1606. They were dragged on wattled hurdles before being "hanged, drawn, and quartered"—hanged until half dead, their innards "drawn" out, and their bodies cut into four. The public were encouraged to light bonfires to celebrate the King's escape.

BEFORE

England was itself the creation of what might be described as colonial expansion. Since the departure of the Romans halfway through the first millennium, it had been occupied by successive waves of settlers.

INVADED ISLAND
Anglo-Saxon raiders **established their own kingdoms ≪ 24–25**. The Vikings came to plunder but the Danes settled and farmed **≪ 46–47**. The Normans **crossed the Channel** from France, making England a colonial conquest of a sort **≪ 68–69**.

OVERSEAS CONQUESTS
Norman lords occupied Ireland in the 12th century. The territories they took there passed to the English kings as (arguably) the country's first overseas colony **≪ 80–81**. That such possessions could bring trouble was already becoming clear. Ireland was the scene for **successive rebellions** in the 16th century **≪ 156–157**. This apparently did nothing to diminish England's appetite for conquests overseas. **Intrepid adventurers** like Frances Drake and Walter Raleigh proved more successful at attacking others' colonies than in establishing outposts of their own **≪ 146–147** in the 16th century.

Penn's treaty with the Indians
The Quaker leader William Penn was granted what became Pennsylvania by King Charles II in 1681, but felt it his duty to reach a separate agreement with the Lenape who actually lived there.

Colonial Expansion

England's earliest ventures into colonial expansion had been ill-fated, and at the beginning of the 17th century that still seemed to be true. The project slowly gathered momentum and successful English colonies were established on North America's eastern seaboard and many Caribbean islands.

The Age of Discovery had been under way for a couple of centuries when James I came to the throne in 1603, but England had not been as successful as Portugal and Spain in conquering new territories. Given the daring shown by so many of its seafarers, it was perhaps surprising that there was no overseas English empire.

Elizabethan adventurers had made many attempts to establish colonies in America. All had met with failure. Sir Francis Drake established a colony at Nova Albion (believed to have been in California) during his circumnavigation

60 **The number of Jamestown settlers who survived the "starving time" of 1609–1610, out of 500. The island had to be abandoned for a time in the spring of 1610.**

of the world. The Roanoke settlement came to a mysterious—and presumably tragic—conclusion later on in the 1580s. What happened to this "Lost Colony" is not known.

Dreams and disillusions
The fate of its founder, Sir Walter Raleigh, seemed somehow to set the tone for exploration in the new century: exaggerated claims, disappointing results—and a grisly end. Raleigh came back from an expedition to Guiana in 1595 with a desire to find the fabled South American kingdom of El Dorado. Queen Elizabeth's favorite was not as popular with her successor: James suspected Raleigh of plotting against him and had the adventurer imprisoned. But in 1616, he allowed himself to be talked around by Raleigh and released him, tempted by the promise of untold treasures.

Raleigh, however, returned from a search for El Dorado without much more to show for a long and expensive expedition than the booty from a Spanish colony he had sacked.

Since James had been trying to cultivate good relations with Philip III, this was the last

thing he had wanted. Raleigh was beheaded in 1618, as a goodwill gesture to the Spanish king.

A faltering start
By this time, James at least had a colony to his name—quite literally: adventurer John Smith had named a settlement "Jamestown." Arriving in the New World in 1607, and faced with the challenge of starting a community from scratch, both he and his genteel companions learned the hard way just how many skills they lacked. Writing home to his financial backers in London, he had called on them to send him colonists of a different kind. "When you send again," he entreated them, "rather send but 30 carpenters, husbandmen, gardiners, fishermen, blacksmiths, diggers up of trees, roots, well provided ... than a thousand of

Pocahontas
Given an Anglicized identity as Rebecca on her marriage to the Englishman John Rolfe, the Powhatan princess became a Christian and worked hard for peace. She even visited England, dying there in 1617 of smallpox.

> "**The next day till noon we traded**: the king feasted all the company; and the afternoon was spent in **playing, dancing, and delight**."

CAPTAIN JOHN SMITH DESCRIBES AN ENCOUNTER WITH THE POWHATAN CHIEF, 1608

such we have." Without such essential workers, the colony had very nearly gone the way of its predecessors, well over two-thirds of its population perishing in the early "starving time," when the colony was also under siege by the native Powhatan Confederacy.

Commerce and conflict

The start of tobacco cultivation brought an economic lifeline—and made a magnate out of one far-sighted settler, John Rolfe. His subsequent marriage to Pocahontas, daughter of Chief Powhatan, brought peace with the Powhatan Confederacy—at least until the 1620s. As Jamestown grew inexorably, however, new settlers extended its boundaries ever further onto Powhatan land.

In 1622, a new young chief, Opechancanough, decided that enough was enough. His warriors attacked the outlying settlements of the English. The raiders came with meat and cereals, as though to trade, and were welcomed into the settlers' homes before falling on their hosts and massacring them: more than 300 men, women, and children were killed.

A port in a storm

In 1609, a ship en route to Jamestown was blown off course in rough weather: it finally made landfall far to the south in the Bermudas. The English seafarers called the island group the Somers Isles for their commander, Admiral James Somers. A new settlement was quickly

established there. Captain Henry Powell stumbled on Barbados in much the same way in 1625; it was settled two years later by employees of Sir William Courten's merchant company. The template for the kind of plantation system, which was to be used throughout the American colonies, was established here: big estates, where cash-crops were cultivated by slave labor. The slaves at this stage were mostly white: many were more properly described as indentured labor, forced into servitude by debt, though others had been transported as punishments for crimes, or in some cases simply abducted from port cities. In the aftermath of the English Civil War, Cromwell sent Royalist POWs to America. Crops included cotton, tobacco, and (from the 1640s) sugar.

Terms of trade
Long in use in the Americas, tobacco was unknown in the Old World until the 16th century. Europeans were soon hooked, and it became a vital currency for trade.

Hudson's horror

The New World was still seen less as an end in itself than as a stepping stone to the riches of the East Indies. The Virginia settlements were established with this goal in mind. The search was on for the fabled Northwest Passage around North America to the Pacific. (This route does actually exist, but is only now appearing thanks to global warming.) Hence the interest of the Muscovy Company, which, after several unsuccessful attempts to find a Northeast Passage around the Northern Cape of Scandinavia and Eurasia's Arctic coast, sent Henry Hudson to sail the other way. After voyages in 1607 and 1608, exploring the waters around Nova Scotia and Greenland, he set out

Pilgrim Fathers
A group of English Puritans set off from Delftshaven, the Netherlands, in 1620. America was a land not only of opportunity but of religious freedom.

in 1610 to chart the Hudson Strait and Bay. The conditions he encountered were truly horrendous; Hudson's crew rose up in mutiny and he himself was lost, presumably murdered.

Religious refugees

The Pilgrim Fathers, a party of Puritan refugees whose ship, the *Mayflower*, arrived on the coast of Massachusetts in 1620 were one of the earliest and certainly the most famous of many groups to flee England's intolerant climate. They were followed by others—and not just Puritan Protestants. A group of Catholics crossed the Atlantic in the 1630s under the protection of George Calvert, Lord Baltimore. The Quakers followed later, settling in Barbados in the first instance; only from 1681 did they arrive in America. The son of a famous general,

50,000 The number of early settlers to England's North American colonies who came as convicts. Thousands more came as indentured servants—debtor-slaves.

peace-loving William Penn was granted territory there by Charles II in return for a debt the King had incurred with his father. The settlement was named Pennsylvania, in honor of Penn and the region's rich forests ("sylvan" deriving from the Latin for "woods"); its capital was Philadelphia—in Greek, the city of "brotherly love."

AFTER

England did not look back: some Scots saw the Act of Union (1707) as another land-grab, but the Britain it produced was unabashedly imperialistic.

EXPANSION OF THE NEW WORLD
Britain's **empire expanded** in the 18th century **212–213 »**. But the American **colonies had been lost** by 1781 **214–214 »**. One of the decisive battles was at Princeton in 1777. New territories were opened up, meanwhile, in Australia and New Zealand **294–295 »**.

BRITISH EMPIRE
In the Victorian period Britain's soldiers and sailors **fought to build an empire** on which "the sun never set" **290–291 »**.

BRITISH FORCES WERE DEFEATED AT THE BATTLE OF PRINCETON, 1777

London and the Thames River, 1611
London in the early 17th century was a huge, bustling metropolis—one of the world's greatest cities. In this panorama by cartographer John Speed, the dominance of the Thames, the city's main commercial artery, is clear. North of the Thames, on the top left of the view, in the City, is old St. Paul's Cathedral. To the right are the piers and arches of London Bridge, then the river's only crossing. In the foreground, on the south bank of the river, Southwark Cathedral is the largest building.

Robert Filmer's book *Patriarcha*
According to the political theorist Robert Filmer, what the father was in his family, the king was in his realm: God's representative, to be given absolute obedience.

Charles I and Parliament

An absolutist king and an increasingly confident Parliament came into collision in the reign of Charles I. With neither side inclined to compromise on basic principles, political turbulence was guaranteed. Yet no one could have predicted quite how completely or how rancorously relations were to break down.

BEFORE

England had always been a monarchy, but since medieval times the Crown had ruled in cooperation with Parliament. Inevitably, there were tensions.

DIFFICULT RELATIONSHIP
England's nobles **reined in royal power** in 1215 when they compelled King John to sign **Magna Carta ❰❰ 86–87**. But difficulties had continued, on and off, since the Reformation. **Parliament looked askance** at King James's mother's Catholicism and his Scottish birth **❰❰ 158–159**.

Commotion in the House of Commons
Charles I bursts into the chamber with his guards, demanding the surrender of five wayward members. The King had violated all convention, and for nothing, since the men were gone. As Charles ruefully remarked: "All the birds have flown."

James I had believed in the divine right of kings, but as a Scots outsider, threatened by Catholics, he had been forced to compromise. His successor, Charles I, felt more secure. This would be his undoing. As Prince Charles, he had traveled to Madrid to seek the marriage of the Infanta. When this unraveled, he made his addresses to Spain's rival Catholic power, France, and married Princess Henrietta Maria, Louis XIII's sister.

On becoming king in 1625, Charles showed his reluctance to reign alongside Parliament. He dissolved it at the slightest provocation, from 1629 dispensing with it altogether. Instead, he introduced a streamlined (and less accountable) executive. A renewed and strengthened Court of Star Chamber (see pp.132–133) dealt with those who opposed his despotic ways.

His style set him against the Puritans. Strict, "pure" Protestants, they rejected the authority of any hierarchy of bishops. They would be ruled spiritually by their individual consciences and by scripture, and saw Charles's Church as Catholic authoritarianism returned. The King's pet clerics, such as William Laud and Robert Filmer, did not disagree. Arguing for Anglicanism's Catholic roots, they rejected the Protestantism of Luther and Calvin, and preached the divine right of kings. Laud was anointed Archbishop of Canterbury in 1633. Charles shared their vision of an English Church whose clear hierarchy

he controlled—not the association of autonomous local congregations the Puritans favored. In 1637, he tried to bring Scotland into line by enforcing the Anglican liturgy, and responded to resistance with the Bishops' Wars of 1639 and 1640. Charles won, but gave way on key demands and saddled England with enormous debts.

Parliament returns
To approve taxes to raise new revenue, he recalled Parliament. Angry at being sidelined for 11 years, it demanded reforms, so three weeks into the "Short Parliament" Charles dissolved it. But, needing money, he swallowed his pride and recalled it again. It passed the Triennial Act, meaning that Parliament had to be recalled every three years, and that the King could not simply decide to do without it. In 1641, he had to agree to a law forbidding him from dissolving Parliament. His Court of Star Chamber was outlawed, too.

In an atmosphere of growing rancor, Charles became convinced that leading MPs had discreetly supported the Scots in the Second Bishops' War. Outraged, in January 1642, he went with his guards to Parliament to arrest key MPs. He found them gone—warned of his arrival. But the King's invasion of the chamber trampled all over the tradition of royal respect for the rights of Parliament's House of Commons. Trust broke down completely: King and Parliament were at war.

KEY MOMENT
RIOT AT ST. GILES'

Charles I's attempts to bring the Kirk (Scottish Church) into line with Anglican liturgy and institutional organization were deeply resented in Scotland. In 1637, these feelings flared up into open revolt in St. Giles' Cathedral, Edinburgh's High Kirk, after market trader Jenny Geddes threw a footstool at James Hannay, the minister reading out the Collect from the Book of Common Prayer. Widespread rioting resulted, followed by thousands signing a defiant National Covenant in Greyfriars Kirkyard in February 1638. In 1643, the English Parliament was to join with its Scots equivalent in signing a Solemn League and Covenant, respecting the autonomy of the Kirk.

AFTER

The disagreement between Charles I and Parliament was too profound to be easily smoothed over. It was too bitter to have anything other than a tragic end.

CONTINUING STRUGGLE
In 1642, **relations between Crown and Parliament broke down** entirely and the nation was plunged into civil war **168–169 ❱❱**. After Charles I's execution in 1649 **170–171 ❱❱**, an attempt was made to govern England **without a monarchy 172–173 ❱❱**. However, the new Commonwealth collapsed, resulting in a **restored Crown** in 1660 **176–177 ❱❱**. In 1688, with the Glorious Revolution, it seemed that **at last a solution** to the differences between Crown and Parliament had been found with the overthrow of James II and the installation of William III as a **constitutional monarch 188–189 ❱❱**. But the Stuarts were not finished, and tried repeatedly to reclaim the throne for James's successors **202–203 ❱❱**.

Charles I
Anthony Van Dyck's 1637 equestrian portrait of Charles I shows the King as an armored knight, the protector of his subjects. Less than a decade later, however, the King was to drag his subjects into a hugely destructive civil war.

BEFORE

England's medieval rulers had dominated their peers through their courage and charisma. All that had changed by the outbreak of the Civil War in 1642.

CENTRALIZED POWER

The **seething rivalries** of late-medieval England's great aristocratic houses eventually boiled over into the Wars of the Roses **‹‹ 122–123**, but Henry VII's **accession brought this conflict to an end**. To prevent further outbreaks of civil strife, he and his Tudor successors set about constructing a centralized English state **‹‹ 132–133**. Henry VIII also established royal control over the country's religious life **‹‹ 136–137**. The first Stuart ruler, James I, inherited sweeping royal powers.

AN OVERBEARING MONARCH

Too rigid an imposition of order can, paradoxically, promote disorder. The system is liable to break down when there is **no sense of give and take**. When Charles I's **arrogant absolutism** proved more than Parliament could stand, he reacted by dispensing with Parliament altogether **‹‹ 166–167**. Finally, in 1642, any sense of **government by consent** collapsed completely. The King and his Parliament were not just at odds but actually at war.

Feeling his authority imploding, Charles I was forced to flee his own capital. He traveled into the country to drum up support. Charles raised his standard at Nottingham on August 22, 1642: 2,000 noble followers rallied to the royal flag. Called Cavaliers, from the French *chevalier*, meaning "horseman" or "knight," they expected to fight on horseback; far fewer infantry—traditionally drawn from the lower classes—heeded the call.

Expensively mounted and dressed, the Cavaliers wore their hair long and flowing—in stark contrast with the severely cropped Roundheads recruited by Lord Essex to oppose them.

Early encounters

The Cavaliers had the advantage at Edgehill, Warwickshire, on October 23, yet still contrived to throw away the victory. They scattered the King's enemies with ease only to lose their focus and fall to plundering. The Roundheads were able to regroup. In the end, this early encounter was inconclusive.

The King continued toward London, attracting new recruits as he went: Essex was waiting for him, west of the city at Turnham Green. His army, too, had grown with the addition of local volunteer militias from across southern England—so many that Charles did not dare attack. The two armies spent several months circling around one another, shrinking from anything but the briefest of attacks. Gradually, through these skirmishes, the Royalists were gaining ground, but at Newbury, in September 1643, their fortunes were reversed. Again, after a successful charge, they dissipated their advantage and the Parliamentarians secured the victory. Even so, neither side could really consider itself victorious and a lengthy stalemate ensued.

New Model Army

A significant voice in earlier political controversies, but marginalized once the shooting started, Oliver Cromwell now came into his own as a military

Oliver Cromwell

The inexperienced Cromwell proved an instinctive general and able military administrator. He masterminded the Roundhead victory in the Civil War.

The Civil War

"We are so many frighted people," wrote Margaret Eure in June 1642. "For my part, if I hear but a door creak I take it for a drum." The Civil War may have divided England—and, ultimately, the entire British Isles—down the middle, but it brought desperate terror, death, and suffering to all alike.

Battle of Marston Moor

A turning point in the Civil War, the combined forces of Scottish Covenanters and English Parliamentarians defeated Royalist forces at Marston Moor on July 2, 1644.

Matchlock musket
The Civil War saw the widespread use of firearms for the first time on British soil. Lit by a match or fuse, the matchlock was slow to fire, and most effective used in large-scale volleys.

commander. Having raised his own mounted militia in his native Cambridgeshire, he proved an able commanding officer and had been appointed Lieutenant-General of Horse by the time of the Battle of Marston Moor, in July 1644.

Even then, the battle could not have been won had it not been for the presence of Lord Leven's Covenanting Scots and the discipline they showed under heavy fire. From 1644, a Scots Civil War was continuing in parallel with the English conflict. The Royalists were led by former-Covenanter James Graham, 1st Marquess

New Model Army's catechism
Protestant faith, moral idealism, and ruthless practicality combined in Cromwell's idea of his New Model Army. Its rules were recorded in a "catechism."

of Montrose. Although he had his eye on the bigger British picture, his allies, clan chieftains, were pursuing local rivalries, and their efforts were fatally unfocused.

Back in England, Cromwell was establishing a New Model Army of 20,000 troops. Most were cavalry—Cromwell's speciality by now—but there were also foot-soldiers and artillery. They were known as Ironsides because of the iron breastplates that they wore. They were trained and drilled—and enthused with the justice of the cause.

Cromwell's efforts paid off at Naseby, Northamptonshire, in June 1645. Defeated, Charles was captured and imprisoned.

A second civil war
Charles reached a secret deal with Scottish nobles and succeeded in starting a second civil war. Under the

New Model Army helmet
Cromwell's Roundheads protected their shaven crowns with helmets like this. Other armor was light—usually little more than a simple breastplate.

"Engagement" of 1647, he offered to establish the Presbyterian Church (in both Scotland and England) for three years in return for their support. The deal split the Kirk: powerful figures were against getting involved. Even so, in 1648, the Duke of Hamilton led an invasion, prompting a Royalist revival south of the Border.

Cromwell's defeat of the Scots at Preston caused this to collapse quickly. Some members of the Long Parliament still wanted an accommodation with the King, fearing the power of the New Model Army. Pride's Purge amounted to a military coup: officers led by Colonel Thomas Pride prevented moderates from entering the Commons chamber to vote. The hard-line "Independents" had their way, and Charles was tried and executed.

Mopping up
Cromwell put down Catholic resistance in Ireland in no uncertain terms, perpetrating notorious massacres at Drogheda and Wexford. In his absence, in 1650, the late King's son, Charles II, led the Scots Royalists in another invasion of England. Cromwell returned, headed north, and laid siege to Edinburgh. Although forced by a shortage of supplies to withdraw to Dunbar, he defeated the pursuing Royalists there on September 3. He delivered the final blow in England at Worcester a year later.

The immediate consequence of the Civil War was a traumatized nation. The conflict killed a higher percentage of the population of the British Isles (anything up to 10 percent) than any other hostilities, before or since.

CROMWELL'S RULE
Cromwell's victory led to the creation of a kingless Commonwealth **172–173 ≫**. Hopes that it would prove a utopia of freedom were quickly dashed. The **rule of the Lord Protector** turned out to be as despotic as Charles I's had been. His death—and the **Restoration of royal power** with the accession of Charles II in 1660—came as a relief to most **176–177 ≫**.

THE GLORIOUS REVOLUTION
England was marked in the long-term by the conflict between king and Parliament. The claims of these two institutions were debated furiously. It was no abstract discussion. **At stake were political power and opportunity**, while religious feeling lent the arguments a special spiritual and moral edge. There was a fear that James II would restore absolutist monarchy. This was the background that made **the accession of William III** in 1688 a Glorious Revolution, rather than a mere coup **188–189 ≫**.

WILLIAM III AND THE CONVENTION PARLIAMENT

FEAR OF REVOLUTION
The deep and disturbing fear in England of a repetition of the Civil War was perhaps in part responsible for the **caution with which most of the population reacted to the French Revolution** of 1789 **236–237 ≫**. However, the (broadly) **democratic ideals** its victors had fought for **remained strong**, informing the 19th-century movement for electoral reform **268–269 ≫**.

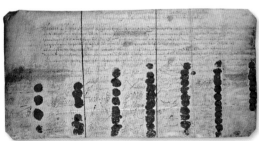

Death warrant of Charles I
Whether from a thirst for justice or for the sake of safety in numbers, 59 Parliamentarians signed this document in January 1649.

The **Execution** of the **King**

England had already seen the world turned upside down in its Civil War: that any man should rise against his ruler could hardly have been imagined. What, then, was the country to make of a trial, which having convicted the King of treason, went on to claim the right to take his life?

To say that Charles I's situation was unprecedented barely begins to do it justice; it was revolutionary. The idea that a monarch, who was seen as the head of the state, might be tried for treason challenged conventional wisdom. Yet times had changed, and common assumptions had been shifting subtly. The King's enemies, the Parliamentarians (see p.166), argued that Charles's first duty was to his country—a country they claimed to represent. For them, the King of England was "not a person, but an office" whose holder had to govern the country according to English law.

A criminal King

A special court of commissioners was created by an Act of Parliament for Charles's trial. It went without saying that they all supported Oliver Cromwell, Parliament's most powerful military leader. The trial opened on January 20, 1649, at Westminster Hall. Led by Parliament's chief attorney, John Cooke, the prosecution charged

Charles not only with breaches of England's constitution, but with betraying England itself. By soliciting the Scots' invasion during the Civil War (see pp.168–169), he had effectively conspired against his country. The King, Cooke insisted, had to take responsibility not only for these crimes, but for all the resultant bloodshed.

Defiance and death

Charles I never agreed to recognize the court, and refused to plead one way or the other. Whatever he might or might not have done, he was answerable only to God, he said. He was asked to plead three times, and each time he refused on the same grounds. It was no surprise when, at the end of a hearing that lasted a week, he was found guilty on all charges. Charles's death warrant was signed by 59 commissioners. Having been imprisoned in St. James's Palace, he was taken out to a public scaffold in front of the Banqueting House in Whitehall on January 31. There, before an awestruck crowd, he was beheaded.

> "I would know by what **power** I am called **hither** … by what … **lawful authority?**"

KING CHARLES I TO THE PARLIAMENTARY COURT THAT PRESUMED TO TRY HIM

The King loses his head
"I shall go from a corruptible to an incorruptible Crown, where no disturbance can be," reportedly said Charles I on the scaffold prior to his execution. He was then cleanly beheaded by his anonymous executioner with a single stroke of the ax.

BEFORE ‹‹

The execution of Charles I was the crowning outrage of a chaotic and traumatic period, which, in the words of the ballad of 1643, had left "the world turned upside down."

A DESPOTIC KING

Charles I's **despotic ways** undoubtedly upset many of his countrymen, and the controversy he caused **divided Scotland and Ireland,** too ‹‹ **166–167**. Even so, most had been horrified to find their country convulsed by civil war. The quarrel was in itself upsetting, but the scale of the **carnage seen during the Civil War** grew far beyond what anyone could have imagined ‹‹ **168–169**.

CROMWELL'S VICTORY

The **victorious Parliamentarians** held the Stuart King responsible for the bloodshed. The King himself appeared **entirely unrepentant** for his part in what had happened. He contemptuously refused to cooperate in a trial ‹‹ **170–171**.

The Commonwealth

Following the Civil War, England headed out into uncharted waters, constitutionally and politically. What had been a kingdom was now effectively a republic. Many believed passionately that they were building a new and better society; others felt alienated by the new elite with their righteous tone.

The dispute between Parliament and the King was brutally resolved. The Long Parliament (called by Charles I in 1640) had been reduced by Pride's Purge of December 1648 (see p.169). What remained was jokingly called the Rump Parliament, and this was itself divided. While the aristocracy had been ousted, along with the King, those members who remained still belonged to the gentry and had their interests at heart.

Cromwell dissolving the Long Parliament
On April 20, 1653—apparently unconscious of the irony that Charles I had gone down this path before him in 1629—Oliver Cromwell decided to dispense with the services of Parliament altogether.

With a balance to strike between upholding tolerance and maintaining social order, the Rumpers opted for safety-first conservatism. The clamorous demand for reform of the legal system was crystallized by Matthew Hale's commission of 1652, which called for protection for poor defendants against abuse by the authorities or wealthy litigants. Parliament quickly lost its nerve and none of the commission's recommendations made it into law.

In religious policy, too, Parliament wanted to send reassuring signals to the English elite and European governments. The Church of England remained the established religion, though the Act of Uniformity of 1559

was repealed. This, at least in theory, meant freedom of worship for all Englishmen and women—although its scope did not include Catholics or the wilder nonconformists.

Religious sects

The Rump was concerned lest it should be thought that the country had collapsed into anarchy. There is no doubt that, in the ferment unleashed by the bringing down of the monarchy and the pinning back of the Church's authority by Protestant "people power," small and self-willed sects of every sort were flourishing. Their "enthusiasm" (a derogatory expression at the time) in bearing witness to their beliefs

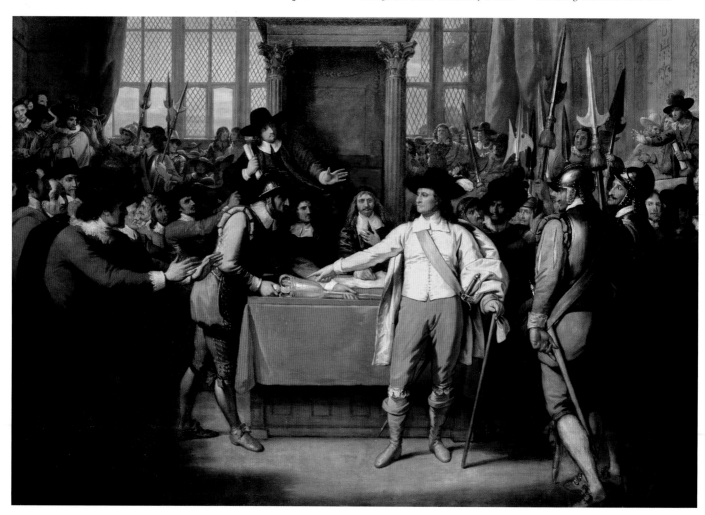

The Commonwealth Laureate
The creator of *Paradise Lost* (1667), John Milton, is regarded as the Commonwealth Laureate, inspired by Puritan principles to produce his greatest work.

unnerved more conservative Christians. The Quakers were typical of these new groups—and the threat they posed. From the late 1640s on, they spoke out for social justice. A strict interpretation of the commandment against murder meant that they condemned all war and military service—a profoundly problematic attitude for the state. The Levellers, though not themselves a sect, were also driven by religious convictions to denounce all inequalities in society.

Mad or menacing?
The Fifth Monarchists placed their trust in the prophecy of the Book of Daniel, which holds that a fifth monarchy, with Christ as King, would succeed those of Assyria, Persia, Macedonia, and Rome. It was to become at least partly real in 17th-century England after 1666 (the year whose number would of course contain the "number of the beast" from the Book of Revelations).

As their nickname suggests, the Ranters were regarded by respectable society as mad. They saw God in all creation; and so completely did they consider themselves to have been "justified by faith," in Luther's theological terms, that they believed themselves to be completely without

sin. While some groups threatened English social structures, sects such as the Ranters seemed to be stepping outside society altogether.

A puritan aesthetic
There was a literary reawakening, too. Parliamentary supporter Andrew Marvell wrote lyrics in a witty, sometimes knotty "metaphysical" style, harking back to Elizabethan poets such

> **COMMONWEALTH A term from the early English concept of the common** *weal*—**meaning "good" or "welfare." It suggested a community of interests ruled not by a king, but by collective considerations of the public good.**

as John Donne. But his friend John Milton, a sometime aide of Cromwell, was clearly inspired by Commonwealth values (though he was not to complete *Paradise Lost*, his epic of Man's creation and fall, until after the Restoration).

The Pilgrim's Progress
John Bunyan's allegorical account of Christian's long and hazardous journey to reach the salvation of the Celestial City is utterly simple in its conception, but has endured, a classic of Commonwealth literature.

John Bunyan's *Pilgrim's Progress* (1678) was a vividly realized allegory of Christian salvation. The former Parliamentarian soldier became a preacher and was jailed after the Restoration for attending nonconformist meetings.

Tax burden
The economic outlook during the Commonwealth was gloomy, with huge liabilities left from the Civil War, and continuing conflicts in Scotland and Ireland. Beleaguered by hostile Catholic powers, England embarked on a major program of shipbuilding from 1649. This was backed up by the Navigation Act of 1651 (see pp.178–179). Ironically, in 1652, this crudely protectionist measure precipitated war—not with Catholic Spain or France, but with the Protestant Dutch.

The Protectorate
The general disillusion found a focus in Parliament, which Cromwell upbraided in ringing terms on April 20, 1653. "Ye sordid prostitutes," he cried, "have ye not defil'd this sacred place, and turned the Lord's temple into a den of thieves? … In the name of God, go." The tone may have been moralistic, but the intent was cynical enough: Cromwell was seizing power in a coup. For a few months, a Barebones Parliament, directly appointed by Cromwell and the leaders of the New Model Army, went through the constitutional motions. No one was convinced, and this assembly was dissolved in December 1653, and Cromwell appointed Lord Protector—or dictator.

Intolerance for all
Although strongly religious, Cromwell was, in principle, more indulgent to the sects than the Rump had been. As dictator, however, he found dissent threatening. The flow of Puritan emigrants from England not only continued but intensified. Not that non-Puritans could be any happier in an England whose government had puritanized every aspect of everyday life. Sacred images and statues in the old cathedrals were destroyed. Theaters, inns, and other haunts of immorality were closed, and restrictions placed on Sunday games and "pagan" festivals. Christmas was not abolished as such, although so many of the associated celebrations were indeed outlawed that Christmas Day became a day like any other day.

Playing cards
Cromwell plays the pipe for his morris-dancing military commander, Lord Thomas Fairfax, on one of a set of satirical "cavalier cards." The Puritans' distrust of all such pagan pleasures was notorious.

AFTER

The mass of the population was not disposed to mourn the passing of the Commonwealth. Charles II's return was welcomed with relief.

A TIME OF CELEBRATION
The "Merry Monarch" seemed determined to continue celebrations throughout his reign. The Restoration period became as much **a byword for decadent revelry** as the Commonwealth had become for seriousness and sobriety **176–177 》**. Over time, public disapproval at royal decadence would be deepened by renewed anger at Stuart intransigence (and suspected Catholic leanings). Charles II's younger brother James, was to be ousted in the Glorious Revolution of 1688 **188–189 》**.

TRADE AND SCIENCE
In some respects, life continued as it had done under the Commonwealth. Britain's **commercial interests** were unchanged and **conflict with the Dutch** came quickly **178–179 》**. Meanwhile, major **intellectual and scientific advances,** made with royal support, suggested that, despite the stereotypes, all seriousness had not been entirely set aside **184–185 》**.

> **"Where is that good, or where is that liberty** so much pretended, so **dearly purchased** …?"

LEVELLER PAMPHLET *ENGLAND'S NEW CHAINS DISCOVER'D*, FEBRUARY 1649

Scotland and Ireland Subdued

BEFORE

The English Revolution did not happen in isolation. Both Scotland and Ireland had to some extent been involved.

SYMPATHY AND HOSTILITY

Scotland's Presbyterians felt a **close kinship** with England's Puritans and shared their vexation at Charles I's **interference** in their Church. Their disputes with Charles had eventually led to the Bishops' Wars **《 166–167**. While their High Church opponents had supported the Stuart King, Charles had eventually done a deal with a powerful Presbyterian group, who in 1648 **invaded England** on his behalf **《 168–169**.

Catholic Ireland had by contrast viewed the rise of the Parliamentarians with alarm—even rising up in **rebellion in 1641**. England's new regime felt a particular contempt for the "popish superstition" under which they saw the Irish as laboring, but they felt much as any other recent rulers of the English state had done. Ireland was the same **poor and uncivilized** province that had rejected Henry VIII's modernizing attempts and had later risen up against Elizabeth I in the Nine Years' War **《 156–157**.

The Parliamentarians could not allow either country to continue in open rebellion—or even as a haven for the disaffected and a **base for future attacks** against England.

MAP OF THE BRITISH ISLES, PUBLISHED 1640

Edinburgh Castle

The Scottish version of the Union Flag flutters proudly in the sky above the Scottish capital, Edinburgh, but it took a century or more of wrangling to get it there.

Locked into their life-and-death struggle, the two sides in the English Civil War spared little concern for the other countries of these islands. Yet Scotland, Wales, and Ireland had all been involved. If not yet a "united kingdom," these were clearly countries whose historical destinies were closely interwoven.

One less obvious consequence of the English Civil War was its underlining of English preeminence in the British Isles. The conflict could even be seen as part of a wider War of the Three Kingdoms, which started with the First Bishops' War in 1639, when Charles I invaded Scotland to impose the Anglican liturgy on the Scottish Kirk (Church). Wales was swept up in England's internal conflict in 1648, but its half-hearted revolt against Parliament that year was quickly put down.

Divine slaughter

The Irish revolt of 1641 had been both a trigger for the English Civil War and a tragedy for Ireland. At first, Catholic Royalist forces remained secure while the Parliamentarians were occupied with fighting in England. But the Irish were eventually trounced at Rathmines by the Parliamentarian commander Michael Jones (a Welshman) in August 1649. Soon after, Oliver Cromwell arrived, and what followed was really an extended mopping-up—and, in Cromwell's eyes, a divinely ordained punishment for earlier rebellion. Hence the gloating tone of his reports of massacres at Drogheda (September 1649) and Wexford (October 1649). Further victories were achieved at Duncannon, Clonmel, and Galway.

And so to Scotland

To Cromwell, the Scots were more "godly" than the Catholic Irish. Scots Presbyterians had fought alongside his men at Marston Moor, so the hatred he had for the Irish was not seen in his Scottish dealings. Although appalled by the Presbyterian lords' "Engagement"

2,000 The number of men "put to the sword" in a single night at Drogheda in 1649, by Cromwell's own account. Most historians believe that hundreds more—including many women and children—were also massacred.

with the King in 1647 (see p.169), he felt more sorrow than anger. In 1649, Scots Presbyterians had proclaimed Charles I's son as King Charles II, and in 1650 allied with him in the shape of a Solemn League and Covenant. With Ireland now subdued, Cromwell felt

Battle of Dunbar

"Praise the Lord, all ye nations!" Oliver Cromwell led his men in the singing of the 117th Psalm before the Battle of Dunbar in 1654. Most historians have ascribed to Cromwell's generalship the fact that his Ironsides went on to win against overwhelming odds.

compelled to invade Scotland. The Scots' army, led by the Earl of Leven, dug in around Edinburgh and stopped Cromwell and his New Model Army in their tracks. Cromwell's ragged retreat to Dunbar almost became a rout before he managed to regroup his forces. His Scots pursuers allowed him to tempt them down from the high ground, on which they would have been impregnable, after which he outflanked them to secure an improbable triumph.

An uncomfortable union

Victory against the odds at Dunbar convinced Cromwell (yet again) that God was on his side. Many Scots were becoming unhappy about their alliance with a king whose beliefs and principles they distrusted. But they were still determined to resist the English invader. Yet Cromwell prevailed, and Scotland was effectively conquered. A face-saving show of free union was put on: leading officers and Presbyterian nobles were scapegoated so ordinary Scots could be said to have been misled. Their lands confiscated, they were sent into slavery in Barbados and America. Scots members

were welcomed into the now weakened English Parliament. Meanwhile, those of Ireland's Catholics not already transported to Barbados and other Caribbean islands—more than 50,000 in all—were told by Cromwell that they could go "to Hell or Connaught." Under the punitive terms of the Act of Settlement of 1652, some 50 percent of the Irish adult male population was at least technically living under a death sentence. Catholic landowners, and a few Protestants deemed disloyal, lost their lands and were granted smaller leases in western Ireland. In

the newly confiscated lands, a sort of informal plantation policy was carried out, with parcels handed to retiring veterans of the New Model Army. Some of these were sold on to speculators. Ironically, of the 10,000 or so who stayed, many adopted the customs of the country, either they or their descendants eventually converting to Catholicism.

Cromwell currency

The only individual other than a reigning monarch to appear on a British coin, Cromwell wears the laurel wreath of the Roman emperor on this English shilling.

‹‹ BEFORE

Britain had survived without a monarchy for a decade since the reign of Charles I was cut short in 1649.

DEATH OF THE KING
Charles I's quarrels with his Parliament had ended with his execution ‹‹ **170–171**. His son, who had fought with him in the Civil War, led a Scottish army into England in 1650, with the intent of bringing about his own restoration of the Stuart monarchy. This **invasion was beaten back**, and Cromwell defeated the Scots at the Battle of Dunbar ‹‹ **168–169**. Charles II fled to France and remained in exile.

COLLAPSE OF THE PROTECTORATE
Cromwell's Commonwealth ended up offering all the rigidity of the most absolutist Stuart rule with none of the fun ‹‹ **172–173**. He died in 1658 and bequeathed the Protectorate to son Richard. His father had **governed through fear**, and when he was unable to inspire that, his authority quickly crumbled. "Tumbledown Dick" was deposed within two years.

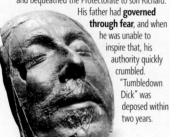

CROMWELL'S DEATH MASK

The Restoration

Rejoicing greeted the Restoration of the monarchy in 1660 as the atmosphere of the Commonwealth had become oppressive. However, moralists deplored the moral license liberation brought by the return of fun and fashion and the mood darkened as Charles II seemed to revert to absolutist Stuart type.

General John Lambert moved to fill the vacuum left by Richard Cromwell's collapse, attempting a second New Model Army coup. General George Monck rose in resistance: he had served both the Royalist and Commonwealth causes. Now, however, he openly courted the exiled King.

It was probably at his suggestion that on April 4, 1660, Charles made the Declaration of Breda. It offered an amnesty to his and his father's old enemies (the "regicides" excepted). Charles undertook to be guided by Parliament if restored, implicitly waiving any claim to a divine right to rule. Under Monck's protection, those MPs expelled in Pride's Purge of 1648 (see p.169) were recalled. This Convention Parliament invited Charles II back to take up his throne.

The monarchy restored
The end of the Interregnum (period between monarchs) came on May 8. Cheering crowds greeted the restored King when he arrived in London on May 28. The Convention Parliament passed the Indemnity and Oblivion Act, delivering on Charles' promise of forgiveness, before its replacement by an elected (though overwhelmingly Royalist) Cavalier Parliament. This rolled back resented Commonwealth reforms, reinstating maypoles, mince pies, and other festive treats. Charles wanted to restore popular celebrations.

Reign of revelry
Charles II was notorious for his mistresses: Nell Gwynn, Barbara Villiers, and Molly Davis were only the most famous. Puritan sobriety was banished—at least at court and in fashionable London, where men and women vied to outdo one another in flamboyance and flair. The moral tone was free and easy: the stereotypical Restoration rake was by no means mythical, and was represented not only by the King but by other brilliant libertines, such as George Villiers and John Wilmot, Earl of Rochester. The reopened theaters offered much raunchier fare than had ever been seen before on the English stage.

13 The number of the regicides— signatories of Charles I's death-warrant—who were executed. Three more, including Cromwell, were already dead but were exhumed and "executed," their half-decomposed corpses hanged, drawn, and quartered.

For the first time, women's roles were played by actresses rather than boys in drag. Playwright Aphra Behn became England's first known professional woman writer.

Taking liberties
Meanwhile, however, Charles was quietly clawing back some of the religious freedoms he had promised, introducing measures restricting the freedoms of nonconformist Protestants. Charles was eager to boost England's overseas trade, but this brought

Return of the monarch
Charles rides through London on the eve of his coronation in 1661. The Restoration of the monarchy was a restoration of pomp and splendor; a dash of much-craved color for a country sunk in drabness.

The Merry Monarch
They called him the "Merry Monarch," but the glint in his eye was not just of lust. Charles had a steely side, and the absolutist inclinations of his Stuart forebears.

England into conflict with the Dutch—hence the Second Anglo-Dutch War, 1665–1667 (see p.179). However, there were fears that Charles was too outward-looking. His marriage to the Portuguese (and Catholic) Catherine of Braganza hardly helped.

A secret treaty
Charles went too far for Parliament when he made his Declaration of Indulgence in 1672, offering religious toleration to Nonconformists. Parliament was furious, guessing that his real aim was to ease the situation for Catholics.

They would have been more enraged still had they been aware of the secret treaty Charles had made with Louis XIV at Dover in 1670, stating his long-term intention of embracing Catholicism and reestablishing it as state religion. He also committed himself to an alliance with France against the Dutch Republic in return for lavish payments.

Charles went to war without involving Parliament, but the Third Anglo-Dutch War proved far more expensive than anticipated. Louis' grants did not begin to cover the costs; the Dutch refused to be defeated, and Charles had to recall Parliament to introduce new taxes. They refused.

Anxiety became hysteria when news broke of the King's brother James's conversion to Catholicism. Charles's officially stated disapproval scarcely mattered. Given his lack of legitimate children, his crown would go to James. In 1679, 1680, and 1681, MPs brought in an Exclusion Bill to cut James out of the succession, but Charles dissolved Parliament before it could be passed.

> **" ...** such a Restoration **was never seen** in the mention of any history, ancient or modern."
>
> DIARIST JOHN EVELYN, 1660

Rebirth of theater
The Cavalier aesthetic was flamboyantly elegant, witty, and risqué. All these qualities were on show in the comedies of William Wycherley, John Vanbrugh, Aphra Behn, George Farquhar, William Congreve, and others.

AFTER »

Charles had been welcomed back on to the throne, but his death was disquieting—not because he would be missed—but once again because of familiar anxieties that a Stuart king was taking the country back to Catholic absolutism.

THE POPISH PLOT
Such anxieties stalked the latter part of Charles' reign. The supposed **Popish Plot of 1679** might have been a hoax got up by the arch-Protestant **mischief-maker Titus Oates**, but it had been believed (and 15 innocent priests and lay-Catholics executed) because it corresponded to existing fears.

FEAR OF CATHOLICISM
Fear of a Catholic monarch loomed so large in the reign of James II that his Protestant subjects felt they had to oust him in the **Glorious Revolution** of 1688 **188–189** ». This fear was to return in 1715 and 1745 **202–203** » **TITUS OATES**

Commerce and War

Trade and conflict had been seen as mutually exclusive, but the world was entering a new and more dangerous age. Whatever else divided them, the Commonwealth and Restoration governments of England shared a conviction that commerce was something worth fighting for.

BEFORE

Trade had always been important to Britain. Since the Tudor period the world had expanded, offering new resources and new markets to exploit.

OVERSEAS TRADE

In Tudor times, **the wool trade** with the Continent brought great prosperity **« 142–143**. During Elizabeth I's reign England's navigators began to travel further afield **« 146–147**. Even then, serious colonial expansion had to wait until James I's reign **« 162–163**. In 1623, 20 English merchants were **massacred by Dutch traders** in Amboyna, Indonesia, in conflict over the trade of spices.

AMBOYNA MASSACRE

The Commonwealth government under Oliver Cromwell (see pp.172–173) worked hard to build its naval power. Distinguished for their contributions to the land campaigns during the Civil War, George Monck and Robert Blake became preeminent as "Generals at Sea."

At stake was not only England's defense, but its commercial interests: trade was key for a small nation with big aspirations. Naval power was needed to safeguard trade with existing colonies and to secure new ones. In the mercantilist thinking of the time, it was crucial for a country to take the biggest share it could of what was assumed to be a finite international market.

Competitors were kept at bay by obstructionist regulation and tariffs.

To protect a merchant fleet recovering after the Civil War, the Navigation Act (1651) stipulated that imports to England be brought direct, without the involvement of foreign shipping.

Difficulties with the Dutch

The Dutch knew that this legislation was aimed at them, as northern Europe's leading traders. After a

Michiel de Ruyter

The Dutch admiral scored major victories against the English, including the Medway Raid. Personally unassuming, his daring was that of the consummate sailor who had served half a century at sea.

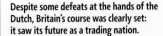

Despite some defeats at the hands of the Dutch, Britain's course was clearly set: it saw its future as a trading nation.

NEW ECONOMIC IDEAS
Britain's role as a trading nation was given impetus by the introduction of **new financial mechanisms** in the early 18th century **210–211 »**. Capitalism was becoming not just a way of doing things, but an article of faith. The **advent of modern economics** was heralded by the work of Adam Smith and other **thinkers of the Scottish Enlightenment 224–225 »**. The Industrial Revolution gave entrepreneurs the chance to put their theories into practice **232–233 »**. In the decades that followed, Britain broke new ground—an economic experiment on a massive scale.

A FREE MARKET
When Britain took action to **end the international slave** trade in the early 19th century, the freedom of the market loomed as large as the liberation of men and women. The campaign by caring members of the public also made a difference to the outcome **234–235 »**. The same contradiction would be seen in the **aggressive promotion** of "free trade" alongside widespread support for the **regulation of working conditions** in the factories and mines **268–269 »**.

Attack on the Medway
England was still dazed from the shock of the Great Plague and Fire of London when, on June 9, 1667, during the Second Anglo-Dutch war, Dutch ships calmly sailed into Chatham and destroyed the English fleet.

chance encounter at Goodwin Sands on May 19, 1652, flared into fighting, the advantage during this First Anglo–Dutch war seesawed back and forth. The shock of several defeats was salutary. Although England's navy triumphed at Portland in March 1653, the shipbuilding program was intensified and Blake's new "Instructions" for war at sea were issued in response to failures in English tactics there. Rather than engaging in a free-for-all, ships filed past the enemy in a "line," maximizing the impact of their cannonades. At the Battle of the Gabbard in 1653, the Dutch were forced back and besieged, but the English retired exhausted and the war ended inconclusively.

Hostilities restored
Charles II's England felt the same commercial imperatives as the Commonwealth had. Anti-Dutch fever was stoked by the great trading companies. Charles's younger brother James, Duke of York, was involved with the Royal Adventurers—in 1672 renamed the Royal African Company. The slave trade was growing in importance, as prisoners-of-war and indentured labor were replaced by Africans, and Dutch trading posts in West Africa and the Caribbean coveted.

In 1663, the Duke of York sent a fleet to Guinea; a separate expedition took the New Netherlands (now the northeastern US). The Dutch admiral Michiel de Ruyter quickly took back the African colonies, before heading west to attack the English in America. Open war erupted in 1665, the Dutch suffering a shock defeat at Lowestoft that June, but turning the tables a year later in the Four Days' Battle off the

> £1,300,000 **The amount of the Crown debt** reneged upon by Charles II in the "Great Stop of the Exchequer," 1672, to enable him to finance the Third Anglo–Dutch War.

Dutch East India Company insignia
Formed in 1602, the Dutch East India Company became Britain's most powerful trading competitor in Asia during the 17th century.

coast of Kent. De Ruyter followed through with his daring Medway Raid. England was brought to terms: under the Peace of Breda, it received the former New Netherlands as New England (New Amsterdam was named New York in James's honor) but had to climb down over its Navigation Act.

Third time lucky?
Neither the Netherlands nor England wanted another war. But a secret treaty with Louis XIV tied Charles II into mounting Franco–Dutch tensions. The navy's role in the Third Anglo–Dutch War (1672–1674) was initially just as seaborne back-up for a French land invasion. The war at sea became central when Louis' army was thwarted by Dutch defenders, who opened their

dykes to flood the countryside. The English were spared defeat at Solebay (June 1672) by a sudden change in the wind, but divisions within the French navy led to reversals at the Schooneveld and then Texel, and Charles II had to sue for peace.

The **Great Fire** of **London**

This great conflagration decimated 80 percent of the City of London, destroying familiar landmarks. New buildings would fill the gaps, including Christopher Wren's St. Paul's Cathedral— transforming the skyline, and establishing new building patterns and standards that helped to create modern London.

On September 5, 1666, famous diarist Samuel Pepys climbed the tower of All Hallows Church, close by his home in Seething Lane, and beheld a terrifying sight: raging fire as far as he could see. It seems the fire first sparked into life in the small hours of Sunday, September 2 at Thomas Faryner's bakery in Pudding Lane, near London Bridge. By the following day, it had advanced west and north. King Charles II tasked his brother, the Duke of York, with controlling the fire-fighting operation—there was no true fire service at this time.

The summer had been hot and dry, the level of the Thames River was low, and a brutal wind blew from the east. Closely packed buildings, many largely timber, easily caught fire. For days, the flames ripped down narrow, twisting streets and through wooden warehouses stuffed with flammables such as oil, brandy, and pitch.

Buildings were pulled down and blown up with gunpowder to provide windbreaks. On September 4, old St. Paul's was engulfed and its lead roof melted "down the streets in a stream,"

according to diarist John Evelyn. Many of London's hysterical citizens suspected arson. Some foreigners were lynched and the Spanish ambassador gave refuge to others. The fire was finally extinguished on September 6. The next year, it was officially declared an accident caused by the hand of God, heat, and wind.

A new city

After the disaster, Christopher Wren, John Evelyn, and Robert Hooke presented the King with ambitious rebuilding plans. Wren wanted to raise a magnificent Renaissance city with wide streets, but his ideas were deemed too costly and impractical. The new city arose slowly on the old plan, with some wider streets, new sewers, and (for the first time) sidewalks. Buildings were made of brick rather than wood.

Wren's St. Paul's Cathedral, completed in 1711, became one of the world's most-admired buildings. Along with his jointly designed monument to the fire, and a number of satellite churches, he helped shape the City's new profile and create an iconic skyline.

> **" The churches, houses,** and all on fire and flaming at once; and **a horrid noise** the flames made, and the **cracking of houses** at their ruins."

SAMUEL PEPYS'S DIARY, 1666

The fire by night
This painting, called *The Great Fire of London in 1666,* was created by 17th-century Dutch maritime artist Lieve Verschuier (c. 1630–1686). Many contemporary paintings depicted the event, providing historians with an important strand of evidence for what happened

Inquiring Minds

A great change took place in scientific thinking in the 17th century. New institutions such as the Royal Society and the Greenwich Observatory, and scholars including Newton and Hooke, helped push scientific inquiry toward the rational and methodical. Modern science was born.

Flamsteed House
Named after Charles II's first Astronomer Royal and designed by Sir Christopher Wren, Flamsteed House was the original Observatory building at Greenwich, London.

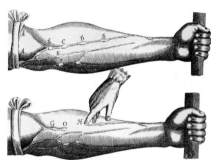

17th-century blood circulation experiment
The milestone discovery by William Harvey (1578–1657) that blood circulated around the body drew on observation, reasoning, and experimentation.

The 17th century was an exciting time for British science. It aroused public interest and saw many groundbreaking demonstrations. Wealthy gentlemen made a hobby of it. New ideas spread rapidly via the universities, scientific organizations, and coffeehouses, and the rising tide of printed matter. Measuring things, and developing instruments to do so, was central to 17th-century science and London grew into a major center for scientific instruments.

British statesman and philosopher Sir Francis Bacon (1561–1626) was a pivotal figure. He valued observation, experience, and experimentation over the Aristotelian methodology of making deductions from assumptions (see pp.152–153). Another English philosopher who advocated reasoned experimentation was John Locke (1632–1704).

Scientific laws

The Baconian school asserted that science should establish rules and laws by a thorough cataloging of phenomena, including variations and negative examples. Suggestions arising from this process should be tested via experiments. Bacon believed that science should have practical applications, for "the relief of man's estate."

British scientists were influenced by many European developments. German mathematician and astronomer Johannes Kepler (1571–1630) devised his laws of planetary motion around 1610. Italian astronomer and physicist Galileo Galilei (1564–1642) employed quantitative experiments and systematic analysis, and produced work on falling bodies and on the telescope, which he also used to study the heavens. French thinker and scientist Descartes (1596–1650)

"Mathematical Demonstrations ... are **the only Truths.**"

CHRISTOPHER WREN, 1657

Light from an oil lamp (left) passed through this glass and diffused and projected onto the specimen.

Compound microscope
This is a replica of Robert Hooke's compound microscope. Hooke's *Micrographia* (1665) was the first important work in its field, detailing the many observations and discoveries of his microscopy.

◀◀ BEFORE

The roots of scientific rationalism, with its stress on "method" can be found in different places, from the Renaissance humanists to the Reformation.

REJECTING THE OLD

The new scientific revolution could be said to have grown from the **rejection of classical and medieval ideas** by European Renaissance humanists **◀◀ 152–153**. Other factors include the growth of vernacular languages **◀◀ 110–111**, and the rise of Protestantism. Prior to the Protestant Reformation **◀◀ 136–137**, Rome was the **ultimate authority** in matters concerned with religion, and scientific matters seen to relate to religion. When Luther questioned this, he opened the field up to other systems of thought.

MAPS AND MATHEMATICS

Another strong influence leading into the 17th century was exploration. The **expansion of exploration** in the 16th century **◀◀ 146–147**, in which England played a major role, drove a great need to improve math and astronomy in order to devise better maps—for example, the pioneering 16th-century Mercator projection, improved significantly by English mathematician Edward Wright (c. 1558–1615). Math, essential for any meaningful scientific inquiry, made significant strides by the start of the 1600s, while interest in astronomy was aroused by events such as the appearance of the **comet of 1532**, visible for more than 100 days, which Edmund Halley later cited in his theories.

THE COMET OF 1532

Eye cup keeps the distance between eye and eyepiece correct. The eyepiece lens was at the top and the objective lens was next to the specimen. Between the two lay a field lens, which increased the field of view.

Body of wood and vellum-covered pasteboard.

competitive spats with fellow scientist Robert Hooke (1635–1703), chief curator of the fledgling society. Newton was elected society president in 1703 (until his death), from which point he dominated affairs there.

Leading scientists of the age had an astonishing array of talents. Newton became Master of the Mint (1690s), organizing the great replacement of old hammered coinage with coins with milled edges. Architect Sir Christopher Wren (1632–1723) was also a formidable mathematician and general scientist

1664 The year Robert Hooke was granted a salary for the diverse demonstrations and discussions he offered for the Royal Society. He had been made curator of experiments for the new society in 1662, but remained unsalaried while the society found its feet.

helped establish scientific method with his 1637 *Discourse on the Method* and his concept "I think therefore I am," using deduction by logic.

Royal patronage

Charles II played a major role in the British scientific revolution, backing two new crucial institutions. The Royal Society was founded in 1660 by Bacon's followers as a forum for scientific ideas, true to his belief in the importance of openly exchanging knowledge. The first of its kind in Britain, and still prestigious today, it is also the world's oldest surviving scientific body. It was given a royal

highly regarded by Newton, a founding member and president of the Royal Society (early 1680s), and an Oxford professor of astronomy. His brilliant intuition for the new experiment-based approach, and for geometry, produced such feats as St. Paul's great dome (see pp.186–187) and the span of Oxford's Sheldonian Theatre (1669)—showing his ability to fuse beauty with a sense of proportion, which expressed this new age of rationalism.

Equally diverse in talent was Robert Hooke, whose continuous talks and demonstrations across multiple fields in the Royal Society's first years produced incredibly fertile results. Hooke's roll call of breakthroughs includes introducing the term "cell" to biology and formulating a law of elasticity. He

INNOVATION
NEWTON'S LAW

Isaac Newton's gravitation law states that there is an attraction between two bodies that depends on their mass and the distance between them. He realized that something must make an apple fall downward from its tree, keep objects close to earth, and hold planets in their orbits. There would have been no exploration of space without Newton's discovery of gravity's laws. There is a famous tale that this revelation came after Newton saw an apple falling off a tree around 1665. The law is contained in *Principia* (1687), and is one of the most important contributions to the modern world.

NEWTON UNDER AN APPLE TREE IN HIS LINCOLNSHIRE BIRTHPLACE

"If I have seen further it is by **standing on the shoulders of giants**."

NEWTON, IN A LETTER TO ROBERT HOOKE, 1676

Focusing was done by moving and turning the microscope on a screw thread, rather than moving the specimen.

charter in 1661. In 1675, Charles founded the Royal Greenwich Observatory in London.

The mathematician, philosopher, and academic Sir Isaac Newton (1643–1727) dominated this era of thinking. His work included breakthroughs on gravitational pull (see right), mathematical calculus, and optical principles—he invented a pioneering reflecting telescope and showed that white light was made up of a rainbow of colors.

The spirit of his age

Newton was a key figure in early Royal Society circles. A man of difficult temperament, he is famed for his

also fitted in acting as a chief surveyor for the City's rebuilding after the fire of 1666 (pp.182–183).

Plotting the stars

Another Royal Society member, in the mold of Bacon and the practical application of science, was Edmund Halley (1656–1742). Encouraged to pursue astronomy by the Observatory's Astronomer Royal, John Flamsteed, Halley worked on planetary motion and helped Newton formulate his gravitational theories. His star catalog of 1678–1679, using observations he had taken at sea, was the first account of its kind for the southern stars. He is best known for his work on comets.

AFTER

The 17th-century scientific revolution laid foundations for the 18th-century Enlightenment and later social theories.

THE AGE OF REASON
In the Enlightenment, or Age of Reason, figures such as poet Alexander Pope (1688–1744) stressed a rational approach in all things 208–209 >>, 224–225 >>.

SOCIAL SCIENCES
Seventeenth-century scientific breakthroughs and philosophical thought showed the **potential of the human mind** and human progress. This anticipated the work of

JOHN STUART MILL

figures such as Jeremy Bentham (1748–1832) and John Stuart Mill (1806–1873), with their rigorous social theories of Utilitarianism 282–283 >>.

St. Paul's Cathedral
St. Paul's Cathedral, completed in the early 1700s, is the masterpiece of architect Sir Christopher Wren. Its dome is one of the largest in the world and is made up of three layers—the inner dome, the brick cone, and the outer dome or "skin." The inner dome measures 103 ft (31 m) across and 225 ft (69 m) in height. The murals inside the dome, showing the life of St. Paul, are by the English painter Sir James Thornhill.

The **Glorious Revolution**

The 17th century had already seen one king killed by order of "the people" and the country plunged into bloody civil war. When a second Stuart monarch, James II, seemed determined to shape the nation to his despotic will and dictate its religious beliefs, his throne was soon under threat.

BEFORE

Tensions between the monarchy and those who considered themselves the representatives of the country were nothing new.

THE MONARCHY AND THE PEOPLE
Magna Carta curtailed the power of the monarchy, although it did not benefit the people as a whole **‹‹ 86–87**. The **Tudors redressed the balance**, aiming to centralize power **‹‹ 132–133**. James I viewed the matter in philosophical, even theological terms, presenting learned arguments for the **divine right of kings** to rule **‹‹ 158–159**. His son, Charles I, was prepared to go to war with his Parliamentary opponents **‹‹ 170–171** over this theory, and to defy them to the death when he was defeated. Parliament's victory was a mixed blessing: it was hard to see how the cause of

CHARLES I AS CHRISTIAN MARTYR

democratic representation or accountability was advanced by the **dictatorship** into which the Commonwealth quickly descended **‹‹ 172–173**. Charles II's **Restoration was welcomed**, but the King's absolutist inclinations soon became evident **‹‹ 176–177**.

ROYAL RELIGION
Charles II's apparent **leanings toward Catholicism** also caused tension between the monarchy and the people, while his younger brother, James II, **was an avowed Catholic ‹‹ 177**. In the eyes of English Protestants, that (clearly hierarchical) faith was the natural accompaniment to Stuart absolutism. It was not one they wanted anything to do with.

William III landing at Torbay
Seen in this painting from c.1680 as a heroic deliverer, many regarded William as a usurper, and James II's ousting as the most cynical of coups.

The Duke of York was a controversial figure even before he became King James II: his conversion to Catholicism upset many; his marriage to Mary of Modena made matters worse. The object of Exclusion Bills (see p.177) and assassination plots, he had no illusions as to his popularity. Yet he was unflappable in his arrogance or, as he saw it, his consciousness of his divine right as king.

Some later historians have tended to see James as an inadequate, cowardly, and weak man. In fact, he was courageous and experienced in battle.

> **7** The number of nobles— the "Immortal Seven"—who democratically decided that William of Orange should occupy the British throne.

During his French exile, he saw front line service against the Fronde—an uprising of disenchanted nobles in the 1650s.

Monmouth's folly

Resistance to James II was quick in coming. The Duke of Monmouth was Charles II's illegitimate son and James's nephew. However, he was also a Protestant and hoped to take the throne. Landing in Lyme Regis with a small force in June 1685, he marched inland through a strongly Protestant region, recruiting supporters at a series of pretend coronations. Failing to take Bristol, he tried Bath before moving on to Warminster. An attempt to open a second front in Scotland having failed, Monmouth's men fell back before being defeated at Sedgemoor on July 6. Judge Jeffreys' Bloody Assizes followed: more than 300 rebels were executed.

James's decision to raise a standing army, rather than recruiting soldiers ad hoc, sent out the message that he was at war with his subjects. His Declaration of Indulgence toward Catholics caused outrage in 1687 and the birth of a son, and legal successor, provoked panic.

By invitation

A group of Protestant nobles, already in negotiation with William of Orange, Stadtholder (the chief of state) of the Dutch Republic, became even more

eager for him to depose James and reign as William III. His wife, Mary (James II's daughter), had the better claim, but William wanted to be more than Prince Consort.

His first invasion fleet was dispersed by winds in October 1688; he later landed at Torbay. James was unfazed until he found his officers defecting in droves. He fled for France, but was captured. William turned a blind eye while they escaped, so James could not become a focus for royalist unrest.

A Convention Parliament in January 1689 issued a Declaration of Rights, asserting that James's attempt to flee amounted to abdication and branding his actions as king unconstitutional. William III and Mary II were (unusually) made joint corulers in his place.

Draft for democracy

The Declaration of Rights was primarily a stick to beat James II with. As formalized in December 1689 as the Bill of Rights, however, it became the blueprint for a constitutional monarchy. The King and Queen would be held in the highest respect as heads of state, but would not be allowed to disregard the wishes of the people's parliamentary representatives.

Mary and William
Shown here enthroned in heaven, William and Mary reigned over England together. At Mary's insistence, theirs was a partnership of equals.

AFTER

James's overthrow was first described as a Glorious Revolution in 1689, and since then, its centrality to the modern British identity has never been in doubt.

ELECTRESS SOPHIA OF HANOVER

LAST OF THE STUART KINGS
The Stuarts, unsurprisingly, believed that an outrageous injustice had prevailed. James fought unsuccessfully to win back his throne **196–197 ››**. William's **failure to leave a dynasty** merely prompted Parliament to seek out another ruler, Sophia, Electress of Hanover (granddaughter of James I), whose successors were to reign into the 19th century **200–201 ››**.

JACOBITE SUPPORT
Stuart supporters—known as Jacobites from *Jacobus*, the Latin form of James—continued to keep faith, in Scotland especially. **A number of unsuccessful uprisings** were staged in the decades that followed **202–203 ››**.

NO REVOLUTION
The French Revolution of 1789 **did not spark a similar overthrow** of the British state **236–237 ››**. Possibly the **constitutional upheavals of 1688** and after had satisfied the desire for moderate democratic change in Britain.

Birth of James Francis Edward Stuart
In this letter of June 24, 1688, Louis XIV of France congratulates James II's wife Mary of Modena on her son's birth. "James III" was seen by Stuart supporters as rightful king of England.

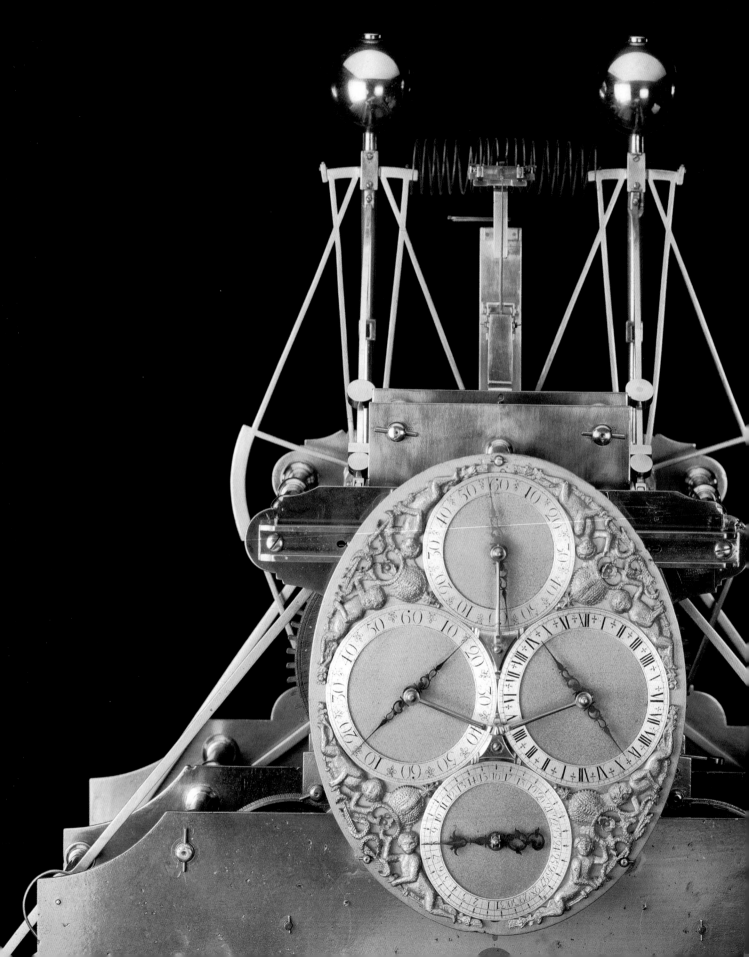

4

RISE OF POWER
1688–1815

As England and Wales united with Scotland, the British realm grew into a powerful trading nation that expanded financially and commercially. It acquired new territories, markets, and sources of raw materials, while inaugurating the Industrial Revolution and eventually defeating the mighty French foe.

Marine timekeeper
In 1735, English clockmaker John Harrison unveiled a precision timekeeper that was unaffected by the motion of a ship; it was the first step in his successful bid to solve the problem of determining longitude at sea.

William and Mary
Mary looks on as her husband, William of Orange, receives the royal crown of England from the assembled lords. The crowning of the joint monarchs was the culminating moment of the Glorious Revolution of 1688.

A British kingdom

The writer Daniel Defoe had a day at the races in 1724, on Epsom Downs, Surrey, where the famous Derby would be run from 1780 onward. Even then, the spectacle was something to comment upon. Defoe was exhilarated by the sight of so many carriages, all the smartly turned-out gentlemen, the ladies in their finery, and, of course, "the racers flying over the course as if either they touched not, or felt not the ground they run upon." Summoning up all of his poetic powers to find an image glorious enough to do justice to the occasion, he wrote: "I think no sight, except that of a victorious army, under the command of a Protestant king of Great Britain could exceed it."

For England, Wales, and Scotland now constituted a collective kingdom of Britain, under a Protestant Hanoverian monarchy. (Ireland was a kingdom of its own, although under the same monarchy as Britain.) And to the British, religious allegiance had become an inseparable aspect of political loyalty. To be patriotic was to be Protestant: it was that simple.

Struggle to unite

Yet it had by no means been a straightforward process reaching this point of unity, and it had assuredly not been easy. If the Glorious Revolution of 1688, in overthrowing the Stuart king James II, had resolved the opposition between the monarchy and the representatives of the people which had so dominated the Tudor and Stuart period, it had brought new and bitter conflicts in its wake.

To some extent, the early tumults were about clearing up unfinished business from the period before. James II, a Roman Catholic, still had claims on the Crown, and still had hopes of returning to power. Yet his defeat in the early 1690s was a defeat also for Catholic Ireland, as well as for like-minded groups in Scotland. Scotland, however, remained the more immediate threat for the new

Hanoverian line in the 18th century, but, again, victories over Stuart pretenders in Scotland in 1715 and 1746 were triumphs for both the state of Britain and for Protestantism.

Empire and industry

The struggle to sort out its own domestic settlement was only the start for the new British state. It had to establish a position for itself, both in Europe and in the wider world. It also had to find a suitable function, and Britain saw its future as that of a major trading nation.

The building of the financial structures that would make this possible from 1694 onward went in parallel with the acquisition of numerous overseas possessions. These lands were to be both sources of raw materials and potential markets for the future. Britain met an early setback in its loss of the American colonies in 1783, but there was consolation to be had in the territorial gains which continued to be made in India.

Britain was extending its horizons in other ways as well. In Scotland, in particular, writers and thinkers were coming to a new understanding of the world, in what became known as the Scottish Enlightenment. Meanwhile, more literal explorations were taking place, as great navigators such as James Cook and Matthew Flinders opened up the exotic lands of the Pacific and Oceania. Just as remarkable in their way also were the new developments taking place in such apparently mundane spheres as farming and industrial manufacture. A revolution swept British agriculture in the 18th century. This in turn, by freeing up resources for the towns, did much to make possible the extraordinary explosion of economic and technological creativity which we now think of as the Industrial Revolution.

When real revolution came in France in 1789, a constitutionally stable Britain proved more-or-less immune to its effects, and strong enough to fight off the menace of a marauding Napoleon Bonaparte as the 19th century began.

Battle of Waterloo, 1815
The narrow victory of the Duke of Wellington's British-led army over Napoleon Bonaparte at the Battle of Waterloo in 1815 left Britain as the dominant power in Europe. For Britain, it also heralded a lengthy era of peace and prosperity.

RISE OF POWER
1688–1815

1688–1708	1709–1738	1739–1767

SEPTEMBER 1688
Britain and its partners in the Grand Alliance (or League of Augsburg) go to war with France. The hostilities will not end until 1697.

MARCH 1689
James II begins his fight back, landing with supporters at Kinsale, Ireland.

FEBRUARY 1692
Government-supporting Campbells massacre the MacDonalds at Glencoe, in the Scottish Highlands. More than 70 die.

1701
Jethro Tull invents his horse-drawn seed drill.

1709
Abraham Darby builds the first blast furnace that uses coke for manufacturing pig-iron.

SEPTEMBER 1709
The Duke of Marlborough prevails at the Battle of Malplaquet, but at considerable cost.

APRIL 1721
Robert Walpole becomes Britain's first prime minister—though this title does not yet exist.

JUNE 1727
George II succeeds his father on the throne.

⌄ King George II

JULY 1690
The English and Dutch fleets are badly beaten by the French at the Battle of Beachy Head.

MAY 1701
The War of the Spanish Succession starts. Britain and its old Grand Alliance partners take on France.

JUNE 1701
Act of Settlement states that after William's successor, Anne, dies, Sophia, Electress of Saxony, will be next in line.

⌄ Battle of the Boyne

APRIL 1713
Treaty of Utrecht brings the War of the Spanish Succession to a close.

AUGUST 1714
Queen Anne dies and, as the Electress Sophia had died a short while before, her son becomes King George I of Britain.

OCTOBER 1715
A Jacobite rising fails.

DECEMBER 1718
Britain joins the Dutch Republic, France, and Austria in the War of the Quadruple Alliance against Spain.

⌃ Bonnie Prince Charlie with Flora MacDonald

APRIL 1739
John Wesley begins his open-air Methodist mission at a meeting outside Bristol.

OCTOBER 1739
The so-called War of Jenkins' Ear begins between Britain and Spain.

SEPTEMBER 1740
George Anson sets out on his four-year circumnavigation of the globe.

DECEMBER 1740
Hostilities become part of a wider War of the Austrian Succession, which will go on until 1748.

APRIL 1746
Jacobite hopes for Bonnie Prince Charlie are effectively ended at Culloden.

APRIL 1756
The Seven Years' War gets under way. This time Britain is allied with Prussia, Portugal, and others against France, its ally in the recent war.

1757
The Sankey Canal, near Warrington, is opened.

OCTOBER 1760
George II dies, to be succeeded by his grandson, George III. Difficulties with the American colonies cast a shadow over the early years of his reign.

JULY 1690
William III wins his pivotal victory at the Battle of the Boyne. James flees soon after, leaving his followers in disarray.

MARCH 1702
William III dies, to be succeeded by his sister-in-law and cousin, Queen Anne.

AUGUST 1704
John Churchill, Duke of Marlborough, wins a dazzling victory at the Battle of Blenheim.

⌄ Duke of Marlborough at the Battle of Blenheim

1733
John Kay's Flying Shuttle enhances the productivity of the hand-operated loom.

1735
John Harrison invents the first chronometer.

« Harrison's H4 chronometer of 1759

AUGUST 1745
Prince Charles Edward Stuart (the "Young Pretender" of the Jacobites) lands in Scotland. He will win a stirring victory at Prestonpans, east of Edinburgh, a few weeks later.

⌄ Parliament, 17th century

1764
James Hargreaves' Spinning Jenny enables one person to operate multiple spinning spools.

APRIL 1764
Parliament passes the Sugar Act: the first of a series of measures designed to raise revenues by levying taxes on the American colonists.

MAY 1707
England and Wales and Scotland become the Kingdom of Great Britain under the Act of Union.

MARCH 1708
"Old Pretender" James Stuart tries to take the throne, but the Royal Navy head off his French fleet at the Firth of Forth.

JUNE 1719
An abortive Jacobite rising is quickly quashed at the Battle of Glen Shiel in the Scottish Highlands.

AUGUST 1720
Shares in the South Sea Company reach their peak price and the "bubble" bursts.

1736
Increased tax on gin causes rioting on the streets of London. The tax is reduced, then removed altogether in 1742.

> "It is ridiculous to imagine, that **the friendship of nations**, whether kind or barbarous, can be gained and kept but **by kind treatment**."
>
> DR. JOHNSON, INTRODUCTION TO *THE POLITICAL STATE OF GREAT BRITAIN*, 1756

1768–1776

AUGUST 1768
Captain Cook sets out on his first voyage to the Pacific.

1769
Thomas Newcomen's Atmospheric Engine, as improved by James Watt, revolutionizes mining, allowing deep workings to be pumped free of water.

MARCH 1770
British soldiers kill five protesters against "taxation without representation" in the Boston Massacre.

JANUARY 1772
Granville Sharp wins a court case on behalf of escaped American slave James Somersett.

JULY 1772
Captain Cook's second voyage—in search of a mysterious "Southern Continent"—begins.

DECEMBER 1773
The Boston Tea Party: angry colonists throw cargoes of tea into the city's harbor.

SEPTEMBER 1774
First Continental Congress of American colonies begins in Philadelphia.

1775
Richard Arkwright's Spinning Frame improves on the Spinning Jenny (1764), yielding stronger yarns and opening the way to mass production of textiles.

APRIL 1775
Fighting breaks out between colonists and the British at the battles of Lexington and Concord, both in Massachusetts. In the weeks that follow, the British are besieged in Boston.

JUNE 1775
British soldiers win the Battle of Bunker Hill, just outside Boston, but fail to lift the siege upon the city.

DECEMBER 1775
American colonists are badly defeated at Quebec.

❯ A sextant

1776
Adam Smith's *An Inquiry into the Nature and Causes of the Wealth of Nations* is published.

❯ A coin to commemorate Adam Smith

1776–1792

JULY 1776
The Declaration of Independence is approved by the Continental Congress.

JULY 1776
Cook's third voyage to the Pacific begins. It will take him via Hawaii to western coasts of North America.

DECEMBER 1776
George Washington crosses the Delaware River on the eve of the Battle of Trenton—an important American victory.

FEBRUARY 1779
Stopping in Hawaii on his homeward voyage, Captain Cook is killed in a fracas with islanders.

JUNE 1780
The army has to be called out to deal with the Gordon Riots—an outbreak of anti-Catholic violence in London.

AUGUST 1780
Cornwallis defeats the Southern Continental Army at Camden, South Carolina.

⌃ William Pitt at Westminster

OCTOBER 1781
General Cornwallis is forced to surrender after the Siege of Yorktown.

DECEMBER 1783
William Pitt the Younger becomes Britain's youngest-ever prime minister, at 24.

MAY 1787
The Society for the Abolition of the Slave Trade is established at a Quaker meeting in London.

❯ Anti-slavery poster

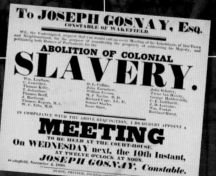

NOVEMBER 1790
Edmund Burke's *Reflections on the Revolution in France* is published. Thomas Paine tried to refute his arguments in his *Rights of Man* the following year.

APRIL 1791
William Wilberforce introduces his first (and unsuccessful) anti-slavery bill in Parliament.

1793–1815

FEBRUARY 1793
Revolutionary France declares war on Britain, which joins the First Coalition.

AUGUST 1793
A Royal Charter is granted to the Board of Agriculture to promote best, most modern practice in British farming.

OCTOBER 1795
An angry mob attacks the King's coach as it takes him to the State Opening of Parliament.

APRIL 1797
Mutiny by sailors of the Royal Navy at Spithead. A second mutiny started at the Nore a few weeks later.

MAY 1798
United Irishman's rebellion breaks out, beginning with an attack on Kildare.

OCTOBER 1805
Nelson wins the Battle of Trafalgar, but dies in the hour of victory.

JANUARY 1809
General John Moore dies during unsuccessful defense of La Coruña, Spain, during the Peninsular War.

JUNE 1798
Irish rebels are crushingly defeated at Vinegar Hill, County Wexford.

AUGUST 1798
Nelson defeats the French fleet at Aboukir Bay in the Battle of the Nile.

DECEMBER 1798
William Pitt the Younger introduces Britain's first-ever income tax.

❯ Cartoon protesting the new income tax

MAY 1811
Wellington defeats the French at Grijó, driving them out of Portugal.

JUNE 1815
Wellington's British army and its allies defeat Napoleon once and for all at Waterloo.

BEFORE

The Glorious Revolution of 1689 left unfinished business to be sorted out.

SCOTTISH RESENTMENT
England may have been happy that it had made Protestant succession sacrosanct, but the other nations did not share the same view. Most Scots approved of England's **efforts at ensuring a Protestant monarchy**, but many were uneasy at England's unquestioning assumption that it could take the lead. **Resentment of English arrogance** had been bred into the Scots for centuries—and certainly since the days of the Independence Wars **≪ 92–93**. Moreover, there were still some Scots who had not been happy to see James II overthrown. They wanted to see the **restoration of the Stuarts**—originally a Scottish dynasty **≪ 158–159**.

IRISH ANGER
Ireland, after fighting England for years, had lost its elite to the Flight of the Earls **≪ 156–157**, only to experience **cruel repression under Oliver Cromwell ≪ 174–175**. The view that the Stuarts stood for despotism and their enemies for freedom struck no chord with those who had suffered so much at Protestant England's hands. They might have no reason to be grateful to an English king, but they neither had they any reason to rejoice when James II was toppled in the Glorious Revolution **≪ 188–189**.

Succession Wars

Scotland and Ireland became battlegrounds as rival factions fought for James II or for William III. The victory of the "Williamites" spelled an end to an immediate Stuart restoration. Protestant triumphs at Derry, Enniskillen, and the Boyne became a foundation-myth for Ulster's Unionist tradition.

The Protestant powers of Europe feared the strength and ambition of Louis XIV of France, though Catholic states such as Spain, Portugal, and Bavaria felt threatened by him as well. The Dutch were immediately threatened when, in 1688, Louis XIV's designs on the Palatinate of the Rhine became clear.

William III of England was still the Stadtholder, or "steward," of Holland. He approached Emperor Leopold I, who formed the League of Augsburg, or "Grand Alliance." The War of the Grand Alliance is also known as the Nine Years' War—though it was different from the Irish conflict of the same name (see pp.156–157).

The orange and the green
With fighting erupting in Europe, Ireland's fate could hardly have loomed large for Louis. But James II hoped for his support in a bid to recover his throne. That the deposed Stuart should

Battle of the Boyne
James II's defeat at the 1690 Battle of the Boyne ended his hopes of reclaiming his throne. William's triumph is celebrated yearly on July 12 by the Orange Order.

see Catholic Ireland as a natural staging post for a reconquest of Britain was logical enough, for many Irish had never accepted William's accession. James landed at Kinsale in the far southwest in March 1689.

A month later, James laid siege to

7,000 The number of combatants killed at the Battle of Aughrim (1691), considered to mark the final collapse of the Jacobites in Ireland. William's army lost around 3,000 men, but the Jacobites also lost crucial officers.

Derry. While the authorities in the city made plans for its surrender, a group of apprentice boys put them to shame by unilaterally locking the gates. The citizens rallied, and a few months later the Royal Navy came and relieved the city. Although Protestant irregulars in the north scored successes, William's forces became bogged down. William himself came to break the stalemate.

A French naval presence could have prevented William from aiding his forces, and a belated fleet was sent up the Channel. An ill-prepared England

Louis XIV of France
The "Sun King" had his own agenda, in which Britain's Wars of Succession were a small and incidental part.

SCOTTISH NOBLEMAN (1648–1689)

"BONNIE DUNDEE"

John Graham of Claverhouse and 1st Viscount Dundee, won fame and his nickname for his fidelity to the Stuart cause. However, in his loyalty to Charles I during his Bishops' Wars (see pp.166–167), such was the energy and ruthlessness with which he had hunted down the Covenanters (Protestant signers of Scotland's National Covenant), that he was widely remembered in the Lowlands as "Bluidy Clavers."

Duke of Marlborough
Included among the furnishings at Blenheim Palace, Oxfordshire, this tapestry shows John Churchill issuing orders at the Battle of Blenheim in 1704.

was caught out in its turn, and a hastily assembled Anglo-Dutch fleet was badly mauled at the Battle of Beachy Head on July 10, 1690.

The twelfth and after
Protestant pride was restored when William led a force to victory at the Battle of the Boyne. The engagement's anniversary on July 12 marks the climax of the Orange Order's marching season, though in fact it was fought on the first of the month according to the Julian calendar then in use. The battle was fought over a ford in the Boyne River: William's army was not only larger (with more than 35,000 men to James' 23,000) but also better trained.

James fled in panic back to France. Led by Patrick Sarsfield, the Earl of Lucan, those left behind fought on bravely. They defeated William at the First Siege of Limerick (1690), but were badly beaten at Aughrim. William's Second Siege of Limerick was successful, forcing the Jacobites to surrender. Both sides signed the Treaty of Limerick in 1691.

Scottish slaughter
In Scotland John Graham of Claverhouse, Viscount of Dundee, had stayed loyal to the Stuarts when James II (James VII in Scotland) was deposed. The rebellion of "Bonnie Dundee" (see BOX) lifted Jacobite hopes with victory at the Battle of Killiecrankie (July 1689). They were dashed again soon after by defeat at Dunkeld that August and at the Haughs of Cromdale the following year. From the first, a nasty cocktail of religious enmity and clan rivalry informed the conflict. This came to a head at Glencoe in 1692. There a group of Campbells in King William's service fell upon the MacDonalds who had taken them into their homes as guests, killing 38. Dozens more died of exposure after fleeing into the snow. The Campbells' justification was the reluctance of their hosts to make an oath of allegiance to the Protestant King—though they seem to have been as interested in settling their own old scores.

Back into battle
Britain had it all to do again in Europe: the Grand Alliance was recreated in 1701 for the War of the Spanish Succession. This time, Britain fought on the Continent, with John Churchill, the Duke of Marlborough, demonstrating his dash and flair. In 1704, he threw the French completely off their guard by marching 50,000 men from the Low Countries to the Danube in just five weeks. His victories at Blenheim on August 14, 1704, and Ramillies in May 1706 were crucial; he won again at Malplaquet in 1709.

The War of the Spanish Succession was also fought in North America. Known as Queen Anne's War, it took its name from William's successor, Anne, who reigned from 1707. It was only in 1713 that Louis XIV was defeated. France ceded to Britain its claims in the Hudson Bay territories in the Treaty of Utrecht.

> " The **action began** at a quarter past ten, and was so hot till **after eleven** that a great many old **soldiers** said they **never saw brisker work**. "

CONTEMPORARY ACCOUNT OF THE BATTLE OF THE BOYNE

AFTER ⟩⟩

A sideshow of the European conflicts of which they formed a part, the Succession Wars were crucial in the development of the modern British and Irish identities.

THE HANOVERIAN DYNASTY
It took a particular context to make a German dynasty into British kings and queens, but the Hanoverians were **quickly accepted by their subjects**. They were also accepted in Scotland once it had come together with England into a united Kingdom of Great Britain 200–201 ⟩⟩. In both countries there were those who fought on for James II's Stuart successors 202–203 ⟩⟩.

A LEGACY OF HATRED
It was in **Ireland** that the legacy was to be most bitter. The country **rose in rebellion** in 1798 238–239 ⟩⟩. It was an enduring legacy as well: Ulster's Protestant Unionists drew inspiration from "King Billy" and his victories as they made their stand against Irish independence early in the 20th century 332–333 ⟩⟩. They did so again at the time of the "Troubles" when they rejected the **nationalist aspirations** of their Catholic neighbors 378–379 ⟩⟩.

Franciae et Hiberniae Regina Fidei Defensor &c
Breve nostrum de Certiorand e Cur Cancellar
nostrorum direct vnarum quodam Retorno sive
retornatum et in filarijs ibm de Record resid
sibi Matheo Johnson Ar Clic Parliamentor

Parliamento nostro apud Westm fact et ordinat intitulat An Act for an
Actus predict cum omnibus it tangentibus Nobis in Cancellar viam sub
Magn̄ Anno Rni nri quinto Wrighte Executio huius Ẅris patet in qu
Parliamentor JUPPRIMUS etiam Stedulam premeaironatam tc
Signat et Sigillat in Cancellar vram preditam sibi retornavit in fila
Westmonaster decimo quarto die Junij Anno Domini Millesimo Se
Franr: Hibniae Regin Fidei Defensor tc Quarto Comuni omnium Duor t
inter alia Sanctum Inactitatum et Stabilitum fuit hoc sequens Statu

Most Gratious Soveraigne Whereas Articles of Uni
the Commissioners nominated on behalfe of the Kingdom of England vnder your
fast in pursuance of an Act of Parliament made in England in the third year of
vnder Your Majesties Great Seal of Scotland bearing date the Twenty seventh da
Third Session of the present Parliament of Scotland to treat of and conernin
of Scotland at Edinburgh the Sixteenth day of January in the fifth year
the said Articles of Union of the two Kingdoms had agreed to and approved
with Advice and Consent of the Estates of Parliament for Establishing the Prot
passed in the same Session of Parliament an Act Intituled Act for securing o
was appointed to be inserted in any Act ratifying the Treaty and expressly
times towing The Tenor of which Articles as Ratified and Approved of with
That the two Kingdoms of England and Scotland shall vpon th
for ever after be Vnited into one Kingdom by the Name of Great Bri
Majesty shall appoint and the Crosses of Saint George and Sa
and vsed in all Flaggs Banners and Standards and Ensigns both at Sea
Kingdome of Great Britain and of the Dominions thereto belonging
and continue to the most Excellent Princess Sophia Electoress an
vpon whom the Crown of England is setled by an Act of Parliament i
the third Intituled An Act for the further limitation of the Crown and bett

Treaty of Union
The parliaments of Edinburgh and London approved this agreement, which led to the creation of the United Kingdom of Great Britain. It began its passage through the Scottish assembly in October 1706 and was ratified by English MPs in March 1707. Scotland was entitled to have 45 members of the Commons and 16 peers in the new British Parliament.

BEFORE ‹‹

The Stuart family had started out in medieval times as stewards to the Scottish kings, but since then their ideas had become much more exalted.

RIGHT TO RULE

James VI firmly believed in his **"divine right" to rule**, and he took the same conviction into his reign as England's James I ‹‹ **158–159**. His son, Charles I, was prepared to go to war with his Parliament ‹‹ **168–169**, finally giving his life for his principles—and pride ‹‹ **170–171**. His son, Charles II, managed to take back the throne after years of exile ‹‹ **176–177**.

A SECOND RESTORATION?

Charles II was succeeded by James II, whose **Catholicism and absolutism alienated powerful Protestant subjects**. In 1688 he was toppled. ‹‹ **188–189**. James and his supporters—the Jacobites—fought back to win the throne, but to no avail ‹‹ **196–197**; though a Stuart did succeed William III, it was the Protestant Queen Anne ‹‹ **200–201**.

SON OF JAMES II (1688–1766)

THE OLD PRETENDER

James Francis Edward was the man who would have been King James III (James VIII of Scotland)—the rightful "King Over the Water" as far as Jacobites were concerned. Others claimed that James II's son had actually been an imposter from birth; that he was smuggled into Mary of Modena's bedchamber in a warming pan after her own baby was stillborn.

James grew up in France. He returned to Scotland in 1708 to reclaim his throne, but his French invasion fleet was beaten back before he could land. He fared little better when he returned for the rebellion in 1715.

Scottish Jacobites

The struggles of the Stuarts to reclaim the Crown—for themselves and for Catholicism—continued through the early decades of the 18th century. The ousted dynasty came back to haunt the Hanoverians in a series of rebellions that rocked the state, reminding Britain of what had so nearly been.

The Jacobites' hopes rested with James Francis Edward Stuart, or James III, though his attempted invasion of 1708 had failed. A Jacobite rebellion in 1715 started promisingly with the capture of Perth, but the Duke of Argyll held Stirling. The Scottish clans were divided: the Earl of Seaforth was with the rebels, but his army was harassed by hostile clans. A small force invaded England, hoping to attract sympathizers along the way; but on November 14, the Jacobites were defeated at Preston. Measures to prevent future risings were introduced.

Taming the Highlands

The Disarming Act did what its name implies, depriving the Highlanders of their weapons. This was a cultural attack as well as a military one, since the dirk (long dagger), claymore (broadsword), and target (small round shield) were part of Highland dress.

British commander General George Wade inspected Scotland in 1724 and recommended large-scale infrastructure improvements to help control the region, with new roads and barracks, and the founding of Fort William, Fort

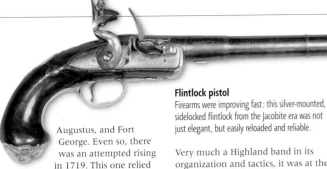

Flintlock pistol
Firearms were improving fast: this silver-mounted, sidelocked flintlock from the Jacobite era was not just elegant, but easily reloaded and reliable.

Augustus, and Fort George. Even so, there was an attempted rising in 1719. This one relied on Spanish help, the French having now made their peace with England. The invasion force was dispersed by the weather; a few hundred men were landed and managed briefly to occupy Eilean Donan Castle, but were defeated at Glen Shiel on June 10. Efforts to "domesticate" the Highlands continued with the establishment of the Black Watch regiment in 1725.

Very much a Highland band in its organization and tactics, it was at the same time firmly loyal to the Crown.

The Young Pretender

"Bonnie Prince Charlie," Charles Edward Stuart, was the son of "Old Pretender," James Francis Edward. With the War of the Austrian Succession in 1743, the French were again looking to make mischief for the British. They agreed to provide naval backing for an invasion of England, but this fleet was broken up by storms. France lost interest, but Charles kept planning. In July 1745, he showed up virtually unannounced (and without French troops) on the Scottish island of Eriskay. His standard was raised at Glenfinnan a few weeks later, despite skepticism among the Highland chiefs.

Charles mustered 3,000 troops, and took Perth and Edinburgh. He lingered there, posing as monarch, while many of his troops dribbled away. He led what was left of his force to an unexpected triumph at Prestonpans, East Lothian, on September 21. There was still no sign of a popular rising in his support. By now, the Crown was organizing its forces.

Dissension split the Jacobite camp: army general Lord George Murray disagreed with Charles on just about everything, including the idea of invading England. Even so, in November the Jacobites headed south via Carlisle and Manchester, where a group of English supporters joined them. However, there was no rush to rally to the Jacobite banner. At Derby, a government agent told Charles that a staunch defense had been prepared in London (which was untrue). To Charles's disgust, the chiefs voted to withdraw to Scotland to consolidate their position.

Bonnie Prince Charlie
After months on the run, the "Young Pretender," lying low on the island of Benbecula in the Outer Hebrides, met Flora MacDonald. A supporter's daughter, she helped him escape, disguising him as her maid Betty Burke.

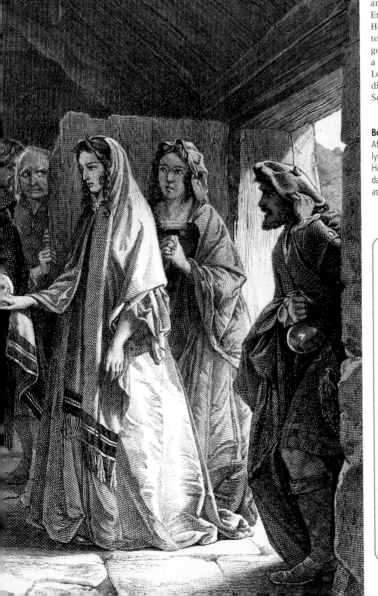

> "We are sadly convinced that they are **not such raw ragamuffins** as they was represented."

WILLIAM WALPOLE IN A LETTER, AFTER PRESTONPANS, SEPTEMBER 27, 1745

Execution of Scottish clan chief
Simon Fraser, chief of the Fraser clan and Jacobite supporter, was the last man to be beheaded on London's Tower Hill on April 9, 1747.

AFTER

In the Highlands, whole communities mourned their dead and surveyed the smoking ruins of their homes and fields. They would have to rebuild their lives—without the support of cultural traditions barred by vengeful and oppressive laws.

REACHING A SETTLEMENT

Many felt used and abandoned by those whom tradition had set above them. They were to feel the same **sense of betrayal** subsequently. Clan chiefs, who turned into strutting aristocrats, started **clearing whole communities off their ancestral lands 294–295 >>**.

For most in Scotland and England, though, the crushing of the Jacobite rebellion in 1745 was welcome. It brought a period of taking stock. The Jacobites' downfall confirmed for Britons that their **future was to be Hanoverian and Protestant**. Most were happy enough with the settlement. The **flowering of intellectual and artistic culture** in Glasgow and Edinburgh in the late 18th century suggested that in some ways the Union with England suited Scotland **224–225 >>**.

FORT GEORGE, INVERNESS

The Battle of Culloden

The Young Pretender's pretensions were unceremoniously ended in a scrappy encounter against professional British troops in open country near Inverness. Culloden has the status of myth, but it was a series of disastrous decisions that ensured the Jacobite cause had to content itself with a romantic gesture of heroic failure.

Prince Charles and his supporters were backed into a corner at Culloden, but they did not have to fight a pitched battle, particularly on such disadvantageous ground. Both tactics and field were the Prince's choice, against the objections of Lord George Murray, his senior general, who favored a low-level guerrilla war.

Futile attack

Murray's own idea for a night attack on the British camp at Nairn, on April 15, was badly botched. The Jacobites were exhausted, hungry, and in disarray as the British, led by the Duke of Cumberland, advanced early on April 16. Confusion among the Jacobite commanders led to their front line being overstretched. Then the Prince left his men standing, exposed to fierce artillery fire, while he waited for the right moment to attack. When it came, the Highlanders' charge quickly lost its cohesion over the rough and marshy ground. Most were shot as they pressed forward. By the time Murray could bring up the French-trained Royal Écossois, his left wing had broken and fled. Victory was out of the question now, though the professional Écossois allowed an orderly retreat, and gave Prince Charles a chance to flee.

The rising collapsed. The Prince, a wanted man, had a price of £30,000 on his head. Even so, he was helped by loyal supporters, and was on the run for months before he slipped away (disguised, notoriously, as Jacobite supporter Flora MacDonald's maid).

Bloody retribution

Reprisals across the Highlands by "Butcher" Cumberland saw suspected Jacobites killed, cattle stolen, crops burned, and villages destroyed. Clan culture was suppressed, with traditional weapons and Highland dress outlawed.

> " Their front had **nothing left to oppose us** but their pistols and broadswords … "

CAPTAIN JAMES-ASHE LEE, OF CUMBERLAND'S ARMY, ON THE JACOBITE CHARGE

Annihilation at Culloden
The heroic charge of the Jacobite's Highland infantry, with broadswords raised, was nullified by the rough and marshy ground across which they had to struggle, under a hail of cannon and musket fire from the disciplined ranks of red-coated British troops.

« BEFORE

The power struggle between the monarch and representatives of the general populace has long been a feature of British history.

POLITICS OF POWER

Efforts to **curb the king's power** were made in medieval times in the Magna Carta **« 86–87**. The Tudors tipped the balance the other way, by **centralizing authority in the sovereign « 132–133**.

The Stuarts took this philosophy to extremes, with James I subscribing to the **divine right of kings « 158–159**. His son, Charles I, felt so strongly on the subject that he went to war with his Parliament **« 168–169**. Charles engaged in a **struggle for power with the Parliament** of England, attempting to obtain royal revenue while the Parliament sought to **curb his royal prerogative**, which Charles believed was divinely ordained. After his execution in 1649 **« 170–171**, his son, Charles II, regained the throne **« 176–177**, which was subsequently snatched away from his younger brother, James II **« 188–189**. The real winner in the Glorious Revolution was not William III but Parliament, in cooperation with which he had agreed to rule. Similarly, the defeat of the Stuart Pretender Bonnie Prince Charlie in 1745 **« 204–205** was a victory not just for the Hanoverians but for the whole **principle of constitutional monarchy**.

After the Act of Union, the English and Scottish assemblies were dissolved to be replaced by a single British Parliament. The power of the Parliament increased—the Glorious Revolution reaffirmed the importance not only of Protestantism, but of Parliamentary democracy.

20 Number of complete years served by Robert Walpole as prime minister, Britain's first such administration—and still easily the longest. In total, Walpole was premier for 20 years and 314 days.

The rise of Walpole

Whig politician Robert Walpole was elected to his father's old Norfolk constituency in 1701 and quickly made his mark, being appointed Secretary of War in 1708. Surviving a politically inspired impeachment, he emerged as First Lord of the Treasury and Chancellor from 1716. He came unscathed and (through no virtue of his own) emerged untainted through the South Sea Bubble crisis of 1720 (see pp.210–211).

As the last man standing in a discredited administration, he assumed unchallenged preeminence as First Lord of the Treasury, Chancellor, and Leader of the House. Walpole was asked by King George I to sort out the crisis,

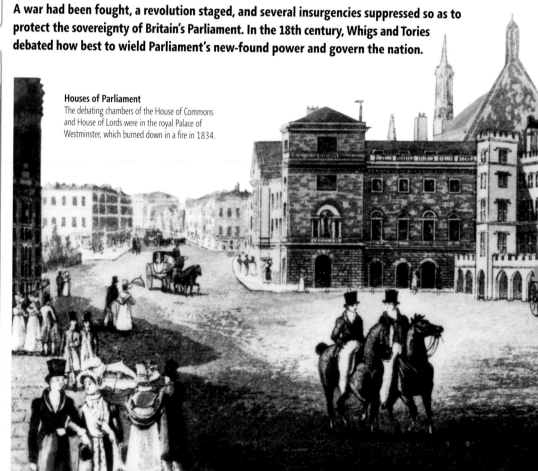

Debating chamber
By the 18th century, the Commons chamber could be seen as the beating heart of British politics. The Hanoverian monarchs were content to let the politicians have their way.

Politics and Prime Ministers

A war had been fought, a revolution staged, and several insurgencies suppressed so as to protect the sovereignty of Britain's Parliament. In the 18th century, Whigs and Tories debated how best to wield Parliament's new-found power and govern the nation.

Houses of Parliament
The debating chambers of the House of Commons and House of Lords were in the royal Palace of Westminster, which burned down in a fire in 1834.

John Wilkes was not content with the King being accountable to Parliament. He fought to make Parliament accountable to the people by printing its proceedings. Already in trouble for publishing satirical material, he was stripped of his seat as an MP in 1769. He persuaded Middlesex voters to assert their democratic rights by reelecting him (though they were promptly overruled by the courts). Wilkes' life and writings helped inspire the American Revolution.

which he did most effectively. In the decades that followed, he favored peace and prosperity over aggression, inaugurated a sinking fund to reduce the national debt, and helped secure the Hanoverian succession.

First prime minister

George II had fallen out with Walpole by the time of his accession in 1727, but Walpole's position was too strong to be assailed. Relations were mended: the King tried to give Walpole 10 Downing Street as a gift, but he would accept it only as an official prime minister's residence.

The title "Prime Minister" did not yet exist, and would not really do so until the 20th century. However, Walpole is generally held to have shaped the office around himself. Even so, his position differed from that of the modern prime minister. He was appointed by the King, not by Parliament; and it was the King (rather than the prime minister) who

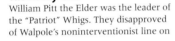

Robert Walpole
It would be no exaggeration to say that Robert Walpole (1676–1745) created the office of prime minister around himself, though the title would not be used until later.

chose his cabinet. The role was to remain controversial—and fluid in definition—under his successors.

Whigs win out

Walpole's ascendancy was good news for the Whig party he led. The Whigs' whole purpose was the defense of constitutional rights, and this period saw a strengthening of the role of Parliament. The Tories were marginalized, with their respect for royal and aristocratic privilege out of favor. The Whig supremacy went on almost without a break until 1756. But the Whigs also generated their own internal opposition groups based around particular causes or personalities. Rapidly changing coalitions therefore meant that political power could change hands under the broader banner of Whig power.

The family firm

William Pitt the Elder was the leader of the "Patriot" Whigs. They disapproved of Walpole's noninterventionist line on

a series of European conflicts. Coming to the fore during the Seven Years' War (1756–1763), Pitt was arguably the real premier in Lord Newcastle's administration from 1758; he took over as prime minister in 1766, but was forced out of public life by ill-health.

William Pitt's son—William Pitt the Younger—was Britain's youngest prime minister ever. He was just 24 when he took office in 1783, and served for more than 17 years before resigning in 1801, but was back in power between 1804 and 1806. He tried to clean up public life and (in the aftermath of an expensive American war) sought to increase revenues through taxation. He also clamped down on smuggling, which was practically an industry at the time.

> **2** The number of pence in the pound paid at the basic rate for the first income tax in 1798. At the time, a pound had 240 pence, giving a taxation rate of just over 0.8 percent.

Taxes! Taxes! Taxes!
Income tax was an utterly alien idea when William Pitt the Younger introduced it in 1798. In this contemporary cartoon the taxman tries to convince John Bull that he is his friend.

AFTER

The opposition between Whigs and Tories was to become a foundation of the British political debate, establishing the parameters of parliamentary business for generations.

CHANGE IN WHIG SUPREMACY
The main point of debate was not the **two-party system**, but the number of voters who were to have a say in bringing the winning party to power **224–225 »**. From the 1890s, the **Labour Party** threatened what workers had increasingly come to see as a **cozy accommodation between different factions of the ruling class 310–311 »**. The Whigs— now the Liberals—were marginalized thereafter.

PARLIAMENT BURNING DOWN, 1834

« BEFORE

The critical, satirical writing that flourished in the 1700s stretches back to ancient times.

CLASSICAL INSPIRATION

Satire was common to ancient classical literature, and certainly among the **Roman writers so admired** in 18th-century Britain. These include Juvenal (c. 60–c. 140 CE), whose 16 famous **"Satires"** attacked the vices of Roman society.

HOME-GROWN SATIRE

In the Middle Ages, Chaucer's *Canterbury Tales* **« 110–111** created **a very English satirical tone**. The Restoration era, freed from Commonwealth restrictions, reveled in an **irreverent exposure of human folly** that characterized 17th-century work such as John Dryden's comic play *Marriage à la Mode* (1673) and his verse satire, *Absalom and Achitophel* (1681). The 17th-century work of **dramatist William Congreve** (1670–1729), such as *Love for Love* (1695), provided another precedent.

Power of the Pen

As the 18th century got underway, a rapidly rising number of tracts, journals, and newspapers dissected every aspect of British politics, manners, and thought. Satire and a questioning spirit defined the times, whose leading figures included Alexander Pope, Jonathan Swift, and Daniel Defoe.

The 1700s was a highly productive time for British thinkers, scientists, artists, and writers in general; it was the Age of Reason and Enlightenment, fed by a new rationality and spirit of exploration (see pp.184–185, 224–225).

The first half of the 1700s was a particularly fertile literary period, often labeled the new Augustan Age after the great Classical writers—Virgil, Livy, Horace, and Ovid—that flourished during Roman Emperor Augustus's reign (27 BCE–14 CE). Eighteenth-century writers made this comparison themselves and looked to this ancient era for inspiration.

There was much political activity in the early 1700s, with factions still nursing grievances from the 1600s and kicking against the established order—the 1715 Jacobite rebellion (see pp.202–203) was a key event. This made it an apt time for writers questioning the order of things—literary, political, religious, and social. The

> **"Satire** is a sort of **glass**, wherein beholders do generally **discover** everybody's face **but their own."**
>
> JONATHAN SWIFT, PREFACE TO *THE BATTLE OF THE BOOKS,* 1704

ways in which they did this were heavily influenced by the satires of Roman writers Horace and Juvenal, which exposed hypocrisy, weakness, folly, and corruption.

Defining satire

Satire as a label for a kind of writing first came into being in ancient Rome. In Latin, *satura/satira* means "medley," as ancient writings that analyzed society were often a medley of miscellaneous poems and prose fragments. Although satire soon became identified with the humorous exposé, its original meaning remained in the minds of 18th-century writers, making it slightly different to our view of it today.

Irish writer and clergyman Jonathan Swift (1667–1745) was the master satirist of the 1700s. His satirical tracts covered topics from religion and poverty to literature and England's unfair treatment of the Irish. Early works include two published in 1704: *The Battle of the Books* (dealing with ancient versus modern learning) and *A Tale of a Tub* (comparing different religions). His prose satire on human society, *Gulliver's Travels* (1726), is presented as an autobiographical account by a ship's surgeon of travels to fantastical lands, and allowed Swift to comment on reason, civilization, and certain political issues.

English poet Alexander Pope (1688–1744), another leading contemporary satirist, is known for his biting wit and skill with heroic couplets—pairs of

rhyming lines in iambic pentameter (see pp.154–155) that were a popular form in his time. His works include *The Rape of the Lock* (about a lock of hair; 1712–1714), *The Dunciad* (in which he attacks the dullness of much contemporary writing; 1728), and *An Essay on Man* (analyzing humans' relationship with God and the universe; 1733–1734).

Club culture

Men's clubs in the 18th century were melting pots for literary trends and political gossip. The infamous Kit-Kat (or Kit-Cat) club, strongly linked with the rise of satire, was named after Christopher Catling, proprietor of the tavern in which members first met. A dining and discussion establishment founded in early 18th-century London by leading Whigs, its members included William Congreve, Alexander Pope, Robert Walpole, writer and politician Joseph Addison, and Irish writer Richard Steele.

Kit-Kat members Addison and Steele were active in another major literary trend of the time—the rise of magazines, journals, and newspapers. Here society gossip, heated issues of the day, poetry, and opinions about current plays and books took printed form. Their contents were much discussed in clubs and coffee shops, and played a major role in spreading new ideas as well as news. Steele founded the *Tatler* periodical (1709–1711) and, with Addison, the *Spectator* (1711–1712).

Samuel Johnson, a leading light in literary circles, who went on to create the first real English dictionary (1755), was a regular contributor to publications such as Edward Cave's

KIT-KAT A term for a painting measuring 36 x 28 in (91 x 71 cm). It comes from more than 40 portraits of the Kit-Kat club's members, painted by Sir Godfrey Kneller. The size worked well for upper-body images.

Jonathan Swift

Swift's work includes his 1729 pamphlet *A Modest Proposal*, in which he uses satire with full force by ironically suggesting that Irish poverty might be eased by feeding poor children to the rich.

The art of caricature
In this late 18th-century image, cartoonist Thomas Rowlandson satirizes the practice whereby rich people paid to have teeth from a poor person transplanted into their own mouths.

British satire remains a powerful way of questioning tradition.

CONTINUING THE TRADITION
Lord Byron carried on the 18th-century tradition with his satirical poem, *English Bards and Scotch Reviewers* (1809). The 1820s saw a **torrent of satire attacking George IV's policies**. In 1841, *Punch* was founded. At its height, this weekly illustrated periodical's radical cartoons and articles were highly influential. Charles Dickens also used satire very effectively to make **comments about social conditions** in his novels.

THE AGE OF TV
The 1960s brought fresh blood to satire and **television became an important forum 372–373 »**. The magazine *Private Eye*, founded in 1962, has continued the tradition of printed political satire into the 21st century.

century. Samuel Johnson's early satirical work *London* (1738) attacked Prime Minister Robert Walpole's policies, while John Gay's *The Beggar's Opera* (1728) and dramatist–novelist Henry Fielding's *The Historical Register for 1736* also poked fun at Walpole. In 1737, Walpole issued the theater Licensing Act, a censorship system that remained until 1968. Defoe's pen brought him plenty of trouble, too: he was imprisoned after producing anti-Jacobite pamphlets in 1712–1713.

Revolutionary writer
Anglo-American political writer Thomas Paine (1737–1809) fled to France at one point after being indicted by the British government for treason. His pamphlet *Common Sense* (1776) supported, and helped to move along, American independence (Benjamin Franklin sponsored Paine's emigration to America in 1774), and his *The Rights of Man* (1791) defended the French Revolution. *The Age of Reason* (1794), in which Paine criticized Christianity, caused widespread outrage.

William Hogarth
Painter–engraver Hogarth (1697–1764) is one of the most famous satirical artists of all time. His famous moralizing series *Marriage à la Mode* (c. 1743) points out the hypocrisies of upper-class marriage.

very popular *Gentleman's Magazine* (1731–1907), possibly the first journal to use the word "magazine." Johnson also wrote most of his own *Rambler* periodical (1750–1752). Important Irish writer Oliver Goldsmith (1728–1774), whose writing includes the comical play, *She Stoops to Conquer* (1773), wrote for a dizzying array of periodicals and also produced his own publication, *The Bee* (in 1759).

The age of the newspaper
British news-sheets had started gathering momentum in the 17th century—the *London Gazette* was founded as the *Oxford Gazette* in 1665 and is the world's oldest surviving periodical. However, newspaper floodgates burst open in the 1700s, helped greatly by Parliament's decision in 1695 not to renew a previous Licensing Act—thus establishing a free press. Soon there were numerous national and provincial papers—dailies, evening papers, and even Sunday papers. The first daily, the *Daily Courant*, arrived in 1702, and the first evening paper, the *Evening Post*, four years later. In 1737, came the *Belfast Newsletter*, the world's oldest surviving general daily newspaper. The Scottish press was also

getting established—the *Edinburgh Gazette* had been founded in 1699, and 1747 brought the *Aberdeen Journal*. In 1791, the oldest surviving Sunday paper, the *Observer*, was born.

Daniel Defoe (1660–1731), talented essayist, satirist, poet, and pamphleteer, was a major figure in this flood of print, and one of the earliest examples of an investigative journalist and feature writer. Defoe's short-lived *Weekly Review* (founded 1704) covered leading contemporary events, while the historical fiction *A Journal of the Plague Year* (1722) shows great investigative skills. Defoe's *Robinson Crusoe* (1719), based on the true story of a shipwrecked sailor, is often said to be the first English novel.

The power of the word
The pen became a mighty weapon and a thorn in politicians' sides in the 18th

50 **The number of provincial (that is, non-London) newspapers going strong in 1782; this was double the number in existence in 1723, and the number would double again to more than 100 by 1808.**

Birth of *The Times*
This shows the day—January 1, 1788—on which the *Daily Universal Register*, founded by John Walter I in 1785, became *The Times*. It is Britain's oldest surviving newspaper with continuous daily publication.

> ## "**Proper words** in proper places, make the **true definition** of a **style**."
>
> JONATHAN SWIFT, *LETTER TO A YOUNG GENTLEMAN LATELY ENTERED INTO HOLY ORDERS*, JANUARY 9, 1720

Commercial Expansion

In the early 18th century, the British economy took a great leap forward—though not because of any major boom in manufacturing or farming. Instead, what has been described as a financial revolution made new ways of making money possible. And then, of course, there was the trade in slaves.

A slaving company
The coat of arms of the Royal African Company—a slave trading company—shows the chief commodity that was traded by it. It was earlier known as the Royal Adventurers.

BEFORE

Britain built its power and prosperity on trade, the lifeblood of its island economy for centuries.

TRADE AND ECONOMY
Trade played its part in securing the relative **affluence of medieval England << 88–89**. The **mercantile economy** was developed both by the **monasteries << 108–109** and the **city guilds << 120–121**. Henry VII promoted overseas trade **<< 132–133**, and his Tudor descendants built on this success. The **colonization of North America** opened up new possibilities **<< 162–163**.

The Glorious Revolution (see pp.188–189) was all very well, but Britain's economic situation was anything but glorious. Scottish merchant William Paterson proposed opening a subscription among entrepreneurs who were prepared to invest money. Collectively, they were to become the governors of a Bank of England, founded by royal charter in 1694.

Market forces
The new national bank gave promissory notes in return for gold deposits. By 1725, these were part-printed, then completed by cashiers, so they could be

1.2 MILLION The amount of loan (in pounds) raised by William Paterson and his partners in 1694 to endow the new Bank of England they were founding.

sold on and circulated to some extent. By 1759, £10 notes circulated freely as currency. The trend took off, although British banking—still in its infancy—was extremely localized: every town had its own bank, issuing its own bills. Money was a working metaphor, standing in for gold in the first instance, but after that for products or labor—whichever the holder chose.

Joint-stock companies, although not altogether new, grew rapidly in importance. These offered a way of sharing risks and profits—investors bought stocks in a company on the open market and partook in the profits, even if they were not directly involved in the company's trading activities. An investor could also sell his share in the company's stock to another buyer at an agreed price. The stock exchange had been established during

Royal Exchange of London
The original Royal Exchange, founded in 1565, had been destroyed in the Great Fire of 1666. Its successor was an architectural statement, a declaration of capitalist intent.

Elizabeth I's reign, but the volume of business was dramatically increasing. The freedom with which cash could now circulate in note form and stock could be traded in share certificates made everything more fluid, freeing up what economist Adam Smith (see pp.224–225) would refer to as the "invisible hand" of the market.

South Sea Bubble
The risks were classically illustrated by the speculative frenzy of the South Sea Bubble. Shares in the South Sea Company soared in value (from about £100 to £1,000 at their peak in August 1720) on the back of claims that the firm had secured a monopoly on the *asiento*—the regular contract for selling slaves to the Spanish Americas. Members of the public who had borrowed heavily to buy shares came catastrophically

unstuck when the company crashed and share prices collapsed.

Expanding horizons

By the early 18th century, the English East India Company was shipping tea, silk, porcelain, and other luxuries from China. It also had bases in Thailand and Vietnam, and a network of contacts in the Spice Islands of Malaysia and Indonesia—although here it lost the major share of the trade to the Dutch. The wealth of the Indian subcontinent was a consolation: the East India Company established a toehold in the 17th century, founding

40,000 **The number of slaves carried by British ships from Africa to the Americas each year in the 1780s; more than 10 million Africans were transported over the four centuries of the Atlantic slave trade.**

posts at Madras (now Chennai, 1640), Bombay (Mumbai, 1668), and Calcutta (Kolkata, 1690), which grew into major cities.

Rule, Britannia!

The reliance on a strong Royal Navy for protection on the seas was crucial in maintaining confidence in overseas trade. The fiasco at Beachy Head (see p.197) in 1690 took some of the gilt off the Glorious Revolution, and Britain was determined to avoid any repetition. This concern influenced the founding of the Bank of England in 1694, which

was seen as an important way of raising some of the funds needed for a major ship-building program. Thereafter, the navy grew in size, while also improving its fighting capability. The policy paid off in the War of the Spanish Succession (see pp.196–197), notably in the capture of the strategically vital Rock of Gibraltar, which became a long-standing possession. The British Empire (see pp.212–213) did not exist yet, but the idea that Britannia might "rule the waves" did: the famous song was published in 1740.

Tragic triangle

The new, more flexible financing methods lent fresh impetus to a long-standing slave trade. London and Bristol took the lead, but were overtaken by Liverpool in the 1740s. Ships from that port alone transported 1.5 million men, women, and children to the Americas. The "triangular trade" was profitable on all three legs: cheap trinkets, textiles, and weapons sent to West Africa were exchanged for slaves, who were sold for profit in the Americas; the traders then loaded up slave ships with cotton, tobacco, and sugar to be sold back home.

The slaves had to endure the agonies of being torn from their homes and families, then forced to suffer the

Rule, Britannia!
Thomas Arne's music and James Thomson's lyrics came together in a stirring (and Anglo-Scottish) partnership in this immensely popular song. Britannia's rule was more aspirational than real, at least for the time being.

miseries of the "Middle Passage" (the journey from Africa across the Atlantic), crammed into fetid and filthy holds for weeks before being sold as beasts of burden on the other side.

> ## "**Trade**, without enlarging the British territories, has given us a kind of **additional empire** …"
>
> JOSEPH ADDISON, ON THE ROYAL EXCHANGE, IN *THE SPECTATOR*, 1711

AFTER

Britain was rich, or at least an important minority of its people were, and the economy as a whole surged ahead at an exhilarating rate.

INVESTING IN THE FUTURE

Now that new mechanisms were in place for making money, **new ways of spending money** were also found—and these were not always wasteful. Suddenly, newly rich landowners found themselves with the

financial security and the leisure time that enabled them to be creative.

This first manifested itself in the construction of stately homes in ornamental grounds, and was quickly followed by more significant innovations—experiments that transformed British farming in the 18th century **230–231** ❯❯. Then, of course, came that time of financial entrepreneurship and technological invention known as the **Industrial Revolution 232–233** ❯❯. With the financial and technological tools it now had its disposal, Britain was ideally placed to be the **workshop of the world 276–277** ❯❯.

INDUSTRIALIZED MANCHESTER SEEN FROM KERSAL MOOR, 1857

« BEFORE

England and Scotland, both island nations, had long depended on seagoing trade. They needed trading partners to secure their own prosperity.

EARLY COLONIES

While Scotland stuck largely to the North Sea routes, England looked beyond, but lagged far behind Spain and Portugal when the **Age of Discovery** got underway in the 15th century **« 146–147**. Its first attempts at colonizing North America were sporadic. **Elizabeth I's adventurers** had done a great deal better by **raiding the New World cities** of the Spanish kings. Under her successor, James I, settlements started in Virginia and New England **« 162–163**. After difficulties, these early colonies prospered.

A SUCCESSION OF WARS

In recent centuries, however, Britain had been beset by problems closer to home: most notably a bitter series of **succession wars « 196–197**. Its armed forces had barely been able to get their breath back before a new round of fighting began over **Maria Theresa's claim** to the Austrian succession **« 200–201**. This conflict had in theory been ended by the signing of the **Treaty of Aix-la-Chapelle** in 1748, but— with so much still to fight for—few diplomatic observers in Europe were convinced.

Colonial Conquests

The middle of the 18th century saw Britain acquiring new territories to the east and west—in India, and in Canada. Its good intentions were quickly tested, as it became clear how immense the possibilities were for England's commercial development—and for the personal enrichment of those in charge.

The Seven Years' War was a European conflict, pitching Britain and Prussia against France and Austria and their allies (see pp.206–207). This inevitably brought about a North American dimension, as both Britain and France had transatlantic colonies. The British settlers coveted Ohio, currently claimed by the French Canadians, who traded with the native tribes for furs.

North American acquisitions

General James Wolfe sailed up the St. Lawrence River in June 1759 with 9,000 men on almost 50 ships to attack Quebec, but this dramatic entrance was followed by an anticlimactic siege. It ended, on September 13, with the hour-long Battle of the Plains of Abraham, in which the generals from both sides sustained fatal wounds. France's Louis Joseph de Montcalm died the next day, but General Wolfe's death in the moment of victory was heroic. His dying proclamation, "Now, God be praised, I die contented …" has become legendary.

Death of General Wolfe
The British Empire did not yet exist, but a mythology of imperial self-sacrifice was taking shape. Wolfe's heroic death, shown in this painting by Benjamin West of 1771, foreshadowed that of Nelson and Captain Scott.

Canada became a British possession when the Treaty of Paris was signed in 1763. George III promptly made a Royal Proclamation, attempting to control the pace and scope of settlement and secure good relations with the Native peoples.

Birth of British India

European companies setting up among "savage" peoples took it for granted that they had a policing role, if only to safeguard their own activities. The East India Company had been chartered by the British Crown, and essentially acted on its behalf. It even had its own army.

The Company's competition with its French rivals soon spilled over into fighting, before getting caught up in the wider conflict of the Seven Years' War. Robert Clive, later the Governor of Bengal, commanded the British force. His

troops smashed the army of the *Compagnie des Indes* and its local ally, the Nawab of Bengal, at the Battle of Plassey (1757). Britain then commenced the Carnatic War in the southeast, capturing the French headquarters at Pondichéry (modern Puducherry) in 1761.

Company consolidates

With the Battle of Buxar (1764), the Company tightened its hold over eastern India, shattering what remained

Growing borders
From the 1770s, the map of India tells a story of continuous British expansion. The fires of the Mutiny were little more than a flash in the pan (see pp.292–293).

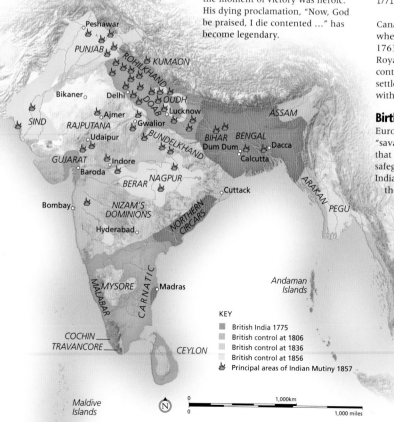

Peshawar
PUNJAB
ROHILKHAND
KUMAON
Bikaner
Delhi
OUDH
Ajmer
Lucknow
DOAB
SIND
RAJPUTANA
Gwalior
ASSAM
Udaipur
BUNDELKHAND
BIHAR
BENGAL
GUJARAT
Indore
Dum Dum
Dacca
Baroda
Calcutta
BERAR
NAGPUR
Cuttack
Bombay
NIZAM'S
DOMINIONS
NORTHERN
CIRCARS
ARAKAN
Hyderabad
PEGU

MYSORE
Madras
MALABAR
CARNATIC

Andaman
Islands

KEY
- British India 1775
- British control at 1806
- British control at 1836
- British control at 1856
- Principal areas of Indian Mutiny 1857

COCHIN
TRAVANCORE
CEYLON

Maldive
Islands

N

| 0 | 1,000km |

| 0 | 1,000 miles |

KEY MOMENT
BLACK HOLE OF CALCUTTA

Perceiving a threat to the independence of the area, the rebellious Nawab of Bengal, Siraj ud-Daulah, laid siege to Fort William. His troops crammed a large number of men, women, and children into the fort guardroom through the night of June 19, 1756. More than 120 of them suffocated in the tropical heat. So, at least, the legend has it. However, most historians warn that this is at the very least an exaggeration. The story was used in Britain as propaganda.

THE FORT WILLIAM IMPRISONMENT

Tipu's tiger
This wind-up automaton, featuring a life-size tiger savaging a prostate redcoat, completed a colonial wish-fulfilment fantasy. The life-size device was made for Tipu Sultan in the late 18th century.

of Mughal power. The Mughal emperor Shah Allam II was still nominally in charge, but the Company became his official agents in the region.

Resistance continued in the south of the subcontinent. Four Anglo-Mysore Wars were fought between 1766 and 1799. The rise of the ruler of the kingdom of Mysore, Tipu Sultan ("Tiger of Mysore"), took Britain by surprise, and he won some initial victories. He was killed in 1799 during the Battle of

Seringapatam, and most of Mysore's territory was annexed by the British. The Anglo-Maratha War in the west was to continue into the 19th century, but Britain's ascendancy over much of the subcontinent had been established.

Controversies followed the rise of the East India Company in the region. The Company was accused of stripping India of its assets by its taxation policy, and pressing for productive land to be turned over from food to cash-crops, such as opium poppies. British officials oversaw policies that led to a collapse in the agricultural economy in Bengal in 1769–1773. This brought about a devastating famine, which caused several million deaths.

Colony expands
Lord Cornwallis takes receipt of two hostage princes of Mysore in this oil painting from 1793. Scenes like this cheered a nation still reeling from the loss of the American colonies.

Imperial status seemed to suit Britain. The power and prestige were the least of it: the possession of colonies was a vital boon to what was first and foremost a trading nation.

SHIFTING SANDS
Britain's status as an imperialist power was soon called into question. Within a generation, the settlers of the original English colonies were in revolt; ultimately, they **broke away completely 214–215 ⟫**. By the end of the 19th century, Britain was more concerned with its own survival, with the **real threat of a French invasion** looming on the horizon **240–241 ⟫**.

EMPIRE BUILDING
The East India Company kept up the fight to **retain its grip on India** until the late 1850s **290–291 ⟫**. With the Victorian Age, Britain continued to build the greatest empire the world had ever seen **296–297 ⟫**.

Surrender at Yorktown

Even a few months before, the British had seemed to have the upper hand against the American insurgents. Lord Cornwallis's withdrawal to Yorktown, on the coast, had been an orderly regroup. Defeat, entirely unexpected, would stun the British establishment, and launch the newly independent United States on a euphoric tide.

Cornwallis found himself isolated, with no support coming from his commander, General Clinton, who was convinced that Yorktown faced no threat. Led by the Marquis de Lafayette, the Virginia army besieging Yorktown was indeed not large, but it held out the hope of reinforcements arriving from the northern colonies. These included both Americans, under General Washington, and a French force led by the Comte de Rochambeau, which had landed at Rhode Island.

Support from the sea
At this point, crucially, Washington and Rochambeau heard that the Comte De Grasse, France's admiral operating in the Caribbean, had agreed to move up the coast in their support. (He had been tied up until now in the Caribbean, but was freed by Spain's agreement to mind French merchant shipping.) Spurred by this, the Americans and French moved south, as though to attack New York, but then continued south to Virginia. Soon, with Lafayette's army, there were almost 17,000 men outside Yorktown, hitting it relentlessly with heavy guns.

Left high and dry
Cornwallis still expected support, and the Royal Navy was indeed on its way. But De Grasse's fleet was waiting when it got there. On September 5, just outside the mouth of Chesapeake Bay, battle began. It was a ragged affair, both fleets being short-crewed, while shoals hampered the formation of lines. The outcome was inconclusive—but that was good enough for the French and the Americans. The British fleet was forced to continue north. Cornwallis, marooned with his men at their base, under ferocious bombardment, felt he had no alternative but to surrender. The American Revolution was now effectively over, although it would take the signing of the Treaty of Paris two years later to make this official.

> **"I have the mortification to inform your Excellency that I have been forced to … surrender the troops under my command …"**
>
> DISPATCH FROM LORD CORNWALLIS TO GENERAL CLINTON, OCTOBER 20, 1781

Surrender at Yorktown
With Cornwallis claiming to be ill, Brigadier Charles O'Hara took the sword of surrender out on his behalf. Rochambeau refused it, pointing to Washington, who in turn indicated Major-General Benjamin Lincoln, who had suffered the humiliation of surrendering at Charleston.

‹‹ BEFORE

Significant changes took place throughout 17th-century Britain, which would make the following century a mixture of tradition and new ideas.

FOUNDATIONS OF WEALTH

Britain in the 1600s was **largely rural**, and presided over by the nobility, but change was on the way. The Bank of England, set up in 1694, provided **sound public finances** and a source of government borrowing, helping to encourage commerce, while the gradual **establishment of an empire** augmented this with new markets and sources of trade **‹‹ 210–213**. The growth of trading towns and cities broadened people's horizons as they moved there in **search of work**. But huge numbers of people still lived in rural areas where lifestyles were taking **much longer to change**, and many farming implements were little different from medieval times.

PEASANT'S CART

Georgian Society

Life in 18th-century Britain could be very enjoyable indeed for those of the better-off classes. There were jobs in London and country retreats for wealthy men, and new professions for those of a more modest means. Fashionable women reveled in the elegance of the social season, while a rising middle class sought out the many stores now proliferating everywhere.

Although there were wars for about half of the century, and economic problems for some of the time, the 1700s were generally a period of stability and prosperity. Wealth, however, was spread unevenly, with around one-third controlled by five percent of the population. Inheriting land was still the way to achieve any position of power, as in the century before. To be an MP, a man had to hold land worth around £500 per annum, and most men couldn't vote unless they owned some property. A country squire with property would be the local magistrate,

and those with money set the day's tone and tastes. One taste was for the social season, which increased in popularity throughout the 1700s. As London grew as a more important commercial and political center, men of substance would spend much time there, with stays often dictated by the sitting of Parliament. Life at their country residences was often linked with the hunting season. A whole social season arose around time spent in London, lasting from April or May to the start of August, and was filled

with parties, theater trips, and sporting events such as the races. Similar seasons arose in Dublin and Edinburgh.

Outside London

Provincial towns and cities were growing, especially the "spa" towns, where the wealthy would stay a while, as part of the annual social rounds, to partake of supposedly health-giving waters from natural springs. Bath was the most fashionable spa,

Jane Austen
With great wit and observation, Jane Austen chronicled the social lives of the middle and upper classes around 1800 in books such as *Pride and Prejudice* (1813).

Elegant Bath
Much of Georgian Bath was created by architects John Wood the Elder and Younger. The younger Wood designed the much-imitated Royal Crescent, seen here.

Early game of cricket
Sports were important male leisure pursuits. Cricket, popular by Restoration times, became a national sport in the 1700s. The Marylebone Cricket Club was founded in 1787. Other male pastimes included hunting, shooting, watching bear-baiting, and the races.

Employment also began to change. Traditional careers for men, had they not been squires, included the Church, army, or navy, often in modest roles, but options now grew. Journalist Daniel Defoe listed a hierarchy of social classes, mentioning "the middle sort, who live well." The rise of professions now saw a growing body of men working as clergy, doctors, lawyers, or—as commerce and industry expanded—businessmen and merchants. They were usually based in towns and were not wealthy landowners, but earned reasonably well. The rising middle classes and their leisure pursuits and growing spending power helped feed new industries and create a consumer revolution. Shopping for everything from cutlery to china to buttons became all the rage.

The Regency and beyond saw some instabilities and class divisions, while the social season continued.

WIDENING GAP
The 1800s brought **uncertainties** arising from wars with France, and the Regency saw a contrast between the extravagance of the rich and the poverty of the urban poor **222–223 »**. The middle classes continued to rise; commerce made headway into the **Industrial Revolution**.

QUEEN VICTORIA'S SEASON
By Victoria's reign **270–271 »**, the **social season** had become highly structured. For families with links to aristocracy, a young debutante's first social season marked her coming of age, and she was presented, dressed in an **extravagant gown**, to the Queen, before embarking on the season's entertainments.

and its population grew markedly in the 18th century. It was a place of fashion and manners, and its season, as in London, was an opportunity for both sexes to show off new clothes, learn new dances, and attract suitable wives and husbands. This might occur at the perennially popular ball, often a lavish affair with added entertainments such as fireworks. At smaller parties, young women might be admired for their singing or piano playing—suitable pursuits along with accomplishments such as sketching. As other towns expanded, also gaining theaters, assembly rooms, and coffeehouses, people from the surrounding areas enjoyed "mini seasons" there, too. It meant that many people moved around

regularly, helped by greatly improved roads that by mid-century reduced traveling times to hours not days. This movement, as well as the greater exchange of goods between town and country, meant that the social classes did start to intermix more.

" I was **three days** … in the race ground, and **danced every night** at the assembly."

JOHN COURTNEY, BEVERLEY SOCIAL SEASON, 1764

Landed gentry
In the mid-18th century, power in Britain was held by an increasingly confident landed gentry. It was a power that was based upon ownership of land and the income it provided. *Mr. and Mrs. Andrews*, painted by Thomas Gainsborough in 1750, is a commentary on the social status of this landowning class, and portrays a married couple presiding over their land. While Mrs. Andrews appears fashionable, her husband's shotgun brutally underlines his proprietorship over the countryside.

Disorder and Religious Revival

Peaceful rural rhythms overseen by a benevolent squire and parson often masked social turmoil. In the cities especially, authority seemed remote; pastoral care and spiritual support still more so. As crime and disorder raged, thousands turned to religious belief for help.

« BEFORE

The stresses and strains of the social order always found a way of expressing themselves, whether in eruptions of unrest or in outbursts of religious enthusiasm.

UPHEAVAL AND UNREST

In the context of a feudal system in mounting crisis, the **Peasants' Revolt** « **104–105** and the Lollards' spiritual rebirth « **108–109** may be understood as two sides of the same coin. In the period that followed, **disorder descended onto the kingdom from above**: it was the country's ruling families who brought chaos and confusion through the Wars of the Roses « **122–123**.

While the drift of the population to the cities through the Tudor period was accompanied by a rise in crime « **132–133**, religious upheaval was introduced by the king and by a clerical elite « **136–137**. With **industrialism** poised to transform the overall economic scene in Britain, **a new round of social and spiritual unrest seemed inevitable**.

Britain was growing wealthier by the year, with its trade and commerce (see pp.210–211) expanding as the country's colonial reach extended (see pp.212–213). Enormous fortunes were being made in the slave trade in particular. Not all shared the prosperity, although everyone had been affected by the transformation of the countryside, as the enclosure process had gathered pace during the 17th century. Thousands, uprooted from the relentlessly poor but essentially orderly life of the country, were living in squalid city slums, where a certain amount of social anarchy—crime, prostitution, and drunkenness—were rife.

Demonized drink

One of William of Orange's less welcome introductions had been gin, a liquor distilled from wheat and flavored with juniper berries.

Thousands relied on so-called "Dutch courage" to help them through their hard and unrewarding lives. In pursuit of its mercantilist goals (see pp.178–279), the government eased restrictions on domestically distilled spirits while hiking up the duties on imported drinks. So gin was a readily available tipple—and the most visible in its effects on the urban poor.

Even so, the Gin Craze that took hold of the nation in the middle of the 18th century seems to have existed more in the minds of the media and those respectable citizens who saw "mother's ruin" as the ruination of society at large. Gin-drinking was associated

Armed police

A Bow Street Runner carried this pistol, made in 1763, but the authorities were fighting a losing battle against street crime, in the capital and elsewhere.

with an urban underclass already regarded with deep suspicion. Then as subsequently, the poor were clearly stereotyped: idle, shiftless, slatternly, criminal, promiscuous, and insubordinate; their potential for violent disorder always feared.

Riotous assembly

Outbreaks of public violence were in any case a feature of this period. There was invariably trouble in naval ports

Gordon Riots

In 1780, armed troops were deployed on the streets of London to break up serious rioting, whipped up by the anti-Catholic rhetoric of Lord George Gordon and his Protestant Association.

Gin Lane

William Hogarth's notorious satire clearly expressed the exaggerated fears of the Establishment. But there is no doubt that the gin craze wreaked havoc among large sections of the urban poor.

A cheap and cheerful literature celebrated the exploits of the most notorious criminals in handbills or broadsides. Crime became a source of sensational entertainment. Thief-taker-turned-criminal Jonathan Wild inspired a novel by Henry Fielding (1743) and the "fair parricide" Mary Blandy inspired a play (1752).

Moral concern

With concern mounting about the moral effect this glamorization of crime and punishment was having in society as a whole, transportation—to Van Diemen's Land (Tasmania) or Botany Bay (New South Wales)—was increasingly seen as an alternative. Early efforts to toughen up law enforcement came with the formation of the Bow Street Runners by the writer and magistrate Henry Fielding. They were known as Robin Redbreasts for the distinctive bright red waistcoats that they wore.

There was a growing sense that religion was not reaching most of the population, especially in the cities. Religious apathy was seen as underpinning immorality and indiscipline of every sort. It was this feeling which prompted the Wesley brothers and George Whitefield to launch their Methodist revival movement, revitalizing what had become a deadened faith.

John and Charles Wesley had already developed disciplines of prayer and contemplation, creating what was mockingly called the Holy Club, during their time at Oxford University. They then went off to the American colonies to spread the word.

Another Holy Club member, George Whitefield (1714–1770), who had also spent time in America, was, by the 1730s, back in England carrying his Christian message to large open-air congregations. Impressed, the brothers joined forces with him: they and a growing band of followers made forays out into the country, preaching in churches and, when allowed, in fields and open spaces.

Crime raged on, regardless of the Bloody Code: fears of punishment were overridden by need, but also criminals realized they were unlikely to be apprehended by a ramshackle system of law enforcement.

METROPOLITAN POLICE

Law enforcement by parish was grossly inadequate, underfunded, and disorganized. The **first major step forward** came in 1829 when Home Secretary Robert Peel established a Metropolitan Police Force for London **278–279 >>**.

MAKING PROGRESS

More hopeful signs of **a moral awakening among the emergent middle class** was evident in the **anti-slavery campaign** of the late 18th century **234–235 >>**. Moreover, while the failure of discontent to translate into action in the aftermath of the French Revolution might have disappointed radicals, conservatives could see this as a sign that **Britain was getting something right 236–237 >>**.

PEELERS MAKE AN ARREST

The name of "Methodism" suggests a dry, mechanical religion: that preached by the Wesleys was anything but. They believed the individual was free either to accept or reject the salvation offered him or her by God. Its acceptance was a joyful embrace of faith. This was why hymn-singing was so important: not only did it enable an uneducated congregation easily to absorb the key tenets of their faith, it allowed a collective belief to be celebrated in a way that was pleasurable for all.

> # "This **wicked gin**, of all Defence bereft, and guilty found of Whoredom, Murder, Theft …"

LONDON EVENING POST, MARCH 1751

---

225 **The number of criminal offenses that were deemed punishable by the death penalty under the Bloody Code operating in Britain at the end of the 18th century and the beginning of the 19th century.**

1740s, was "Gentleman Highwayman" James MacLaine. Executions became a show, with carnivalesque scenes on the road from Newgate prison to the gallows at Tyburn, as swaggering desperadoes joked and postured to the delight of drunken crowds.

when the fleet was in. Rioting by demobilized soldiers and sailors marred the peace after major wars.

The mob—a monstrous entity—loomed large in the nightmares of the elite, but was this many-headed monster really just the "people" by another name? Was its violence the only way they had of registering their feelings in a system which offered them no representation? Bread riots would not have broken out if hunger had not taken hold. The Gordon Riots of 1780 articulated real anger at the passing of the Papists Act, which had eased the penalties against Catholics prepared to swear their loyalty to the Crown.

Punishing criminals

Taming the monster brought ever more draconian punishments: by the 1800s more than 200 offenses were punishable by death. These included stealing a sheep, shoplifting or pickpocketing an item worth more than five shillings, and identity theft.

Punishment had to be done publicly, to send out a message. Often, the policy backfired, making celebrities of colorful criminals. Jack Sheppard, a habitual thief who also made a habit of escaping prison in spectacular style, was briefly idolized in the 1720s; so, too, in the

KEY MOMENT
ORDERING ENGLISH LAW

In 1765 William Blackstone (1723–1780) started a quiet revolution with the first volume of his *Commentaries on the Laws of England*. Blackstone brought order to an impenetrable forest of obscure (and often apparently contradictory) legislation that had been passed over centuries. For the first time, ordinary people could, if they wished, consult a clear and authoritative guide to the law.

SIR WILLIAM BLACKSTONE

‹‹ BEFORE

Earlier development of a tolerant humanism was key to Scottish 18th-century thought.

RELIGIOUS EXTREMISM
In the 16th century, Scottish humanist George Buchanan (1506–1582) preached **resistance to religious tyranny**. Scotland in the 17th century was rife with **superstition and intolerance**, but many were shocked by the execution of a young student for **blasphemy** in 1697.

NEW TOLERANCE
In the early 1700s, a **more moderate outlook** developed. Ulster-born philosopher Francis Hutcheson (1694–1746) was a major figure. His students at Glasgow University included Adam Smith and future Church leader Alexander Carlyle.

The Scottish Enlightenment did much to forge Scotland's sense of history and identity. It centered on Edinburgh, where people gathered in taverns, debating clubs, and the salons of poet Alison Cockburn to share ideas. Edinburgh's university became the most-revered worldwide.

Ideas-wise, there was a stress on human potential, improvement, reason, and on finding underlying principles. Leading figures shared a widespread admiration for French philosopher Jean-Jacques Rousseau (1712–1778), who believed that humans had been constrained by civilization. The most important thing was to think for oneself.

Shaping society
Social and economic improvement and organization were central issues, and Scottish Enlightenment theory was

Walter Scott
Scott's evocative tales of Scotland were popular in his own day, placing Scotland on the international map. He is said to be the father of historical fiction.

very influential in France and America. Theorist David Hume (1711–1776), author of *A Treatise of Human Nature* (1739–1740), believed in challenging conventional wisdom and, in true rationalist style, valued experience (see pp.184–185). Adam Smith (1723–1790), often cited as the father of modern economics, stood against strong state economic controls. Philosopher Adam

Ferguson (1723–1816) was a sociology pioneer who characterized humans as sociable, naturally progressive beings.

The power of song
Ayrshire-born Robert Burns (1759–1796) has become, for many, Scotland's eternal poet laureate. Popular in his day, he collected traditional Scottish songs (including *Auld Lang Syne*) and wrote poetic favorites such as *Tam o' Shanter* (1791) in Scots dialect.

In a similar vein, James Macpherson (1736–1796) collected Gaelic literature and claimed that his *Poems of Ossian* (1760–1763) was a long-lost Celtic epic. Despite this being false, the work was a huge contemporary success worldwide.

Burns and Macpherson might be seen as attempting to find a new identity for post-Union and post-Culloden Scotland, as was poet and novelist Sir Walter Scott (1771–1832). His romantic

New Town, Edinburgh
Edinburgh and Glasgow grew enormously in the 18th and 19th centuries. Edinburgh gained the extensive New Town, a masterful example of city planning.

Scottish Enlightenment

Scottish intellectual, scientific, and artistic life flourished in the 18th century, and Edinburgh became an internationally important, stylish center. Leading figures included poet Robert Burns, thinkers Adam Smith and David Hume, engineer James Watt, and Romantic historical novelist Walter Scott.

historical novels began in 1814 with *Waverley*, set during the 1745 Jacobite rising. The novels mix nostalgic Scottish tradition with the Enlightenment's desire for progress.

Art and architecture

In late 18th-century Edinburgh, the lively, natural portraits of Sir Henry Raeburn (1756–1823) captured the major players of the Scottish Enlightenment. Raeburn was the first Scotland-based artist to gain worldwide acclaim. Allan Ramsay (1713–1784) was another renowned Scottish portraitist, known for sensitive images of women. Edinburgh-based Alexander Nasmyth (1758–1840), famed for landscapes that brought a natural air to classical conventions, is seen as the source of the Scottish landscape tradition.

The 1700s brought increasing prosperity and rapid population growth to Edinburgh. The city's 18th-century New Town, with its elegant, spacious Georgian terraces and squares, was created to cope with some of this. Influential worldwide, it includes Charlotte Square, a gem by Scots-born architect Robert Adam (1728–1792).

Science and engineering

There was considerable scientific activity. William Cullen (1710–1790) and Joseph Black (1728–1799) pioneered chemistry as a discipline, as did James Hutton (1726–1797) with geology. James Watt (1736–1819), and John McAdam (1756–1836), made their names as engineers. Watt invented the condensing steam engine and gave us the terms "watt" and "horsepower."

James Hutton
A pioneering natural scientist, Hutton developed controversial views (since vindicated) on the Earth's aging in works such as *Theory of the Earth* (1795).

Adam Smith
This 1797 coin commemorates Adam Smith, author of *The Wealth of Nations* (1776), which outlined the "division of labor" theory.

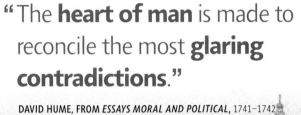

> " The **heart of man** is made to reconcile the most **glaring contradictions**."

DAVID HUME, FROM *ESSAYS MORAL AND POLITICAL*, 1741–1742

AFTER

Scottish Enlightenment thought reverberated through many fields, notably signaling the social sciences and socialist theories of the future.

SMITH AND THE FREE MARKET

Adam Smith's ideas about the **division of labor** helped to create **modern western capitalism**. The **division of labor** deals with the way in which various tasks are shared among different parties in society. Smith believed that, if unconstrained by state controls, a **free market encourages specialization** and society benefits. His ideas influenced economics well into modern times. The Adam Smith Institute, a **British think-tank**, was founded in 1977, and Margaret Thatcher **382–383 »** cited him as an inspiration. Adam Ferguson's views on the division of labor anticipated those of communist Karl Marx (1818–1883) and French sociologist Émile Durkheim (1858–1917).

MOVING ON

Historian and political philosopher **Thomas Carlyle** (1795–1881) **282–283 »** inherited much of the forthright, challenging spirit of the Scottish Enlightenment and was an important influence on 19th-century British culture.

New Horizons in the Pacific

Successive voyages by George Anson, James Cook, and Matthew Flinders gave Britain an important presence in the Pacific Ocean. Cook's explorations in particular brought scientific and geographical discoveries, and gave opportunities for the creation of new colonies, opening up new realms to the imagination and extending Britain's imperial horizons.

BEFORE

The British people had been intrepid seafarers for many centuries, but were slow in starting colonies around the world.

VOYAGES OF DISCOVERY
Elizabethan adventurers accomplished great **voyages of discovery ‹‹ 146–147**, but successful **settlements** were not established until the reign of James I **‹‹ 162–163**.

FULL AHEAD
By the 17th century, England was a trading nation, **prepared to fight for its commercial interests ‹‹ 178–179**. The country was also a developing center of science: advances were to translate to the world of navigation, making a **systematic exploration of the globe** a possibility **‹‹ 184–185**.

By the 18th century, the study of science had advanced. New inventions and insights (see pp.184–185) both fostered and facilitated the desire to investigate the world, inspiring explorers and giving them better navigational instruments and investigative aids. Britain was in the forefront of these new researches.

Booty came first, though: George Anson's circumnavigation of the globe did not start out as a voyage of discovery. His intention was to attack the Spanish treasure fleets that brought home the riches of the colonies.

Anson's voyage
Leaving Portsmouth in September 1740, Anson's flagship HMS *Centurion* led a flotilla of five warships across the Atlantic and around Cape Horn, braving ferocious storms, only to find

Cook's sextant
A relatively new invention, the sextant allowed Cook to plot his geographical position with accuracy.

the weather in the Pacific Ocean even worse. They stopped for repairs before setting out to search for treasure-laden Spanish shipping.

Only a couple of minor vessels came their way until, after stops in China, on June 20, 1743, they encountered the galleon *Nuestra Señora de Covadonga*. Sailing westward from Manila, it was

Cook arrives in Hawaii
Cook's second visit to what he called the Sandwich Islands in 1779 was ill-fated. He was killed by islanders in a fracas over a stolen boat.

almost defenseless—despite being laden with silver coins. After capturing it, Anson made his way home. His share of the booty was more than £90,000.

Cook's tours
Born in Yorkshire in 1728, James Cook served as a merchant seaman on a coaster in the coal trade before joining the Royal Navy at the start of the Seven Years' War. In 1768, his ship, *Endeavour*, took an expedition to the South Pacific, from where a Transit of Venus (the passage of the planet across the face of the sun) could be observed. While the expedition's scientific leader Joseph Banks oversaw the recording of astronomical observations, Cook and

his crew observed with astonishment the ways of the Pacific Islanders. These were captured by the expedition's artists (notably Sydney Parkinson), while botanist Daniel Solander collected a wealth of undiscovered plants.

Endeavour sailed south to New Zealand before heading west to Australia, where it made landfall at what Cook called Botany Bay, with its many specimens for Solander to collect. The ship then rounded Cape York and passed through the Torres Strait to New Guinea and Indonesia, finally reaching England again in 1771.

Southern search

In 1772, Cook led a second voyage in HMS *Resolution*, accompanied by a ship aptly named *Adventure*. The expedition was charged with finding *Terra Australis* (Latin for "Southern Land"), an undiscovered southern continent whose existence had been proposed since ancient times. The theory was that *Terra Australis* would somehow "balance out" the vast landmasses of the northern hemisphere. Of course, Cook did not find it—though he would have reached Antarctica if he had ventured even a little further.

His third voyage, from 1776, was once again on *Resolution*. Cook discovered the Sandwich Islands (Hawaii) before going north along the western coast of North America to the Bering Strait. Their goal was to find the fabled Northwest Passage (see p.163) from the "other"—Pacific—side.

Meeting with no success, Cook turned back, heading south to Hawaiian waters again. He put in to rest at Kealakekua Bay in January 1779. On February 14, during a clash with local warriors, he was killed in rather confused circumstances on the beach.

Around Australia

If Matthew Flinders (1774–1814) had never done anything else, he would have had a place in history for popularizing the use of the name "Australia" (from *Terra Australis*), for what had previously been called New Holland. The earlier name testified to the pioneering role of Dutch adventurers in opening up these waters in the 17th century. Captain James

Chronometer
By keeping accurate time, seafarers could calculate longitude by figuring out the difference between local noon and noon at Greenwich.

Cook established Britain in the region, but the competition from French navigators such as Louis de Bougainville (1729–1811) was stiff. The first Frenchman to circumnavigate the globe, Bougainville explored the Pacific Ocean a couple of years before Cook, and claimed several island groups for France. By 1800, the British were at home in New South Wales: the rest of the continent remained mysterious, however, with even its coastal outline uncharted. Matthew Flinders helped complete the picture by the successive surveys he undertook on his naval sloop, *Investigator*. Setting out from England in December 1801, he took a course well to the south of what was then customary, arriving off Cape Leeuwin (the southwestern tip of Western Australia) and following the southern coast, all the way around to Sydney. After a period in port, between 1802 and 1803 he took to sea again, heading north up the Queensland coast, ultimately circumnavigating the continent completely.

Tahitian lady
In the 18th century, English voyagers were staggered by the exoticism and beauty of the indigenous cultures they came upon in the lands of the Pacific.

> "**Several of the Natives came to us in their canoes, but more to look at us** than anything else."

CAPTAIN JAMES COOK, ON HIS ARRIVAL IN TAHITI, 1769

AFTER ⟫

Britain's explorers did much to extend their country's global reach—of crucial importance to becoming a great commercial and imperial power.

TRADING NETWORK
The worldwide trading network that resulted from extending the country's reach was to stand industrial Britain in good stead when it came to **finding raw materials and markets for its exports 266–267 ⟫**. Further major explorations of the world were made in Victorian times **286–287 ⟫**. In the meantime, Britain built up its presence in India **290–291 ⟫**, while **sending emigrants into its new dominions** around the world **294–295 ⟫**.

BRITAIN'S FIRST SETTLERS IN AUSTRALIA

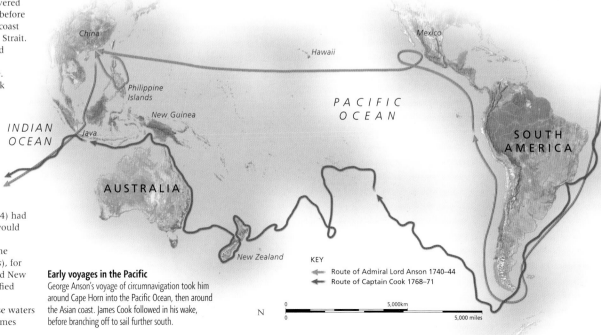

Early voyages in the Pacific
George Anson's voyage of circumnavigation took him around Cape Horn into the Pacific Ocean, then around the Asian coast. James Cook followed in his wake, before branching off to sail further south.

China • Hawaii • Mexico • Philippine Islands • New Guinea • PACIFIC OCEAN • INDIAN OCEAN • Java • SOUTH AMERICA • AUSTRALIA • New Zealand

KEY
← Route of Admiral Lord Anson 1740–44
← Route of Captain Cook 1768–71

N

0 — 5,000km
0 — 5,000 miles

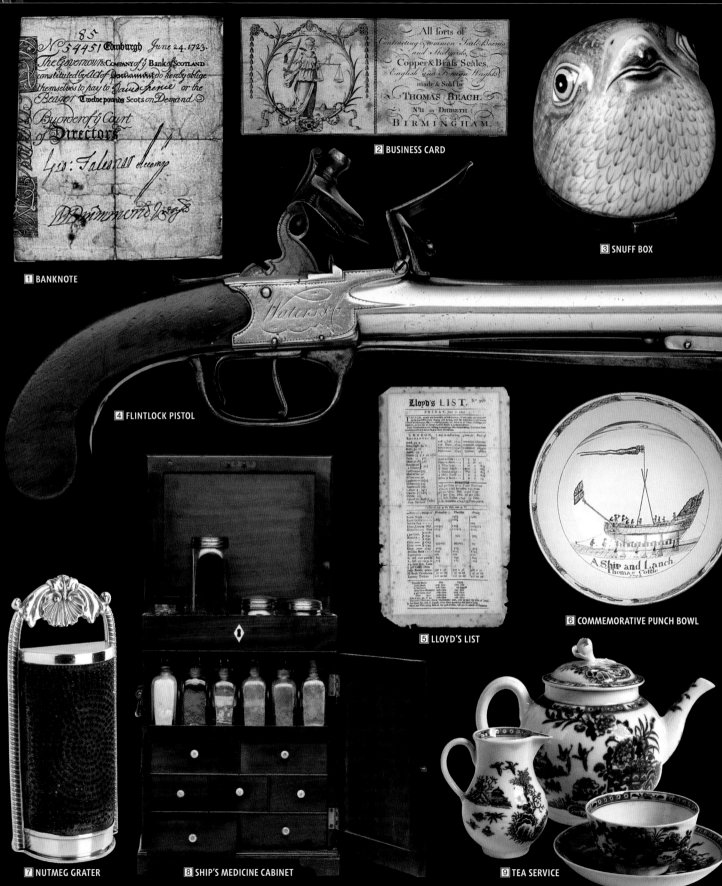

1 BANKNOTE

2 BUSINESS CARD

3 SNUFF BOX

4 FLINTLOCK PISTOL

5 LLOYD'S LIST

6 COMMEMORATIVE PUNCH BOWL

7 NUTMEG GRATER

8 SHIP'S MEDICINE CABINET

9 TEA SERVICE

Georgian Trade

The Georgian age brought a boom in Britain's domestic and international trade, supported by a fast-expanding financial sector and an increasingly professional merchant navy. Britain was in business, bringing in raw materials from North America and the Far East, and making high-quality luxuries for export. Other trades were less glamorous—notably a cruel and squalid traffic in slaves from Africa.

1 Banknote, issued by the Bank of Scotland in 1723. One of the earliest British banknotes in existence. The individual's details were filled in by hand. **2 Business card**, 1754, printed by a maker and seller of scales in Birmingham. **3 Enameled copper snuffbox** made in Staffordshire in 1775. **4 Blunderbuss flintlock pistol** made in 1785. It has a brass barrel and two triggers. **5 Lloyd's List**, Friday, June 7, 1745, details the day's shipping news. First published in 1734, when London's port and financial markets were both beginning to boom, it has appeared regularly ever since. **6 Hand-painted delftware punch bowl**, 1752, decorated with a ship sliding down the slipway to mark a successful launch. As the vessel has no guns, it is likely to be a merchant brig. **7 Silver nutmeg grater** made in London in 1810. **8 Foldaway medicine chest**, c. 1800, belonging to a ship's doctor. **9 Worcester blue tea service**, 1750s,

showing the clear influence of Chinese design. Itself a Chinese invention, porcelain was first made in Europe in the 18th century. **10 A roll of snuff, some clay pipes, and a wallet** dated 1761. **11 Samuel Wyatt's plan for the Isle of Dogs** (1796) was one of several such designs proposed. The port of London was expanding rapidly at this time. **12 Ship's biscuit** inscribed with the date April 13, 1784. Made of flour and water, hard tack kept for years. **13 Iron ankle band** used to shackle a slave, 18th century. **14 Ceramic creamware pitcher**, c. 1780, painted with a scene of a sailor's farewell to his girl. A title above lines of text reads "Poor Jack." **15 Sextant**, mid 18th century, used to plot a ship's latitude from the angle between the horizon and the sun or a given star. **16 Slave ship plan** from the 1790s illustrating the stowage of slaves for the Middle Passage—the leg from Africa to America—of the "triangular trade" of slaves.

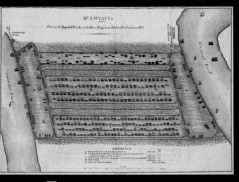

10 SNUFF, PIPES, AND WALLET

11 PLAN FOR THE PORT OF LONDON

12 SHIP'S BISCUIT

13 ANKLE BAND

14 CERAMIC PITCHER

15 SEXTANT

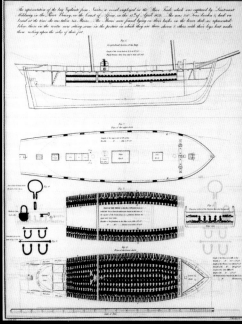

16 SLAVE SHIP PLAN

Modernizing Agriculture

Rural life had long been idealized as a blessed state: man toiled hard, and the earth gave its abundance by God's grace. In the 18th century, however, landowners asked whether it was giving enough and whether the application of scientific methods might not make agriculture more rewarding.

The idea was catching on that agriculture might be an industry; that its skills and equipment might be bettered, its yields improved. The feudal serf had been a subsistence farmer, tied to his land and loyal to his lord. His situation was defined by a cosmography in which he would no more have questioned his place than that of the sun or the stars circling in their spheres. His role was not to change things, but to accept them stoically. This medieval outlook became a memory, however, as cash payment took the place of the feudal bond.

The farmer was a paying tenant now, or at least a paid laborer on an employer's land.

The coming of enclosures

Key to this changing relationship was the accelerating trend toward enclosure, which dated back to Tudor times (see pp.142–143) but had sped up in the 17th century. Large numbers of the rural population, dislodged from lands they and their

Plow of wood and iron
Ancient technology was reinvented in the Agricultural Revolution of the 18th century. Wood-and-iron plows offered the perfect compromise between robustness and lightness for ease of use.

forebears had farmed for centuries, drifted to the cities. The enclosures were a tragedy for thousands of poor families.

The advantage from the landlord's point of view—and for the economy overall—was the opportunity enclosure brought to make improvements. Until then, agriculture had been traditional and inherently conservative. Now, however, a new confidence was apparent in landlords; a new readiness to try out innovations and to take risks. Crop rotation was not new in itself, but it was improved. The three-field system used (though gradually refined) since late medieval times was replaced with a four-field system. After a cereal crop, legumes such as clover, or root crops such as turnips, would be planted. Both helped recharge the earth with nitrogen, while producing food for livestock (whose manure was widely used as fertilizer).

This and other improvements were made possible by pioneers such as Robert Bakewell, who from the 1760s adopted a more scientific approach to agriculture. He set aside designated plots on his Dishley estate, in Leicestershire, and tested combinations of rotation, fertilizers, and livestock.

Taking stock

Bakewell's method of stockbreeding involved keeping males and females apart, so that he could manage their breeding much more carefully than had been done before. This way he was able to develop the much larger and more luxuriantly fleeced New Leicester sheep and the Dishley Longhorn cow (big and chunky, and so purpose-bred for beef). He also produced a more powerful

The Country Housewife
Science came to the kitchen when Richard Bradley, Cambridge University's Professor of Botany, wrote *The Country Housewife* in 1736. This manual, on every aspect of cooking, food preservation, and brewing, became an indispensable housekeeper's companion.

◀◀ BEFORE

In Britain, as in most of Europe, the medieval economy was overwhelmingly agrarian and was changing only very slowly.

A FEUDAL SYSTEM
The Domesday Book shows an England dominated by the feudal system: most people **toiled in serfdom on the land ◀◀ 74–75**. Efficiencies over the centuries that followed gradually increased agricultural productivity, without radically changing the feudal system **◀◀ 88–89**, though growing tensions were registered in the Peasants' Revolt **◀◀ 104–105**. The cities came into their own, and **merchant companies and guilds organized** urban economic life **◀◀ 120–121**.

CHANGES BEGIN
Tudor enclosures made England's farmland yet more productive, albeit at considerable social cost **◀◀ 132–133**. The **enclosure process gathered momentum** through the 17th century. So, too,

however, had researches into science and the study of humanity's relations to its world. While Isaac Newton was mapping out the universe, others were **inquiring into just about every other aspect of the natural environment ◀◀ 184–185.**

PEASANT WORKING THE LAND

ulif ef nomnat lefeies.

LANDSCAPE AS ART

Enlightened landowners saw their profits soaring as their lands became more productive. With their wealth they could afford to improve not just their working farms, but their homes as well. Their confidence was rising, too: they believed implicitly that they could improve on nature, and set about creating numerous picturesque settings.

Landscape architects such as Charles Bridgeman (1690–1738) and William Kent (c. 1685–1748) led the way in establishing the taste for a natural look which, while offering an enticing hint of wildness, was reassuringly domesticated in its overall effect.

This sensibility reached its height in the rolling parkland vistas conjured up by Lancelot "Capability" Brown (1716–1783). Where a previous generation might have rejoiced in the self-conscious artificiality of an ornamental garden with fountains, lawns, and symmetrically laid-out walks, now the emphasis was on a carefully contrived spontaneity. Great as the contrast with earlier styles was, such scenes were to fall foul of later Romantic judges, who believed that natural beauty should not be landscaped, but should be wild and uncontrolled.

Improved Black Cart Horse, the ancestor of the modern Shire.

A disciple of Bakewell's, Thomas Coke developed his ideas at Holkham Hall, in Norfolk, from 1776. His Holkham Clippings, open to the public, made his annual shearing into what we would nowadays call an agricultural show. It served as a sort of trade fair for improvement-minded farmers, stockbreeders, and engineers.

The consequences of these local experiments were felt nationwide. Statistics kept by London's Smithfield Market give the average weight of a bullock in 1710 as 370 lb (168 kg); by 1795 it was more than twice that at 800 lb (363 kg). Over that same period the weight of sheep actually more than doubled, from 29 to 79 lb (13 to 36 kg).

Technological transformation

Farming was transformed by innovations such as Jethro Tull's seed drill (1701) and Joseph Foljambe's

Scientific agriculture

Selective breeding allowed the scientific landowner to achieve constant improvements—and aspire to even more. While genetic science was not yet understood, it was clear that mating animals with special strengths offered the chance of a benefit in the next generation. Animals could be bred bigger, meatier, or woollier.

Rotherham plow (1730), which was lighter, yet more robustly made than earlier models. Andrew Meikle's threshing machine (1786) made the annual harvest much easier to manage, making light of one of the most labor-intensive tasks.

Technological development in agriculture helped to create a climate in which technological advances could be harnessed in other areas, too. The growth in profits helped fund amateur research and experimentation, and rapidly rising yields meant that a growing urban population could be fed, setting things in place for the now-incipient Industrial Revolution.

AFTER

The Agricultural Revolution was profoundly significant in itself; yet its indirect results were still more far-reaching.

DRIFT TO THE CITIES

Brutal though the process may have been, enclosure—and the evictions it brought—helped clear the way for the great advance that

CITY SLUM DWELLERS, 1861

was to be represented by the Industrial Revolution. Those dislodged from the land, drifting to the cities, **constituted a ready-made labor force**, grateful for the chances offered to them by the new entrepreneurs 232–233 ≫.

URBAN NEEDS

The transition was by no means painless. Living conditions in the industrial cities were frequently horrific; work was exacting (and often dangerous) and the hours were long. Soon, **political discontent found expression** in popular protest 264–265 ≫. But there was to be no turning the clock back. In time and as industrialization gathered momentum **276–277 ≫**, the **greater output from the countryside** allowed a large and (in food terms) nonproductive urban population to be supported. As the 20th century began, Britain was well on its way to becoming a predominantly urban society.

Inventors and Entrepreneurs

In the space of a few generations, the Industrial Revolution was to utterly transform the British scene—from its landscape to its social assumptions and sense of identity. Invention and entrepreneurship went together in bringing about these changes. Neither could have taken place without the other.

« **BEFORE**

Trade was always important to the nations of Britain. In the preceding centuries, it became more vital still.

CONDITIONS FOR ENTERPRISE
In Tudor times, **the wool trade brought great prosperity** « 142–143. Flourishing commerce (cultural and mercantile) with northern Italy ensured that England shared in the benefits of the Renaissance « 152–153. **Trade expanded rapidly during the Commonwealth and Restoration**, with England even going to war to defend its market share « 180–181. Scientific advances through the 17th century led to new technologies « 184–185. Just as important was **the financial ingenuity that made their development possible** through the introduction of more sophisticated banking and of joint-stock companies « 210–211. Meanwhile, **increased agricultural productivity was freeing up a huge potential workforce** to work in industry « 230–231.

INNOVATION

A NEW POTTERY

Founded in 1736, Josiah Wedgwood's Staffordshire stoneware was industrialized elegance, bringing gracious living within reach of the middle class. A readiness to innovate in kiln and glaze technology was matched by resourcefulness in marketing, especially in securing the approval of Queen Charlotte in 1765. Although it was mass produced, it was made to exacting standards, was beautifully colored in white, blue, or black, and was tastefully decorated—often with classically influenced designs.

WEDGWOOD TEAPOT

The early 18th century found a still overwhelmingly rural Britain poised uncertainly between a fast-receding past and an unknown future. Thousands of agricultural workers were left unemployed by a labor surplus that resulted from high rates of population growth; often their families were uprooted by enclosures, which were gathering pace throughout the decades of the Agricultural Revolution (see pp.230–231).

With a sole dependence on agriculture seemingly gone, manufacturing, mainly in textiles, offered an alternative, or at least additional work. Some people had established themselves as spinners or weavers, processing wool on wheels or handlooms in their own homes, often combined with farming work. Yet such "cottage industries" were by definition small in scale. There was no suggestion that production could be stepped up sufficiently to supply anything more than the most modest local trade.

Productivity and factories

Technological innovation was to change all that. Inventions, such as John Kay's flying shuttle, in 1733, made even handloom weaving more productive. The realization that these devices automated the processes of manufacturing offered to manufacturers the possibility of replicating them, perhaps many times over, to bring output to unprecedented levels. Yet productivity was still limited by the capacity of the individual man or woman to work, marrying strength and stamina with manual skill.

External sources of power were not new: horses had pulled carts and coaches from time immemorial; windmills and watermills had been used for centuries in grinding grain. The challenge facing 18th-century inventors was to harness the brute power of water to the delicate tasks of textile manufacture. In 1738, Lewis Paul and Edward Baines invented a roller-spinning machine, which allowed yarns to be made on a much larger

The new industrial landscape

The Industrial Revolution excited not just the economic, but the artistic, imagination. A new kind of landscape that both attracted and repelled was born at the Ironbridge Gorge, in Coalbrookdale, Shropshire.

scale. Paul's carding machine of 1748 allowed the clumps and tangles to be teased out of the raw wool with ease, enabling the worker to produce far more usable fiber. James Hargreaves' spinning jenny (1764) was quickly eclipsed by Richard Arkwright's spinning (later, water) frame, in 1775.

Arkwright was arguably responsible for a more important innovation: modern factory production. At his five-story mill in Cromford, Derbyshire, he used water power to drive whole rows of carding machines, spinning

500 **The number of horses whose work Newcomen's first steam engine of 1711 was able to perform. Steam power was quickly to become much stronger still, performing the work of thousands of horsepower.**

frames, and mechanical looms, under the supervision of some 200 local workers—men, women, and children. Serving in shifts, they kept the factory running day and night. Arkwright's system meant that the output of thousands of highly skilled artisans could now be surpassed by that of a few, mainly unskilled, workers.

Arkwright achieved enormous economies of scale, but water power was not available everywhere, and even where it was, capacity was limited by difficulties of access and river flow. The first steam pump was developed by Thomas Savery, in 1698, although its poor performance gave no suggestion that a technological revolution was under way. Thomas Newcomen's atmospheric engine, in 1712, was an improvement, although Scottish engineer James Watt was to make it better still. Watt saw how inefficient Newcomen's engine was, particularly in its condenser. Using cold water, this condensed steam in

its chamber to produce a vacuum, which had the effect of pulling a piston down to raise the pumping beam. Then more steam was produced, driving the piston up once more, until the chamber cooled down and the condensing cycle could begin again. Heated and cooled at every stroke, the process was hugely wasteful in energy. Watt's separate condenser allowed most of the heat to be retained and reused in successive strokes; his steam pump also had an efficient rotating engine. Watt was sponsored by Matthew Boulton, who was one of the new breed of entrepreneurs. With no personal pretensions to technical mastery, he was driven instead by a dream of industrial power; a desire to realize the potential of new technologies. His Soho Manufactory, in Birmingham, made

Marketing technology
Richard Trevithick's 1808 locomotive, named *Catch Me Who Can*, raced a horse around a specially built circular track in Bloomsbury, London, in order to prove the value of this new invention. It was not enough to invent technology, it had to be sold as well.

" I sell here, sir, what all the world desires to have—**POWER**."

MATTHEW BOULTON, TO DIARIST JAMES BOSWELL, 1776

everything from toys to buttons and, from 1788, had a steam-powered mint for the mass production of coins.

A new age of iron

Steam was used where water power was used before, but now with new applications, especially in mining for coal and Cornish tin. Steam pumps raised rainwater from previously inconceivable depths, allowing a rapid expansion in the industry, and—since Abraham Darby had found a way of using coke in iron production—meeting a soaring demand for coal. In 1709, ending centuries of charcoal-fueled forest-smelting, Darby built a gigantic blast furnace at Coalbrookdale, making possible the large-scale production of pig-iron. It also made its mark on the Shropshire landscape, a diabolical one, many felt. Belching smoke by day, it cast an infernal glow at night, while ringing with the din of its machinery. The Industrial Revolution was everywhere. Even where mills and mines did not stud the skyline, canals crisscrossed the country. With huge quantities of raw materials and manufactured goods to be moved, canals were vital. The Sankey Canal, near Warrington, was built in 1757; the Bridgwater Canal four years later; and the Leeds and Liverpool Canal followed in 1774.

AFTER »

Britain led the way as the world's first industrial nation. The challenge now was to manage that advantage.

DRAMATIC CHANGE
The **pace of change was startling**: the sense, at once exhilarating and alarming, was of an entire country rushing onward like one of the new steam trains that were careering across the countryside **258–259** ». Many of the population felt left behind, however: **uprooted from the traditions of rural life**, they found themselves disorientated, struggling to find their way in sprawling cities. At this time of progress and prosperity, **poverty was rife and living and working conditions frequently atrocious**. It seemed that political turbulence, including a Luddite backlash against machines and industry, could hardly now be avoided **264–265** ».

NO WAY BACK
Britain's course was established, and with other competitive nations racing to catch up, there was no turning back, or any great desire to. Despite the problems, **most took pride in the industrial preeminence** of what remained the workshop of the world **276–277** ».

ANTI-INDUSTRY LUDDITE

The Anti-Slavery Movement

The institution of slavery did not seem self-evidently wrong to many in 18th-century England, much of whose prosperity depended on the trade. The success of the abolitionist cause represented not just the righting of a historic wrong, but a rare example of sustained persuasion producing a real change of heart.

In 1765, Bristol-born sugar planter John Pinney wrote: "I can assure you that I was shocked at the first appearance of human flesh exposed for sale." He recovered from his discomfort

BEFORE

Slavery was a part of Roman and early medieval life, but for the British, trading in slaves on a large scale was relatively recent.

THE NEED FOR SLAVES
The 17th century brought **colonial expansion on a significant scale**, opening up new North American and Caribbean territories for exploitation **«« 162–163**. True, people there could be exploited, but American Indians were not the answer. Epidemiologists estimate that, within a century of the Europeans' arrival, about 90 percent of the indigenous population were carried off by **Old World diseases** to which they had no inbred immunity. As commerce became increasingly the mainstay of British economic life, **the slave trade played an ever more central part «« 178–179**.

quickly enough, however, and was able not merely to accept but to justify the trade in Africans: "Surely God ordained them for the use and benefit of us."

A lucrative trade

How much easier was it for those in England who simply profited second- and third-hand? That group was not restricted to the merchant communities of Liverpool and Bristol. The slave trade

Anti-slavery poster
Campaigners successfully mobilized middle-class opinion: this meeting was called by prominent clergy and other pillars of the community in Wakefield, Yorkshire.

AFRICAN SLAVE SHIP

underpinned Britain's general prosperity. The trade brought tobacco from the Chesapeake, rice from the Carolinas and Georgia, and sugar from the Caribbean. The profits from the trade contributed to some of the ventures and infrastructure projects of the Industrial Revolution.

British and black
A small but significant Black-British population had by this time become established. Some were freed slaves—often former personal servants—but there were also US seafarers from the northern states who had decided to stay on in the (sometimes only slightly) more tolerant climate they found in

seaports such as Liverpool and Bristol. London had Britain's biggest black community, though: it was a major port and the nation's economic powerhouse. Most of the new Black-British population worked in menial trades, but some were more educated and prosperous. These included Ignatius Sancho (a shopkeeper who was also a composer and playwright), Ottobah Cugoano, and Olaudah Equiano.

"Am I not a man ...?"
The last two became important—as examples of what black people might become—for a new but growing abolitionist movement. "Am I not a man and a brother?" asked the kneeling

Slaves thrown overboard
In 1781, the Liverpool slave ship *Zong* threw 122 slaves overboard to relieve overcrowding, and then made an insurance claim—later contested in court—for their lost cargo. Such indifference to life horrified many in Britain.

black slave on the medallion issued by Josiah Wedgwood in 1787. White Britons found this rhetorical question easier to answer in the affirmative when faced by articulate and presentable figures such as Cugoano and Equiano.

Some voices (such as those of the Quakers) had been raised against the outrage of slavery since the end of the 17th century. The Society for the Abolition of the Slave Trade was

In Britain itself, the immediate impact of the abolitionists' eventual success was to raise questions about how Britons were being treated by their fellow Britons.

GREATER DIGNITY AND CHOICE

Slavery might not have existed officially in Britain, but countless thousands toiled in **terrible conditions in mines and factories**, and in the **sweatshops** of the garment trade. Caring members of the richer classes took a new interest in their plight, while radicals attempted to **mobilize the poor** themselves 264–265 ».

The recognition grew that bound up in their wage-slavery was **a genuine lack of democratic participation**, and this added momentum to the campaign for electoral reform 268–269 ». A desire to have greater dignity and choice in their lives spurred many in the working classes to strenuous efforts in self-education 278–279 ».

Gustavus Vassa
Nigerian-born Olaudah Equiano was renamed by his Virginia owner after a 16th-century Swedish nobleman. It seems to have been an act of sheer facetiousness. However, Gustavus Vassa later became an important abolitionist campaigner.

American slave James Somersett, who ran away during a visit to London. He was captured, but Sharp took legal action to prevent his return to Virginia.

Final victory

Their court victory effectively established that slavery was prohibited in Britain; though some ambiguity existed until the end of the century. The Society developed a new kind of political activism, including rallies, petitions, and popular tie-in items such as jewelry and medallions.

Abolitionists drew attention to an outrage most were unaware of, and ultimately succeeded in changing the moral climate. It took them a long time, though, and while the trade was abolished throughout the British Empire in 1807, slavery was not outlawed until 1833.

founded in 1787. Its leaders included James Ramsay (a Royal Navy surgeon, who had seen conditions on slave ships), Elizabeth Heyrick, Thomas Clarkson, Granville Sharp, and, most famously, William Wilberforce. The latter's key contribution was in Parliament where he introduced his first bill in 1791, though it was roundly rejected.

The Society was strongly Christian: three-quarters of its founders were Quakers; others belonged to Anglican, Methodist, Baptist, and other groups. Christian views did not automatically ensure abolitionist views. John Newton, since famous as a reformed slaver and as author of the hymn *Amazing Grace*, did not end his involvement in the

trade until some years after his spiritual rebirth of 1748. A non-Christian case against slavery was also emerging—and not just a post-Enlightenment view that it was inhumane. Since Adam Smith (see pp.224–225), there had been a prejudice against anything that hindered the free functioning of the market economy.

Granville Sharp scored an early victory in 1772 with his support for

William Wilberforce

Christian conviction inspired this Yorkshire-born MP to take up the cause of abolitionism in the 1780s. Religious groups took the lead in the campaign that called for an end to the slave trade.

BEFORE

Political violence had been seen in Britain, although nothing matched the scale of the revolution in France (1789–1799).

BRITISH UPRISINGS

The **Peasants' Revolt** of 1381 set the establishment trembling **« 104–105**. Two centuries later, **Henry VIII's Reformation** sparked not just religious but social unrest **« 136–137**. Charles I's problems with his Parliament **« 166–167** started a struggle between elites, but the whole country got caught up in the **horrors of the Civil War « 168–169**. The Glorious Revolution, despite its name, had been more of a palace coup, though its repercussions were felt by all **« 188–189**.

FRENCH REVOLUTION

INTELLECTUAL (1737–1809)

THOMAS PAINE

Born in Norfolk in 1737, Thomas Paine immigrated to America in his mid-thirties, and experienced the tumults and the triumph of the American independence struggle. A friend of founding fathers such as George Washington and Thomas Jefferson, he discovered a calling in the radical cause, and went to France to join the fight for freedom there. His book *The Rights of Man* (1791), an eloquent counterblast to Burke's *Reflections* won him widespread admiration as the prophet of revolution, but he found little honor in his homeland, where he was roundly vilified.

Reaction to the Revolution

"Bliss was it in that dawn to be alive," wrote the Romantic poet William Wordsworth, recollecting his experiences as a young student in revolutionary Paris. But many of his countrymen were not convinced—especially as hope turned to disillusion, and tumult to terror.

The French Revolution did not directly involve Great Britain. On the other hand, it was happening less than 30 miles (48 km) from Dover. Prime Minister William Pitt the Younger was concerned, but felt that it was not Britain's quarrel. He found he could not ignore it altogether, though. Pitt was no radical, but in a spirit of good-housekeeping he had been trying to clean up British public life (see pp.206–207). However, events in France produced a conservative backlash in Britain, and the merest hint of reforming intent was taken as revolutionism. The new mood was articulated by the Irish statesman and thinker Edmund Burke, in his pamphlet *Reflections on the Revolution in France* (1790). *Liberté, egalité et fraternité* ("freedom, equality, and brotherhood": the French revolutionary slogan) would only lead to tyranny and bloodbath, Burke prophesied.

Pamphlet war

Burke's book kicked off a major debate over the issues raised by the Revolution: what place (if any) the monarchy should have; what freedom should mean; the relative importance of individual and collective rights. More than 300 further publications appeared in the "pamphlet war" that followed. Tom Paine, long-standing cheerleader for change (see BOX) responded with his *Rights of Man* (1791), although Mary Wollstonecraft had beaten him to it, her

Pitt the Younger at Westminster

As Britain's youngest-ever prime minister—just 24 when he came to office—William Pitt the Younger did much to reform the assembly whose committees he graced and whose debates he electrified.

236

FRENCH LIBERTY.   BRITISH SLAVERY.

French Liberty, British Slavery
James Gillray's satirical swipe takes a familiar line: Britain's cautious conservatism delivered more to the people than France's radicalism. There was something in the claim.

AFTER »

Britain showed every sign of riding out the revolutionary storm. Its constitutional regime was flexible enough to cope with and contain a degree of unrest.

MOVEMENTS FOR CHANGE
In the decades that followed, **industrialization placed enormous strains on the social order.** Workers started organizing to win their rights. One early movement was that of the **Chartists 264–265** », who campaigned for electoral reform **268–269** ».

CHARTISTS MEETING, 1848

Government alarm, meanwhile, led to a crackdown on radicalism. At the Treason Trials of 1793–1794, a series of writers and speakers were charged with sedition, first in Scotland, then in London. The Scottish trials were kangaroo courts; radicals Thomas Muir and Thomas Palmer being found guilty and transported as a formality. London jurors would not be cowed: a couple of defendants (including Paine) were convicted, but most were not. In some cases their prosecutions were quite literally laughed out of court, although the Conservative press and "Loyal Britons" were not amused.

Vindications of the Rights of Men appearing just weeks after Burke's *Reflections*. She went one better in 1791 with a *Vindication of the Rights of Woman*, a bold articulation of the case for feminism.

Terror and treason
Whatever the rights and wrongs of the argument, events on the ground in France were bearing out Burke's gloomy prognosis. By 1792, the revolutionary government was calling on others to emulate their example. Then, in January 1793, Louis XVI and his family were executed; centralized despotism and the beginnings of the Terror followed. Relations with Britain were frosty even before France, as part of its aim to export revolution, declared war on February 1. After this, what had been a fear for the country's political stability became a concern for its immediate security.

While respectable England was haunted by the specter of the *sans culotte* (the "knee-breech-less" hooligan of the Paris streets), the first riots in Britain were by reactionary "Church-and-King" mobs. These attacked dissenters and intellectuals over their supposed sympathy with the French Revolution. A particularly nasty attack occurred in Birmingham in 1790.

Mutiny!
Although most of the violence in Britain up until this point had come from those the radical thinkers were now branding "reactionaries," the threat of revolution was not altogether imaginary. "Corresponding Societies" called for universal male suffrage, schools for all, and other measures which would undoubtedly have transformed society. A famine in the mid-1790s inevitably heightened popular unrest. In 1795, George III's coach was mobbed by a crowd up to 200,000 strong, shouting "No King, no war, no famine, and no Pitt!" Rushed through in response to this outrage against the Crown itself, the Two Acts (against Seditious Meetings and Treasonable Practices respectively) promised to make life all but impossible for the radicals.

A shudder ran down respectable spines when the insurrectionary spirit

300 The number of effigies of Tom Paine burned across Britain by members of the Association for the Protection of Liberty and Property against Republicans and Levellers, November–December 1792.

now showed itself in the very force that was supposed to be protecting Britain. April 1797 brought a naval mutiny at Spithead, off Portsmouth.

It was, in truth, barely a mutiny at all, although it suited a Conservative press to see it that way: the participants, seeking better pay and conditions, bent over backward not to be disruptive and promised that they would not refuse to fight if called upon to do so. This dispute was resolved by negotiation.

The following month, however, a second, more serious, mutiny took place off the Nore at the mouth of the Thames. While this started as a copycat protest, it quickly got out of hand—partly because the Admiralty cracked down on it so harshly, clearly seeing it as a sign of the rot setting in. The Navy's tougher line was met with violence—and escalating demands. Ultimately, indeed, quite ludicrous demands: the dissolution of Parliament, for instance, and an end to the war with France. The Nore mutineers were starved into submission, and when the protest finally collapsed, ringleader Richard Parker was hanged from the yardarm as a warning to others; 28 of his followers were also executed, while others were flogged or transported to Australia.

" But what is **liberty without wisdom**, and **without virtue**? It is the greatest of all possible evils … "

EDMUND BURKE, *REFLECTIONS ON THE REVOLUTION IN FRANCE*, 1790

Rebellion in Ireland

Among those looking to the French example in their thirst for freedom were those in Ireland, both Protestant and Catholic, who believed that it was time to break the British connection, once and for all. In May 1798, the moment came for the United Irishmen. Thousands rose in open rebellion.

Ireland appeared stable as the end of the 18th century approached. But this stability was based on the rule of an essentially Anglican Ascendancy: northern Presbyterians shared the Catholics' sense of disenfranchisement.

United for Ireland

This was the logic behind the formation of the Society of United Irishmen, which held its first meeting in Belfast in 1791. Its founders Samuel Neilson,

Vinegar Hill
General Lake looks on as his cannons cut a swathe through the rebel ranks. They made a valiant last stand atop this hill in County Wexford.

Theobald Wolfe Tone, and Thomas Russell were all Protestants, as was their early leader James Napper Tandy. They were "patriots"—in the specialized sense that they were Protestants who favored Irish independence. They were also unabashedly influenced by both the American and French Revolutions. Yet it was only Wolfe Tone who favored universal suffrage—Catholics included.

His comrades felt the peasantry was (in William Drennan's words) "unfit for liberty"—too much influenced by its clergy to be trusted with democratic responsibilities. The issue was energetically discussed at meetings and in the United Irishmen's newspaper, the *North Star*.

Theobald Wolfe Tone
Wolfe Tone believed that Ireland's Protestant "patriot" gentry could make common cause with the Catholic peasantry. He committed suicide after he was captured in 1798.

BEFORE

The story of the previous two centuries in Ireland was one of English overlordship, often brutally enforced.

FLIGHT OF THE EARLS
Finally prevailing in the Nine Years' War, England demanded the **loyalty and obedience** of the old Catholic elite, who for the most part chose instead to leave their homeland, in the Flight of the Earls. The Plantation of Ulster established Protestant settlers in the north **«** 156–157.

DRIVEN UNDERGROUND
Meanwhile, a series of penal laws **restricted the religious freedoms of Catholics**, barring them from public office. Cromwell's atrocities made clear his contempt for the Irish and their religion **«** 174–175, driving Catholicism underground. Not surprisingly, the Catholic Irish sided with the Stuarts in the Succession Wars **«** 196–197.

ANGLO-IRISH ATTITUDES
Calm was assured in the 18th century when a Protestant Anglo-Irish "Ascendancy" **felt secure in its hold** over a powerless, impoverished, and overwhelmingly Catholic peasantry.

ANGLO-IRISH STATELY HOME, WICKLOW

The ultra-Britishness of the Protestants in Ulster is taken for granted now, but as the example of the United Irishmen shows, this was not always so.

Even at the time, however, some Protestants took a different direction. The edge of the Ulster Plantation was a natural flash point for sectarian violence. The Orange Order, which was named after William of Orange, whose victories in the Succession Wars (see pp.196–197) were rallying-points, was established at Loughgall, Armagh, in 1795, after the Battle of the Diamond. This sectarian brawl at the Diamond crossroads sparked off the Armagh Outrages, in which many Catholic homes were attacked. Membership of the Order overlapped with that of the Peep o' Day Boys, who attacked in the dawn, ruthlessly driving out many hundreds of Catholic families.

Crackdown
Meanwhile, a crackdown by the authorities in 1793 had driven the United Irishmen underground. By 1796, Wolfe Tone and Lord Edward FitzGerald were meeting French revolutionary officials in Paris.

A son of the Duke of Leinster, FitzGerald, the "Citizen Lord," was potentially a powerful advocate for the United Irishmen's cause. In the end, his impetuosity and indiscretion made him a liability, alienating moderates in the Irish ascendancy and rattling the French. Even so, France did put together an invasion fleet that same

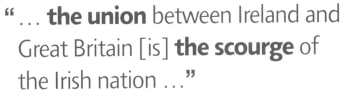

" ... **the union** between Ireland and Great Britain [is] **the scourge** of the Irish nation ... "

THEOBALD WOLFE TONE, TO HIS COURT-MARTIAL, NOVEMBER 10, 1798

year, only for it to be dispersed by a "Protestant Wind." Despite this, the United Irishmen had 280,000 members by the beginning of 1798. Again, government reaction left them no peaceful recourse: the imposition of martial law in March 1798 precipitated a rising. This time, however, the French dragged their heels and sent only a small force.

In Ireland, a new group of rebels, known as the Croppies, were ready for the fight. The Croppies took their name and style from the French Jacobins, who had close-cropped hair to show their contempt for the aristocratic powdered wig. Across the country, though, support for a fight was patchy. Brutal campaigns by General Gerard Lake in Ulster and around Dublin weakened the United Irishmen in what should have been their heartlands. Further south, the Catholic peasants were far more exercised by their poverty—and by the penal laws.

90 The number of days after the start of the rebellion when the first French forces arrived in support, but they were too late. The Irish rebels had been, to all intents and purposes, crushed two months before.

Vinegar Hill
On May 24, 1798, Kildare was taken in a surprise attack by the British. It all turned very dirty as a string of tit-for-tat massacres ensued. The high-minded nonsectarianism of the United Irishmen went by the wayside, especially in the south. The murderous feeling was mutual as British armies converged on the county of Wexford. A force that was 20,000 strong defeated the inadequately armed rebels at Vinegar Hill on June 21. Up to 1,000 people, including women and children, were killed in the aftermath.

Toward union
The French sent a disappointingly small force under General Humbert, which arrived on the coast of Mayo in August 1798. With their help, the local rebels established a Republic of Connaught—which lasted all of 13 days. In October, Wolfe Tone tried to land in Donegal with a larger French force, but he did not even make it to the shore before being captured by the British.

Up to a point, the justice of the rebels' cause was implicitly acknowledged in the 1800 Act of Union, which came into effect in January 1801. William Pitt the Younger viewed Ireland's exclusion from full union as an anomaly and the direct cause of much disaffection among the island's ruling class. In his eagerness to enlist support, he strove to further the cause of Catholic emancipation. This upset George III, who took seriously his role as patron and protector of the Church of England. The prime minister was forced to resign in 1801, and Catholic emancipation progressed slowly, finally arriving only in 1829.

AFTER

The harsh suppression of the rebels guaranteed that Ireland's 18th century would end just as its 16th and 17th centuries had: in a burning sense of grievance against the English.

UNDERCURRENT OF ANGER
Violent unrest continued to be part of Irish life in the decades that followed, but for the most part on a small and local scale. The Famine of the 1840s, **266–267** ≫, did nothing to reduce **Irish resentments**, though sheer want and exhaustion produced passive stoicism, rather than violent eruption. A deep, continuing undercurrent of anger ensured that, despite the best efforts of O'Connell and Parnell, a wholly **peaceful campaign for Home Rule** would be difficult to sustain **300–301** ≫.

THE FENIAN FIGHT
If the Fenians—formed by the Irish diaspora in America in the 1850s— looked to ancient Ireland and the warriors of Finn MacCool's Fianna for their name, they looked to the Croppies of 1798 for **political inspiration**. They were a model for Irish Republicans down to the troubled years of the 20th century **378–379** ≫.

FENIAN BANNER, 1866

BEFORE

Antagonism toward France was for centuries an established constant of English, and then British, history.

WARS WITH FRANCE

Close ties in the Norman era later gave way to the Hundred Years' War **« 96–97**, **« 118–119**. Conflict flared again in Tudor times **« 138–139**. A united kingdom now, Britain built **an empire at France's expense**, taking territories in North America and India **« 212–213**. France in its turn tried to thwart Britain's plans, **supporting rebellious colonists** in America, **« 214–215**, and the Jacobites in Scotland **« 202–203**. The French Revolution and ensuing Terror caused consternation across the Channel, **« 236–237**, especially when the French **backed the United Irishmen's uprising « 238–239**.

GUILLOTINE OF THE TERROR

The Napoleonic Wars

A whole continent could not contain the vaunting ambition of Napoleon Bonaparte, the "Little Corporal" who seized an emperor's crown. For Britain, as for other European countries, the need to handle the threat from France overshadowed the end of the 18th and start of the 19th centuries.

France in the early 1790s was ebulliently aggressive: this was a way for the revolutionary regime to maintain momentum and keep the people's spirits high. French soldiers were repulsed on invading the Austrian Netherlands in 1790, but fared far better when they tried again two years later. Britain joined Austria, Spain, Prussia, and the Kingdoms of Sardinia and Naples in a First Coalition against France in 1793, but this alliance did not faze the French. With reason: the defeat of an Austro-British army at Tourcoing in May 1794 left the First Coalition in disarray, and by 1795 France appeared to be secure. But war was a way of life now for France; the first resort of a government which preferred to seek enemies abroad than to tackle its difficulties at home.

Little Corporal to emperor

The Italian island of Corsica had been ceded to France in 1768, so when Napoleone di Buonaparte was born the following year, he was French, and it was to a French military academy that he went a decade later. He came to prominence as a young artillery commander at the Siege of Toulon, in 1793, after that city had sought, with British backing, to throw off France's Convention government. He had then

The Battle of Waterloo, 1815

The Battle of Waterloo, in which the French were beaten by an Anglo-Prussian force, finally finished Napoleon (see pp.246–247). It took place after Napoleon had escaped from his exile on the island of Elba.

625 **The percentage rise (from 40,000 to 250,000 men) in the size of the British Army between the start of the Revolutionary Wars (1793) and the height of the Napoleonic Wars (1813).**

saved the new Directory government, thwarting a coup attempt in 1795. Now a general, from 1796 he fought a triumphant campaign against Austria in Italy. Austria was brought to terms in 1797, though the following year, it became a member (with Britain, Russia, Portugal, Sweden, and the Ottoman Empire) of the Second Coalition.

In 1798, Napoleon invaded Egypt. Though the Canal was not yet built, Suez was vital to Britain's links with its empire in India. The British therefore supported the Ottoman Turks, Egypt's then rulers. Although the Royal Navy,

under Horatio Nelson, failed to stop the French landing, in 1799 its guns helped push them back at the Siege of Acre, preventing a French conquest of Syria. However, Napoleon still controlled Egypt, and, from November 10, he was a preeminent member at home of the Consulate, a dictatorial government. Yet he remained a field commander, leading a reorganized army to dazzling victories at Marengo and Hohenlinden. In 1802, with Austria once more forced to surrender, Britain agreed its own reluctant peace at Amiens.

Both sides broke the Treaty of Amiens, the French by interfering in Switzerland, the British by seizing Malta. When a Third Coalition brought Britain into

alliance with Austria, Russia, and others, Napoleon demonstrated his defiance by crowning himself Emperor of France on December 2, 1804.

Defending the "ditch"

In 1805, resolving to invade England, Napoleon marshalled 180,000 troops on France's northern coast. It was almost as many soldiers as the British Army had in total (about 200,000, to France's 2.5 million). The English Channel, Napoleon notoriously observed, was "a mere ditch," which it would take only a little courage to cross. It turned out to be a more formidable barrier, however, especially when it was patrolled by a determined Royal Navy.

Vice-Admiral Robert Calder thwarted Villeneuve's French fleet at Finisterre that July; Nelson won famously (albeit tragically) at Trafalgar three months later. In the longer term, the Royal Navy also helped to protect Britain's overseas trade (and damage France's). This was crucial for an industrializing nation. As Napoleon, despairing of dominance at sea, imposed his Continental System, British trade was barred from French-controlled areas, which by this time meant much of western Europe. Thanks to the Royal Navy, this "nation of shopkeepers" (Napoleon's gibe) was able to stay in business—not least by providing economic support to other nations struggling against Napoleon.

On land, however, Napoleon's victories went on: December 2, 1805, brought his culminating triumph over an Austro-Russian army at Austerlitz. Again, Austria was forced out of the coalition. It was unable to join the Fourth Coalition, now hastily formed by Britain in conjunction with Prussia, Russia, Saxony, and Sweden. Events followed the familiar pattern: Britain won significant victories at sea, but the Coalition as a whole was soon defeated.

France invaded Portugal in 1807 with Spanish assistance. The Peninsular War began when the ungrateful French occupied Spain itself in 1808. Britain sent troops to help Spanish regular and irregular forces in what was to be a long and dirty war. They made some progress—so much so that Napoleon decided to come and take charge himself. He swept through Spain in the now-customary way. The moment he returned to France, however, his armies became bogged down again. General John Moore's death at La Coruña, in January 1809, provided an iconic

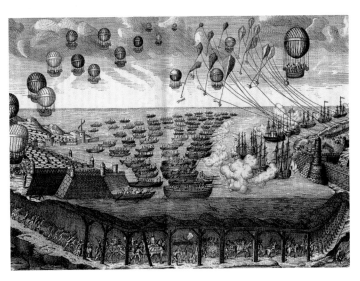

Napoleon's invasion plan
This cartoon jokingly imagines coordinated attacks over, under, and across the English Channel as Britons faced up to the threat of a French invasion in 1805. All these approaches were feared as real possibilities.

> # "Destiny urges me to a goal of which I am ignorant. Until that goal … I am invulnerable …"

NAPOLEON BONAPARTE, *MAXIMS OF NAPOLEON*

moment for patriotic Britons: he had not won, but he had saved his country from a crushing defeat. In May, Arthur Wellesley (later the Duke of Wellington) effectively expelled the French from Portugal at the Battle of Grijó. It was by no means a rout, however. Indeed, a lengthy stalemate ensued. An attempt by Britain to open a second front in central Europe in a Fifth Coalition with Austria failed in the face of now-familiar defeats.

The tide turns

The year 1812 changed everything. Wellesley was already back on the offensive (having taken Badajoz in April) when Napoleon invaded Russia in June. Wellesley took Salamanca in July, in a decisive victory for the allies, and with no Napoleon to reverse it. Emboldened by the Emperor's disastrous defeat in Russia, the European powers joined Britain in a Sixth Coalition. With Napoleon's army exhausted after its Russian nightmare, and under unrelenting pressure in Spain, France was defeated at the Battle of Leipzig in October 1813. Britain, though not directly involved in that fateful engagement, played its part in Iberia, finally expelling the French from the peninsula in April 1814. By then, Napoleon had been forced to abdicate and sent to Elba, an island off Italy's western coast.

AFTER

The Napoleonic Wars, and the Battle of Waterloo that followed in 1815, gave Britain a nasty scare, but the country emerged as a great power.

EUROPEAN LEADER
The reign of Queen Victoria, **270–271 »**, was to be something of a **golden age**, as Britain opened up a technology gap—and an economic lead—over its continental neighbors. This **preeminence found a showcase** in the Great Exhibition of 1851 **272–273 »**.

FRENCH FRIENDS
That a **degree of complacency** crept in became evident in the Crimean War, where the military, which had gone **more-or-less untested** since the Napoleonic era, struggled to make its advantages of technology and resources tell **274–275 »**. Britain was **an ally of France** in that conflict and, as Germany emerged as a major (and increasingly aggressive) power, the **alliance was renewed** in World War I, **320–321 »**, and then again in World War II **346–347 »**.

YOUNG QUEEN VICTORIA

BRITISH NAVAL COMMANDER Born 1758 Died 1805

Admiral **Nelson**

> ## "Our country **will** … **forgive** an officer for **attacking** an **enemy** than for **leaving** him alone."
>
> CAPTAIN HORATIO NELSON, 1794

Born in Norfolk to a country clergyman, Horatio Nelson grew up to be Britain's most famous admiral. He was not just admired but extravagantly feted, attracting such interest and excitement that his status came close to that of a celebrity. While his sense of duty was strong, he showed an audacity that bordered on indiscipline and a dashing courage that kept him in the public eye. His

Emma Hamilton
The wife of Britain's ambassador to Naples, Emma Hamilton met Nelson in the aftermath of his triumph at the Nile. Neither tried to conceal their relationship.

romantic life was equally reckless, with his long-standing affair with Lady Emma Hamilton arousing scandal and admiration in equal measure.

Nelson joined the Royal Navy in 1771, aged only 12. Starting his career as an ordinary seaman, he soon became a midshipman, the lowest officer rank. In 1773, he volunteered to serve on HMS *Carcass* in a journey in search of the Northwest Passage (see pp.286–287). It was on this voyage that the 14-year-old encountered a polar bear on an ice floe. His musket misfiring, Nelson had

to fight the beast off with the weapon's butt. His Arctic foray was followed by a venture to the tropics, when Nelson sailed with HMS *Seahorse* to the East Indies. The late 1770s and the American Revolution and associated battles with France brought great opportunities for an able officer and Nelson attained several commands.

Hero of Cape St. Vincent

In 1783, now a captain, Nelson married Frances "Fanny" Nisbet, the daughter of a wealthy West Indian planter. Though they appeared to have been happy together, Nelson had more time than he wanted with his wife. Peace had left him bored and it was only after the outbreak of the French Revolutionary Wars in 1792 that the Admiralty finally gave him a new command.

Nelson quickly showed himself worthy—displaying, moreover, a readiness to put his own safety on the line. He lost the sight in one eye in action in Corsica in 1793. Four years later, he disobeyed orders in leading a boarding party at the Battle of Cape St. Vincent, off the Portuguese coast. Fortunately, the gamble paid off and, the Spanish fleet defeated, Nelson returned to England a hero, especially after having lost an arm in a later battle at Tenerife. Nelson was idolized as a dashing rule-breaker who led from the front.

Battle of the Nile

Napoleon, the French general, was one of Nelson's strongest rivals. In May 1798, Napoleon set sail with his fleet from Toulon, France. His plan was to invade Egypt as a first step in a

Admiral Nelson
Devotion to duty and individualistic swagger vied for supremacy in Nelson's style. He became the ultimate British hero for the Romantic age.

> " To leave off action ... **damn me** ... I have only one eye—I have a right to be **blind sometimes** ... "

NELSON, NOT SEEING THE WITHDRAW SIGNAL AT COPENHAGEN, 1801

campaign against the British in India. Although Nelson narrowly failed to intercept Napoleon, he found the fleet a few months later at Aboukir Bay, Egypt, completely destroying it in the brief Battle of the Nile that followed. Nelson's victory influenced the course of the entire war and he was awarded the title "Baron Nelson of the Nile."

Nelson now broke another rule by embarking on a long affair with Lady Emma Hamilton, who was the wife of the British ambassador to Naples. Yet, however scandalous his conduct, he seemed to have a special license. At Copenhagen in 1801, where the Danish and Norwegian fleets had been defying the British blockade on French trade,

Battle of Trafalgar

An audacious battle plan to split Villeneuve's fleet brought Nelson a vital edge against the Franco-Spanish; the final flourish of an unconventional career.

Nelson famously put his telescope to his blind eye and "did not see" Admiral Parker's signal to withdraw. In the battle that ensued, he forced the Danes to ask for a cease-fire and surrender. Victory, it appeared, vindicated any misconduct, and at home Nelson was made a viscount.

Battle of Trafalgar

HMS *Victory* was to be Nelson's flagship as a commander-in-chief of the Mediterranean Fleet, locked in conflict with the navy of a France now led by Emperor Napoleon. By 1804, the French were trying to destroy the Royal Navy, or at least entice it away from the English Channel to give an invasion force a clear run at Britain. But Admiral Villeneuve's Franco-Spanish fleet was trapped at Toulon. Breaking out eventually, it was pursued south to Cádiz, in Spain, by Nelson, who finally confronted it near Cape Trafalgar.

Breaking the rules for the final time, Nelson formed his fleet into smaller squadrons in order to outmaneuver Villeneuve's traditional line formation. He had the signal flags spell out the message "England expects every man to do his duty." He was no exception, walking openly on the deck throughout, an inspirational presence to his men—and an irresistible target for the French sniper who finally felled him with a shot. His hero's death, in the hour of victory, became emblematic of the British spirit of self-sacrifice. His body, having been taken home, was borne up the Thames River on a barge and he was given a splendid state funeral at St. Paul's Cathedral.

Nelson's death

The admiral's heroic death at the Battle of Trafalgar took on iconic significance, endearing him to the masses during Britain's imperial age.

TIMELINE

- **September 29, 1758** Horatio Nelson born in Burnham Thorpe, Norfolk, the son of clergyman Reverend Edmund Nelson and wife Catherine.
- **1771** The 12-year-old Nelson enlists in the Royal Navy.
- **1774** Nelson joins HMS *Seahorse* for a voyage to the East Indies. He experiences action for the first time in a clash with vessels belonging to Hyder Ali, King of Mysore, in southern India.
- **1783** Commanding a small flotilla in the Caribbean, Captain Nelson leads a daring, but unsuccessful, attempt to capture the Turks Islands from the French.
- **August 1793** A Royal Navy expedition captures Corsica. Nelson loses the sight of his right eye during the preliminary bombardment.

HMS VICTORY

- **March 14, 1795** The French plan to retake Corsica is frustrated when Nelson defeats their fleet at the Battle of Genoa.
- **February 14, 1797** Nelson disobeys orders in defeating the Spanish off Cape St. Vincent, southwestern Portugal.
- **July 22–27, 1797** Nelson loses his right arm after it is struck by a musket ball in the course of the capture of Santa Cruz de Tenerife.
- **August 1–3, 1798** "By this time tomorrow I shall have gained a peerage or Westminster Abbey," Nelson jokes before leading his fleet to triumph over the French in the Battle of the Nile.
- **April 2, 1801** After ignoring his commander's order to withdraw, Nelson defeats the combined fleets of Denmark and Norway at Copenhagen.
- **October 21, 1805** Nelson is victorious at the Battle of Trafalgar, but is hit by a sharpshooter's bullet and killed. In 1843 his life is immortalized by Nelson's Column, in Trafalgar Square, London.

NELSON'S COLUMN

The Battle of Waterloo

Just when the European powers had thought they were safe, Napoleon Bonaparte was back to torment them. Escaping the Mediterranean isle of Elba in March 1815, the ousted emperor set about reconquering the Continent. By June, he seemed poised for a lightning and final triumph.

While Britain and its allies mobilized, Napoleon assembled a volunteer army of seasoned, and besottedly loyal, troops. Deeming attack the best form of defense, he marched into Belgium (then part of the United Kingdom of the Netherlands), hoping to prevent the British and Prussian forces assembled there from linking up and attacking.

The fighting begins

The British, led by the Duke of Wellington, moved south from Brussels, meeting the left wing of the French army, led by Marshal Michel Ney, on June 16. Holding Ney's attack, they fell back to a ridge above the Brussels road. On June 18, its numbers now swollen to 68,000 by the arrival of Dutch and German allies, Wellington's force faced Napoleon's experienced army of 72,000 and twice as many cannons. However, Wellington set up fortified outposts in farms on the ridge, and established his own artillery and sharpshooters there. Wellington kept his main force behind the ridge so a relentless French bombardment was largely wasted, moving his men up only when the French infantry charge began. Despite devastating musket volleys, Napoleon's troops kept on coming until forced back by Wellington's heavy cavalry. Ney's cavalry now charged—again and again; the British infantry formed squares and held firm. Finally, the vital farm of La Haye Sainte, in the center of the battlefield, was seized by the French. Napoleon's victory seemed imminent.

Defeat and exile

However, the 50,000-strong Prussian army, led by Marshal Blücher, was now approaching. While the main French army tried to hold it back, Napoleon's Imperial Guard made one last attempt to break the British line. Wellington's army stood firm and the French fled, having suffered 25,000 casualties and 8,000 captured. Napoleon abdicated his throne on June 24, surrendering to the British on July 15. He was exiled to St. Helena, in the South Atlantic.

> " It has been a **damned nice thing**—the **nearest-run thing you ever saw** in your life."
>
> THE DUKE OF WELLINGTON, AFTER THE BATTLE OF WATERLOO, JUNE 18, 1815

Battle of Waterloo
French cavalry charge a tightly packed British square at the Battle of Waterloo. Marshal Ney's cavalry came very close to breaking through the British by the time that Blücher and his Prussians came to Wellington's rescue.

5
INDUSTRY AND EMPIRE
1815–1914

In the 19th century, Britain dominated the world with an Empire ruled by Queen Victoria and built on industrial might, economic power, and imperial muscle. In the early 20th century, the threat of war overshadowed the bright prospects of an Edwardian era that witnessed innovation, justice, and hope.

James Watt's steam engine
Scottish mechanical engineer James Watt developed a steam engine that was more efficient than Thomas Newcomen's pioneering invention: it transformed the generation of steam power and opened the way for the Industrial Revolution.

INDUSTRY AND EMPIRE
1815–1914

1815–1831

AUGUST 16, 1819
Fifteen unarmed protestors are killed and hundreds injured in the Peterloo Massacre, Manchester.

JANUARY 29, 1820
King George III dies. His son and regent replaces him as George IV.

» Prince Regent, later George IV

1815
Corn Laws introduced by Parliament. Designed to protect British agriculture, they set a minimum price below which grain may not be imported.

FEBRUARY 23, 1820
The Cato Street Conspiracy to assassinate PM Lord Liverpool is broken up as arrests are made.

MARCH 5, 1824
First Anglo-Burmese War begins. Britain will take much of northeastern India over the next two years.

FEBRUARY 1818
Final defeat of the Maratha Empire leaves the British East India Company in power across most of India.

MAY 24, 1819
Princess Alexandrina Victoria is born. Since she is the daughter of George III's fourth son, it seems unlikely she will ever reign.

MARCH 24, 1829
Catholic Relief Act allows Roman Catholics to sit in Parliament.

JUNE 26, 1830
George IV dies. His daughter Princess Charlotte having predeceased him, he is replaced by his younger brother, William IV.

SEPTEMBER 15, 1830
The Liverpool and Manchester Railway is opened.

DECEMBER 27, 1831
HMS *Beagle* sets out from Devonport with naturalist Charles Darwin on board.

» Stephenson's *Rocket*

1832–1843

MARCH 18, 1839
British ships arrive off Guangzhou and start the First Opium War. The inevitable victory yields important trading concessions.

FEBRUARY 6, 1840
The British and the Maori in New Zealand sign the Treaty of Waitangi.

⌃ Great Reform Act cartoon

JUNE 7, 1832
The Great Reform Act receives Royal Assent, becoming law.

MARCH 1834
A group of agricultural laborers in Tolpuddle, Dorset, are tried for starting a trade union.

» Queen Victoria

NOVEMBER 1837
Rebellion in Lower Canada (Quebec) by settlers threatens US-style breakaway until revolt is suppressed.

1838
Richard Cobden and John Bright found the Anti-Corn Law League, attracting support from both industrialists' and workers' groups.

FEBRUARY 10, 1840
Queen Victoria marries Prince Albert of Saxe-Coburg and Gotha. The two will become inseparable companions.

JANUARY 1842
Britain's retreating army is almost completely wiped out as the First Afghan War ends.

⌄ Chartists' meeting

MAY 1838
The People's Charter is published, calling for fair representation for all people in Britain.

DECEMBER 1838
British troops based in northwestern India invade Afghanistan at the start of the First Afghan War.

MAY 1842
A Chartist petition, calling for universal male suffrage, and signed by more than 3 million people, is rejected by Parliament.

MARCH 1843
General Sir Charles Napier wins the Battle of Hyderabad and annexes Sind.

1845–1855

1845
Benjamin Disraeli's novel *Sybil* introduces the idea that Britain is "Two Nations: the Rich and the Poor."

MAY 19, 1845
Sir John Franklin's ill-fated expedition to find the Northwest Passage departs from Greenhithe, Kent.

SEPTEMBER 1845
Phytophthora infestans, or potato blight, is reported in Ireland.

DECEMBER 1845
First Anglo-Sikh War begins. By February 1846, Britain has taken much of the Punjab.

» Famine Memorial, Dublin

OCTOBER 23, 1853
The Ottoman Sultan declares war on Russia. Britain and France send troops to Crimea in support.

JUNE 25, 1846
An Act repealing the Corn Laws is passed in the House of Lords.

JULY 1, 1847
Lord Shaftesbury's Factory Act limits to 10 the number of hours to be worked each day by women and children.

OCTOBER 25, 1853
The Battle of Balaclava brings Russian defeat—but also disaster for Britain's Light Brigade.

SEPTEMBER 1854
British, French, and Ottoman troops lay siege to the Russian Black Sea naval base of Sebastopol.

APRIL 10, 1848
A major Chartist meeting is held on Kennington Common, London: the size of the turnout is hotly disputed.

SEPTEMBER 9, 1855
The capture of Sebastopol effectively ends the Crimean conflict, though peace will not formally be agreed until the following February.

APRIL 18, 1848
Anti-British violence in Punjab triggers the Second Anglo-Sikh War. The East India Company cements its hold on Punjab and takes the Northwest Frontier region.

» Surgeon's kit

> "Were we required to **characterize this age of ours** by any single epithet, we should be tempted to call it … **the Mechanical Age**."
>
> THOMAS CARLYLE, *SIGNS OF THE TIMES*, 1829

1856–1887

OCTOBER 8, 1856
Chinese action against a vessel suspected of smuggling sparks the Second Opium War.

MAY 10, 1857
The Indian Mutiny erupts in Meerut, India. It will be more than a year before the British put down the uprising.

JANUARY 26, 1885
Governor Charles George Gordon is killed by Islamic rebels in Khartoum, Sudan, prompting a punitive expedition commanded by General Kitchener.

» Edward VII and Queen Alexandra

« Indian Mutiny

MARCH 4–5, 1867
The Fenian Rising in Ireland attracts little support and is quickly quashed by the authorities.

OCTOBER 27, 1871
Henry Morton Stanley meets the explorer David Livingstone (not heard from for some years) by Lake Tanganyika.

JUNE 8, 1886
Gladstone's Government of Ireland Bill is thrown out by the House of Commons. There will be no Home Rule for the Irish—yet.

MAY 1, 1876
Queen Victoria is proclaimed Empress of India. She will be officially enthroned in Delhi in 1877.

JANUARY 22, 1879
British forces are overwhelmed by the Zulus at the Battle of Isandhlwana, but they will go on to win the war.

⌃ Indian postage stamp

DECEMBER 16, 1880
The First Boer War breaks out. Four months later, the British will have to concede defeat.

MAY 2, 1882
Charles Stewart Parnell wins concessions for the Irish Land League movement in the so-called Kilmainham Treaty.

JUNE 20, 1887
Queen Victoria celebrates her Golden Jubilee—half a century on the throne.

1888–1902

AUGUST 25, 1888
The Scottish Labour Party is founded.

JANUARY 22, 1901
Queen Victoria dies, to be succeeded by her scapegrace son, Edward VII.

AUGUST 14, 1889
London dock strike begins. The dockers' victory lends enormous impetus to the trade union movement.

JANUARY 14–16, 1893
The Independent Labour Party is launched at a Bradford conference.

SEPTEMBER 19, 1893
New Zealand's parliament passes legislation making the country the first in the world to grant the vote to all adult women.

DECEMBER 29, 1895
The ill-fated Jameson Raid attempts to take back Transvaal from the Boers.

⌃ Pretoria yields

SEPTEMBER 2, 1898
Kitchener's army wins the Battle of Omdurman against the Sudanese, losing just under 50 lives to the rebels' 10,000.

OCTOBER 11, 1899
The Second Boer War begins. Britain will grind out a victory, albeit at some cost to its reputation.

JULY 22, 1901
Law Lords judge the union is responsible for company losses in the Taff Vale Railway dispute, which amounts to the outlawing of strike action.

MAY 31, 1902
The Treaty of Vereeniging ends the Boer War.

1904–1914

APRIL 8, 1904
The Entente Cordiale is signed, promising friendship between Britain and France.

MARCH 31, 1905
The German Kaiser's sudden visit to Tangiers sparks a diplomatic crisis.

MARCH 1906
The Trade Disputes Act upholds the right of trade unions to strike without liability for losses caused.

DECEMBER 2, 1906
HMS *Dreadnought* is commissioned, a new kind of battleship, both swift and strongly armored.

⌃ Union banner

AUGUST 31, 1907
The Anglo-Russian Treaty is signed in St. Petersburg.

SEPTEMBER 9, 1907
A Royal Proclamation announces New Zealand's dominion status.

JULY 1, 1911
The presence of a German gunboat provokes a second Morocco Crisis.

JUNE 28, 1914
Archduke Franz Ferdinand of Austria is assassinated by the Serbian anarchist Gavrilo Princip, precipitating the July Crisis.

MAY 6, 1910
Edward VII dies and his son George V succeeds him.

MAY 31, 1910
The Union of South Africa is created as a self-governing dominion.

JULY 28, 1914
Outbreak of war between the Central Powers (Austria and Germany) and Serbia makes Russian involvement inevitable.

AUGUST 4, 1914
Germany invades Belgium and so Britain goes to war.

⌄ Weapons factory

BEFORE «

When a monarch came to the throne when he or she was too young to reign with mature judgement, or when a king or queen was incapacitated by an illness, the tradition was for a trusted counselor to act as Regent, reigning on their behalf. It had not happened for centuries, however.

OVERSEEING THE KINGDOM

William Longchamp, Richard the Lionheart's Lord Chancellor, administered England during **his King's absence at the Third Crusade** and after **« 82–83**. More typically, a regent would be appointed to oversee the kingdom while the monarch was a minor.

TRUST MISPLACED?

This position of regent was clearly open to abuse. In 1330, the 17-year-old Edward III had to **rise up and seize his own throne** from the regent Roger Mortimer, Earl of March (his mother's lover), who had abused his position. In 1453, Richard Plantagenet, the Duke of York, stepped in **to run the kingdom** as Lord Protector when Henry VI had a mental breakdown **« 122–123**.

Such precedents came to mind in the 1780s as George III's unstable health raised the question of whether a regent was going to be needed—particularly because this would mean **replacing a King who had by common agreement reigned wisely and well « 200–201** with a profligate and somewhat irresponsible Prince of Wales.

The Regency

As his father's regent and, subsequently, as king in his own right, George IV brought the monarchy— and to some extent his kingdom—into disrepute. The Regency is rightly celebrated for its fashions, art, and architecture, but this historic spree was to have a hangover, both political and social.

George III was quiet and staid. His son could hardly have been more different. The King was angered early on by the Prince of Wales's radical airs and his friendship with Charles James Fox, the leader of the Whig party.

The profligate prince

The Prince was witty, scandalous, and a spendthrift. Setting himself up in sumptuous style at Carlton House, he ran through the £100,000 per year (about £5 million/$6.5 million by today's values) he received from his father and from Parliament. Partying heroically, he kept a series of expensive mistresses (including actress Mary Robinson and Grace Elliott, a rich physician's wife).

The situation became even worse once he decided to settle down, secretly marrying Maria Fitzherbert—a widow twice over and a Catholic. Marriage did nothing to dull his enthusiasm for taking mistresses. In 1787, after his father refused to bail him out, the Prince had to leave his royal residence and move in with Maria. As the Prince

Prince Regent
A socialite, a spendthrift, and a sexual adventurer, the Prince Regent showed no sense of seriousness or responsibility. Many thought that he did not represent much improvement on his now unstable father.

> **630,000** Amount in pounds of debt owed by the Prince of Wales, as of 1795. This is in the region of £50 million ($65 million) at 21st-century values. These (and subsequent) debts were paid by Parliament.

had perhaps anticipated, an embarrassed Parliament paid off his debts, enabling him to return to Carlton House.

Regency crisis

By 1788, the King was slipping toward physical and mental collapse, though his so-called madness may have been the rare blood disease porphyria. Fox saw the crisis as an opportunity, urging the prince's adoption as Regent; Tory leader William Pitt the Younger was naturally opposed. Finally, he agreed, but insisted that the Prince's powers as regent must be restricted.

In the end, George III recovered and was determined to sort out his son. So, in 1795, by once more withholding his financial support, he forced him to wed

> # "Dundas attempted to make himself known to the K, but … the **King was fully occupied** with his own ideas …"

PRINCESS MARY, LETTER TO THE PRINCE REGENT, DECEMBER 28, 1812

his cousin, Caroline of Brunswick. The Prince was physically repulsed by her from the start. Caroline was just as disappointed in a husband who, she confided, was "very fat and … nothing like as handsome as his portrait." The Prince was drunk at the wedding ceremony that April.

They produced a daughter, Charlotte (born the following January), after which Caroline considered her marital duty done. They lived apart and had their own lovers from that time on. While a noisy press took Caroline's part, young Princess Charlotte had to be taken into the care of her paternal grandfather, George III. (Caroline returned to Europe in 1814.)

The Regency begins

The Prince's actual Regency dated from January 5, 1811. Parliament repeated its procedures of 1788, but this time followed through. There followed a golden age of glamour, albeit shot through with a certain sleaziness—and largely funded by the public purse. The Prince Regent was a lavish patron of the arts—especially of John Nash's architecture, which remains a lasting monument to the Regency and its values. It was a great time for fashions and furnishings, too, though most of all it was an age of glittering parties.

Not everyone was having so much fun. Poverty was rife in the country at large, a problem aggravated by the economic slump that followed the end of the Napoleonic Wars. The slump's impact was redoubled by the imposition of protectionist Corn Laws to keep up the price of grain.

A rapidly radicalizing working class and a frightened elite made a combustible mixture. Fears of sedition were to some extent self-fulfilling: rioting broke out across the north in the months that followed the Peterloo Massacre of August 16, 1819. At St. Peter's Field in Manchester, a mounted militia of local gentry charged a mass meeting calling for parliamentary reform. Fifteen were killed and hundreds hurt.

There was real sedition, too: the Cato Street conspirators hoped to murder Prime Minister Lord Liverpool and his Cabinet in February 1820. They were infiltrated by a government agent and apprehended, but still gave the Establishment a nasty scare.

King George IV

Just weeks before, George III had died and George IV succeeded as King in his own right. Caroline returned, resolved

The high life
Regency London was celebrated for its glamour and glitz. The Cruikshank brothers ,Robert and George, created this caricature in 1825. George, in particular, was destined to achieve great fame for his comic art.

Luddites attack a machine
A spate of attacks on new machinery swept industrial England from 1811. Named for Ned Ludd, the (maybe mythical) hand weaver who started the craze, the Luddites feared the new technology was destroying jobs.

to be Queen Consort. A public outcry prevented George from officially excluding her from this position. Still barred from the Coronation, she fell ill and died a few weeks later.

Things went downhill fast from here. George refused to support his old Whig friends in their long-cherished plan of Catholic emancipation. He increasingly identified with the Tories—though he was hardly the greatest of assets from their point of view. Grotesquely obese by now, he attracted public ridicule. He died in 1830. Princess Charlotte and George's brother Frederick had both died, so the succession passed to a younger brother, William IV.

AFTER

George IV left the country in some chaos—political, social, and to a certain extent economic. The monarchy was bankrupt, both financially and morally. Yet industrial development, quietly continuing in the background all this while, meant that the economic outlook was rather better than it may have seemed.

RESTORING STABILITY
Political turbulence continued into the reign of George IV's successors **264–265 》**, only partly allayed by the introduction of electoral reform **268–269 》**. Yet time was on Britain's side: the lengthy reign of Queen Victoria would be a chance for stability to be restored **270–271 》**. It was at this time that Britain emerged as the world's leading industrial nation **276–277 》** and a strong (and increasingly assertive) imperial power **296–297 》**.

Brighton Pavilion
Begun in 1787 as a seaside bolt-hole for the Prince of Wales
(later George IV), Brighton Pavilion was successively
redesigned until 1822. John Nash, who created this final
form, knew the Prince's tastes and produced an awe-inspiring
monument to frivolity. Even so, it has its serious aspect,
hinting at as yet barely acknowledged British ambitions
in Asia. In contrast with the Indian theme of the exterior,
with its suggestion of the Taj Mahal, the interior is a riot
of Chinese-style ornamentation.

Steam and Speed

Speed became the watchword of 19th-century Britain. A railroad mania pulled Britain out of its rural past, and sent steam locomotives hurtling around an expanding national network. Great steamships also rode the waves. Amazed Victorians found their horizons instantly broadened.

chimney

piston

boiler

firebox

footplate

It was the steam engine that revolutionized Britain's transportation system forever. It is hard to imagine how incredible railroad travel must have seemed in the 1800s. At the beginning of the 19th century, British life for many was slow, rural, and provincial. Travel was by horse and the greatest distance that could be covered at a full gallop in one day was approximately 80 miles (130 km).

First steps

In 1804, Cornish mining engineer Richard Trevithick (1771–1833) demonstrated the world's first railroad journey by steam at Penydarran. By this time, there was a large amount of colliery track across the country, and people were beginning to see the potential for national passenger services.

The first major landmark in British railroad history was the opening of a rail line between Stockton and Darlington, in 1825. Originally intended to link coal mines, its first locomotive was George Stephenson's *Locomotion No. 1*. This carried passengers at the line's grand opening demonstration, and did so subsequently, marking it as the world's first steam locomotive–pulled public railroad. The next milestone was the 1830 opening of the Liverpool to Manchester line, linking two great, rapidly expanding industrial cities. *Rocket*, George

> **272** Acts of Parliament were passed at the height of the railroad mania in 1846, creating new rail companies.

Stephenson's best-known locomotive (1829), ran on this line at speeds of up to around 29 mph (47 kph).

Railroad mania

After the Liverpool–Manchester line opened, numerous other lines followed at a dizzying speed. By the 1840s, Britain was in the grip of a railroad "mania." All kinds of people joined the mad scramble to make money from the railroads. A lot of ordinary, inexperienced middle-class investors got caught up in a mess of poor practice, fraud, and chaos, and many lost large amounts of money, as did railroad companies. Everywhere there was a frenzy of uncontrolled rail expansion.

By mid-century, most areas of Britain were close to a rail line and trains were giving the country's Industrial Revolution a massive boost, propelling it into position as a world leader. The canals soon became overshadowed by the railroads for rapid freight transport, and trades such as mining and the production of iron, textiles, and manufactured goods prospered as a result. Coal could be taken speedily from collieries to major ports for onward transportation; Welsh coal was transported through great tunnels in the Malvern Hills to Birmingham's expanding factories.

The prices of many goods fell in places linked by rail, letters arrived quicker, and people's horizons widened. Building trains, tracks, tunnels, and bridges provided work, and increased the country's engineering and construction expertise—now in demand worldwide.

Steam ships

Taking people and goods by ship was important to Britain. There was already a good system of internal waterways,

Stephenson's *Rocket*
The *Rocket*, built by George Stephenson and his son Robert, was the model for all future steam locomotives. Its main features include a multitube boiler that improves heat transfer.

but looking farther afield, Britain—an island—needed to be able to trade with as many other countries as possible.

Early steam-engine technology was adapted for the first British steamships, such as William Symington's small wooden paddle-steamer, *Charlotte*

> **"** … the **desire of gain** has become so strong, that a **Railway to the Moon** would have found **speculators** … **"**
>
> ALFRED CROWQUILL, *ILLUSTRATED LONDON NEWS*, NOVEMBER 1, 1845

BEFORE

CHALDRON WAGON

While the history of railroads is firmly rooted in mining, by the 1700s, large quantities of freight were being transported by water.

EARLY INNOVATIONS

Between the 1500s and 1700s, wooden, then cast-iron, tracks were used for **mining wagons**—horse-drawn coal wagons called chaldrons were common in northeastern England. In the 1700s, Thomas Newcomen, James Watt **‹‹ 224–225**, and Matthew Boulton developed the **steam engine**. Early locomotives were used in collieries.

In the 1700s, much freight was moved around British waters; large wooden sailing boats plied the coasts and oceans with both cargo and passengers. In 1783, the French *Pyroscaphe* became the **first successful steamboat**, and in 1794, the Earl of Stanhope built the *Kent*, an influential prototype.

INNOVATION

BESSEMER PROCESS

As the 1800s progressed, steel rails became a feature of the railroads. Steel was increasingly used in place of iron in large ships. In the 1850s, English engineer Sir Henry Bessemer (1813–1898) patented the process that made mass steel production possible. Molten pig-iron is placed in a furnace called a Bessemer converter, air is blown in, impurities are removed, carbon is added, and molten steel is then poured off. This process made steel cheaper and contributed to the 19th-century boom in British transportation, manufacturing, and industry.

Dundas, in which the steam engine drove a single paddle wheel located in the stern. In 1801–1802, she was put to the test on the Forth and Clyde canal, near Glasgow, and traveled 20 miles (32 km) in six hours, towing two 70-ton barges, making her the first operational steam tugboat. She became the first vessel in the world to use steam propulsion commercially (although her life was short-lived).

Vying for trade

By the 1820s, British steamships were an alternative to stagecoach travel for better-off people, and by 1840 they were common on Britain's rivers and around its coasts. Rather like railroad mania, competition heated up among the major steamship companies founded in the late 1830s, especially to make the fastest crossing of the Atlantic. In 1838, the flagship of the Great Western Steamship Company, Brunel's *Great Western*, sailed into New York 14 days and 12 hours after leaving Bristol (see pp.260–261). It arrived just 12 hours behind *Sirius*, its rival from the British and American Steam

The Cunard Line

Canadian-born British shipowner Sir Samuel Cunard founded one of the early competitive transatlantic steamship companies. In 1840, he won the contract to carry mail from Britain and Canada on a fleet of four 1,000-ton ships made in Scotland.

Navigation Company, which had sailed from Ireland and had taken longer to cross the ocean. A regular transatlantic service ensued and steamships became very important for passenger and freight trade alike.

In the 1840s, paddle wheels were replaced with screw propellers, which were much more efficient. Larger engines were needed, but these were too heavy for wooden boats, so iron was introduced, and later steel, supplied by Britain's flourishing metals industry, which gained further strength

as a result. Places such as the Clyde, the Tyne, and Belfast became famed for their shipyards and supplied the world, with other jobs created by the maintenance and building work on harbors and ports.

The telegraph

The electric telegraph was another enormously important communications development and it was closely associated with both trains and steamships. Developed in 1837 by British scientists William Cooke and Charles Wheatstone, the railroads were used for the telegraph system and, from the mid-1800s, telegraph cables were laid across the Channel and North and Irish seas. Later, Brunel's *Great Eastern* steamship was used to lay a transatlantic cable.

The Liverpool–Manchester line

This contemporary engraving shows excited crowds gathered at Edge Hill, Liverpool, for the grand launch of the Liverpool–Manchester line, on September 15, 1830. This was the world's first timetabled intercity passenger railroad, also transporting large amounts of freight.

AFTER ≫

The march of rail and ship was unstoppable in the 19th century, experiencing some dramatic reversals in the 20th century.

EXPANDING NETWORK

By the 1890s, British railroad companies **owned 10 percent of urban land**. The railroads increasingly established a vital link between the south and north. In 1934, Locomotive number 4472, the most famous of the *Flying Scotsman* service, became the first locomotive to travel nonstop from London to Edinburgh and the first steam engine to reach 100 mph (160 kph). In 1963, the controversial **Beeching Report** initiated a massive cost-cutting closure of more than 2,000 local stations.

In 1900, Britain had the world's **largest navy** and a flourishing **shipbuilding industry**. The Edwardian age produced massive stylish **steamship liners** carrying wealthy vacationers and ordinary people seeking to emigrate. Cunard's speedy RMS *Lusitania* and RMS *Mauretania* were the world's first quadruple screw liners, and by 1912, it took just five days to cross to New York from Southampton. From the 1960s, British shipbuilding **gradually declined**.

PIONEERING ENGINEER Born 1806 Died 1859

Isambard Kingdom
Brunel

"… **great things** are **not done** by those who **count the cost** of every thought and act."

BRUNEL'S COLLEAGUE, DANIEL GOOCH, ON BRUNEL'S DEATH, 1859

Brunel was one of history's most inspired engineers, with a unique instinct for materials and artistic design. Ambitious and entrepreneurial, he epitomized industrial Britain's spirit. Brunel was the son of talented engineer Sir Marc Isambard Brunel, who fled revolutionary France and arrived in England in 1799. Educated in engineering and mathematics in Paris, the younger Brunel worked with his father from 1825–1828 on constructing the first tunnel beneath the Thames. He sustained a serious injury there when the tunnel flooded.

By bridge and rail

While recovering, Brunel drafted plans for a great bridge across the Avon Gorge, at Bristol. Leading Scottish engineer Thomas Telford also submitted a proposal, but a suspension design by Brunel, for the longest single-span yet built, was adopted.

Man of the moment

The chain-cigar-smoking Brunel was a driven, often impractical workaholic, who constantly juggled projects. A celebrity in his day, he raised the status of engineering as a profession and lent it glamour and excitement.

SS *Great Eastern*

The massive ship was designed partly to cater to the immigration encouraged by 1851's Great Exhibition (see pp.272–273). Although the ship could carry 4,000, she proved too costly to run as a passenger ship.

Flying on the Firefly
This 19th-century image shows a Firefly class steam locomotive, designed by Brunel's designer Daniel Gooch, on the track between Bath and Bristol. These achieved speeds of more than 70 mph (113 kph) by the late 1840s.

Brunel built railroads all over Britain and in Italy, and advised on railroad line construction in Australia and India. His numerous rail structures include Maidenhead bridge (the world's flattest brick arch), Saltash Bridge (see pp.262–263), and Box Tunnel.

100 Roughly the number of workmen killed during the construction of the Box Tunnel through solid rock between Bath and Chippenham. The project took five years to build.

By this time, Brunel was living well, with a pleasant London home-office at Duke Street, Westminster. He started building a grand retreat at Torquay (which was never finished). Married in 1836, he and his wife had two sons and a daughter.

Brunel at sea
Steamships were another record-breaking area for Brunel. Each of his ships was the world's biggest when unveiled. In 1838, his wooden paddle ship, the SS *Great Western*, became the first steamship to run a regular transatlantic passenger service. This massive vessel could cross the Atlantic without refueling. His SS *Great Britain*, the first large vessel to have an iron hull and a screw propeller, first crossed to New York in 1845; it later carried 16,000 emigrants to Australia. The SS *Great Eastern* (1858), with both a screw and paddles, was the first ship with a double iron hull. The 32,000-ton ship proved to be one too many exhausting, difficult projects. Brunel died shortly after its maiden voyage.

Construction began in the 1830s, but was dogged by financial and other problems and did not finish until 1864, after Brunel's death. Many doubted that such a bridge would hold, but it is now considered one of the greatest engineering achievements in the world. In 1833, Brunel was remodeling Bristol's docks and also started work on the ambitious plan to build a railroad between Bristol and London. The Bristol to Paddington line opened in 1841, with an extension to Exeter by the mid-1840s. Although successful, this technical miracle cost many construction workers' lives and greatly exceeded its budget.

Beauty in structure
Brunel's design sense brought a new beauty to engineered structures. He oversaw all design aspects of the Great Western Railway's line, including the original Bristol terminal building at Temple Meads.

CLIFTON SUSPENSION BRIDGE, BRISTOL

Royal Albert Bridge
Cheering crowds acclaim the opening of the Royal Albert Bridge by Prince Albert, consort of Queen Victoria, on May 2, 1859. Much patriotic pride was taken in major projects such as this one, recognizing the part they could play in promoting prosperity. The bridge, which was one of Isambard Kingdom Brunel's greatest engineering achievements, crosses the Tamar River, linking Plymouth, Devon, with Saltash, Cornwall.

« BEFORE

The Industrial Revolution made its mark on British society, but many people still struggled to adapt to a new situation.

SOCIAL CHANGES

Parliamentary enclosure and new crop systems increased agricultural productivity, while also marginalizing rural workers, many of whom **sought employment in towns «« 230–231**. Gradually, technology brought further social changes, as it reinvented some types of work, such as textile spinning and weaving, and ironmaking **«« 232–233**. **Older forms of work persisted** in small workshops, but thousands of the new **industrial workers were exploited** in a system akin to servitude.

LEAD ORE WASHERS

Years of Change

Few doubted that the Industrial Revolution was changing the nature of work and the diversity of British workplaces. From 1820 to 1850, the industrializing areas witnessed new ways of working that started to alter everything, from timekeeping and housing to family dynamics and class relations.

The impact of machines such as the spinning frame and steam engine on many workplaces is easily exaggerated. Most British people still worked on the land and—outside key regions such as Lancashire, West Midlands, and central Scotland—much manufacturing took place mainly in the home (spinning and hand-weaving) or in small establishments such as blacksmith's shops and iron foundries.

Petition by trade unionists to the King

Up to 100,000 protestors registered their opposition to the transportation of the Tolpuddle Martyrs in April 1834. Although the demonstrators petitioned in a deferential manner, the protest was a show of potential strength.

Where the factory system was in place, however, work was redefined. Physical strength was less important. Women did the same work as men (for less money). Children tended the machines—reaching in to clear snags, or crawling underneath to recover objects. Mine owners also preferred employing women and children—they were good in confined spaces and cheap to employ. Employers took on families: the male head was responsible for the behavior of his wife and children.

Pay was often docked for disobedience or perceived lack of effort. Employers had other holds over workers and their families. Many factories and mines

17 The average life expectancy in years in Liverpool during the 1850s. High infant mortality depressed the figure, as did the city's unhealthy cellar dwellings and an influx of famine-weakened Irish immigrants.

provided accommodation, but charged high rents. Often workers were paid in tokens exchangeable only in company-owned "truck" shops—where cheap goods were sold at high prices.

All change

The rhythms of life were changing. While the agricultural day was geared to the sun and the seasons, urban trades

Chartists' meeting
How many people came to Kennington Common on April 10, 1848, to support the Chartists' cause is contentious. The authorities' estimate of 15,000 was low, but Chartist claims of 300,000 were fanciful.

involved careful timekeeping. In fact, the advent of railroads and their travel timetables increasingly encouraged the observance of a "standard" time across the country.

Highly regimented employees worked regular shifts in factories running 20 hours a day or more. Gas lighting made this possible. It had, for example, been in use at Matthew Boulton's Soho ironworks since the 1790s.

City life had always been more anonymous than country life, but there was a sense that workplace relations in the coming age of automation might become more impersonal; workers feared that as factory hands they might be mere cogs in the machine.

United we stand
From 1838, there was a clamor for a People's Charter, enfranchising the working class (or at least the males). Millions signed petitions demanding votes in annual elections. Chartists held mass protests, some of which ended violently, shocking the establishment.

Workers tried to come together to exert influence on their employers, but their scope for action was very circumscribed. The Combination Laws of 1799 and 1800 prohibiting trade unions were abolished in 1824, but, since this triggered a spate of strikes, a tough new act was passed in 1825. When six farm workers in Tolpuddle, Dorset, formed a union

in 1832, they were sentenced to transportation. The Tolpuddle Martyrs soon become icons for those who sought to expand the trade union movement and its influence later in the century.

Changing opinions
Many opinion-formers were worried about the effects of changes taking place. Elizabeth Gaskell called one of her novels *North and South*—the two were a world away, economically and culturally. Her north and south were stereotypes: much of Lancashire and Yorkshire was agrarian still; while factories operated in southern England, in centers such as Swindon and around the capital. However, Gaskell's title reflects the growing feeling that, society-wide, the ties that bound people together were loosening.

Those who invested in the free market were not dissuaded by the thought that it created want as well as wealth. No one was to blame for the poverty of the masses; nor should the wealthy be swayed by their plight. *The Times* was notoriously to claim it was "the result of Nature's simplest laws."

Many reformers were as inhuman as the capitalists, insisted writers such as Charles Dickens and Elizabeth Gaskell, for they believed in systems and theories and overlooked the individual. The criticism was harsh, given that individuals were to benefit from the reformers' work, not just in bringing in factory acts and other humanitarian legislation, but in embarking on a new kind of systematic social study—the Blue Book, in which statistics collected by government inspectors in particular places or industries were published.

Other social work set out to improve people's lives. John Snow's research on the distribution of cholera outbreaks in London in the 1850s, brought a breakthrough in medical understanding. Philanthropists founded Ragged Schools for street children, offering basic skills in reading, writing, and arithmetic, and—since many founders were clergymen—Bible study. In New Lanark, Scotland, Robert Owen tried to run a factory community that provided comfortable accommodation for his workers and education for their children.

ENGLISH NOVELIST (1812–1870)

CHARLES DICKENS

Victorian England's most popular novelist, Charles Dickens was first and foremost an entertainer who created a wonderful cast of characters—adorable, eccentric, and grotesque. Beguiling as they were, his stories also took readers into a Britain they might never otherwise have visited—from slums to factories and from workhouses to back-offices.

Thanks to his unique ability to bridge the gulf between the classes, his readers were deeply moved by what they read. Many people were inspired into action: Dickens' great novels worked their influence on many aspects of Britain's changing society, from poverty and penal policy to sanitation and schooling.

AFTER

Britain marched on in apparent prosperity and peace, but the injustices persisted, too; so did the deep resentment of the poor.

STILL EXCLUDED
The Great Reform Act of 1832 expanded the electorate and made the **electoral system more accountable 268–269** ❯❯. However, the mass of people were still excluded, their helplessness underlined by a sense that they were now the only group that did not have a stake in the nation's fortunes, which had never been better, as Britain reigned supreme as the **world's leading industrial nation 276–277** ❯❯.

WORKING-CLASS VOICE
The **plight of the poor** and its reflection on society at large influenced, explicitly or implicitly, everything from **architecture to literature and theology 282–283** ❯❯. This interest and concern could hardly compensate for **lives of toil and chronic hardship**—or the lack of any **democratic voice**. As the 19th century approached its close, living standards for most working people improved, while British workers became better organized, making their presence felt in workplace action and finding their voice in party politics **310–311** ❯❯.

> " If **something** be not done, something will do itself **one day**, and in a **fashion** that will **please nobody**."

THOMAS CARLYLE, OF THE CONDITION OF THE WORKING CLASS, IN *CHARTISM*, 1840

BEFORE

In the Tudor age, England had taken violent possession of Ireland. Since then, Ireland had come through a difficult few centuries.

VIOLENT UNION

Elizabeth I's armies brutally crushed the country, and James I (James VI of Scotland) established a **plantation to pacify the north** that included many Scots ❮❮ **158–159**. But the Irish took advantage of the English Civil War to rise up themselves, although Oliver Cromwell **put their rebellion down** ❮❮ **174–175**. The Succession Wars brought renewed resistance, though William III's victory at the **Battle of the Boyne was decisive** ❮❮ **196–197**. With the United Irishmen's defeat, it seemed the British had finally prevailed: since 1800, **Ireland had belonged to the Union** ❮❮ **238–239**.

The Irish Famine

***Phytophthora infestans*, a water mold, struck potato fields in Ireland in 1845, and destroyed the all-important potato crop, but the famine that ravaged Ireland in the years that followed was as much the result of human mismanagement as nature.**

Ireland was outwardly prosperous at the start of the 19th century. This was hardly the whole story, though. The Irish had undergone successive displacements since the old landowners were condemned by Oliver Cromwell "to Hell or Connaught" (to either be killed or move to the barren lands in western Ireland). Many of the Anglo-Irish had displaced themselves, becoming familiar figures in Dublin and London society. Known as "absentee landlords," they received regular remittances from their agents, and the middlemen often leased their estates, subdividing them into smallholdings for renting on short leases with inflated rents.

Tenants were also displaced to higher, more marginal land, to make way for lucrative livestock. They often had to bid for their own plots at auctions as each lease ended, and the rents rose dramatically every time.

A miracle food

By the 18th century, the masses were living a life of abject poverty, sustainable only because of potatoes. This New World crop had been introduced in the 16th century. The Irish had traditionally lived mainly on cereals (wheat and oats). Now, any grain they could grow went to the market, along with any dairy products: people subsisted entirely on potato. They were also paid in potatoes for the work they did on larger farms. Yet, remarkably well-nourished, they thrived. Between 1687 and 1791, the population more than doubled, from 2.16 to 4.75 million. By 1841, it had risen by 3.4 million, not counting the 1.75 million who had emigrated.

A blighted country

By 1845, a population of more than 8 million was completely dependent on the potato. It was not much of a life,

perhaps, but it allowed the country's richer land to be fully productive from the point of view of a landowning class who were largely disengaged.

The "blight," as the mold was also called, showed itself in black blotches on the leaves of the plant, but did its real damage underground. The potato first discolored, and then turned into a watery, rancid mush. All of Europe was affected by the blight, but elsewhere, potato was just one among many different food crops grown. In Ireland, the potato dominated agriculture. Approximately half the Irish crop was destroyed in 1845, and this rose to 75 percent the following year.

Remembering the dead
Rowan Gillespie's haunting Famine Memorial, created in 1997 in Dublin, records Ireland's tragedy.

Deserted village
This empty ruin, on Achill Island, Mayo, stands in a former village that was abandoned in the Famine.

°Londonderry

°Belfas

°Dublin

°Limerick

°Cork

0   100 km
0   100 miles

KEY
Decrease in population 1841–51
More than 30% decrease
20 to 30% decrease
10 to 20% decrease
0 to 10% decrease
Area of rise in population

Extent of the famine

The west of Ireland, largely comprising the province of Connaught, became a "hell of hunger" as a result of the famine, and saw significant depopulation, as the map shows. Other rural areas fared little better, while the main cities saw the desperate influx of the hungry.

Since the Act of Union in 1800, Ireland had not had its own parliament, and Britain, untroubled by the blight and dominated by free-trade thinking, was deaf to pleas for protectionist measures. These might have stopped other food exports from Ireland, which were still proceeding on a massive scale.

Tory Prime Minister Robert Peel discreetly shipped in maize from America, but the facilities for making it

1.1 MILLION

An estimate of the number of deaths attributable to the Irish Famine, not including those who died during emigration to another country.

edible did not exist in Ireland. In 1846, his Whig successor, Lord John Russell, set up programs to create work, but his Assistant Secretary to the Treasury, Charles Trevelyan, believed the Famine was a divine judgement on the

rebellious and feckless Irish. They were thus cast as idle charity-cases, despite the fact that they were still highly productive, and that throughout the Famine, Ireland continued to export food to the world.

Final toll

Britain, the world's leading economic nation, was embarrassed by the international response to this tragic failure. Offers of help to Ireland came from everyone from American Indian groups to the Ottoman Sultan. All were indignantly rejected by London. In Ireland, many suspected the motives of those who helped—especially of the British Protestant missionary groups, a minority of whom served religious instruction with their food. The much-exaggerated idea of the "souper"—the desperate, starving individual who converted from Catholicism to Protestantism in return for soup—took hold throughout.

Mortality figures for the Famine are difficult to establish and inevitably contentious. While many could be said simply to have starved to death, many more died of diseases related to famine. Others died as a result of a cholera epidemic. A reasonably cautious estimate would be about 1.1 million dead, and a further 1 million pushed into emigration. There was a cultural cost as well. If the memory of the Famine became a major rallying point for the Irish diaspora worldwide, its effect in Ireland was to weaken the sense of national identity, or of the Gaelic identity at least. Rural Irish speakers bore the brunt of the disaster. An ancient culture was destroyed.

Searching for potatoes

As depicted—part sympathetically, part disdainfully—in *The Illustrated London News* in 1849, Irish families sought frantically for any sustenance.

AFTER

The legacy of the Famine in Ireland was to be both bitter and enduring: Irish emigrants carried their resentment with them around the world.

MASS EMIGRATION

Many Irish went to **Britain's overseas dominions 294–295 »**, though most ended up in the United States. Across this new diaspora, as in Ireland itself, **the mood was rancorous**.

SHIPS TAKING EMIGRANTS

AN ANTI-BRITISH VOICE

The Irish had **little influence** in US society at first, but as they became established, they were able to raise a powerful **anti-British voice**. From the 1850s, US-based Fenians fought for Irish freedom, but the Home Rule campaign was mainly peaceful **300–301 »**. In the 1970s and 1980s, Irish-Americans lent support to the IRA in its **armed struggle 378–379 »**.

The Triumph of Reform

While some were asking why the poor should suffer to underwrite Britain's booming wealth, a rising middle class was questioning the justice of the electoral system—and demanding change.

The urban middle class had already shown their strength in the success of the Abolitionist movement (see pp.234–235), compassion reinforced by a steelier sense that slavery was a brake on the free market.

Parliament abolished the slave trade throughout the Empire in 1807 and the Royal Navy enforced the policy at sea. Again, idealism and economic realism went together. Britain, the inevitable winner in trials of economic strength, opposed all kinds of anticompetitive practice.

Corn Laws

Yet a certain ambivalence was evidenced by the introduction of the Corn Laws in 1815. They barred all wheat imports unless the domestic price reached a certain level. Unabashedly protectionist, the laws guaranteed the income of an aristocratic

The House of Commons

Rebuilt since the fire of 1834, the Palace of Westminster made an impressive home for Britain's Parliament. Yet democracy had its limits: there was no place in the Commons for representatives of the working poor.

landed interest, which was represented by the Tories. The Whigs, to whose cause the class of newly wealthy industrialists had naturally gravitated, favored a free market in food so cheaper produce could be imported and wages kept down.

> **5** The number of electors who, in the constituency of Old Sarum, Wiltshire, sent two members to Parliament in the 1802 elections. Gatton, Surrey, had seven voters, while Camelford, Cornwall, had 25.

Wage slaves

In general, the Whigs had come to have the interests of the industrialists at heart, so it was the Tories who took the lead in trying to ease conditions for the working poor. The 1802 Factory Act stipulated a maximum eight-hour working day for children aged 9–13 years; 12 hours for those aged 14–18. But the repeated outlawing of the employment of children under the age of nine in textile mills thereafter underlined how often legislation was ignored. Besides, the law could influence only the most readily regulated industries—chiefly textiles. Others—including mines and garment-making sweatshops—were unaffected.

Lord Shaftesbury, a Tory, and Radical MP John Fielden fought for a new Factory Act, though they were not to prevail until 1847. Others were campaigning, too. In 1838, Richard Cobden and John Bright launched their Anti-Corn Law League, providing a powerful focus for the Free Trade lobby.

Electoral absurdity

Social injustice was perpetuated by political inequality. Only those owning a property could vote, so a mere 200,000 out of more than 10

◀◀ **BEFORE**

The people of Britain had learned to take pride in their perceived tradition of liberty, courageously—but moderately—upheld.

PEOPLE POWER
Tyranny was successfully resisted during the Civil War **<< 168–169** and the Glorious Revolution of the 17th century **<< 188–189**. Yet the **dangers of "people power"** when taken to extremes were all too clear from France's recent Reign of Terror **<< 236–237**.

AN END TO SLAVERY
Ordinary people took heart from the fact that, as the 19th century began, **their voices were being heard** and their opposition spurred an end to the cruel slave trade **<< 234–235**.

million adult males were eligible. Of more significance to the property-owning middle classes, however, were the glaring geographical inequities in the system. Many constituencies were "pocket boroughs," their electors voting at the behest of the local lord. Several "rotten boroughs" had only a handful of electors, but still sent members to Parliament on the landowner's say-so.

The Industrial Revolution had demographically transformed Britain. Cities such as Manchester and Leeds grew, and with them substantial, new (and predominantly Whig-supporting) electorates. A system that placed a major conurbation on par with a quaint cathedral city (or even Oxford and Cambridge Universities, which both had their own MPs) appeared to them to be crying out for reform.

Lord Grey's Whig government, elected in 1830 after George IV's death, tried twice to bring in reform, but both times it was rebuffed—when they got legislation through the Commons, it was thrown out by the Lords.

The Great Reform Act

The Tories tried to block yet another attempt in 1832, but gave in to William IV's threat to create more lords who would vote the bill through. So the Great Reform Act was duly passed. It abolished the worst rotten boroughs and extended the electoral franchise—though not as much as working-class campaigners had hoped. Parliament was far more cleanly

1832 Reform Act
Whig leaders attack the Old Rotten Tree with the axes of reform—while frantic Tories try to keep the whole tottering structure standing. Rural magnates sit pretty in their nests while, from nearby Constitution Hill, the smaller British nations—and the aristocracy—look on.

elected by a much larger electorate, but a property qualification remained, so only about one in six men (and no women at all) could vote.

British politics looked different, even so. Having long since won the fight for parliamentary power under a constitutional monarchy, the Whigs were moving on to the battle for free trade and for limits to government intervention in the economy: increasingly they called themselves "Liberals." The Tories, too, were changing. Robert Peel's Tamworth Manifesto (1834) laid the foundations for the modern Conservative Party. Endorsing the Great Reform Act, Peel promised to support change where truly needed.

As good as his word, in 1846 he sacrificed his second term as prime minister to repeal the Corn Laws. And it was to be a Conservative prime minister, Benjamin Disraeli, who introduced a Second Reform Act in 1867; the Liberal William Ewart Gladstone brought in the Third Reform Act in 1884.

AFTER

It was in the 1840s that philosopher Karl Marx made "bourgeoisie" the dirty word it has remained for writers and thinkers on the left. Whether by accident or design, the electoral reforms of the 1830s drove a wedge between the middle class and the working class.

FIGHT FOR CHANGE
Professional men, who had been excluded, now had their place in Parliamentary democracy, but working-class men (and all women) were still out in the electoral cold. Even so, **many in the middle class strove to improve social conditions 278–279 》**. Among the workers, however, the conviction was growing that if they wanted change they were going to have to fight for it themselves. **310–311 》**.

VOTING BY BALLOT

BRITISH MONARCH Born 1819 Died 1901

Queen Victoria

"I shall do **my utmost** to fulfil **my duty** towards **my country**."

QUEEN VICTORIA, ON HER ACCESSION, 1837

Queen Victoria
For some years after Albert's death, it seemed that the Queen had all but abdicated, but she resumed her duties, and her dignity and decorum were much admired. She is seen here in 1899, still in mourning for the Prince Consort.

Both of William IV's daughters had died soon after birth, leaving him with no immediate successor. Of the King's younger brothers, none of the next three in line had lived long enough to ascend the throne, and only the late Duke of Kent (formerly next in line after William) had a legitimate surviving child. So it was that, on William's death in June 1837, his young niece, Victoria, came to the throne. She was ill-prepared in many ways for the responsibility of monarchy.

Hers had been an isolated childhood: she had been closely protected—possibly overprotected, many felt—by a manipulative mother, the Duchess of Kent, from whom she was eventually to become estranged. There had been some question that the Duchess might become regent, acting on behalf of her daughter, but Victoria had just reached the age of 18 when her uncle died, and Lord Melbourne, the Whig Prime Minister, took the new Queen under his wing, winning her eternal gratitude and affection in return.

Queenly bearing

"I may call you Jane," she had told a childhood playmate, "but you may not call me Victoria." Britain's longest-serving monarch felt a strong sense of regal entitlement from the start. While in many ways Victoria is rightly taken as a model of the modern constitutional monarch, she had a distinctly despotic streak at the same time. Her strong favoritism for Melbourne and the Whigs was quickly established, and she took very little trouble to conceal it. Tory Prime Minister Robert Peel,

having defeated Melbourne, resigned in 1839 when she refused to go along with changes he proposed to her royal household. (This despite the fact that the appointment of new personnel was at that time customary with incoming administrations.) Far from feeling embarrassment,

Prince Albert
Victoria's public image was of austerity, even coldness, but her love for her Prince Consort was clear. She never got over his death in 1861.

Queen Victoria and her family, 1890s
Victoria's family was the center of her life; her children married many of the crown heads of Europe. Her grandson Kaiser Wilhelm II is seen here (front row, left).

Victoria was only too delighted when Peel's resignation cleared the way for Melbourne and the Whigs to return to office. However, her hostility toward Tory governments was only a short-lived feature of her reign.

Wife and mother

Queen she may have been, but as an unmarried woman Victoria still had to live with her mother, according to the convention of the time, and the Duchess still bullied her the way she had when she was a girl. This in part may have driven her in her desire to marry Prince Albert of Saxe-Coburg and Gotha, for this relationship does not appear to have been a case of love at first sight. The attachment became legendary,

however, once the Queen fell madly in love with her Prince Consort, who also became her key adviser. They had nine children, who were destined to make matrimonial connections with all the leading royal houses of Europe.

Victorian morality

The idea of a "royal family" became celebrated at this time. The sanctity of the home and the joys of domestic life were widely idealized; sober respectability was much prized. Traditionally, the ruling class had been conspicuously lax in their sexual conduct: if Victoria's uncles had been short of legitimate children, they had produced plenty on the "wrong side of the blanket." However, "Victorian Morality" had no better exemplar than the Queen herself. A devoted (even passionate) wife to Albert, she was seriously prudish and intolerant of anything that smacked of sexual license.

Albert and after

As her Prince Consort, Albert further developed the role of the monarchy in promoting all-around good works. He was an important patron of the Great Exhibition in 1851, and encouraged the Queen's own close identification with the armed forces, underlined by her introduction of the Victoria Cross for valor in 1856, against the background of the Crimean War. However, tragedy struck in December 1861, when Albert died from typhoid fever while at Windsor Castle. He was only 42.

The Queen was left desolate. She wore mourning from that time on, and shunned public appearances where she could. While she always met minimum requirements, her failure to go further caused public muttering (gossip about her attachment to her Balmoral gillie John Brown did not help). There was some serious anger at what some saw as a dereliction of duty. On the other hand, her retreat from the political front line was welcomed by those in government. She slipped back into the largely ceremonial role that is now expected of monarchy.

Musical queen
From childhood, Victoria was an enthusiastic pianist, particularly loving works by Beethoven, Schubert, and Mendelssohn, who wrote pieces especially for her.

Imperial monarch

In the latter part of her reign, Victoria regained her popularity as the symbol for a successful and ever-more powerful imperial nation. More experienced now, she also regained the confidence to act on her own initiative. As a result, she was a much greater influence over (and nuisance for) senior politicians. In 1876, Tory Prime Minister Benjamin Disraeli arranged for her to be given the additional title of Empress of India.

Whatever Victoria's personal flaws, they were rendered insignificant by her sheer longevity as reigning monarch. There was a huge outpouring of joy at her Diamond Jubilee in 1897.

TIMELINE

- **May 24, 1819** Princess Alexandrina Victoria is born to Princess Victoria of Saxe-Coburg Saalfeld and Prince Edward, Duke of Kent and Strathearn, George III's fourth son.

- **June 20, 1837** Princess Victoria becomes Queen at the age of 18.

- **February 10, 1840** Victoria marries Prince Albert of Saxe-Coburg and Gotha in the Chapel Royal of St. James's Palace, London.

- **May 1, 1840** The Queen's profile appears on the world's first postage stamp, the Penny Black.

- **November 9, 1841** The Queen gives birth to Prince Albert Edward, the future King Edward VII.

- **1845** The Queen and Albert buy Osborne House, on the Isle of Wight, to redevelop as a holiday home.

- **April 1848** Victoria and her family leave London for Osborne House, amid fears of revolutionary violence in the capital.

- **April 7, 1853** The Queen is anesthetized with chloroform for the birth of her seventh child, Prince Leopold of Albany, giving this medical innovation an important boost.

- **October 1853** Outbreak of Crimean War. The hostilities do not cease until February 1856.

- **January 29, 1856** The Victoria Cross for valor is introduced.

OSBORNE HOUSE

- **April 24, 1857** Outbreak of Indian Mutiny. After it has been put down, the Crown takes direct charge of administrating India.

- **May 1, 1876** Victoria is awarded the additional title of Empress of India; it is formally proclaimed in Delhi the following year.

- **March 2, 1882** After seven earlier attempts, would-be poet Roderick MacLean tries to assassinate the Queen with a pistol. He is finally confined to an insane asylum.

- **March 27, 1883** Victoria's personal attendant John Brown dies. His passing, the Queen's letters suggest, leave her feeling almost as though she has been widowed a second time.

- **June 8, 1886** Gladstone's Government of Ireland Bill, proposing Home Rule for Ireland, is voted down in the House of Commons, to the Queen's ill-concealed relief.

- **June 20, 1887** The Queen's Golden Jubilee—50 years on the throne—is celebrated. Celebrations are intensified by news that an Irish Fenian plot to kill her has been discovered.

- **June 20, 1897** Victoria's Diamond Jubilee—60 years on the throne—sparks general celebration.

- **October 11, 1899** The Second Boer War begins. It ends in a British victory—although British tactics cause controversy and the war lasts until May 31, 1902.

- **January 22, 1901** Victoria dies at Osborne House at the age of 81.

The Great Exhibition

At 11:45 a.m. on May 1, 1851, Queen Victoria arrived to officially open The Great Exhibition of the Works of Industry of all Nations, in Hyde Park, London—the first-ever international industrial exhibition. It announced Britain as the foremost nation battling for manufacturing supremacy in an increasingly industrialized, modern world.

The world had never seen a trade fair this large before. Such was the public's enthusiasm that on its first day up to 30,000 crammed into its purpose-built venue, a massive airy greenhouse designed by Joseph Paxton and nicknamed "The Crystal Palace" by *Punch* magazine. Among the crowd, alongside Victoria, was Prince Albert, whose pet project this had become.

Empire on the rise

By the mid-1800s, Victoria headed an empire on such a rapid rise that it would embrace a quarter of the world's population by the end of her reign. The Great Exhibition was conceived as a way of showing that Britain was now the "workshop of the world" and its leading industrialized nation, and so this great fair displayed a dizzying array of extraordinary, impressive, and innovative goods and machinery from throughout its lands. Items from potential competitor countries were also on show, following Albert's desire to promote healthily competitive free trade and diplomatic links.

Science, industry, and artistry

The 100,000 exhibits ranged from the huge Koh-i-Noor diamond to Sir David Brewster's stereoscope, and from steam locomotives and mechanical toys to an envelope-making machine and a garden seat for the Queen carved from coal. Exotic items, such as North African tapestries and metalwork and shawls from India, influenced Victorian tastes, and the sheer array of goods fed the growing mania among middle-class Victorians for shopping.

By the time the Great Exhibition closed, on October 11, 1851, around 6 million people had seen it, many of them several times—the Queen herself made 34 visits. The Crystal Palace was dismantled and moved to Sydenham, south London, where sadly it perished in a fire in 1936.

> "God bless my **dearest Albert**, and my **dear Country**, which has shown itself **so great today**."
>
> QUEEN VICTORIA'S JOURNAL, MAY 1, 1851

Paxton's Crystal Palace
Joseph Paxton's Crystal Palace exhibition hall covered about 26 acres (10 hectares) of Hyde Park, in London, and was designed to be later dismantled and moved. It was the world's first true prefabricated building made from mass-produced parts.

BEFORE «

As the 19th century reached its midpoint, Britain was strong and confident.

FULL STEAM AHEAD

The country had been quick to translate **technological advance** into entrepreneurial opportunity since the start of the Industrial Revolution **«« 232–233**. It had led the way in developing steam power, on the railroads, and at sea **«« 258–259**. With all its **economic strength**, however, its military might had **not been substantially tested** since the Battle of Waterloo in 1815 **«« 246–247**.

SAFEGUARDING SUEZ

India's importance to Britain had been growing since the 18th century **«« 212–213**. Hence the need to ensure stability on the isthmus of **Suez, a vital junction** on the route to India. With the Ottoman Empire clearly in terminal decline, Czar Nicholas I of Russia had **designs on the Dardanelles**, the straits linking the Black Sea with the Mediterranean and Suez.

RUSSIAN AGGRESSION

At the beginning of 1853, Nicholas **proclaimed himself protector** of the Ottoman Sultan's Christian subjects, with rights over Jerusalem and its pilgrimage sites. The **Sultan appealed to** France and Britain, and when Russia invaded his Danube provinces of Moldavia and Wallachia that summer, **they responded**. After the Russian Navy had destroyed the Turkish fleet at Sinop, the focus shifted to the Crimean peninsula.

FLORENCE NIGHTINGALE

Moved by press reports of the wounded in the Crimean War, well-connected Florence Nightingale pulled strings and secured permission to take 38 volunteer nurses out to help. In October 1854, her party arrived at the military hospital at Scutari, Turkey. They found a tumbledown facility built above broken sewers. Rats and flies were everywhere; no artificial light or anesthetics, or even bandages, were available. The wounded lay directly on the floor or on soiled straw. Florence took it all in hand, got it clean and orderly, and sorted out the administration. Strongly proprietorial, she walked the wards in the darkest watches of the night earning herself the reverential nickname, the Lady with the Lamp.

The **Crimean War**

The expectation was that Crimea would see a powerful industrialized Britain sweep aside all opposition, a "Great Exhibition" for the military. The reality was different. Organizational limitations let the armed forces down, and they found themselves in a wretched stalemate for many months, killing thousands.

A Franco-British force was sent to Crimea in the spring of 1854, largely to neutralize the Russian Black Sea naval base of Sebastopol. British naval power was crucial, and a base for it was established near the Ottoman capital, Constantinople (Istanbul).

Industrial might

Britain's industrial output was 10 times Russia's and its army much better equipped. Its standard musket range was five times that of the Russian equivalent. Russia's infrastructure was almost completely undeveloped. It took three months to get weapons and materiel to Crimea by horse and cart. Britain and France could ship supplies by sea in just three weeks. Crimea anticipated later wars in hinging as much on logistics as on fighting itself. One in three Russian troops did not even make it to the front. But Britain's advantages were offset by poor training and provisioning.

Surgeons kit
These instruments were used in Crimea by a military surgeon, Dr. Evans. Supply problems meant that most operations had to be carried out without anesthetics, although chloroform, for example, was now in use.

In the public eye

Previous wars had seemed remote to those not involved. The Crimean War was modern in having an important media presence. William Howard Russell went on behalf of *The Times* newspaper, becoming the first known war correspondent. Since his copy was substantially uncensored by the authorities, war's sufferings were literally brought home to the public in their morning papers. They became available almost instantly through telegraph technology. Photos were published for the first time, too. Russell had plenty to write about.

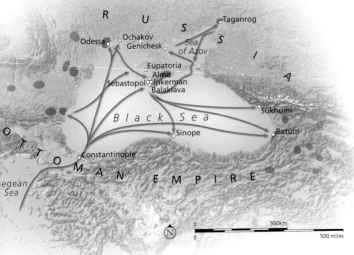

Map of the Crimean War
After fighting took place along the Russo-Ottoman borders, the focus moved to Crimea and Sebastopol, from where Russia's navy attacked Ottoman shipping.

KEY
- British, French, and Ottoman forces
- Russian forces

British artillery officers with cannon
Officers of the 14th Artillery Regiment pose casually around a gun in a photograph taken by Roger Fenton toward the end of 1853. Stagey as they may seem today, images like this one made a powerful impression on the public back in Britain, beginning to bring home to them the awful realities of war.

In September 1854, after defeating the Russians at the Battle of Alma, the Allies besieged Sebastopol. The Russians tried unsuccessfully to lift the siege on October 25 at the Battle of Balaclava, but Britain's victory was marred by the misunderstanding that led to the Charge of the Light Brigade. Almost 300 men were needlessly killed when the wrong target was attacked.

This kind of thing had happened before, but now Russell was on hand to give his unsparing report. The tragic charge was presented as a heroic failure, but the official incompetence was unmissable. A fresh attempt by the Russians to dislodge the Allies failed at the Battle of Inkerman on November 5.

However, the Allies' siege had so far failed, too. They dug in for months of miserable trench warfare and artillery bombardment. Freezing conditions became more wretched when winter storms interrupted seaborne supplies: cholera and typhus, rife since summer, tore through the army. In January 1855, while about 83 men died of wounds, 2,761 died from disease. Russell was scathing in his criticism of provision for the wounded and of the general incompetence with which the war was being waged.

A victory ... of sorts

The final victory was one for both British logistics and British capitalism. Engineers Thomas Brassey and Samuel Morton Peto built the Grand Crimean Central Railway to bring up men and artillery to Sebastopol, swinging the fortunes of the siege.

However, it was fairer to say that Russia had lost the war than Britain had won. The Czar could not keep up the struggle, having lost more than 100,000 men compared to Britain's 17,500 dead, France's 90,000, and Turkey's 35,000. The death of Nicholas and the succession of Alexander II allowed an opportunity for peace talks to be held in Paris in 1856.

Battle of Sebastopol
Painter Jean-Charles Langlois had served as a soldier himself. He went to Crimea with war photographer Léon-Eugène Méhédin. His panoramic scenes of the conflict are beautiful but unsparing.

AFTER »

The immediate outcome of Crimea for Britain was a great deal of soul-searching. Its self-confidence and, more specifically, competence were called into question. The war had boosted the prestige of the press, even as it lowered that of the army and the administration, and the newspapers led the ensuing outcry.

VITAL CHANGE
Reforms were introduced in nursing and the army. Officers' commissions once sold to wealthy young gentlemen now went to professionals on merit. Confidence recovered, restored by easy triumphs against China in the Second Opium War and some harder-won campaigns against the Zulu and Ashanti in Africa **296–297** »

INDUSTRIALIZED WARFARE
These colonial wars were unequal struggles, fought against poorly armed and primitively equipped adversaries. The Crimean War provided at least a foretaste of what might happen when great modern armies met. Only much later would it become clear how far the dismal conditions of the armies dug in around Sebastopol foreshadowed the trench warfare of the Great War of 1914–1918 **320–321** »

《 BEFORE

Britain's Industrial Revolution gave it a head start over the competition in the race for economic dominance.

LARGE-SCALE INDUSTRY

As early as the 18th century, British inventors were building the **technological foundations** on which future prosperity would be built **《 232–233**. The **cottage industries** of the past were giving way to large-scale production, much of it in fully mechanized, meticulously organized factories.

British know-how enabled industrial and economic development to surge forward full steam ahead in some of the most **modern factories** and on the most modern **transportation infrastructure** in the world **《 258–259**.

HANDLOOM WEAVER

Workshop of the World

If the 18th century had seen an Industrial Revolution, it was the 19th that saw Britain totally transformed into what was to be the world's first industrial power. This second phase of transition was as much economic and social as it was technological, touching almost every aspect of British life.

The Great Exhibition had been a wonderful store window for the products of the Industrial Revolution, but Britain was busier than ever behind the scenes. For a brief moment, it had been not just the foremost but the only industrial nation, producing two-thirds of the world's coal, half its iron, almost three-quarters of its steel, and about half of its commercially manufactured cotton. Rival nations were reacting fast. For the moment, though, they were struggling to catch up.

Workers in a textile factory

Processes once done painstakingly by hand by highly skilled workers were now carried out mechanically—and on an enormous scale. Much of the work could be done by women and children, who were cheaper to pay and easier to manage than male labor.

A world city

While industry was associated with the Midlands and North, London—a city of manufacturing itself, although mainly in smaller workshops—was growing as a financial center underwriting much industrial enterprise. The skills it developed served entrepreneurs internationally. By 1800, it was the modern world's first city with a population of a million; by 1900, it would have more than six times that number. Railroads made it a transportation hub, the main stations having been built from the 1830s. The Underground (subway system) was under construction from 1863.

Textiles, toys, and tools

The more familiar industrial activities also continued. The Lancashire cotton mills flourished. Cotton products accounted for more than half Britain's exports by value by 1830. By 1860, Lancashire alone had 440,000 cotton workers, employed in 2,650 mills. Wool was enjoying comparable fortunes across the Pennines in Yorkshire. Bradford, a small town of 16,000 people in 1800, had 182,000 by 1850. Leeds emerged as a

major trading and communications center. Birmingham was booming, too: a miscellany of mostly small-scale concerns here made everything from buttons to toys and tools. England's second city soon had an impressive collection of public buildings to advertise its new wealth and status in a golden age of civic pride.

King coal

The early industrial heartlands in Lancashire and Yorkshire were fueled by the availability of coal supplies so close to the surface that they could simply be dug out from handy hillsides. Many other seams could not be mined, owing to access problems, though the demand was not so great that this really mattered. From about 1800, deep-mining technology developed, including wooden pit props, winding gear, and engine-driven fans for ventilation. The Davy lamp made mining much safer from 1816.

From iron to steel

Welsh coal had been extracted since very early in the Industrial Revolution. Passages could be dug more or less horizontally into the valley sides. The coal extracted was used in the local iron industry. Later, shafts were sunk vertically to depths of 2,600 ft (800 m) or more. Tramways, and later railroads, were built to take coal to the coast for export (mainly from Cardiff) and use in local steelworks. Centers like Merthyr were already important in ironmaking, but production took off during the railroad boom. The great blast furnaces built at Dowlais and Cyfartha were the most important in the world by the 1840s. Much iron from Welsh works was exported through Swansea to support rail construction elsewhere.

The large-scale switch to steel (an alloy of iron with carbon for extra toughness) was made possible by the

THE CONVERTERS

introduction of the Bessemer Process in 1858. This used jets of air to remove the impurities from the molten metal and allowed mass production for the first time. Sheffield, the traditional steelmaking center, still used a small-scale crucible method. It was overtaken by big steelworks elsewhere, but had a role making high-quality steel for cutlery and weapons.

Prospering ports

All these products had to be shipped to their export destinations, and in many cases raw materials had to be brought in. Seaports boomed along with the general prosperity. London was the world's largest port by 1802: it was linked to the canal network with the construction of the Limehouse Basin in 1820. Wapping Dock (from 1805) could accommodate 300 ships at a time. The East India Docks handled £30 million worth of tea a year by the 1860s. Frozen meat was brought in from Australia by the 1880s.

Other ports flourished, too. The boom enabled Liverpool to take the loss of the slave trade in its stride. Already a major port in 1800 (Britain's first wet dock was built here in 1715), it had just over

1,000 The percentage rise in UK iron production between 1800 and 1850, from around 250,000 tons to 2.5 million. Steel production went from 60,000 tons in 1850 to 5 million in 1900.

2 miles (3 km) of quays, taking £130,000 dues per year. By 1857, it had 15 miles (24 km) of quays, and dock dues of £250,000; it almost doubled in size again by 1900.

Shipbuilding

The first steam seagoing ship, the *Comet*, was built in Glasgow in 1812. An estimated 42 steamships had been built along the Clyde by 1820. In general, iron hulls were built on the Lower Clyde and machinery built upriver in Glasgow. Shipbuilding in Belfast began in the 18th century: Harland & Wolff was founded in 1862, although its heyday would not be until the early 20th century. Newcastle, a long-standing port for shipping coal in the coastal trade, emerged as another important shipbuilding center.

Enfield carbine rifle
British industrial might translated easily into military dominance in the early 19th century, particularly over the peoples of Africa and Asia. Britain's colonial conquests were in part driven by the need for both new markets and supplies of raw materials for its industry.

Steelmaking
The Bessemer Process made possible the manufacture of high-quality steel on a massive scale: here steel is seen being fired in the converter (above) and cast into ingots (below).

AFTER

Britain's industrial dominance could not go on for ever: too many competitors wanted their share of the economic spoils.

CHANGING WORLD
Britain's workers wanted their share of the spoils, too. The **rise of trade unions and the Labour Party** in the early 20th century meant that managers could no longer arrange things on their own terms **310–311 ≫**. If the conflict of 1914–1918 brought Europe its **first industrialized war 320–321 ≫**, the peace that followed brought a war of a different sort, as industry battled to progress against the power of an **ascendant United States 330–331 ≫**.

DEPRESSION AND DECLINE
The **Great Depression** after 1929 was deep and worldwide **334–335 ≫**, but for a Britain already bruised by the experience of World War II **354–355 ≫**, the loss of its empire came as another blow **364–365 ≫**. While the **chronic labor unrest** that afflicted Britain in the 1970s **376–377 ≫** may have been arrested by the Conservative governments of Margaret Thatcher in the 1980s **382–383 ≫**, it was at the expense of the industrial economy as a whole.

NEW INDUSTRY IN BRITAIN, 1920S

Shipbuilding
Prosperous industrialists in top hats pose in front of a large ship under construction. Enmeshed by supportive struts, the ship looms above the river with factory chimneys behind.

Victorian Values

Hard work, progress, and self-improvement were important in Victorian Britain. Society's values were increasingly in the hands of an expanding middle class that was growing wealthy through industry. Home, hearth, and family life were central to well-being, while there was a great drive to raise living standards for all.

In Victorian Britain, the home became a powerful symbol of what every right-thinking citizen should aspire to. Here, everyone knew their place, all was kept in pristine order, and family life was nurtured. Having a strong family unit within this home, the Victorians believed was to be the aim of all. The model home was middle-class, fashioned by money from 19th-century industry, rather than inherited aristocratic wealth. Domesticity was a virtue encouraged in all women and a middle-class wife absorbed herself in homemaking or genteel pursuits, such as needle skills. For poorer girls and women, working as a domestic servant was seemly because it supported family life or helped them prepare for their own married lives.

Part of making society an ordered Christian place was sexual restraint. Ladies were expected to behave with decorum and to be accompanied by male chaperones until they were married. At the same time, prostitution was rife because many women who needed to earn money had few other ways available to them for supporting themselves.

Victorian institutions
The Victorians set up a number of institutions to control or care for the population. Workhouses were set up in 1834 for those who were unable to work. The idea was that people should work for their food and accommodation, rather than relying on handouts. Conditions in the workhouses were such that many would go to any lengths to avoid going there.

Family values
Dollhouses like this one helped girls prepare for the role of running a home, as well as being cherished toys and family heirlooms.

‹‹ BEFORE

The Victorian era reacted against some moral aspects of the previous century while developing others.

SOCIAL REFORM
Victorian primness was partly **a reaction against the decadence** and sexual openness of their Georgian forebears, as caught in Thomas Rowlandson's caricatures of Georgian aristocrats. However, the Victorians also inherited some of their **zeal for social reform** from some notable Georgians, including William Wilberforce **‹‹ 234–235**.

SELF-PORTRAIT BY THOMAS ROWLANDSON

The basis of the modern police force was started by Sir Robert Peel. He created the Irish Constabulary in 1822 and London's Metropolitan force ("bobbies") in 1829. The aim was to provide a centralized and ethical crime prevention force. By 1857, there were regional police forces in England, Scotland, and Wales. Jails and asylums were also built on a grander scale than before—the 1845 Lunacy Act ordered all counties to build asylums. Mental illness sufferers had previously been treated as criminals—the Act was seen as a force for good, enabling people to receive treatment.

Household advice
The Victorians loved strict rules. Mrs. Beeton's best seller, *Book of Household Management* (1861), included instructions on food preparation and medical advice.

Education for all
In the drive to educate the nation, hundreds of schools opened. A series of Education Acts between 1870 and 1891 brought "board" schools (run by boards of governors) and compulsory free education. Discipline was highly valued and schoolchildren were often beaten. Dickens, who campaigned for better education before these Acts were enforced, portrayed several cruel schools in his novels. At the same time, Acts limiting child labor and reducing working hours for all were also introduced. Numerous public lectures and evening classes at Working Men's and Working Women's colleges further raised levels of education.

Social improvement
There was social improvement of many other kinds, too. In an age when diseases such as cholera tore through industrial slums, better drains, and

REFORMER (1812–1904)

SAMUEL SMILES

Scotsman Samuel Smiles was the quintessential Victorian. A doctor, campaigning journalist, and chief executive of various railroad companies in their golden age, he was a true middle-class professional. He was also a political and social campaigner, and was interested in self-improvement. Smiles admired prominent self-made men, such as George Stephenson and Josiah Wedgwood. Potted biographies of such figures, along with Smiles's general reflections, filled his best-known book *Self-Help* (1859), which sold more than 250,000 copies during his lifetime. This hugely influential work helped shape the typical middle-class Victorian values of hard work and thrift, the drive to rise from humble origins, self-reliance, duty, and strength of character.

Hub of the home
This typical Victorian parlor sums up middle-class values perfectly. Crowded with possessions, it was where families gathered to read and enjoy their hobbies.

> " The **spirit of self-help** is the root of all genuine growth in the individual."

SAMUEL SMILES, *SELF-HELP*, 1859

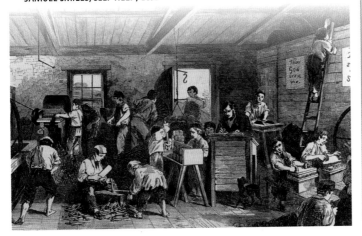

sewage systems came into existence: the first part of Joseph Bazalgette's great new London sewer system opened in 1865. Gas street lighting increased throughout the 1800s and in the late 1800s, Mosley Street, Newcastle, became Britain's first street to be lit by electricity. Model middle-class suburbs were built around the larger cities, such as Ealing in west London, and, thanks to increased train links, bankers, doctors, and lawyers led healthier lives far from city smog in new houses with indoor toilets. Public parks and gardens were laid out at the same time in these suburbs, with the aim of improving the health of the nation.

Ragged schools
This illustration shows a Birmingham ragged school set up in 1843. This institution was set up for the poor to provide a basic education and teach skills such as shoe-making, carding wool, or making firewood.

AFTER

Victorian values continued to be a touchstone against which new ideas were measured into later periods.

POST-WAR BRITAIN
In 1950s Britain, many Victorian buildings were demolished as **society looked to the future** rather than the past. Later in the century, Victorian architecture was preserved and became much-loved. **Many Victorian creations**, including buildings, sewers, and museums, are **still in use today**.

LATER VIEWS OF THE VICTORIANS
Consumerism, **self-improvement**, and **competition** are still at the heart of British society. Some politicians continue to use "Victorian" as shorthand for family values and law and order—or narrow-minded repression if you have a different set of views. In the 1980s, Margaret Thatcher **382–383** >> famously praised the "Victorian values" of **self-reliance and betterment**, and of being one great nation.

« BEFORE

WORDSWORTH'S HOME, DOVE COTTAGE

Religion and Romanticism were two major pillars of the cultural conflicts that engaged many 19th-century thinkers and artists.

PRE-REFORMATION RELIGION
The **Oxford Movement** looked back to the ideals of the pre-Reformation Church **« 136–137**. They saw it as **a pious and pure religion**, untainted as yet by the liberalism and **rationality of subsequent centuries**.

PRE-RAPHAELITE ART
The Pre-Raphaelite artists **admired the art** prior to High Renaissance painters such as Raphael (1483–1520), whom they deemed **too polished and idealized**. They favored early 15th-century Italian and Flemish work, such as the Arnolfini Portrait by Jan van Eyck.

ROMANCE VERSUS REASON
The *Lyrical Ballads* (1798) of William Wordsworth and Samuel Taylor Coleridge are often seen as **starting the high point of English Romanticism**. The Romantics fought against the 18th-century Age of Reason. Influenced by French thinker Jean-Jacques Rousseau (1712–1778), **they promoted beauty, unconstrained nature, and human emotion and liberty**. They were a huge influence on 19th-century figures, such as the critic John Ruskin (see box), who greatly admired Wordsworth.

Cultural Conflict

Running through the self-confidence of the 19th century were currents of conflict and dissent. Religious believers underwent crises of faith, while writers and artists criticized the status quo. All kinds of ideas circulated, from the Romantics' call for freedom, to the return to medievalism of the Pre-Raphaelite artists.

Spurred by political revolutions across Europe, a Romantic cultural rebellion took hold in Britain in the early 19th century. Escaping from 18th-century reason, poets William Wordsworth, John Keats, Percy Bysshe Shelley, and the dissolute Lord Byron, stressed nature and the emotional expression of the individual. Notable works included Keats' "Ode on a Grecian Urn" (1820) and Byron's epic *Don Juan* (1819–1824). Another cultural strand, Romantic medievalism, turned away from the mass materialism of Victorian culture, whose values many found superficial. The Pre-Raphaelite Brotherhood of young English artists, founded in 1848, rebelled against what they saw as the artificial, pompous, and academic art of the day, and sought an anti-dogma truth to nature. They

Madox Brown and, later, Edward Burne-Jones. The frequent mix of realism and religion, rejection of

> **UTILITARIANISM The moral theory of creating the greatest good for the greatest number of people. Also known as the "greatest happiness principle," utilitarianism was a popular theory in the Victorian period.**

Renaissance styles, and Rossetti's sensual female portraits (such as *Bocca Baciata*, 1859) all caused initial outrage, although leading art critic John Ruskin championed them.

Dissatisfaction with mechanistic Victorian industrialization spawned two other historical revivals: the Gothic Revival and the Arts and Crafts Movement. Ruskin played a major part

and Crafts Movement. This reacted to mass production by promoting a medieval-influenced idea of the craftsman and of handmade goods.

Faith, radicalism, and hard times
The 1830s onward saw a revival of High Anglican and Catholic ideas as a way of reinvigorating a stagnating Church of England. It was led by Oxford churchmen John Newman, John Keble, and Edward Pusey. Often called the Oxford Movement, or Tractarianism (after a series of written tracts), it greatly affected Anglican theology. Though some feared a return to papacy, it saw instead a general religious revival, with new churches built and a desire to help the needy. It was also an age when people, including Ruskin and novelist Thomas Hardy, questioned their faith.

> " I seek **antiquity not novelty**. I strive to **revive not invent**."
>
> AUGUSTUS PUGIN, LETTER TO JOHN BLOXAM, SEPTEMBER 13, 1840

harked back to medieval art prior to the work of Raphael and the High Renaissance, which was revered by the Victorians. Their founding members were Dante Gabriel Rossetti, John Everett Millais, and William Holman Hunt. Associated artists included Ford

in both. His love of what he saw as the beautiful Christian spiritualism of medieval architecture was shared by numerous British architects, notably Augustus Pugin, author of *The True Principles of Pointed or Christian Architecture* (1841), whose Victorian Gothic work includes detailing on the Houses of Parliament. George Gilbert Scott became the most successful Victorian Gothic architect, completing London's St. Pancras Station in 1865. Pugin wrote that "all ornament should consist of enrichment of the essential construction of the building." This functionalist idea, that art and design should honestly express its purpose and construction, rather than being superficial decoration, was also a guiding principle of William Morris, who was at the forefront of the Arts

Symbolic realism
John Everett Millais' *Christ in the House of His Parents*, c.1850, believed to be influenced by Oxford Movement caused great controversy for showing the sacred as ordinary.

ENGLISH ACADEMIC, CRITIC, AND SOCIAL REFORMER (1819–1900)

JOHN RUSKIN

London-born Ruskin had a claustrophobic childhood framed by a Romantic-spirited father and a religious mother, and he struggled with the oppositions of sensuality, intellectualism, and religious propriety. In the 1870s, "aesthetic" artist James McNeill Whistler sued Ruskin for accusing him of "flinging a pot of paint in the public's face" with an abstract work. The ensuing court case thrust Ruskin, and the era's artistic values, into the spotlight. Ruskin emotively championed the landscapes of J. M. W. Turner in *Modern Painters* (1843–1860) and Gothic architecture in *Stones of Venice* (1851–1853).

The ideas of Charles Darwin on natural, not divine, evolution (see pp.288–289) had a profound effect, and an increasing agnosticism pervaded this age of scientific inquiry.

While some looked to the past, others faced the present head on. Modern industrial society had highlighted poverty and many social inequalities. Ruskin became a social reformer, and taught at London's Working Men's College (see pp.278–279). Morris formed the Socialist League in 1884 and outlined a socialist utopia in *News from Nowhere* (1891). Europe's 1848 revolutions furthered radical thought. Karl Marx and Friedrich Engels wrote the *Communist Manifesto* (1848), and founded modern communism. Engels, author of *The Condition of the Working Classes in England in 1844* (1845), worked in a Manchester cotton mill run by his German family. Marx was a German economist and philosopher, based in England after

Hard Times
In novels such as *Hard Times* (1854) and *Oliver Twist* (1839), Charles Dickens highlighted the plight of the dispossessed of Victorian Britain.

1849. His *Das Kapital* (1867–1894) predicted capitalism's collapse.

The writings of Charles Dickens championed the downtrodden and sought social reform in areas such as sanitation and poor law. Dickens was a contradiction typical of this age of cultural conflicts. The society that he critiqued, albeit often fondly, gave him great success. One of his targets, notably in *Hard Times* (1854), was the utilitarianism of Jeremy Bentham and John Stuart Mill, central to Victorian thinking.

Through all of this, ran the influence of Thomas Carlyle, a Scots historian–philosopher, based in London after 1834, and author of *Sartor Resartus* (1833–1834). Carlyle disliked Victorian materialism and utilitarianism, and promoted social reform. Doubting conventional Christianity, he developed an unorthodox spiritualism and a belief in the power of strong individuals.

Form and function
This modern-looking chair by Philip Webb came from Morris & Company. It is simple but functional, and covered with fabric in a nature-inspired design. Typical Morris items were furniture, fabric, wallpapers, and beautiful medieval-style, handmade books.

MORRIS & COMPANY William Morris's company was founded in 1861. Its carefully crafted products were designed by artists such as Dante Gabriel Rossetti and Edward Burne-Jones.

AFTER

In the 19th century, cultural trends forged major modern ideas, from the cult of the individual to the Welfare State.

INDIVIDUALISM
The Romantics' stress on the **unfettered individual**, rather than on the needs of the group or society, **often ran counter to Victorian utilitarianism** and fed the 20th-century "cult of the individual." The Romantic poets' image also did much for the **concept of the tortured artist** and the special qualities of being creative.

MODERNISM
The idea, embraced by Morris and the Arts and Crafts Movement, that **form should express function** prefigures the form-follows-function mantra of 20th-century Modernist design. The stylish minimalist chairs of the 1930s owe much to Morris. Even Pugin's Gothic designs, with their **functionalist ethos**, connects in the unlikeliest of ways with modern British architects.

THE WELFARE STATE
The **socially conscious** and campaigning work of figures such as Dickens, Ruskin, and Morris aided the **rise of socialism** and the Labour Party. Ruskin, with his passion for making lectures and courses available to the working class, and his **general interest in social reform**, is often said to have influenced the creation of the Welfare State 360–361 >>.

Victorian workhouse, 1900

At this Marylebone workhouse in London, men sit in regimented rows to receive their evening meal. Women were kept separate from the men, for the sake of decency. As charity was regarded by many Victorians as being morally corrupting and encouraging idleness, hard (if pointless) labor was prescribed in order to reduce its harm. The resemblance to a prison of the day is inescapable—as it was to its inmates, for whom it was clear that poverty was considered a crime.

Exploring the World

Explorers had always experienced the desire to chart the unknown wildernesses of the Earth, but they had never felt so well-equipped as they did now. They were often driven by other motives, too: a desire to spread the word of Christ or, perhaps unconsciously, that other gospel—the Anglo-Saxon way.

British explorers in Africa were often impelled by a pious desire to bring salvation to the "savages." It seemed only natural that, along with the good news of Christianity, they should bring tidings of black Africa's divinely ordained subservience to white Europe. Explorer James Richardson's visit to the Sahara oasis of Ghat, in 1845, was a case in point.

Presumed Livingstone

Another missionary-explorer, David Livingstone (1813–1873) traced the course of the upper Zambezi River from 1851; he then walked to the Atlantic coast at Luanda. Retracing his steps to the source of Zambezi, he followed it down to the Indian Ocean, becoming the first European to cross the African continent from west to east.

He was also the first westerner to see one of the largest waterfalls in the world—local people knew it as the "Smoke that Thunders"; Livingstone named it Victoria Falls.

The Queen's name was also given to the lake discovered by Richard Burton and John Speke's expedition in 1856. Speke's claim that Lake Victoria was the source of the Nile was correct, though little more than an educated hunch. An 1860 expedition intended to furnish proof was beaten back by hostile tribes.

Livingstone, back in Africa from 1865, disappeared into the interior, causing a media outcry in Britain. An American newspaper, the *New York Herald*, sent Welsh journalist and explorer Henry Morton Stanley in search of him. In 1871, finding a frail and elderly European in a village by

The Northwest Passage
Navigators were still tantalized by the idea of this tempting short-cut to the riches of the east. It was there, but severe ice made it impassable.

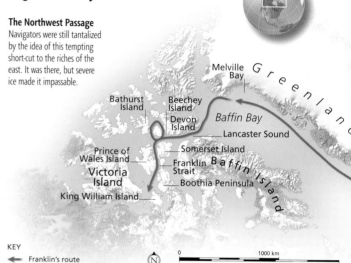

Melville Bay
Greenland
Bathurst Island
Beechey Island
Devon Island
Baffin Bay
Lancaster Sound
Prince of Wales Island
Somerset Island
Franklin Strait
Baffin Island
Victoria Island
Boothia Peninsula
King William Island

KEY
← Franklin's route

0   1000 km
0   1000 miles

N

> ## "During the whole day, we had not seen a **single drop of water** or **blade of grass**."
>
> CHARLES STURT, IN THE AUSTRALIAN INTERIOR, 1829

« BEFORE

The timeless urge to travel was accompanied by a new-found sense of scientific exploration.

EXPLORATION AND DISCOVERY
Mungo Park, a product of post-Enlightenment Scotland **« 224–225**, traveled up the Gambia River to the Niger in 1795. **Cook's voyages « 226–227**, were inspired by a hunger for adventure and knowledge.

NEW PURPOSES
The **anti-slavery campaign** generated an interest in Africa **« 234–235**. Industrial Britain began to regard the world as a source of raw materials, and as a **potential market « 276–277**.

VOYAGE
DANS L'INTÉRIEUR
DE L'AFRIQUE,
FAIT EN 1795, 1796 et 1797;
PAR M. MUNGO PARK,
ENVOYÉ PAR LA SOCIÉTÉ D'AFRIQUE
ÉTABLIE À LONDRES;
Avec des éclaircissemens sur la Géographie
de l'intérieur de l'Afrique, par le Major
RENNELL.
Traduit de l'Anglois sur la seconde édition
PAR J. CASTÉRA.
TOME PREMIER.

A PARIS,
...
AN VIII.

MUNGO PARK'S BOOK, 1816

Burke and Wills explore Australia

Robert Burke and John Wills approach Coopers Creek on what was both a successful expedition and an ill-fated one. The explorers crossed the continent, but only one of the group returned.

Lake Tanganyika, Stanley hailed him with the iconic words, "Dr. Livingstone, I presume …."

Australia opens up

The Sydney Cove settlement (see pp.294–295) sat on the doorstep of an enormous continent, so did colonies at Melbourne (from 1835) and Adelaide (1836). Not much was known even of New South Wales before the first forays by farmer-explorer Gregory Blaxland from 1813. Subsequent explorations revealed the Lachlan and Macquarie Rivers flowing north and west, away from the ocean. Working around the

David Livingstone

A complex mixture of wanderlust, curiosity, Christian evangelism, and a desire to stop the slave trade drove Livingstone. This 19th-century lithograph shows him arriving at Lake Ngami in Botswana.

coast in opposite directions, navigators Matthew Flinders and Nicolas Baudin managed to miss the mouth of the Murray River. The assumption remained that the rivers to the north drained into some inland sea.

From 1829, Charles Sturt began exploring the Darling Basin, finally finding the Murray and tracing it down to the ocean. He struck deeper into the interior during his Central Australian Expedition of 1844–1846. Suffering from scurvy, heat, and dehydration, he was lucky to make it back alive.

Explorers Robert O'Hara Burke and William John Wills were not so fortunate. In 1860, they left Melbourne to cross the continent from south to north. They took camels, which they felt would cope well with the conditions. Even so, only four out of 20 men made it to the Gulf of Carpentaria in northern Australia. Nine dropped out in the early stages; then seven died, three on the homeward journey,

> **29,000** The estimated total distance, in miles (47,000 km) covered by Livingstone in Africa, opening up some 1 million sq miles (2.6 million sq km) of territory.

including Burke and Wills themselves. Only one—John King—returned home, but the expedition had achieved what it set out to do.

Arctic agony

Meanwhile, the centuries-old search for the Northwest Passage (see pp.226–227) continued. Sir John Franklin mapped much of North America's northern coastline from the 1820s. His final expedition in 1846–1847 ended grimly, with his ship getting trapped in ice off King William Island in northern Canada. What happened to Franklin and his crew will probably never be known, though rumors of murder and cannibalism circulated at the time.

Heroic failure was the order of the day for British exploration of the North and South Poles, most famously in the case of Captain Scott (see BOX). But Ernest Shackleton turned objective setback into triumph when, having first failed to reach the South Pole in 1908, he undertook a new expedition six years later. His ship *Endurance* ice-bound and his men forced ashore, Shackleton took a small party by boat to South Georgia island, 800 miles (1,300 km) away across rough seas, to summon help.

ROBERT FALCON SCOTT

Born near Devonport, Robert Falcon Scott joined the Royal Navy in 1888, working his way up the ranks over the years. By 1897, Scott served as lieutenant and torpedo officer, and led an Antarctic expedition from 1901–1904. His second expedition to the South Pole though, ended in tragedy. Setting out in 1910, Scott and his companions lost out to Roald Amundsen's Norwegian expedition through sheer ill-luck and—it was later suggested—poor organization and obstinacy. Reaching the Pole only to find they had been beaten, they then faced a terrible homeward trek. Their bodies were found in their tent by a subsequent search party, along with Scott's journal—a moving record of their final days.

AFTER

The idea gained ground that adventurers were running out of places to explore—that the remaining challenges were more about endurance than exploration.

FEAR OF THE UNFAMILIAR
For many Britons, the feeling that the world "out there" was dark and dangerous was only underlined by news of the **Indian Mutiny 292–293 »**. Paradoxically, though, thanks to a **steady flow of emigrant families**, many other far-flung places were becoming British homes away from home **294–295 »**.

RISE AND FALL OF THE EMPIRE
For better or worse, the country became accustomed to interacting with large parts of the outside world mainly through the medium of its warships, its soldiers, and its colonial officials **296–297 »**. The responsibilities imperial power brought proved troublesome **342–343 »**. In the decades following **World War II**, it became clear that the sun was slowly setting on the **British Empire 364–365 »**. While, for some, Mrs. Thatcher's **Falklands** adventure brought back Britain's self-respect; to others it seemed an incongruous show of bravado by a fading force **382–383 »**.

British India

For better or worse, Britain's sense of its imperial destiny came of age in 19th-century India. Lives were devoted to the Empire's service—and colossal fortunes were made. The occupiers believed that they had brought their Indian subjects a golden age of good governance, order, civilization, and prosperity.

Indian postage stamp
Introduced in 1857, the postal service was one of many benefits brought to India by the Raj. The British were slower to acknowledge the immeasurable benefits—economic and strategic—they received.

« BEFORE

Britain's position as an island nation had, paradoxically, prevented it from ever growing too insular. Reliant on trade, it always had to look beyond its own shores.

COLONIAL EXPANSION

After something of a false start in the reign of Elizabeth I **«« 146–147**, England's **first colonial ventures** were across the Atlantic in North America **«« 162–163**. The 18th century brought territorial gains in Canada, and **the establishment of outposts** in the Indian subcontinent by the **East India Company «« 212–213**. The Company's fortunes expanded under British officer Robert Clive when Mughal Emperor Shah Alam granted it the revenue rights to Bengal. These acquisitions went some way toward making up for the **loss of the American colonies «« 214–215**. With industrialization proceeding apace **«« 232–233**, **colonial expansion** became **ever more essential** to Britain, which needed new sources of raw materials and potential markets for its manufactured products **«« 276–277**.

ROBERT CLIVE RECEIVING THE DIWANI (REVENUE RIGHTS) OF BENGAL, 1765

ritain carried its policy of arm's-length imperialism in India into the new century, with the East India Company acting as an occupying power. The conquests continued: the Mughal Emperor Shah Alam II, an old man with his authority already much reduced by his defeat at Buxar (see pp.212–213), was forced to accept British protection in 1804. He was reduced to no more than a puppet of the Company. The power of the Maratha Empire was broken in 1818, but still the Company kept up its program of expansion.

Taking hold

The expansion started in 1824 with the conquest of Burma, which proceeded smoothly. Company troops took Assam, Manipur, and adjacent territories by 1826, but there were setbacks. The First Afghan War (1839–1842), intended as a war of conquest, ended up an unmitigated disaster. Of the 4,500 men (and 12,000 civilian followers) who went to Kabul, only one man—military surgeon William Brydon—survived.

Soon, though, the British were back on the offensive. They took Sind (1843) and Gwalior (1844) before going on to fight two Sikh Wars (1845–1846 and 1848–1849). These consolidated the Company's hold on the Punjab, while a Second Burma War (1852) secured Lower (southern) Burma.

Tax and trade

By 1856, 70 percent of the subcontinent was directly under British rule. In reality, though, British dominance was more or less complete. Treaty arrangements with local rulers typically respected their ceremonial authority, while reserving actual power for the Company itself.

Slowly, the Company's role changed from that of a commercial operation doing the minimum policing required to ensure stability, to something very much like a government. Increasingly, its profits were derived more from taxation than from trade.

British officer in India
Even averagely important officers could live like little viceroys in British India. Thronged by servants, they ignored the wider realities, encountering only deference from those Indians they came into contact with.

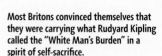

British Indian railroads
A locomotive pulls into a railroad station near Calcutta in 1867. Originally built to boost trade and for military purposes, the Indian railroad network soon saw rapid growth in passenger services.

AFTER

Most Britons convinced themselves that they were carrying what Rudyard Kipling called the "White Man's Burden" in a spirit of self-sacrifice.

INDIAN INDEPENDENCE
There was some anger then, when the 1920s and 1930s brought an intensifying campaign on the part of Indians, who wanted to be free of British rule **>> 342–343**. World War II changed attitudes—and Britain's position in the world— and in 1947 **India became independent >> 364–365**. Built for the British Viceroy, Delhi's Rashtrapati Bhavan is now the official residence for the president of the Republic of India.

THE IRON GATES OF
RASHTRAPATI BHAVAN

thousand British officers had charge of huge numbers of native sepoys. In 1857, the entire edifice very nearly came crashing down—when sepoys rebelled against their officers and a full-scale mutiny erupted (see pp.292–293). The mutiny threatened the very continuance of British rule.

The British Raj
The aftermath saw a wholesale reorganization of the army in India, with more native-British troops brought in. The East India Company's role as intermediary was replaced with direct rule from Westminster. Queen Victoria was proclaimed the Empress of India. Britain was proud of this "jewel in the crown": Indian chic influenced everything from furnishings to cuisine.

Its future now apparently secure, the Raj (the new official name for British rule) went on with its routines. Officers' families could enjoy elegant rounds of picnics, balls, and banquets. They escaped the heat for cooler hill stations in summer and commanded a large complement of servants, thanks to the abundance of cheap labor.

Corruption was endemic either way, although there were intermittent crackdowns, as in the case of Warren Hastings. In 1788, Hastings, the Governor of Bengal, was impeached on corruption charges. Although acquitted by the House of Lords, he was disgraced.

Western ways
Britain made great play of its "civilizing" mission—and did try to stamp out *suttee* (the burning of Hindu widows on their husbands' funeral pyres) and female infanticide. It also suppressed the *Thuggee* (Thugs) a cult whose members lived as bandits, strangling innocent travelers as sacrifices to the goddess Kali. And, of course, it gave India the benefits of western technology and infrastructure. Roads—of obvious military use—were at the same time beneficial to all. The Company spent £400,000 per year on its road building program during the late 1840s: this included a tarmac highway between Delhi and Calcutta. Railroads, vital for British business, could also be presented as a boon for Indians. Soon the whole subcontinent was crisscrossed by railroads.

Rebellion flares up
Many Indians viewed the educational opportunities made available to members of its elite with suspicion. They sensed that the British were intent on educating them out of their Indian ways, and schooling them in subservience to Company rule.

Cultural sensitivity was all-important, given the extent to which the British were outnumbered. Tiny in number compared with the indigenous population, they may have enjoyed immense power but it was precariously poised. Even in the army, a few

Tiger hunt
Viceroy Lord Curzon poses with his prize and his party (including wife Mary Victoria) in this 1902 photograph. Wild and beautiful, but subdued by British power: that was how the Raj liked to see India.

> " I know nothing at all about them … I think **the less one sees** and knows of them **the better**."
>
> ENGLISH LADY ON INDIANS, REPORTED BY JULIA CHARLOTTE MAITLAND, 1837

Indian Mutiny

The initial flare-up was over the use of greased gun cartridges, but the sepoys' sense of outrage went much further. The ensuing mutiny threatened to consume the British Raj. Asked to oppress their own people, the native soldiers were shocked to find themselves despised—and exhilarated to appreciate the power they possessed.

It is hard, in hindsight, to pinpoint when the uprising started, as a series of minor incidents marked an escalating crisis. The first major outbreak came at the Meerut cantonment where, on May 9, several troops refused on religious grounds to use gun cartridges greased with pork or beef fat. The next day, they were court-martialed and sentenced to long prison terms. The punishment provoked a general mutiny on the base and rioting in the nearby city.

Escalating violence
The uprising at Meerut fueled similar insurrections across much of north and central India. The rebels reached Delhi on May 11, and attempted to set up Bahadur Shah II (the last of the Mughal line) as the emperor of India. By July, the British forces placed the city under siege—although they were besieged themselves from behind by Indian forces. At Lucknow, the British garrison

kept the rebels at bay, but a prolonged fight for the control of the city continued for many months.

In June, the rebel forces besieged the British garrison in Cawnpore (now Kanpur). Despite the British surrender, 100 of their wives and children were captured and massacred.

Outrage and retribution
The barbaric killings fueled mounting anger in Britain. The country erupted in jingoistic rage and stridently called for dire punishment. Bloody retributions followed, as British troops regained their hold over the colony through 1858. Reports of genuine atrocities, compounded by more exaggerated tales, helped foster a deep-seated sense of racial superiority and distrust toward Indians among the British population. As a precaution, the British Parliament ended the East India Company rule and put India under the direct administration of the British Crown.

> **"We heard dreadful shouting and screaming in the city; it was fearful to think how close the wretches were to us."**
>
> *DIARY OF LADY JULIA INGLIS*, UNDER SIEGE IN LUCKNOW, JULY 4, 1857

Storming of Delhi
British troops, with loyal Sikh sepoys, storm the gates of Delhi, while the rebel sepoys defend their positions. One of three coordinated attacks, it began just before daybreak on September 14, 1857. Even then, it took days of fighting to secure the city.

BEFORE

Britain had been sending people to America for some time—often unwillingly as convicts or indentured labor.

NEW COLONIES
After a difficult start, Britain's colonies along North America's **Atlantic coast << 162–163** flourished. Much of **eastern Canada << 212–213** was **colonized**, and more colonies were acquired from the French in 1763. Although the loss of the American colonies **<< 214–215** hit Britain hard, **new possibilities** opened up **in the Pacific << 226–227**. In the 19th century, men such as Gregory Blaxland and Charles Sturt ventured into the **Australian interior << 286–287**.

EMIGRATION
If new lands exerted a pull as potential colonies, a definite push for emigration already existed. The **Agricultural Revolution produced slow-motion turmoil** in the British countryside over generations **<< 230–231**. An **Ireland still shattered by the famine** of the 1840s **<< 266–267** saw **people emigrating** in their thousands every year.

Dominions and Emigrants

Britain started to think of itself as an imperial power, but with that status came responsibilities. This unprecedented situation required innovative thinking: how was such a large empire to be run? As the 19th century wore on, British power and people were making their presence felt around the world.

Even as America's colonies were breaking free, Britain had been extending its influence to the north. Naturally, though, there were fears that the Canadian colonists might follow their American neighbors. Rebellions broke out in Lower and Upper Canada in 1837–1878, general dissatisfaction compounded in what was formerly French Lower Canada (now Quebec) by a nationalistic impulse. Upper and Lower Canada were in 1840 brought into a single Province of Canada—French-speakers were now outnumbered. However, from 1848 steps were taken to allow a limited degree of autonomy under a system known as Responsible Government.

A better England
Edward Gibbon Wakefield, who founded the New Zealand Company in 1837, said that New Zealand was destined to be "a better England." His vision enthused thousands, and British emigrants flocked there. Difficulties early on with the warlike Maori were apparently settled with the Treaty of Waitangi in 1840. Some 500 chiefs signed the treaty—although it is not clear if they understood the terms they were agreeing to. In any case, new arrivals quickly encroached beyond the boundaries appointed for settlement, causing continuing conflict. Even so, more Maoris were killed by diseases from which they had no immunity. An indigenous population estimated at around 140,000 in 1840 had fallen to 42,000 by 1890.

161,700 The number of people who were transported to Australia (New South Wales, Tasmania, and Western Australia) between 1788 and 1868. An estimated 25,000 of these were women.

First settlers
Believed to be the first photograph to be taken in Australia (in 1855), this image shows the racial hierarchy already well established. The white man quite literally has the whip-hand.

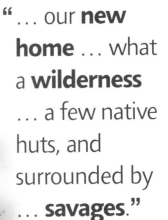

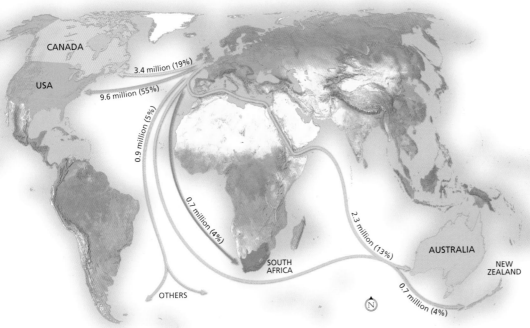

CANADA

USA

3.4 million (19%)

9.6 million (55%)

0.9 million (5%)

0.7 million (4%)

2.3 million (13%)

0.7 million (4%)

SOUTH AFRICA

AUSTRALIA

NEW ZEALAND

OTHERS

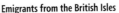

"… our **new home** … what a **wilderness** … a few native huts, and surrounded by … **savages**."

HARRIET LONGFORD, IN A LETTER TO HER MOTHER, FROM PORT AURORA, NEW ZEALAND, JANUARY 27, 1840

Initially an outpost of New South Wales, New Zealand was its own colony from 1841. It won what amounted to Responsible Government status in 1852. It was certainly a "better England" as regards electoral representation—extending the vote to women in 1893.

Gold rush

New South Wales got its first, unwilling, settlers on January 18, 1788, when Captain Arthur Phillip's First Fleet arrived in Sydney Cove, bringing 700 convicts. The green countryside was more arid than it seemed, its soils obstinately uncultivable, but the convicts had to make it work to survive, and ultimately they succeeded.

Soon immigrants were coming voluntarily, not just to New South Wales, but to the other colonies of what from 1817 was called Australia. Tasmania (or Van Diemen's Land), first settled in 1802, was a separate colony from 1825; Western Australia followed in 1832; South Australia in 1836; and Victoria in 1851. These, too, started gaining Responsible Government status. Queensland (1859) and Northern Territory (1863) received this status from the start.

"Wherever the European has trod death seems to pursue the aboriginal," wrote Darwin when the *Beagle*

Ornate Maori club
The Maoris used hooked clubs in the wars of the 1830s. The immediate impact of white settlement sparked trouble between native tribes.

sailed into Australia in 1836. Australia's native population fell by 90 percent through the 19th and early 20th centuries. Some were massacred; many more died of Old World diseases.

Spectacular gold finds in the 1850s brought fortune hunters flocking in from around the world. In a single decade, Australia's population rose from 400,000 to more than 1 million. The gold rush was quick, but many disappointed prospectors stayed on. Australia was starting to feel like its own nation, but it was not until 1901 that it became a self-governing dominion.

Striking out

"The great tide of emigration flows steadily westward," reported the *Illustrated London News* in 1850, although this was because the main current of emigration was from an Ireland still reeling from the Famine (see pp.266–267). The Irish made up the overwhelming majority of

Rebelling emigrants
The defeat of the *Quebecois Patriotes* at Saint-Eustache December 14, 1837, meant the Lower Canada Rebellion was all over—bar extensive reprisals by the British.

Emigrants from the British Isles
This map shows the principal areas of the world to which people from the British Isles immigrated between 1821 and 1911. Colored arrows show the number of immigrants as well as the percentage of the total number of immigrants.

the hundreds of thousands of emigrants from the British Isles to the United States during the 1840s. Paradoxically, this rural people settled mainly in the big cities.

English, Welsh, and Scottish emigrants mostly made their way to existing British colonies—arriving in Canada at a rate of 35,000–40,000 a year through the 1840s.

The Scottish Highlands were undergoing a sort of speeded-up version of English Enclosures in the shape of the "Clearances." As traditional chiefs reinvented themselves as aristocrats, with the authorities' encouragement, they needed cash to sustain their newly lavish lifestyles. Many decided to clear land—which had supported subsistence farming—for grazing by sheep. Whole communities were evicted, sometimes brutally, and many had little choice but to emigrate.

AFTER

The white-dominated dominions continued to maintain the closest of connections with the mother country. This continues to the present day.

CANADIAN INDEPENDENCE
The restive spirit lingered in the French-speaking areas of Canada; a **Quebecois separatist movement** sprang up in the 1970s, although calls for **secession** were **rejected in referendums** of 1980 and 1995.

FRIENDS IN NEED
Despite a posture of **impatience with the "Poms"** (a mildly offensive word used by Australians and New Zealanders for an English person) of Britain, Australia remains close to Britain, both at an official level and in the **informal contacts** between family members across the world. Both Australia and New Zealand sent floods of **volunteers to support Britain** in World War I. ANZAC (the Australia and New Zealand Army Corps) suffered terrible casualties in the Gallipoli Campaign (April 1915–January 1916) **320–321 》**. Both countries came to Britain's aid again during World War II **348–349 》**.

THE BRITISH MONARCHY ABROAD
The **independence movement** of the **post-war period** was noticed in Australia, New Zealand, and English-speaking Canada, but their white populations had far more **positive feelings toward Britain** than the colonized peoples of Asia and Africa **364–365 》**. There was, correspondingly, less pressure to break the connection, in particular with the Crown, still held in high affection thanks to the **popularity of Queen Elizabeth II**. Moves to abolish the monarchy have so far been thwarted.

Imperialist Muscle

The world's first industrial power, Britain was a pace-setter in technology, trade, and agriculture. Its navy ruled the waves and its army occupied vast areas of dry land. It is no surprise then that Britain was walking tall. Increasingly, indeed, it was swaggering—a self-appointed policeman, supremely arrogant in its "civilizing mission."

Britannia began life as a colony—the bleakest and most remote of the Roman Empire. At least, after the cruelties of conquest, its people had been able to enjoy several comparatively untroubled centuries of the *Pax Romana*—"Roman Peace" (see pp.31–32). Britain's imperial apologists liked to talk of a *Pax Britannica*, bestowed on the fortunate peoples of Africa and Asia.

The Opium Wars
Britain's addiction to tea, and to its trade in Chinese silk and ceramics for the European market, was at first paid for with silver. Once America was lost, however (see p.214–215), and the price of silver rose, opium was found to be a perfect substitute. High in value and easy to ship, it grew well in the hilly areas of India where labor was also cheap. There was one small problem though—opium had been illegal in

6 MILLION The number of opium addicts in China by the end of the 1820s, their habits supported largely by illegal imports from British India. Britain took violent exception to a Chinese crackdown.

BEFORE

Britain's forces had fought abroad for centuries, but taking territories for colonization belonged to a comparatively recent stage in the country's history.

COLONIAL EXPANSION
England's adventurers missed the boat when the **Age of Discovery** began in the 15th century. While Portugal and Spain built vast empires, England's early attempts at establishing **New World colonies** were half-hearted **‹‹ 146–147**. Not until **James I's reign** had serious settlement begun **‹‹ 162–163**. Since then, however, England made great strides, the **Thirteen Colonies** in North America going from strength to strength while the merchant companies took huge areas of **Canada and India** under British administration **‹‹ 212–213**. More territories were taken from the French (and from the Dutch) at the time of the **Revolutionary Wars ‹‹ 240–241**. Further conquests were made in the **Indian subcontinent** after the defeats of the Mughal and Maratha empires **‹‹ 290–291**.

Second Opium War
Chinese tents await the arrival of the British delegation in Tientsin (Tianjin) in 1858. So disadvantageous was the agreement reached here that the Emperor had second thoughts and tried to resist.

China since 1729. Britain used "independent agents" (or, more bluntly, smugglers) to conduct its trade, and it did so on an extraordinary scale. In 1729, 200 chests of opium were brought into China. By 1828, the figure rose to 13,131 despite repeated crackdowns. Quite apart from the social cost of mass addiction, this was a huge drain on the Chinese economy.

Another anti-opium drive was mounted in China in 1836. The Chinese Emperor wrote politely to Queen Victoria asking her to stop the traffic, but was ignored. In May 1839, officials confiscated 20,000 crates of opium at Guangzhou (Canton) and destroyed it. British officials demanded that full payment be made. When the Chinese instead turned back foreign vessels approaching the port, Britain dispatched a punitive expedition of 16 warships, with 4,000 men. These clashed with the Chinese fleet that November, destroying 71 junks and capturing 60 coastal batteries. Having consolidated its hold on this section of coast, the expedition headed north to Shanghai and smashed another war fleet, before heading up the Yangtze River, destroying property and killing thousands of civilians.

Opening of the Suez Canal, 1869
Britain displaced the French in India—which only made their presence in Suez more disconcerting. The French-built canal was of strategic significance. Britain went part of the way to relieving its anxieties by buying out the heavily indebted Ottoman Egypt's share in 1875.

Forced to sue for peace, under the Treaty of Nanjing, the Emperor had to hand over Hong Kong, open key ports, and accord Britain "most favored nation" status. This meant that any privilege given to any other nation would automatically apply to Britain, too. The Emperor also had to allow the opium trade to continue. Other powers, including the United States and France, then demanded their own treaties. Christian missionaries arrived in China and started preaching.

All this foreign interference—and the continuing opium problem—pushed China too far. The murder of a French missionary and the arrest of a Chinese ship, previously registered as British, for opium-smuggling became the pretext for joint Franco-British hostilities. This Second Opium War (1856–1860) was designed to wring further concessions from a thoroughly humiliated China. When the Emperor dragged his feet, the allies attacked with Russian and American support. They sacked Beijing,

13 MILLION The extent in sq miles (33.7 million sq km) covered by the British Empire in the early 20th century. More than 450 million people lived under British rule.

including the Summer Palace. China was carved up into tranches for exploitation by the foreign powers.

African upstarts
Zulu power, built by King Shaka through the 1820s, had carried all before it in southern Africa, but it came up against a technology-gap at Blood River in 1838. More than 3,000 Zulu warriors were cut down here by the rifles of 500 Boers. Things did not always go the white man's way though: on January 22, 1879, at Isandhlwana in South Africa, King Cetshwayo's Zulus inflicted a shattering defeat on a bigger and much better-armed British army. The shock to morale back home was tempered by the

Zulu War 1879
A British delegation returns from talks with the Zulu king Cetshwayo. At Isandhlwana his warriors had earned him the right to be treated with respect. Even in defeat, he demanded careful handling.

However successful the British were in persuading themselves that their empire-building was altruistic in intent, their subject nations were harder to convince.

DEMAND FOR AUTONOMY
The **desire for autonomy** among British colonies was strong. By the 1930s, Indians were looking to a future free of British domination **342–343** ≫. **British high-handedness** was remembered then—just as it was to be in the period after World War II when the **"Wind of Change"** began blowing through **Africa**. It would also be remembered by the Chinese as they negotiated the arrangements for **Hong Kong 364–365** ≫. Its arrogance would blow up in Britain's face in its humiliation over the **Suez Canal 366–367** ≫. Some would say that Britain had been badly served by the unchallenged supremacy it enjoyed at its imperial noon in the 19th century. The entire post-war period was overshadowed by a **sense of long-drawn-out decline**.

stirring heroism of a handful of troops who maintained a gallant last stand at Rorke's Drift. European firepower ultimately proved overwhelming: within six months, the Zulu capital Ulundi fell and Cetshwayo was forced to sue for peace.

Britain also clashed with its former partners in the slave trade, the Ashanti. The Ashanti had built a powerful empire centered on present-day Ghana. Britain tried to take it over in the First Anglo-Ashanti War of 1823, but was badly mauled before beating the Ashanti back into the interior. A second war in 1863–1864 was inconclusive. Britain won the Third Ashanti War (1873–1874) convincingly, burning the

> " Whatever happens, **we have got**/The Maxim gun and **they have not**."
>
> HILAIRE BELLOC, *THE MODERN TRAVELLER*, 1898

47 **The number of British casualties at the Battle of Omdurman, September 2, 1898.** Kitchener's British force cut down 9,700 Sudanese rebels with their artillery and their Maxim guns.

Ashanti capital Kumasi. After further wars (1894–1896 and 1900), the Ashanti territory was finally absorbed into Britain's Gold Coast colony.

Egypt had long been important as a crossing-point between the Mediterranean Sea and the Indian Ocean. It had been still more vital since the opening of the French-built Suez Canal in 1869. Not quite a British colony, it

was nominally a part of the Ottoman Empire but ruled by Ismail Pasha, the Khedive—a sort of viceroy or governor. It was on his behalf, at least in theory, that Britain's General Charles George Gordon made an expedition southward up the Nile into Sudan.

Here the Islamic teacher Muhammad ibn Abdalla announced he was the *Mahdi*, a Messiah-like redeemer prophesied in certain traditions of Islam.

Zulu regiments carried shields covered in dried cow hide. Experienced soldiers had white shields with black markings.

Carved buffalo horn
Carved around 1880, this horn shows scenes of the recent Zulu Wars. The Zulus favored battle tactic was inspired by the buffalo horn—two wings extended outward, moving in to enfold the enemy as the *impi* (regiment) as a whole attacked.

British soldiers used cannons to attack Zulu warriors armed with spears.

Thousands flocked to join him, and by 1882 the Egyptian authorities had lost their grip.

Last stand
George Gordon had gone to Khartoum in Sudan to restore order, but since his presence only inflamed the situation, he was ordered to evacuate his troops. Instead, he made the personal decision to stay on and defend the city and Sudan against the *Mahdi*'s forces. By March 1884 he was under siege. A popular clamor in Britain led to the dispatch of a relief expedition from Egypt. But on January 26, 1885—just a few days before help arrived—the rebels stormed the city, and Gordon had his heroic end, cut down by his attackers.

Fury erupted back home and Lord Herbert Kitchener began a long and arduous campaign to take back Sudan. The battles of Omdurman (1898) and Umm Diwaykarat (1899) were both victories for Britain's Maxim gun and heavy artillery. Might prevailed: Sudan was declared a condominium—jointly ruled by Britain and Egypt, but with the former in charge.

> " Remember that you are an **Englishman**, and have drawn **first prize** in the lottery of life."
>
> CECIL RHODES, IN *THE INDEPENDENT*

Railroad station
New transportation technologies such as the railroads and the steamship shrank the world and extended people's horizons in the 19th century. They could travel for business or for pleasure, and to find fresh work opportunities. William Powell Frith's painting, *The Railway Station* (1862), teems with colorful characters from all social classes in 19th-century London's Paddington Station.

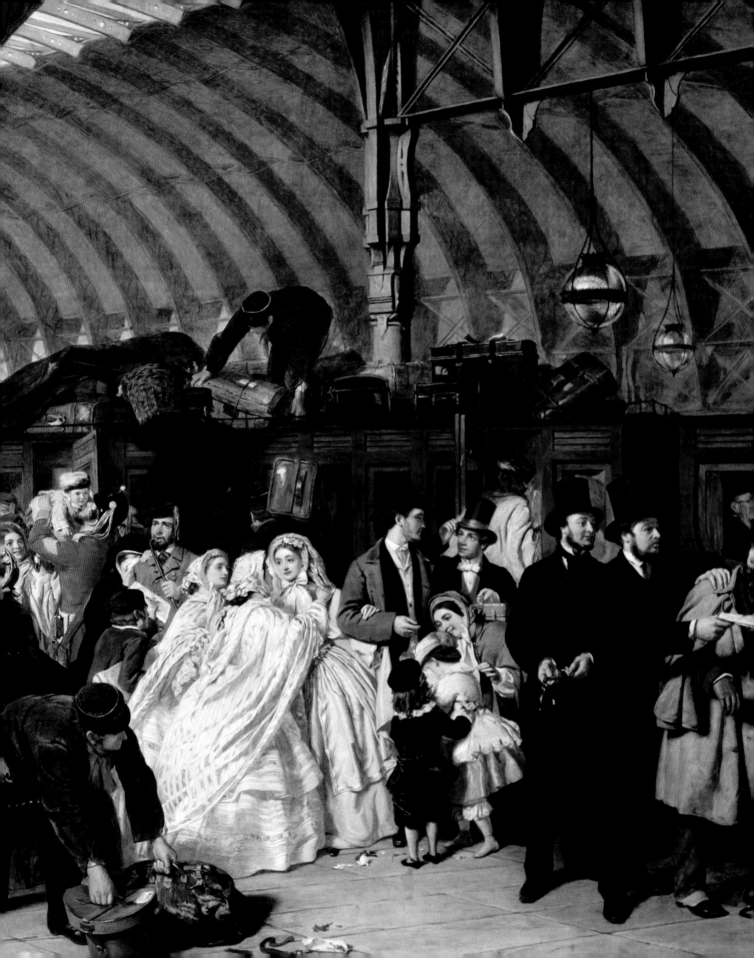

BEFORE ◄◄

Ireland had always seemed alien to England in a way that Scotland had not, however strong its enmity. It persisted with a foreign religion and culture despite the best efforts of British administrators, Protestant clerics, and armies.

IRISH REBELLION
Nine years of fighting in Elizabeth I's reign subdued the Irish without reconciling them to their subjection; the **Plantation of Ulster** was at best only a partial success **◄◄ 156–157**. Cromwell crushed the Irish, **◄◄ 174–175** but he could not make them renounce their rebellious ways, a fact that became clear in the **Succession Wars** of the late 17th century **◄◄ 196–197**.

ACT OF UNION
A wholesale rebellion in 1798 was ruthlessly put down **◄◄ 238–239**. The Act of Union of 1800 established **Ireland's official status as one of the four nations of the United Kingdom**. Far from providing an answer, though, the new arrangement called into question the integrity of the British state—the very phrase "the Irish Question" dates from this time. Any idea the Irish may have had of belonging to Britain—except in the sense of being a colonial possession—was destroyed by their experiences during the **Great Famine** of the 1840s **◄◄ 266–267**.

Irish Home Rule

The United Kingdom was never going to be truly united as long as an unwilling Ireland remained a member. The campaign for autonomous Home Rule might have seemed philosophical to a people mired in poverty, but Daniel O'Connell and Charles Parnell inspired a mass-movement for real change.

Ireland was still trying to recover after the overwhelming experience of the potato famine in the 1840s. The old problems remained unresolved, yet the people were in no position to organize. The campaign for Catholic emancipation launched by Daniel O'Connell, a noted Irish lawyer and political leader, had from 1805 changed an elite preoccupation into a mass-movement. Once emancipation was achieved in 1829, the next step was to agitate for repeal of the Act of Union of 1800. Britain sent a battleship to counter O'Connell's "monster meeting" near the coast at Clontarf in 1843. As so often in Irish nationalist history, British overreaction fed unrest.

A violent alternative

O'Connell's peaceful strategies and limited demands increased Irish impatience. He saw a self-governing Ireland as remaining under the British monarchy. A more radical Young Ireland alliance was established in 1842, and in 1847 an avowedly violent Irish Confederation broke away from that.

> " No man has the right … to say to his country: ' **Thus far shalt thou go and no further** … ' "

CHARLES STEWART PARNELL, JANUARY 21, 1885

Its leader, Protestant landowner and MP William Smith O'Brien, was fired by the revolutionary ferment sweeping Europe in 1848, but his uprising ended in fiasco.

The Fenians

A decade on, Young Ireland veterans reformed as the Irish Republican Brotherhood (IRB), behind James Stephens in Ireland, and John O'Mahoney and James Doheny in New York. The IRB is now generally known as the Fenian Brotherhood, the name taken by its American arm. It referred to the Fianna, a war-band of the legendary Fionn mac Cumhail, a hunter-warrior from Irish mythology. The Fenians included Irish-American troops demobilized after the Civil War (1861–1865) in the United States. In a raid on

Canada (May–June 1866), they briefly captured Fort Erie, defeating the Canadians at the Battle of Ridgeway.

In Britain and Ireland, however, the authorities quickly swung into action, arresting most of the rebels. Those still free felt their hand forced, so they mounted a hastily conceived Fenian Rising on March 4–5, 1867. The action invited a draconian British response. Five men were hanged over a policeman's accidental killing. Although the Fenians failed militarily, their movement injected a new radicalism

200,000 The number of people who turned out for the funeral of Charles Stewart Parnell at Glasnevin, Dublin, on October 11, 1891. He was mourned as another Irish martyr.

into mainstream nationalism—and a new urgency into the British Establishment's response.

Home Rule

The 1870s saw O'Connell's Repeal campaign reinvented by Isaac Butt, his former opponent and a Protestant: his "Home Government" slogan was soon changed to a snappier-sounding call for "Home Rule." An admirer of Britain, Butt preferred devolution—with the Irish Parliament responsible for domestic affairs and Westminster handling bigger issues such as foreign policy and defense. In 1875, Home Rule candidate Charles Stewart Parnell was elected to Parliament, where his flamboyant filibustering and points of order amused the press and public as much as they irritated the government.

Such constitutional discussions did not appeal to an impoverished peasantry. Prime Minister William Gladstone's Liberal government passed a Land Act in 1870 to address their problems, but the situation remained intolerable. From 1879, the Land

Widow McCormack's Cabbage Patch
In 1848, rebel leader William O'Brien, along with 40 supporters, cornered a group of policemen in Widow McCormack's farmhouse. A stand off ensued, resulting in an epic military engagement.

Fenian leaders snatched from police, 1867
A policeman was shot when Fenians in Manchester attacked a prison van to free a couple of comrades. Though his death had clearly been accidental, five men—the "Manchester Martyrs"—were hanged.

AFTER

The "Irish Question" had still to be answered. And, sadly, much more blood would be shed. The stronger the Nationalist impulse; the more resolute the Unionist reaction.

ULSTER PROTESTANTS
While Republicans fought for freedom, **Protestants in Ulster** opposed Home Rule **332–333 >>**: their freedom could only be guaranteed in the context of the United Kingdom, they insisted. Thousands of them went to the trenches of **World War I**, laying down their lives for the Britain they felt was theirs **322–323 >>**. The compromises made to accommodate Ulster's Protestants came back to haunt Britain—and the Irish "Free State" (and later Republic)—most seriously in **the Troubles** of the late 20th century **378–379 >>**.

"NO HOME RULE" BANNER, 1910

League—set up by former Fenian Michael Davitt—campaigned for fairer tenancy agreements. Parnell was made the League's first president. He had the unique ability to charm the political classes while reaching out to the downtrodden. Even neutrals saw the mismatch between the League's prosaic aims and the popular enthusiasm it awakened. It attracted radical elements and, at a local level, tenants angry at the conduct of (often absentee) landlords and agents. Tenants took the law into their own hands during a long period of unrest that became known as the Land Wars. In 1881, Gladstone's government passed a Second Land Act, which made things marginally better.

Parnell proved adept in walking the tricky tightrope between constitutionalism and radicalism. Even so, he was arrested and taken to Dublin's Kilmainham Jail that year. From prison he negotiated the Kilmainham Treaty. Agreed with Gladstone on May 2, 1882, it regulated rent-arrears for tenant farmers. Parnell received a hero's reception upon leaving jail and the campaign went on.

Charles Stewart Parnell
A Protestant landowner, Parnell made an improbable hero for Ireland's Catholic poor.

Fall of Parnell
Just a few days later, however, the Irish Chief Secretary Lord Frederick Cavendish and Undersecretary

T. H. Bourke were knifed to death in Dublin's Phoenix Park. This single action of an IRB splinter group, the Invincibles, created an outrage, giving new impetus to the constitutional movement and the growing partnership between Parnell and Gladstone. The Home Rule campaign grew rapidly. Gladstone introduced a bill in 1886, though this was defeated in the Commons and he lost the general election he called in response.

Political scandal
Parnell's reputation was badly damaged by the following year's purported "revelations." In 1887, *The Times* published a letter in which Parnell expressed sympathy with the Phoenix Park murderers—a cynical smear, but not easily shaken off. He was still, however, working toward Home Rule with Gladstone, and his popularity in Ireland was at its height when news broke of his long-standing relationship with a married woman. Parnell's credibility was shot, as far as his supporters were concerned. Parnell died a broken, marginalized figure in 1891, aged 45. Gladstone went on alone, trying again with the Irish Government Bill of 1893. This made it through the Commons before being thrown out by the House of Lords.

Fighting Gladstone
Gladstone, the boxing kangaroo, defends his Second Home Rule Bill (1893), an Irish "Joey" peeping from his pouch, in this cartoon by Franz Jüttner.

BEFORE

Conflict with the Boers was a feature of Cape life from 1795, with the Boers finally establishing their own republics.

BOER REPUBLICS
The British seized Cape Colony during the French Revolutionary Wars, **« 240–241** as they feared that France would snatch it from a Dutch Empire in decline. The Boers, Dutch-descendents who had farmed the region since the 17th century, were increasingly irked by British interference. The abolition of slavery **« 234–235** was the last straw: the Boers **undertook a Great Trek into the interior**, establishing **new Boer Republics** in Transvaal and Natal.

THE GREAT TREK

The **Boer War**

Years of tension between the British and the Boers came to a head in 1899, plunging South Africa into a bitter—and often dirty—guerrilla war. The victory that was eventually wrested was welcomed more with relief than with rejoicing in Britain, and with a good deal of soul-searching on the public's part.

A s the music-hall song of the 1870s suggested, "We don't want to fight, but by jingo if we do/ We've got the men, we've got the ships, we've got the money, too!", Britain was in a bullish mood as its imperial power expanded in the late 19th century. It met with one significant setback, though, in 1880, when Transvaal's Boers rose up against the 1877 annexation of their state by the British. After 10 weeks of sporadic fighting, a truce was declared and Britain restored the Boers' independence in 1881, but with the Boers accepting nominal British control.

Empire builder
Meanwhile, Cecil Rhodes (1853–1902) was carving out his own territory within the British Empire. A mining magnate,

he founded De Beers in 1880 and the British South Africa Company in 1889. To describe Rhodes as a businessman, however, does not do justice to the extraordinary—even exorbitant—scope of his activities or ambitions. His racial philosophy proclaimed the natural fitness of the Anglo-Saxon peoples to dominate and civilize the rest of the world, reflecting the fact that the imperial mission was becoming quasi-religious in some quarters. Rhodes hoped for a corridor of British-ruled territory to extend the length of Africa "from the Cape to Cairo," but his vision

for the Empire was greater still. One day, he believed, it would take back the United States and become the supreme government of the world.

In such a context, Rhodes' exploits in southern Africa seem relatively modest, but they were outrageous. Effectively, he was licensed by the British government to extend his company's control as a colonial government over enormous

27,927 The number of Boer women and children who died in British concentration camps; it is not known how many native African internees died in the camps, but it was, at the very least, 14,000.

Battle of Elands River
The "Death or Glory Boys" of the 17th Lancers live up to their nickname in Richard Caton Woodville's iconic painting. A press and public hungry for heroics turned defeats into patriotic victories.

Boer soldiers in battle
The Boers mishandled the Mafeking siege: though far outnumbering the British garrison, they allowed commander Baden-Powell to keep them at bay with a series of cunning bluffs until reinforcements came.

territories to the north of Cape Colony. Malawi and Botswana managed to avoid his interference, making their own protectorate deals directly with London. He was beaten in his bid for Katanga by King Leopold II of Belgium, who incorporated it into his Congo Free State. But Rhodes still took over the whole of what are now Zambia and Zimbabwe: this territory was named Rhodesia in his honor in 1894.

All this time Rhodes was a member of the Cape parliament, and was elected its prime minister in 1890.

Rhodes was determined to expand Cape Colony into Transvaal, as gold finds there had sent British prospectors rushing to the territory. To Rhodes, the obvious way of legitimizing the situation was to make this Boer Republic a British territory by force. Led by one of his men, Leander Starr Jameson, a group of irregular soldiers attacked Transvaal in 1895, hoping to trigger an uprising among the English *Uitlanders* (British residents in the former republics of the Transvaal and Orange Free State). The Jameson Raid was a disaster, and Rhodes was forced to resign.

Collision course
Tensions grew until, on October 12, 1899, the Boers ambushed a British armored train, capturing weapons and ammunition. In the following weeks, the Boers invaded Cape Colony, making rapid headway against an unprepared enemy. They were held at Elandslaagte on October 21, but British forces then fell back, allowing the Boers to advance and besiege the towns of Ladysmith and Mafeking. The Boers were soon besieging Kimberley as well. Further defeats for Britain came at Magersfontein and Colenso. The latter began with a botched attempt to lift the Siege of Ladysmith.

Pretoria won
After the Relief of Mafeking came the relief of seeing Pretoria fall: the British public was weary of a war that had gone on much longer, and been more unpleasant, than expected.

A subsequent effort on January 23, 1900 saw British forces taking the summit of Spion Kop in a dawn attack—only to find themselves under fire from Boer artillery on overlooking hills.

However, the Boers had now pinned themselves down. The ensuing stalemate allowed Britain to regroup and bring in reinforcements, resulting in the mobilization of the largest British army yet sent abroad, with almost 200,000 in the field. Ultimately, the advantage in numbers and resources won out. The Siege of Ladysmith was finally lifted on February 27. Amidst jubilant celebrations back in Britain, Mafeking was relieved on May 18, while Transvaal's capital, Pretoria, was taken on June 5.

War of attrition
Rather than surrender, though, the Boers took to the hills to wage another guerrilla war. Britain reacted ruthlessly, with a scorched-earth policy (see BOX), creating its own small forces of mounted troops to counter the Boer raiding parties. Trains were used to whisk men and munitions around the country. Controversially, Lord Kitchener, the British Chief-of-Staff, confined more than 100,000 Boer civilians in concentration camps.

The mood in Britain was somber. There was little glory to be gained in warfare of this kind. Like the Crimean conflict, this was a very well-publicized war, swarming with special correspondents (including the young Winston Churchill). Radicals such as Lloyd George and the Labour Party leader Keir Hardie made opposition to war an important rallying point for their supporters. Some maverick Conservatives also came out on the pro-Boer side.

For what it was worth, the war had been won. The Boers were forced to sign the Treaty of Vereeniging in 1902, giving up their territory—though they were to be given a degree of autonomy five years later. For now, the Boers agreed to come under British sovereignty. In 1910, South Africa became a self-governing dominion, comprising Cape Colony, Natal, Transvaal, and the Orange Free State. It would have to wait until 1961 to be totally free of British rule and become a republic.

INNOVATION
CONCENTRATION CAMPS

Lord Kitchener pursued a scorched-earth policy, killing the livestock, destroying the crops, and contaminating the water supplies the Boers depended on. To him it seemed only logical that he should also remove the families and communities who were helping sustain their struggle. More than 40 tented concentration camps were prepared, into which women, children, and elderly men were herded. Food supplies and sanitation were hopelessly inadequate and thousands died of dysentery, typhoid, and other diseases. The British did not want to risk keeping Boer prisoners of war in the country: they were sent to St. Helena, Ceylon, and other offshore islands.

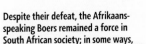

AFTER

Despite their defeat, the Afrikaans-speaking Boers remained a force in South African society; in some ways, indeed, the dominating force.

RECRUITMENT DRIVE
Britain put the Boer War behind it: with a **belligerent Germany arming fast,** it had more pressing concerns to attend to **312–313 ≫.** Kitchener was to gain immortality as the face of Britain's recruiting campaign for World War I **320–321 ≫.**

SOUTH AFRICAN MATTERS
Back **in South Africa, defiance of Britain continued.** The country became a self-governing dominion from 1910. Afrikaans was given parity with English as official language in 1925, while full independence was gained in 1931.

Racist discrimination against the black majority was enshrined in law with **the introduction of apartheid** (literally "apartness": segregation) in 1948. **Protests against its injustices marked the student unrest** of the 1960s and the 1970s.

AN APARTHEID NOTICE IN CAPE TOWN

◀◀ **BEFORE**

Over many years waiting to accede, Bertie, as Edward was commonly known, developed the habits of a lifetime that would also color his reign.

NOT GROOMED TO RULE

Born on November 9, 1841, in Sandringham, Norfolk, the future Edward VII was the second child and eldest son of Queen Victoria. Bertie served as **heir apparent longer than anyone else** in British history. Failing to flourish in the army or at university, he lacked focus or any outstanding abilities. As Prince of Wales, Bertie became a **playboy, famed for a string of indiscretions**, including a divorce and gambling scandals. His extravagant habits formed a model for the wealthy leisured people of the day. **Lavish country house parties**, especially shooting weekends at Sandringham, were his speciality. In 1863, he married the Danish Princess Alexandra (1844–1925), but his philandering continued, including a high-profile affair with actress Lillie Langtry. Appalled by him, Victoria **kept him away from affairs of state**, so he was badly prepared for kingship.

LILLIE LANGTRY

The **Edwardian Age**

The Edwardian era was one of extravagance and elegance—for the wealthy. Edward's short reign saw a transition between Victorian and post-Great War values. Aspects of the modern world were forged, with achievements and novelties ranging from motorcars and tabloid newspapers to airplanes and cinemas.

The dawn of a new century after Victoria's death brought a new, if not youthful (at almost 60 years), monarch in Edward VII, whose persona was far more fun loving than that of his mother. It felt like a fresh start, filled with technological innovation.

However, Victorian attitudes persisted (see pp.278–279 and pp.282–283). Wealthy industrialists still contributed large sums toward art galleries and museums. Civic authorities proclaimed their importance with impressive buildings in an overblown Baroque style. In 1903, the Workers' Educational Association (WEA) was founded for working adults, and military officer Robert Baden-Powell founded the Boy Scouts in 1908, to teach boys citizenship and leadership skills.

King and country

A racier edge to life also developed. Immediate precedent came from decadent tastes during the turn-of-the-century years, spearheaded by figures such as writer Oscar Wilde (1854–

1900) and Art Nouveau–Aesthetic artist Aubrey Beardsley (1872–1898), with his stylized, daring illustrations.

A long time in waiting for the throne, Edward had grown outgoing and hedonistic, and stamped his reign with that trait. He could be charming, pleasant, and diplomatic. Always

Pomp and circumstance
Edward is seen here with Queen Alexandra in an image celebrating his coronation. He injected great pomp and ceremony into royal life and raised the profile of the monarchy.

> " I never in my life met with such a **thorough and cunning lazybones**."

PRINCE ALBERT ON HIS SON BERTIE

impeccably dressed, he pursued open philandering and headed the pleasure-seeking country house party set. Yet he was popular despite his lavish lifestyle.

Edward's more serious interests lay in the armed forces, foreign policy, and European diplomacy, although he is seen as having exercised little real political power. Some of his views were liberal,

Motoring in style
The Rolls Royce Silver Ghost was a British car that captured the spirit of the times. Charles Rolls and Henry Royce formed the Rolls Royce company in 1906. Their ambition was to create English-made cars that were the best in the world.

others not—he was against votes for women (see pp.308–309). His son George V, much quieter and not a party-goer, nevertheless continued the monarchy's popularity with the public. The early part of his reign is often included under the Edwardian era.

Faster and faster

Life in Britain was speeding up. There were car rallies and record-breaking flying contests. For the wealthy, motorcars became far more common. Modern cars first appeared in the late 1800s. In 1909, John Moore-Brabazon became the first resident Englishman to make an officially recognized airplane flight in England.

Electric trams replaced the Victorians' horse-drawn trams, transforming life and leisure for urban working people in the expanding towns and cities. The Victorians' railroad system continued to flourish (see pp.258–259). For the wealthy, this was the heyday of luxury transatlantic passenger liners, such as the Cunard Line's *Mauretania* and *Lusitania* (both 1906), and competition for the coveted Blue Riband award for fastest transatlantic crossing. People emigrated abroad as third-class passengers on these liners in increasing numbers.

Popular pursuits

These less stern times saw a huge rise in popular culture. Music hall had evolved in the late Victorian era and now moved into more lavish theaters, such as the London Palladium (1910). Queen of Edwardian music hall was Marie Lloyd (1870–1922), with songs such as *The Boy I Love is Up in the Gallery*.

Lloyd's colorful private life, and scandals such as that of wife-killer Dr. Crippen, hanged in 1910, were splashed across tabloid newspapers, thanks to the rapid growth of the popular press under Lord Northcliffe. The first British press baron, Northcliffe founded the *Daily Mail* in 1896 and the *Daily Mirror* in 1903.

Crippen was the first criminal to be caught using wireless telegraph. In 1901, Italian Guglielmo Marconi sent

A PARTICIPANT IN THE NATIONAL ROUND ARCHERY EVENT

London stepped up when, in 1906, Rome backed out of hosting the fourth Olympic Games in 1908, due to an eruption of Mount Vesuvius. The 1908 London event breathed new life into the Games, with the help of Britain's solid Amateur Athletics Association and British Olympic Association (formed 1905). It also gave birth to the current international marathon distance—arrived at arbitrarily, after members of the British royal family extended the course so that they could observe it better.

the first transatlantic radio message from England. In 1908, the first English cinema opened, in London, with early silent stars including Charlie Chaplin.

Home habits

The middle class, supported by business and industry, continued to grow, demanding large, airy homes within easy reach of towns and cities. Spacious, well-planned suburbs sprang up on the urban fringes close to railroad lines. Garden suburbs and garden cities, inspired by models such as Liverpool's Port Sunlight (see pp.278–279), founded in late Victorian times, included London's Hampstead Garden Suburb (begun 1907), with contributions by Edwin Landseer Lutyens (1869–1944). Cottage-like Arts and Crafts house styles were popular (see pp.282–283). Inside homes, electricity became more widespread for the better-off, although many poor families had to wait until the 1920s to enjoy this benefit.

Divided Britain

Edwardian Britain saw a great gap between the extravagant aristocracy and the poor, and an economic downturn relative to Victorian times was felt in some quarters. The rise of socialism and demands for reform continued, responded to in part after the Liberal victory of 1906. Despite problems, there was some greater social mobility and improved literacy.

1900 **The year the Prince of Wales bought a Daimler Phaeton. This purchase was soon to make him the first British monarch to own a motorcar.**

Artistic differences

This was a fertile period for the arts, reflecting the era's shifting attitudes. Traditional, patriotic writers such as Rudyard Kipling (1865–1936), famed for his children's *Just So Stories* (1902), jostled with people like H.G. Wells (1866–1946), whose *Tono Bungay* (1909) satirized Edwardian society. Irish Fabian George Bernard Shaw's plays, such as *Pygmalion* (1913), questioned contemporary conventions. Two other Irishmen, W.B. Yeats (1865–1939) and James Joyce (1882–1941), ushered in Modernism with works including Yeats's *The Green Helmet and Other Poems* (1910) and Joyce's short stories, *Dubliners* (1914).

Visual art embraced the glamorous society portraits of Anglo-American John Singer Sargent (1856–1925) and the seedy Camden Town paintings of Walter Sickert (1860–1942). Critic–painter Roger Fry's (1866–1934) Post-Impressionist exhibitions at London's Grafton Galleries (1910–1912), featured work by Cézanne, Gauguin, van Gogh, and the Cubists that shocked Edwardians with their bold areas of flat color and strange perspectives.

Edward's reign saw the last flourishing of an old order; its innovations helped to forge a very different future world.

A POST-WAR WORLD

During George V's reign, there were **growing shifts in society**—such as the increasingly strident calls for female suffrage **308–309 »**. After the horrors of World War I, the Edwardian era looked impossibly outmoded and distant.

TOWN PLANNING

One of the defining threads of 20th-century Britain was the **creation of new towns**, with almost 40 built in the UK between the mid-1940s and mid-1970s. Edwardian garden cities—the world's first was at Letchworth, Hertfordshire (1903)—prepared the way. Their pioneer was Ebenezer Howard (1850–1928).

THE MARCH OF MODERNISM

Modernism came into full force after World War II. Modernist writers included T.S. Eliot, James Joyce, W.B. Yeats, Virginia Woolf, W.H. Auden, Aldous Huxley, and D.H. Lawrence. Edwardian Art Nouveau, with its strong flowing lines and stylized forms, often nature-inspired, fed into 1920s and '30s **Art Deco**.

The social season

The social season of the wealthy included the Henley Regatta, where these Edwardians are heading, Epsom, Ascot, Lords, Cowes, and Wimbledon—all good opportunities to meet a wealthy spouse.

Sinking of the Titanic

More than 1,500 lives were lost when RMS *Titanic* hit an iceberg and sank on her maiden voyage—a truly dreadful tragedy in human terms. But the disaster also dealt a shattering blow to British prestige and pride, denting the confidence of the world's first industrial power.

The luxury liner RMS *Titanic* set out from Southampton on its maiden voyage with all the fanfare that might be expected for the largest passenger ship ever built. Unfortunately though, it was never to reach New York. Just four nights into the journey, the White Star liner hit an iceberg and—despite a seemingly impressive array of safety features—swiftly sank. Of the 1,517 people who died, many must have been condemned by the fact that there were only 1,178 lifeboat places for the 2,227 souls on board.

True or false?

Rumors ran rife in the days after the disaster—and the myth-making has hardly abated even now. Some said the first-class passengers were given precedence in the lifeboats. According to others, the makers had claimed that the *Titanic's* watertight compartments made it "unsinkable." It was also believed that the ship was speeding to satisfy a whim of the White Star chairman, J. Bruce Ismay; it fell victim to a curse; and so on. While none of these are backed by evidence, it is true that the lifeboat davits were a great deal closer to the first-class accommodation. One of the more inspiring stories turned out to be true: many survivors attested that the saloon band kept on calmly playing as the ship went down.

New standards for safety

Inquiries in both the United States and Britain revealed that the *Titanic* had actually carried fewer lifeboats than maritime law required. The regulations were quickly tightened up. The US Hydrographic Office established a permanent "Ice Patrol" in the North Atlantic shipping lanes.

Radio also had a part to play: reports of ice in the area had been received and could have been passed on to the *Titanic's* crew. Ironically, though the vessel had been fully fitted with the latest Marconi telegraph receiving and transmitting equipment, this had been kept as a luxury option for first class passengers.

The sinking of the *Titanic* quickly took on all but mythic status, but another myth was punctured by her loss. Britons could no longer feel quite so complacent about their industrial and technological preeminence. The 20th century saw them struggling to stay ahead.

> **"** The loss ... was due to **collision with an iceberg**, brought about by the **excessive speed** with which it was being navigated.**"**

JUDGEMENT OF THE OFFICIAL BRITISH INQUIRY INTO THE *TITANIC'S* SINKING, 1912

The story of the century
A newsboy does a roaring trade as Londoners stop to read all about the *Titanic's* tragedy. Newspapers abounded with stories of the disaster, and people were eager to get the latest information.

Emmeline Pankhurst arrested
On May 21, 1914, toward the end of the militant campaign, Emmeline Pankhurst was arrested yet again. She had been trying to present a petition to the King at Buckingham Palace. World War I would soon overtake suffragette hostilities.

The **Suffragettes**

During the early 1900s, enraged by Parliament's failure to introduce female suffrage and give voting rights to women, "suffragettes" took matters into their own hands. With leaders such as Emmeline and Christabel Pankhurst, they began a campaign of demonstrations and escalating direct action.

As the 20th century began, women were increasingly making their presence felt in society, especially in higher education and some professions, although a continuation of Victorian values meant women still had no vote, vital for true progress. Despite some support in Parliament for female suffrage (extending the franchise to women), many men still thought the murky, boisterous business of politics too complex and indelicate for the female mind and constitution. Male-dominated medical opinion at the time often painted women as emotionally unstable, incapable of reasoned decision-making on weighty matters. There were even women who agreed—in 1908, novelist Mrs. Humphry Ward

Forcible feeding
This issue of *Suffragette*, founded in 1912 and edited by Christabel Pankhurst, focuses on the controversy of force-feeding while in prison.

formed the National Anti-Suffrage League. The word "suffragette" seems to have been coined sarcastically by the *Daily Mail* in an article on January 10, 1906. After this, the term suffragette tended to be used for someone taking militant action.

Fighting the fight

Angered by the blocking of reform bills, politically active middle-class socialist Emmeline Pankhurst (1858–1928), and daughter, Christabel (1880–1958), set up the Women's Social and Political Union (WSPU) in 1903, adopting the slogan "Votes For Women." At first, their campaigning was fairly moderate. Meetings were held and campaigning literature was handed out in the street. Gradually, they gathered enormous support from women around the country.

In 1905, after Christabel was arrested and imprisoned for assaulting a policeman attempting to remove her from an election meeting for being disruptive, the campaign gathered militancy. At the end of 1906, 21 suffragettes were in prison. By 1911, after the Parliamentary campaign failed yet again, militancy moved far beyond rallies and demonstrations. Suffragettes chained themselves to railings, poured acid on golf courses, invaded Downing Street, and, in March 1912, smashed windows across London's West End and Knightsbridge.

Emmeline was establishing a reputation as a highly skilled, rousing orator. In a speech at the Albert Hall, London, on October 17, 1912, she declared: "I say to the Government: You have not dared to take the leaders of Ulster for their incitement to rebellion. Take me if you dare."

Militant suffragettes in prison resorted to hunger strikes as a protest, and attempted to resist force-feeding as a way to get their message across. Meanwhile, the National Union of Women's Suffrage Societies continued a more moderate campaign, and had more than 50,000 members by 1913.

Suffragette hunger-strike medal
Hunger-strike medals were first presented to suffragettes in August 1909, at St. James's Hall, London. The lower bar shows the date of arrest, and the disk has the presentee's name on the other side.

organized marches through London.

By 1914, society was becoming more horrified at seeing women involved in these actions. Politicians were nervous, especially with an election imminent, although this made the suffragettes hopeful that something might finally be done. In another dramatic protest, Mary Richardson slashed Velázquez's *Rokeby Venus* painting in the National Gallery. Then, with female suffrage still unresolved, World War I broke out. The issue passed into a kind of limbo.

BEFORE

Victorian women's lives were restricted, but vital strides toward improving their rights were made in the 1800s.

INEQUALITY AND DISSATISFACTION
In Victorian times, **poorer women sought paid work**, while better-off women focussed on nurturing home and family **《 278–279**. Women had **no vote**, and before 1883 could not even retain their own property once married.

GETTING ORGANIZED
In 1866, a group of women petitioned JS Mill, Liberal MP and supporter of women's rights, to push for female suffrage, but his **amendment to the 1867 Reform Bill was defeated**. From the 1860s, barrister Richard Pankhurst, who married Emmeline Goulden in 1879, drafted early women's rights bills, but the government always **blocked voting reforms**. In 1888, Annie Besant organized the matchgirls' strike at Bryant & May's factory in London's East End; it won **better pay** and recognition of the health risks to workers. The next

year, the Pankhursts founded the Women's Franchise League, winning some local voting rights for **married women**. In 1897, Millicent Fawcett helped form the **more moderate** National Union of Women's Suffrage Societies (NUWSS).

MATCHGIRLS' STRIKE AT BRYANT & MAY

The Cat and Mouse Act

People were deeply shocked by the imprisonment and force-feeding, especially at a time when women were still considered by many to be fragile creatures. Herbert Asquith's Liberal government decided they must tackle the hunger-striking issue decisively. In 1913, they passed an Act nicknamed the "Cat and Mouse Act," which released suffragettes prior to the desperate stage where force-feeding might become necessary, and then reimprisoned them when their health had recovered. The year saw a crescendo of extreme action. Emmeline was detained in New York while fund-raising there, and there was an attempt to blow up Chancellor of the Exchequer Lloyd George's house. Suffragette Emily Wilding Davison was killed after throwing herself under the King's horse at the Derby on June 4, 1913. Thousands packed London's streets for her funeral procession. Also that year, Sylvia (1882–1960), another of Emmeline's daughters, formed the East London Federation, which

---

AFTER »

World War I would prove a watershed in the battle for female enfranchisement, and the 1920s saw equal voting rights for all.

GREAT WAR AND AFTER
At the outbreak of war **320–321 》**, all imprisoned **suffragettes were released**. Emmeline campaigned to recruit women for the **war effort**. Many were impressed by how well women filled the roles of absent men and this helped **change attitudes** further. In 1918, **women over 30** gained the vote (men could vote at 21), but it was debatable whether it was the militant or the moderate approach that had been **the key to success**. In 1919, Nancy Astor became the first woman to sit in the House of Commons. All **women over 21** finally got the vote in June 1928, a few weeks short of Emmeline's death.

NANCY ASTOR MP

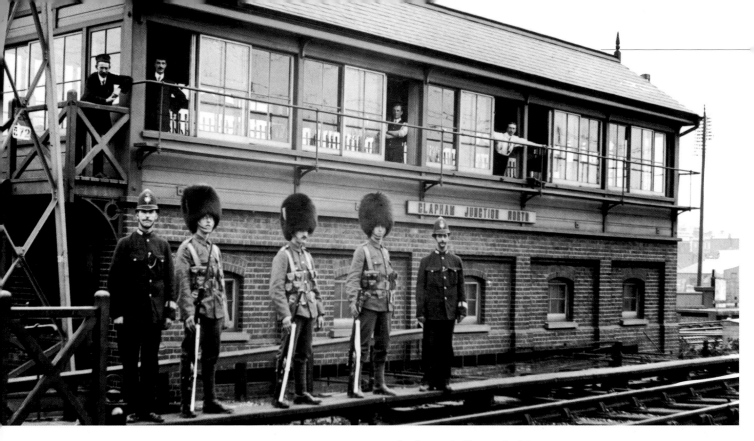

Trade Unionists and Socialists

Political developments in the late 19th century brought Britain's most marginalized and ground-down communities a sense of new possibilities, optimism, and hope.

Guardsmen and police on sentry duty
National security was at stake, it seems, in the railroader's dispute of 1911: this London railroad signal box was to be protected at all costs. The authorities had no compunction about suggesting that strikers were shameless criminals and national enemies.

BEFORE

The poor had learned early that, weak as they might be individually, collectively they could represent a powerful force.

UNITED FORCE
The **Peasants' Revolt** of the 14th century **« 104–105** was the most celebrated of the early shows of strength by the marginalized, a powerful **statement of defiance** against their oppressors. Since then, the structure of society had changed completely, most notably with the advent of industrialization **« 232–233**. The **Chartists** made attempts to find **strength in unity « 264–265**, but the high hopes placed in electoral reform had not been realized **« 268–269**. Britain was the world's most successful industrial nation, but the question of the workers getting their share remained unanswered.

For Britain's working class, the Great Reform Act of 1832 (see pp.268–269) had been a huge disappointment—a collective workers' voice had still not emerged. From 1874, the trade unions financed the campaigns of a series of Liberal candidates for Parliament. The trend peaked in 1885, when 12 such MPs were elected.

Striking out

Any improvement in the lot of the working class through Parliamentary legislation was clearly going to be slow in coming. They did, however, have muscle in the mass. Individually, workers hardly came poorer or more powerless than the matchgirls of Bryant & May's factory in London's East End. When Annie Besant (see pp.308–309) led them in a strike in 1888, they showed the way to other workers.

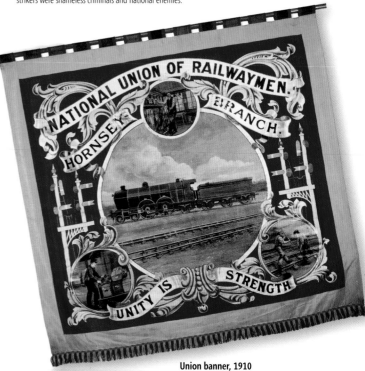

Union banner, 1910
The slogan on the banner says "Unity is strength," but equally important is the implication of the dignity of labor. All swirling scrolls and symmetry, this banner, ironically, carries the suggestion of an aristocratic coat of arms.

The first big show of union might came in 1889 on the London docks. The dockers, poorly paid casual workers, demanded greater security and higher wages. The dispute was spontaneous—unions were formed as the action went on, spreading quickly to other ports. The employers' uncompromising stand was defeated by the determination of the dockers, supported by their comrades in foreign ports as far as Australia.

James Keir Hardie
The first leader of the Labour Party, Hardie's pragmatic moderation—much criticized at the time—helped ensure the party's appeal beyond a Marxist fringe.

Striking back

Employers could take collective action, too. In 1897, machine-operators' demand for a maximum eight-hour day was met by a national lockout. The men were barred from their workplaces (unpaid, of course) until the Amalgamated Association of Engineers agreed to management's terms.

Just how badly the workers' power had frightened the Establishment was evident in the judge's ruling in the Taff Vale Railway Dispute (1901)—it held the railroader's union liable for the loss of revenue caused to the South Welsh railroad company by its members' strike. The union was fined £3,000 plus £19,000 expenses, sparking a series of similar suits from employers.

Even middle-class liberals were uneasy about this ruling, which effectively outlawed strike action. Sir Henry Campbell-Bannerman's Liberal government brought in the 1906 Trade Disputes Act, explicitly removing any question of such liabilities on the part of unions.

Liberal treatment

His successor, Herbert Asquith, and Chancellor David Lloyd George tried to alleviate conditions for the working class. Limited provision was made for free school meals and pensions for those over 70 years of age. Their "People's Budget" (1909) increased taxes for the rich, whose outrage was expressed in an enraged press—and an obstructive House of Lords.

Even so, a National Insurance Act was passed in 1911. People paid into a fund while they worked. In return, they received sick pay and medical treatment or maternity care. Labor exchanges were opened and some unemployment

44,325 The total number of votes cast for the Independent Labour Party in the 1895 election. All 28 candidates came last in their respective polls, including Keir Hardie in London's West Ham South.

benefit paid. The Conservatives as well as the hard-line free market Liberals criticized these measures.

Labor pangs

The left wing of the labor movement also attacked these measures for being inadequate. The strikes continued, especially in the mines and the transportation sector. The Scottish Labour Party was founded in 1888, and Scottish-born workers helped create the Independent Labour Party in England in 1893. The election of James Keir Hardie as an Independent to the seat of West Ham South in 1892 was a milestone.

The Labour Party grew slowly, but the caution and vague idealism so derided by more sophisticated left-wing thinkers ultimately brought it popularity and strength. Even so, with only 30,000 members by 1914, it showed little sign of shaking the foundations of the system.

BEATRICE WEBB

Born into a middle-class family, Beatrice Potter married the socialist Sidney Webb (1859–1947) in 1890. Together they helped give the growing labor movement an intellectual arm. During the 1890s, they led the Fabian Society, which had been founded in 1884. Named for Quintus Fabius Maximus, a Roman general who had used what was called "softly-softly" delaying tactics to defeat his enemies, the Society argued for a nonrevolutionary road to socialism. Its members included writers such as Virginia Woolf, George Bernard Shaw, E. Nesbit, and H.G. Wells. The Webbs founded the London School of Economics in 1895, to advance social studies, and a left-wing magazine, the *New Statesman*, in 1913.

> " The Labour Party is **in league with life**, and works for **liberty** that **men may live**."

ACTIVIST KATHARINE GLASIER IN HER DIARY, JANUARY 1893

AFTER »

Garment workers' strike, 1914
Internationalism was central to socialist thinking: it was said that the British workers had more in common with their comrades in Italy or Russia than with an exploitative upper class in the UK.

The 20th century was to see the fortunes of the labor movement rise and fall, a prey to fluctuations in the economy—and the public mood.

GROWING MILITANCY

The Great Depression **334–335 »** left workers in a weak position. The Jarrow March **336–337 »** was more an appeal for action than a defiant stand. Much as the nation revered its wartime leader Winston Churchill, it cheerfully ditched his Conservative Party in 1945, sweeping Clement Attlee's Labour government into office with a **mandate to construct a socialist Welfare State 360–361 »**. In hindsight, however, this was to seem something of a high water mark for the movement. The student radicalism of the 1960s and the union militancy of the 1970s **376–377 »** produced a profound reaction in the country as a whole. Amid claims that the trade union "barons" were "holding the nation to ransom," **Margaret Thatcher won a milestone election victory 382–383 »**.

CLEMENT ATTLEE WINS THE 1945 ELECTION

The **Road** to **War**

Britain began the 20th century in a position of considerable economic strength, and with its imperial authority felt around the world. Yet clouds were gathering as a new European power emerged. Germany was still an unknown quantity, but Britain did not like what it was seeing.

Germans rejoiced to see their nation unified, but heartwarming as their story was, their leaders had not necessarily seen it the same way. To Bismarck, unification had not been about the brotherhood of man but "Blood and Iron."

A similar tone was taken by Kaiser Wilhelm II, who ascended the throne in Berlin in 1888 determined to bring back "glorious times" and secure Germany the "place in the sun" that it deserved. He was speaking literally, perhaps, hinting at the need to acquire African and Asian colonies, but his meaning had been understood as mainly figurative. His Germany was to take its rightful place at the forefront of

« BEFORE

The latter half of the 19th century saw a shift in power in Europe, with Germany emerging as a strong, new nation.

EUROPE'S CHANGING AGGRESSORS
British enmity with France was more or less an established tradition since the Hundred Years' War of medieval times **« 96–97**, **« 118–119**, and the Napoleonic wars were a real threat **« 240–241**. However, times had changed, and through the 1860s, behind the banner of **Otto von Bismarck, the Prussian Chancellor**, the miscellaneous little kingdoms, statelets, and duchies of Germany came together to form a **powerful new nation at the heart of Europe**. Bismarck secured his goal in the face of French opposition in 1871, after inflicting a humiliating defeat in the Franco-Prussian War.

OTTO VON BISMARCK

European states. Sending his troops to China to help put down the 1900 Boxer Rebellion that had risen up against the European powers there, he bade them to be as ruthless as Attila's ancient Huns, thus bestowing on his countrymen an enduring, if ugly, nickname.

Strange bedfellows
Other nations were naturally wary of Germany's new ambition. In 1902, Britain made an alliance with Imperial Japan, so that the Royal Navy might concentrate on waters closer to home. The new threat trumped even long-standing enmities. An unprecedented Entente Cordiale (Friendly Agreement) was reached with France in 1904. Russia already (since 1892) had its own treaty with France, so the signing of the Anglo-Russian Treaty in 1907 produced a Triple Alliance between these three powers. Mere agreement would not be enough, though, in the face of the unabashed and growing militarism of the German regime.

Germany sought its own allies. Already (since 1879) allied with Austria-Hungary, it now wooed the Ottoman Empire. Afraid of Russian expansion, the Ottoman Turks responded. Despite its historical antipathy for the Turks, Bulgaria feared Russia even more, so it, too, moved into an alliance with these Central Powers.

Arms race
Wilhelm, sardonically known in Britain as Kaiser Bill, was a grandson of Queen Victoria (and, some said, her favorite grandson), as well as the nephew of King Edward VII. He had also been something of an Anglophile, especially with regard to the Royal Navy. The story went that the humiliation of seeing his country's paltry showing at the British naval review staged for his

£398 MILLION
The total military expenditure of Britain, France, Russia, Italy, Austria-Hungary, and Germany in 1914. In 1870, it was £94 million; in 1910, £289 million.

grandmother's Diamond Jubilee in 1896 left him resolved to catch up at any cost. He placed Admiral Alfred von Tirpitz at the head of the Imperial Naval Office with explicit orders to build up the German navy.

Britain had a head start, but clearly had to respond. In 1906, the Admiralty commissioned its latest battleship, HMS *Dreadnought*. Steam turbine-driven, it was much faster than its predecessors. It also carried much bigger guns, enabling it to engage its enemies at a distance, beyond torpedo range. It transformed naval warfare to such an extent that a whole generation of warships was named after her. Germany, inevitably, got its own equivalent, the *Nassau*, in service by 1908. Just as inevitably, this produced a clamor from British Conservative campaigners for more dreadnoughts: "We want eight, and we won't wait!," the slogan went.

A logic of war
Build-ups were under way in other arms of the military as well, and other European states joined in the arms race. The result was that nobody really felt safe. One of the worst-kept secrets of the period, the Schlieffen Plan (drawn up at Wilhelm's orders by Count Alfred von Schlieffen in 1904, although subsequently modified) envisaged simultaneous invasions of Russia in the east and France (via neutral Belgium and Luxembourg) in the west.

German militarism prompted answering moves toward militarism abroad, bringing the top brass into the very heart of government. In Britain, the Liberal government of Herbert Asquith was busy with important welfare reforms, but armament proceeded apace at the same time. War seemed an inevitability: the only question was exactly when.

There had already been a couple of nasty moments. Berlin had been alarmed at the implications for colonial Africa of Franco-British friendship. In March 1905, the Kaiser paid a much-publicized visit to Tangiers, promising the Moroccan King his support against French domination. France and Britain both reacted angrily to this, the First Morocco Crisis. A second was caused six years later by the deployment of the German gunboat *Panther*, off Agadir, in July 1911. The threat of war in Europe was again averted, though. On November 4, 1911, a face-saving territorial exchange was

Entente Cordiale, 1904
French soldiers and British sailors fraternize: a magazine takes an upbeat view of Anglo-French relations, though the new friendship was going to take getting used to.

British armaments factory
With years to prepare for a war that many believed was coming, nations had plenty of time to build up vast quantities of weapons for their growing armed forces. There had never before been such an arms race.

agreed. Germany withdrew its claims in Morocco and instead received territory in Equatorial Africa to add to its existing protectorate in Cameroon.

Spiraling into destruction

The problem with complex alliances was that they produced many potential flash points. In the end, the spark that set off the explosion came from Sarajevo, in Bosnia. The Serbian anarchist Gavrilo Princip's assassination

of Archduke Franz Ferdinand, heir to the Austrian throne, on June 28, 1914, precipitated the July Crisis and, as of July 28, war between Austria and Serbia, a Russian ally. As Russia mobilized for war with Austria, their respective allies France and Germany also mobilized as committed. Britain went through the form of demanding a promise from Germany that it would respect Belgian neutrality. This was not forthcoming. Instead, the Germans put the latest revision of the Schlieffen Plan into action, invading Belgium on August 4. Britain had no alternative now but to declare war. Many genuinely believed that the war would all be over by Christmas.

AFTER ⟫

SARAJEVO ASSASSINATION

Gavrilo Princip's bullets at Sarajevo set in motion a meat-grinder of a war; millions suffered in a nightmare of mud and slaughter.

EUROPE'S TRAGEDY
Britain prevailed in the Great War—later known as World War I—but at enormous cost **322–323 ⟫**. And even then, the "war to end wars" did not live up to its billing. **The writing was on the wall** from the moment of the Versailles Treaty **330–331 ⟫**, but it took the rise in Germany of Hitler and the Nazis to make **a second catastrophe** a reality **346–347 ⟫**.

MODERN TIMES
1914–present

In the 20th century, the rich, proud, and powerful British nation heroically fought two world wars, but inexorably lost its empire, and saw its global influence diminish. Its strong parliamentary democracy and constitutional monarchy persisted, and the country developed a pioneering welfare state and a worldwide reputation for culture, science, and technology.

The Morris Mini-Minor
As the appetite for large cars waned and the threat of German "bubble cars" loomed, the British Motor Corporation unveiled its "proper miniature car." Known affectionately as the "mini," it quickly became a modern British icon during the 1960s.

War of attrition
British soldiers sent to fight in France and Belgium in World War I found themselves engaged in static trench warfare along the Western Front. Three-quarters of a million Britons were killed in four years of conflict.

A global zenith

In 1914, Britain ruled the largest empire in history, and the City of London was the hub of global finance. Much of the world's trade was carried in British ships, the Royal Navy dominated the oceans, and British industry was still a force to be reckoned with. The story of Britain over the following century is inevitably a tale of decline—the loss of empire and the dwindling of economic, financial, and military power. In 1997, Britain's colony of Hong Kong was handed over to China; in 2008, an Indian company took over Jaguar and Land Rover factories in Britain. Both these events show a shift in power and status that, from the perspective of 1914, is awesome. Yet through times when the world was racked by warfare and revolution, Britain's liberal institutions of parliamentary democracy and constitutional monarchy were extraordinarily robust, and the country performed a heroic role in two world wars.

Conflict and decline

Britain's entry into World War I in 1914 stands as a watershed in the nation's history. That epic conflict, with its massive losses of young men's lives in the often inglorious warfare of the trenches, was a shock to the British psyche, using up long-accumulated reserves of patriotic sentiment that were never to be fully restored. Britain may have won the war, but its finances were undermined by war debts, and its core industries fundamentally weakened. High levels of unemployment disfigured areas of Britain well before the onset of the worldwide Great Depression in 1929. Southern Ireland broke away from the United Kingdom after a traumatizing conflict. Yet a more modern Britain also took shape in the 1920s and 1930s, a country in which women had the vote on the same basis as men, and electricity pylons and arterial roads became symbols of progress. Despite Britain's best efforts for peace, a second war with Germany broke out in 1939. World War II was truly, in Prime Minister Winston

Churchill's words, Britain's "finest hour." The social solidarity and collective sacrifice that carried the British people through early disasters to eventual victory brought irresistible demands for a more democratic, egalitarian future, embodied in the welfare state created by a Labour government after 1945.

Post-war Britain

Britain's efforts to maintain "great power" status in the post-World War II period failed. Over 20 years, the British Empire was disbanded, and Britain's subservient status to its American ally was tacitly accepted. Domestically, a combination of welfarism, consumerism, and full employment made the 1950s and 1960s a secure and satisfying time for many Britons. While car and home ownership increased, Britain became a global force in popular culture, especially the worlds of popular music and fashion. Mass immigration, mostly from former colonies, transformed Britain into a multiracial, multicultural society, but commitment to the post-imperial Commonwealth declined in importance, as Britain moved toward closer economic and political integration with Europe. The failings of the British economy were at times humiliating, with sterling crises underlining the country's financial weakness, and in the 1970s, trade union action leading to temporary breakdowns of power supplies and public services. Terrorism became a fixed feature of British life after Northern Ireland descended into a state close to civil war.

The 1980s saw a change of direction. Economic liberalization made employment less secure and society less equal, while increasing opportunities for enterprise and wealth creation. Britain experienced the benefits and occasional severe shocks of being tied into an expanding but unstable globalized economy. Whatever the future held, in the early 21st century the British people were more prosperous, healthier, better educated and housed, and arguably more tolerant and open-minded than ever before.

21st-century London
The glittering office towers of the modern capital reflect the leading role of the financial and service industries in Britain's economy, after the long-term decline of the country's once-dominant manufacturing sector.

MODERN TIMES
1914–PRESENT

1914–18

1919–1938

1939–1945

AUGUST 4, 1914
Britain declares war
on Germany.

AUGUST 23, 1914
The British Expeditionary Force
fights its first battle with the
Germans at Mons.

☆ British 6-in howitzer gun

JULY 1, 1916
The Somme offensive is
launched in France; almost
20,000 British soldiers are
killed in a day.

DECEMBER 7, 1916
David Lloyd George
becomes Prime Minister.

JUNE 28, 1919
The Treaty of Versailles is
signed, imposing peace
terms on Germany.

1919–1922
Anglo-Irish War leads to the
partition of Ireland between
the independent Irish Free
State and Northern Ireland.

OCTOBER 1932
Oswald Mosley forms the British
Union of Fascists.

OCTOBER 1936
Unemployed workers from
Tyneside march to London
in the Jarrow Crusade.

≪ A child's gas mask

JUNE 6, 1944
Allied troops invade Normandy
in the D-day landing.

MAY 8, 1945
Germany surrenders;
VE Day is celebrated
in London.

SEPTEMBER 3, 1939
Britain declares war on Germany.

MAY 10, 1940
Winston Churchill becomes Prime
Minister, forming a coalition
government.

MAY–JUNE 1940
The British Expeditionary Force
is evacuated from Dunkirk.

JULY 26, 1945
Churchill is defeated in
a general election; Labour
wins a landslide victory.

JANUARY 24, 1924
Ramsay Macdonald forms
the first Labour government.

MAY 3–12, 1926
General strike brings Britain
to a standstill.

DECEMBER 1930
Unemployment in Britain
tops 2.5 million.

≫ King Edward VIII

**JULY–SEPTEMBER
1940**
The Battle of Britain is fought in
the air over southern England.

**SEPTEMBER
1940–MAY 1941**
The Blitz by German Luftwaffe
carries out intensive night
bombing raids on British cities.

≫ H2S Mk IIc radar

☆ British war graves
in Somme, France

APRIL 25, 1915
British and ANZAC troops land
at Gallipoli, Turkey.

MAY 7, 1915
The ocean liner *Lusitania* is
sunk by a German U-boat.

MAY 31, 1915
London is bombed by
a German airship for the
first time.

JULY–NOVEMBER 1917
The Battle of Passchendaele
is fought in Flanders, Belgium.

≫ Dance troupe

DECEMBER 10, 1936
Edward VIII abdicates to marry
divorcée Wallis Simpson.

SEPTEMBER 1938
Prime Minister Neville
Chamberlain averts war with
Germany in the Munich Crisis.

≪ Gandhi in London

DECEMBER 1942
The Beveridge Report
outlines a postwar
welfare state.

AUGUST 15, 1945
Japan surrenders; the
war ends in Asia.

APRIL 24, 1916
Irish republicans stage the
Easter Rising in Dublin.

**MAY 31–JUNE 1,
1916**
The British and German fleets
clash at the Battle
of Jutland.

FEBRUARY 1918
The Representation of the
People Act gives women over
30 years the right to vote.

NOVEMBER 11, 1918
An armistice ends the
fighting in World War I.

**AUGUST–SEPTEMBER
1931**
Economic crisis leads to
formation of a National
Government.

SEPTEMBER 1931
Indian Congress leader
M.K. Gandhi comes to Britain
for a Round Table Conference.

**OCTOBER 23–
NOVEMBER 5, 1942**
General Bernard Montgomery's
Eighth Army defeats Axis forces
in the Desert War at El Alamein.

≫ World War II poster

HOLDING THE LINE!

"Let us therefore … so bear ourselves that if the **British Empire** and its **Commonwealth** last for a thousand years, men will still say, 'This was **their finest hour**'."

WINSTON CHURCHILL, JUNE 18, 1940

1946–1969

THE BRITISH COMMONWEALTH OF NATIONS

TOGETHER

⌃ Commonwealth poster

AUGUST 15, 1947
Britain grants independence to India and Pakistan.

JUNE 22, 1948
West Indian immigrants arrive in Britain on board *Empire Windrush*.

JULY 5, 1948
The National Health Service is founded.

1950–1953
British troops fight in the Korean War.

⌃ Beatlemania

OCTOBER 3, 1952
Britain tests its first atom bomb.

JUNE 2, 1953
The coronation of Elizabeth II takes place.

OCTOBER–NOVEMBER 1956
The Suez Crisis: an Anglo-French invasion of Egypt fails.

FEBRUARY 3, 1960
Harold Macmillan's "Winds of Change" speech announces Britain's intention to withdraw from its African colonies.

1963
The Beatles emerge as Britain's leading pop group.

OCTOBER 16, 1964
Labour leader Harold Wilson becomes Prime Minister, ending 13 years of Conservative government in Britain.

JULY 30, 1966
England's soccer team wins the World Cup.

AUGUST 14, 1969
British troops are deployed in cities in Northern Ireland to halt rioting.

1970–1989

JUNE 19, 1970
Ted Heath becomes Prime Minister after a surprise Conservative election victory.

1972
The Troubles in Northern Ireland are at their peak, causing 476 deaths in a year.

≫ Ulster mural

JANUARY 22, 1972
Britain joins the European Economic Community.

FEBRUARY 28, 1974
Heath is defeated in an election after declaring a "three-day week" to face down a miners' strike.

JULY 1975
Annual inflation in Britain reaches 26 percent.

JANUARY–FEBRUARY 1979
Widespread strikes undermine James Callaghan's Labour government in what is known as the Winter of Discontent.

≫ Women's liberation

MAY 4, 1979
Margaret Thatcher is elected Britain's first woman Prime Minister.

APRIL–JUNE 1982
Britain fights Argentina in the Falklands War.

MARCH 1984–MARCH 1985
A miners' strike is defeated by tough government action, ending the era of trade union power.

OCTOBER 12, 1984
Thatcher narrowly escapes assassination by an IRA bomb in a Brighton hotel.

NOVEMBER 1984
The sale of British Telecom begins the privatization of major nationalized industries.

JUNE 11, 1987
Thatcher wins a third consecutive general election victory.

1990–2019

NOVEMBER 28, 1990
Thatcher resigns as Prime Minister after losing the support of her own party.

JANUARY 16–FEBRUARY 28, 1991
British forces take part in a US-led campaign to drive Iraqi troops out of Kuwait.

MAY 6, 1994
The Channel Tunnel link with France is inaugurated.

MAY 2, 1997
Tony Blair becomes Prime Minister after a landslide Labour victory.

≫ British troops in Iraq, 2006

APRIL 10, 1998
The Good Friday agreement provides for power-sharing between Protestants and Catholics in Northern Ireland.

JULY 1, 1999
The devolved Scottish Parliament is opened.

MARCH 2003
British forces support the United States in a controversial invasion of Iraq.

JULY 7, 2005
Suicide bombers kill more than 50 people in attacks in London.

SEPTEMBER 14, 2007
The Bank of England bails out Northern Rock bank, signaling the start of a major financial crisis.

MAY 11, 2010
David Cameron becomes Prime Minister at the head of a Conservative-Liberal Democrat coalition government.

APRIL 29, 2011
Prince William marries Catherine Middleton in Westminster Abbey.

JULY 27, 2012
Athletes from across the world converge on London for the 2012 Summer Olympic and Paralympic Games.

JUNE 23, 2016
The United Kingdom votes in a Referendum by 51.9 percent to 48.1 percent to leave the European Union.

≫ London skyline

<< **BEFORE**

Britain had developed an isolationist tradition, depending on its navy to ensure national security and avoiding alliances with European powers. But in August 1914 the country was caught up in the rush to war.

WAR IN EUROPE
Germany declared war on Russia on August 1, 1914, and on France two days later. Britain's Liberal government was divided over whether to enter the war on the side of France. Britain had made secret military commitments to the French but there was **no formal alliance**. However, the German invasion of Belgium on August 4 provided a clear justification for a declaration of war, since Britain was a **guarantor of Belgian independence**.

LONG STRUGGLE ENVISIONED
The British Army had **prepared for a European war**. A force of six infantry divisions and one cavalry division was available for **rapid mobilization** and dispatch to the Continent. On August 9 the first elements of this British Expeditionary Force (BEF) left for France. Lord Kitchener, newly appointed Secretary of State for War, told the Cabinet that they would have to prepare for a **three-year war** and raise an army numbering **millions of men**.

Britain Enters the Great War

Britain declared war on Germany on August 4, 1914. At first, popular expectation that it would be "over by Christmas" did not seem absurd, but with the stalemate of trench warfare on the Western Front, the country was soon committed to fielding a mass citizen army in a merciless war of attrition.

Although the outbreak of war with Germany was greeted by a cheering crowd in Trafalgar Square, London, most British people did not enter the conflict in a spirit of flag-waving jingoism—diaries and private letters of the time reveal anxiety, resignation, and dismay. But the average Briton was intensely patriotic and believed that the cause was just. When the government requested volunteers for the army, it triggered what historian John Keegan called "a spontaneous and genuinely popular mass movement." The initial request was for 100,000 men to come forward; in September 1914, about 175,000 volunteered in a single week.

In Ireland, the Protestant Ulster Volunteer Force and the majority of the Catholic Irish Volunteers both offered their services to the British Army. Volunteers also responded to the call to arms in Australia, New Zealand, and Canada, which unhesitatingly supported the British cause.

Early setbacks
However, the daunting task of organizing, training, and equipping a mass citizen army would take many months, and in the meantime Britain depended upon its small regular army, augmented by reserves and part-time Territorials.

Lining up for war

High-spirited volunteers, responding to the call to serve "King and Country," wait outside a recruiting office. More than 3 million men had entered the British armed forces as volunteers by the end of 1915.

Arriving in Europe through August 1914, the British Expeditionary Force (BEF) took up position on the northern end of the French line. There they found themselves directly in the path of Germany's main offensive, delivered in a right hook through Belgium. After fighting holding actions at Mons and Le Cateau, they were soon in full retreat, along with their French allies. Germany looked set for a swift victory. By the end of August, the commander of the BEF, cavalry general Sir John French, had decided to withdraw his forces from a campaign he considered lost, but he was overruled by Lord Kitchener, the War Minister, in London. Thus the British supported France in its decisive counteroffensive at the Battle of the Marne in September. The Germans were driven back and pursued northward. The culminating battle of 1914 was fought at Ypres, in northern Belgium, in October and November. At immense cost, the British and French armies fought the German Army to a standstill. Exhausted, both sides dug in to a series of heavily fortified trenches along a line from the English Channel coast to Switzerland, which became known as the Western Front.

Determined spirit

The losses in the fighting in 1914 were unprecedented. Britain's pre-war regular army had been wiped out, but despite some fraternization with enemy troops at Christmas, Britain's commitment to the war remained unshaken. German massacres of civilians and wanton destruction during the occupation of Belgium—real, if exaggerated by Allied propagandists—had convinced most of

Imperial strength

Britain relied on its Empire to provide much of its manpower. These Sikhs were among more than 1 million Indian troops who served during the war.

the British public that they were fighting for civilization against barbarism. During 1915, German use of poison gas on the Western Front, the sinking of the ocean liner *Lusitania* by a German submarine, and the first Zeppelin (airship) bombing raids on London all served to confirm hatred of "the Hun" and the British determination to fight. Britain's military and political leaders, however, struggled

> **89,864** The number of British casualties on the Western Front in the first three months of the war. It is more than the total number of troops in the British Expeditionary Force at the start of the war, which was 84,000.

in vain to find a path to victory. The war at sea was in effect a stalemate, with Germany unable to break a British naval blockade of their ports, but the Royal Navy suffered unexpected losses to German submarines and mines. This stand-off was most unsatisfactory to a British public brought up on tales of Nelson's heroic victories. There was also

trench stalemate on the Western Front. Through 1915, mass infantry assaults on the German trench line, from Neuve Chapelle in the spring to Loos in the fall, cost tens of thousands of British lives for minimal gains.

Further frustration

The entry of Ottoman Turkey into the war on the German side in October 1914 provided a potentially easier target for Britain to attack. However, in March 1915, an Anglo-French naval force failed to force a passage through the Dardanelles straits and capture Constantinople (Istanbul), the Ottoman capital. The following month, the Allies landed troops at Gallipoli, to the west of the Dardanelles. The force included a large Anzac (Australian and New Zealand) contingent, but again Turkish resistance was unexpectedly strong and, as on the Western Front, the fighting became bogged down in static trench warfare. Despite landings at Suvla Bay in August, the Gallipoli campaign was another failure. By the time the Allied troops were pulled out in January 1916 it had cost more than 21,000 British and almost 9,000 Australian lives. The innocence and enthusiasm of August 1914 was by then left far behind.

> Early failures brought changes in political and military leadership, but Britain remained committed to a war of attrition.

EFFECTIVE GOVERNMENT

Asquith's Liberal government was criticized for failing to provide **sufficient munitions** for the army (the "shell scandal") and for the Gallipoli fiasco. In May 1915, Asquith brought the Unionists (Conservatives) into a **coalition government**, with a token place for Labour. **Winston Churchill**, blamed for Gallipoli, was fired as **First Lord of the Admiralty**. Lloyd George, the Chancellor of the Exchequer, took up a new role as **Minister of Munitions**, rapidly increasing weapons output.

MAJOR MILITARY CHANGES

In December 1915, the British **military command** was shaken up. In London, General William Robertson, appointed Chief of the Imperial General Staff, pushed Kitchener into the sidelines. In France, Sir John French, **blamed for serious errors** at Loos, was replaced by General Douglas Haig. Robertson and Haig were convinced that the war could only be won by **even larger offensives** on the Western Front 322–323 ≫.

WAR GENERAL DOUGLAS HAIG

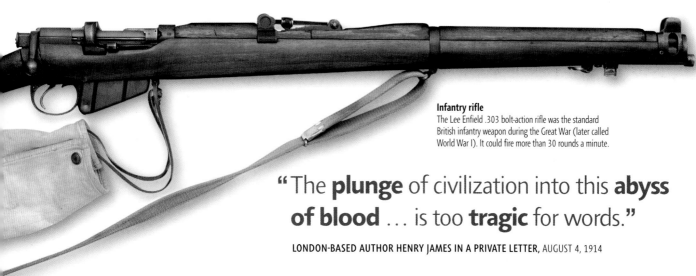

Infantry rifle

The Lee Enfield .303 bolt-action rifle was the standard British infantry weapon during the Great War (later called World War I). It could fire more than 30 rounds a minute.

> "The **plunge** of civilization into this **abyss** of blood … is too **tragic** for words."
>
> LONDON-BASED AUTHOR HENRY JAMES IN A PRIVATE LETTER, AUGUST 4, 1914

Victory through Slaughter

The battles on the Western Front in France and Flanders in the years 1916 to 1918 were industrialized warfare at its most destructive. Drawing on deep reserves of patriotism, courage, and stoical endurance, British and Empire troops ultimately triumphed, but at the cost of almost 1 million lives.

BEFORE

By 1916, the demands of Britain's war effort were leading to the abandonment of cherished freedoms. The Liberal Party split under the strain and David Lloyd George emerged as a decisive war leader.

FILLING THE RANKS

By the end of 1915, about 2.5 million men had **volunteered for military service**, but the demand for soldiers was insatiable. Many Liberal and Labour politicians were strongly opposed to compulsory military service, but in January 1916, the government introduced **conscription for single men**, extended to married men four months later. A small number of conscientious objectors were, however, allowed to assert their right not to fight for their country.

NEW ENERGY

Herbert Asquith, Liberal Prime Minister since 1908, was widely seen as **lacking the drive** to energize the war effort. In December 1916, Lloyd George rebelled against Asquith, taking part of the Liberal Party with him. A five-man **War Cabinet** was formed, headed by Lloyd George as Prime Minister, along with three Conservatives and Labour's Arthur Henderson.

DAVID LLOYD GEORGE

O n the Western Front in 1916, General Haig commanded about 2 million soldiers in the largest army that Britain had ever known. It comprised patriotic volunteers, many in "Pals battalions" from their own neighborhood, workplace, or sports club, as well as Canadians, Australians, and New Zealanders, who were to earn an outstanding reputation for fighting skill and aggression. British industry provided vast quantities of artillery shells and weapons of decent quality, and an expanding Royal Flying Corps provided air support.

An Anglo-French offensive was planned for summer 1916 at the Somme River. With France's armies already overstretched by the epic Battle of Verdun, the British took the dominant role. Haig hoped for a breakthrough that would win the war. Instead, the initial attack on July 1 was a military disaster (see pp.324–325), and the operation degenerated into attritional warfare. Lasting more than four months, it did at least inflict around half a million casualties

> **"** I suppose to people **at home** it is a **fine victory**. Well, so it is, but they don't see **the dead**. **"**
>
> LIEUTENANT FIRSTBROOKE CLARKE, PASSCHENDAELE, 1917

on the Germans, almost as many as the British and French, but the maximum advance made in return for this terrible loss was 7.4 miles (12km).

Through 1917 the burden of the Allied war effort fell increasingly on Britain, as the French army was racked by mutinies, and Russia collapsed in revolutionary upheaval. Although conscription proved a disappointment, with fewer men conscripted during 1916 than had volunteered in the previous year, the British Army continued to grow and British industry supplied ever more shells and guns. Haig mounted further large-scale offensives against the Germans' heavily defended trench systems, at Arras in April 1917 and at Third Ypres (Passchendaele) from July to November. These operations had their successes—the seizure of Vimy Ridge by the Canadians in April, the momentary breakthrough of tanks at Cambrai in November—but, as at the Somme, little ground was gained and casualties were massive.

Fighting at Passchendaele was especially grim because of the persistent rain and waterlogged terrain that made conditions for troops atrocious—the mud was sometimes so deep that men who slipped into it sank without trace. A dispute over strategy raged as Lloyd George demanded his military commanders come up with a more imaginative, less costly way of fighting the war. Although British imperial forces took over German colonies in Africa, and fought the Turks in Iraq and Palestine, these remained sideshows. Haig was probably correct in believing that there was no alternative to winning the war other than fighting on the Western Front.

Meanwhile, the sea war had not met British expectations. The British and German battleship fleets, focus of such patriotic enthusiasm before the war, clashed only once, at Jutland on May 31–June 1, 1916. However, the battle was, for Britain, unsatisfactorily inconclusive, although the Royal Navy retained control of the North Sea.

Submarine threat

More important than battleships were the German submarines (U-boats). A serious nuisance earlier in the war, in 1917 U-boats became a menace to Britain's survival as they were unleashed in large numbers against merchant shipping bound for or leaving British ports. Unrestricted submarine attacks on their ships helped bring the United States into the war, but threatened to starve Britain into defeat before the Americans could mobilize an expeditionary force. In April 1917, around one in four merchant ships that set sail from a British port was sunk. The crisis was overcome when the

> **78** British generals were killed during the war. This makes it evident that senior officers did not always fight the war from the safety of a comfortable chateau well to the rear, as is sometimes imagined.

Royal Navy began to organize and escort merchant convoys, and losses to U-boats fell to a sustainable level.

Toward final victory

In 1918, the trench stalemate came to an end. The United States, at war with Germany since April 1917, took more than a year to organize and train a mass army to fight in Europe. In March 1918 Germany imposed a harsh peace upon revolutionary Russia's Bolshevik government. It released huge German forces for an offensive on the Western Front that they hoped would win the

Trench hitter
Howitzers were essential in trench warfare as they lobbed a shell in a high trajectory. This 6-in (15.2-cm) British howitzer was one of the smaller howitzers to be used.

AFTER »

Contemporaries called the 1914–1918 conflict "the Great War" with good reason. It cost the lives of 956,703 British Empire military personnel, of whom 704,803 were from the British Isles.

NATION IN MOURNING

The vast majority of dead were victims of enemy action—a contrast to earlier wars when disease was the major killer. **Medical advances** ensured that many of the **seriously wounded survived**. About 40 percent of the 5 million British soldiers who served received disability pensions. Mental hospitals housed tens of thousands of victims of "shell-shock." In terms of total British population, the loss was actually lower than the 300,000 people who had been emigrating annually before 1914. But the **deaths were shockingly selective**—almost one in three men born between 1890 and 1895 were killed.

Although a Victory Parade was held in London after the Versailles peace agreement in 1919 **330–331** », the ceremonial emphasis after the war was on the **memory of the fallen**. For many years, the two-minute silence on Armistice Day (November 11) was assiduously observed. **Commemoration** focused upon the **ordinary servicemen**, epitomized by the funeral of the Unknown Warrior on Armistice Day 1920. Towns and villages throughout Britain erected **war memorials** that still stand today—sadly, often with the dead of World War II added on.

The killing fields

British troops cope with the horrors of war on the battlefield at Passchendaele in 1917. Although poison gas was the most notorious weapon in World War I, artillery bombardment caused the majority of casualties, as well as creating a wasteland of shell craters and mud.

war before the Americans arrived to neutralize their numerical advantage. Launched on March 21, it was initially a great success. German forces tore through British trenches and advanced across the old Somme battlefields. After a follow-up offensive in Flanders in April, Haig issued an appeal to his troops on April 11: "With our backs to the wall and believing in the justice of our cause, each one of us must fight to the end ...." The Allies created a joint command, with French General Ferdinand Foch becoming supreme commander. Resistance stiffened and the Germans stalled 62 miles (100 km) short of Paris. In June, the first American troops entered the fighting, beginning to tip the advantage away from the Germans.

Contrary to myth, British soldiers did not spend the war walking in lines into machine-gun fire under the orders of uniformly stupid officers. By 1918 the British Army had developed a set of fighting techniques that combined

precision use of artillery with flexible infantry tactics and support from tanks and ground-attack aircraft. Many lower-level officers had been promoted on merit from the ranks and senior commanders had learned from

170 MILLION

The number of artillery shells manufactured in Britain during the Great War. In one day in September 1918, the British Army fired 943,000 shells at a cost of £3,871,000.

experience. On August 8, 1918, the British launched a counteroffensive at Amiens, inflicting heavy casualties and taking many prisoners. German General Erich Ludendorff called it "the black day of the German army" and told the Kaiser the war was lost. Over the

following two months, Allied forces drove the demoralized Germans back in attack after attack, penetrating territory that had been under German occupation since 1914. Wanting to end the fighting before Allied armies entered Germany, the Germans sought an armistice. They tried to obtain lenient terms by negotiating with US President Woodrow Wilson, but Britain and France insisted on, in essence, a German surrender. With their Turkish and Austro-Hungarian allies defeated, and their cities in the grip of a revolutionary upheaval, the Germans had no choice but to submit. The guns fell silent at 11 a.m. on November 11, 1918. The presence of increasing numbers of Americans was important, and the French had fought well, but it was above all a British victory.

> " I hope **we may all say** that thus, this **fateful morning,** came to an **end all wars**. "
>
> DAVID LLOYD GEORGE, HOUSE OF COMMONS, NOVEMBER 11, 1918

INNOVATION

BRITISH MK IV TANK

The British Army made the first-ever use of tanks in warfare during the Battle of the Somme. Employed at Flers-Courcelette in September 1916, Mark I tanks failed to achieve the hoped-for impact. The Mark IV, used successfully on the opening day of the Battle of Cambrai in November 1917, still had severe defects. It was slow and prone to mechanical failures; the crew suffered from poor visibility and arduous conditions. Nevertheless, more than 400 tanks led off the significant Amiens offensive in August 1918.

MARK IV TANK

First Day of the Somme

The opening of the Somme offensive was the worst disaster in British military history. In a single day, the British Army suffered 57,740 casualties, including the death of more than 19,000 men. The majority of those who fell were volunteers of the New Armies recruited in 1914–1915. Entering battle for the first time, thousands were cut down without even having fired their weapons.

General Douglas Haig doubted the fighting worth of the clerks and factory workers who joined up so enthusiastically at the start of the war. He believed that they would be incapable of flexible infantry tactics, in which soldiers exploited cover and rushed forward, while colleagues gave supporting fire. The order was given by Haig that: "The assaulting troops must push forward at a steady pace in successive lines …."

The battle begins
In Haig's view, the task of the infantry would merely be to occupy devastated German trenches. For a week before the offensive, more than 1,000 British guns pummeled the German lines. Moreover, 21 mines tunneled under the enemy positions were exploded just before the attack. But the German trenches at the Somme were deep and well constructed. The bombardment neither killed the defenders, nor cleared away the dense barbed wire behind which they sheltered.

At 7:30 a.m. on July 1, British troops, many of whom were carrying up to 60 lb (27 kg) of equipment, clambered out of their trenches and walked in line across "no man's land." When German machine-guns opened fire, men fell in swathes. If they could not penetrate the enemy barbed wire, they were trapped in a killing ground. In some places German positions were taken—the 36th Ulster Division, which adopted more sophisticated infantry tactics, was able to penetrate to the German second line of trenches.

German counterattacks were fierce, and most ground gained was lost again. "Pals" battalions, such as the Accrington Pals and the Grimsby Chums, formed by colleagues and neighbors, suffered grievously in the attack. Another unit, the Newfoundland Regiment, went into the battle with 780 men; the following day 68 answered roll call. Haig's conclusion about the day's events was that the Germans had "undoubtedly been severely shaken" and that the offensive should resume immediately.

> " … magnificent display of trained and **disciplined valor** … only failed … because **dead men can advance no further**."

MAJOR-GENERAL SIR BEAUVOIR DE LISLE, DESCRIBING THE NEWFOUNDLAND REGIMENT ON THE FIRST DAY OF THE SOMME, JULY 1, 1916

Going over the top
British soldiers go into action at the Battle of the Somme. Once "over the top" of their own trenches, they were encouraged to push forward toward the German lines, as the British commanders feared that if they were allowed to take cover during the attack, they would "go to ground" and never resume their advance.

« BEFORE

The outbreak of war in 1914 temporarily brought a remarkable degree of unity to a country deeply divided on many social and political issues.

STRIKERS' COOPERATION

In the years just before World War I, the government and employers were challenged by **mass strike action** organized by militant trade unions **« 310–311**. In mid-1914, the coal miners, transport workers, and railroaders negotiated a Triple Alliance that threatened a general strike. The war, however, showed that the **patriotism of most British workers** was far stronger than their class allegiance. The trade union movement called for "an immediate effort … to terminate all existing trade disputes." Although socialists theoretically believed in international solidarity between workers, the majority of the **Labour Party supported the war**. The most prominent exceptions were Ramsay Macdonald and the veteran Keir Hardie.

SUFFRAGETTE SUPPORT

The militant campaign for **women's suffrage** was vehement in 1914 **« 308–309**. The leaders of the Women's Social and Political Union (WSPU), Emmeline and Christabel Pankhurst, responded to the war by ordering an immediate **suspension of the campaign**. They instead began agitating for the "women's right to serve."

IRELAND'S CONTRIBUTION

Although Ireland was on the brink of **civil war**, after the declaration of war on Germany, both Protestants and Catholics **volunteered for service** in the British Army. A minority of Catholic radicals, however, believed a German victory would **further their interests**.

The Home Front

World War I made Britain a more democratic society. Although the authorities curtailed freedoms and used propaganda and censorship to show the war in a favorable light, they recognized that Britain could achieve victory only through the efforts of all its citizens and that social solidarity was an ideal to pursue.

The war brought an unprecedented expansion of the powers of the state in Britain. By and large, this was readily accepted by a population committed to the single-minded goal of defeating the enemy.

The Defence of the Realm Act (DORA), introduced four days after the start of the war, gave the government the power to introduce regulations "for securing the public safety and the defense of the realm." This blanket measure was used to authorize the censorship of newspapers, and the compulsory takeover of ships, land, or factories. It also allowed the government to introduce a variety of relatively minor limitations on freedom.

In the course of the war, bans were applied to mundane activities, ranging from the buying of rounds in pubs and the ringing of bells, to the purchase of binoculars and the lighting of bonfires.

Restrictions on pub opening hours, imposed in an effort to increase war production in 1915, were not relaxed until the 1980s. The change of the clocks for British Summer Time introduced in 1916 has continued to the present day.

The government had an ideological aversion to state interference in the running of the economy—"business as usual" was a popular slogan early in the conflict—but found itself carried along the path of state intervention by the demands of total war.

New changes

Paper banknotes for sums of £1 and 10 shillings were issued to replace the use of gold sovereigns. Railroads and coal mines were taken under government control. With millions of men subtracted from the nation's workforce to fight in France, and a massive increase in armaments production required, new workers had to be found for the factories. Almost 800,000 women were recruited for munitions work. Trade union objections were overcome by the promise of limits on the profits of employers. Women also worked in large numbers as bus conductors, military nurses, office clerks, and farm laborers in the Women's Land Army. Price inflation, wages, and taxes rose sharply. There were winners and losers: a working-class couple in well-paid jobs

> **30** The standard percentage rate of income tax collected by the British government in 1918. In 1914, at the start of the war, it had been 6 percent.

Calling for support
A government poster calls on civilians to support the nation's servicemen by their efforts. Propaganda engaged newly developed advertising techniques.

could enjoy prosperity, while a family with the breadwinner away in the forces may be impoverished due to the rising prices. However, new works' canteens at least improved the diet of those in factory employment.

Outrage against Germany

Soldiers returning home from the front often felt that civilians were hopelessly out of touch with the realities of the war. Censorship and propaganda hid the horror of the trenches, while promoting a hearty jingoism and savage hatred of "the Hun" (the Germans). Yet most families and communities had an intense emotional involvement in the conflict, and painfully grieved the mutilation and death suffered by so many of their friends, sons, and brothers. Popular feeling against the Germans was strong. In May 1915, the liner *Lusitania* was sunk by a German U-boat (submarine), killing more than 1,000. In response, rioting mobs attacked German businesses in British towns and cities, or any corporation

Air raids
A damaged London house shows the effects of a German airship raid. Air attacks killed 1,400 people in Britain during the war, most of them civilians.

Women munitions workers
The presence of women in munitions factories was the starkest symbol of the abandonment of traditional limits on female roles. The work was hard and hazardous, but the women earned status and good money.

with a foreign name. The royal family were later obliged to demonstrate their Britishness by changing their name of Saxe-Coburg and Gotha to Windsor.

The government was sensitive to criticism from demagogues, such as Horatio Bottomley, who accused it of failing to prosecute the war with enough energy, and for being soft on "traitors" who advocated peace.

Air raids on civilians

British civilians came under direct enemy attack in December 1914, when east coast towns including Scarborough, Hartlepool, and Whitby were shelled by German warships, killing more than 100 people. *Zeppelin* and *Schütte-Lanze* airships conducted nighttime bombing raids on London in May 1915.

A blackout was enforced, and the capital ringed with gun batteries and searchlights. Night-flying aircraft armed with incendiary ammunition eventually provided the answer to the airships, which became too vulnerable to continue their campaign. In 1917, the German Gotha bomber aircraft took

over, with a raid on Folkestone, Kent, in May killing 95 people. Their first attack on London, arriving without warning in the middle of the day on June 13, killed 162. Night raids by Gothas led Londoners to seek shelter in Underground stations. Popular demands for improved air defense, and for revenge raids against German cities, helped lead to the formation of the Royal Air Force in April 1918.

Opposition and inclusion

The war inevitably placed immense strain upon the social and political system. In 1917, with no end to the conflict in sight, and the German U-boat campaign creating food shortages, discontent expressed itself in strikes with a distinct political edge. Siegfried Sassoon, a serving officer who had won the Military Cross in France, publicly appealed to the government to seek peace, arguing

that the conflict was being prolonged unnecessarily, making it "a war of aggression and conquest." News of the Russian Revolution excited the hopes of socialists and the fears of the Establishment. Yet, outright opposition to the war remained limited to a minority in socialist and pacifist circles. In response to popular discontent, the government brought in measures to control rents and hold down prices of essential foods. It eventually introduced rationing, although on a much smaller scale than in World War II.

Meanwhile the Representation of the People Act, passed by Parliament in March 1918, conceded the largest extension of franchise in British history. Giving the vote to all men over the age of 21, and to all women above 30 years, it increased the electorate from under 8 million to more than 21 million. The war made Britain a true democracy for the first time in its history.

AFTER ≫

At the end of the war there was a move to return to prewar "normality," but the change in women's status was accepted, at least in part, as irreversible.

WOMEN'S PROGRESS

Women were **immediately evicted** from traditional male jobs in industry and transportation, but the Sex Disqualification (Removal) Act in 1919 **lifted formal barriers** to women's progress in professions and the civil service. Women over 30 voted in the December 1918 general election, and in 1919 Nancy Astor became the **first woman MP** to sit in Parliament. The extension of the vote to women, on the same basis as men, had to wait until 1929.

SPANISH FLU

In mid-1918, Britain was ravaged by **the Spanish flu**, which killed 250,000 people. Preventive measures, such as wearing masks and using anti-flu sprays on public transportation, were slow to be adopted. It was by far the **worst epidemic** in modern British history, yet was overshadowed by memory of the war.

PREVENTING SPANISH FLU

"Master had gone to war and Missis ruled the household."

ROBERT ROBERTS, DESCRIBING WOMEN IN SALFORD IN THE GREAT WAR, *THE CLASSIC SLUM: SALFORD LIFE IN THE FIRST QUARTER OF THE CENTURY*, 1971

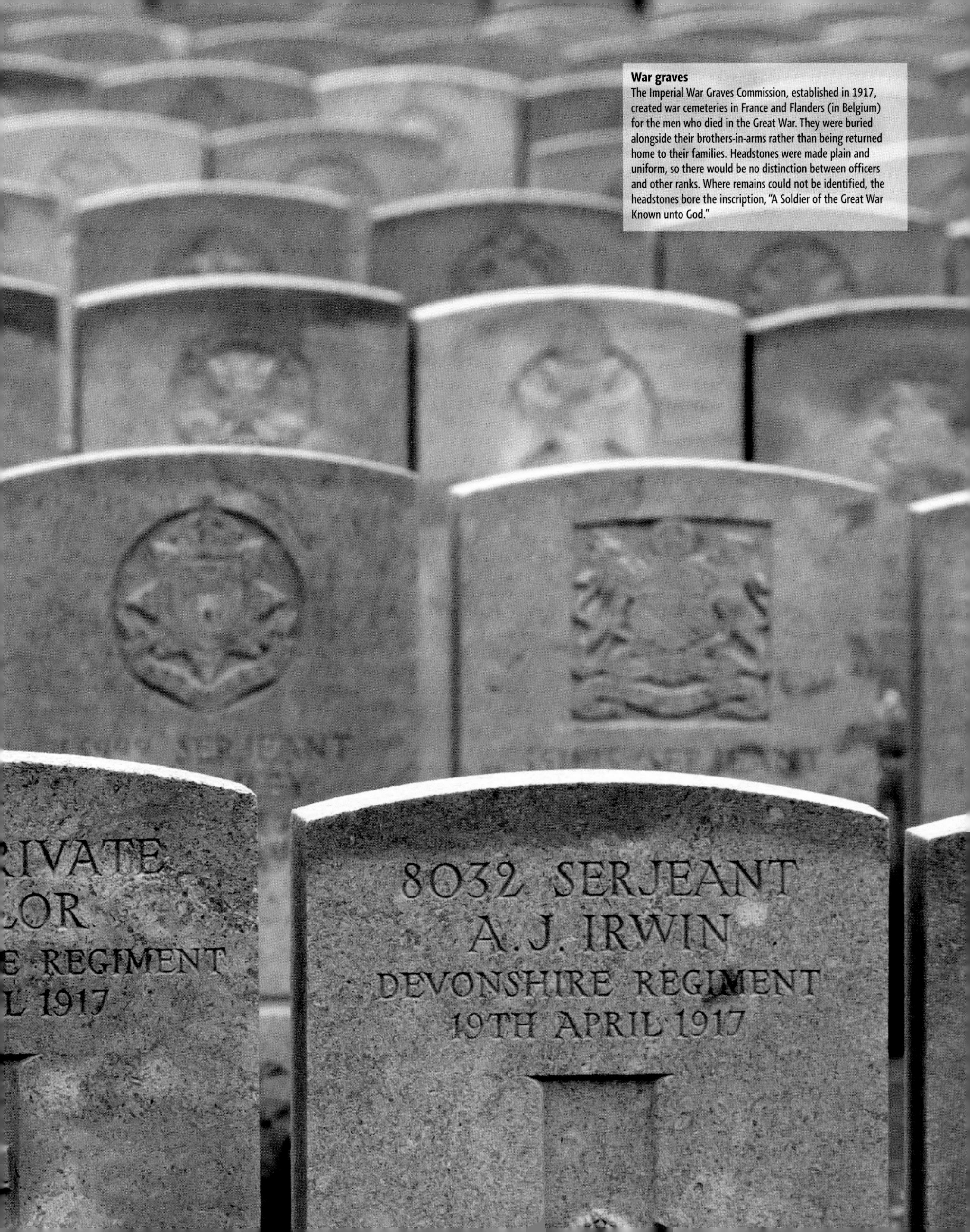

RIVATE
OR
E REGIMENT
L 1917

8032 SERJEANT
A.J. IRWIN
DEVONSHIRE REGIMENT
19TH APRIL 1917

Armistice Day
Servicemen on leave and joyful civilians celebrate peace and victory in Trafalgar Square, London, on November 11, 1918. Street parties were held and church bells rung across Britain.

Peace and After

British celebrations on the signing of the armistice in November 1918 were overshadowed by awareness of the human cost of victory and of the difficulties that lay ahead on the path to a durable peace. For many people the transition from war to peace was to prove a thoroughly disillusioning experience.

Although the armistice of November 11, 1918, ended the fighting in World War I, it did not end the war. A conference was convened to meet in Paris, where the victorious powers determined the peace terms to be presented to Germany. Also on their agenda were issues arising from the collapse of the Austrian, Russian, and Ottoman Turkish empires. Meanwhile, Britain maintained its naval blockade of Germany. When the peacemakers met in 1919, Britain's Lloyd George balanced the cynical realism of France's Georges Clemenceau with the lofty idealism of US President Woodrow Wilson. Lloyd George supported Wilson's pet plan for an international organization to maintain peace, the League of Nations, and also attempted to moderate Clemenceau's demands on Germany.

Dinner's ready
This 1916 cartoon denounces wartime deals to reward Britain's allies with enemy territory. Many people wanted a peace based on just principles, rather than on profit for the victors and the plunder of the defeated.

Britain and France agreed in demanding reparations payments from the Germans to cover the immense cost of the war, which had put both countries heavily in debt. Protesting, Germany signed the peace treaty at Versailles in June 1919.

It severely restricted German armed forces, put the Rhineland under Allied military occupation for 15 years, imposed unspecified reparations payments, and declared Germany guilty of having caused the war. German reaction was swift: sailors of the German High Seas Fleet, interned at Scapa Flow in the Orkneys under the armistice agreement, scuttled their warships in protest. The British intellectual elite soon turned against the peace agreement. Economist John Maynard Keynes's 1919 best-seller, *The Economic Consequences of the Peace,* helped generate a widespread impression in Britain that the Germans had been unfairly treated.

Britain's troubles

Conflict rather than peace was the keynote of both domestic and foreign affairs in the immediate aftermath of the war. In 1919, British forces were in action from Afghanistan to Arkhangelsk, where they briefly intervened against the Bolshevik government in the Russian Civil War. Ireland was in revolt (see pp.332–333), and in Britain trouble also flared. Demobilization of the wartime armed forces proceeded too slowly. Thousands of soldiers eager to return to civilian life demonstrated in central London in early 1919. Protests by Canadian troops at Rhyl, in north Wales, were suppressed violently. When they eventually returned to their homes and families, the ex-servicemen faced an uncertain world.

Industrial disputes proliferated. In January 1919, Glaswegian workers inspired by the Bolshevik Revolution led a strike on "Red Clydeside" that had to be suppressed by troops. The army was also called in when a police strike in Liverpool unleashed rioting in August 1919. Further strikes were provoked when the railroads and mines, nationalized during the war, were returned to private ownership against the wishes of their workers. At the 1918 general election, Lloyd George promised to build "a fit country for heroes to live in." His government tried to respond to discontent and reward wartime loyalty. Unemployment benefits were extended and government housing accorded a priority. However, a brief post-war economic boom soon collapsed and by 1921, there were 2 million workers without jobs. The era of mass unemployment had begun in Britain. The British had won the war, but it did not feel like a victory.

BEFORE

Britain entered World War I with the sole declared aim of protecting Belgian independence. Other aims later appeared.

EVOLVING IDEALS
In the first two years of the war, various **secret agreements** were made with Britain's allies that would, for example, have allowed Czarist Russia to annex Constantinople (Istanbul) from Turkey. Partly through pressure from the United States, Britain later evolved **more idealistic war aims**. In January 1918, Prime Minister David Lloyd George denied that Britain was fighting a "war of aggression," embraced the **cause of self-government** for the Poles and the Slav peoples of the Austrian Empire, and committed Britain to support founding an "international organization," which would be "an alternative to war." This became the **League of Nations**.

ANTI-GERMAN SENTIMENT
Fighting a general election in December 1918, however, Lloyd George felt the need to appeal to **popular hostility against Germany**. Supporters of his Liberal-Conservative coalition reacted favorably to slogans such as "Hang the Kaiser" and "Make the Germans Pay." On a tide of **aggressive patriotism**, the coalition won a crushing majority in Parliament, taking 475 seats.

AFTER

With a coalition of Conservatives and Liberals in government from 1918, the Labour Party was able to establish itself as the leading opposition force in Parliament.

CONTRASTING FORTUNES
Post-war discontent **fueled support for Labour**, which won 142 seats in Parliament in 1922, and 191 seats in 1923. This was enough for Ramsay Macdonald to finally form the **first of two minority Labour governments** in the 1920s, although the first lasted less than 10 months. The **Liberal Party was reduced** to a third-party status and Lloyd George's political career went into decline. The Labour Party condemned the Versailles Treaty in 1919 and remained **strongly pacifist** throughout the 1920s and 1930s.

12 MILLION The number of workers eligible for unemployment benefits under new 1920 legislation. This was five times the number covered by the unemployment insurance program introduced in 1911.

Down but not out
A former soldier turns street performer to earn a living. Such scenes were common in much of Britain during the economically depressed 1920s and 1930s.

DISCHARGED SOLDIER. NO PENSION
Wife & 4 Children to support
Served Overseas
I Thank You !

« BEFORE

In 1914, the confrontation between Ulstermen and Catholic Nationalists over Home Rule threatened civil war. This was averted by the outbreak of World War I.

HOME RULE OPPOSED
The **Home Rule Bill** of 1912 would have given a devolved Irish parliament great powers. The House of Lords delayed its passage but by August 1914 it only awaited **Royal Assent**. Protestants, who formed a majority in most parts of Ulster, opposed Home Rule. Supported by senior figures in the Conservative Party and the British Army, they formed the Ulster Volunteers, an armed militia to **resist Home Rule**. The Nationalists responded by founding and arming the Irish Volunteers.

HOME RULE POSTPONED
At the outbreak of war **« 320–321**, Home Rule was **postponed for the duration** of the conflict. The Ulster Volunteers enrolled in the British Army, most forming the 36th Ulster Division. The majority of the Irish Volunteers also chose to serve Britain, forming the 10th and 16th Irish Divisions. Around 30,000 Irishmen **died fighting in the British armed forces** in World War I.

The war on the streets
British troops, brought in to suppress the Easter Rising in April 1916, man a makeshift barricade in a Dublin street. The British Army suffered almost 500 casualties in a week's street fighting, including 116 soldiers killed.

Irish Independence

A failed uprising by Irish Republicans in Dublin at Easter 1916 set in motion a chain of events that led to the independence of southern Ireland six years later. The six counties of Northern Ireland received Home Rule, remaining a part of the United Kingdom under a sectarian Protestant government.

The decision of Irish Nationalist leader John Redmond to support the British war effort in August 1914 split the Nationalist movement. A minority of the Irish Volunteer militia rejected the call to join the British Army. They were to a large degree under the control of the radical Irish Republican Brotherhood (IRB). The IRB saw the war as an opportunity to overthrow British rule. They established contact with the Germans, who agreed to supply arms. An uprising was set for Easter 1916. Nothing went as planned. A ship carrying German rifles arrived off the Irish coast, but was intercepted by the British. Orders were distributed to the Irish Volunteers canceling the uprising. However, a hard core of the IRB in Dublin, led by Padraic Pearse, went ahead regardless. Supported by James Connolly's Citizens Army, a small socialist group, the IRB launched an insurrection on Easter Monday. They took over buildings in Dublin, including the General Post Office where Pearse declared Ireland an independent republic. The rebels numbered around 1,600 men, and were armed with rifles and shotguns. The Dublin population was either indifferent or hostile. The British rushed troops to the city and suppressed the uprising with the use of artillery. More than 400 people died in the fighting, before Pearse agreed to surrender on April 29.

Belfast volunteers
Belfast shipyard workers volunteering for service in the British Army in August 1914. More than 200,000 Irishmen, Protestant and Catholic, fought for Britain in World War I.

"**Ireland, through us, summons her children to her flag and strikes for her freedom.**"

PADRAIC PEARSE, PROCLAMATION OF THE IRISH REPUBLIC, APRIL 1916

By their behavior after the uprising, the British authorities turned a victory into a defeat. Outraged at this "stab in the back" in wartime, they executed 15 leaders of the uprising, including Pearse and Connolly. It made martyrs of the republicans and won widening support for their cause. Sinn Féin, previously insignificant, became the political embodiment of Republicanism. In April

47 The number of the 73 Sinn Féin MPs elected in the December 1918 general election who were in jail at the time. They had been arrested in a British crackdown on Republicans. The British released them all the following April.

1918, faced with a crisis in the war with Germany, the British government proposed extending conscription to Ireland. The Republican response was hostile. Conscription was denounced by Catholic priests and Irish Nationalist MPs withdrew from Westminster.

Rise of Sinn Féin
The British backed down, but too late to save the situation slipping beyond their control. When a general election was held in December 1918, 73 Irish seats were won by Sinn Féin. Rejecting the Westminster Parliament, the Sinn Féin MPs set up an Irish Parliament, the Dáil Éireann, to rule the republic that

had been proclaimed in Easter 1916. In January 1919, the Irish Republican Army (IRA), led by Michael Collins, began a campaign of ambush and assassination, to which the British responded with an equally unscrupulous use of force. Recently demobilized British soldiers were recruited as Black and Tans, and auxiliaries, to aid the army and police in suppressing the rebellion. These often ill-disciplined irregulars

Easter Rising medal
In 1941, on the 25th anniversary of the 1916 Easter Rising, a medal was created for those Republicans who claimed to have taken part in the rebellion.

terrorized the Catholic population, while the IRA shot village policemen in the back. The British government sought a political solution in a variant on Home Rule. The 1920 Government of Ireland Act established separate devolved parliaments for southern Ireland in Dublin and for the six largely Protestant counties of Ulster in Belfast. The Protestants accepted the deal, and a Northern Ireland Parliament opened in Belfast in June 1921. Sinn Féin rejected this devolution, but in July agreed to a truce and opened negotiations with the British government.

Agreement reached
In December 1921, the Irish delegation, led by Michael Collins, signed an agreement in London with the British government, which gave effective independence to all Ireland except the six counties of Ulster as a dominion within the British Commonwealth. The Anglo-Irish Treaty split Sinn Féin. Eamonn de Valera, the leader of both the party and of the Republican government, led the opposition to the agreement, chiefly over symbolic issues such as the requirement for members of the Dáil Éireann to swear fidelity to the British monarch. Pro- and anti-Treaty republicans then embarked on a civil war, but this did not stop the new Irish Free State from being formally founded on December 6, 1922.

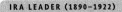

Led initially by Michael Collins, pro-Treaty Irish republicans fought a civil war against anti-Treaty republicans, while Catholics in Northern Ireland came under Protestant rule, creating an issue for future conflict.

CIVIL WAR
The **Irish Civil War** lasted from June 1922 to May 1923, killing several thousand, before the IRA "irregulars" were **defeated by the Irish Free State** government. **Eamonn de Valera**, the most prominent anti-Treaty politician, later emerged as Ireland's **dominant political figure**, after his Fianna Fáil party won a Dáil majority in 1932.

DE VALERA'S IRELAND
De Valera combined conservative Catholic social policies with **anti-British** nationalism. In 1937, he changed the constitution, renaming the Irish Free State "Éire" or "Ireland" and claiming the whole of the island as national territory. In World War II **348–349 »**, he kept **Ireland neutral**.

UNRESOLVED DIVISIONS
Northern Ireland's borders enclosed a **large Catholic minority**, while ensuring permanent Protestant domination. Its **government** harshly repressed the IRA and **intimidated Catholics**. The partition of Ireland continued to be regarded by the IRA as a casus *belli* with Britain. In 1939–1940, an **IRA bombing campaign** on the British mainland caused great damage and loss of life.

348–349 »

IRA LEADER (1890–1922)
MICHAEL COLLINS

Collins was born in County Cork in 1890. He joined the Irish Republican Brotherhood and took part in the 1916 Easter Rising. As an IRA leader during the war of independence he was responsible for the assassination of 13 people, including British intelligence officers, on "Bloody Friday," November 21, 1920. In December 1921, he negotiated the Anglo-Irish Treaty that ended the war, and in June 1922 led the attack on anti-Treaty IRA forces in Dublin, leading to civil war. Commander-in-chief of the government forces, he was shot dead in an anti-Treaty ambush in Cork on August 22, 1922.

Crisis and Depression

In the 1920s and 1930s, Britain faced a decline in industrial output, a general strike, worldwide depression, financial crisis, and unemployment. While it struggled to cope with a troubled new world, the nation did not succumb to the political extremism that destroyed democracy through much of Europe.

The London crash
A crowd gathers outside the London Stock Exchange after the collapse of the financial empire of speculator Charles Hatry in October 1929.

The crisis in the world economy, known as the Great Depression, is generally dated to 1929, but the economic woes of the inter-war period started much earlier in Britain. Mass unemployment struck in 1920–1921, following a brief inflationary boom. After that, the number of jobless never fell below 1 million until World War II.

Production levels of coal mining, shipbuilding, and textiles decreased, turning areas dependent on such traditional industries into persistent unemployment black spots. Agriculture

violence. After a week-long stalemate, a compromise was negotiated with the government, which allowed the trade union leadership to call off the national strike. The miners, however, maintained their stance. They continued the strike for six months, but were ultimately starved into submission.

In the end, it was not the workers' militancy that rocked the established order, but a worldwide economic catastrophe. The crash of the New York Stock Exchange in October 1929 signaled the beginning of the Great

Macdonald won a general election in May 1929, unseating Stanley Baldwin's Conservatives. The new government now faced the consequences of global economic turmoil. Macdonald and his Chancellor of the Exchequer, Philip Snowden, were under pressure to slash government spending. Then in 1931, a banking collapse in Austria and Germany had an effect on Britain. The Bank of England advised budget cuts to the government in order to avoid the collapse of Sterling.

Altered politics

When Snowden proposed cutting unemployment benefits as part of a package of austerity measures, nine Labour ministers resigned. Macdonald stayed on as Prime Minister, forming a coalition government with the Conservatives and Liberals, while the Labour Party went into opposition. The move ate into the pay of all public employees, including sailors of the Royal Navy, who staged protests at Invergordon. Inflated accounts of this "mutiny" led to renewed pressure on Sterling and the Gold Standard had to be abandoned.

The pound devalued sharply. The long-term effect of this devaluation was beneficial, but the shock of the crisis to

> ## " … **ordinary decent people** … to whom an **extraordinary misfortune** has happened."
>
> SIR WILLIAM BEVERIDGE, BBC RADIO BROADCAST, 1931

BEFORE

World War I did irreparable damage to the British economy. The country entered the post-war period heavily in debt and with key industries vulnerable to foreign competition.

A COSTLY AFFAIR
The war cost Britain more than £11 billion. Only a fraction of this expenditure was covered by increased taxation. The national debt rose from £650,000 to £8 billion, mostly owed to investors by way of war loans. After the war, about a **half of the government's income from taxation** was spent on **servicing the debt**. Britain also came out of the war owing £850 million to the United States, although the British were in turn owed money by other wartime allies. This chain of debts **complicated international financial relationships**, blocking the return to a stable global economy.

INDUSTRIAL DECLINE
British industry coped well with the demands of war, but while its **factories focused on war production**, exports suffered. In the post-war period, it proved **impossible to recover** the lost markets. Britain's **industrial production** had been **falling for decades**, but in 1914 its shipyards, for example, had built more ships than the rest of the world combined. By the 1920s, such traditional industries had simply lost their competitive edge.

was also thrown into crisis by falling prices and global overproduction. Yet Britain's government, bankers, and industrialists continued to dream of returning to the life of the pre-war world, with the City of London as the financial center of the global economy. It was this vision that lay behind the economically irrational decision to return to the Gold Standard in 1925, a system under which the nation's currency could be exchanged for a fixed weight of gold on demand at the central bank. This fixed the value of Sterling well above its natural exchange rate. The move raised the cost of British exports, depressed wages, and worsened the fate of struggling industries.

Escalating tensions
In 1926 a crisis in the coal-mining sector led to the General Strike, the era's most famous challenge to the established order. Mine-owners responded to foreign competition and declining profits by demanding wage cuts and longer working hours. When the country's million-strong coal miners refused to accept the owners' terms, they found themselves locked out of the pits. The trade union reluctantly embarked on a national strike in support of the miners. The government, aided by volunteers, undertook emergency measures to maintain essential services. Moderation and good sense on both sides largely averted

Depression. World trade shrank, currencies were devalued, banks collapsed, industrial and agricultural output plummeted, while unemployment figures soared. By December 1930, the number of people left jobless rose above 2.5 million in Britain. The Labour Party, led by Ramsay

Keeping working
A poster for the London and North Eastern Railway advertises its role in keeping blast furnaces working during the prolonged lock-out of the coal miners in 1926.

> **62** **The percentage of unemployed in the working population of Merthyr, a mining district of South Wales in 1934. This compared with a rate of 5 percent in Coventry, a center for new industries.**

national self-confidence was palpable. By 1932, more than half the working population remained idle in regions such as South Wales, Tyneside, and parts of Scotland. The government took timid measures to revive local economies, providing funding under the Special Areas program, while attempting to limit the cost of unemployment.

The apparent bankruptcy of the existing system seemed to validate new social and political beliefs. Young people flocked to embrace socialism and Marxism, providing a ready audience for works such as George Orwell's *The Road to Wigan Pier*, distributed by the Left Book Club. The British Communist Party, founded in 1920 in the wake of the Russian Bolshevik Revolution, never won a mass following, but was

Blackshirt salute
British fascist leader Oswald Mosley receives a Nazi-style salute from his blackshirted followers during a rally in Hyde Park in 1934. The banning of such military-style parades two years later punctured Mosley's popular appeal.

BUF march through a predominantly Jewish area of London's East End led to violent clashes with anti-fascists. This "battle of Cable Street" stirred the government to ban political uniforms and limit rallies. After this, the influence of Mosley and the BUF sharply declined.

50,000 The number of members claimed by the British Union of Fascists in the 1930s. In the late 1930s, the Communist Party had a membership of about 16,000.

nonetheless influential. At the other end of the political spectrum, Oswald Mosley, a disillusioned former member of the Labour government, established the British Union of Fascists (BUF) in 1932. The membership of the party was never large, but the aggressive posturing of Mosley's supporters ensured plentiful publicity. In October 1936, a provocative

Democracy intact
In truth, unlike many other countries in Europe, Britain in the 1930s remained a remarkably stable parliamentary democracy. While there were some local protests by the unemployed, the majority of the population remained largely contented. The deflationary slump produced stable or falling prices, while wages tended to rise, improving living standards. The introduction of advanced coal-cutting machines also stemmed the decline of the old industries. A general election in 1935 confirmed the Conservatives as the largest party in the House of Commons under Stanley Baldwin. The British economic, social, and political system survived the Depression surprisingly intact.

In retrospect, mass unemployment was the dominant image of the inter-war years. This bred a determination among Britain's policy makers to ensure it would not happen again.

RISE IN INDUSTRIAL PRODUCTION
With strong growth in new industries such as motor manufacture and electrical goods, British industrial production in the late 1930s was 75 percent higher than it had been before World War I. However, unemployment remained stubbornly high in the areas most affected by the Depression 338–339 ≫. It was not until 1940 that nationwide unemployment fell below 1 million for the first time in 20 years. By 1941, though, labor shortages posed a serious threat to the war effort 354–355 ≫.

THE KEYNESIAN METHOD
Fearing that unemployment would return at the end of the war, British politicians came under the influence of economist John Maynard Keynes. During the 1930s, Keynes had argued that governments should abandon their obsession with balancing their budgets. Instead, they should run budget deficits to **stimulate the economy during a slump**. He explained how governments could use spending and interest rates to manage demand in the economy and **maintain full employment**. There was interest in Keynes's ideas during the 1930s, but the government **did not abandon traditional economic policy**. After World War II, however, Keynes's ideas became the basis for successful efforts by post-1945 British governments to maintain full employment 360–361 ≫.

Eviction protest
The eviction of poor families from their row houses for nonpayment of rent is the occasion for a spontaneous protest in a Chelsea street. Such small-scale protests against poverty and unemployment, although common in the 1930s, were politically ineffectual.

The Jarrow March

In October 1936, 200 unemployed men from the Depression-hit Tyneside shipbuilding town of Jarrow marched to London to present a petition to Parliament. Their protest was brushed aside by the government and ultimately had no practical effect.

The closure of Palmers shipyard, Jarrow's major employer, in 1933 had devastated the local economy. By 1936 unemployment in the town had risen to more than 70 percent. Jarrow's Labour MP, Ellen Wilkinson, later called it "the town that was murdered." After a project to build a new steel works at Jarrow was canceled, local councillors organized the march to draw attention to the town's desperate plight.

The marchers

Throughout the Depression years, "hunger marches" had been staged by masses of unemployed workers tramping from industrial areas to the capital. Regarded as a communist-inspired threat to the social order, these marches were ignored or disparaged by the media, and the marchers were often harassed by the police. But the organizers of the Jarrow "crusade" ensured that no communists took part, and even won the backing of the local Conservatives. To avoid disorder, the march was kept small, with 200 men picked out of 1,200 volunteers. Their petition, couched in respectful terms, carried 11,572 signatures.

The marchers set off on October 5, 1936, with the blessing of the Bishop of Jarrow and led by their mayor. Press coverage was copious and largely favorable. The marchers encountered a generous and enthusiastic reception at their stopping points along the 300-mile (480-km) route. So much food was provided that, coming from a community in which malnutrition was rife, the men found themselves gaining weight.

The impact of the march

The popular sympathy that the march evoked was not echoed in government circles. When the marchers reached London, Prime Minister Stanley Baldwin ignored them. On November 4, the petition was delivered to Parliament and representatives of the marchers, including Ellen Wilkinson, met MPs in the House of Commons. The practical impact of the march was minimal. Only the need for ships during World War II ended mass unemployment in Jarrow.

> **"** We didn't know we were entering **the history books**. We did it because we were **desperate for work …"**
>
> JARROW MARCHER CORNELIUS WHALEN, 2001

On their way to London
Presented sympathetically by the press, the Jarrow marchers moved the British public with the dignity of their protest. The marchers asked only for a chance to work for a living. The instruments for their mouth-organ band were paid for by journalists.

‹‹ BEFORE

Major social and technological changes that characterized British society in the period between the wars were a continuation of developments visible in the Edwardian era.

POPULATION CHANGES

Probably the biggest change in society was a **fall in the birth rate**. Women who married in the 1880s had on average 4.6 children. By the 1900s, the standard British family had just over three children, and in the 1920s the **average dropped** to 2.2. Contrary to a long-established myth, low birth rates in the 1920s and 1930s were not the result of a lack of husbands caused by World War I. **A lower proportion of women remained unmarried** in the 1920s–1930s than in the pre-war period, but couples were **choosing to have smaller families**, and achieving this aim despite limited availability of contraceptives.

AN URBAN SOCIETY

The **consumerism** of the 1920s and 1930s was also rooted in pre-war Britain. Movie theaters, motor vehicles, professional spectator sports, and mass newspapers were **all part of the urban society** of the 1900s, but were on a significantly smaller scale than between the wars. **Electricity generation** existed on a local basis, but only one house in 17 had electric power by 1920. In 1939, the Central Electricity Board was supplying two-thirds of the homes in Britain.

Carry on smiling
Glamorous dance troupes were a staple of West End shows and movie musicals in the 1930s, providing a hard-working living for young women escaping poverty.

Life in the Twenties and Thirties

In the years between the two World Wars, British social life underwent rapid change that, for many people, brought greater freedom, comfort, and fun. It was a time of picture palaces, dance halls, and wireless radio. While the unemployed survived "on the dole" in the old industrial towns of the north, a new home-owning, car-owning British society was beginning to take shape in much of the south.

In 1933, author J.B. Priestley went on a journey through England, writing an account of the state of the nation. In the depressed, old industrial areas of the north he found jobless men in cloth caps loitering in boarded-up streets, and poverty mitigated only by the solidarity of long-established working-class communities. In the south he found a wholly new England. It was, Priestley wrote: "the England of arterial and by-pass roads, of filling stations and factories that look like exhibition buildings, of giant cinemas and dance halls and cafes, bungalows with tiny garages, cocktail bars, Woolworths,

motor-coaches, wireless, hiking, factory girls looking like actresses, greyhound racing and dirt tracks, swimming pools and everything given away for cigarette coupons." This was a new world that angered opinion-forming intellectuals. They railed against the spread of pebble-dashed cheap housing in "ribbon development" along roads outside towns and cities. They denounced the corruption of British culture by the

Life in the suburbs

A suburban home was an ideal for many middle-class families. About 2.5 million new houses were built for private sale in the period between the wars.

influence of American movie celebrities, popular music, and dance crazes. But even the critical left-wing author George Orwell admitted that, for a young person in the 1930s, "indulging in a private daydream of yourself as Clark Gable or Greta Garbo … compensates you for a great deal."

An Idea for your Holiday - BELGIUM.

BRUSSELS. The Grande Place. By Leonard Richmond, R.O.I.
Travel via DOVER–OSTEND or DOVER–CALAIS.
Details from Continental Enquiry Office Victoria Station, London, S.W.

Class differences and modernization

British society was, of course, deeply divided by class and income. Men signing on the dole (unemployment), children with rickets, people on welfare harassed by "means-test" snoopers enquiring into the details of their life, and families crowded into insalubrious slums were a world away from the middle-class life of suburban houses and commuting by electric train. Yet many advances of the 1920s and 1930s were widely shared. Housing improved

Foreign travel
While working-class people took paid vacations at British seaside resorts, a growing number of more affluent people could now afford to travel abroad.

for some poorer people with slum clearance plans and new government home building. The national grid spread electricity supply across the country.

The radio, a state monopoly run by the BBC from 1922, provided home entertainment. About 10 million newspapers were sold daily. Movie-going was near universal, with the northern town of Bolton boasting 14 cinemas for its population of 260,000. The making of cheap, stylish clothing and cosmetics marketed through chain stores such as Marks & Spencer and Woolworths helped banish archaic items such as clogs and shawls. Young people strutted their finery to big band music at dance halls on Saturday nights.

Spectator sports attracted huge crowds. Wembley Stadium was first used as a venue for soccer's FA Cup

The job hunt
Desperate men scrutinizing job advertisements were a familiar sight in northern industrial towns, but less so in prosperous southern England and the Midlands.

750,000 more women in employment than 20 years earlier. Many refused to go into domestic service, instead working in offices and light industry. The middle classes had difficulty finding servants, and the shortage was permanent. Many middle-class women were forced to do housework, their chores mitigated by labor-saving devices, such as electric vacuum cleaners and electric irons. Bearing fewer children than previous generations, they enjoyed better health. Women also had more freedom to develop relations with the opposite sex, while the introduction of disposable menstrual pads contributed to their comfort. Marie Stopes's popular books, especially *Married Love*, published in 1918, encouraged marriage in which a man was attentive to a woman's sexual needs. They were indicative of changing attitudes. Society still had no doubt that a woman's true place was as a wife and mother, but there were now exceptions.

For the lower middle classes and more prosperous working class, it could be a good time to live. A £25 deposit and easy credit from a building society could buy a

new house. Unemployment and poverty marked the era, but suburban streets, family cars, and affordable consumer goods showed the way of the future.

> " Fish and chips … the movies, the radio, strong tea, and the Football Pools have **between them averted revolution**."

GEORGE ORWELL, *THE ROAD TO WIGAN PIER*, 1937

DIXIE DEAN

final in 1923, its capacity of 127,000 swamped by the number of fans clambering to see the game. Active participation in sports flourished. Open-air pools were built for swimming in many towns, and hiking across the countryside became popular. Only the better-off could afford a car, but British factories were building 300,000 a year, and by 1939 there were about 2 million private cars in Britain.

Women empowered

The position of women—granted the vote on an equal basis with men in 1928—changed as well. They lost many of the work opportunities that had opened up for them during the war, but in 1931 there were almost

Sporting heroes
Everton and England soccer star Dixie Dean was one of many sports celebrities of the era. Yet the high status of sports heroes was not matched by their pay, which remained that of a skilled factory worker.

AFTER »

Many social trends of the 1920s and 1930s continued through World War II and reached their apogee in the post-1945 period.

SPENDING MORE
Working-class **incomes rose** in the late 1930s. This was magnified during World War II, so real wages in 1945 were 20 percent higher than in 1938. **Mass entertainment** peaked in the late 1940s, while increasing **car sales**, delayed by gas rationing during the war, resumed in the 1950s. **Home ownership** became more and more prominent in the 1960s 370–371 ».

THE FEMALE WORKFORCE
The slow growth in **female employment** during the 1920s and 1930s gathered pace in the 1940s. By 1951, there were almost 7 million women in employment compared with 5.5 million in 1911. The high number of **women going out to work** became a feature that distinguished Britain from continental Europe.

INNOVATION
SUPERMARINE SEAPLANE

Britain's aircraft industry was one of the success stories of the inter-war years. The streamlined Supermarine seaplanes, designed by Reginald Mitchell, were built to compete in the prestigious Schneider Trophy, an international speed trial, which attracted large crowds in the 1920s. In 1931, Britain was given the trophy to keep after Supermarine won its third consecutive contest. It was the first aircraft to fly at more than 400 mph (650 kph). Mitchell went on to design the Supermarine Spitfire, one of the most successful of the World War II monoplane fighter aircraft.

2 FOOD PROCESSOR

3 ELECTRIC STOVE

4 TELEPHONE

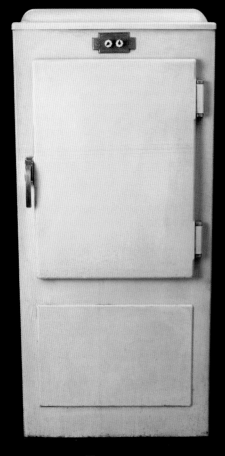
1 REFRIGERATOR

5 DRY SHAVER

6 ELECTRIC TOASTER

Domestic Appliances

Appliances for household use grew in importance as domestic servants became less common. The arrival of plastics and of electricity in the home in the 1930s opened the way for a boom in the sale of consumer durables of all kinds.

1 Refrigerator marketed by the Thomson-Houston company in the 1930s; a time when few British homes had fridges. **2 Food processor**, the first made by Kenwood, dating from 1948. It was a chunky appliance made mostly of metal. **3 Electric stove** from 1900 with resistance wires that heated up iron plates. **4 Telephone** from the 1930s with a cradle design and rotary dial. A classic style of the period, almost invariably made in standard black. **5 Dry shaver** marketed in the 1950s as a contrast to the traditional "wet" shaving, requiring hot water and foam. **6 Electric toaster** in chrome from the early 1950s. A drop side allowed for inserting and removing the bread, a design that was soon superseded by the pop-up toaster. **7 Cona coffee maker**, first made in 1910, and designed to make the "perfect" coffee. Its glass structure allowed infusion to take place at the correct temperature. This model dates from the 1950s. **8 Star vacuum cleaner** from around 1920—a hand-pumped machine for use in pre-electric households. **9 Kettle and urn** with a handle and feet of Bakelite, one of the first plastics, valued for its heat-resistant properties. **10 Electric heater** dating from

1913. **11 Television,** known as a "televisor" and invented by John Logie Baird in 1926. It showed a "visual wireless" image in black-and-white on its small screen from the beginning of the television age. **12 Can opener**, bulls-head style, made in the 1920s. This style was first developed in the mid-19th century. **13 Electric hair drier** dating to the 1920s; this model has a wooden handle. **14 Goblin teasmaid** dating from the 1950s. This machine was designed to wake a sleeper with a fresh cup of tea automatically prepared—as its name suggests—performing the function of the live-in maid that many could no longer afford to employ. **15 Gramophone** of a wind-up portable variety that was widely used through both world wars. **16 Electric kettle**, made of stainless steel with a Bakelite handle and whistling spout. **17 Cabinet wireless radio** by the British electronics company Ekco, dating from 1932. This boldly modernist style was made out of Bakelite. **18 Washing machine**—the English Electric Liberator was an expensive front-loader washing machine introduced in the 1940s; it was designed to "liberate" the housewife from one of the heaviest household chores.

8 STAR VACUUM CLEANER

7 CONA COFFEE MAKER

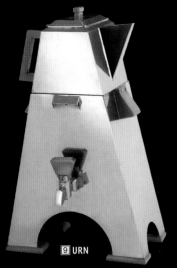

9 URN

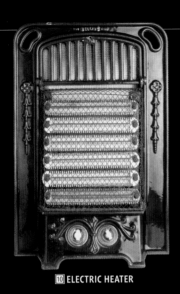

10 ELECTRIC HEATER

11 TELEVISION

12 CAN OPENER

13 HAIR DRIER

14 GOBLIN TEASMAID

15 GRAMOPHONE

16 ELECTRIC KETTLE

17 CABINET WIRELESS RADIO

18 WASHING MACHINE

341

About 230,000 troops from the British Empire died fighting for Britain in World War I. This sacrifice had a decisive impact on relations between Britain and the dominions and India.

GROWING INDEPENDENCE

The British government tried to use the war to **strengthen ties** between the white dominions and the home country. In 1917, the prime ministers of Australia, Canada, South Africa, and New Zealand were invited to London to serve in an **Imperial War Cabinet**. However, pride in their role in the war made the **dominions more assertive** of their independence after 1918 than they had been before. India, who **suffered heavier losses** in the war than any dominion, was promised in 1917 that it would be rewarded with "responsible government"—that is, **very limited self-rule**—within the British Empire.

Imperial Issues

In the 1920s and 1930s, the British Empire reached its greatest extent, expanded after World War I by German colonies in Africa and part of the former Ottoman Empire. Yet Britain ruled with declining confidence, its authority challenged in particular by a vigorous independence movement in India.

Gandhi in London
Indian Congress leader Mohandas Gandhi visits London for a Round Table Conference in 1931. Gandhi's rejection of western dress codes was a calculated political gesture.

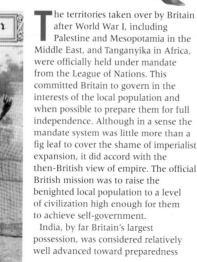

England cricketer Harold Larwood
Larwood was part of a diplomatic incident in 1932–1933, when his "bodyline" bowling, directed by his team captain, Douglas Jardine, was objected to by Australia.

The territories taken over by Britain after World War I, including Palestine and Mesopotamia in the Middle East, and Tanganyika in Africa, were officially held under mandate from the League of Nations. This committed Britain to govern in the interests of the local population and when possible to prepare them for full independence. Although in a sense the mandate system was little more than a fig leaf to cover the shame of imperialist expansion, it did accord with the then-British view of empire. The official British mission was to raise the benighted local population to a level of civilization high enough for them to achieve self-government.

India, by far Britain's largest possession, was considered relatively well advanced toward preparedness for limited self-government under a British-educated elite. Instead of benignly conducting a slow, peaceful progress toward a degree of self-rule, however, Britain found itself faced with a clamorous independence movement that provoked confrontation and fed off the repressive measures taken by the authorities in response. At Amritsar in April 1919, troops commanded by General Reginald Dyer fired on Indian demonstrators, causing heavy loss of life. It triggered widespread protests against British rule, during which Mohandas Gandhi, a master of political propaganda, emerged as the leader of the main independence movement, the Indian National Congress. In 1929, Britain undertook to make India a

458 MILLION
The population of the British Empire in 1922—about a quarter of the total world population at the time. Its land area was 13 million sq miles (34 million sq km).

self-governing dominion at some time in the future, but this only redoubled Congress pressure for immediate independence. Gandhi led a famous march to the sea in spring 1930, to challenge a British tax on salt. When he visited Britain for a Round Table Conference on India's future in 1931, he was given a hero's welcome by some British workers, and denounced by arch imperialist Winston Churchill as "a seditious middle temple lawyer, now posing as a fakir …." Despite Churchill's opposition, and the noncooperation of Congress, a Government of India Act was passed by the Westminster Parliament in 1935, giving India some self-government. The Act kept Britain's viceroy in control, however, and was a compromise, which settled nothing and satisfied no one.

At the heart of the question was race: Britain recognized the right of white people to self-determination, but was reluctant to extend that right to non-whites. In 1926, Britain formally recognized the independence that the white dominions had long exercised in practice. Britain and its dominions were now "equal in status, in no way subordinate to one another … freely associated as members of the British Commonwealth of Nations." This was embodied as the 1931 Statute of Westminster. The dominions were thus distinguished from colonies in the West Indies, southeast Asia, and Africa, although where there were substantial white populations—in Southern Rhodesia (now Zimbabwe) and Kenya—colonies were accorded a degree of self-government.

A new closeness

Formally, the Commonwealth of Nations was linked by allegiance to the monarchy. Serious efforts were also made to nourish sentimental, cultural, and practical bonds between the Commonwealth's equal and independent members, as well as between Britain and its colonies. As commercial aviation developed, the routes of Britain's Imperial Airways were consciously planned with this in mind; traveling by luxury flying-boat from London to Cape Town or Sydney via Kenya or India in the late 1930s, showed the global reach of empire. Sports had an essential part to play in imperial bonding. The first Empire Games were held in 1930, as legal ties between the dominions were loosening. Cricket was seen as embodying important British values. Australia and South Africa had played against England since the 19th century, but in the inter-war years this was extended to the West Indies, India, and New Zealand. However, the most important links were economic. The Depression struck the Commonwealth and colonies hard, chiefly through the sharp fall in prices of the primary products they exported. A British Empire Economic

Imperial airways
A poster advertises passenger flights to Europe, Africa, India, and the Far East. Imperial Airways extended its air routes across the globe, to countries under British influence.

> ## "We are **engaged** in an entirely new experiment in the world's history and empire building."

LORD BALFOUR, SPEECH IN PARLIAMENT, NOVEMBER 24, 1925

EMPIRE EXHIBITION IN WEMBLEY

The British Empire Exhibition, held at Wembley, London, in 1924–1925, was a large-scale celebration of Britain's imperial past and present. It was opened in April 1924 by King George V, who gave the first royal broadcast, his speech relayed by radio. Attended by more than 27 million visitors, the exhibition was a striking success. Its attractions included a model of the Prince of Wales made from Canadian butter, and reenactments of World War I battles. The exhibition was a conscious attempt to revive imperial sentiment, and its great popularity suggested that the British remained very much attached to the idea of having a huge empire spread throughout the world.

Arab protests

British authorities attempt to control a rioting Arab crowd in Palestine in November 1933, during protests against Jewish immigration. Opposed by both Arabs and Jews, the British found the Palestinian problem intractable.

Conference at Ottawa in 1932 instituted "imperial preference", which encouraged trade within the Empire while erecting a tariff barrier against trade with the rest of the world. By the late 1930s, Britain was the destination of more than half of Australia's exports and of more than four-fifths of New Zealand's.

Imperial bonding was by no means a total success. The economic downturn stimulated discontent with colonial rule in the West Indies and in Britain's West African colonies. Canada was being drawn into the economic and cultural orbit of the United States—it was the only dominion that did not join a British-led Sterling zone in the 1930s. South Africa's Boers—the majority of the dominion's whites—remained of doubtful allegiance. Perhaps most significant, if apparently trivial, was the furore caused by the England cricket team's tour of Australia in 1932–1933. The English adopted "bodyline" bowling tactics to counter the Australian batting hero Don Bradman. Seen as dangerous and unfair, it led to both informal popular and formal diplomatic protests in Australia. The message was that both the governments and the people of the dominions were ready to assert their independence against the British.

Middle East problems

The extension of British imperial interests in the Middle East after the collapse of the Ottoman Empire in 1918 brought complex problems. Out of its League of Nations mandated territories, Britain crafted the new states of Iraq and Jordan, soon given nominal independence under pro-British Arab rulers—similar to the independence granted to Egypt in 1922, which did not preclude the maintenance of British troops there. In Palestine, however, no such arrangement could be made. By the Balfour Declaration of 1917, Britain committed itself to "the establishment in Palestine of a national home for the Jewish people." After World War I, Jewish immigration increased, and so did tension with the Arab population. The British authorities were caught in a trap. Their efforts to limit Jewish immigration earned them the hostility of the Jews, while their failure to end Jewish immigration roused the wrath of the Arabs. From 1936, the British faced a full-scale Arab revolt that was repressed by armed force. A British proposal for the partition of Palestine between Arab and Jewish states was rejected by both sides. The issue remained unresolved.

AFTER

Five million soldiers from the dominions and colonies fought with British troops in World War II. It confirmed the Empire's importance, but also advanced its downfall.

END OF EMPIRE APPROACHING

In 1939, Australia and New Zealand joined Britain at war **without hesitation**, quickly followed by Canada. In South Africa, a neutralist prime minister was ousted by the pro-British veteran Jan Smuts. South Africa **remained divided**, the Afrikaner Nationalist Party supporting Hitler. Despite talk of self-government, India was brought into the war by the viceroy **without consultation** with Indian political leaders.

Britain's **early defeats in the war**, and especially the loss of Singapore to the Japanese in February 1942, **undermined its status** as an imperial power, as did the attitude of Britain's ally, the United States. The **Atlantic Charter**, an Anglo-American statement of war aims, declared "the **right of all people** to choose the form of government under which they live." Britain's Prime Minister **Winston Churchill** remained a **convinced imperialist**, announcing he did not intend "to preside over the dissolution of the British Empire," but by 1945, pressure for an **end to colonialism** was mounting **364–365 ≫**.

Edward, Prince of Wales
As heir to the throne, the future Edward VIII was a glamorous figure, at least by the standards of British royalty, and the formal pose shown here contrasted to the informality he would bring to the role of king.

The **Abdication** of **Edward VIII**

In December 1936, Britain was threatened with a constitutional crisis when the young King Edward VIII declared his intention of marrying twice-divorced American Wallis Simpson. The government considered the King's choice of consort unacceptable. The issue was resolved when Edward abdicated, choosing love and exile over duty and the throne.

BEFORE

King George V died on January 20, 1936. His eldest son was to be crowned Edward VIII on May 12, 1937, but it never happened.

THE PRINCE

George V's reign had been one of **moral conservatism** in private life, and a rigid adherence to the principles of **constitutional monarchy** in the execution of public duties. Edward had shown while Prince of Wales that he was **unlikely to be so restrained** in either sphere. He had on occasion commented publicly on political issues, such as unemployment.

CORONATION CUP

A "FAST" SOCIAL SET

Considered handsome and, at 41 years old, still **relatively young at his accession**, Edward was used to mixing with a "fast" social set, where such modern trends as cocktails and jazz were enjoyed, and **extra-marital affairs were normal**. This was ultimately to be his undoing.

American divorcée
Born Bessie Wallis Warfield, Wallis Simpson was a well-off socialite from Pennsylvania, who had been divorced twice. In 1930s Britain, few people considered divorce morally or socially acceptable.

At his accession Edward VIII was a popular King. He brought a fresh breath of modernity, glamour, and relative youth to the stuffy image of the British monarchy. However, the Conservative Prime Minister Stanley Baldwin and other key Establishment figures, such as the Archbishop of Canterbury, Cosmo Lang, disapproved of him. The British press shielded the public from knowledge of the Prince of Wales's private life, but insiders knew that Edward—like his grandfather Edward VII—did not conform to contemporary standards of rectitude in sexual morality. Baldwin was also troubled by the fear that the new King, who had loose sympathies with Nazi

British Establishment, however, the idea of an American divorcée as queen was unthinkable. Baldwin won backing from his own government and party, as well as from the opposition and heads of Britain's Dominions, for an absolute rejection of the King's planned marriage. A proposal for a morganatic union—with Simpson the King's wife, but not his queen—was equally unacceptable. Edward was told to choose between marriage to Simpson and the throne.

The storm breaks

Early in December, the British press at last broke its self-imposed silence and the issue exploded into the headlines. There was much popular sympathy for the king, but politically he won the support only of extremists and eccentrics,

" I **renounce** the throne for myself and my **descendants**."

KING EDWARD'S MESSAGE ANNOUNCING HIS ABDICATION, 1936

Germany and Oswald Mosley's Fascist BUF, would refuse to be governed by his ministers on political issues.

A marriage crisis

A far greater storm than Edward's political views was brewing from a quite different direction. On November 16, Edward informed Baldwin that he was determined to marry Mrs. Wallis Simpson, who was already in her second marriage.

From 1934, she was his constant companion, a fact widely reported in the American and other foreign press, but ignored by British newspapers, partly because they respected the privacy of the royal family, and partly because the major press barons, Lords Rothermere and Beaverbrook, were well disposed toward Edward.

So the crisis was at first played out entirely behind closed doors. Simpson had been granted a decree nisi at a divorce court in Ipswich on October 27, so there was no legal obstacle to her eventually marrying Edward. To the

Duchess memorabilia
Since the Duchess of Windsor's death in 1986, many of her possessions have been sold at auction, including the handbag and gloves shown here.

including the Communist Party, Mosley's BUF, and the maverick Conservative backbencher Winston Churchill.

Ignoring pleas from Simpson, who had fled abroad, that he should abandon her and keep the throne, on December 10 Edward abdicated. The abdication was confirmed by Act of Parliament the following day. Edward's brother Albert, Duke of York, became King George VI. In a dignified, moving radio broadcast that evening, Edward, now Duke of Windsor, said: "I have found it impossible to carry the heavy burden of responsibility and to discharge my duties as King as I would wish to do without the help and support of the woman I love." That night he sailed from Portsmouth into exile.

The British people, whatever diverse opinions they held in private, docilely accepted this reassertion of the values of the British Establishment. The shy and stuttering George VI inherited the coronation arranged for Edward.

The abdication document
The Instrument of Abdication was signed by Edward and witnessed by his three brothers at Fort Belvedere in Windsor Great Park on December 10, 1936.

AFTER

Edward's reign lasted 327 days. His subsequent life as Duke of Windsor lasted 35 years, during which he made only rare and fleeting visits to Britain.

DUKE AND DUCHESS

On June 3, 1937, the **Duke of Windsor married** Wallis Simpson at the Château de Condé, in France. No member of the British Royal

CHÂTEAU DE CONDÉ

Family attended. Wallis Simpson became Duchess of Windsor, but George VI would **not accord her the right** to be styled "Her Royal Highness."

GOVERNOR OF THE BAHAMAS

Edward made no secret of his **admiration for Nazi Germany**. In World War II **348–349 ≫**, he was made Governor of the Bahamas to remove him from possible **contact with Germans**, who saw him as a future king of a fascist Britain.

BEFORE

After World War I, Britain felt secure and took part in international efforts to promote disarmament and find peaceful methods of resolving disputes.

SEARCH FOR PEACE
Britain was a founding member of the **League of Nations** **‹‹ 330–331**, which undertook to deter any act of aggression by collective action. This, and the **absence of any powerful enemies**, enabled Britain to slash defense spending to 2.5 percent of national income. In 1928, Britain signed the Kellogg-Briand Pact, **renouncing war** "as an instrument of national policy."

COUNCIL OF THE LEAGUE OF NATIONS

Digging air-raid trenches
Children at Harrow, near London, prepare primitive air-raid shelters in their school playground during the Munich Crisis of September 1938.

Slide to War

The rise of Adolf Hitler's aggressive Nazi regime in Germany from 1933 posed a challenge that the British did not want to face. Seeking peace at almost any price, Neville Chamberlain's government followed a policy of appeasement, which at least bought the country time to rearm. In the end, Hitler's actions made it impossible for Britain to avoid war.

On January 30, 1933, Adolf Hitler became Chancellor of Germany, determined to overthrow the 1919 Versailles Treaty (see p.331) and restore Germany as a great power. Ten days later, Oxford Union students voted that they would "in no circumstances fight for [their] King and Country." The unpatriotic vote led to outrage in much of the British press, but it reflected a widespread anti-war sentiment—a heartfelt desire to avoid a repetition of the slaughter of World War I.

Britain's response to Hitler's insistent provocation was inhibited from the outset by the belief that Germany had a genuine grievance over the Versailles Treaty. It was also confused by the Conservative Party's perception of the Nazis as a useful barrier to the spread of Soviet communism. The Labour Party and the trade union movement were also implicated in the failure to stand up to Hitler, opposing British rearmament until the late 1930s.

Public opinion in Britain would never have supported military action to uphold the Versailles Treaty in 1935–1936, when Hitler openly embarked on rapid rearmament and sent troops into the demilitarized Rhineland. The League of Nations proved incapable of decisive action against Japanese aggression in

Manchuria in 1931, and the Italian invasion of Ethiopia in 1935. By the second half of the 1930s, the idea of collective security through the League was dead. Traditional balance of power diplomacy stumbled amid European ideological divides between dictatorships and democracies, fascists and communists. Britain tried to make an ally of Italy, but fascist dictator Benito Mussolini found Hitler more accepting of Italy's aggressive ambitions. Soviet Russia, an obvious potential ally against Germany, was shunned because of British dislike of Stalin's communist regime. The same ideological complications paralyzed the British government response to the Spanish Civil War of 1936–1939. While Germany and Italy intervened militarily on behalf of Francisco Franco's right-wing nationalists, Britain's only involvement came from

Vital war material
Britain raced to produce shells and other munitions as war approached. Defense budgets more than tripled 1935–1939.

individuals joining the communist-organized International Brigades.

Appeasement
By the time Neville Chamberlain took over from Stanley Baldwin as Prime Minister in 1937, Conservative backbencher Winston Churchill's warnings against giving in to German aggression were sounding uncomfortably convincing. Chamberlain believed that Britain lacked the military strength to stand up to the Germans. He accelerated the rearmament program that Baldwin had tentatively begun two years earlier, while simultaneously pursuing appeasement—the satisfaction of Germany's "legitimate claims." After absorbing Austria in the "Anschluss" of March 1938, Hitler turned his attention to Czechoslovakia, which had a German minority in its Sudetenland region. Faced with a possible German attack on the Czechs, in September 1938, Chamberlain embarked on a diplomatic initiative, flying

twice to meet Hitler in Germany. However, each concession made was followed by Hitler raising the stakes. War looked inevitable, but at the last hour, an agreement reached at Munich saw the Sudetenland region detached from Czechoslovakia, and Chamberlain returned home to triumphantly announce "peace for our time."

Euphoria was short-lived, however, and a sense of having given in to aggression through fear was confirmed in March 1939 when Hitler sent troops into the Czech capital, Prague—to which he had no "legitimate claim."

Invasion news
London's *Evening Standard* announces the German invasion of Poland, and Britain's subsequent mobilization, on September 1, 1939. Britain declared war on Germany two days later.

Britain responded by guaranteeing to defend a number of countries, including Poland, against German aggression, and by seeking a military accord with Soviet Russia. They were preempted by the Nazis, who concluded their own pact with Stalin in August, clearing the way for a German attack on Poland on September 1.

Munich Pact
Returning from the Munich Conference to cheering crowds on September 30, 1938, Prime Minister Neville Chamberlain waves a paper bearing Hitler's signature and his own. He later declared he had returned from Germany "bringing peace with honor," but Winston Churchill called the agreement a disaster.

Evening Standard

GERMANS INVADE AND BOMB POLAND BRITAIN MOBILISES
Warsaw, Cracow, Nine Other Towns Bombed: Danzig is "Annexed"

600,000 An estimate of the number of civilian deaths expected through German bombing in the first two months of fighting. The actual civilian death toll was 60,000 in more than five years of war.

Because of Britain's commitment to defend Poland, on September 3, 1939, Chamberlain grimly informed the British people that they were "at war with Germany."

FIRST DAYS OF WAR
The war had been long expected. The authorities were prepared for the immediate **bombing of British cities**, and assumed there would be mass casualties. On September 1, two days before the declaration of war, the **evacuation of cities** began and a **blackout was enforced**. Some 1.5 million Anderson air-raid shelters had already been distributed for people to erect in their yards, but the **bombing did not happen immediately**. In September 1939, most casualties were caused by **road accidents in the blackout**. Conscription was already in place when the war began, but Britain did not have any plans for giving military assistance to Poland, which was **left to fight alone**.

BRITISH PRIME MINISTER Born 1874 Died 1965

Winston **Churchill**

"In war, **resolution**;
in defeat, **defiance**;
in victory, **magnanimity**;
in peace, **goodwill**."

WINSTON CHURCHILL, *THE SECOND WORLD WAR*, 1948–1953

Winston Leonard Spencer Churchill was born into an aristocratic family and grew up in a late-Victorian Britain that saw imperialism in full flood. His father was a senior Conservative politician, and his beautiful mother an American heiress. As a young cavalry officer and war correspondent, Winston Churchill developed a love of empire and a delight in warfare. After seeing military service in British India, he took part in the Battle of Omdurman in 1898 in the Sudan, where the Mahdists were slaughtered by British firepower, and in 1900 witnessed the British military disaster at Spion Kop, during the Boer War. A gifted writer and natural self-publicist, he wrote articles and books that showcased his experiences, describing his participation in a cavalry charge at Omdurman or his escape from a Boer prisoner of war camp in the style of boys' adventure stories. By the time he entered Parliament as a Conservative MP in 1900, following in his father's footsteps, he was already a recognized public personality. Too restless and ambitious to settle comfortably in the Tory ranks, in 1904 he "ratted" to join the Liberal Party, whose interest in radical reform offered more scope for dramatic action. Along with David Lloyd George, he made himself the most newsworthy

The British bulldog
This American poster dating from 1942 shows Prime Minister Winston Churchill as a bulldog. It was a familiar image for a British wartime leader determined to defend the nation he loved.

minister in the pre-World War I Liberal administration. Home Secretary in 1910, at the age of 35, he found plenty of outlet for his bellicosity in confrontations with striking trade unionists, pro-Union Ulster Protestants, and militant suffragettes intent on votes for women. As First Lord of the Admiralty from October 1911, he drove forward the "naval race" with Germany. Embracing technological innovation, he gave the Royal Navy oil-fired battleships with 15-in (38-cm) guns, and created the Royal Naval Air Service to exploit the potential of aircraft—just as he would later promote the development of the first tanks for the army.

The Great War
As war with Germany approached in the summer of 1914, Churchill described his emotional state as "interested, geared up, and happy." Yet the first year of the war proved a personal disaster. The Royal Navy failed to live up to the British public's expectations. Churchill's fascination with imaginative schemes led him to back the disastrous Gallipoli campaign against Germany's Ottoman ally in 1915. When it failed, with huge British casualties, he was ejected from the

Master of war
Churchill is photographed in North Africa in 1944, a still vigorous leader approaching his 70th birthday. He was not a warmonger—he did his best to preserve peace—but it was his nature to be thrilled by armed conflict.

Welcome visit
Churchill visits bomb-damaged Bristol after a raid in April 1941. His walkabouts were designed to raise morale among the hard-pressed British. Despite some skepticism, his presence seems to have been genuinely welcomed by the majority.

TIMELINE

November 30, 1874
Churchill is born at Blenheim Palace, Oxfordshire, son of Lord Randolph Churchill and Jennie Jerome. He is educated at Harrow (1888–1893) and the Royal Military College, Sandhurst (1893–1894).

1895–1900 Cavalry officer and war reporter in Cuba, India, Sudan, and South Africa.

YOUNG CHURCHILL

October 1900 Elected Unionist (Conservative) MP for Oldham. Crosses the floor of the House of Commons in 1904 to join the Liberal Party.

1908 Enters Cabinet in the Liberal government of Herbert Asquith; marries Clementine Hozier.

1911 Appointed First Lord of the Admiralty; holds post as Britain enters World War I in 1914.

May 1915 Ousted from Admiralty after failed Gallipoli landings. Serves on Western Front from November 1915 to March 1916. Becomes Minister of Munitions in July 1917.

1919–1922 Secretary of State for War and the Colonies. Loses seat in 1922 general election.

October 1924 MP for Epping. Rejoins the Conservative Party and becomes Chancellor of the Exchequer to June 1929.

1929–1939 Out-of-office backbencher. Critical of Conservative policy on India and appeasement.

September 1939 Outbreak of World War II. He is again appointed First Lord of the Admiralty.

May 1940 Churchill replaces Chamberlain as Prime Minister, leading a broad coalition government through World War II.

July 1945 Defeated in general election, but remains leader of the Conservative Party.

October 1951 Wins general election and resumes as Prime Minister, serving to April 1955.

January 24, 1965 Churchill dies in London. He is accorded a state funeral on January 30.

Admiralty. Shocked and humiliated, Churchill struggled to achieve political rehabilitation. By July 1917, after a spell in the army at the front line in France, he was back in the Cabinet, now led by Prime Minister Lloyd George, but although he continued to hold high office into the post-war period, his reputation had taken a hard knock. His talents and energy were admired, but he was widely distrusted, even by his own party members, as an irresponsible adventurer.

Wilderness years
Churchill "re-ratted" to join the Conservative Party in 1924. In the unlikely role of Chancellor of the Exchequer, he was responsible for Britain's disastrous return to the Gold Standard in 1925—a decision based on the advice of financial experts that was designed to return stability to a jittery post-war international financial system. When Wall Street crashed and the world economy nosedived in 1929, Churchill was among the victims, losing

> " … what is **our aim**? I can answer in one word: Victory. **Victory** at all costs …"
>
> **WINSTON CHURCHILL**, MAY 13, 1940

much of his personal wealth. Relegated to the backbenches, in the 1930s, his career was saved by the rise in Germany of Adolf Hitler and the Nazi Party. Churchill's ominous warnings of the growing German threat, advocacy of British rearmament, and opposition to the appeasement of Hitler looked increasingly prescient as the European situation worsened. It was inevitable that he should be asked to join the government by Prime Minister Neville Chamberlain when war broke out again in September 1939.

War leader
Churchill's rise to Prime Minister in May 1940 was paradoxical. He had been more responsible than anyone else for the fiasco of the Norwegian campaign that had brought down the Chamberlain government. Yet his warlike spirit and his sheer desire for the job made him the natural choice to lead the country in its greatest crisis. He told the British people "we shall never surrender," and convinced them that he meant it. His old-fashioned, high-flown speeches, broadcast on radio, touched a chord with their stirring, if daunting, promise of "blood, toil, tears, and sweat." The impact on the nation's morale was immediate. Less successful was Churchill's impact on military operations. He wanted to run the war himself, overriding the military professionals, but had lost none of his

Presidential gift
This medallion was presented to Churchill in 1955 by US President Dwight Eisenhower. Churchill always stressed the bond between the two "English-speaking peoples."

propensity for ill-judged offensives. His work rate was phenomenal for a man beyond retirement age. He flew around the world to Allied summits, from Tehran and Yalta to Casablanca and Quebec. His total commitment to defeating Hitler made him a loyal ally of Joseph Stalin, despite his hatred of Soviet communism, and he assiduously courted President Roosevelt, both before and after America's entry into the war in December 1941. In the long run, he was ill-rewarded for his pains, as both Roosevelt and Stalin intended to end the British Empire that Churchill loved, and British influence was increasingly sidelined.

Post-war years
After the heroic days of 1940, Churchill's hold on the British public waned. He could not identify himself with the popular desire for social change. His defeat in the 1945 general election was not a judgment upon his war leadership, but on the policies he was expected to follow in peace. In 1946, he alerted the Americans to the danger of Soviet expansion in his "Iron Curtain" speech at Fulton, Missouri. Publication of his war memoirs won him the Nobel Prize for Literature. His second spell as Prime Minister from 1951 was marred by his worsening health, and his reluctant resignation in 1955 was a relief to his colleagues (he stayed an MP until 1964). But his place in British hearts was never lost, and his state funeral in 1965 was an occasion of deep-felt national mourning.

FUNERAL CORTEGE OF WINSTON CHURCHILL

Life during the Blitz
A milkman carries out his duties the morning after a German bombing raid over London during the winter of 1940–1941. This period of intense bombing, which became known as the Blitz, was devastating, but most were determined to remain defiant in the face of the enemy.

Life in Wartime Britain

The authorities in Britain recognized that the war for national survival could not be won without enlisting the support of the whole population. Civilians in Britain's cities and factories were in the front line of the war against Hitler.

The British entered World War II without enthusiasm, but with a better understanding of the demands of total war than in 1914. They accepted conscription with barely a murmur of dissent, and the government introduced rationing when it discovered that the public favored it. The distribution of gas masks, the imposition of blackouts, and the mass evacuation of children from cities reflected expectations of immediate aerial bombardment. The evacuation of children from urban slums to rural England, where there was less risk of air raids, was a shock for everyone—some of the children had never seen a cow, while many people who housed them had never seen children who slept without pyjamas. The experience is credited with making the British middle class more aware of the realities of urban poverty.

Preparing for war

The war did not take on urgency and drama until spring 1940. After the establishment of a coalition government under Winston Churchill in May and the fall of France in June, a sense of social solidarity and common endeavor was forged. This was not only exaggerated by official propaganda, but also truly felt by a population with its back

79 London Underground stations acted as bomb shelters during the Blitz. Some 177,000 people were sleeping in them every night at the height of the bombing.

to the wall. More than a million men, most too old for the army, enrolled in the Home Guard militia in summer 1940 and prepared to fight until death if the Germans invaded. When the Blitz, the long-awaited German bombing of towns and cities began in September, civilian morale held up far better than the authorities had expected. Of course, bombed civilians were terrified. In London, many took refuge in Underground stations or in

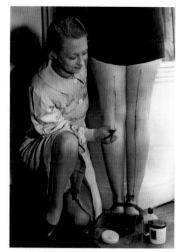

Missing luxuries
Some women painted seams on their legs to create the illusion of stockings—the kind of luxury goods almost unobtainable under austerity regulations.

« BEFORE

World War II brought a vast extension of the powers of the British state over its citizens. From the outset, some basic liberties were suspended.

THE PRICE OF WAR
The **Emergency Powers Act** authorized the government to make regulations that it thought necessary for the defense of the country, or for the prosecution of the war. In October 1939, a **National Register** of British citizens was compiled and **identity cards** were issued.

INTERNMENT OF ENEMY ALIENS
At first, **German nationals** in Britain were **assessed by tribunals** and those identified as pro-Nazi were interned. In 1940, almost all enemy aliens were interned. About 1,500 **British Fascists were imprisoned** without trial, including their leader Sir Oswald Mosley.

Bomb shelter
Anderson shelters were structures of corrugated steel that people erected in their backyards. Half-buried and covered with a layer of earth, they offered good protection for a family. More than 3 million shelters were distributed by the government.

INTERNMENT CAMP AT LIVERPOOL

"This war, whether those at present in authority like it or not, has to be **fought as a citizens' war**."

J.B. PRIESTLEY, *OUT OF THE PEOPLE*, 1941

communal shelters, although more remained in their home. In smaller cities people decamped to the countryside. There were instances of breakdown of order—looting of bomb-damaged buildings and theft of valuables from the dead. These acts were wholly outweighed by the everyday heroism of air-raid wardens, firefighters, medical personnel, police, and ordinary citizens, who carried on with their daily lives amid the devastation. By the end of the second year of the war, more British civilians had been killed by enemy action than British servicemen. Yet popular support for the war effort remained intact—members of the government or the royal family were able to visit recently bombed streets with minimal security and with the expectation of a warm response.

Consensus and sacrifice

The high level of consensus in support of the war allowed the state to exercise control over people's lives without being seen as oppressive. Aware that the battle for production was as important as the clash of armies, the government in effect extended conscription to civilian life. The Ministry of Labour, under leading trade unionist Ernest Bevin, was vested with the power to direct "any person in the United Kingdom to perform any service required in any place." The blurring of the distinction between military and industrial service was exemplified by the Bevin Boys, young conscripts chosen by lot in 1944 to work in understaffed coal mines instead of battlefronts. Even more than in World War I, women were called upon to carry out jobs traditionally occupied by men. The conscription of women, first introduced in December 1941, was the subject of much soul-searching for the government, but readily accepted by the population at large. Productivity rose steeply, not only in factories but also in

agriculture, where fertilizers and tractors pushed up yields. There was little trade union resistance to the direction of labor or measures taken to increase output, partly because industrial wages rose by around 10 percent above inflation through the war. The middle classes by contrast did badly, hard hit when the standard rate of income tax was raised to 50 percent in 1941.

8 MILLION The number of women in work by 1943. Around 2 million women were employed in arms factories and 500,000 in noncombat roles in the armed forces.

The involvement of the whole population in the war effort was one of the key purposes of government propaganda. Campaigns for people to hand in their unwanted aluminum pots and pans to be recycled as Spitfires, or to "Dig for Victory" by growing vegetables in their flower beds, were important not for their practical effect, but for the sense of participation they encouraged.

Rationing and austerity were the order of the day for the British people, but were made bearable by apparent equality of sacrifice. Government regulations set the size of the lapels on a jacket and the length of shirt-tails, the recipe for a loaf of bread, the style and wood content of furniture, the maximum price of a restaurant meal, and the size of a pencil. The state also provided people with cheap food in work canteens and national restaurants (communal kitchens), cod liver oil and free school meals for children, and useful advice on how to cook nutritious vegetables. Despite shortages, such as the lack of bananas, the British people, in general, ate more healthily during the war than before it.

The American influence

The later stages of the war were in many ways different from the heroic period of the invasion scare and the Blitz. The huge influx of foreign troops, primarily Americans, in 1943–1944, had a significant impact on British

Not these shells...

... but THESE

"STAY PUT" THIS SUMMER
In peace-time the Railways welcome holiday crowds. This summer holidays should be spent at home.
RAILWAY EXECUTIVE COMMITTEE

society. It opened up new perspectives for people, many of whom had rarely, if ever, met a foreigner before the war. American soldiers and airmen were only partly responsible for the extraordinary rise in the illegitimate birth rate, which tripled during the war. Nevertheless, the attraction that the proverbially "overpaid and oversexed" allies exercised upon British women was reflected in the 80,000 "GI brides," who eventually sailed

Stay-at-home vacations
A government poster tells people to vacation at home, to lessen pressure on the railroad system. This advice was rejected by the people, who continued leisure travel despite the cancellation of some train services.

to the United States. The subjection of the war-weary London population to attack by V-1 flying bombs and V-2 rockets in 1944 was psychologically harder to bear than the Blitz. By 1945, people were yearning not only for peace, but for a better future. There was a widespread desire that Britain should not go back to the way it had been before—that unemployment and poverty had to be left behind. This mood underlay the landslide Labour victory in the 1945 general election, contested while the country was still at war with Japan. It conveyed the sense that people deserved decent lives for patiently bearing the risks and sacrifices of the path to victory.

Child's gas mask
Gas masks were distributed not just to adults, but also children and babies. They weren't of much use, as neither side resorted to the use of chemical weapons.

AFTER

The foundations of a post-war welfare state were laid by Churchill's coalition government during the war, most famously through the conclusions of the 1942 Beveridge Report.

THE BEVERIDGE REPORT

In 1941, economist and social reformer Sir William Beveridge was appointed chairman of a government committee on social insurance. The report he published the following year was an instant best seller. It advocated **"cradle to grave" social security** to be funded by **national insurance**, with contributions from individual employers and the state. There was to be a national health service and an end to mass unemployment. The new plan would slay the hostile "giants on the road of reconstruction," which Beveridge capitalized as: Want, Disease, Ignorance, Squalor, and Idleness.

The Beveridge report was welcomed by Labour members of the governing coalition. In 1944, the government issued white papers

with proposals for a **national health service**, full employment, and social insurance **360–361 >>**. Meanwhile the President of the Board of Education, the Conservative politician, R.A.B. Butler, produced an Education Act that instituted **free, universal secondary schooling**.

WILLIAM BEVERIDGE

The Battle of Britain

In the summer of 1940, Royal Air Force (RAF) pilots in Hurricanes and Spitfires fought to deny the German Luftwaffe command of the skies over southern England. If the RAF had failed, Germany might have mounted a cross-Channel invasion of Britain, with the Royal Navy unable to intervene because of a lack of air cover.

On June 18, 1940, Prime Minister Winston Churchill told the House of Commons that "The Battle of France is over. The Battle of Britain is about to begin." However, his statement was premature.

The duel begins

Into mid-July, as preliminary skirmishes between the RAF and the Luftwaffe commenced over the English Channel, Adolf Hitler continued to hope that Britain would agree to a humiliating peace settlement with Germany. It was not until August 13 that the Germans launched a sustained campaign to destroy Britain's air defenses.

Fortunately for Britain, this was a battle the RAF had long prepared to fight. A system of radar stations linked to central control rooms allowed RAF fighters to scramble in time to intercept incoming German bombers and their Messerschmitt fighter escorts. Hugh Dowding, the head of RAF Fighter Command, cleverly conserved his forces, while the Luftwaffe wavered in its objectives, never sufficiently systematic in targeting radar stations, aircraft factories, or airfields.

The RAF also benefitted from an influx of pilots from the dominions and from across occupied Europe. This was essential, for although there were always sufficient aircraft, experienced pilots were particularly in short supply.

On September 7, with RAF Fighter Command hard pressed, the Luftwaffe switched from attacking airfields to the daylight mass bombing of London.

The battle climaxes

On September 15, now known as Battle of Britain Day, around 1,000 German aircraft attacked in two waves. The RAF responded in strength, claiming to shoot down 186 enemy aircraft on the day. Although this is now discounted as exaggerated, Britain's air defenses had not broken, and while daylight raids continued into October, any invasion plans were indefinitely postponed.

"Never in the field of human conflict was so much owed by so many to so few."

PRIME MINISTER WINSTON CHURCHILL, HOUSE OF COMMONS, AUGUST 20, 1940

Hurricanes in flight

RAF Hawker Hurricanes fly in tight formation in the skies over southern England in the summer of 1940. Although its role in the Battle of Britain is often overshadowed by that of the Supermarine Spitfire, the Hurricane actually accounted for most of the RAF's kills in the battle.

Celebrating victory
The inhabitants of a street in Bristol—without most of their young men, who were still away in the armed forces—celebrate victory in 1945. The British were determined that winning the war would be followed by building a fairer society.

The array of forces aligned with Britain in 1942 was impressive. As well as the US and the Soviet Union, there were the Commonwealth countries that had stood by Britain from the start, and governments-in-exile and the freedom fighters of defeated European countries—the Free French and the Polish resistance making some particularly notable contributions. Yet the tide of the fighting flowed against the Allies for a long while. By the summer of 1942, the Japanese advance reached the borders of India, and German armies continued to push deep into the Soviet Union. In North Africa, the Axis forces under General Rommel invaded Egypt, placing the Suez Canal at risk. In the Atlantic, the sinking of Allied merchant ships by U-boats rose steeply. Churchill's popularity slumped and his leadership came to be questioned as the sequence of military disasters appeared unstoppable. Then, in October–November 1942, General Bernard

committed themselves to seeking the "unconditional surrender" of their enemies. The Allies were divided on strategy, though. Churchill successfully resisted American pressure for a speedy invasion of France—his attitude was based on a pessimistic estimate of the risks involved—and convinced the US to devote resources to the Mediterranean. Meanwhile, British and American air forces undertook a joint bombing offensive against Germany, with the RAF attacking by night and the US Army Air Force (USAAF) by day. They achieved

two notable acts of mass devastation— of Hamburg in July 1943, killing more than 40,000 German civilians, and of Dresden in February 1945, killing around 25,000. The merits or otherwise of the bombing of German cities remains one of the war's most controversial aspects.

Britain's weakening control
Britain's waning influence on the war was evident when Churchill met Stalin and Roosevelt at Tehran in 1943, where he had to accept an invasion of France in 1944.

> "These are **not dark days**: these are great days—the **greatest days** our country has ever lived."
>
> WINSTON CHURCHILL, SPEECH GIVEN ON OCTOBER 29, 1941

An **Allied Victory**

Between 1942 and 1945, Britain fought as part of an alliance dominated by the United States and the Soviet Union. The British could be rightly proud of their role in the victory over Germany and Japan, but the supreme effort of war exhausted the nation's resources.

 BEFORE

The United States entered World War II as an ally of Britain after the Japanese attacked Pearl Harbor on December 7, 1941. Hitler obligingly declared war on the Americans four days later.

ANGLO-AMERICAN ALLIANCE
The foundation for a wartime Anglo-American alliance had already been somewhat laid. The **Atlantic Charter**, agreed between Churchill and President Roosevelt in August 1941, provided **a principled statement of war aims**, including "no territorial gains," "self-determination," and "freedom from want and fear." The **American lend-lease program was already established** as the basis for providing Britain and other allies of the United States with war supplies.
　On December 13, 1941, British and American leaders met in Washington at the Arcadia conference and thrashed out terms for military cooperation. They set up the **Combined Chiefs of Staff as a joint supreme command**. Britain also handed the Americans the fruit of its atom bomb research. Although the Soviet Union had been fighting alongside Britain since June 1941, no such close-knit relationship existed.

Montgomery's Eighth Army defeated Rommel in the Egyptian desert at El Alamein. Churchill later wrote, "Before Alamein we never had a victory. After Alamein we never had a defeat."

The Allies fight back
In 1943, the enemy was pushed back on all fronts. The U-boat menace in the Atlantic was finally subdued, and the

1 MILLION The total weight in tons of the bombs dropped on targets in Germany by the RAF during World War II. More than 55,000 airmen of RAF Bomber Command were killed in the war.

Soviet Red Army defeated the Germans at Stalingrad and Kursk. Italy was invaded and had to surrender, although the Germans continued the fight in the Italian peninsula. Japan was also pressed back by the Americans and Australians in the Pacific. At a summit in Casablanca in January 1943, Churchill and Roosevelt

Liberation march
British soldiers march through the French port of Cherbourg, captured from the Germans less than a month after the Normandy landings in 1944. Everywhere they went, Allied troops were welcomed as liberators.

TO-DAY IS V-E DAY
Germany Signs Final Unconditional Surrender

PREMIER TO BROADCAST AT 3 p.m.: THE KING AT 9

4.7 MILLION The number of men in the British armed forces in June 1945, comprising 2,920,000 in the Army, 783,000 in the Royal Navy, and 950,000 in the Royal Air Force.

Triumph in Europe

A newspaper announcement on May 8, 1945, declares that "Victory in Europe" has officially arrived. VE Day had been frustratingly delayed as a series of German surrenders took six days to complete.

England was turned into a massive armed camp in preparation for landings in Normandy, which took place on D-Day (June 6). The Allied invasion force was under the command of the American General Dwight D. Eisenhower, although many of the troops were British and Canadian. In the hard fight to break out of Normandy, relations between Britain's war hero Montgomery and Eisenhower deteriorated rapidly. They remained acrimonious during the eventful and costly campaigns that took the

Allied armies across France and Belgium, and eventually over the Rhine in spring 1945.

In the last months of the war, British troops drove the Japanese out of Burma, advanced into northern Italy, and occupied the Ruhr, while the RAF laid waste to German cities. Yet the country's financial resources were exhausted and so were its people. The German surrender, finalized on May 8, 1945, was greeted with relief and enthusiasm. When the Allied leaders met at Potsdam, Germany, in July—with the newly elected Prime Minister, Clement Atlee, replacing Churchill during the conference—Britain still commanded its place at the top table, and was accorded occupation zones in Germany alongside America, Russia, and France. But the United States dropped atom bombs on Hiroshima and Nagasaki in August and accepted the subsequent Japanese surrender with only the most cursory reference to its allies.

The Big Three at Yalta
Churchill, Roosevelt, and Stalin meet in February 1945 to discuss the war and post-war arrangements. Britain's influence on key decisions was, by this stage, waning.

> "In defending ourselves, we were **defending the liberties** of the **whole world** ..."
>
> KING GEORGE VI, SPEECH GIVEN ON VE DAY, MAY 8, 1945

AFTER »

In August 1945, the Treasury warned that Britain was facing bankruptcy, described by economist J.M. Keynes as "a financial Dunkirk." Victory had been won at a heavy cost, in terms of both lives and cash.

COST OF WAR
About 400,000 British people lost their lives in the war, including more than 300,000 members of the armed forces, 60,000 civilians, and more than 30,000 merchant seamen.

The war **placed Britain in deep debt**. When Japan surrendered, American aid under lend-lease was abruptly cut off. Britain was obliged to enter into negotiations for a loan, which was accorded by the Americans on harsh terms in December 1945.

BEFORE

The 1945 general election was a victory for the Labour Party, which won 3 million more votes than the Conservatives and took 393 seats in Parliament.

LABOUR'S REFORM POLICIES
Many of the reforms of the new Prime Minister, Clement Attlee, and others were **influenced by Churchill's** wartime government **‹‹ 350–351**, in which they had served. These included **proposals on welfare reform.**

AND NOW—
WIN THE PEACE

VOTE LABOUR

LABOUR PARTY POSTER FOR
THE 1945 GENERAL ELECTION

The **Postwar Years**

The Labour government, elected in 1945, set itself a Herculean task. It had to rebuild a war-devastated country, simultaneously create a welfare state, and mitigate the injustices of a capitalist economy. In spite of its partial failures, the Labour government was successful in its efforts.

Whereas in the wake of World War I many people had longed to return to the certainties of the pre-war world, the prevalent mood in 1945 was captured by the slogan: "Never again!" The 1930s had been a time of poverty and unemployment, and World War II was seen as a "people's war" fought for a better future.

The Labour government encouraged the continuation of the war-time spirit of shared sacrifice and collective effort. In truth there was little alternative, for Britain's economic situation was dire. The nation was impoverished and had to pay for the war—foreign debts totalled £25 billion and only a grudgingly accorded US loan kept government finances afloat. There were worldwide

Nationalization of the mines
Miners read a notice announcing the nationalization of coal mines. In practice, the state-owned pits were run by bureaucrats rather than by "the people."

Free medical care
This National Health Service hospital opened in Wiltshire in July 1948. Free medical care was the most durable and popular innovation of Attlee's postwar Labour government.

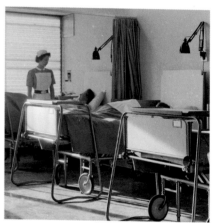

food shortages and Britain lacked the foreign currency to pay for imports. Wartime rationing was not only maintained, but tightened and extended—even bread was rationed in 1946. Black-market "spivs" flourished, satisfying the desire for small luxuries, from restricted foodstuffs to nylon stockings.

The early months of 1947 were perhaps more depressing than any part of the war. A winter of freezing temperatures and heavy snowfalls—including the coldest February on record at the time

and a three-week period in which no sunshine was recorded in London at all—coincided with a critical shortage of coal. Some coal-fired power stations shut down, factories closed, and

THIS COLLIERY IS NOW
MANAGED BY THE
NATIONAL
COAL BOARD
ON BEHALF OF THE PEOPLE
JANUARY 1 1947

110,000 The number of houses in London that were destroyed during the war by the Luftwaffe and the V-weapons.

families huddled in unheated homes by candlelight. Shortages remained normal into the 1950s. When London hosted its first postwar Olympic Games in 1948, foreign athletes were encouraged to bring their own food.

A socialist commonwealth

Against this background of austerity, the Labour government forged ahead with welfare reforms in education and health care. When the new Parliament met in 1945, their election manifesto promised a "socialist commonwealth." A wave of nationalization brought the Bank of England, the railroads, gas and electricity supply, telephones, road transportation, and the coal mines under state control.

This did not, in reality, create socialism, but a mixed economy, in which bureaucratically managed state monopolies existed alongside private enterprises. Efforts to create the socialist panacea, a planned economy, were tentative. However, there was no return to the mass unemployment of prewar years. Government measures to boost depressed areas succeeded and, by the end of 1947, there were labor shortages.

Reform measures

Meanwhile, welfare reforms aimed to ensure freedom from want "from the cradle to the grave." They provided more security from life's misfortunes than British people had ever known before. The National Health Service was guided into existence by Health Minister Aneurin Bevan, in 1948. It was popular with everyone except doctors, who fought against it until they were able to continue private practice alongside their state duties.

The problem of substandard living conditions was compounded by the war. A practical and popular temporary solution was the erection of "prefabs"— simple prefabricated houses. By 1948, as a long-term measure, 200,000 council houses (public housing) were being built every year. The 1946 New Towns Act began a drive to relocate people from overcrowded inner cities to rural locations such as Stevenage in Hertfordshire and Basildon in Essex.

School Milk Act
Children enjoy free school milk, provided to all pupils under the Act passed in 1946. This health and welfare measure was repealed by Margaret Thatcher during her tenure as an Education Secretary in 1971.

The working classes consolidated wage rises they had achieved during the war, gaining ground on the middle classes, whose salaries tended to fall relative to the cost of living. A high level of income tax—45 percent was the standard rate—helped further narrow the gap between better-paid professionals and manual workers.

The building of houses for sale to owner-occupiers virtually ceased and gasoline rationing restricted private motoring. Yet the middle class were also among the beneficiaries of the welfare state, as they did not need to pay for health care or education—their children made up the majority of those who passed the 11-plus entrance examination and attended the free grammar schools.

Continuing austerity
Ration books were introduced during World War II and remained a part of people's everyday life until the 1950s.

Growth of the leisure industry
With austerity the order of the day, a drabness infected much of daily life. People chafed at the irritations of petty bureaucracy, lines, and shortages. But the lack of goods to

buy in the shops paradoxically left people of all classes with money in their pockets to spend on leisure and entertainment. Movie-going reached a pitch never equaled before or since, with one in three of the population going to the movies every week. Sporting events also drew enormous crowds. The taste for collective leisure found its most typical expression in the burgeoning of campgrounds, especially popular with workers who enjoyed at least a week's paid vacation a year.

Relaxing restrictions
Some Labour leaders, notably Sir Stafford Cripps, believed austerity was a good thing. They disapproved of consumerism and luxury on moral and political grounds. On the whole, though, the government was keen to relax rationing and lift restrictions on people's daily lives. However, Britain's poor economic situation delayed the country's return to normal peacetime conditions. Export-led manufacturing growth had gained strength by 1949–1950, but the potential benefits of this were lost through financial shocks—an enforced devaluation of the pound in 1949, and the strain on government finances from Britain's decision to enter the Korean War in 1950 (see pp.368–369). Labour tried to prove that it could offer fun as well as security by mounting the Festival of Britain in 1951, intended to highlight progress and provide an entertaining day out. However, the Attlee government, for all its durable achievements, was on its way out.

In 1951, the Labour government was forced out of power by the Conservatives. This did not, however, herald any radical change in economic or social policies.

LABOUR VS CONSERVATIVES
In the early 1950s, **the Labour government was running out of energy and ideas.** The drive to transform Britain through nationalization and welfare reform had been succeeded by a policy of "consolidation." The Labour government came to power with a narrow majority in the February 1950 general election. Aneurin Bevan resigned from the Cabinet in April 1951, following the **party split over introducing payment** for National Health eyeglasses and dentures. In the election of October 1951, the Labour Party attracted the largest share of the popular vote—about 49 percent—but Churchill's Conservatives won a working majority of seats in the House of Commons.

CONSERVATIVE MEASURES
Winston Churchill's Conservative government denationalized the iron and steel industry, but left the other nationalized industries untouched. It also **endorsed the welfare state**, including the National Health Service, which **continues to be the main provider of health care** in Britain to this day. With more favorable economic conditions, the Conservatives were **able to end rationing** in June 1954 370–371 ➤➤.

> " The **Labour government** has ensured **full employment** … contrast with prewar days!"
>
> LABOUR PARTY ELECTION MANIFESTO, 1950

Time to celebrate
The Festival of Britain in 1951 was organized by the Labour government to celebrate British achievement and bring some color and enjoyment into the lives of the war-torn population.

The **Modern Monarchy**

The accession of Elizabeth II to the throne in 1952 was greeted by optimistic admirers of royalty as the start of a second glorious Elizabethan era. With traditional deference in decline, the monarchy experienced a rough ride through the latter half of the 20th century. Its survival into the new millennium showed an impressive ability to adapt to changing times.

Princess Elizabeth and Prince Philip were on a safari in Kenya when George VI died on February 6, 1952. The new Queen was a calm, self-possessed, and reticent young woman, with an absolute commitment to her royal duties. The preparations for her coronation revealed that she had a clearer sense of what was expected of a modern monarchy than her advisers. The government and experts on royal protocol had agreed that the televising of the event should stop at the doors of Westminster Abbey. The Queen, however, insisted that the coronation ceremony itself should be televised, so that the moment could be shared with her people.

Held on June 2, 1953, the coronation was a demonstration of the power of archaic ceremony and modern technology. Three million people lined the streets in the rain to see Elizabeth pass by in her fairy-tale coach, while more than 20 million watched on televisions, with neighbors crowding the front rooms of those lucky enough to possess a set. The event was a spectacular costume drama, with lords in ermine and coronets, bishops in copes, and Prime Minister Winston Churchill bizarrely garbed as the Lord Warden of the Cinque Ports. The public loved it all, and left-wing intellectuals, who had hoped the working class would scorn at such royalist nonsense, were confounded.

Elizabeth grasped the need for a modern monarch to be seen by the people very early in her reign. Soon after the coronation, she embarked on a round-the-world tour during which she became the first reigning monarch to visit Australia and New Zealand. This trip was the first of many royal visits to the Commonwealth countries. They were conscious attempts to foster a popular sentiment of loyalty among former colonies, the queen's status as head of state being the only surviving political link between the now fully independent countries. At home, the Queen gave her first televised Christmas speech in 1957—the royal Christmas broadcast on radio was a long-established tradition. Her manner was impeccably bland—the lack of evident personality or opinion suiting the role of a constitutional figurehead.

Family troubles

As at the time of the abdication of King Edward VIII in 1936, the troubles of the modern monarchy came from

The young monarch
Queen Elizabeth II was 27 years old at the time of her coronation in June 1953. The traditional regalia of the monarchy, such as the orb and scepter, were deployed during the ceremony.

BEFORE

Albert, Duke of York, acceded to the throne in December 1936 after the abdication of his elder brother, Edward VIII ❮❮ 344–345. He took the regal name George VI.

KING GEORGE VI
King George VI was a shy and inhibited man, who suffered from a speech impediment that, although partly cured by therapy, made public speaking a trial for him and for his listeners. He had none of the glamour of his brother Edward, but he had a **strong sense of duty**. He followed the example of his father George V in reigning as an **impeccable constitutional monarch**. During the war he stayed in residence with his family at Buckingham Palace throughout the German bombing. His visits to bomb-damaged streets and munitions factories won him respect and affection.

ELIZABETH'S EARLY YEARS
George VI's eldest daughter Elizabeth **joined the Auxiliary Territorial Service** (ATS) toward the end of the war, driving trucks. With her sister Margaret, she mingled with celebrating crowds in London on VE Day in 1945. Two years later she **married Prince Philip** of Greece and Denmark, who was granted the title of Duke of Edinburgh.

Coronation souvenir
A gold-luster earthenware teapot in the shape of the royal coach was one among many souvenirs of the coronation. The image of Elizabeth on the coach recalls her war service in the ATS.

The success of the Queen's Silver Jubilee in 1977 demonstrated the nation's continued readiness to celebrate the monarchy—even if the Sex Pistols' ironic punk anthem *God Save the Queen* topped the charts. The marriage of Prince Charles, the heir to the throne, and Lady Diana Spencer in 1981 was, like the coronation, a romantic spectacle for the vast majority of the population. By the early 1990s, the messy disintegration of Charles and Diana's union, accompanied by detailed revelations of adultery by both parties, seriously undermined royalist sentiment. With the marriages of two of Elizabeth's other children, Princess Anne and Prince Andrew, also heading

the collision between the demands of private life and public role. Elizabeth herself, like her father and grandfather, seemed immune to this conflict; her

Remembering Diana
Thousands of bouquets, cards, and other tributes were left outside Kensington Palace by mourners after Princess Diana's death in August 1997. The Queen was criticized by many of Diana's admirers for her cool public response to the death.

AFTER »

In the first decade of the 21st century, the royal family entered a relatively tranquil phase after the troubles of the 1990s, with the new generation taking center stage.

ROYAL WEDDINGS

Prince Charles, himself divorced, married the divorcée Camilla Parker Bowles in a civil wedding in 2005. The **ending of resistance to divorce** on the part of the Church of England and the Establishment in general enabled the marriage to take place without Charles renouncing his right to inherit the throne.

Prince William and Prince Harry, Charles's sons from his marriage to Princess Diana, continued the royal family's **tradition of service** in the armed forces. In 2011 the **wedding of William and Kate Middleton** (who then became the Duke and Duchess of Cambridge) was well received by the public and the media. They welcomed their third child, Prince Louis, in April 2018. The same year also witnessed the wedding of **Harry and Meghan Markle**, the couple becoming the Duke and Duchess of Sussex. In May 2019 they had their first child, Archie.

> "Throughout all my life and with all my heart I shall **strive to be worthy of your trust**."

QUEEN ELIZABETH II, RADIO BROADCAST, JUNE 2, 1953

personal life was erased by the demands of royal duty. But members of her family were not. The first crisis of the modern monarchy concerned Elizabeth's sister, Princess Margaret. She wished to marry Group Captain Peter Townsend, who was divorced. The government, the Church of England, and the rest of the royal family were united in opposition to the marriage, and in 1955 Margaret called it off. She was not reconciled, however, to a life of duty. She married photographer Antony Armstrong-Jones in 1960,

for divorce, the royals were subjected to investigation of their private lives, personal attacks, and caricature. Such disrepute of the monarchy had not been seen in Britain since the Regency scandals of the early 19th century.

The extraordinary outpouring of grief that followed Diana's death in a car crash on August 31, 1997, developed a distinct anti-monarchist edge. The Queen's lifelong reticence and reliance upon formal protocol played badly with the public in the grip of heightened emotion. Realizing that she needed to

portray a less aloof image, Elizabeth was soon seen chatting with her people on carefully stage-managed visits to pubs and council flats, while the media were offered behind-the-scenes access to life at Buckingham Palace.

Present-day monarchy

In 2012, the 60th anniversary of the Queen's accession was celebrated throughout the Commonwealths and in 2015 she became Britain's longest reigning monarch. Her longevity and the emergence of a new, younger generation of royals, who were accepted both as celebrities and ordinary human beings, helped to restore the popularity of the monarchy both in the UK and abroad. In Australia, a referendum to make the country a republic was defeated in 1999.

THE DUKE AND DUCHESS OF CAMBRIDGE ON THEIR WEDDING DAY

16 The number of independent countries of which the Queen is head of state, the largest being Britain, Canada, and Australia. The 16 countries have a combined population of about 130 million.

drifted into a number of affairs, and finally divorced in 1978. This was a foretaste of much to come.

In the early years of Elizabeth's reign the media was respectful and protective toward the royal family. A rare criticism of the Queen's manner of speaking—an article in 1957 that described her as having the manner of a "priggish schoolgirl"—was greeted with united outrage by the press. From the 1960s, this deference progressively eroded and was slowly abandoned—but this change was slow to have effect.

Head of the Commonwealth
The Queen appears on an Australian postage stamp from the 1960s. Elizabeth takes her role as head of the Commonwealth most seriously, frequently visiting Commonwealth countries.

> "It's vital that the monarchy **keeps in touch with the people**. It's what I try and do."

DIANA, PRINCESS OF WALES

Retreat from Empire

After World War II, Britain had neither the means nor the moral authority to continue ruling a quarter of the world's population. Within 20 years of the war's end, Britain almost ceased to be a colonial power and its Commonwealth was an international organization of limited practical importance.

The last viceroy and the lost leader
Mohandas Gandhi, leader of the Indian independence struggle, stands between Lord and Lady Mountbatten. Mountbatten was the last viceroy of the Indian Raj; Gandhi was assassinated by Hindu extremists soon after independence.

« BEFORE

World War II delivered body blows to Britain's imperial authority from which the Empire never recovered. A series of defeats by Japan in 1941–1942 fatally undermined British prestige in Asia.

TUMULT IN THE COLONIES

When **war with Japan** erupted in December 1941, Australia announced it would "look to America" as its prime ally. Australian troops were **withdrawn from fighting for the British** in the Mediterranean to defend their own country. The **surrender of the British base at Singapore** to the Japanese in February 1942, in which many Australians were taken prisoner, confirmed the **realignment of Australia** with the United States.

In India, 2.5 million men **volunteered to fight for Britain** in the war, but Subhas Chandra Bose's Indian National Army fought for the Japanese. The Indian National Congress declared a **campaign of civil disobedience** in July 1942 under the slogan "Quit Now," which was **harshly repressed** by the British authorities.

WEAKENED BRITAIN

Britain fought the war as an ally of the United States and the Soviet Union; both were **hostile to British imperialism**. They emerged from the war strengthened **« 358–359**, while Britain was much weakened.

INDIAN PROTESTORS BEING PUNISHED, 1942

The Labour government elected to power in 1945 had no intention of dismantling the British Empire. Foreign secretary Ernest Bevin described himself as a "genuine enthusiast for empire." But India was a special case. The Labour Party had long supported Indian self-rule. The issue was not whether India should become independent, but how the transfer of power was to take place. Lord Mountbatten was appointed viceroy with instructions to reach a swift agreement with the conflicting Indian political movements. The difficulty of reaching a satisfactory deal with Muhammad Ali Jinnah's Muslim League resulted in partition. At midnight on August 14, 1947, India celebrated independence, and so did Muslim Pakistan. Partition on independence led to immediate large-scale population movements and massacres, and to a series of wars over the following decades. However, both India and Pakistan remained members of the Commonwealth, maintaining generally friendly relations with the former imperial power.

Britain begins to withdraw

Withdrawing at the same period from Burma and Ceylon (Sri Lanka), Britain had divested itself of the largest part of its empire. This had remarkably little impact on Britain's self-image, however, because the dominions and colonies remained central to the country's status as a world power and to its hopes of post-war economic recovery. Between 1945 and 1955, around half of Britain's trade was with the colonies and Commonwealth. The United States relaxed its hostility to British imperialism in the context of the Cold War, recognizing British rule as a barrier to the spread of communism. Yet shrunken British resources and emboldened independence movements turned the imperial experience into a fighting withdrawal. Palestine was abandoned to warring Jews and Arabs in 1948. In Malaya, Britain conducted a successful military campaign against communist insurgents, granting independence to a pro-British government in 1957. In Kenya,

Colonial conflict
British troops arrest a demonstrator in Aden in 1967, during one of the many colonial conflicts that occurred during the retreat from empire.

> " Great Britain **has lost** an empire and has **not yet found** a role."
>
> **US SECRETARY OF STATE DEAN ACHESON,** DECEMBER 5, 1962

the Mau Mau uprising by the Kikuyu was suppressed with considerable brutality between 1952 and 1960, while during the same period British troops fought a guerrilla movement in Cyprus. After the Suez Crisis of 1956 (see pp.366–367), however,

Britain began to reevaluate its position as a colonial power. The realization dawned that it no longer possessed the financial and military resources to impose its will on far-flung parts of the globe.

Rapid dissolution

The Gold Coast became the first of Britain's African possessions to be granted independence, as Ghana, in 1957. Cyprus became independent in 1960. Most other colonies were moving toward representative government. In 1960, while visiting South Africa, Prime Minister Harold Macmillan announced: "The wind of change is blowing through this continent. Whether we like it or not, this growth of national consciousness is a political fact." It showed that Britain intended to hand over its colonies to the African independence movements. Between 1960 and 1968, all remaining British

Commonwealth united
This optimistic image of multiethnic comradeship dates from World War II. The term "Commonwealth" came to be preferred to "Empire," because it implied free cooperation between equals, instead of subjection.

territories in Africa were granted independence, except in Southern Rhodesia, where whites made a Unilateral Declaration of Independence (UDI)—not recognized by Britain—to avoid black-majority rule. Most of the West Indian colonies also became independent. A campaign was fought

23 **The number of new independent countries created by the dissolution of the British Empire. The number of people outside Britain under British rule fell from around 700 million in 1945 to about 5 million in the 1970s.**

against insurgents in Aden, in Arabia, between 1963 and 1967, before British troops were precipitately withdrawn. With this, the era of colonial wars was over. The British Empire ceased to exist except for a few outposts, the most important of which, Hong Kong, was handed back to China in 1997.

Kenyan independence

Prince Philip stands alongside Jomo Kenyatta at the celebrations for Kenya's independence in December 1963. Kenyatta had been imprisoned by the British in the 1950s for allegedly masterminding the Mau Mau uprising.

Britain retreated from empire with a good measure of dignity in most places. Many in power in newly independent states, including Jawaharlal Nehru in India and Jomo Kenyatta in Kenya, kept good relations with Britain as members of the Commonwealth. British involvement, both political and economic, in former colonies was considerable—Britain backed Nigeria resolutely through the Biafra secession war of 1967–1970. Yet some former colonies became hostile to Britain, as when Uganda was ruled by the brutal Idi Amin in the 1970s. South Africa also opposed British policies. Its white government withdrew from the Commonwealth in 1961 to pursue its racist apartheid policies. South Africa supported the white government of Southern Rhodesia, allowing its UDI regime to survive until 1980, when at last it became formally independent as Zimbabwe under black-majority rule.

After Britain joined the European Economic Community (EEC) in 1973, its economic links with the Commonwealth inevitably declined.

DECLARING INDEPENDENCE

In both Australia and Canada, **new patterns of immigration** from the 1970s created an ethnically mixed population. The Canada Act of 1982 and the Australia Act of 1986 affirmed the **complete independence** of the two countries.

MULTIETHNIC BRITAIN

While Britain was disbanding its empire, **large numbers of immigrants** from former colonies came to live in the old "mother" country. One of the main legacies of empire is the **ethnic diversity of modern British society.**

SIGNING THE EEC TREATY OF ACCESSION

The Suez Crisis

The military intervention at Egypt's Suez Canal in 1956 was the moment Britain's ambition to remain an imperial power foundered. The humiliating climb-down forced upon the British government by economic weakness and international disapproval showed it could no longer carry out a foreign policy independent of the United States.

In July 1956, the United States announced it was withdrawing funding from the Aswan High Dam construction project in Egypt. Egyptian ruler Gamal Abdel Nasser reacted on July 26 by nationalizing the Anglo–French–owned Suez Canal, intending to fund the dam with revenue from the waterway. British Prime Minister Anthony Eden was savagely hostile to Nasser, describing him as a "Muslim Mussolini." He feared that, once in control of the Canal, Nasser would block European oil supplies carried by tanker from the Middle East.

Eden wanted both to wrest the Canal from Egyptian control and to engineer Nasser's downfall. He was drawn by France into a secret agreement with Israel. The Israelis would attack Egypt in the Sinai, giving Britain and France an excuse to send in troops to "protect" the Canal. The Israeli operation began on October 29 and Anglo-French bombing raids struck Egypt the following day. On November 4, British troops landed by air and sea to occupy the Suez Canal zone.

The attack on Egypt provoked a torrent of criticism in Britain, the opposition Labour Party denouncing it as illegal aggression. There was a mass anti-war protest in Trafalgar Square in London on November 4. More importantly, the United States and the United Nations denounced the invasion. After the United States encouraged the selling of Britain's currency on the international money markets, thus threatening the British economy, Eden agreed to a cease-fire on November 6. On December 22, British troops handed over the Canal zone to a UN peacekeeping force. Despite the volume of protest, however, opinion polls suggest that British voters were indifferent to the debacle. Nonetheless, Anthony Eden's health broke under the strain, and the Prime Minister resigned in January 1957.

> "They have **besmirched** the name of Britain. They have made us **ashamed** [where] formerly we were proud."

LABOUR MP ANEURIN BEVAN SPEAKING OF THE BRITISH GOVERNMENT AT AN ANTI-WAR RALLY IN TRAFALGAR SQUARE, LONDON, NOVEMBER 4, 1956

Blocked Suez Canal
In response to the British invasion, Egypt blocked the Suez Canal by sinking ships in the waterway. The resultant interruption of oil supplies from the Middle East led the British government to introduce gas rationing in December 1956. Rationing remained in force until spring 1957, when the Canal reopened.

Prepared for nuclear attack
Dressed in full gear, members of the Civil Defence Corps' Technical Reconnaissance Unit test for radiation as part of a civil-defense exercise at Bristol on February 10, 1951. Such rehearsals were undertaken in anticipation of nuclear strikes.

The **Cold War**

After World War II, Britain tried to retain its independent status as a great power, but in practice became a subordinate ally of the United States in its confrontation with the Soviet Union. The British now lived with the risk of annihilation in a nuclear war.

BEFORE

Britain's relationship with its major World War II allies, the United States and the Soviet Union, rapidly changed after the war. By 1948, the Soviets were identified as Britain's enemies.

RELATIONS BEGIN TO FREEZE

In March 1946, former Prime Minister **Winston Churchill, ‹‹ 350–351**, warned an American audience in Missouri of an **"Iron Curtain"** dividing Europe. Britain supported US President Truman's fight against communism in 1947. In 1948–1949, Britain and the United States staged **the Berlin airlift to West Berlin**, which had been placed under Soviet blockade. In April 1949, Britain became a founding member of the **North Atlantic Treaty Organization** (NATO), which committed the United States to defend western Europe against Soviet aggression.

Britain's Labour government of 1945, and in particular its fiercely anticommunist Foreign Secretary Ernest Bevin, feared a Soviet invasion of western Europe. Although Bevin also encouraged cooperation between European countries, he saw the support of the United States—the world's only nuclear power at the time—as vital. The North Atlantic Treaty Organization (NATO), founded in 1949, was a triumph for British diplomacy. The payment in return for Britain was that it support the United States when the Korean War broke out in 1950, contributing substantially to the US-led United

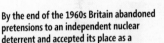

KEY MOMENT

THE ALDERMASTON MARCH

The Campaign for Nuclear Disarmament (CND) was founded in 1957. It hoped that by persuading the British government to renounce nuclear weapons it could trigger general disarmament worldwide. At Easter 1958, CND mounted a march from London to the Atomic Weapons Research Establishment at Aldermaston, Berkshire. Later, the march was reversed in direction, and became an annual ritual of protest, attracting a growing number of mostly young demonstrators. The last significant Aldermaston march was in 1963, though CND itself remains active today.

Cambridge spies

Four of the Soviet agents recruited at Cambridge University in the 1930s included, clockwise from top left, Anthony Blunt, Donald Maclean, Kim Philby, and Guy Burgess.

Nations forces that fought North Korea and China to a standstill in the costly three-year conflict.

Despite cultivating its "special relationship" with the United States, Britain also intended to remain a great power. Thus, in January 1947, a secret Cabinet committee decided that Britain would develop its own atom bomb. Britain's first nuclear device was exploded in 1952. A nuclear strike force, the V bombers—Valiants, Victors, and Vulcans—came into service during 1955–1958, capable of destroying Russian cities. Meanwhile, British civil defense planners produced estimates of Britain's inevitable near-extermination in the event of a nuclear war.

Espionage

The secrecy surrounding nuclear weapons and the brinkmanship of nuclear confrontation encouraged espionage, and Britain was shown to have been penetrated by Soviet agents at the heart of its Establishment. In 1951, Guy Burgess and Donald Maclean, who had both worked at the British Embassy in Washington, fled to Moscow to avoid arrest. Their associate, Kim Philby, once a leading figure in Britain's Secret Intelligence Service, also defected to the Soviet Union in 1963. Much later it was revealed that Anthony Blunt, once Keeper of the Queen's Pictures, had also been a spy. Whether or not this was evidence of the decay of Britain's ruling elite, it certainly annoyed Britain's US allies.

The purpose of Britain's independent nuclear deterrent was to maintain great power status, but in the 1960s Britain's subordination to the United States was

12 MILLION The number of people in Britain who might be killed in the first few days of an all-out nuclear war, according to a worst-case estimate by the Ministry of Defence in 1968.

British nuclear missile

The Avro Blue Steel air-launched missile was built for Britain's V bombers in the 1960s. Its effectiveness was fortunately never tested in action.

The NATO agreement
Signed on April 4, 1949, the North Atlantic Treaty Organization (NATO) bound member states—the United States, Canada, and 10 European countries—to collectively defend against attacks on member nations.

obvious. Unable to afford its own nuclear ballistic missiles, Britain had to beg the US for its Polaris missile to arm British submarines. During the Cuban Missile Crisis of October 1962, the most dangerous moment of the Cold War, the United States effectively ignored the British government. Britain was in the front line of US nuclear defenses against the Soviet Union, without any control over United States' policies.

AFTER

By the end of the 1960s Britain abandoned pretensions to an independent nuclear deterrent and accepted its place as a subordinate in an American-led alliance.

BRITAIN SIDELINED

When the United States and the Soviet Union embarked on **arms limitation talks** in 1969, Britain was sidelined. In the 1980s, Cold War tensions flared as US cruise missiles stationed in Britain provoked protests. Prime Minister Margaret Thatcher, **382–383 ››**, aggressively opposed Soviet communism, yet negotiations from 1986 that ended the Cold War were held exclusively between the Soviets and the US.

IRONIC DECLASSIFIED NUCLEAR BUNKER SIGN

"We've **got to have** [the atom bomb] … We've got to have the bloody **Union Jack** on top of it."

BRITISH FOREIGN SECRETARY ERNEST BEVIN, OCTOBER 1946

RUSH FOR CANDY AT THE END OF RATIONING

The Conservative Party won the general election in 1951, just when Britain was emerging from post-war austerity. It took credit for improving living standards.

END TO RATIONING
The **end of austerity** was symbolized by the end of wartime rationing. Gas rationing came to an end in 1950. The Conservatives **ended rationing** for tea, candy, sugar, and meat, which was the last item to be de-rationed, in July 1954.

LESS NATIONALIZATION
The Conservative government **denationalized the iron and steel industry** in 1953 and road haulage in 1954. It left unchanged the **Welfare State** and the mixed economy created by the Labour government « **360–361**, with much of British industry still under **state control**.

HAROLD MACMILLAN AS PRIME MINISTER

Harold Macmillan was educated at Eton, fought in the trenches in World War I, and represented a northern constituency during the Depression. His experiences made him a "one-nation" Tory, committed to full employment and welfare. He was also a flamboyant showman, a quality that served him well as Britain entered the age of television. Taking over as Prime Minister after the Suez debacle, he won an impressive election victory in 1959. He retired as premier in 1963, due to illness. In the 1980s, he was critical of Margaret Thatcher's abrasive brand of Toryism.

Never had it so Good

The catchphrase "You've never had it so good!," adapted from a speech by Harold Macmillan in 1957, sums up how many British people felt about life in the 1950s and early 1960s. Rising wages and near full employment brought security and growing prosperity, expressed in ownership of consumer goods.

In 1951, the average wage of an adult male in Britain was £8 6s (£8.30) a week; a decade later it had risen to £15 7s (£15.35). With price inflation modest, this near doubling of pay, combined with full employment, brought a striking change in living standards for most Britons. Seeking to win a general election in 1957, Prime Minister Harold Macmillan rightly described Britain as enjoying "a state of prosperity such as we have never had in my lifetime—or indeed in the history of this country." Living conditions were still austere by the standards of the

6.9 MILLION The number of households across Britain that owned a television set in the late 1950s.

21st century—only a minority owned a refrigerator or a telephone—but to those who had lived through the Depression and the war, financial security and new consumer goods were highly satisfactory and liberating, and most people were immune to the easy sneers of intellectuals railing against shallow materialist aspirations.

For the better off, the drive for home ownership of the 1930s resumed in the 1950s. Houses were affordable, and by 1961, more than 40 percent of the population owned their own homes. Few well-off people fulfilled a more

modest aspiration to rent a home with an inside toilet and a bath—in 1951, one-third of British homes had no bathroom. The Conservative (Tory) governments of the 1950s built a higher volume of public housing than their Labour predecessors, although with some sacrifice of quality. Old inner-city slums were demolished, and their population was emptied into freshly built suburban public housing or New Towns such as Corby, Harlow, and Hemel Hempstead. Although this move was criticized for breaking up working-class communities, it transformed living conditions and was broadly popular with those rehoused, who could now enjoy a new-found privacy, cleanliness,

Election victories in 1955 and 1959 kept the Conservatives in power for 13 years, but in 1964 Harold Wilson led Labour back to government with a promise to transform Britain in the "white heat of technology."

CHANGE NEEDED
The need for the **modernization of Britain** was an important theme of public debate in the early 1960s. Sir Alec Douglas Home, who succeeded Macmillan as Prime Minister in 1963, was **out of touch** with the modern world and modern technology. Nevertheless, **Labour won** only a **small majority** of the popular vote and seats in Parliament in October 1964. It won a larger majority in another election in 1966.

LABOUR POLICIES
The Wilson government made little attempt to follow socialist policies. Labour's commitment to **economic planning proved ineffectual**. Instead, the government was preoccupied with Britain's **deteriorating financial position**, which led to a devaluation of the pound in 1967, and with the need to keep wage rises down to an affordable level. An attempt to curb the **power of the trade unions** failed **376–377 »**.

Road to progress
The M1 motorway opened in 1959, and it became a symbol of the modernization of Britain at this period. Although car ownership was rapidly expanding, only one in three families had a car, leaving plenty of space on the road.

Family viewing
By the end of the 1950s, television had replaced the radio as family entertainment in a majority of British homes. Concerns were frequently expressed about the influence of TV on children.

New arrivals
West Indian immigrants arrive at Victoria Station in London in 1956. By then, almost 50,000 West Indians were settling in Britain each year, drawn by the availability of jobs in understaffed public services.

and a yard. Economies from the late 1950s saw apartments built instead of houses, and the unpopular tower blocks transformed the skyline of British cities.

Culture and conflict
The values of a secure home-centered family life were celebrated, and the ideal "housewife and mother" image of womanhood was promoted by magazines and advertising. There had been a brief bulge in the birth rate in 1947 as men returned from war, but it was from the late 1950s that Britain experienced the "baby-boom." By 1964, every woman was, on average, bearing three children.

The focal activity for the nuclear family was watching television. Kick-started by the televised coronation in 1953, owning or renting a television had become common in all classes by the late 1950s. Movie audiences halved in the decade. The advent of commercial television in 1955 was a crucial moment, breaching the BBC monopoly on broadcasting that had lasted since the 1920s. Although independent television was at first careful to court respectability, for example with some serious drama programs, competition for viewers inevitably led to more of mass entertainment and less "worthiness."

In the 1950s, labor shortages led to the recruitment of West Indians to staff National Health Service hospitals and public transportation. The immigrants were granted right of entry to Britain with the 1948 British Nationality Act. In 1958, white mobs spearheaded race riots by attacking black residents in the Notting Hill district of London. An Immigration Act passed in 1962 failed to stem the inward flow from the Commonwealth or halt racial tensions.

In the 1950s, homosexuals were targeted by the police in a draconian campaign that brought more than 5,000 prosecutions for consensual sex acts. The liberal Wolfenden Report of 1957 was a reaction against this wave of persecution, but it would be another 10 years before its call for decriminalization was embodied in legislation.

Low economic growth
Despite the 1950s being a period when many Britons were doing well for themselves, due to the Welfare State and a nascent consumer society, growing prosperity was no antidote to an increasing sense of national decline. British industry was not performing well in comparison to its German and French competitors.

Falling exports led to a deficit in the balance of payments. Restrictive working practices imposed by trade unions and old-fashioned attitudes of management were blamed for stunting the growth of British productivity.

Conservative governments had adopted the basic tenets of Keynesian demand management economics, accepting a measure of inflation as the price to pay for maintaining full employment. Despite the apparent success of this approach, budgetary policy developed into an ever-more stuttering stop-go alternation of the brake and accelerator, and the economy cooled or stimulated as inflation or unemployment threatened. By the 1960s, it was obvious that satisfying popular expectations of rising living standards was going to be problematic, and that the performance of the British economy was not going to be good enough.

Kitchen convenience
The Kenwood mixer is a classic design from the 1950s. It was the sort of kitchen equipment coveted by middle-class housewives, who were living in a world in which live-in domestic servants had become rare.

"No more running out for a bag of chips to eat with your bread. Now, you got fair wages …"
ALAN SILLITOE, *SATURDAY NIGHT AND SUNDAY MORNING*, 1958

Britain goes Pop

Britain's image was transformed in the 1960s. The land of the bowler hat, tea, and the "brolly" became identified with popular culture, stylish art, and loose morals. Change was apparent, a genuine liberalization underlying the clichés of the swinging sixties.

The defining characteristic of Britain in the 1960s was the blend of a welfare state with a consumer society, of "cradle-to-grave" social security and full employment with enterprise and social mobility. Society was more egalitarian than it had been in the past and people were more prosperous than they had ever been. The spread of home and car ownership was accompanied by consumer spending, evident in the growing popularity of package vacations to Europe. The country's popular leisure activities centered around the home: television, gardening, and do-it-yourself home improvement. Despite growing prosperity, Britain did not become complacent. Instead, a modest but growing affluence was accompanied by innovation in culture and lifestyles.

The decline in respect for authority was one of the most obvious changes in the British mentality. In the 1950s, the mass media banned jokes about religion or the monarchy, and government ministers never faced hostile interviews or inquiries into their private lives. This was abandoned in the satire boom of the early 1960s. The theatrical review *Beyond the Fringe*, the magazine *Private Eye*, and the TV program *That Was the Week That Was* breached traditional restraints—for example, by having an actor caricature the Prime Minister.

In 1963, the burgeoning culture of disrespect was gifted a first-rate political scandal, revolving around War Secretary John Profumo's involvement with Christine Keeler. The unravelling of this complex affair brought explicit sexual references to news broadcasts and considerable disrepute to the ruling classes. The defeat of the much-ridiculed Conservatives in a general election in 1964 brought no relief to politicians, for the Labour

400 MILLION The number of people who watched the worldwide TV broadcast of The Beatles' *All You Need Is Love* in June 1967. It was the first global satellite TV program.

government of Harold Wilson was subjected to a torrent of ridicule through its six years in office.

Popular culture

Britain's youth and pop culture displayed the same spirit of irreverence that animated political satire. Youth was a burgeoning market, not because most young people had a lot of money, but because they were prepared to spend all the money they had on records and clothes. Bright young working-class men and women, beneficiaries of new educational opportunities in the postwar grammar schools and art colleges, found openings for ambition in pop music, acting, fashion, or photography. However, the relevance of class was limited—Mick Jagger and John Lennon were from middle-class backgrounds, and many prime movers of pop culture were private-school educated.

The mass hysteria of Beatlemania in 1963 was the point at which the world began to picture a different Britain. The Beatles took the United States by storm the following year, opening the way for a series of other creative British bands.

Swinging London

In 1966, *Time* magazine created the label "Swinging London," and the fashion shops of Carnaby Street became a tourist attraction. Fashion designer Mary Quant's mini-skirt became an icon of the decade.

Fashion icon

Lesley Hornby, better known as Twiggy, became Britain's most prominent fashion model in 1966, aged 16. Her working-class origins and androgynous figure made her a perfect icon of Swinging London.

The Rolling Stones
Marketed as a more rebellious alternative to The Beatles, The Rolling Stones seemed genuinely subversive and threatening to many conservative parents in the mid-1960s. Forty years later, lead singer Mick Jagger was awarded a knighthood.

BEFORE

There were stirrings of a new spirit in Britain from the mid-1950s. Established conventions of public decency and respect for authority were increasingly challenged.

ANTI-CONVENTION
In 1956, the success of John Osborne's play *Look Back in Anger*—a tirade against the hypocrisy of British society—led to the invention of the label "Angry Young Men" for **writers critical of the established order**. In the same year, the **arrival of American rock 'n' roll** in Britain occasioned some un-British riotous misbehavior by young fans. In 1960, **censorship was challenged** by the publication of an unexpurgated Penguin edition of D. H. Lawrence's *Lady Chatterley's Lover*. The book was cleared of obscenity in a landmark trial.

Now **YOU** can read it

LADY CHATTERLEY'S LOVER

In many British households the generation gap between the attitudes and tastes of children and their parents was a daily reality. Schools resisted the fashions for long hair for boys and short skirts for girls.

The Pill became widely available in the later 1960s, but there is little evidence of a sexual revolution. Recreational drugs circulated—pills early in the decade, pot later—but alcohol remained the most widely favored intoxicant. The drug-fueled world of free love and psychedelic style that centered around London "underground" magazines and music clubs of the late 1960s was very much a minority scene.

Protests and legislation

As in other countries, Britain underwent a large-scale expansion of university education in the 1960s. British students singularly failed, however, to form the revolutionary force seen in Europe and the United States. An anti-Vietnam War demonstration in London, in March 1968, was the sole example of violent protest. Real liberalization did come,

The swinging sixties
The film *Blow-Up,* directed by Michelangelo Antonioni in London in 1966, is a typical foreigner's view of Britain at the time, and focuses on fashion photography, casual sex, and recreational drugs.

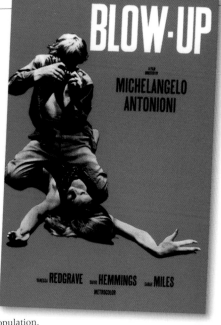

through due parliamentary process. The House of Commons voted to abolish capital punishment in 1965, homosexual acts between consenting adults were decriminalized in 1967, abortion was legalized, and by the end of the decade, the divorce laws had been liberalized. Also important were the first Race Relations Acts, which banned all forms of discrimination against Britain's growing immigrant population.

These reforms were hotly contested by those with more conservative attitudes. Groups such as Mary Whitehouse's National Viewers' and Listeners' Association campaigned against the relaxation of censorship and general moral decadence. In 1968, Conservative MP Enoch Powell articulated white fears about immigration in an infamous speech foreseeing "rivers of blood" in Britain's streets.

Even though this period brought bitter social conflict to much of Europe and the United States, a general benevolence reigned in Britain—typified by the support expressed by *The Times,* a newspaper of the Establishment, for members of The Rolling Stones arrested on drug charges in 1967. Essentially secure, Britain accepted youthful rebellion for what it mostly was—fun.

Anti-Vietnam War demonstration
Actress Vanessa Redgrave addresses anti-Vietnam War protestors in Trafalgar Square on March 17, 1968. The demonstration ended in violent clashes with police outside the US Embassy in Grosvenor Square.

In a general election held in June 1970, the Labour government suffered a shock defeat to Ted Heath's Conservatives. This did not, however, mark any sharp change of direction in society or culture.

CONTINUITY OF POPULAR CULTURE
The end of the 1960s cultural moment could be symbolized by the breakup of The Beatles in 1970, or by the trial of radical journalists of the "underground" magazine *Oz* for obscenity in 1971. Britain continued to earn its reputation as an **innovative center of pop music and fashion**. Political policies were not reversed. For example, the **transition from grammar and secondary modern schools to comprehensives** initiated by the Labour government accelerated under Conservative Education Secretary Margaret Thatcher.

RISE OF REVOLUTIONARY GROUPS
However, a relatively liberal Conservative government faced a **sharp rise in political radicalism**. As well as suffering the overflow from violence in Northern Ireland **378–379 》**, Britain had its own urban terrorist group in the Angry Brigade, which carried out a score of bombings from 1970 to 1972. Various revolutionary Marxist groups, barely present in British universities in 1968, attracted substantial support among students in the 1970s. The **women's movement, gay liberation, and ecology movement** also flourished after 1970 from limited beginnings in the previous decade.

> "Years of revolt, **years of** carefree, sinless excess, of **drugs**, **music**, **revolution** … of the ever-exciting **tomorrow**."
>
> JONATHAN GREEN, *DAYS IN THE LIFE,* A 1960s RETROSPECTIVE

Beatlemania
Policemen struggle to restrain Beatles fans outside Buckingham Palace as the "Fab Four" receive their MBEs on October 26, 1965. The decoration of pop stars—officially for services to exports, though some said it was to improve Prime Minister Wilson's popularity—was unprecedented and widely criticized. Some older recipients returned their MBEs in protest.

After 1945, the government and employers in Britain bought social peace with pay rises, full employment, and welfare payments. However, by the start of the 1970s, this deal was breaking down.

UNION MILITANCY
From World War II onward, governments began treating the trade union movement as legitimate representatives of the working people of Britain. But the second half of the 1960s brought a **rise in union militancy**. In 1966, the seamen's union called for a damaging nationwide strike and stoppages at the local level proliferated. Faced with **mounting economic problems**, the Labour government legislated to hold down prices and wages, but **limits on pay rises** were **opposed by**

trade unions. In 1969, opposition from union leaders blocked proposals to impose legal limits on strike action. The election of the Conservative government of Edward Heath in 1970 led to **redoubled confrontation** with the unions.

EQUAL PAY FOR EQUAL WORK
One industrial action of particular significance was a 1968 strike by women machinists at Ford's Dagenham plant in England. They demanded the **same pay as men**, for doing the same job. The strike stimulated the Labour government to pass an **Equal Pay Act** outlawing pay discrimination between men and women. It was one of the earliest displays of the women's movement that flourished in Britain in the 1970s.

Conflict in Society

Britain entered choppy waters in the 1970s as the postwar economic boom stalled, with high inflation and rising unemployment. Social and political conflicts raged against this background of economic uncertainty. Militant trade unions humiliated governments, while political activists demanded various kinds of liberation and equality. Some people expressed fears of a breakdown of liberal democracy.

The Conservative government led by Ted Heath from 1970 to 1974 had to deal with a world economic crisis. It also faced the hostility of trade unions determined to win large pay rises, regardless of the government's efforts to control inflation. In 1972, the first national coal miners' strike since the 1920s blacked out cities with daily power cuts. Mass picketing prevented the use of fuel stocks, and the miners only went back to work after winning a substantial wage increase. In the winter of 1973–1974, a cut in oil supplies resulting from the Yom Kippur War in the Middle East coincided with more industrial action by miners. Heath

declared a three-day week to save fuel and called a general election, which he narrowly lost. Harold Wilson's incoming Labour government bought the miners' cooperation with large pay rises.

Left-wing militancy
Ideas emerging from the international student revolt in France during the late 1960s inspired trade union militancy. Marxism returned to fashion, and notions of revolutionary socialism and workers' power inspired influential minority groups, such as the Socialist Workers Party (SWP). However, the right-wing National Front also increased its membership and staged provocative

Women's liberation
Feminist demonstrators imaginatively represent a woman as crucified by the demands of sexual objectification, housework, and shopping.

Anti-Asian demonstration
Protestors oppose the government decision to admit Asians expelled from Uganda to Britain, in 1972. Their hero was Enoch Powell, an MP noted for opposing a multiracial society.

Grunwick strike

A picketer is arrested in one of many clashes with police during the prolonged Grunwick dispute of 1976–1978. The British tradition of a lightly equipped, good-humored police force was on the wane.

marches that led to violent clashes with anti-fascists.

Race and immigration were crucial issues. Despite a Race Relations Act in 1975, which tightened existing law banning racial discrimination, racial abuse and racially motivated attacks against Britain's black and Asian population were commonplace. In 1976, musicians mounted a Rock Against Racism campaign, and the following year the SWP initiated an Anti-Nazi League to oppose the activities of the National Front.

12.9 MILLION

The average number of working days lost to strike action in Britain annually, in the 1970s. During the 1990s, this figure was 660,000 working days.

Grunwick strike

A strike by Asian women workers at the Grunwick factory in London in 1976, seeking recognition for a union, became a focus for left-wing militancy. More than 500 arrests took place in various clashes between supporters of the strikers and police,

but the employers refused to yield and the strikers were defeated after a long struggle.

Flourishing feminism

The resurgence of militant feminism, which had not been in force since the time of the suffragettes, was in some ways the most radical feature of the 1970s. The first National Women's Liberation Conference was held in 1970,

and the feminist magazine *Spare Rib* was first published in 1972. The "women's lib" attack on male supremacy and patriarchy went beyond the pursuit of equal pay and fair treatment at work—both subjects of 1970s legislation. It raised issues such as the division of work in the household, domestic violence, and the representation of women in the media. Like the movement for gay rights in the same period, militant feminism faced an uphill struggle. A mere 23 women MPs were elected to

Parliament in February 1974 and trade union leaders were uniformly male.

To many observers, the ferment of 1970s Britain looked more like terminal decline than the building of a fairer society. From the violence of soccer gangs to the raw sound and outrageous styles of punk rock, they found plentiful evidence of anarchy. Faced with mounting public disorder, the police began to adopt tougher tactics. In April 1979, Blair Peach, a member of the Anti-Nazi League, was killed by police at an anti-racist demonstration in Southall. A certain gentleness, long taken to characterize the British, was disappearing into the past.

AFTER »

From 1974, Labour governments sought to rule in close collaboration with trade union leaders. This policy ended disastrously in the 1978–1979 "winter of discontent."

PACIFYING UNIONS

Labour agreed to a **"social contract"** with the unions. In return for government policies promoting social equality, unions accepted limits on wage rises. Inflation was cut sharply, but Britain's **financial problems remained acute.** In 1976, the government was forced to cut spending. Unemployment rose above 1 million for the first time since World War II.

MOUNTING FRUSTRATION

In the winter of 1978–1979, union frustration at the government's **tight wage policy** boiled over. A nationwide stoppage by truck drivers threatened food and fuel supplies. Strikes by public service workers followed. This period **ruined Labour's reputation** as the party that could handle the unions, leading to the election of **Margaret Thatcher** as Prime Minister in 1979 382–383 ».

"The **cozy world** we were told would go on forever … **is gone**."

JAMES CALLAGHAN, SPEECH TO LABOUR PARTY CONFERENCE, 1976

Punk style

The 1970s punk movement outraged conservative opinion with its raucous music and unruly posturing, but punk fashions soon became a London tourist attraction.

TRASH PILED UP IN A LONDON STREET DURING A GARBAGE COLLECTORS' STRIKE, 1979

Celebrating violence
A mural on a house in Northern Ireland celebrates the Ulster Volunteer Force, a Protestant paramilitary group that killed more than 400 people during The Troubles.

From the 1920s to the 1960s, British governments paid little attention to Northern Ireland. The Protestant majority was allowed to discriminate against Catholics in areas such as public housing and employment. In 1967, to oppose discrimination, the Northern Ireland Civil Rights Association was founded. Its demonstrations met a brutal response from Protestant police and extremists. In January 1969, a vicious attack on marchers at Burntollet Bridge led to battles between Catholics and police in the Bogside area of Derry. The Northern Ireland government failed to halt the rise of Protestant extremism or Catholic protest. On August 12–14, 1969, violence in Derry spread to Belfast, with Protestant police and rioters attacking Catholic districts. On August 15, British troops were sent in to halt the violence, in which eight

KEY MOMENT

BLOODY SUNDAY

On January 30, 1972, the Northern Ireland Civil Rights Association marched in Derry to protest against internment. Soldiers from the British Parachute Regiment were sent to keep order. After reports of sniper fire and youths throwing stones, the "Paras" opened fire, killing 14 unarmed people. The report of the Saville Inquiry in 2010 described the killings as "unjustified and unjustifiable," and British Prime Minister David Cameron issued an official apology in Parliament the same year.

Troubles in Northern Ireland

The deployment of British troops on the streets of Belfast and Derry in 1969 marked a breakdown of order in Northern Ireland. Over the following 30 years, more than 3,000 people, including 763 British soldiers, were killed in massacres and atrocities that scarred the reputation of the United Kingdom.

Hunger-strike riots
The death of IRA hunger striker Bobby Sands in May 1981 led to rioting by Northern Ireland Catholics. During his fast, Sands was elected a British MP in a by-election.

 BEFORE

In 1922, six counties of Ulster became Northern Ireland, a part of the United Kingdom under a devolved Protestant-dominated government at Stormont.

GROWING REPUBLICANISM
In 1949, the Irish government in Dublin declared **Ireland a republic**. Britain promised Northern Ireland would stay in the UK as long as Stormont wished it. In 1956–1962, the Irish Republican Army (IRA) mounted an **armed campaign** "to drive the British invader from the soil of Ireland," but both the Irish and Northern Ireland governments **suppressed it**. In the late 1960s, a largely Catholic civil-rights movement **challenged Protestant domination** of Northern Ireland.

CIVIL RIGHTS MARCH, 1969

people had been killed and hundreds wounded. At first, British soldiers were welcomed by Catholics as impartial protectors. Britain's Labour government was hostile to the Protestant Unionists and envisaged radical reforms, but political progress was too slow.

Escalating violence
In the summer of 1970, events spiraled out of control. Tough army action in Catholic Belfast, with house-to-house searches and a curfew, stirred up old hostility to the British. Extremists benefited. Frustrated by the inaction of the "official" Irish Republican Army (IRA), the breakaway Provisional IRA planned an armed campaign to drive the British out of Northern Ireland. Amid the general breakdown of order, many Catholics welcomed this new IRA as their best defense against Protestants and British troops. Protestant armed groups, such as the Ulster Volunteer Force (UVF), also grew in strength. In February 1971, the first British soldier was killed. Sniping and bombings became daily occurrences. In August, internment was introduced. The arrest without trial of hundreds of Catholics, some grossly ill-treated by interrogators, led to a rapid escalation of violence. In the last five months of 1971, 143 were killed, including 46 soldiers and police. Some Catholic districts of Belfast and Derry became barricaded no-go areas openly controlled by the IRA.

Bloody Sunday, in January 1972 (see BOX), increased Catholic support for the IRA. It seemed that nothing could stem the rising violence.

New strategies

Desperate for a solution, the British government placed the province under direct rule from Westminster, and in early July flew IRA leaders to London for secret peace talks. No agreement was reached and mayhem followed. Fifteen British soldiers were killed in eight days, and, on July 21, the IRA exploded 19 bombs in central Belfast. Catholic opinion was shocked by the bombings, which killed and maimed Catholic and Protestant alike. Britain seized the moment as support for the gunmen flagged and launched a large-scale military operation to reoccupy the no-go areas. From July 1972, the rate of bombings and shooting halved, and compared with the 467 killed in 1972, the 1973 death toll was down to 250. This was seen an "acceptable level" of violence by the British government. Increasingly, the killings were sectarian, with gruesome murders of Catholics by Protestants and vice versa. The IRA

extended its terrorist campaign to mainland Britain. The worst incident, in November 1974, saw 19 killed in the bombing of two pubs in Birmingham; six men were soon arrested and convicted, but were later proved innocent. Meanwhile, Britain tried a political solution: a Protestant and

Anti-riot duty
British soldiers in riot gear prepare for action in Northern Ireland. Rubber bullets and CS gas were among weapons deployed against rioters.

Catholic power-sharing executive was installed at Stormont, and in May 1974 the Irish government's right to a say in Northern Ireland's affairs was recognized by the Sunningdale Agreement.

Protestants responded with a general strike, while UVF bomb attacks in the Republic of Ireland killed 33. Unable to overcome Protestant resistance, Britain resumed direct rule and abandoned the political settlement.

From 1975, the intensity of the killings subsided. The IRA, well organized and well armed, was capable of sustaining a terrorist campaign indefinitely, as it proved by occasional spectacular acts, such as the murder of Lord Mountbatten in August 1979, on the same day as killing 18 British soldiers at Warrenpoint. However, it was a different kind of IRA pressure that radically altered the Northern Ireland political scene in the 1980s. In 1981, IRA inmates at the high-security Maze prison began a hunger strike in pursuit of political-prisoner status. While Prime Minister Margaret Thatcher refused to negotiate, first Bobby Sands and then nine other IRA prisoners starved themselves to death. For the first time, Sinn Féin, the political wing of the IRA, won mass support among Northern Ireland Catholic voters. Although not evident at the time, this shift was to open the way to a Northern Ireland settlement.

In the 1990s, the deadlock over Northern Ireland was broken. The Good Friday agreement of April 1998 raised hopes of an end to terrorism and sectarian violence.

TOWARD PEACE

Buoyed by **electoral support** from Northern Ireland Catholics, Sinn Féin leader Gerry Adams began to seek a **political route to achieving nationalist aims**. The IRA continued its terrorist campaign—for example, in a mortar attack on Downing Street in 1991, and the bombing of the City of London in 1993. John Major's **British government entered into negotiations** with both Sinn Féin and the Irish government. Much progress had been made by 1997, when Tony Blair was elected British Prime Minister. His appointment of Mo Mowlam as Secretary of State for Northern Ireland **started a decisive peace offensive**. For the first time, Catholic and Protestant extremists, many serving life prison sentences, were included in negotiations.

The 1998 Good Friday Agreement reprised the **power-sharing arrangement** of 1973–1978, but with a plan for disarming nationalist and loyalist terrorists, and setting up a devolved Northern Ireland Assembly. The killing of 28 people in a bomb attack by IRA dissidents in Omagh in August 1998 highlighted the dangers of a return to violence.

« BEFORE

Throughout the postwar period, governments pursued economic policies designed to guarantee full employment, while supporting rising living standards and a welfare state.

TROUBLES
In the 1970s, however, high inflation, balance of payments crises, and pressure on the value of

CARS WAITING FOR GASOLINE

the pound made full employment impossible to sustain and forced **cuts in government spending «« 376–377**. One key problem was reliance on imported oil from the Middle East, which led to lines at gas pumps in 1973–1974.

Miners' strike
Strikers confront police during the miners' strike of 1984–1985 at the Orgreave coking plant in June 1984. The government made ruthless use of police powers in crushing the strike.

Turn to the Right

Margaret Thatcher's election as Prime Minister in May 1979 marked a decisive change in direction for Britain. A long-term trend toward equality was reversed as the celebration of wealth and enterprise replaced belief in social solidarity and security. Much of British industry was consigned to the trash can of history, while the City of London was awash with easy money.

The most distinctive feature of Thatcher's years in power, from 1979 to 1990 (see pp.382–383), was the abandonment of any effort toward consensus. Her government's style was confrontational and opponents were to be overcome, not won over. During her early years in power, she presided over a widespread collapse of British manufacturing. High interest rates, a strong pound, and cuts in public spending combined to destroy struggling businesses. As factories closed, the number of unemployed more than doubled to over 3 million. Working-class communities that had been created by the Industrial Revolution of the 19th century and had survived the Depression were finally ruined.

Curbs on unionism
Trade unions might have been expected to lead resistance to this process, but from the outset Thatcher ended the convention of consulting union leaders

on policy. New trade union legislation outlawed mass picketing and introduced financial penalties for illegal strikes. In 1981, Thatcher made concessions to avoid a confrontation with the powerful National Union of Mineworkers (NUM), but by 1984 she welcomed a national miners' strike as a chance for a decisive confrontation.

The defeat of the miners in a year-long strike inspired a change of attitude in employers. Strikes were resisted, with ruthless use of the new legal powers, and terms and conditions were increasingly imposed on employees without negotiation. The discontent of the unemployed, especially black youths who were also victims of racism, spilled over into riots in Brixton and Toxteth.

The Conservatives' ability to carry through a radical program was helped by a split in the Labour Party in 1981, when the Social Democrats were founded. They were also able to exploit widespread popular disillusion with the

> **397** The number of seats in Parliament won by the Conservatives in the election of 1983, giving them an overall majority of 144. The opposition was split; Labour won only 28 percent of the popular vote.

Bang and crash
Worried traders on the stock exchange watch fortunes disappear in the crash of October 1987. The crash came just a year after the deregulation of the London stock market in the "big bang."

condition that Britain had reached in the 1970s (see pp.376–377). The crackdown on strikes was quite widely welcomed and few people regretted the mass privatization of the nationalized industries in the mid-1980s—better-off members of the working class lined up to buy shares in British Telecom or British Gas. Working-class families also

responded to the "right-to-buy" policy that gave them a chance to purchase rented government properties. Some people felt enlivened by a sense of opportunity and competition, while others were angered by loss of security and an end of "jobs for life." The deregulation of the financial sector, climaxing in the "big bang" in the City of London in 1986, allowed individuals who were not necessarily from

> **5,000** The number of coal miners employed in South Wales by the end of 1989; the South Wales coalfields had once employed 250,000 men.

traditional moneyed backgrounds to make large sums of money. Cuts in income tax—compensated by rises in indirect taxation—left people on good incomes with far more money in their pockets. The obsessively consumerist yuppie was a symbolic figure of the period. The contrast between the rampant consumerism and evident prosperity of many areas

> **" It is certainly safe … to pronounce the brain death of socialism."**
>
> NORMAN TEBBIT MP, 1988

ARTHUR SCARGILL

Born into a Yorkshire mining family, Arthur Scargill started work at a pit at the age of 15. As a left-wing militant in the National Union of Mineworkers (NUM), he orchestrated a crucial mass picket at Saltley Gate during the 1972 miners' strike. He was elected President of the Yorkshire section of the NUM in 1973 and national NUM President in 1981. He sought a chance for strike action against the Thatcher government, which he believed intended to destroy the coal industry and the NUM. He refused to hold a national ballot of members when a strike began over pit closures in Yorkshire in March 1984, splitting the union. His attempt to use mass picketing, so successful in 1972, failed in the face of the ruthless policing. The defeat of the strike in March 1985 was followed, as he had predicted, by large-scale pit closures.

"I have to caution you. The BT3 Share Offer closes soon."

It is my duty to inform you that applications for the BT3 Share Offer must be in soon.

If you haven't registered there's no need to look so worried, as there's still time for you to apply.

You can pick up a prospectus that contains an application form at branches of NatWest, Lloyds, Royal Bank of Scotland and Ulster Bank.

Application forms will also appear in the national press.

The very last opportunity to submit completed applications is 10.00 am on Wednesday 14th July. Application deadlines do vary and yours may well be earlier. Please check your application form for details.

Remember, don't loiter.

IT COULD BE WORTH INVESTIGATING. **BT3** Share Offer

Privatization

The trend-setting privatization of British Telecom in 1984 not only reversed state ownership, but also sought to make ordinary people into shareholders. Shares were sold at a price that guaranteed investors a profit.

of southern England and the urban decay of northern industrial towns and inner cities was as stark as in the 1930s.

Boom and bust

Britain's image on the world stage improved in the 1980s. Once perceived as the "sick man of Europe," Britain

> **4,500,000** The number of people who bought shares in British Gas when it was privatized in 1985. The sale raised £5.4 billion for the government coffers.

was now seen as economically dynamic and financially sound. Whether the changes carried out merited this response is more doubtful. The Thatcherite allegiance to thrift applied only to government spending. From the mid-1980s, easy credit made possible a boom in house prices and a rapid rise in private debt. Inflation was far from conquered, reaching almost 9 percent in the late 1980s, forcing a rise in the base interest rate to a punishing 15 percent. Unemployment remained stubbornly high throughout the decade. Rising output from North Sea oil fields helped with the balance of payments and public finances, but the cost of unemployment benefits absorbed a good deal of revenue from oil. A stock market crash in October 1987 revealed the instability that deregulation brought in its wake, and put in question the wisdom of encouraging ordinary citizens to invest their savings in shares.

Thatcher's influence

Yet, if Britain's financial problems were not solved, a definite change in attitudes was nonetheless achieved for better or for worse. Those who continued to believe in raising direct taxes to reduce inequality, or those who thought that economic activity should have any other goal besides maximizing profits, found themselves swimming against the tide. Thatcher fell from power in 1990, but her policies were set to continue.

> **" Let Labour's Orwellian nightmare … spur us … to rebuild the fortunes of this … nation."**
>
> MARGARET THATCHER, CONSERVATIVE PARTY CONFERENCE SPEECH, OCTOBER 10, 1980

Oil rig in the North Sea
The exploring of North Sea oil fields, beginning in the 1970s, reached its full effect in the 1980s and 1990s. It strengthened Sterling, which made British exports expensive, and encouraged the switch from coal to oil.

AFTER

The fall of Margaret Thatcher from power in 1990 followed a sharp drop in popularity in her final term in office. She was succeeded as Prime Minister by her protégé John Major.

NO MAJOR CHANGE

Thatcher's **unpopularity resulted from mounting economic problems** in the late 1980s and from her persistence in introducing a **poll tax to replace the council rates**, a measure that provoked serious riots and was regarded as unjust by many of the government's own supporters. There was also dissension within the Conservative Party over Europe, with **Thatcher's anti-European stance** being highly divisive.

Taking over as Prime Minister after Thatcher was unseated by a Conservative Party revolt, John Major replaced the poll tax with a fairer council tax and ensured that Britain took part in the founding of the European Union (EU) in 1992. His subsequent general election victory, the **fourth consecutive Conservative win**, forced the Labour Party to begin a fundamental rethink of its policies.

Major's government soon found the strain of coordinating its currency with other EU countries unsustainable. The result was an enforced **devaluation of the pound**, which inflicted a damaging humiliation on the government, but unexpectedly resolved Britain's most pressing economic difficulties. By the mid-1990s, both **unemployment and inflation were falling**.

BRITISH PRIME MINISTER Born 1925 Died 2013

Margaret Thatcher

"With huge **courage** and **perseverance**, she turned **Britain** into a **different country**."

DAVID CAMERON, SPEECH, JANUARY 30, 2006

Margaret Thatcher was Britain's most controversial prime minister of the 20th century. Her personal influence on the direction taken by British society and the British economy in the 1980s was decisive. She was a person of narrow views and limited sympathies—even one her closest aides and greatest admirers, Ferdinand Mount, admitted that he "never became fond of her." But she was a fiercely effective political

unemployment was a sign of idleness. Neither the sufferings of the Depression nor the collectivist sentiment of wartime affected her attitudes. Winning a place at Oxford University from grammar school, she later became president of its Conservative

12.5 The percentage at which unemployment in the United Kingdom peaked under the Thatcher government in January 1982.

operator, ready to make concessions to avoid defeat, but ruthless and uncompromising once in a position of strength. Outspoken and direct where other politicians were evasive, she was hated by her opponents, and eventually alienated many within her own party, but she also commanded loyalty and admiration. Winning three consecutive general elections for the Conservatives was made easier by a split within the Labour Party, but it was also a tribute to her strength of leadership and, in a sense, the success of her policies.

Early life

Thatcher's father was a shop owner in Grantham, Lincolnshire, prominent in local politics, and a great influence on her. Like him, she felt none of the sentimental affection for the British working classes found among many Tory grandees of the upper classes. To her, poverty was a personal failing, and

Prime Minister Margaret Thatcher
Britain's first woman Prime Minister poses for an official photograph in 1985. Margaret Thatcher turned Britain into a more dynamic and enterprising country, although at the expense of social solidarity.

Return from the Falklands War

Crowds greet the returning Task Force after victory in the Falklands War of 1982. Thatcher's unwavering response to Argentinian aggression aroused patriotic fervor and transformed her standing in opinion polls at the time.

Association. Progress for a woman in the Conservative Party was hard, but persistence and talent saw her win the parliamentary constituency of Finchley in the 1959 general election.

As Education Secretary in the early 1970s, she displayed her ability to infuriate opponents. For abolishing free school milk, she was abused as "Margaret Thatcher, Milk Snatcher," ironically making her name memorable to a broad public. After Ted Heath had been humiliated by the trade unions, and lost two general elections in 1974, she was put forward as a candidate by Conservative MPs seeking to challenge him and sharply change policy. To general astonishment, she beat not only Heath, but also the experienced and moderate William Whitelaw. Choosing the first-ever woman party leader surprised the Conservatives, who had hardly intended to make a statement about gender and politics. It also wrong-footed militant feminists, confronted with the singular success of a woman with whose views they almost entirely disagreed.

Election victory

Through the 1970s, Thatcher absorbed the ideas of thinkers who rejected the post-war consensus built around the welfare state, Keynesian economics, and full employment. Control of the money supply, unfettered free-market capitalism, and an end to state interference in the economy were to provide an answer to Britain's persistent economic problems. As Thatcher later said, the roots of her beliefs lay rather in the principles that her small-town background had taught her: "an honest day's work for an honest day's pay; live within your means; pay your bills on time; support the police." Neither Thatcher's personality nor her policies were especially attractive to voters in the 1979 general election, but

the clear failings of the Labour government of Jim Callaghan helped her win a comfortable majority. At first, her tenure of office looked set to be brief. As unemployment and

Brighton bombing

In October 1984, an IRA bomb exploded in the Grand Hotel, Brighton, where Conservatives attending a party conference were sleeping. Thatcher, the main target of the bomb, escaped, but five other people died.

inflation soared in 1980–1981, her popularity ratings dropped to among the lowest ever for a Prime Minister. It was typical of Thatcher that her response was an intransigent speech to a Conservative Party conference declaring: "The lady's not for turning!" Then came the Falklands War (see pp.384–385). Thatcher's resolute nationalism won her a military victory and a popular following that she never lost in virtually all of her years in office.

> "There is **no such thing as society**: there are **individual men and women**, and … families."

MARGARET THATCHER, INTERVIEW, SEPTEMBER 1987

As her hold on power tightened from 1983 onward, Thatcher initiated radical change. The privatization of nationalized industries, tax cuts, and the freeing of capital markets changed the face of Britain. She convinced a new generation that the pursuit of wealth was good, and that dependence on the welfare state was bad. She had no sympathy for those made jobless by her economic policies, or for the miners and other workers crushed by her crusade against trade unions. Her instincts were authoritarian, and she employed police power ruthlessly in the suppression of strikes and riots. When the Greater London Council became a center of opposition to her rule, she abolished it. Her willpower and courage were unquestionable, whether shrugging off an attempt by the IRA to assassinate her at Brighton in 1984, or facing down revolt by members of her Cabinet. Like no Prime Minister since Winston Churchill, she cut a figure on the world stage, convincing foreigners that Britain was again a power to be reckoned with. Her downfall came through her stubborn persistence in introducing the poll tax, which alienated much public opinion, and her anti-European gestures, which alienated leading members of her Cabinet and party. By the time a party revolt unseated her in 1990, however, she had changed Britain for good.

Thatcher puppet

This puppet of Margaret Thatcher, from the TV show *Spitting Image*, was typical of the hostile caricature to which she was subjected. Her opponents disliked her demeanor as much as her policies.

TIMELINE

- **October 13, 1925** Born Margaret Hilda Roberts in Grantham, Lincolnshire.
- **1943–1947** Studies chemistry at Oxford University.
- **1950–1951** As the Conservative candidate for Dartford in two general elections, she fails to win a seat in Parliament.
- **1951** Marries divorced businessman Denis Thatcher.
- **1953** Qualifies as a barrister. Gives birth to twins.
- **October 1959** Enters the House of Commons as Conservative MP for Finchley, the constituency she would represent until 1992.
- **1970–1974** Serves as Secretary of State for Education and Science in the Conservative government of Edward Heath.
- **February 11, 1975** Elected as leader of the Conservative Party.

CAMPAIGNING IN THE 1950S

- **January 19, 1976** Makes a speech accusing Soviet Union of attempting world dominance, leading a Soviet publication to dub her "the Iron Lady."
- **May 4, 1979** Becomes Prime Minister after winning a 43-seat majority in the general election.
- **1981** Soaring inflation and unemployment and collapsing industrial output, make Thatcher's government immensely unpopular.
- **April–June 1982** Leads Britain to victory over Argentina in the Falklands War.
- **June 9, 1983** Reelected as Prime Minister with a landslide 144-seat majority in Parliament.
- **March 1984–March 1985** Defeats a strike by the National Union of Mineworkers (NUM) (see pp.380–381), ending the era of trade union power.
- **October 12, 1984** Escapes unscathed from an IRA attack on her hotel at the Conservative Party conference in Brighton.
- **November 1984** Begins privatizing nationalized industries, beginning with British Telecom.
- **June 11, 1987** Thatcher wins her third general election, with a working majority of 102 seats.
- **April 1990** Proposes a Community Charge, or poll tax, causing riots across England and Wales.
- **November 22, 1990** Announces her resignation and is replaced as Prime Minister by John Major.
- **April 8, 2013** Dies in her lodgings at the Ritz Hotel in London.

« BEFORE

Britain retained conscription—renamed National Service—for 15 years after the end of World War II, before making a transition to a slimmed down, highly professional armed force.

COSTS OF WAR

After World War II, Britain's **military commitments were extensive**, including fighting colonial wars, contributing to the North Atlantic Treaty Organization (NATO) alliance, and developing an independent nuclear deterrent. In 1963, Britain spent **10 percent of its national wealth on defense** (the comparable figure for 2008 was 2.5 percent). This level of **cost was unsustainable**. Commitments were reduced by granting independence to colonies and abandoning a global role to **concentrate on Europe and the contribution to NATO**.

MILITARY DOWNSIZING

Since the late 1960s, the **Royal Navy** faced **drastic spending cuts**, while the **Army became a much smaller body of regulars**. The Army's elite units, such as the **SAS and the Paras, gained an international reputation**. Though trained to fight as part of NATO forces, its **combat role** in the 1970s was **mostly to quell the "Troubles"** in Northern Ireland « 378–379.

Wars in Peacetime

By the 1980s, the training and equipment of British forces were based on expectations of a nuclear war against the Soviet Union or on countering low-level terrorism. Instead they became involved in arduous and often controversial campaigns in the Falklands, the Balkans, Iraq, and Afghanistan.

In April 1980, Britain's Special Air Service (SAS) stormed the Iranian Embassy in London to free hostages taken by Arab gunmen. The following year a group of women set up a peace camp to protest against the planned stationing of American cruise missiles with nuclear warheads at Greenham Common in Berkshire. These events illustrated the primary military preoccupations of the early 1980s: terror attacks, which Britain had developed great expertise in countering, and the nuclear confrontation with the Soviet Union and its allies. When

war came in April 1982, it was from another direction altogether. Argentina, governed by a military junta, occupied the Falkland Islands, a tiny and remote remnant of the British Empire, situated in the South Atlantic.

When Prime Minister Margaret Thatcher dispatched a Task Force to retake the islands, an old-fashioned war proved immensely popular with a surprisingly jingoistic British public. Thatcher avoided a Suez-style diplomatic disaster (see pp.366–367) by carefully securing American support for the military action. Her ruthlessness

in ordering a submarine to sink the Argentinian battleship *Belgrano* as the Task Force approached the islands showed the character of a natural war leader. Although the much reduced Royal Navy was stretched to the limit by the demands of the operation, losing four warships in fierce air and sea battles, British troops were successfully deployed on the island. Once ashore, the Royal Marines and Paras demonstrated outstanding fitness and fighting skills. The Argentinians were defeated in June, with almost 10,000 soldiers surrendering. Thatcher's

Occupying Iraq

British soldiers conduct a long-range desert patrol in Iraq in 2006. Jalal Talabani, Iraqi President from 2005, praised the British for having come "to liberate Iraqi people from the worst kind of dictatorship."

Welcome to Kosovo
British troops entered Kosovo as part of a NATO-led peacekeeping force in 1999 after the withdrawal of Serb forces. They were greeted enthusiastically by the local Kosovan population.

Despite ending its military campaign against Iraq in 2009, Britain's ongoing contribution to the war against the Taliban in Afghanistan severely stretched its military resources.

CAMPAIGN IN AFGHANISTAN
The UN-sanctioned operation in Afghanistan was less controversial than the Iraq invasion, but there were persistent complaints of British forces struggling with **inadequate or outdated equipment**. Almost 9,000 British military personnel were active **in Afghanistan in 2013**. The British Government planned to reduce that number to 5,200 by the end of the year.

ISIS
The **emergence of ISIS** (Islamic State in Iraq and Syria), that captured large parts of western Iraq and eastern Syria, underlined the complex nature of the challenges to Britain's armed forces. As part of an **international coalition to dislodge the group**, the RAF took part in air strikes against ISIS in Iraq from 2014 and in Syria from 2015. To date, more than 400 British army trainers have been deployed to Iraq and a number of special forces to Syria.

popularity with voters soared, guaranteeing her reelection in 1983, and Britain's international standing was on the whole enhanced.

Crisis in the Middle East
Britain's next major military action was in the Middle East. Any illusions that the end of the Cold War in the late 1980s would be followed by an era of world peace were dispelled when Iraqi dictator Saddam Hussein invaded Kuwait in 1990. With the blessing of the United Nations, the United States organized a coalition to counter this act of aggression. Britain made a larger military contribution than any other of America's allies, with more than 40,000 troops deployed, and the RAF and Royal Navy fully involved. Iraqi forces were defeated in 1991. The blatant aggression

750,000
The estimated number of people in London who protested against the planned invasion of Iraq on February 15, 2003. It was one of the largest political demonstrations in British history.

of the Iraqis, the UN endorsement of the use of force, the swiftness of the victory, and the low coalition casualties combined to make the war largely uncontroversial with the British public.

Defending human rights
The break-up of Yugoslavia in the 1990s brought warfare to Europe for the first time since 1945. In early 1999, efforts to find a negotiated settlement between Serbian leader Slobodan Milosevic and a movement seeking independence for Kosovo failed. Faced with the prospect of the massacre of Kosovans by Serb forces, NATO embarked upon the first offensive in its 50-year history, launching bomb and missile attacks on Serb targets. The attacks caused considerable civilian casualties, but the Serbians were induced to withdraw from Kosovo.

British Prime Minister Tony Blair was a leading advocate of the military action against Serbia and enunciated what became known as the "Blair doctrine"—arguing that the "international community" had a right and duty to intervene militarily in any country to uphold human rights and enforce civilized conduct. The term "international community" did not mean the UN, which had failed to support military action in Kosovo, but the United States and its allies.

War on terror
Blair's positioning of himself as America's closest ally was in line with British foreign policy since World War II— the sole exception being the Wilson government's refusal to contribute forces to America's Vietnam War in the 1960s. After the 9/11 attacks on the United States in 2001, there were few

Mourning the fallen
Mourners grieve as a cortege of hearses carry the repatriated bodies of seven British soldiers and Marines killed in Afghanistan through the town of Wootton Bassett, Wiltshire, in June 2010.

dissenting voices when Blair spoke of standing "shoulder-to-shoulder" with the American people against Islamic terrorism. The subsequent American invasion of Afghanistan, in which Britain played a supporting role, was widely accepted as a reasonable action, overthrowing a Taliban regime that was allied to al-Qaeda terrorists and that was oppressive, especially in its treatment of women.

The British government found itself tied into US foreign policy, though with no real influence over its direction. The right-wing administration of President George W. Bush embarked on an aggressive "war on terrorism" that ignored basic human rights and on a policy of intimidation of "rogue states" that led in 2003 to the invasion of Iraq. Blair was pulled along in the wake of American action, for which he proved a more eloquent spokesman than Bush.

SA80 Bullpup assault rifle
The SA80 Bullpup became the standard-issue British infantry rifle in 1987. It has seen combat use in the Gulf War of 1991, the invasion of Iraq in 2003, and operations in Afghanistan.

The commitment of 45,000 British troops to the Iraq invasion provoked massive anti-war demonstrations. Instead of clear-cut victory, the invasion led to a long struggle against insurgency, the collapse of Iraq into civil strife, and disgrace for Anglo-American forces found to have tortured Iraqi prisoners. By the time British troops were

extricated from Iraq in 2009, the situation in Afghanistan had deteriorated radically. Despite the killing of Osama bin Laden by US armed forces on May 2, 2012, the Taliban was resurgent. The war in Afghanistan dragged on, complicated by the appearance of pro-ISIS militia, and as things stand, there is no end in sight.

« BEFORE

The election of Tony Blair as Prime Minister in May 1997 ended 18 years of Conservative rule and ushered in a new era in British political life.

BLAIR'S LEADERSHIP
As leader of the Labour Party from 1994, Blair **abandoned** its long-standing commitment to the **state control of key industries** and embraced the **wealth-creating potential of free enterprise**, in effect accepting the economic changes wrought by Thatcherism **« 380–381**. His "New Labour" won a landslide victory in the 1997 election against John Major's Conservatives. At 43, Blair was the youngest British Prime Minister in the 20th century.

TONY BLAIR CELEBRATES ELECTION VICTORY

London skyline
A panoramic view of the British capital stretches from the center of financial power in the City to the seat of political power in the Houses of Parliament. By 2006, almost one-third of London's citizens were born outside the United Kingdom.

By the late 1990s, Britain appeared to have recovered from the persistent economic and financial problems that had plagued the country for decades. Inflation was below 1.5 percent, the unemployment rate around 5.5 percent, and the British economy grew in every quarter of every year between 1997 and 2007. Although wealth was shared unequally, most British people benefited to some degree by rising living standards, helped by the introduction of a minimum wage. Government spending on the National Health Service and on education also rose.

Labour Prime Minister Tony Blair and his Chancellor of the Exchequer Gordon Brown inevitably took much of the credit for this rosy economic situation, which was the single largest factor in securing further Labour general election victories in 2001 and 2005.

The downside
Some aspects of the economic prosperity provided cause for disquiet, however; British manufacturing continued its seemingly irreversible decline, although it was compensated by rapid growth in the services and financial sector. Increasing inequalities in wealth were exemplified by banks and financial companies, which gave bonuses to employees equivalent to a lifetime's earnings for others. Britain was awash with easy money— consumption was fueled by credit-card borrowing and property prices inflated

Financial meltdown
Investors line up to withdraw their money from the insolvent Northern Rock bank in September 2007. The banking crisis revealed that much of Britain's prosperity was built on shaky foundations.

by the availability of cheap mortgages. The news that the Northern Rock bank was on the verge of collapse in 2007 marked the beginning of the credit crunch and the end of the long period of prosperity. Inheriting the premiership from Blair, Gordon Brown found himself at the forefront of an international effort to stem a global banking collapse, taking failing banks into state ownership at the expense of a vast expansion of budgetary deficit and public debt.

A period of change
The period of Tony Blair's premiership from 1997 to 2007 brought some radical reforms in Britain's system of government. Since the 1970s, the Scottish National Party (SNP) had been a significant force in British politics. Blair was not prepared to accept the SNP's demand for independence, but instead instituted a Scottish Parliament with a devolved government exercising considerable powers in 1999. Wales was also given its own assembly and a Catholic-Protestant power-sharing

Facing the Future

Britain entered the new millennium with its people prosperous, unemployment low, and freedom and democracy intact. In the following two decades, however, terrorism and counterterrorism, a brush with financial catastrophe, and a vote to radically alter Britain's relations with the EU suggest that the present century is shaping up to be as troubled as the last.

London bomb attacks
British-born Hasib Hussain was 18 years old when he blew up this bus on July 7, 2005, killing 14 people including himself. Suicide bombers also targeted three Underground trains in the rush-hour terrorist attacks.

executive was set up in Northern Ireland. There was also a radical change in Westminster. All but 92 hereditary peers lost their seats in the House of Lords in 1999.

Evolving attitudes
One significant aspect of the 1997 election was the number of seats won by female MPs—119 in all, compared to 24 women elected in 1974. This reflected ongoing changes in attitudes toward women and their expectations. In the first decade of the 21st century, 70 percent of British women had paid employment, one of the highest in the world. Although a lot of these jobs were part-time and they remained under-represented in boardrooms, it was true that many barriers to their advancement had crumbled.

Attitudes to homosexuality also underwent a radical transformation. Being gay was no longer a bar to advancement in politics or almost any other area of life, and by 2010 Gay Pride marches had become popular festivals rather than acts of protest. The issues of race and immigration remained contentious, despite the officially adopted ideology of multiculturalism and generally high levels of integration. The West Indian and Asian presence in Britain was long established, but the expansion of the European Union to include the countries of Eastern Europe in 2004 was followed by a fresh influx of immigrants. Recent figures suggest that more than one in 10 of the UK population had been born abroad.

Terrorist threat
The British military involvement in wars in Afghanistan and Iraq were contentious and there has been a rise in radical Islamic terrorism. In July 2005, suicide bomb attacks on Underground trains and a bus in London killed 52 people. The rise of ISIS in Iraq and Syria led to a number of attacks inspired by their Islamist ideology, including a bomb attack on a concert in Manchester which killed 22 people in 2017. The authorities need to use enhanced digital surveillance to combat these terror attacks, leading to fears of an erosion of civil liberties.

Britain and Europe
Although Gordon Brown had steered Britain through the international economic crisis of 2007-2009, the Labour party lost the 2010 General Election. Even so, David Cameron's Conservatives failed to win an overall majority and he was forced to govern in a coalition with the Liberal Democrats, which embarked on rigorous public spending cuts. The majority Conservative government which replaced it in 2015 gave way to demands for a Referendum on Britain's European membership after a rise in the vote of the anti-European UKIP (UK Independence Party). A campaign which focused on immigration, and contested claims that the UK would be financially better-off outside the EU or could make better trade deals on its own, resulted in a narrow vote to leave (by 52 to 48 percent). Subsequently, the UK sought to negotiate its future relationship with the EU, a process that proved to be more complex and protracted than previously thought.

The United Kingdom had never been an enthusiastic participant in the European Union and decades of attacks by right-wing politicians and commentators led to a Referendum on Britain's EU membership in 2016.

BREXIT
Although Britain won opt-outs from elements of an increasingly integrated European Union, including from the Schengen agreement on visa-free travel and use of the Euro currency, **many believed the EU had evolved in a direction contrary to Britain's interests.** UKIP, founded in 1991, gave political voice to this view and its winning of 12.6 percent of the vote in the 2015 General Election led Prime Minister David Cameron to concede a Referendum on Britain's membership. The **vote was narrowly in favor of Britain's exit** (or "Brexit") and an extended period of difficult negotiations ensued to determine the terms for Britain leaving and how it would trade with the EU in the future.

NIGEL FARAGE

Monarchs and Rulers

MONARCHS

MONARCHS OF ENGLAND

HOUSE OF WESSEX

802–839	Egbert
839–855	Aethelwulf
855–860	Aethelbald
860–866	Aethelbert
866–871	Aethelred
871–899	Alfred (the Great)
899–925	Edward (the Elder)
925–940	Athelstan
940–946	Edmund (the Magnificent)
946–955	Eadred
955–959	Eadwig (All–Fair)
959–975	Edgar (the Peaceable)
975–978	Edward (the Martyr)
978–1016	Aethelred (the Unready)
1016	Edmund (Ironside)

HOUSE OF DENMARK

1014	Sweyn (Forkbeard)
1016–1035	Canute (the Great)
1035–1040	Harold I (Harefoot)
1040–1042	Harthacnut

HOUSE OF WESSEX (RESTORED)

1042–1066	Edward (the Confessor)
1066	Harold II

HOUSE OF NORMANDY

1066–1087	William I (the Conqueror)
1087–1100	William II (Rufus)
1100–1135	Henry I (Beauclerc)
1135–1154	Stephen
1141	Matilda

PLANTAGENET (ANGEVIN LINE)

1154–1189	Henry II (Curtmantle)
1189–1199	Richard I (the Lionheart)
1199–1216	John (Lackland)
1216–1272	Henry III
1272–1307	Edward I (Longshanks)
1307–1327	Edward II
1327–1377	Edward III
1377–1399	Richard II

PLANTAGENET (LANCASTRIAN LINE)

1399–1413	Henry IV (Bolingbroke)
1413–1422	Henry V
1422–1461	Henry VI
1470–1471	Henry VI

PLANTAGENET (YORKIST LINE)

1461–1470	Edward IV
1471–1483	Edward IV
1483	Edward V
1483–1485	Richard III

HOUSE OF TUDOR

1485–1509	Henry VII
1509–1547	Henry VIII
1547–1553	Edward VI
1553	Lady Jane Grey
1553–1558	Mary I
1558–1603	Elizabeth I

HOUSE OF STUART

1603–1625	James I (James VI of Scotland)
1625–1649	Charles I

THE COMMONWEALTH

1653–1658	Oliver Cromwell; Lord Protector
1658–1659	Richard Cromwell; Lord Protector

HOUSE OF STUART (RESTORED)

1660–1685	Charles II
1685–1688	James II

HOUSE OF ORANGE AND STUART

1689–1702	William III and Mary II

HOUSE OF STUART

1702–1707	Anne

MONARCHS OF BRITAIN

HOUSE OF STUART

1707–1714	Anne

HOUSE OF HANOVER

1714–1727	George I
1727–1760	George II
1760–1820	George III
1820–1830	George IV
1830–1837	William IV
1837–1901	Victoria

HOUSE OF SAXE–COBURG–GOTHA

1901–1910	Edward VII

HOUSE OF WINDSOR

1910–1936	George V
1936	Edward VIII
1936–1952	George VI
1952–	Elizabeth II

MONARCHS OF SCOTLAND

HOUSE OF ALPIN

843–858	Kenneth I (Kenneth MacAlpin)
858–862	Donald I
862–878	Constantine I
878–879	Aedh
879–889	Eochaid
889–900	Donald II
900–942	Constantine II
942–954	Malcolm I
954–962	Indulf
962–966	Dub (or Duff)
966–971	Cuilean (or Culen or Colin)
971–995	Kenneth II
995–997	Constantine III
997–1005	Kenneth III
1005–1034	Malcolm II

HOUSE OF DUNKELD

1034–1040	Duncan I
1040–1057	Macbeth
1057–1058	Lulach
1058–1093	Malcolm III
1093–1094	Donald III
1094	Duncan II
1094–1097	Donald III
1097–1107	Edgar
1107–1124	Alexander I
1124–1153	David I
1153–1165	Malcolm IV
1165–1214	William
1214–1249	Alexander II
1249–1286	Alexander III

NO HOUSE

1286–1290	Margaret (Maid of Norway)
1290–1292	Interregnum
1292–1296	John Balliol
1296–1306	Interregnum

HOUSE OF BRUCE

1306–1329	Robert I
1329–1371	David II
1332–1341	(with interruptions) Edward Balliol

HOUSE OF STUART

1371–1390	Robert II
1390–1406	Robert III
1406–1437	James I
1437–1460	James II
1460–1488	James III
1488–1513	James IV
1513–1542	James V
1542–1567	Mary (Queen of Scots)
1569–1625	James VI (James I of England)

PRINCES OF WALES

1137–1170	Owain Gwynedd (or Owain ap Gruffydd)
c. 1230–1240	Llywelyn the Great (or Llywelyn ab Iorwerth)
1240–1246	Dafydd ap Llywelyn
1258–1282	Llywelyn ap Gruffudd
1282–1283	Dafydd ap Gruffudd

MONARCHS OF IRELAND

846–860	Máel Sechnaill mac Maele Ruanaid
861–876	Áed Findliath (or mac Néill)
877–914	Flann Sinna
915–917	Niall Glúndub
918–942	Donnchad Donn
943–954	Congalach Cnogba
955–978	Domnall ua Néill
979–1002	Máel Sechnaill mac Domnaill
1002–1014	Brian Boru
1014–1022	Máel Sechnaill mac Domnaill
died 1064	Donnchad mac Briain
died 1072	Diarmait mac Máel na mBo
died 1086	Toirdelbach Ua Briain
died 1119	Muirchertach Ua Briain
died 1121	Domnall Ua Lochlainn
died 1156	Toirdelbach Ua Conchobair
died 1166	Muirchertach Mac Lochlainn
died 1198	Ruaidri Ua Conchobair

PRIME MINISTERS AND PRESIDENTS

PRIME MINISTERS OF BRITAIN

(W) = Whig   (c) = coalition   (T) = Tory
(Li) = Liberal   (C) = Conservative   (L) = Labour

1721–1742	Sir Robert Walpole; (W)
1742–1743	Spencer Compton (W)
1743–1754	Henry Pelham (W)
1754–1756	Thomas Pelham–Holles (W)
1756–1757	William Cavendish (W)
1757–1762	Thomas Pelham–Holles (W)
1762–1763	John Stuart (T)
1763–1765	George Grenville (W)
1765–1766	Charles Watson–Wentworth (W)
1766–1768	William Pitt the Elder (W)
1768–1770	Augustus FitzRoy (W)
1770–1782	Frederick North, Lord North; (T)
1782–1782	Charles Watson–Wentworth (W)
1782–1783	William Petty–FitzMaurice (W)
1783	William Cavendish–Bentinck (W) (c)
1783–1801	William Pitt the Younger (T)
1801–1804	Henry Addington (T)
1804–1806	William Pitt the Younger (T)
1806–1807	William Wyndham Grenville (W) (c)
1807–1809	William Cavendish–Bentinck (T)
1809–1812	Spencer Perceval (T)
1812–1827	Robert Banks Jenkinson (T)
1827–1827	George Canning (T)
1827–1828	Frederick John Robinson (T)
1828–1830	Arthur Wellesley (T)
1830–1834	Charles Grey (W)
1834–1834	William Lamb (W)
1834–1834	Arthur Wellesley (T)
1834–1835	Sir Robert Peel (C)
1835–1841	William Lamb (W)
1841–1846	Sir Robert Peel (C)
1846–1852	Lord John Russell (W)
1852–1852	Edward Smith–Stanley (C)
1852–1855	George Hamilton–Gordon (P) (c)
1855–1858	Henry John Temple (W)
1858–1859	Edward Smith–Stanley (C)
1859–1865	Henry John Temple (Li)
1865–1866	John Russell (Li)
1866–1868	The Earl of Derby (C)
1868	Benjamin Disraeli (C)
1868–1874	William Ewart Gladstone (Li)
1874–1880	Benjamin Disraeli (C)
1880–1885	William Ewart Gladstone (Li)
1885–1886	Robert Gascoyne–Cecil (C)
1886–1886	William Ewart Gladstone (Li)
1886–1892	Robert Gascoyne–Cecil (C)
1892–1894	William Ewart Gladstone (Li)
1894–1895	Archibald Primrose (Li)
1895–1902	Robert Gascoyne–Cecil (C)
1902–1905	Arthur Balfour (C)
1905–1908	Sir Henry Campbell–Bannerman (Li)

1908–1916	Herbert Henry Asquith (Li)
1916–1922	David Lloyd George (Li) (c)
1922–1923	Andrew Bonar Law (C)
1923–1924	Stanley Baldwin (C)
1924–1924	Ramsey MacDonald (L)
1924–1929	Stanley Baldwin (C)
1929–1931	Ramsey MacDonald (L)
1931–1935	Ramsey MacDonald (NLP) (c)
1935–1937	Stanley Baldwin (C) (c)
1937–1940	Neville Chamberlain (C) (c)
1940–1945	Winston Churchill (C) (c)
1945–1951	Clement Attlee (L)
1951–1955	Winston Churchill (C)
1955–1957	Sir Anthony Eden (C)
1957–1963	Harold Macmillan (C)
1963–1964	Alec Douglas–Home (C)
1964–1970	Harold Wilson (L)
1970–1974	Edward Heath (C)
1974–1976	Harold Wilson (L)
1976–1979	James Callaghan (L)
1979–1990	Margaret Thatcher (C)
1990–1997	John Major (C)
1997–2007	Tony Blair (L)
2007–2010	Gordon Brown (L)
2010–2016	David Cameron (C) (c)
2016–	Theresa May (C)

PRIME MINISTERS OF NORTHERN IRELAND

(UU) = Ulster Unionist

1921–1940	James Craig (UU)
1940–1943	John Miller Andrews (UU)
1943–1963	Basil Brooke (UU)
1963–1969	Terence O'Neill (UU)
1969–1971	James Chichester–Clark (UU)
1971–1972	Brian Faulkner (UU)

PRIME MINISTERS OF IRELAND

(CG) = Cumann na nGaedheal   (FF) = Fianna Fáil
(c) = coalition   (FG) = Fine Gael

1922–1932	William Thomas Cosgrave (CG)
1932–1948	Éamon de Valera (FF)
1948–1951	John Costello (FG) (c)
1951–1954	Éamon de Valera (FF)
1954–1957	John Costello (FG) (c)
1957–1959	Éamon de Valera (FF)
1959–1966	Sean Lemass (FF)
1966–1973	Jack Lynch (FF)
1973–1977	Liam Cosgrave (FG) (c)
1977–1979	Jack Lynch (FF)
1979–1981	Charles Haughey (FF)
1981–1982	Garret FitzGerald (FG) (c)
1982	Charles Haughey (FF)

1982–1987	Garret FitzGerald (FG) (c)
1987–1992	Charles Haughey (FF) (c)
1992–1994	Albert Reynolds (FF) (c)
1994–1997	John Bruton (FG) (c)
1997–2008	Bertie Ahern (FF) (c)
2008–2011	Brian Cowen (FF) (c)
2011–2017	Enda Kenny (FG) (c)
2017–	Leo Varadkar (FG)

PRESIDENTS OF IRELAND

(apn) = all-party nomination   (U) = Unionist
(FF) = Fianna Fáil   (LP) = Labour Party
(WP) = Workers' Party   (Ind) = Independents

1938–1945	Douglas Hyde (apn)
1945–1959	Seán T. O'Kelly (U)
1959–1973	Éamon de Valera (FF)
1973–1974	Erskine H. Childers (FF)
1974–1976	Cearbhall Ó Dálaigh (apn)
1976–1990	Patrick Hillery (FF)
1990–1997	Mary Robinson (LP/WP/Ind)
1997–2011	Mary McAleese (FF/Ind)
2011–	Michael Higgins (LP)

FIRST MINISTERS OF SCOTLAND

(LP) = Labour Party   (SNP) = Scottish National Party

1999–2000	Donald Dewar (LP) (c)
2000–2001	Henry McLeish (LP) (c)
2001–2007	Jack McConnell (LP) (c)
2007–2014	Alex Salmond (SNP)
2014–	Nicola Sturgeon (SNP)

FIRST MINISTERS OF WALES

(LP) = Labour Party

2000–2009	Hywel Rhodri Morgan (LP) (c)
2009–18	Carwyn Jones (LP) (c)
2018–	Mark Drakeford (LP) (c)

FIRST MINISTERS OF NORTHERN IRELAND

(UUP) = Ulster Unionist Party
(DUP) = Democratic Unionist Party

1999–2000	David Trimble (UUP)
2000–2001	David Trimble (UUP)
2001–2002	David Trimble (UUP)
2007–2008	Ian Paisley (DUP)
2008–2010	Peter Robinson (DUP)
2010–2015	Peter Robinson (DUP)
2016–2017	Arlene Foster (DUP)

Index

Page numbers in **bold** indicate main entries.

A

abortion 373
Achill Island, Mayo 266–267
Acre, Syria, sieges of 83, 241
Act of Settlement (1652) 175
Act of Settlement (1701) 137, **200**
Act of Supremacy (1534) 135, 137
Act of Uniformity (1559) 172
Acts of Attainder 132, 142
Adam, Robert 225
Adams, Gerry 379
Addison, Joseph **208**, 211
Aden 364, 365
Adrian IV, Pope 81
Áedán, king of Dal Riata 59
Aelle, king of Northumbria 47
Aelle of Sussex 40
Aethelbald, king of Mercia 41
Aethelbert, king of Kent 40, 41, 44
Aethelflaed, lady of the Mercians **52**, 53
Aethelred, king of Mercia 41
Aethelred "the Unready," king of England 57
Aethelwold, king of Northumbria 52
Aetius 35
Afghan War, First 290
Afghanistan **385**, 387
Africa 146, 179, **286**, **296–297**, **302–303**,
   312–313, 343, 364–365
   see also North Africa; South Africa
Age of Discovery **146**, 162, 212
Age of Reason 185, **208**, 282
Agincourt, battle of (1415) 99, **118–119**, 122
Agricola, Julius 30
Agricultural Revolution 193, **230–231**, **232**,
   294
agriculture
   assarts 89
   early 10, 16, 21
   18th century 193, 201, **230–231**
   enclosures 104, 142–143, 222, 230, 232
   field strips 88, 89
   14th century crisis 120
   implements 10, 33, 142, 218, 230, 231
   Irish 266–267
   manors 88–89
   Roman 33
   sheep 89, 142, 231
   20th century 334
   World War II 355
Aidan, bishop of Lindisfarne 44
air raids
   World War I 321, 326, 327
   World War II 347, 349, **352–355**, 358, 361
aircraft 304, 343, **356–357**
   seaplanes 339
airships 321, 326, 327
Alam II, Shah **213**, 290
Alba, duke of 149
Alba, kingdom of 59
Alban, St., shrine of 44
Albany, Robert Stewart, duke of (*earlier*
   Robert of Fife) 116–117
Albert, Prince 262, **270**, **271**, 273, 304
alcohol 222, 373
Alcuin of York 41, 46
Aldermaston March 369
Alexander II, king of Scotland 92
Alexander III, king of Scotland 92
Alexander II, czar of Russia 275
Alexandra, Queen 304
Alfred the Great 47, **50–51**, 52
alliterative style 110
Alnwick Castle 114
Ambassadors, The (Holbein) 152–153
American Indians 162, 163, 212, 214, 234,
   244, 245
American Revolution 209, **214–217**, 242
Amin, Idi 365
Amlaíb, king of Dublin 55, 59

Amritsar massacre 342
Amundsen, Roald 287
anesthetics 271, 274
Anderson shelters 347, **354**
Andrew, duke of York 363
Angevin Empire 76
Anglesey 58
Anglicanism 137, 166, 174, 282
Anglo-Dutch Wars 173, 176–177, 178–179
Anglo-Irish "Ascendancy" 238
Anglo-Mysore Wars 213
Anglo-Saxon Chronicle **40**, 46, 47, 51, 53, 68, 75
Anglo-Saxons 10–11, 33, 34, 35, **40–45**, 58,
   68, 69, 70, 98
   art and craftwork 8–9, 36–37, 40, 42–43,
      44, 45, 48–49
   Christianity 44–45
   jewelry 41, 50
   literature 110
   society 60–61
Angry Brigade 373
Anne, Princess Royal 363
Anne, queen of Great Britain and Ireland
   197, **200**
Anne of Cleves 135
Anne of Denmark 158
Anschluss 346
Anselm, St., archbishop of Canterbury 69,
   72–73
Anson, George 226, 227
Antonine Wall 28, 30
apartheid 303, 365
appliances, domestic **340–341**, 371
apprentices **120**, 121
Aquae Sulis *see* Bath
aqueducts 33
Aquitaine 76, 77, 96, 97, 118, 119
Arabs 343
Arbroath, Declaration of (1320) 93
archery 96, **99**, 101, **118–119**, 125
   as sport 305
architecture
   Georgian 218–219
   Gothic cathedrals 89, 112–113
   Gothic Revival 282
   New Town, Edinburgh 225
   Regency 255, 256–257
   Saxon 60
   Tudor 142
   Victorian 279
   Wren's 182, 184, 185, 186–187
Ardoch Fort, Scotland 24
Argentina 384–385
Arkwright, Richard 233
Armada *see* Spanish Armada
Armagh Outrages 239
armies
   Boer War 303
   Canadian 244
   Civil War 168, 169
   Crimean War 274
   medieval 99, 118
   Napoleonic Wars 240, 241
   New Model Army **169**, 173, 175, 176
   19th century reform 275
   Norman 98
   post-1945 384
   Roman 22, 24, 28, 29, 34–35, 98
   World War I 320–321, 322, 325
   World War II 359
Armistice Day 323, 330
armor 99, **124**, 125
   see also helmets
art
   Anglo-Saxon 8–9, 40, 42–43, 44, 45, 50
   Celtic 21, 39, 48–49, 54
   Edwardian 305
   Georgian 220–221
   industrial landscapes 232–233
   medieval 103, 108–109, 114–115, **152**
   Pictish 59
   portraits 134, 140–141, 167, 208, 225, 305
   prehistoric 15, 16

Pre-Raphaelite 282
   Roman 29
   Scottish 225
   Tudor 134, 140–141, 144–145, **152**
   Viking 46, 55
   war 274–275
Art Deco 305
Art Nouveau 304
Arthur, King 34, 40, 110
Arthur, prince of Wales **128**, 134, 135, 148
Arts and Crafts Movement **282**, 305
Ashanti people 297
Asquith, Herbert 309, 311, 312, 321, 322
Asser 51
assizes 76–77
Assizes of Arms 99
Astor, Nancy 309, 327
astronomy 184, 185, 200, 226–227
Aswan High Dam 367
asylums 278
Athelstan, king of England 11, **53**, 58, 59
Atlantic Charter (1941) 343, **349**, 358
atomic bombs 359, 369
Attlee, Clement 311, 359, 360, 361
Atrebates 24
Augsburg, League of 196
Augustine, Saint 44
Augustus, Emperor 23, 208
Austen, Jane 218
Australia **227**, 277, **287**, **294–295**, 343,
   362–363, 364–365
   transportation to 223, 237, 294, 295
Austria 200–201, 212, 240, 241, 313, 346
Avebury, Wiltshire 17

B

Babington Plot (1585) 138, 141
"baby boom" 371
Bacon, Francis 152, 153, 155, **184**, 185
Baden-Powell, Robert 303, 304
Baines, Edward 232–233
Bakewell, Robert 230
Baldwin, Stanley 334, 335, 337, 345, 346
Balfour Declaration (1917) 343
Ball, John 104, 105
Balliol, Edward 92, 93
Balliol, John 92
Bank of England 181, **210–211**, 218, 334, 361
banking crisis 386
banknotes **210**, 228, 229, 326
Banks, Joseph 226–227
Bannockburn, battle of (1314) 65, 93,
   94–95, 138
Banqueting House, London 159, 170–171
Barbados 163, 175
barbarians 34, 35
Barebones Parliament 173
barons 64, 73, 76, 77, 84–85, 86, 123
barrows **16**, 20, 21
Bath, Somerset 218–219
   Roman (Aquae Sulis) 29, **33**
Battersea Shield 20–21
battles
   Agincourt (1415) 99, **118–119**, 122
   Aughrim (1691) 196, 197
   Austerlitz (1805) 241
   Balaclava (1854) 275
   Bannockburn (1314) 65, 93, **94–95**, 138
   Barnet (1471) 65, **122–123**
   Beachy Head (1690) **197**, 211
   Blenheim (1704) 197
   Bosworth (1485) 123
   Bouvines (1214) 84, 86
   the Boyne (1690) **196–197**, 266
   Britain (1940) 349, **356–357**
   Brunanburh (937) 53, 55, 59
   Builth (1282) 91
   Bunker Hill (1775) 214
   Buxar (1764) **212–213**, 290
   Cambrai (1917) 322, 323
   Cape St. Vincent (1797) 242

Castillon (1453) 119
   Castledermot (848) 54
   Clontarf (1014) **55**, 81
   Crécy (1346) 96, 99, **100–101**, 116
   Culloden (1746) 204–205
   Dettingen (1743) 200
   the Diamond (1795) 239
   Dunbar (1654) 175
   Edgehill (1642) 168
   El Alamein (1942) 358
   Elands River (1901) 302
   Falkirk (1298) 93, 99
   Flodden (1513) 134, 135, **138**, 158
   Formigny (1450) 119
   Halidon Hill (1333) **93**, 96
   Hastings (1066) 68, 70–71
   Hattin (1187) 83
   Homildon Hill (1402) 115, **117**
   Inkerman (1854) 275
   Killiecrankie (1689) 197
   La Coruña (1809) 241
   Lake Erie (1813) 244–245
   Lewes (1264) 85
   Marston Moor (1644) 169, 174
   Mons Badonicus (500) 40
   Mons Graupius (83) 24
   Naseby (1645) 169
   Neville's Cross (1346) 116–117
   New Orleans (1815) 245
   the Nile (1798) 242–243
   Omdurman (1898) **297**, 350
   Otterburn (1388) 115, **116**, 138
   Passchendaele (1917) 322, 323
   the Plains of Abraham (1759) 212
   Plassey (1757) 212
   Poitiers (1356) **97**, 114
   Preston (1648) 169
   Preston (1715) 202
   Prestonpans (1745) 203
   Princeton (1777) 163
   Ramillies (1706) 197
   Rorke's Drift (1879) 297
   Sebastopol (1854) 274–275
   Sedgemoor (1685) 189
   the Somme (1916) 322, 323, **324–325**
   Stamford Bridge (1066) 68
   Stirling Bridge (1297) 93
   Tippecanoe (1811) 244
   Tourcoing (1794) 240
   Towton (1461) 122, 123
   Trafalgar (1804) 241, **243**
   Vinegar Hill (1798) 238–239
   Waterford (1650) 175
   Waterloo (1815) 240–241, 246–247
   Widow McCormack's Cabbage Patch
      (1848) 300
   Ypres (1914) 321
Baudin, Nicolas 287
Bayeux tapestry 11, 61, **70–71**
Bazalgette, Joseph 279
BBC (British Broadcasting Corporation)
   339, 371
Beagle, HMS **288**, 289, 295
Beaker People 17
beakers, claw 40
Beardsley, Aubrey 304
Beatles, The 372, 373, **374–375**
Becket, Thomas 62–63, **77–79**, 81, 108, 110
Bede, The Venerable 30, **45**
Beeching Report 259
Beeton, Mrs. **278**, 280, 281
Beggar's Opera, The (Gay) 209
Behn, Aphra 176, 181
Belfast 277, 332, 333, 378, 379
Belfast Newsletter 209
Belgium 303, 313, 320, 321, 349
Belgrano, sinking of the 384
Benedict Biscop, Saint 45
Bentham, Jeremy 185, 283
Beowulf 35, **40**, 110
Berlin airlift 369
Bermudas 163
Berwick, siege of (1332–1333) 92–93

Besant, Annie 309, **310**
Bessemer process **258**, 277
Bevan, Aneurin 361, 367
Beveridge Report (1941) 355
Bevin, Ernest 355, 364, 369
Biafra 365
Bible, translations of 109, 158
"big bang" 380, 381
Bill of Rights (1689) 189
Birmingham 233, 237, 258, 277, 379
birth rate 338, 371
bishops 69, 72–73, 108, 158
Bishops' Wars **166**, 174, 196
Bismarck, Otto von 312
Black and Tans 333
Black Death **102–103**, 104, 117, 120, 142
Black Hole of Calcutta 213
Black Watch regiment 203
Blackstone, William 223
Blair, Tony 379, 385, **386–387**
Blake, Robert 178, 179
Blandy, Mary 223
Blaxland, Gregory 287
Blitz 349, **352–353**, **354–355**
Blitzkrieg 349
blood circulation 184
"Bloody Assizes" 189
Bloody Sunday 378–379
Blow Up (film) 373
Blücher, Gebhard Leberecht von 247
Boccaccio, Giovanni 110
bodkins 96
"bodyline" controversy 342, 343
Boer War 271, **302–303**, 350
Boers 296, 302–303, 343
Boleyn, Anne 134, 135, 140
Boniface, Saint 45
bonus culture 386
Book of Kells, The 48–49, 54
books
    early 39, 45, 48–49, 57
    medieval 89, 106–107
Boston massacre 214
Boston Tea Party 215
Botany Bay 227
Bothwell, James Hepburn, earl of 138
Bougainville, Louis de 227
Boulton, Matthew 233, 265
Bow Street Runners 222, 223
Box Tunnel 261
Boxer Rebellion 312
Boxgrove, West Sussex 14
Bradford, Yorkshire 276
Bradley, Richard 230
Breda, Declaration of (1660) 176
Brendan, Saint 38
Bretwaldas 40–41
Brian Boru 55, 81
Bridgeman, Charles 231
bridges 165, 260–261, 262–263
Bright, John 268
Brighton bombing 383
Brighton Pavilion 256–257
Bristol 211, 234, 260–261, 351, 358, 368
Britain, origins of name of 21
British Empire **212–213**, 251, 273, 287,
    290–297, 302–303, 316, 317
    decline and end 342–343, 364–365
    see also colonial expansion
British Empire Exhibition 343
British Expeditionary Force (BEF) 321
British Gas 380, 381
British Summer Time 326
British Telecom 380, 381
British Union of Fascists (BUF) 335
Brittany 77, 96, 97
Brixton riots 380
brochs 21, 30
bronze 20, 21
Brown, Gordon 386, 387
Brown, John 271
Brown, Lancelot ("Capability") 231
Bruce, Edward 81, **93**
Bruce, Robert 92, 93, 158
Brunel, Isambard Kingdom 259, **260–263**
Brunel, Marc Isambard 260, 261
Buchan, Alexander Stewart, earl of ("Wolf of
    Badenoch") 117
Buchanan, George 224

BUF *see* British Union of Fascists
Bunyan, John 173
burgage rights 89
Burghal Hidage 51, 72
Burgundy 38, 118, 119
burhs 51, 52, 72
burials, ancient 16, 17, 19, 20, 21
Burke, Edmund 236–237
Burke, Robert O'Hara 287
Burma 290, 359
Burne-Jones, Edward 282, 283
Burns, Robert 224
Burton, Richard 286
Bush, George W. 385
Butt, Isaac 300
Byrd, William 152
Byron, Lord 209, **282**
Byzantine Empire 82, 83, 102

C

Cable Street, battle of 335
Cabot, John 146
Cade, Jack 105
Cadiz, sack of 148–149
Cadwallon of Gwynedd 58
Caesar, Julius 22–23
Cahir Castle 156–157
Calais, France 65, 118, 119
    siege of 96, 97, 101
calendar 200
Callanish stone circle 10
Cambridge, University of 89, 108, 369
Cameron, David 382, 385, 387
Campaign for Nuclear Disarmament 369
Campbell-Bannerman, Henry 311
Camulodunum *see* Colchester
Canada 212, 244, 245, 294, 295, 296, 300,
    343, 363, 365
canals **233**, 277
cannon 99, **119**, 146, 275, 297
Canterbury 47, 120
    archbishopric of **44**, 45, 60, 79, 103
Canterbury Cathedral 69, 109
    Becket's murder 62–63, **77**, **78–79**, 110
Canterbury Tales (Chaucer) 98, 108,
    110–111, 208
Canute, king of England **56**, **57**, 60, 61
Cape Colony 303
capital punishment 223
    abolition of 373
    last Tower Hill execution 203
capitalism 179, 210, 225, 283, 383
Caractacus 13, **24**
Caribbean *see* West Indies
Carlyle, Thomas 225, 253, 265, **283**
Carnaby Street, London 372
Caroline of Brunswick 254–255
Carrick, John Stewart, earl of 116
cars 277, 304, 314–315, 316, 339, 371
Carthusians 108
Cartimandua, queen of the Brigantes 24
cartoons, satirical 209, 237, 269, 289
Cassivellaunus 22–23
castles 68, **69**, 72–73, 76, 114
    French 82, 84
    Irish 81, 156–157
    Scottish 58, 174–175
    sieges 92–93, **97**, **99**
    Welsh 64, **90–91**
Cat and Mouse Act (1913) 309
catechism 109
Catesby, Robert 161
cathedrals 69, 89, 112–113, 117, 164–165
    role of masons 121
    see also Canterbury Cathedral; St. Paul's
        Cathedral
Catherine of Aragon 128, 134, 135, 137, 148
Catherine of Braganza 177
Catholic Emancipation 255, 300
Catholicism *see* Roman Catholicism
Cato Street conspiracy (1820) 255
Cattle Raid of Cooley 31
Catuvellauni 22, 23, 24
causewayed camps 16
Cavaliers 171
cavalry 22, 98, 99, 168, 169
Celts 11, **20**, 29
    art 21, 39, 48–49, 54

Christianity 44, 45
    gods 33
    language 29, 30, 31
censorship 209, 326, 372, 373
Cetshwayo, king of the Zulus 296–297
Chamberlain, Neville **346–347**, 349, 351
chantry chapels 108
Charge of the Light Brigade 275
chariots 21, 22
charity 108
Charlemagne, king of the Franks 39, 41
Charles IV, king of France 96
Charles VI, king of France 97, 118–119
Charles VII, king of France 119
Charles I, king of Great Britain and Ireland
    128, 138, 158, **166–167**, **168–169**, 174,
    189, 196
    execution **170–171**, 172, 176
Charles II, king of Great Britain and Ireland
    129, 163, 169, 173, 174, **176–177**, 179,
    189, 200
    and London 180, 181, 182
    and science 185
Charles, prince of Wales 363
Charles Edward Stuart, Prince ("Young
    Pretender"/"Bonnie Prince Charlie")
    158, **203–205**
Charlotte, Princess 255
Charlotte Dundas (paddle-steamer) 258–259
Chartists 237, **265**, 310
Chaucer, Geoffrey 98, 108, **110–111**, 208
Cheddar, Somerset 53
Chester 52, 68–69
Chichester, Arthur 156, 157
child labor 264, 268, 276, 278
China **296**, 297, 312
Chinon Castle 84
chivalry **98**, 146
chloroform 271, 274
cholera 265
Christianity 11, 136
    Anglicanism 137, 166, 174, 282
    Anglo-Saxon 44–45
    Celtic 44, 45
    Church reform 69, 108–109
    clergy 76, 89, 108–109
    in Ireland **38–39**
    and Latin language 29
    medieval 108–109
    missionaries 39, 45, 267, 286, 296
    Oxford Movement 282
    questioning of 282–283, 289
    revival movement 223
    and slave trade 235
    Vikings and 45, 47, 51, 57
    see also Protestantism; Roman Catholicism
Christmas 237, 281, 362
chronometers 190–191, 227
Church *see* Christianity
"Church-and-King" mobs 237
churches 60, 83, 121, 282
    see also cathedrals
Churchill, Winston **350–351**
    early career 303, 321, 345, **350–351**
    as imperialist 319, 342, 343
    and World War II 346, 347, 349, 351, 354,
        355, 357, 358, 359
    after World War II 311, **351**, 361, 362, 369
churls 60–61
cinema 305, 339, 361, 371, 373
circumnavigations 146, 226, 227
cities *see* towns and cities
Civil War, English 163, 166, **168–172**, 173,
    176, 178, 180
Civil War, Irish 333
Civil War, Spanish 346
class divisions 305, 339
Claudius, Emperor 23, **24**, 25
Clement VII, Pope 137
clergy
    reform 108–109
    special courts for 76
    urban 89
Clifton Suspension Bridge, Bristol 260–261
Clive, Robert 212, 290
clubs, men's 208
CND *see* Campaign for Nuclear Disarmament
coal mining
    bad conditions 235

Bevin Boys 355
    decline 381
    nationalization 360, 361
    production levels 276, 334
    strikes 376, 380, 381, 383
    technology 233, 258, 277, 335
Coalbrookdale, Shropshire 232, 233
coalition governments 331, 334, 354–355, 387
Cobden, Richard 268
coffeehouses **180**, **181**, 184, 219
coins
    Anglo-Saxon 37, 41, 53
    Cromwell's 175
    French 96
    Iron Age 21, 32
    medieval 76, 89
    Newton's innovations 185
    Norman 68
    Roman 30, 33, 34–35
    Scottish 93, 225
    Tudor 126–127, 144
coke 233
Coke, Thomas 231
Colchester, Essex 20, 21, 23, 24, 25, 28,
    32–33
Cold War 364, **368–369**, 385
Collins, Michael 333
colonial expansion 143, 147, **162–163**, **212–
    213**, **226–227**, 234, 290, **294–295**, 296
    see also British Empire
Columba, Saint 38
Columbanus, Saint 38
Columbus, Christopher 146
Combination Laws (1799/1800) 265
comets 184, 185
Comgall, Saint 38, 54
Commius 22
Commonwealth (Cromwell's) 129, 166, 169,
    172–173, 176, 178–179
Commonwealth of Nations, British 317, **343**,
    362, 363, 364
communism **283**, 346, 351, 358, 364
Communist Party, British 334, 335
Comyn, John 93
concentration camps, Boers in 302, **303**
Confirmation of the Charters 85
Congo Free State 303
Congreve, William 208
Connolly, James 332–333
conscientious objectors 322
conscription 322, 333, 347, 354, 355, 384
Conservative Party 269, 303, 312, 334, 335,
    346, 361, 370, 371, 372, 373, 382, 387
    see also Tories
Constantine III, Emperor 35
Constantine I, king of the Picts and Scots 59
Constantine II, king of Alba 53, **59**
Constantinople 83, 121, 274
Constitution, USS 244
consumerism 338, 370, 372
contraception 373
Convention Parliament 176
Conwy Castle 90, 117
Cook, James **226–227**, 286
Cork, Ireland 54, 156
Corn Laws 255, **268**, 269
Cornwall 16, 20, 233
Cornwallis, Lord Charles 213, 215, 217
coronations 122, 133, 201
Corresponding Societies 237
Corsica 240
cotton industry 276
Country Housewife, The (Bradley) 230
courtly love 110
courts 76–77, 121, 132, 166
Covenanters **166**, 169, 174, 196
craftsmen 89, 103, 121
crannogs 30
Cranmer, Thomas, archbishop of Canterbury
    135, 137
Crécy, battle of (1346) 96, 99, **100–101**,
    116
credit crunch 386
cricket 219, 342, 343
Crimean War 241, 271, **274–275**
criminous clerks 76, 77
Crippen, Hawley Harvey 304–305
Cromwell, Oliver 129, 157, 163, **168–169**,
    171, **172–173**, 176, 178–179
    and Ireland 169, 174, 175, 266

and Scotland 174–175
Cromwell, Richard 176
Cromwell, Thomas 135, 136, 156
crop rotation 230
Croppies 239
Cross of Cong 81
crossbows **99**, 101, 125
Crusades 77, **82–83**
Crystal Palace 273
Cuban Missile Crisis 369
Cubism 305
Culloden, battle of (1746) **204–205**
Cumberland, William Augustus, duke of 204
Cunard Line 259, 304
Cunedda 31
Cunedda 31
cursuses 16
Curzon, George Nathaniel, Lord 291
cutpurses 143
cycling 280–281
Cyprus 364
Czechoslovakia 346–347

D

Dafydd of Gwynedd 90, 91
Dáil Éireann 333
Dal Riata (Dalriada) 31, 38, 59
Danebury hillfort, Hampshire 20, 21
Danegeld 57
Danelaw 47, 52
Danse Macabre 103
Darby, Abraham 233
Darnley, Henry Stuart, Lord 138
Darwin, Charles 283, **288–289**, 295
Davenant, William 181
David, Saint 58
David I, king of Scotland 92
David II, king of Scotland 93, **116**, 117
Davison, Emily Wilding 309
Davy lamp 277
de la Pole, Michael 114
de Lacy, Hugh 81
de Valera, Eamonn 333
de Vere, Robert 114
Dean, Dixie 339
death penalty *see* capital punishment
Decameron (Boccaccio) 110
Declaration of Independence 214–215
Declarations of Indulgence 177, 189
Defence of the Realm Act (1914) 326
Defoe, Daniel 192, **209**, 219
Delhi, India 291, 292–293
democracy 335
depopulation 120
Depression, Great 277, 311, 316, **334–335**, 337, 343, 351
Derby, Epsom 192
Derry (Londonderry), Ireland 157, 196, 378
Descartes, René 185
Desmond Rebellions 156
Despard, Charlotte 251
devaluation 334, 361, 381
devolution 333, 387
Diana, princess of Wales 363
Diarmait of Leinster 55
Dias, Bartolomeu 146
Dickens, Charles 209, **265**, 278, 280–281, **283**
disease
  in native peoples 234, 295
  Roman Britain 33
  Stone Age 16
  Victorian age 265, 278–279
Disraeli, Benjamin 269, 271
Dissolution of the Monasteries 135, 142, 152
divine right of kings 128, 158, 166, 189, 202
divorce laws 373
doctors 103
dollhouses 278
Domesday Book 69, 72, **74–75**, 89, 142, 230
dominions **294–295**, 342, 343
  see also British Empire
Domitian, Emperor 24
Donne, John 153, 173
Douglas, William, earl of 116, 117
Dowland, John 153
Downing Street, No. 10 207
Drake, Francis **146**, 149, 150, 162
Dreadnought, HMS 312

Dresden, Germany 358
Drogheda, massacre at 169, 174
drugs, recreational 373
Dryden, John 181, 208
Dublin 81, 218, 266
  Easter Rising 332–333
  Phoenix Park murders 301
  Viking 53, **54–55**, 81
Duchess of Malfi, The (Webster) 153
Dudley, Robert *see* Leicester, Robert Dudley, earl of
Dumbarton Castle 58
Dundee, John Graham, 1st Viscount 196–197
Dunkirk 348, 349
Durrow monastery, Ireland 39
Dutch *see* Netherlands
Dyfed 58

E

Eadred, king of Wessex 53
Eadwine Psalter 89
ealdormen 53, 57, **60**
earls 60
earthworks 10, 16, 20, 21
East Anglia 37, 40, 44, 47, 57, 69
East India Company **211**, **212–213**, **290–291**, 292
Easter, date of 45
Easter Rising 332–333
economy
  Adam Smith's influence 224, 225
  18th century 179, **210–211**
  Great Depression 277, 311, 316, **334–335**, 337, 351
  Keynesian theory **331**, 335
  post-1950 317, 371, 376, 380–381, 383, 386
  Tudor 133
  World War I and after 326, 331
  World War II and after 355, 359, 360
Eden, Anthony 367
Edgar, king of Wessex 53
Edgar Aetheling 68, 69
Edinburgh, Scotland 166, 169, 218, 224–225
Edinburgh Castle 95, 174–175
Edinburgh Gazette 209
Edmund, king of Sicily 84, 85
Edmund, king of Wessex 53
Edmund Ironside, king of Southern England **57**, 72
Edric the Wild 68
education
  in India 291
  medieval 89, 108
  20th century 355, 373
  Victorian 265, 278, 279
Edward the Confessor, king of England, 57, **60–61**, 68, 72, 85
Edward the Elder, king of Wessex **52–53**, 72
Edward the Martyr, king of England 57
Edward I, king of England ("Hammer of the Scots"/"Longshanks") 83, 85, **90–91**, **92–93**, 99, 116, 158
Edward II, king of England (*earlier* Edward of Caernarvon) 91, 92, 93, 95
Edward III, king of England 83, 92, **93**, **96**, 99, **101**, 104, **110**, 114, 116, 117, 254
Edward IV, king of England 122–123
Edward V, king of England 123
Edward VI, king of England **133**, 135, 136–137
Edward VII, king of Great Britain and Ireland 271, **304**, 312
Edward VIII, king of the United Kingdom, *later* duke of Windsor **344–345**, 363
Edward, the Black Prince **97**, 114
Edwardian society and culture 304–305
Edwin, Earl 68
Edwin, king of Northumbria 44, 58
EEC *see* European Economic Community
Egbert, king of Wessex 41, 46
Egbert's Stone 50, 51
Egypt 240–241, 242–243, 297, 343, 358
  Suez Canal 296, 297, 358, 366–367
Eisenhower, Dwight D. 351, 359
El Dorado 162
Eleanor of Aquitaine 76, **77**
electoral reform 235, 237, **268–269**
  see also suffragettes
electricity 279, 305, 338, 339, 340–341

Elgin Cathedral 117
Elizabeth I, queen of England and Ireland 126–127, 135, 137, **140–141**, 143, 158, 180
  arts and literature 152–153
  and Ireland 157
  and Mary, queen of Scots 138–139
  and seafarers **146–147**, 162, 212
  stock exchange 210
  war with Spain and defeat of Armada 141, 147, **148–151**
Elizabeth II, queen of the United Kingdom 295, **362–363**
Ely Cathedral 112–113
emigration 163, 173, 294, 295
  from Ireland 267, 294, 295
Empire Games 343
enclosures 104, **142–143**, 222, 230, 232
Endeavour (Cook's ship) 226–227
Engels, Friedrich 283
Enlightenment 185, 208
  Scottish 179, 193, **224–225**
Entente Cordiale 312
entertainment 280–281, 304, 338, 339, 361
epidemics 327
  see also plague
Equal Pay Act (1970) 376
Equiano, Olaudah *see* Vassa, Gustavus
Eric Bloodaxe, king of York 53
Essex, Robert Devereux, earl of 140, 141, 149, 156, 157
Ethiopia 346
European Economic Community (EEC) 365
European Union (EU) 381, 387
evacuation 347, 354
Evelyn, John 177, 182
evictions 335
evolution, theory of 283, **288–289**
Exchequer 73
  Irish 81
excommunication 109
executions 203, 223
exploration **146–147**, 162, 163, 184, 193, **226–227**, **286–287**

F

Fabian Society 311
factories **232–233**, 235, **264–265**, 355, 380
  munitions 313, 326, 327, 334, 346
Factory Act (1802) 268
Faerie Queene, The (Spenser) 141, 153
fairs, trade 121
Falklands War 287, 383, **384–385**
famine
  Irish 251, **266–267**, 295, 300
  1790s 237
Fascism **335**, 345, 354
fashion 142, 145, 181, 219, 339
  1960s 372–373
Fawcett, Millicent 309
Fawkes, Guy 161
feasting 21, 40
feminism 377, 383
Fenians **239**, 267, **300**, 301
Ferguson, Adam 224, 225
Festival of Britain 361
fetes 143
feudalism 64, **73**, **88**, 98, 120, 222, 230
  in Ireland 81
fiefs 73
Field of the Cloth of Gold 135
Fielden, John 268
Fielding, Henry 209, **223**
Fifth Monarchists 173
Filmer, Robert 166
Fire of London, Great 121, **129**, 180, **182–183**
Fitzgerald, Edward ("Citizen Lord") 239
Fitzherbert, Maria 254
Fitzroy, Robert 288
Flamsteed, John 185
Flanders 89, 121
Flinders, Matthew 227, 287
flint tools 14, 15, 16
Flodden, battle of (1513) 134, 135, **138**, 158
flu, Spanish 327
Flying Scotsman (locomotive) 259
flying shuttle 232
Foljambe, Joseph 231
football 280, **339**

footpads 143
force-feeding 309
Ford, John 153
forests 76, 88, 89
Fort George 203
Fort William, India 213
Fort William, Scotland 203
forts, Roman 24, 34
Fox, Charles James 254
France
  "Auld Alliance" with Scotland 134, 138
  Charles II's alliance with 177, 179
  colonies of 212, 227
  Entente Cordiale/Triple Alliance **312**, 313
  Field of the Cloth of Gold 135
  Huguenots 181
  Hundred Years' War 65, **96–101**, 104, 115, **118–119**
  and Jacobites 203
  Napoleonic Wars **240–241**, 242–243, 244, **246–247**, 255
  Norman and Plantagenet power in 64, 77, 132
  other wars with 122, 134, 135, 138, 141, 148, 197, 212, 237, 240
  relations with USA 244
  Revolutionary Wars **240**, 242, 244
  sends force to aid Ireland 239
  and World War I 321, 322, 331
  and World War II 349, 354, 358–359
  see also French Revolution
Francis I, king of France 135
Franco, Francisco 346
Frankish rulers 39, 41, 44
Franklin, Benjamin 209
Franklin, John 287
Franks Casket 42–43
Franz Ferdinand, Archduke 313
Fraser, Simon, Lord Lovat 203
Free French 358
free market 225, 235, 265, 268, 269, 383
freemen 89
French, John 321
French Revolution 169, 193, 209, **236–237**, 238–239, 240
friars 108
Frobisher, Martin 146
Froissart, Jean 100–101
Fry, Roger 305
furniture design 283

G

Gaillard Castle 82
Gainsborough, Thomas 220–221
Galápagos Islands 288–289
Galen 103
Galileo Galilei 184
Gall, Saint 39
Gallipoli campaign 295, **321**, 350
Gama, Vasco de 146
Gandhi, Mohandas 342, 364
garden suburbs and cities 305
gardens 231, 279
gas, poison 321, 323, 355
gas lighting 265, 279
Gaskell, Elizabeth 265
Gaul 22, 23, 29, 34, 35, 38
Gay, John 209
General Strike 334
generation gap 373
Gentleman's Magazine 209
George I, king of Great Britain and Ireland **200**, 206–207
George II, king of Great Britain and Ireland **200**, 207
George III, king of Great Britain and Ireland 200, **201**, 212, 237, 239, 254–255
George IV, king of Great Britain and Ireland (*earlier* the Prince Regent) 201, 209, 250, **254–255**, 256
George V, king of the United Kingdom **304**, 305, 343, 345
George VI, king of the United Kingdom 345, 359, **362**
Georgian period
  society **218–223**, 278
  trade 193, **210–211**, 227, **228–229**
Gerald of Wales (Giraldus Cambrensis) 90

Germanus, bishop of Auxerre 44
Germany
  Berlin airlift 369
  medieval fairs 121
  Nazis 345, 346, 347, 351
  reparations imposed on 331
  see also World War I; World War II
Ghana 297, 364
Gibraltar 211
Gildas 40, 58
Gillray, James 237
gin 222, 223
glacial periods 14–15
Gladstone, William Ewart 269, 300–301
Glasgow, Scotland 277
Glencoe massacre 197
Globe Theatre 152, 154, 155
Glorious Revolution 129, 166, 169, 173,
  177, **188–189**, 192, 196, 206, 210, 211
Gloucester 120
Glyn Dwr, Owain 117
Godwin, earl of Wessex 57, 60, 61
gold rushes 295, 303
Gold Standard 210, **334**, 351
Goldsmith, Oliver 209
Gooch, Daniel 260, 261
Good Friday Agreement (1998) 379
Gordon, Charles George 297
Gordon Riots 222, 223
Gothic style 89, 112–113, 152, 282
Gower, George 140, 152
Gower, John 110
Grand Alliance, War of the 196
grave goods 17, 21, 35
gravitation law 185
Great Britain, SS 261
Great Eastern, SS 259, 260, 261
Great Exhibition 271, **272–273**, 276, 280
Great War *see* World War I
Great Western, SS 259, 261
Greater London Council 383
Greenham Common protest 384
Greenwich, London 104–105, 184
Greenwich Observatory 184, 185
Gregory I, Pope 44, 51
Grenville, Richard 149
Grey, Charles, Lord 269
Grey, Lady Jane **133**, 137
Grosseteste, Robert, bishop of Lincoln 108
Gruffudd of Gwynedd 90
Grunwick strike 377
guilds **120–121**, 142, 180
Gulliver's Travels (Swift) 208
gunpowder 99
Gunpowder Plot 158, **160–161**
guns 99, 169, 203, 222, 228, 277, 321
Guthrum 47, **50–51**
Gwynedd, Wales 58–59, 90–91
Gwynn, Nell 176, 181

H

haberdashers 120
Hadrian's Wall 10, 23, 24, **26–27**, **28**, 32, 34
Haig, Douglas 321, 322, 323, 325
Halfdan 47
Halley, Edmund 184, 185
Hamburg, Germany 358
Hamilton, Emma 242, 243
Hampstead Garden Suburb 305
Hampton Court 135
Hanover, house of 192, 197, **200–201**
Hansa 121
Harald Bluetooth, king of Denmark 47, 57
Harald Hardrada, king of Norway 57, 68
hard labor 285
Hard Times (Dickens) 283
Hardie, Keir 303, 311, 326
Hardy, Thomas 282
Harfleur, siege of 118, 119
Hargreaves, James 233
Harlech Castle **90–91**, 117
Harold Godwinson, king of England 57, 60,
  61, 68, 70
Harold Harefoot, king of England 57
Harrison, John 191
Harrison, William Henry 244, 245
Harry, Prince 363
harrying of the north 68

Harthacnut, king of England 57
harvests, bad 89, 102, 107, 142
Harvey, William 184
Hastings, battle of 68, 70–71
Hastings, Warren 291
Hathaway, Anne 154
Hawaii *see* Sandwich Islands
Hawkins, John 146
Heath, Edward (Ted) 373, 376, 383
Hebrides 10, 92
helmets 21, 36, 68, 99, 125, 169
henge monuments 17, 18–19
Hengist and Horsa 40
Henri IV, king of France 141
Henry I, king of England **72–73**, 84, 96
Henry II, king of England 64, **76–77**, 79, 81,
  82, 83, 96
Henry III, king of England 65, 83, 84, **85**,
  90–91, 96
Henry IV, king of England 109, 114, 115,
  117, 118, 122, 132
Henry V, king of England 109, 115,
  118–119, 122
Henry VI, king of England 65, 119, **122–123**,
  254
Henry VII, king of England 65, 105, 117, 123,
  128, **132–133**, 134, 138, 142, 146, 148
Henry VIII, king of England 128, 133,
  134–137, 138, 140, 142, 148, 152
  and Ireland 156
  and the navy 133, 146, 147
  and Reformation 136–137
Henry, Prince ("the young King") 77
Henry Grace a Dieu (ship) 147
Henry the Navigator 146
Henslow, John Stevens 288
Hereford, William FitzOsbern, earl of 68
Herschel, William 200
Hilliard, Nicholas 152
Hiroshima, Japan 359
Hitler, Adolf 346–347, 349, 351, 357
Hogarth, William 209, 223
Holbein, Hans, the Younger 134, 135, 152–153
Holkham Bible 94–95
Holkham Hall, Norfolk 231
Holy Cross Abbey 80–81
Home, Alex Douglas 371
Home Guard 354
Home Rule, Irish 157, 239, 251, 267, 271,
  300–301, 332
Homo heidelbergensis 14
Homo sapiens sapiens 15
homosexuality 371, 373, 387
Hong Kong 296, 297, 316, 349, 365
Hood, Robin 85
Hooke, Robert 182, 184, 185
Hospitaller, Knights 83
House of Commons 85, 166, 206, 268–269
House of Lords 206, 387
household manuals 230, 278, 280, 281
housing
  "right to buy" 381
  Roman Britain 29, **33**, 34
  20th century 338–339, 361, 370–371
  Victorian 278
Howard, Catherine 135
howitzer 322
Hoxnian interglacial 14
Hudson, Henry 163
Hudson's Bay Company 181
Huguenots 181
humanism 153, 224
Hume, David **224**, 225
Hundred Years' War 65, **96–101**, 104, 115,
  118–119
hunger marches 337
hunger strikes 309, 378, 379
Hunt, William Holman 282
hunter-gatherers 15, 16
hunting 88, 291
Hurricane aircraft 356–357
Hus, John 109
Hutcheson, Francis 224
Hutton, James 225
Huxley, Thomas Henry 289
Hywel Dda (the Good) 58–59

I

iambic pentameter 155
Ice Age 14–15
Iceni 24
Idwal Foel of Gwynedd 58–59
immigrants 181, 317, 365, 371, 373, 376–377
  early black community 234
  21st century 387
Imperial Airways 343
income tax 207, 355, 361, 381
Independent Labour Party 311
India 211–213, 274, 290–291, 296–297,
  316, 321
  independence 291, 342–343, 364, 365
Indian Mutiny 212, 271, 287, 291, 292–293
Indian National Congress 342
individualism 283
Industrial Revolution 193, 211, 231, 232–233,
  250, 258–259, 264–265, 269, 274, 276–277
industry, 20th century 334, 335
Ine of Wessex 41
inflation 371, 381, 386
Innocent III, Pope 84, 86, 108
interest rates 381
internment 354, 378
Invergordon mutiny 334
Invincibles 301
Iona monastery 38, 44, 46
IRA *see* Irish Republican Army
Iranian Embassy siege 384
Iraq 343, 384, 385, 387
Ireland 11, 59, 65, 115, 192, 251, 316
  Act of Union (1800) 239, 267, 300
  Christianity in 38–39
  Civil War (1922–1923) 333
  Cromwell and 174, 175, 266
  Edward Bruce in 81, **93**
  emigration from 267, 294, 295
  English conquest of 77, **80–81**
  famine 251, **266–267**, 295, 300
  Flight of the Earls 238
  Home Rule 157, 239, 251, 267, 271,
    300–301, 332
  independence and prior events 332–333
  Iron Age 30–31
  monarchs and rulers 388, 389
  monasteries 38–39, 46, 54, 55, 80–81
  Nine Years' War **157**, 238
  Normans in 156, 162
  plantations of 156–157, 175, 266, 300
  police force 278
  raiders from 31
  rebellions 141, 156–157, 162, 174, 175, 197,
    238–239, 300, 332–333
  republicanism 378
  Romans and **30–31**, 34
  1798 revolution 157, **238–239**
  Spanish support for 149
  Stone Age 16, 17
  support for Jacobites and war with William
    III 196–197
  Swift's tracts on 208
  Tudors and 156–157
  Vikings and 53, **54–55**
  and World War I 320, 326, 332
  writers 305
  see also Northern Ireland; Ulster
Ireton, Henry 175
Irish Confederation 300
Irish Free State 333
Irish Republican Army (IRA) 333
  Provisional 378, 379, 383
Irish Republican Brotherhood **300**, 332
  see also Fenians
Irish Volunteers 320, 332
Iron Age 10, **20–22**
Iron Curtain 369
iron production 233, 276, 277
Ironbridge Gorge, Shropshire 232–233
Ironsides 169
ISIS 385, 387
Islam 82–83, 387
Ismail Pasha 297
Israel 367
Istanbul *see* Constantinople
Italy 121, 346, 349, 358
Ivar the Boneless 47

J

Jackson, Andrew 245
Jacobite rebellion (1715) 193, 200, **202**,
  208
Jacobite rebellion (1745–1746) 193, 201
Jacobites 189, 196–197, **202–203**
Jagger, Mick 372
James II, king of Scotland 117
James IV, king of Scotland 132, 138
James V, king of Scotland 138
James I, king of England (James VI of
  Scotland) 128, 131, 138, 141, 149, 152,
  158–159, 161, 162, 166
James II, king of Great Britain and Ireland
  (*earlier* Duke of York) 129, 158,
  169, 175, 177, 182, **189**, 192,
  196–197, 200, 202
James Francis Edward Stuart, Prince ("Old
  Pretender") 189, **202**
Jameson Raid (1895) 303
Jamestown, Virginia 162–163
Japan 312, 346
  in World War II 349, 358, 359, 364
Jarrow March **336–337**
Jarrow monastery 45, 46
Jean II, king of France 97
Jedburgh Abbey 92
Jefferson, Thomas 215, 236
Jeffreys, Judge 189
Jelling runestone 47
Jerusalem **82–83**, 274
jewelry 41, 44, 46, 50, 54, 144
Jews 343
Jinnah, Muhammad Ali 364
Joan of Arc **119**, 122
John, king of England 64, 77, 81, 82,
  84–87, 90, 108
John of Gaunt, duke of Lancaster 97, **104**,
  105, 109, 114, 115, 122
John the Fearless, duke of Burgundy
  118–119
Johnson, Samuel 195, **208–209**
joint-stock companies 210
Jonson, Ben **152**, 154, 155
Jordan 343
jousting 98–99
Joyce, James 305
Julian of Norwich 109
juries 77
justices 76–77
Justinian, Emperor 102
Juvenal 208

K

Kay, John 232
Keats, John 282
Keeler, Christine 372
Kempe, Margery 109
Kenneth MacAlpin, king of the Picts and
  Scots 11, 59
Kent 40, 41, 44, 104, 105
Kent, William 231
Kenya 343, 364, 365
Kepler, Johannes 184
Kett's Rebellion 133
Keynes, John Maynard **331**, 335,
  359, 383
Kidwelly Castle 64
Kilkenny Castle 81
Killigrew, Thomas 181
Kilmacduagh tower 55
King's Men 154, 155
Kingston Brooch 44
Kinsale, siege of 156
Kipling, Rudyard 291, **305**
Kit-Kat (Kit-Cat) club 208
Kitchener, Horatio Herbert, Lord 297,
  303, 321
knights 88, 89, **98–99**
  Templars and Hospitallers 83
Knox, John 137
Korean War 361, 369
Kosovo 385
Kuwait, invasion of 385
Kyd, Thomas 153

L

La Tène culture 20, 21, 30
labor
  child 264, 268, 276, 278
  division of 225
  poor conditions 231, 235
  surplus 232
  waged 143
  see also unemployment
Labour Party 207, 277, **311**, 367, 373, 380
  first governments 331, 334
  post-1945 governments 355, 360, 361,
    364, 369, 371, 372, 376, 377, 378, 386
  and world wars 326, 346
Lady Chatterley's Lover (Lawrence) 372
Ladysmith, siege of 303
Lafayette, Marquis de 217
Lake, Gerard 239
Lamarck, Jean Baptiste de 288
Lancashire 276, 277
Lancaster, House of 115, 122
Land Acts 300–301
Land League and Land Wars 301
landlessness 143
landlords 103, 104, 230
  absentee 266, 301
landscaping 231
Lanfranc, archbishop of Canterbury 69
Langland, William 109, 110
Langlois, Jean-Charles 275
Langton, Stephen, archbishop of Canterbury
  84, 86, 108
Langtry, Lillie 304
language
  English 69
  French 88
  Germanic 110
  Latin 28, 29, 33, 45, 69, 89
  Old English and Middle English 110
  vernacular 110
  Viking 47, 55
Larwood, Harold 342
Lateran Council (1215) 108
Latin language 28, 29, 33, 45, 69, 89
Laud, William 166
law
  Anglo-Saxon 41
  reforms 172, 223, 373
Lawrence, D.H. 372
lay investiture 72–73
lead mining 29, 264
League of Nations 331, 342, 343, 346
Leeds, Yorkshire 269, 277
Leicester, Robert Dudley, earl of 140–141, 149
Lennon, John 372
Leo X, Pope 135, 136–137
Levellers 173
Liberal Democrats 387
Liberal Party 269, 305, 310, 311, 322, 331,
  334, 350
  see also Whigs
lidos 339
life expectancy 16, 264
Limerick, sieges of 197
Lindisfarne 41, 44, 46
Lindisfarne Gospels 45
literature 208–209, 265, 305
  vernacular 110, 152
  see also books; poetry; theater
Little Moreton Hall, Cheshire 142
Liverpool 211, 234, 264, **277**, 305, 354
Liverpool to Manchester railroad 258, 259
Livery Companies 121
Livingstone, David 286–287
Lloyd, Marie 304
Lloyd George, David 303, 309, 311, 321,
  322, 323, 331, 350, 351
Lloyds of London 181, 228, 229
Llywelyn ap Gruffudd 90–91
Llywelyn ap Iorwerth (Llywelyn Fawr) 90
Locke, John 184
lockouts 311, 334
Lollards 109, 222
London
  air raids 327, 349, 352–353, 354, 355, 360
  Armistice Day 330
  Banqueting House 159, 170–171
  battle of Cable Street 335

Bermondsey fete 143
black community 234
  dock strikes 311
City and finance 276, 316, 334, 381, 387
  Georgian 218
  Great Fire 121, **129**, 180, **182–183**
  Greater London Council 383
  medieval 120–121
  men's clubs 208
  Metropolitan Police 223, 278
  1960s 372–373, 374–375
  Norman 89
  Olympic Games 305, 361
  panoramas 164–165, 386–387
  Peasants' Revolt 104–105
  plague 103, 180, 181
  as port 229, **277**
  Roman 24, 28, **33**
  17th century **164–165**, **180–181**, 184
  slave trade 211
  Southwark 33, 152, 155, 165
  stations 282, 298–299
  suburbs 279, 305
  Temple Church 83
  terrorist attacks 387
  theaters 152, 154, 181
  Trafalgar Square 243, 330, 373
  Treason Trials 237
  21st century 317
  underground 276, 354, 355
  Viking raid on 47
  West End shows 338
  workhouse 284–285
  see also Greenwich; St. Paul's Cathedral;
    Tower of London; Westminster Abbey
London Bridge 165
London Gazette 209
London Palladium 304
London School of Economics 311
Londonderry see Derry
Long Parliament 169, 172
longbows 99, 101, **118–119**, 125
Longchamp, William 254
longitude 191, 227
Look Back in Anger (Osborne) 372
Lord Chamberlain's Men 155
Lords Appellant **114–115**, 118
Louis VII, king of France 77
Louis IX, king of France 85, 90
Louis XIV, king of France 177, 179, 196, 197
Louis XVI, king of France 215, 237
Louis, Prince (son of Philip II) 85
Lucknow, siege of 292
Luddites 233, **255**
Luftwaffe 357, 361
Lusitania, RMS 304, 321, 326
lute 153
Luther, Martin 109, **136**, 148, 173, 184
Luttrell Psalter 88, **106–107**
Lutyens, Edwin Landseer 305
Lyell, Charles 289

M

Macbeth, king of Scotland 59, 60
MacDonald, Flora 203
Macdonald, Ramsay 326, 331, 334
MacLaine, James 223
Macmillan, Harold 364, 370
MacMurrough, Dermot, king of Leinster 81
Macpherson, James 224
Madison, James 244
madrigals 153
Maeatae 29
Máel Sechnaill, (9th century Irish king) 54
Máel Sechnaill (11th century Irish king) 55
Mafeking, siege of (1899) 303
magazines 208–209
Magna Carta 64, 67, 84–85, **86–87**, 128, 189
Magnus, king of Norway 60
Mahdi 297
Major, John 379, 381
Malaya 364
Malcolm II, king of Scotland 59
Malcolm III, king of Scotland 69
Malcolm IV, king of Scotland 76, 92
Maldon causeway, Essex 57
Malthus, Thomas 289

mammoth 15
Manchester 211, 258, 259, 269, 301
Mandubracius 22
manors 88–89
Maori 294, 295
maps 30, 85, 174, 181, 184
marathon 305
Marconi, Guglielmo 305
Margaret, Princess 363
Margaret, the "Maid of Norway" 92
Margaret of Anjou **122**, 123
Margaret Tudor 138
Markle, Meghan 363
Marlborough, John Churchill, duke of 197
Marlowe, Christopher 152, **155**
Marvell, Andrew 173
Marx, Karl 269, **283**
Marxism 334, 376
Mary I (Mary Tudor), queen of England 133,
  137, 140, 141, 148
Mary II, queen of Great Britain and Ireland
  (with William III) **189**, 192
Mary Queen of Scots 137, **138–139**, 141, 158
masons 121
matchgirls' strike 309, **310**
materialism 282, 283, 289
mathematics 184, 185
Matilda (Maud), queen of England 64, **73**, 76,
  96
Maximus, Magnus 31, 34
Mayflower (ship) 163
medals 271, 309, 333
medical care 103, 228, 360, 361
  nursing 274, 275
  surgery 33, 274
Medway Raid 178–179
megaliths 10
Meikle, Andrew 231
Melbourne, William Lamb, Lord 270–271
mental illness 278
  shell-shock 323
Mercator projection 184
merchants 89, 101, **118–119**, 125
Mercia 40–41, 44, 47, 51, 52, 53, 57, 58
Merciless Parliament 114–115
Methodism 223
microscopy 184–185
middle classes 143, 219, 223, 250–251, 268–
  269, 278–279, 305, 338–339, 355, 361
Middle East **343**, 376, 380
Middleton, Kate 363
Middleton, Thomas **153**, 158
Mildenhall treasure 34–35
Mill, John Stuart 185, 283, 309
Millais, John Everett 282–283
Milosevic, Slobodan 385
Milton, John 153, 173
Mini-Minor 314–315
mining see coal mining; lead mining; tin mining
Mirror, The, or The Glasse of the Synneful 141
missionaries 39, 45, 267, 286, 296
Mithras 32
mob violence 223, 237
Modernism 283, 305
monarchy 388
  constitutional 206
  modern 362–363
monasteries 44, 45, 83, 89, 108, 109, 136
  dissolution of the 135, 137, 142, 152
  Irish 38–39, 46, 54, 55, 80–81
  secularism and reform 39
  Viking raids on 46, 54
Monck, George **176**, 178
money see banknotes; coins
Monmouth, James, Duke of 189
Monroe, James 245
Montfort, Simon de 64, **85**
Montgomery, Bernard 358, 359
Montrose, James Graham, Marquess of 169
Moore, John 241
Moore-Brabazon, John 304
Morcar, Earl 68
More, Thomas 135, 137, 153
Morocco crises 312–313
Morris, William 121, **282**, **283**
Mortimer, Edmund 117
Mortimer, Roger 254
mosaics 33
Mosley, Oswald 335, 354
motorways 371

mounds 16, 19
Mount Grace, Yorkshire 108
Mountbatten, Louis, Lord 364, 379
Mowlam, Mo 379
Mughal Empire **213**, 290
multiculturalism 387
Munich pact 347
Munster, Plantation of 156–157
Murray, George 203, 204
Muscovy Company 163
music 119, 152, 153, 271, 372, 377
music hall 304
musket 169
Muslims see Islam
Mussolini, Benito 346, 349

N

Nagasaki, Japan 359
Napoleon Bonaparte 193, **240–241**, 246–247
Napoleonic Wars **240–243**, 244, **246–247**, 255
Nash, John 255, 256–257
Nasmyth, Alexander 225
Nasser, Gamal Abdel 364
National Covenant **166**, 196
National Front 376, 377
National Health Service 355, 360, **361**, 386
National Insurance Act (1911) 311
National Union of Mineworkers 380, 381
nationalization 360, 361
NATO see North Atlantic Treaty Organization
natural selection, theory of 288–289
navies 22, 51, 146, 179
  German 312
  Tudor 133, 142, 146, 147
  see also Royal Navy
Navigation Act (1651) 173, 178, 179
navigation aids 190–191, 226, 227, 229, 289
Nawab of Bengal 212, 213
Nazis 345, 346, 347, 351
Neanderthals 14–15
Nehru, Jawaharlal 365
Nelson, Horatio 241, **242–243**
Neolithic Age 15, **16–17**
Netherlands (Dutch)
  Elizabeth I's alliance with 141, 148–149
  and exploration 227
  immigrants 181
  Louis XIV and 196
  trade rivalry with 211
  wars with 173, 176–177, 178–179
  in World War II 349
New Model Army **169**, 173, 175, 176
New Statesman 311
New World **146**, 162–163, 179, 212
New Zealand **294–295**, 343, 362
Newcastle-upon-Tyne 277, 279
Newcomen, Thomas 233
Newfoundland Regiment 325
Newgrange, Ireland 16
newspapers 208, **209**, 304, 306–307, 339
  war correspondents 303
Newton, Isaac 179, **185**
Newton, John 235
Ney, Michel 247
Nicholas I, czar of Russia 274, 275
Nigeria 365
Nightingale, Florence 274
Nine Years' War (Grand Alliance) 196
Nine Years' War (Irish) **157**, 238
nonconformists 172–173, 177
Nonsuch Palace 132–133
Nore mutiny 237
Norman Conquest 11, 64, **68–71**, 110, 132
Norman rule **72–73**, 88–89
Normandy 69, 73, 82
Normandy landings 359
North Africa, war in 349, 358
North Atlantic Treaty Organization (NATO)
  369, 384, 385
North Pole 287
North Sea oil 381
Northcliffe, Alfred Harmsworth, Lord 304
Northeast Passage 163
Northern Ireland 317, **378–379**, 387, 389
  see also Ulster
Northern Ireland Civil Rights Association 378
Northern Rock bank 386
Northumberland, earls of 114, 115

Northumbria 40, 41, 44, 47, 52, 53, 57, 59, 61, 76
Northwest Indian War 245
Northwest Passage 146, **163**, 227, 242, 286, **287**
Norwich 109, 121
Nova Albion 146, 162
nuclear weapons 359, 368, 369, 384
NUM *see* National Union of Mineworkers

O

Oates, Titus 177
O'Brien, Muirchertach 81
O'Brien, William Smith 300
Observer 209
O'Connell, Daniel 300
O'Connor, Rory, king of Connaught 81
O'Connor, Turlough 81
Odo, bishop of Bayeux 68, 69
O'Donnell, Hugh Roe 157
Óengus mac Fergus *see* Onuist
Offa, king of Mercia 40, 41
Offa's Dyke **40**, 41
Ogham alphabet 30, 31
oil supplies 367, 380, 381
Olaf Tryggvason 57
Olympic Games 305, 361
Omagh bombing 379
O'Neill clan 156, 157
  see also Uí Néill dynasty
Onuist, king of the Picts 59
Opium Wars 296
oppida 21, 32
Orange Order 197, 239
Order of the Garter 132
orders, religious 108
Ordinance of Labourers (1349) 104
Orkneys 17, 331
Orléans, Louis, duke of 118
Orwell, George 334, 339
Osborne, John 372
Osborne House, Isle of Wight 271
Oseberg ship 46–47
Oswald, king of Northumbria 41, 44
Oswy, king of Northumbria 40, 41, 45, 59
Othello (Shakespeare) 155
Ottoman Empire 83, 241, 274, 297, 312, 321, 323, 343, 350
Outremer 83
Owain of Gwynedd 76
Owen, Robert 265
Oxford, University of 89, 108, 109
Oxford Movement 282
Oz (magazine) 373

P

Pacific region 226–227
pacifism 327
Paddington Station, London 298–299
Paine, Thomas 209, **236**, 237
Pakistan 364
Palace of Westminster 206–207, 268–269
Pale of Settlement 81
Paleolithic era **14**, 16
Palestine 343, 364
Palladius 38
Pankhurst, Christabel **309**, 326
Pankhurst, Emmeline **308**, **309**, 326
Paradise Lost (Milton) 153, 173
Paris, Matthew 85
Paris Peace Conference (1919) 331
Park, Mungo 286
Parker Bowles, Camilla 363
Parliament 236–237
  accountability 206
  after Act of Union 206
  beginnings 64–65
  and Charles I and Civil War **166–167**, 168, 169, 171, 172, 180
  Charles II and 176, 177
  Cromwell and 173, 175
  electoral reform 235, 237, **268–269**
  Gunpowder Plot 158, **160–161**
  Henry III and 85
  James I and 158
  land as qualification for 218

Palace of Westminster 206–207, 268–269
  Pugin's Gothic decor 282
  and Richard II 114–115
  Scottish 93, 387
  and taxation 85, 104
parlor, Victorian 278–279
Parnell, Charles Stewart 300, 301
Parr, Catherine 135
passage graves 16, 17
Patrick, Saint 38, 39
Paul, Lewis 232–233
Paulinus, Suetonius 24
Paxton, Joseph 273
Peach, Blair 377
Pearse, Padraic 332–333
peasants 89, 104, 120, 230
Peasants' Revolt **104–105**, 120, 142, 222, 310
Peel, Robert 223, 267, 269, 270–71, 278
Peep o' Day Boys 239
Pembroke, Richard fitzGilbert de Clare, earl of ("Strongbow") 81
Pembroke, William Marshall, earl of 85
Penda of Mercia 40, 41, 44
Peninsular War 241
Penn, William, and Pennsylvania 162, 163
pensions 311
Pepys, Samuel **180–181**, 182
Percy, Henry ("Hotspur") 115, 116, 117
Percy, Thomas 161
Percy family 114, 115, 118
Perry, Oliver 244–245
Peterloo Massacre 255
Pevensey fort 68
Philadelphia, Pennsylvania 214, 215
Philip II, king of Spain 133, 140, 141, 146, 148, 149, 150
Philip V, king of Spain 200
Philip, Prince, duke of Edinburgh 362, 365
Philip II, king of France 83, 84, 85
Philip IV, king of France 93, 96
Philip VI, king of France 96, 97, 101
Philip the Bold, duke of Burgundy 118
Philip the Good, duke of Burgundy 119
Phoenix Park murders 301
photography 280
  war 275
Picts 11, **30**, 31, 34, **59**
Piers Plowman (Langland) 109, 110
Pilgrim Fathers 163
Pilgrimage of Grace 135, 137
pilgrims, Canterbury 108, 110
Pilgrim's Progress, The (Bunyan) 173
pill, contraceptive 373
Pipe Rolls 73
Pitt, William, the Elder 207
Pitt, William, the Younger **207**, 236, 239, 254
plague 102, 180, 181
  Black Death **102–103**, 104, 117, 120, 142
Plantagenet, Geoffrey, Count of Anjou 73, 76, 96
Plantagenets 73
plantations, slave 163
plantations of Ireland 156–157, 175, 266, 300
plows 10, 33, 230, 231
Pocahontas 162, 163
pocket boroughs 269
poetry
  blank verse 153, 155
  Elizabethan 153, 155
  iambic pentameter 155, 208
  medieval 110–111
  metaphysical 153, 173
  Romanticism 282
  Scottish 224
Poland 347, 358
police force **223**, 278, 377, 383
poll tax 32, 104–105, 381, 383
Poor Laws 143
pop music 372, 377
Pope, Alexander 185, **208**
Popish Plot (1679) 177
popular culture 372–373
population
  London 181
  1920s and 1930s 338, 342
  Norman period 89
  Roman Britain 29
  Stone Age 16
Port Sunlight, Liverpool 305

ports 211, 277
Portugal 146, 241
postal services 271, 290
potatoes 266–267
Potsdam Conference (1945) 359
pottery
  ancient 16, 17
  Roman 33
  Wedgwood 232
poverty 143, 222, 233, 255, 265
  in Ireland 239, 266
  20th century 311, 335, 354, 360
  Victorian 278, 284–285
Powell, Enoch 373, 376
Powhatan Confederacy 163
Powys 58
Prayer Book Rebellion 133
Pre-Raphaelite Brotherhood 282
Presbyterians 169, 174, 175
prices 103, 142, 258, 334
  inflation 371, 381, 386
Pride's Purge **169**, 172, 176
Priestley, JB 338, 355
prime ministers 206–207, 389
Princip, Gavrilo 313
printing 184
prisons 278
Private Eye 209
privateering **146–147**, 149, 226
privatization 380, 381, 383
Privy Chamber 142
professions 219
Profumo, John 372
propaganda 326
prostitution 278
Protestantism
  Hanoverians and 200
  in Ireland and Northern Ireland 238, 239, 267, 301, 332, 333, 378, 379
  in Netherlands 148–149
  Stuarts and 158, 176
  Tudors and 133, **136–137**, 141
  see also Puritans; Reformation
Provisions of Oxford and Westminster 85
psalters 57, 88, 89, 106–107
Ptolemy 30
public houses 326
Pugin, Augustus 282
Punch 209, 289
punishments 143, 161, 223
  death penalty 203, 223, 373
punk movement 377
Puritans 163, 166, 173
Pytheas of Massilia 21

Q

Quakers 162, 163, 173, 234, 235
Quant, Mary 372
Quebec, Canada 212, 294, 295
Queen Anne's War 197

R

Race Relations Acts 373, 377
race riots 373, 380
radar **349**, 357
radicalism 237, 255, 373
radio
  communication 305, 307
  entertainment 339, 341
  information broadcasts 343, 351
Raeburn, Henry 225
Raedwald of East Anglia 40
RAF *see* Royal Air Force
ragged schools 265, **279**
Ragnall 52–53
railroads 250, **258**, **259**, 261, 265, 275, 276, 277, 304, 355
  Indian 291
  South African 303
  stations 259, 282, 298–299
  strikes 310, 311
Raj, British 291
Raleigh, Walter 140, 146, 149, 152, 155, **162**
Ramsay, Allan 225
Ramsay, James 235

Ranters 173
rationing 354, 355, 360, 361, 370
Red Stick confederacy 245
Redgrave, Vanessa 373
Redwald, king of East Anglia 37
Referendum 319, 387
Reform Acts 265, **269**, 310
Reformation 128, 133, **135–137**, 141–142, 184
  in Netherlands 148–149
  in Scotland 137, 138
Regency period 254–255
  see also George IV
religion
  Iron and Bronze Age ritual sites 22
  Roman Britain 29, 32
  17th century sects 172–173
  Stone Age 17
  see also Christianity
reliquaries **38–39**, 52, 62–63, 145
Renaissance 152–153
reparations 331
Representation of the People Act (1918) 327
Restoration 173, **176–177**, 180, 200
Revere, Paul 214
Revolutionary Wars **240**, 242, 244
rhetoric 110
Rhodes, Cecil 297, **302–303**
Rhodesia 303
  Southern 343, 365
Rhodri Mawr (the Great) 58
Rhys of Deheubarth 76
Richard I, king of England ("the Lionheart") 77, **82**, 83, 84, 254
Richard II, king of England **104–105**, 110, **114–115**, 116, 118, 122
Richard III, king of England 123
Richard, duke of York **122**, 254
Richardson, James 286
Richardson, Mary 309
Richborough fort, Kent 34
Rievaulx Abbey 137
riots 222–223, 237, 255, 371, 373, 380
Rising of the North 141
Rizzio, David 138
roads
  Indian 291
  motorways 371
  Roman 29, 32
  Scottish 202–203
Roanoke, Virginia 146, 162
Robert Curthose, duke of Normandy 69, **72**, **73**, 82
Robert the Bruce, king of Scotland 95, 138
Robert II, king of Scotland (Robert Stewart) 93, **138**
Robert III, king of Scotland 116–117
Robertson, William 321
Robinson Crusoe (Defoe) 209
Roche of Montpellier, Saint 103
Rochester Castle 72–73
Rock Against Racism 377
rock 'n' roll 372
Rocket (locomotive) 258
Roger, bishop of Salisbury 73
Rolfe, John 162, 163
Rolling Stones, The 372, 373
Rolls Royce 304
Roman Catholicism 136
  emancipation 255, 300
  Gordon Riots against 222, 223
  in Ireland and Northern Ireland 156, 169, 174–175, 196, 238–39, 326, 333, 378–379
  in New World 163
  Stuarts and 129, 158, 161, 166, 177, 189
  Tudors and 133, 137, 138, 141, 148, 158
  Victorian revival 282
Roman de la Rose 110
Romans 10, 20, **22–35**
  army 22, 24, 28, 29, 34–35, 98
  Christianity 44
  citizenship 28
  end of empire 33, 34–35
  forts 24, 34
  frontiers 28, 29, 30–31
  gods and goddesses 32, 33
  governors and procurators 28, 29
  health and well-being 33
  houses and villas 29, 33, 34
  invasion of Britain 22–25
  plague 102

roads 29, 32
taxation 32
temples 32, 33
towns 28–29, 32–33, 34
trade 29, 30
writers 208
Romanticism 282, 283
Rommel, Erwin 349, 358
Roosevelt, Franklin D. 349, 351, 358, 359
Ros, Richard 110
Rossetti, Dante Gabriel 282, 283
rotten boroughs 269
Roundheads 168
Rousseau, Jean-Jacques 224, 282
Rowlandson, Thomas 209, 278
Royal Adventurers 179
Royal Air Force (RAF) 327, 349, 356–357, 358–359, 385
Royal Albert Bridge, Saltash 261, 262–263
Royal Exchange of London 210–211
royal family, modern 362–363
change of name 327
Royal Navy 133, 142, 146, 196, 211, 240–241, 274, 312, 316, 384, 385
mutinies 237, 334
and US 244–245
World War I 321, 322
World War II 350, 359
Royal Society 181, 185
Rubens, Peter Paul 159
Rule Britannia! (Arne and Thomson) 211
Rump Parliament 172
Ruskin, John 282, 283
Russell, John 267
Russell, William Howard 274–275
Russia 241, 274–275, 312, 313
see also Soviet Union
Russian Revolution 322, 327, 331, 334
Ruthwell Cross 44
Ruyter, Michiel de 178, 179

S

Saddam Hussein 385
sagas, Irish 31
St. Albans (Verulamium) 24, 33
St. Pancras Station, London 282
St. Paul's Cathedral 164–165, 182, 185, 186–187
Saladin, Sultan of Egypt and Syria 83
Salisbury Cathedral 89
Sambourne, Linley 289
Samian ware 33
Sancho, Ignatius 234
Sands, Bobby 378, 379
Sandwich Islands 226, 227
sanitation 33, 120, 278–279
Sarajevo, Bosnia 313
Sargent, John Singer 305
SAS see Special Air Service
Sassoon, Siegfried 327
satire 208–209, 237, 372, 383
Savery, Thomas 233
Saxons see Anglo-Saxons
scalping 244
Scapa Flow, Orkneys 331
Scargill, Arthur 381
Schlieffen Plan 312, 313
scholasticism 153
school meals, free 311
school milk 361, 383
schools
comprehensive 373
medieval 89, 108
Victorian 265, 278, 279
science
and agriculture 230–231
18th century 226–227, 230–231
experimental 153, 184
Scottish 225
17th century 173, 179, 184–185
Victorian 273, 283, 288–289
scientific instruments 184, 200
scorched-earth policy 303
Scotland 11, 58, 59, 65, 69 192–193
Athelstan's invasion 53
"Auld Alliance" with France 134, 138
Battle of Bannockburn 65, 93, 94–95, 138
Battle of Culloden 204–205

Battle of Flodden 134, 135, 138, 158
Christianity 38
Covenanters 166, 169, 174, 196
devolution 387
early settlers 10
Edward the Confessor's campaign in 60
Enlightenment 179, 193, 224–225
Henry II and 77
Highland Clearances 295
House of Stuart 138
independence struggle and subsequent wars 92–93, 116–117
Irish settlements 31
Jacobite rebellions 193, 197, 200–201, 202–203
Mary Queen of Scots 137, 138–139, 141, 158
monarchs and rulers 388, 389
Picts 11, 30, 31, 34, 59
press 209
Reformation and Protestantism 137, 138, 158, 196
Romans in 24, 28, 29, 30
17th century wars 166, 169, 174–175
trade 212
Treason Trials 237
union of the crowns (1603) 138, 149, 158–159
union (full) with England (1707) 138, 158, 175, 198–199, 200
Scott, George Gilbert 282
Scott, Robert Falcon 287
Scott, Walter 224–225
Scott, Winfield 245
Scottish Labour Party 311
Scottish National Party (SNP) 387
Scouts, Boy 304
scutage 84, 86
seafarers 146–147
seals 120, 148
seaplanes, Supermarine 339
season, social 218, 219, 305
Sebastopol, Russia 274, 275
seed drill 231
Segar, William 152
Serapis 32
Serbia 313, 385
serfdom 105, 230
servants 106–107
women as 278, 339
Seven Years' War 201, 207, 212, 214
Severus, Septimius 29
sewage systems 278–279
Sex Disqualification (Removal) Act (1919) 327
Sex Pistols 363
sextants 226, 229
sexual morals 278, 339
Seymour, Jane 135
Shackleton, Ernest 287
Shaftesbury, Anthony Ashley Cooper, Lord 268
Shakespeare, William 110, 123, 143, 152, 154–155, 181
Sharp, Granville 235
Shaw, George Bernard 305, 311
sheep 89, 142, 231
Sheffield, Yorkshire 277
Sheldonian theater, Oxford 185
shell-shock 327
Sheppard, Jack 223
sheriffs 60, 73, 76–77, 85
shipbuilding 173, 179, 211, 259, 277, 334
ships 147, 163, 226–227, 244, 245, 288
passenger liners 304
slave ships 229, 234–235
steamships 258–259, 261, 277
Titanic disaster 306–307
Viking 46–47
World War I 312
see also navies
Short Parliament 166
Sickert, Walter 305
Sidney, Philip 149, 153
siege warfare 92–93, 97, 99
Sihtric Caec, king of Dublin and York 53, 55
Sikh Wars 290
Sikhs 321
Simnel, Lambert 132
Simpson, Wallis see Windsor, Duchess of
Singapore 343, 349
"Singeing of the King of Spain's Beard" 149
Sinn Féin 333, 379

Sir Gawain and the Green Knight 110
Skara Brae, Orkneys 17
slavery and slave trade 146, 163, 175, 179, 200, 210, 211, 222, 277
campaign against 223, 234–235, 268, 286
Roman 33
slave ships 229, 234–235
slums 222, 231, 278–279
Smiles, Samuel 250, 279
Smith, Adam 210, 224, 225, 235
Smith, John 162–163
Snow, John 265
Snowden, Philip 334
SNP see Scottish National Party
Social Democrats 380
socialism 305, 311, 334, 361, 376
Socialist League 311
Socialist Workers Party 376, 377
society
Anglo-Saxon 60–61
Edwardian 304–305
Georgian 218–223, 278
medieval 88–89
1920s and 1930s 338–339
1950s and 1960s 370–373
Tudor 142–145
Victorian 278–279, 284–285
Society for the Abolition of the Slave Trade 234–235
Society of United Irishmen 238–239
SOE see Special Operations Executive
Solander, Daniel 227
Solemn League and Covenant 166, 174
Somersett, James 235
Somme, battle of the 322, 323, 324–325
sonnets 155
Sophia of Hanover, Electress 189
South Africa 296–297, 303, 343, 365
South Pole 287
South Sea Bubble 206, 210–211
Southwark, London 33, 152, 155, 165
Soviet Union
and Cold War 369, 384
communism 346
in World War II 347, 349, 358
see also Russia; Russian Revolution
Spain
Hanoverian wars with 200
and New World 146, 162, 200
Peninsular War 241
Stuarts and 158
Tudors and 134, 135, 141, 148–151
Spanish Armada 141, 147, 149, 150–151
Spanish Civil War 346
Special Air Service (SAS) 384
Special Operations Executive (SOE) 349
Spectator 208
Speed, John 165
Speke, John 286
Spenser, Edmund 110, 141, 153
spices 83, 120
spies 369
spinning 232–233
Spitalfields, London 181
Spithead mutiny 237
Spitting Image 383
sports 145, 219, 280, 339, 342, 343, 361
Stalin, Joseph 346, 347, 351, 358, 359
stamps, postage 271, 290, 363
Stanley, Henry Morton 286–287
Star Chamber, Court of 132, 166
Statute of Labourers (1351) 103
Statute of Wales (1284) 91
steam power 233, 248–249, 258–259
steamships 258–259, 261, 277
steel 258, 259, 276, 277
Steele, Richard 208
Stephen, king of England 64, 73, 76
Stephenson, George 258
Stigand, archbishop of Canterbury 68, 69
stock exchange 210, 334, 380–381
stock market crashes 334, 351, 380, 381
Stone Age 14, 16–19
Stone of Scone 92
Stonehenge, Wiltshire 17, 18–19
Stopes, Marie 339
Stormont, Belfast 379
Straw, Jack (medieval rebel) 104, 105
street lights 279

strikes 265, 309, 310–311, 326, 331, 376, 377
General Strike 334
miners' 376, 380, 381, 383
Strongbow see Pembroke, Richard, earl of
Stuart (Stewart), House of 93, 116, 138, 202
Stuart succession 128–129, 138, 141, 200
Sturt, Charles 287
suburbs 279, 305, 338–339
Sudan 297, 350
Sudbury, Simon, archbishop of Canterbury 104–105
Sudetenland 346–347
Sueno's Stone 59
Suez 240–241, 274
Suez Canal 296, 297, 358, 366–367
Suez Crisis 364, 366–367
suffragettes 251, 308–309, 326, 350
Sulis 33
Sunningdale Agreement (1974) 379
surgery 33, 274
suttee 291
Sutton Hoo ship burial 8–9, 36–37, 40
Sweyn, king of Denmark 57
Swift, Jonathan 208, 209
swords 22, 36, 47, 52, 124
Symington, William 258–259
Synod of Whitby 44, 45
Syria 385

T

Taff Vale Railway Dispute 311
Tahiti 227
Tallis, Thomas 153
tally sticks 73
Tamworth Manifesto 269
Tandy, James Napper 238
tanks 323
Tara, Ireland 31, 39, 54, 55
Tasmania 295
Tatler 208
taxation
in American colonies 214, 215
Charles I and 166
for Crusades 82, 83
East India Company and 290–291
fyrd and heregeld 61, 98
income tax 207, 355, 361, 381
indirect 381
lay subsidies 104
Parliament and 85, 104
poll tax 32, 104–105, 381, 383
Roman 32
Scottish 116
scutage 84, 86
Tudor 135, 142
20th century 311
wool 120
tea 214, 215, 228, 229, 296
Tecumseh 244, 245
telegraph 259, 304–305
telescopes 179, 200
television 362, 371
Telford, Thomas 260
Templar, Knights 83
temples, Roman 32, 33
tenants 73, 77, 89, 143, 230, 266, 301
terrorist attacks 317, 384
Angry Brigade 373
IRA 333, 379
al-Qaeda 385, 387
Tewkesbury Abbey 98–99
textile industry 232–233, 276–277, 334
Thames River 164–165, 260
Thatcher, Margaret 225, 279, 361, 369, 373, 377, 379, 380–385
theater
Edwardian 304
Elizabethan and Jacobean 152–153, 154–155
Licensing Act (1737) 209
Puritans and 181
Restoration 176, 177, 181
thegns 60, 98
Theodore of Tarsus, archbishop of Canterbury 44–45
Thomas of Bayeux, archbishop of York 69
Thorkell the Tall 57
Thorseby, John, archbishop of York 109
Thuggee 291

time, standard 250, **265**
Times, The **209**, 265, 274–275, 301
tin mining 20, 29, 233
Tipu Sultan 213
Tirpitz, Alfred von 312
Titanic, RMS **306–307**
tobacco 163, 234
Togodumnus 24
Tolpuddle Martyrs 264, 265
tools, ancient 14, 15, 16, 21
torcs 20
Tories 200, 201, 207, 255, 268, 269, 270–271
see also Conservative Party
tournaments 98–99
Tower of London 91, 105
"princes in the tower" 123, 132
towns and cities
burhs 51, 52
Georgian 218–219
industrialization 231, 269
medieval 89, 120–121
New Towns 305, 361, 370
oppida 21, 32
Roman 28–29, 32–33, 34
suburbs 279, 305, 338–339
Tudor 143
Ulster 157
Viking 55
Toxteth riots 380
trackways 16–17
Tractarianism *see* Oxford Movement
trade 232
Anglo-Saxon 40
British Empire and Commonwealth 343, 364
Crusades and 83
18th century 193, **210–211**, 227, **228–229**
free market 225, 235, 265, 268, 269, 383
Iron Age 20, 21, 32
London and 180, 181
Napoleon and 241
New World 163, 181
Roman 29, 30
17th century 178–179
slavery and 234
Stone Age 16–17
Tudor 142
urban 89
Viking 46
wars 143
Trade Disputes Act (1906) 311
trade unions 277, **310–311**, 317, 326, 350, 371, 376, 377
General Strike 334
Margaret Thatcher and 380, 383
origins 121
Tolpuddle Martyrs 264, 265
and World War II 346, 355
Trafalgar, battle of (1804) 241, **243**
Trafalgar Square, London 243, 330, 373
trams, electric 304
transportation **223**, 237, 294, 295
Transvaal 303
Traprain Law, East Lothian 30
Treason Trials (1793–1794) 237
treaties
Aix-la-Chapelle (1748) 212
Amiens (1302) 93
Amiens (1802) 241
Brétigny (1360) 97
Edinburgh (1328) 93
Fort Wayne (1809) 245
Ghent (1814) 245
Guerande (1381) 97, 118
Guines (1354) 97
Kilmainham (1882) 301
Limerick (1691) 197
Nonsuch (1585) 141, 149
Paris (1763) 212
Troyes (1420) 119
Utrecht (1713) 197
Vereeniging (1902) 303
Versailles (1919) 331, 346
Waitangi (1840) 294
Windsor (1175) 81
trebuchet 118
Trelleborg, Denmark 57
Tresham, Francis 161
Trevelyan, Charles 267
Trevithick, Richard 233, 258
Tribal Hidage 40

Trinovantes 22, 23
Triple Alliance **312**, 313
troubadours 110
Tudor dynasty **117**, 123, **128–133**, 168, 180
art and craftwork 134, 140–141, **144–145**, **152**
and Ireland 156–157
society 142–145
Tull, Jethro 231
tunnels 260, 261
Turgéis 54
Twiggy (Lesley Hornby) 372
Tyler, Wat 104–105

U

U-boats 322, 326, 327, 349, 358
Uganda **365**, 376
Uí Néill dynasty 31, 38, 39, 54, 55
see also O'Neill clan
Ulster 39, 93, 157, 197, 239, 300, 301, 332, 333, 350
see also Northern Ireland
Ulster Volunteer Force 320, 332, 378, 379
underground railroads 276, 354, 355
unemployment 316, 331, 334, 335, 336–337, 339, 360, 361, 377, 380, 381, 382, 386
benefit payments 311
18th century 232
United Kingdom, creation of 198–199
United Nations 385
United States of America
American Revolution 209, **214–217**, 242
British debt to 334, 359
and Cold War 364, **369**
emigrants to 267, 295
flag and anthem 245
and Iraq and Afghanistan 385
and Suez Crisis 367
War of 1812 244–245
and World War I 322–323, 331
and World War II 349, 351, 355, 358, 359
universities 89, 108, 373
Unknown Warrior 323
Urban II, Pope 82
utilitarianism 185, **283**
Utopia (More) 153
UVF *see* Ulster Volunteer Force

V

V-1 bombs and V-2 rockets **355**, 360
vagabonds 142, 143
Van Dyke, Anthony 167
Vassa, Gustavus 235
Verica 23
Verulamium see St. Albans
Vespasian 24
Victoria, queen of Great Britain and Ireland 219, 241, **270–273**, 282, 291, 296, 312
Victoria, Lake 286
Victoria Cross 271
Victoria Falls 286
Victorian age 250–251
culture 282–283
empire 251, 273, 287, **290–297**
entertainment 280–281
exploration 286–287
industry 276–277
science 273, 283, 288–289
society **278–279**, 284–285
Vietnam War 373, 385
Vikings 11, 41, 44, **46–47**, 50–53, 57
art and craftwork 46, 54, 55
and Christianity 45, 47, 51, 57
Danegeld 57
and Ireland 54–55
language 47, 55
and Scotland 59
and Wales 58, 59
weapons 47, 52
villas, Roman 29, **33**, 34
villeins 73, 89, 120
Viroconium 28
Volusenus 22
Vortigern, king of the Britons 40
Votadini 30
voting rights 218, 251, 308–309, 327, 339

W

Wade, George 202–203
wages 103, 120, 335, 339, 355, 361, 376
minimum wage 386
Wakefield, Edward Gibbon 294
Wales 11, 58–59, 65, 116
castles 64, **90–91**, 117
devolution 387
English campaigns in 76, 99, 174
Irish settlements 31
medieval 90–91
mining and industry 277, 381
monarchs and rulers 388, 389
Owain Glyn Dwr's rebellion 117
Romans and 24
unemployment 334
Wales, princes of 91, 388
Wall Street Crash 334, 351
Wallace, Alfred Russel 289
Wallace, William 93
Walpole, Robert 200, **206–207**, 208, 209
War of Jenkins' Ear 200
War of the Austrian Succession **200–201**, 203, 212
War of the Quadruple Alliance 200
War of the Spanish Succession **197**, 211
Warbeck, Perkin 132
Wars of the Roses 65, **122–123**, 128, 132, 168
Warwick, earl of ("the Kingmaker") **122–123**
Washington, George **214–215**, 217, 236
water power 233
Waterloo, battle of (1815) 240–241, 246–247
Watt, James 225, **233**, **248–249**
WEA *see* Workers' Educational Association
weapons
Anglo-Saxon 36
cannon and artillery 99, **119**, 146, 275, 297, 322, 323
guns 99, 169, 203, 222, 228, 277, 321
Iron Age 21
Maori club 295
medieval 96, 99, 101, 118–119, **124–125**
nuclear 359, 368, 369
Roman 22
Stone Age 16
tanks 323
V-1 bombs and V-2 rockets **355**, 360
Viking 47, 52
weaving 232
Webb, Beatrice and Sidney 311
Webb, Philip 283
Webster, John 153
Wedgwood, Josiah **232**, 234, 288
weights 40, 120
Welfare State 283, 361, 371, 372, 383
Wellington, Arthur Wellesley, duke of 241, 246–247
Wells, H.G. **305**, 311
Wembley Stadium 339
Wesley, John and Charles 223
Wessex 11, 41, 44, 46, 47, **50–53**, 57, 58
West Indies 146, 163, 343, 365, 371
Westminster Abbey 61, 85, 154–155, 201
Wexford, Ireland 81, 169, 174
Wheathampstead, Hertfordshire 22
Whigs 200–201, 207–208, 254–255, 268–271
see also Liberal Party
Whistler, James McNeill 282
Whitby Abbey 45
White Horse of Uffington 22
Whitefield, George 223
Whitehouse, Mary 373
Whittington, Richard 120
Wilberforce, William 235
Wild, Jonathan 223
Wilde, Oscar 304
Wilhelm II, Kaiser 271, **312**
Wilkes, John 206
Wilkinson, Ellen 337
William the Conqueror (William I) 61, **68–71**, 75, 88, 108
William II (William Rufus), king of England 69, 72, 82
William III, king of Great Britain and Ireland 169, **188–189**, 192, 196–197, 200, 222, 296
William IV, king of Great Britain and Ireland 255, 269, 270

William, Prince (son of Prince Charles) 363
William Clito, duke of Normandy 73
William the Lion, king of the Scots 77
Wills, William John 287
Wilson, Harold 371, 375, 376, 385
Wilson, Woodrow 323, 331
Wilton Diptych **114–115**, 152
Winchester 50, 57, 73
Windsor, duchess of (Wallis Simpson) 345
Windsor, duke of *see* Edward VIII
"winter of discontent" 377
witenagemot (witan) **53**, 85
witchcraft 158
Witham pins 41
Wolfe, James 212
Wolfe Tone, Theobald **238**, 239
Wolfenden Report (1957) 371
Wollstonecraft, Mary 236
Wolsey, Thomas 135, 142
women
equal pay 376
MPs 327, 387
strikes by 309, 310, 376, 377
and theater 176, 181
Victorian 278
votes for 251, **308–309**, 326, 339
work 264, 276, 326, 327, 338, 339, 387
in world wars 326, 327, 355
Women's Liberation movement 376, 377
Women's Social and Political Union (WSPU) **309**, 326
Woodville, Elizabeth 123
wool 89, 118, 120, 121, 142, 232, 276
Wordsworth, William 236, 282
Workers' Educational Association 304
workers' rights 251, 255, **264–265**, 268
see also trade unions
workhouses 278, **284–285**
Working Men's colleges 278, 283
World War I 295, 301, 309, 316, **320–331**, 332, 342
events leading to 312–313
Gallipoli campaign 295, **321**, 350
home front 326–327
peace and after 323, **330–331**, 334
secret agreements 331
trench warfare 316, 322
war graves 328–329
World War II 295, 316–317, 339, 343, **346–359**, 364
Battle of Britain 349, **356–357**
Blitz 349, **352–353**, **354–355**
conscription 347, 354, 355
D-Day (Normandy landings) 359
Dunkirk 348, 349
evacuation of children 347, 354
events leading to 346–347
rationing 354, 355, 360, 361, 370
victory 358–359
Wren, Christopher 181–182, 184–187
Wulfstan, archbishop of Canterbury 45, 57
Wyatt, Thomas 153
Wyatt's Rebellion 133, 141
Wycliffe, John 108, **109**

Y

Yalta Conference (1945) 359
Yeats, W.B. 305
yeoman-farmers 143
Yom Kippur War 376
York 28, 44, 45
Viking 47, 52, 53, 55, 57, 68
York, house of 122, 132, 133
Yorkshire 108, 142, 276–277
Yorktown, siege of 216–217
Young Ireland alliance 300
Ypres 321
Yugoslavia 385

Z

Zambezi River 286
Zambia 303
Zeppelin 321, 327
Zimbabwe 303, 343, 365
Zong (slave ship) 234–235
Zulu Wars 296–297

Acknowledgments

Dorling Kindersley would like to thank the following people for their assistance in the preparation of this book:

Susan Kennedy for additional text; Jane Ellis for proofreading; Jackie Brind for compiling the index; Laura Palosuo for coordinating the jacket creation; Peter Radcliffe for additional design; Weishaupt Barbara, Era Chawla, Niyati Gosain, Rajnish Kashyap, Arushi Nayar, Avani Parikh, Divya PR, Ivy Roy, and Neetika Vilas for design assistance; Megha Gupta, Ankush Saikia, and Chitra Subramanyam for editorial assistance; and Jaypal Singh Chauhan, Shanker Prasad, and Tanveer Zaidi for DTP support.

The publisher would like to thank the following for their kind permission to reproduce their photographs:

Key a-above; b-below/bottom; c-center; f-far; l-left; r-right; t-top

Centrale Bibliotheek van de Universiteit, Ghent, Belgium / The Bridgeman Art Library. **122–125 Getty Images:** Danita Delimont (ftl-ftr). **123 The Bridgeman Art Library:** Private Collection / © Look and Learn (bc). **124 Dorling Kindersley:** The Trustees of the British Museum (bl/ Broadsword, bc/Mace); The Board of Trustees of the Royal Armouries (fbl, bc/ Dagger); Warwick Castle, Warwick (br/ Mace); Wallace Collection, London (fbl/ Dagger, cr). **125 Dorling Kindersley:** Robin Wigington, Arbour Antiques, Ltd., Stratford-upon-Avon (tc); The Board of Trustees of the Royal Armouries (cl, cra, fcl); Wallace Collection, London (cr, cb, cb/Bill, cb/ Halberd). **126–127 Corbis:** Hoberman Collection. **128 Corbis:** Historical Picture Archive (tl). **129 Getty Images:** AFP (br). **130 Corbis:** Hoberman Collection (tc); Francis G. Mayer (crb). **Dorling Kindersley:** Charlestown Shipwreck and Heritage Centre, Cornwall (tr); Judith Miller / Woolley and Wallis (cr); Whitbread Plc (bc). **Getty Images:** Hans the Younger Holbein (bl). **Wikipedia, The Free Encyclopedia:** Elizabeth1book (cla). **130–131 Corbis:** Neil Beer (Background). **131 Dorling Kindersley:** The Science Museum, London (cra); Wallace Collection, London (tc). **Getty Images:** John Barker (bl); Dirck Stoop (c); Sir James Thornhill (crb). **Wikipedia, The Free Encyclopedia:** Patriarcha-Book of-Robert Filmer Originally from 1680 (cla). **132–133 Wikipedia, The Free Encyclopedia:** Nonsuch Palace by Joris Hoefnagel. **132 Dorling Kindersley:** Wallace Collection, London (cla). **Getty Images:** (br). **132–138 Corbis:** Angelo Hornak (ftl-ftl). **133 Alamy Images:** World History Archive (cra). **Getty Images:** English School (bl). **134 Getty Images:** English School (bl); Hans the Younger Holbein (cr); SuperStock (bc). **135 Dorling Kindersley:** British Library (cr). **Getty Images:** Friedrich Bouterwek (tl); DeA / G. Nimatallah (fbl); Peter Willi (bl); Hans Holbein the Younger (bc); Hans the Younger Holbein (br). **136–137 Getty Images:** English School. **136 Corbis:** Gustavo Tomsich (br). **137 The Bridgeman Art Library:** His Grace The Duke of Norfolk, Arundel Castle (br). **Corbis:** Robert Harding World Imagery (bc). **138 The Art Archive:** Victoria and Albert Museum London / V&A Images (c). Bibliothèque Nationale De France, Paris: (bl). **Dorling Kindersley:** Whitbread Plc (br). **Getty Images:** (cr). **139 Corbis:** Bettmann. **140–141 Corbis:** The Gallery Collection. **140 Getty Images:** Sarah Countess of Essex (c). **140–147 Corbis:** Angelo Hornak (ftl-ftr). **141 Getty Images:** English School (cr). **TopFoto.co.uk:** 2004 Topham Picturepoint (br). **Wikipedia, The Free Encyclopedia:** Elizabeth1book (tl). **142 Corbis:** Bettmann (cl); Robert Estall (bl). **Dorling Kindersley:** Museum of English Rural Life, The University of Reading (cr). **143 Corbis:** Hoberman Collection (cb). **Getty Images:** Joris Hoefnagel (tc). **144 Alamy Images:** fotolincs (ca/Posy Ring). **The Art Archive:** British Museum (cl); Victoria and Albert Museum London / Sally Chappell (cr/Armada Jewel); Museum of London (tc, tr, br/Watch). **Corbis:** Adam Woolfitt (tl). **144–145 The Art Archive:** Museum of London (bc). **145 Alamy Images:** The Art Archive (br); V&A Images (tc). **The Art Archive:** Museum of London (cla, clb, bl/reliquary, bc, c). **Dorling Kindersley:** Worthing Museum and Art Gallery (tr). **146–147 Wikipedia, The Free Encyclopedia:** AnthonyRoll-1 Great Harry / Anthony Anthony. **146 Alamy Images:** Mary Evans Picture Library (cl). **Dorling Kindersley:** National Maritime Museum (tl). **148–149 Corbis:** Gianni Dagli Orti. **148 Getty Images**. Nasim Tadghighi: (bl). **149 Alamy Images:** The Art Gallery Collection (bl). **Corbis:** Angelo Hornak (ftr). **150–151 Getty Images:** SuperStock. **152–153 Photo Scala, Florence:** The National Gallery, London. **152 Getty Images:** Nicholas Hilliard (cl); Time & Life Pictures (bc). **152–158 Corbis:** Angelo Hornak (ftl-ftl). **153 Alamy Images:** Lebrecht Music and Arts Photo Library (tr). **Corbis:** Burstein Collection (bc). **Dorling Kindersley:** Judith Miller / Woolley and Wallis (bl). **154 Getty Images:** Neale Clark (bl). **155 Corbis:** Bettmann (cl, crb). TopFoto.co.uk: (bc). **156 John McCavitt / Author of Sir Arthur Chichester, Lord Deputy of Ireland, 1605-16 (Belfast, 1998).** : (tr). **TopFoto.co.uk:** Topham Picturepoint (tl). **156–157 Corbis:** Richard Cummins. **157 Getty Images:** (br); English School (tr). **158 Corbis:** Fine Art Photographic Library (tl). **Getty Images:** (cra); English School (cb). **159 Getty Images:** Peter Paul Rubens . **160–161 Getty Images:** German School. **162 Corbis:** Bettmann (cra); Francis G. Mayer (bc). **162–163 Corbis:** Angelo Hornak (ftl-ftr). **163 Corbis:** Francis G. Mayer (br). **Dorling Kindersley:** Charlestown Shipwreck and Heritage Centre, Cornwall (cl). **Getty Images:** Popperfoto (tr). **164–165 Occidental College Library**. **166 The Bridgeman Art Library:** English School, (17th century) / British Library, London, UK (cr). **Corbis:** Angelo Hornak (ftl). **Getty Images:** John Singleton Copley (bl). **Wikipedia, The Free Encyclopedia:** Patriarcha-Book of-Robert Filmer Originally from 1680 (tl). **167 Getty Images:** Sir Anthony van Dyck. **168 Dorling Kindersley:** Wallace Collection, London (cra). **168–169 Corbis:** Angelo Hornak (ftl-ftr). **Getty Images:** John Barker. **169 Dorling Kindersley:** The Board of Trustees of the Royal Armouries (tl, tc). **Getty Images:** English School (br). **TopFoto.co.uk:** Topham Picturepoint (cr). **Wikipedia, The Free Encyclopedia:** New Model Army—Soldier's catechism (cl). **170–171 Corbis:** The Gallery Collection. **172 Getty Images:** Benjamin West (bl). **172–181 Corbis:** Angelo Hornak (ftl-ftr). **173 Alamy Images:** Mary Evans Picture Library (tr). **Corbis:** (cb). **Getty Images:** Time & Life Pictures (tl). **174–175 Alamy Images:** Mary Evans Picture Library. **174 Getty Images:** Nicolas Sanson D'Abbeville (cl). **175 Alamy Images:** Neil McAllister (cr). **Getty Images:** (tc, c). **176 Getty Images:** (cl). **176–177 Getty Images:** Dirck Stoop . **177 Corbis:** (br); Bettmann (tr). Getty Images: DeA Picture Library (tl). **178–179 National Maritime Museum, Greenwich, London:** Pieter Cornelisz van Soest. **178 akg-images:** British Library (bl). **Alamy Images:** Peter Horree (br). **179 Corbis:** Dave Bartruff (br). **180 Alamy Images:** Photos 12 (bc). **Getty Images:** John Hayls (tr). **181 Corbis:** Historical Picture Archive (tr). **Dorling Kindersley:** Stephen Oliver (crb). **Getty Images:** (tl). **182–183 Getty Images:** Lieve Verschuier. **184 Corbis:** Bettmann (cl); Angelo Hornak (tl). **Getty Images:** SSPL (bc). **184–185 Corbis:** Angelo Hornak (ftl-ftr). **Dorling Kindersley:** The Science Museum, London. **185 Corbis:** Leonard de Selva (cr). **Getty Images:** Kean Collection (br). **186–187 Corbis:** Neil Beer. **188 Getty Images:** SuperStock . **189 Alamy Images:** Pictorial Press Ltd (cl); The Print Collector (bc). **Corbis:** Angelo Hornak (ftr); Michael Nicholson (cr). **Getty Images:** Sir James Thornhill (tr). **190–191 National Maritime Museum, Greenwich, London:** Ministry of Defence Art Collection. **192 Corbis:** Bettmann (tl). **193 Corbis:** Stapleton Collection (br). **194 Alamy Images:** Mary Evans Picture Library (c). **The Bridgeman Art Library:** Wyck, Jan (1640-1700) / National Army Museum, London (clb). Corbis: Bettmann (cra). **Dorling Kindersley:** National Maritime Museum, Greenwich, London (cb). **Getty Images:** (br). **194–195 Getty Images:** Thomas Jnr. Malton (Background). **195 akg-images:** North Wind Picture Archives (ca). **Alamy Images:** The Art Archive (bl). **Getty Images:** (cr); SSPL (cl); English School (crb). **196 The Bridgeman Art Library:** Lely, Sir Peter (1618–80) (after) / Private Collection (bl). **Getty Images:** (cr). **196–197 The Bridgeman Art Library:** Wyck, Jan (1640–1700) / National Army Museum, London. **Dorling Kindersley:** The 68th Durham Light Infantry (ftl-ftr)). **197 Corbis:** Michael Freeman. **198–199 The National Archives of Scotland**. **200 Alamy Images:** Mary Evans Picture Library (tl). **Getty Images:** (br); Allan Ramsay (c); George Scharf the Elder (bc). **200–203 Dorling Kindersley:** The 68th Durham Light Infantry (ftl-ftr). **201 Getty Images:** (tc). **202 Getty Images:** (clb). **202–203 Corbis:** Bettmann. **203 Corbis:** Patrick Dieudonne / Robert Harding World Imagery. **Dorling Kindersley:** Judith Miller / Wallis & Wallis (tl). **Getty Images:** (cr). **204–205 Alamy Images:** World History Archive. **206 Alamy Images:** North Wind Picture Archives (tr). **Corbis:** Michael Nicholson (bl). **206–207 Getty Images**. **206–215 Dorling Kindersley:** The 68th Durham Light Infantry (ftl-ftr)). **207 Corbis:** Philadelphia Museum of Art (br). **Getty Images:** (tl, tr). **208 Getty Images:** (bl). **209 Corbis:** The Gallery Collection (cr). **Getty Images:** SSPL (tl); Time & Life Pictures (br). **210 Alamy Images:** North Wind Picture Archives (tl). **210–211 Corbis:** Historical Picture Archive. **211 Alamy Images:** Lebrecht Music and Arts Photo Library (tr); Pictorial Press Ltd (br). **Corbis:** Hulton-Deutsch Collection (tl). **Mary Evans Picture Library:** Glasshouse Images (bl). **212 Getty Images:** Benjamin West (cra). **212–213 Getty Images:** Robert Home. **213 Alamy Images:** North Wind Picture Archives (cl). **Getty Images:** Indian School (tc). **214 Alamy Images:** coin Alan King (cl). **Corbis:** Burstein Collection (bl). **Getty Images:** (tr). **214–215 Getty Images**. **215 Corbis:** Joseph Sohm; Visions of America (cl). **Getty Images:** (tr). **216–217 Alamy Images:** The Print Collector. **217 Getty Images:** SSPL (tc). **218 Dorling Kindersley:** Weald and Downland Open Air Museum, Chichester (cl). **Getty Images:** (cr). **218–219 Dorling Kindersley:** The 68th Durham Light Infantry (ftl-ftr). **Getty Images:** Thomas Jnr. Malton. **219 Getty Images:** Popperfoto (tl). **220–221 Alamy Images:** The Art Gallery Collection. **222 Dorling Kindersley:** Ross Simms and the Winchcombe Folk and Police Museum (tr). **TopFoto.co.uk:** Granger Collection (bc). **222–243 Dorling Kindersley:** The 68th Durham Light Infantry (ftl-ftr). **223 Alamy Images:** Niday Picture Library (bc). **Getty Images:** (tl, cr). **224–225 Mary Evans Picture Library**. **224 Corbis:** (tc). **225 Alamy Images:** The Art Archive (tc); World History Archive (tl). **226 The Art Archive:** (ca). **Getty Images:** SSPL (cb). **227 Dorling Kindersley:** National Maritime Museum, Greenwich, London (cla). **Getty Images:** SSPL (tc); Time & Life Pictures (cr). **228 Alamy Images:** Mary Evans Picture Library (c); V&A Images (tr). **Dorling Kindersley:** The Trustees of the British Museum (tl); The Board of Trustees of the Royal Armouries (ca); Judith Miller / John Bull Silver (bl); National Maritime Museum (bc); Lyon and Turnbull Ltd. (br). **229 Dorling Kindersley:** Judith Miller / Dreweatt Neate (tl); National Maritime Museum (c, bl, bc); Wilberforce House Museum, Hull City Council, UK (cr). **Getty Images:** SSPL (cl). **230 Alamy Images:** The Art Archive (bc). **Dorling Kindersley:** The Museum of English Rural Life, The University of Reading (c). **Getty Images:** (br). **230–231 The Art Archive:** Lincoln Museum and Gallery / Eileen Tweedy. **231 The Art Archive:** Nicolas Sapieha (cr). **Mary Evans Picture Library:** (bc). **232 Dorling Kindersley:** Judith Miller / Woolley and Wallis (bl). **232–233 Getty Images:** SSPL. **233 Alamy Images:** Mary Evans Picture Library (tr). **Getty Images:** (bc). **234 Getty Images:** (bl); English School (c). **234–235 Getty Images**. **235 The Bridgeman Art Library:** Royal Albert Memorial Museum, Exeter, Devon, UK (tc). **Getty Images:** After John Russell (br). **236–237 Alamy Images:** North Wind Picture Archives. **236 Corbis:** The Gallery Collection (cl). **Getty Images:** Time & Life Pictures (bl). **237 Alamy Images:** Mary Evans Picture Library (cra). **Library Of Congress, Washington, D.C.:** LC-USZC4-6088 (tl). **238–239 Alamy Images:** Pictorial Press Ltd . **238 Alamy Images:** Mary Evans Picture Library (tr). **Corbis:** Eye Ubiquitous (bl). **239 Corbis:** Bettmann (br). **240 Corbis:** (cl). **240–241 Corbis:** Stapleton Collection. **241 Corbis:** Stefano Bianchetti (tr); The Gallery Collection (br). **242 Corbis:** Francis G. Mayer (cl). **242–243 Getty Images:** Roger Viollet. **243 Corbis:** Fine Art Photographic Library (tl); Michael Nicholson (br). **Dorling Kindersley:** HMS Victory / Lt Cdr DJ 'Oscar' Whild RN (cr). **Getty Images:** Time & Life Pictures (bc). **244 Library Of Congress, Washington, D.C.:** LC-DIG-ppmsca-10752. **245 Corbis:** (cr); Bettmann (tl); Smithsonian Institution (tc). **Dorling Kindersley:** The 68th Durham Light Infantry (ftr). **Getty Images:** (br); Christie's Images (bl). **246–247 Getty Images:** Hulton Archive. **248–249 Dorling Kindersley:** The Science Museum, London. **250 Corbis:** The Gallery Collection (tl). **251 Corbis:** Hulton-Deutsch Collection (br). **252 Alamy Images:** Alan King engraving (cb); Pictorial Press Ltd (ca). Corbis: (c). **Dorling Kindersley:** Rough Guides (cr). **Getty Images:** Sir Thomas Lawrence (cla); SSPL (bl, br). **252–253 Corbis:** Historical Picture Archive (Background). **253 Alamy Images:** Ivan Vdovin (clb). **Corbis:** Alinari Archives (br). **Getty Images:** Popperfoto (ca); SSPL (cr); Time & Life Pictures (cb). **Photolibrary:** British Library; (cl). **254 Getty Images:** Sir Thomas Lawrence (ca). **254–255 Dorling Kindersley:** National Railway Museum, York / Science Museum / Science & Society Picture Library (ftl-ftr). **Getty Images**. **255 Mary Evans Picture Library:** Tom Morgan (tr). **258 Getty Images:** SSPL (cl, br, tr). **258–259 Dorling Kindersley:** National Railway Museum, York / Science Museum / Science & Society Picture Library (ftl-ftr). **259 Corbis:** (tc). **Getty Images:** SSPL (cb).

Hulton-Deutsch Collection (cr). **Getty Images:** SSPL (bl). **261 Dorling Kindersley:** Rough Guides (cr). **Getty Images:** Otto Herschan / Hulton Archive. **264 Getty Images:** SSPL (cla). **264–265 Photolibrary:** Guildhall Library & Art Gallery. **264–269 Dorling Kindersley:** National Railway Museum, York / Science Museum / Science & Society Picture Library (ftl-ftr). **265 Alamy Images:** Alan King engraving (cr). **Getty Images:** (cr). **266–267 Corbis:** Michael St. Maur Sheil. **266 Dorling Kindersley:** Rough Guides (bl). **267 Corbis:** (tr); Museum of the City of New York (br). **268–269 The Bridgeman Art Library:** Houses of Parliament, Westminster, London, UK. **268 Dorling Kindersley:** Rough Guides (bl). **269 Alamy Images:** Pictorial Press Ltd (tr). **Getty Images:** (br). **270–271 Corbis.** **270 Getty Images:** Popperfoto (c). **271 Corbis:** Hulton-Deutsch Collection (tc). **Getty Images:** James Emmerson (cr). **272–273 Corbis:** Historical Picture Archive. **274–275 Corbis:** The Gallery Collection. **274 Getty Images:** SSPL (ca). **274–283 Dorling Kindersley:** National Railway Museum, York / Science Museum / Science & Society Picture Library (ftl-ftr). **275 Corbis:** (tr). **276 Corbis:** Bettmann (bc). **Getty Images:** SSPL (cla). **277 Corbis:** Bettmann (ca); Hulton-Deutsch Collection (bl). **Dorling Kindersley:** The Board of Trustees of the Royal Armouries. **Getty Images:** Edward Gooch (br). **278 Alamy Images:** Lordprice Collection (bc). **278–279 Corbis:** Blue Lantern Studio. **279 Corbis:** (bc). **Getty Images:** Time & Life Pictures (cr). **280 Dorling Kindersley:** Blists Hill Museum, Ironbridge, Shropshire (tr); The Museum of London (cl); Judith Miller / Hamptons (cr); Peter Radcliffe (c/Cricket, c/Rugby, crb/Cyclist tourist, crb/Cyclist tourist). **Dominic Winter:** (bc). **281 Corbis:** Peter Harholdt (cr). **Dorling Kindersley:** Judith Miller / Biblion (tc, tc/Children's Books); The Museum of London (cl). **Lebrecht Music and Arts:** (br). **Mary Evans Picture Library:** (tr). **282 Corbis:** Bob Krist (tl). **Getty Images:** Time & Life Pictures (br). **282–283 Getty Images:** SuperStock. **283 Alamy Images:** V&A Images (tr). **Getty Images:** Time & Life Pictures (tl). **284–285 Alamy Images:** Pictorial Press Ltd. **286–287 Alamy Images:** The Print Collector. **Dorling Kindersley:** National Railway Museum, York / Science Museum / Science & Society Picture Library (ftl-ftr). **286 Alamy Images:** The Art Archive (bl). **287 Getty Images:** (tc, cr). **288 Corbis:** Bettmann (bl). **Getty Images:** Popperfoto (br). **289 Corbis:** Bettmann (bc). **Dorling Kindersley:** Down House / Natural History Museum, London (cra, tc); Natural History Museum, London (cla). **Getty Images:** (br). **290 Alamy Images:** Ivan Vdovin (tl). **The Art Archive:** India Office Library / British Library (bl). **290–291 Dorling Kindersley:** National Railway Museum, York / Science Museum / Science & Society Picture Library (ftl-ftr). **Getty Images:** Dip Chand (br). **akg-images:** British Library (br). **Corbis:** Hulton-Deutsch Collection (tl). **292–293 Photolibrary:** British Library. **294 Getty Images:** (bc). **294–297 Dorling Kindersley:** National Railway Museum, York / Science Museum / Science & Society Picture Library (ftl-ftr). **295 Dorling Kindersley:** The Trustees of the British Museum (tr); Toronto Public Library: (bc). **296 Alamy Images:** INTERFOTO (ca). **Getty Images:** Otto

Herschan (br). **297 Corbis:** Hulton-Deutsch Collection (tl). **Dorling Kindersley:** Photograph reproduced with the kind permission of the Royal Pavilion, Libraries and Museums (Brighton & Hove) (c). **298–299 Corbis:** Fine Art Photographic Library. **300 Getty Images:** (bl). **300–305 Dorling Kindersley:** National Railway Museum, York / Science Museum / Science & Society Picture Library (ftl-ftr). **301 akg-images:** IAM / World History Archive (tl). **Alamy Images:** Mary Evans Picture Library (br); World History Archive (cl). **Getty Images:** Popperfoto (tr). **302 Mary Evans Picture Library:** (cl). **302–303 The Art Archive:** Eileen Tweedy. **303 akg-images:** World History Archive (cr). **Corbis:** Hulton-Deutsch Collection (tl). **Getty Images:** (br); Time & Life Pictures (bc). **304 Dorling Kindersley:** National Motor Museum, Beaulieu (bl). **Getty Images:** (cl); Popperfoto (cr). **305 Getty Images:** (tl, cb). **306–307 Corbis:** Hulton-Deutsch Collection. **308 Getty Images:** English School. **309 The Art Archive:** London Museum / Eileen Tweedy (tl). **Corbis:** Bettmann (br); Michael Nicholson (cl). **Dorling Kindersley:** National Railway Museum, York / Science Museum / Science & Society Picture Library (bc). **Getty Images:** (bc). **310 Getty Images:** SSPL (ca, br). **311 Dorling Kindersley:** National Railway Museum, York / Science Museum / Science & Society Picture Library (ftr). **Getty Images:** (cr); Popperfoto (br). **312 Dorling Kindersley:** National Railway Museum, York / Science Museum / Science & Society Picture Library (ftl). **Getty Images:** (br); Imagno (bl). **313 Corbis:** Alinari Archives (ca); Leonard de Selva (bc). **316 Corbis:** Hulton-Deutsch Collection. **317 Corbis:** David Bank / JAI. **318–319 Getty Images:** (Background). **318 Alamy Images:** ColsTravel France (cl). **Dorling Kindersley:** Royal Artillery Historical Trust (cla); Eden Camp Museum, Yorkshire (cra). **Getty Images:** (bc, br); Popperfoto (c); SSPL (cr); Sasha (cb). **319 Alamy Images:** Stephen Barnes / Loyalism and Unionism (ca). **Corbis:** Ade Groom / Monsoon / Photolibrary (br); Swim Ink 2, LLC (cla); Carl Schulze / dpa (cr). **Getty Images:** Rolls Press / Popperfoto (c). **320 Getty Images:** (tc). **321 Getty Images:** (tc, cr). **321–323 Corbis:** Ocean (ftl-ftr). **322 Dorling Kindersley:** Royal Artillery Historical Trust (bl); Judith Miller / Hope and Glory (cl). **323 Dorling Kindersley:** Imperial War Museum (br). **Getty Images:** Time & Life Pictures (tc). **324–325 The Art Archive:** Imperial War Museum. **326 Corbis:** Ocean (ftl). **Getty Images:** (bl); SuperStock (tr). **327 Corbis:** Hulton-Deutsch Collection (br). **Getty Images:** Time & Life Pictures (tc). **328–329 Alamy Images:** ColsTravel France. **330 Getty Images:** SSPL. **331 Corbis:** Hulton-Deutsch Collection (br). **Getty Images:** SSPL (ca). **331–335 Corbis:** Ocean (ftl-ftr). **332–333 Getty Images:** Popperfoto. **333 Corbis:** Sean Sexton Collection (br). **Getty Images:** (tr). **334 Corbis:** Bettmann (tl). **Getty Images:** SSPL (bc). **335 Corbis:** Hulton-Deutsch Collection (tl). **Getty Images:** (bc). **336–337 Getty Images:** Popperfoto. **338 Getty Images:** (br); Sasha (tr). **338–343 Corbis:** Ocean (ftl-ftr). **339 Corbis:** Tim Gidal (tr); Stapleton Collection (tl); Museum of Flight (br). **TopFoto.co.uk:** 2000 Topham Picturepoint (bl). **340 Dorling Kindersley:** Algerian Coffee Stores (br/Coffee Maker); The Science Museum, London (tr); Robert Opie (tl, tc, cr).

Etan J. Tal. : (c). **341 Dorling Kindersley:** Glasgow City Council (Museums) (tr); Judith Miller / Woolley and Wallis (tl); The Science Museum, London (tc, cr); Judith Miller / Below Stairs of Hungerford (cla); Judith Miller / Luna (fcr); Robert Opie (br). **342 Corbis:** (tl). **Getty Images:** (ca); Popperfoto (bl). **343 Corbis:** (tr); Swim Ink 2, LLC (bc). **344 Dorling Kindersley:** Judith Miller / Hope and Glory (cl). **Getty Images:** Popperfoto. **345 Corbis:** Marc Dozier (br); Hulton-Deutsch Collection (cr, bl); Max Rossi (cb). **345–347 Corbis:** Ocean (ftl-ftr). **346 Dorling Kindersley:** Royal Artillery Historical Trust (bc). **Getty Images:** (cl, tc). **346–347 Getty Images.** **347 Getty Images:** (tc). **348 Alamy Images:** The Print Collector. **349 Corbis:** Hulton-Deutsch Collection (cb). **Getty Images:** SSPL (bl). **349–351 Corbis:** Ocean (ftl-ftr). **350 Corbis:** Bettmann (cr). **Getty Images:** (c). **351 Corbis:** Bettmann (tl, cl). **Getty Images:** (tr, br). **352–353 Corbis:** Hulton-Deutsch Collection. **354 Getty Images:** (tl, bl, crb). **354–355 Corbis:** Ocean (ftl-ftr). **355 Dorling Kindersley:** Eden Camp Museum, Yorkshire (cr). **Getty Images:** (br); SSPL (tc). **356–357 Getty Images. 358–359 Getty Images. 358 Alamy Images:** Coyote-Photography.co.uk (tl). **358–365 Corbis:** Ocean (ftl-ftr). **359 Dorling Kindersley:** Imperial War Museum (tl). **Getty Images:** (tr). **360 The Art Archive:** Bodleian Library Oxford / C.P.A General Election 1945 (cla). **Getty Images:** (cb); Chris Ware (tr). **361 Alamy Images:** Lordprice Collection (br). **Getty Images:** Kurt Hutton (tc); SSPL (clb). **362 Corbis:** Bettmann (cb). **363 Alamy Images:** Steven May (bc). **Corbis:** Ralf-Finn Hestoft (tr). **Dorling Kindersley:** Judith Miller / Hope & Glory (tl). **Corbis:** Rune Hellestad (br). **364 Alamy Images:** The Print Collector (tl). **Corbis:** Bettmann (bl); Hulton-Deutsch Collection (cra); Swim Ink 2, LLC (bc). **365 Corbis:** Hulton-Deutsch Collection (tr). **Getty Images:** (bc). **366–367 Getty Images:** Joseph McKeown / Picture Post. **368 Getty Images. 369 Corbis:** Hulton-Deutsch Collection (clb). **Getty Images:** (c, crb); AFP (tr); SSPL (br). **369–373 Corbis:** Ocean (ftl-ftr). **370 Corbis:** Bettmann (clb). **Getty Images:** Terry Fincher (tl); Bert Hardy (tr). **371 Corbis:** Hulton-Deutsch Collection (cl). **Dorling Kindersley:** Design Museum, London (tr). **Getty Images:** (tl). **372 Corbis:** Sunset Boulevard (cl). **Getty Images:** (bl); Popperfoto (cr). **373 Alamy Images:** Pictorial Press Ltd (cl). **Corbis:** Bettmann (bc). **374–375 Getty Images:** Central Press. **376 Getty Images:** (bl); Rolls Press / Popperfoto (cr). **376–387 Corbis:** Ocean (ftl-ftr). **377 Alamy Images:** Homer Sykes Archive (tc); parkerphotography (bl); LondonPhotos—Homer Sykes (br). **378 Alamy Images:** Stephen Barnes / Loyalism and Unionism (ca). **Corbis:** Bettmann (tr); Hulton-Deutsch Collection (bl). **378–379 Corbis:** Michel Philippot / Sygma. **379 Alamy Images:** Alain Le Garsmeur (ca). **Getty Images:** (cra); Popperfoto (cla). **Rex Features:** John Rogers (bc). **381 The Advertising Archives:** (tc). **Corbis:** Bob Fleumer (bl). **Getty Images:** (cr). **383 Corbis:** Bettmann (c); Bryn Colton / Assignments Photographers (tl). **Getty Images:** (bc). **TopFoto.co.uk:** 2003 Topham Picturepoint (tr). **384 Corbis:** Carl Schulze / dpa (cb). **385 Corbis:** Anja Niedringhaus / epa (tl). **Dorling Kindersley:** The Board of Trustees of the Royal Armouries (cr). **Getty Images:** (br).

386–387 Corbis: Ade Groom / Monsoon / Photolibrary. **386 Getty Images:** AFP (cl, ca). **387 Corbis:** Peter Macdiarmid / epa (tl). **Getty Images:** (cr). **388–400 Corbis:** Hoberman Collection (ftl/-ftr).

Jacket images: *Front:* **Corbis:** The Gallery Collection bc; National Maritime Museum, Greenwich, London: (background); *Back:* **The Bridgeman Art Library:** Photo © Philip Mould Ltd, London tc; **Corbis:** Bettmann c, cr, Patrick Dieudonne / Robert Harding World Imagery tr, Jason Hawkes ftl, Hulton-Deutsch Collection cl, Stapleton Collection fcl, Peter Turnley fcr, Nik Wheeler tl; **National Maritime Museum, Greenwich, London:** (background); *Spine:* **Corbis:** The Gallery Collection t; National Maritime Museum, Greenwich, London: b; *Front Flap:* **National Maritime Museum, Greenwich, London:** SP; *Back Flap:* **National Maritime Museum, Greenwich, London:** SP; *Front Endpapers:* **Getty Images:** Ashley Cooper / Visuals Unlimited, Inc. 0; *Back Endpapers:* **Getty Images:** Ashley Cooper / Visuals Unlimited, Inc. 0

All other images © Dorling Kindersley
For further information see: www.dkimages.com